Cobb's Legion
Cavalry

Cobb's Legion Cavalry

A History and Roster of the Ninth Georgia Volunteers in the Civil War

HARRIET BEY MESIC

McFarland & Company, Inc., Publishers
Jefferson, North Carolina, and London

The present work is a reprint of the illustrated case bound edition of Cobb's Legion Cavalry: A History and Roster of the Ninth Georgia Volunteers in the Civil War, *first published in 2009 by McFarland.*

LIBRARY OF CONGRESS CATALOGUING-IN-PUBLICATION DATA

Mesic, Harriet Bey, 1937–
Cobb's Legion Cavalry : a history and roster of the ninth Georgia volunteers in the Civil War / Harriet Bey Mesic.
p. cm.
Includes bibliographical references and index.

ISBN 978-0-7864-6432-6
softcover : 50# alkaline paper ∞

1. Confederate States of America. Army. Cobb's Legion. Cavalry Battalion.
2. Confederate States of America. Army. Cobb's Legion. Cavalry Battalion — Biography.   3. United States — History — Civil War, 1861–1865 — Campaigns.
4. United States — History — Civil War, 1861–1865 — Cavalry operations.
5. Georgia — History — Civil War, 1861–1865.   I. Title.
E559.6.C63M47 2011   973.7'458 — dc22   2008050559

BRITISH LIBRARY CATALOGUING DATA ARE AVAILABLE

© 2009 Harriet Bey Mesic. All rights reserved

No part of this book may be reproduced or transmitted in any form or by any means, electronic or mechanical, including photocopying or recording, or by any information storage and retrieval system, without permission in writing from the publisher.

On the cover: Cavalry charge near Brandy Station, Virginia; portrait of Thomas Reade Rootes Cobb, 1823-1862 (Library of Congress); background © 2011 Shutterstock

Manufactured in the United States of America

McFarland & Company, Inc., Publishers
Box 611, Jefferson, North Carolina 28640
www.mcfarlandpub.com

To the memories of

William David Wiggins
of Company A, Cavalry, CSA

Thomas J. Dunnahoo of
Company H, Cavalry, CSA

John William Wesley
of Company C, Infantry, CSA

Acknowledgments

I wish to thank some of the descendents of the Cobb's Legion troopers who spent many years researching the legion and then unselfishly opened their files and shared them with me. Without their help, it would have taken me several more years to finish this book.

The first is James Edward Rowe, who became interested in Cobb's Legion as a child listening to his grandmother's stories about the Civil War. After reading the touching and intimate account of the death of his great-great-grandfather, Thomas J. Dunnahoo, in Wiley Howard's *Sketch of Cobb's Legion*, he became dedicated to researching the history and the biographical data of the men in Companies C and H.

The second is Glen Spurlock, a descendent of John William Wesley. Glen Spurlock is an ardent supporter of research involving all Georgia units. He spent many years researching the biographies of the men in the whole Cobb's Legion — infantry, cavalry, and artillery — studying census, cemetery, pension application, and other historic records. Most of the biographical facts on Cavalry Companies B, D, E, F, G, I, K, and L, and some of the information on the other companies, came from his research.

Bessie Lee Humphreys Gray shares the ancestor William David Wiggins with me. Bessie Gray and my husband, Harry Randolph Mesic, aided me in my original research at the Georgia Archives and in the research of Company A. If I had not had their help in the beginning, this book would never have been written.

I sincerely appreciate all the help that I received from each of these individuals.

Cobb's Legion Cavalry was the best regiment of either army, North or South. Some regiments had one squadron that was better than the others, but the Cobb Legion never failed me no matter what squadron was in front.
— General Wade Hampton, Cavalry Corps Commander
Confederate States of America

Table of Contents

Acknowledgments — vii
List of Maps — xi
Preface — 1

Chapter 1 — Creation of Cobb's Legion Cavalry — 3
Chapter 2 — The Peninsula Campaign — 7
Chapter 3 — The Seven Days Campaign — 11
Chapter 4 — The Second Manassas Campaign — 17
Chapter 5 — The Maryland Campaign — 21
Chapter 6 — Stuart's Raid into Pennsylvania — 32
Chapter 7 — The Blue Ridge Campaign — 41
Chapter 8 — Picketing the Rappahannock — 46
Chapter 9 — The Gettysburg Campaign — 60
Chapter 10 — Late Summer and Fall of 1863 — 88
Chapter 11 — The Bristoe Campaign — 94
Chapter 12 — The Mine Run Campaign — 98
Chapter 13 — Winter of 1864 — 102
Chapter 14 — The Overland Campaign — 106
Chapter 15 — The Trevilian Campaign — 115
Chapter 16 — The Siege of Petersburg — 129
Chapter 17 — The Campaign of the Carolinas — 151

Afterword — 174
Appendix A — Commanding Officers — 177
Appendix B — Roster — 181
Appendix C — Original Members of Cobb's Legion Cavalry — 326
Appendix D — Greensboro Roster — 329
Appendix E — Killed in Action, Mortally Wounded in Action, or Death Attributed to Disease — 331
Appendix F — Prisoners of War — 335

*Appendix G — Those Who Went on Horse Detail to Georgia
with Capt. Bostick on September 20, 1864* 339
Appendix H — Last Record: Deserted or Absent Without Leave 342
Chapter Notes 343
Bibliography 347
Index 351

List of Maps

Seven Days Battle	9
Action at Massaponax Church	15
Second Manassas Campaign	19
Maryland Campaign	22
Stuart's Raid to Chambersburg	33
Blue Ridge Campaign	42
Picketing the Rappahannock	47
Battle of Brandy Station	62
Gettysburg Campaign/Brandy Station to Rowser's Ford	68
Gettysburg Campaign/Rowser's Ford to Martinsburg	72
Gettysburg/East Cavalry Field	82
Late Summer and Fall of 1863	89
Bristoe Campaign	95
Mine Run Campaign	99
Winter of 1864	103
Overland Campaign	107
Trevilian Raid/North Anna River	116
Trevilian Day 1	118
Trevilian Day 2	121
Trevilian Campaign	125
Siege of Petersburg/North of Petersburg	130
Weldon Railroad	132
South Carolina Campaign	152
North Carolina Campaign	160

All maps were created by Harriet Bey Mesic except "Gettysburg/East Cavalry Field," which was created by Hal Jespersen.

Preface

Cobb's Legion Cavalry was considered by many to be the most desirable regiment in which to serve. There were men who willingly gave up officers' commissions in the infantry for the privilege of serving as a private in this superior cavalry unit. These men fought in more than one hundred thirty named engagements during the course of the Civil War, crossing thousands of miles and seven states, and were in most of the major battles in the East.

Often during a cavalry charge, Cobb's Legion was placed in front and led the charge, as was the case at Dispatch Station, Haymarket, White Ridge Road, Barbee's Cross Roads, Little Washington, Dumfries, Brandy Station, Frying Pan Church, Parker's Store, Trevilian Station, and Hatcher's Run in Virginia; Frederick City and Burkittsville in Maryland; Hunterstown in Pennsylvania, and Fayetteville in North Carolina. Not only were the men skilled in fighting, but they could also be depended upon to give their all and hold their ground. They would not turn and run.

When a number of men from Cobb's Legion Cavalry were detached to take part in an action (such as Stuart's Raid to Chambersburg), there is no record of which men were chosen. However, it is possible to identify some of the men in a specific action from the records of those wounded or killed in action, or from diaries, letters, or a claim filed for a horse killed in battle.

Apparently, few of the men wrote diaries, most likely because they were almost constantly on the move. The diary of Col. Frederick Joseph Waring of the Jeff Davis Legion was very valuable in researching Cobb's Legion Cavalry because the Jeff Davis Legion served in the same brigade with them. After the war, Wiley C. Howard of Cobb's Legion Cavalry, Company C, wrote a very descriptive sketch of some of his experiences during the war, and Cobb's Legion Cavalry is mentioned many times in the *Official Records of the War of the Rebellion*.

During the last months of the war, when they were operating against Union Gen. William Tecumseh Sherman in the Carolinas, their records

Pvt. Owen Eugene J. O'Connor of Company I was born in County Cork, Ireland. He gave his age as 18 when he was mustered into service, but he was actually 15 years old. Photograph courtesy Owen Schweers.

were burned to prevent them from falling into the hands of the enemy. Although the details of many of these engagements are missing, the records that exist are nevertheless impressive. Sometimes the date of an action that occurred late in the war varied by a couple of days in various accounts, so an attempt has been made to put the actions in chronological order.

The men who fought with Cobb's Legion Cavalry were idealists, fighting for Southern freedom from Northern tyranny. It has been said,

> But little is known of the story of the cavalry. And yet they endured privation and death on the lonely picket with only the dead for company; they went down, rider and horse, in the desperate charge, the hand-to-hand encounter, in unnamed "skirmishes"; dismounted to fight, [they were] transformed into infantry, as brave and stubborn as ever grasped the rifle, they fell on fields, styled "cavalry affairs," unknown to fame. May a day come when justice will be done to their memory.[1]

The purpose of this book is to do justice to the memory of the gallant and heroic men of Cobb's Legion Cavalry.

CHAPTER 1

Creation of Cobb's Legion Cavalry

Organization

Cobb's Legion (or Cobb Legion) was organized by Colonel (afterwards Brigadier-General) Thomas Reade Rootes Cobb during the spring of 1861. It was mustered into Confederate service for the duration of the war during the month of September 1861 in DuBose's Brigade, Kershaw's Division, Longstreet's Corps.

In the beginning, men — who were promised a bounty of $50 — had to be at least eighteen years of age, enlist for three years or the duration of the war, and serve a year in the legion before they could collect the bounty. In 1864, men who enlisted under the age of 18 were promised a bounty of $50.

Originally, Cobb's Legion was composed of a battalion of cavalry, a battalion of infantry, and a battery of artillery, but the three arms never served together. The theory behind Civil War legions was that they would be capable of a great deal of independent activity. It did not take long to discover that the legion could not move any faster than its slowest unit, which, of course, was the artillery. Almost immediately, the artillery arm of Cobb's Legion was separated from the other two arms.

Within months, it was discovered that the logistics of cavalry and infantry serving in the same unit created impossible problems. Although the cavalry and infantry battalions of Cobb's Legion were not officially separated from one another until March 9, 1863, they actually stopped serving together as a consolidated command in the summer of 1862.

When the cavalry battalion reached regimental strength, it was designated as the 9th Regiment Georgia Volunteer Cavalry but continued to be referred to as Cobb's Legion. The cavalry battalion originally contained only five companies (Companies A, B, C, D, and G) recruited from various locations in the state of Georgia. Later, six additional companies were added (Companies E, F, H, I, K, and L). On July 11, 1864, the eleventh company was detached and transferred to Phillip's Legion, and Cobb's Legion Cavalry served with ten companies for the remainder of the war. Although Cobb's Legion was considered to be a Georgia regiment, men from several of the Southern states served in this unit.

Because of their dependability and many deeds of valor, the cavalry corps commander, Gen. Wade Hampton, often said that Cobb's Legion was "the best regiment of either army, North or South. Some regiments had one squadron that was better than the others, but the Cobb Legion never failed me no matter what squadron was in front."[1] (Squadron was another name for a company. It usually had about eighty men and three officers, although toward the end of the war the numbers dwindled.) Hampton said this in spite of the fact that many gallant regiments served under him from his own native state of South Carolina.

Function of the Cavalry

Southern cavalrymen, most of whom began riding in early childhood, were accomplished horsemen. They were chiefly country-bred, hardy men, who found it easy to make the transition into becoming cavalrymen and performing a fierce and furious charge.

In the Confederacy, the cavalrymen furnished their own horses, and they were the best their families could afford. Many were well-bred pets. Most of the horses cost more than a cavalry trooper earned in a year's time. The finest horses ridden by the most skillful horsemen added up to cavalry units that were surpassed by none.

At the time of a cavalryman's enlistment, he entered into a contract with the government. The contract required that the cavalryman had to supply his own horse, which was mustered into service at a fair market valuation. The government promised to provide feed, horseshoes and a smith to do the shoeing, and to pay the cavalryman forty cents per day for the use of his horse. If the horse was killed in action, the government agreed to pay the owner the muster valuation. If the horse was captured in battle, worn out, or disabled, the loss fell on the owner, who had to furnish another horse under the same conditions or be transferred to another arm of the service.

When a cavalryman's record stated that he was without a horse, or on "horse detail," and there is no record of the man being reimbursed for a horse killed in action, there is no way to tell if his horse died or if it were captured. In those cases, the horse is reported in this book as being "lost." When a record states that the man was on "horse detail," that meant he had been sent home to procure another horse.

The duties of the cavalry were many. They had to discover the points at which the enemy was planning to concentrate for an attack on the army. This meant the cavalry had to picket all approaches, report enemy movements, and skirmish with the Yankee cavalry. They had to do their best to defeat the enemy, and if they failed to stop them, they had to delay them to allow time for their own infantry to come up.

Frequently, they had to fight in order to mask the movements of their own army. They had to keep open the lines of communication through which supplies were obtained and protect the capital city of Richmond from raiding parties. They were always on the alert to capture or destroy the enemy's trains and depots, and to threaten or interfere with his lines of communication, and harass him in every conceivable manner.

During Grant's siege of Petersburg, the cavalry supplemented the infantry in the trenches, protected the exterior flanks, and resisted attacks. Throughout the war, they frequently suffered from a deficiency of clothing, shelter, and food, yet their fighting power was not impaired by these shortages. However, the depleted condition of the malnourished men put them at risk of becoming ill and impaired the healing of their wounds, contributing to their mortality rate.

Their regular daily rations were a half-pound of bacon or salt pork and a pint of cornmeal or flour for each man. Often, this was cut in half, and sometimes the half ration was reduced. After the capture of Federal cattle in September 1864, beef instead of pork was occasionally issued. In the late autumn of 1864, a very small amount of sugar and coffee was infrequently dispensed. There were never any rations of wine, whiskey or any other alcoholic beverage. At rare intervals, tobacco plugs were issued. Because of their numerous and unexpected movements, the cavalry was supplied more irregularly than the other branches of the service. Usually, foraging by the individual was forbidden, but that rule turned out to be pointless because the countryside in which they operated was often already stripped of supplies.

The pay for a private was $24 a month for himself and his horse, scarcely enough to buy a pair of shoes. The depreciated Confederate money had very limited purchasing power. However, the greatest disadvantage the cavalry operated under was not in the area of supplies and equipment, but in the shortage of manpower. They were badly outnumbered in practically every engagement with the enemy. While the enemy had a limitless pool of men, the men lost by the South were irreplaceable. The cavalry was often called the "eyes and ears of the army," but it was also the army's "claws."[2]

Uniforms, Arms, and Accoutrements

The state of Georgia made most of the things needed to arm and equip her men. The soldiers wore gray broadcloth uniforms manufactured in Georgia with C.S.A. buttons, and a two-piece Georgia state belt plate that supported swords made by W.J. McElroy Company of Macon, Georgia. Their revolvers were the Griswold and Gunnison copy of a Colt model manufactured in Griswoldville, Georgia. The Augusta Powder Works manufactured their percussion caps, powder, and bullets, along with the necessary belts and boxes.

The officers had gold sleeve knots and collar stars cut from a brass sheet by local manufacturers. The cavalry members wore yellow stripes on their trousers and yellow cords on their slouch hats. The artillery had red stripes and cords, and the infantry had blue stripes and cords.

The armaments of the Confederate cavalry were sorely inferior to those of their opponents. The Southern troopers generally possessed only muzzle-loaders, mostly Enfield rifles, compared to the breech-loading carbines, chiefly Spencer rifles, of the Union army. Repeating carbines captured from the enemy were useless because of the lack of ammunition. Captured magazine rifles were confiscated from the men in August 1864 because the lack of cartridges made them worthless at critical moments.

A man lying on the ground behind cover could not load an Enfield rifle, necessitating a greater exposure to the enemy. The cartridges were made of paper and subject to damage by dampness and rain and the rifles often misfired. The breech-loading carbines and magazine rifles of the Union troops were free from these defects. The Union troops armed with them should have been equal to twice the number of Southern troops with muzzle-loaders. Yet, the Confederate cavalrymen were often outnumbered two or more to one and still out-fought the Union cavalrymen on the battlefield. In addition, a considerable number of Confederate cavalrymen did not have revolvers, while the enemy was amply supplied with them.

The *Armament Report of the Cavalry Corps, December 15, 1864* stated that the number of men in Hampton's command was 5,552. Of those men, 1,100 were unarmed, 925 did not have long-range guns, and a large proportion were without revolvers. (This report covered only government issued arms and not personal weapons, which were private property and not subject to the inventory count. However, most of the men depended on the government to supply their weapons.) Fortunately, the powder the men used was always good, due largely to the skill and energy of Col. George Raines, the superintendent of the Powder Works of Augusta, Georgia.

Cobb's Legion Cavalry Companies

Staff commanders of Cobb's Legion Cavalry were Pierce Manning Butler Young and then Gilbert J. Wright.

Company A, the Richmond Hussars, was made up of men mostly from the town of Augusta, Georgia, and surrounding Richmond and Columbia counties. Thomas P. Stovall and Thomas B. Archer served as its officers. The original members enlisted on August 17, 1861, at Augusta, Georgia.

Company B, the Fulton Dragoons (also known as Bowden Volunteers, Zachariah Rice's Cavalry, Yancey's Cavalry, and Burr's Cavalry), was made up of men mostly from Fulton County, Georgia. Benjamin Cudworth Yancey, Zachariah A. Rice, Oliver Hazard Perry Juhan, and John Howard Burr served as its officers. The original members enlisted between July 30 and August 14, 1861, at Atlanta, Georgia.

Company C included William G. Delony's Cavalry and Georgia Troopers Company A, and was mostly made up of men from Clarke County, Georgia, with William G. Delony and Thomas C. Williams serving as its officers. The original members enlisted on August 1, 1861, at Athens, Georgia, and their muster rolls show that they were in Richmond, Virginia, by August 15, 1861.

Company D, the Dougherty Hussars (also known as Wright's Cavalry), was mostly made up of men from Dougherty County, Georgia, with Winburn J. Lawton, Gilbert J. Wright, Caleb Halstead Camfield, and Samuel D. Bostick serving as its officers. The original members enlisted on August 10, 1861, at Albany, Georgia.

Company E, the Roswell Troopers (also known as King's Cavalry), was mostly made up of men from Cobb and Gwinnett counties, Georgia, with Barrington S. King and William Choice Dial serving as its officers. The original members enlisted between March 15 and March 24, 1862, at Roswell, Georgia, and April 9, 1862, at Lawrenceville, Georgia.

Company F, Georgia Hussars (also known as Grubb's Hussars) was mostly made up of men from Burke County, Georgia, with Malcolm Daniel Jones and William R. "Bill" Roberts serving as its officers. The original members enlisted March 25, 1862, at Burke County, Georgia.

Company G, the Fulton Dragoons Company B, was mostly made up of men from Fulton County, Georgia, with William M. Williams serving as its officer. The original members enlisted July 3–29, 1861, at Madison, Georgia.

Company H, the Georgia Troopers Company B, was mostly made up of men from Clarke County, Georgia, with Jeremiah E. Ritch serving as its officer. The original members enlisted February 16, 1862, at Lynchburg, Virginia, and February 22–25, 1862, at Athens, Georgia.

Company I, the Richmond Hussars Company B, was mostly made up of men from Fulton and Richmond counties, Georgia, with J. Jefferson Thomas and William B. Young serving as its officers. The original members enlisted from February 13, 1862, to April 21, 1862, at Augusta, Georgia.

Company K, the Richmond Dragoons (also known as Eve's Cavalry) was mostly made up of men from Richmond County, Georgia, with Francis Edgeworth Eve serving as its officer. The original members enlisted February 2–6, 1862, at Camp Maynard, Georgia.

Company L was mostly made up of men from DeKalb County, Georgia, with Alpheus M. Rodgers serving as its officer. The original members enlisted March 17, 1862, at Athens, Georgia.

Civil War units were sometimes known by alternate designations. Often these were the name of the commanding officer. Cobb's Legion Cavalry was also called the Cobb Legion and Young's Cavalry (for Pierce Manning Butler Young).

Chapter 2

The Peninsula Campaign

Richmond

By early September 1861, all the troopers of Cobb's Legion Cavalry had been sent from Georgia to a camp near Richmond, Virginia, where Lt. Pierce Manning Butler Young became their drillmaster. It was a job at which he proved to be very skillful. At age twenty-five Young had lived in Georgia for twenty-three years. He was born in South Carolina. He had lacked three months of graduating from West Point when the war began. The fact that Cobb's Legion Cavalry earned the reputation of being the best regiment in either army, North or South, no doubt had a lot to do with the excellent training they received from Young. On September 11, 1861, Cobb's Legion Cavalry was ordered to Yorktown, Virginia, to join the Army of the Peninsula. Before they left Richmond, Young was promoted to major.

Company Notes
September 1–30, 1861

Company C — Died: Miles A. Anderson

Yorktown

The Army of the Peninsula was a unit of less than 10,000 men, under the command of the ostentatious general John Bankhead Magruder, who was derisively called "Prince John" by his troops. He prided himself on his lordly airs and appearance and did not wear a Confederate uniform, but a uniform he had fashioned for himself that included a black felt hat and a black overcoat with a cape.

The first service for Cobb's Legion Cavalry was at Camp Marion below Yorktown. At the time, Yorktown was considered to be the key to holding the peninsula and protecting Richmond from the east. While they were at Camp Marion, Young was promoted to lieutenant colonel.

On October 3, 1861, they were sent to Camp Washington, located in a place near Yorktown called Cockletown. The cavalry camped with the infantry and artillery units of Cobb's Legion, except when they were detailed for other service, usually vidette duty. (Videttes were mounted sentinels posted in advance of the army.)

By this time, the fall rains typical for Virginia had set in with the accompanying mud and cold. Many sicknesses in the camp accompanied the foul weather, and casualties began to occur. Col. Thomas Cobb found that he did not like Virginia as much as he had hoped.

In November, he and his brother Howell wrote a joint letter to the War Department, requesting the transfer of their commands to Georgia, but their request was not acted on, so Cobb's Legion remained in Virginia.

A roster of the Second Division, Department of the Peninsula, listed Cobb's Legion under the command of Gen. Lafayette McLaws of Georgia. The men continued performing vidette duty, with its accompanying dangers.

Company Notes
October 1861–February 1862

Company A — Died: Uriah Blanchard
Company B — Died: Julius Michael Frix
Company C — Died: Edward A. Anderson, William J. Helton
Company D — Died: William B. Cochran, James N. McCullum, W.W. Mershew, C.W. Wilder

Protecting the Railroads

The leaders of the Confederacy believed that the Union would try to separate Kentucky, Tennessee, Virginia, and North Carolina from the states of the Deep South before attempting to crush the remainder of the Confederacy. Before the Union could seize Virginia and North Carolina, it would first have to control the railroads. To control the railroads, they would have to take Norfolk and Suffolk, Virginia. After Norfolk was evacuated and left to the enemy, holding on to Suffolk became an essential part of the Confederate defense plan.

An order was issued on Tuesday, March 4, 1862, for 5,000 men, including the 350 men of Cobb's Legion Cavalry, to cross the James River at King's Mill at old Jamestown, Virginia, and then proceed to Suffolk, Virginia. They spent just a few days in Suffolk before being ordered to travel on the Wilmington & Weldon Railroad to Goldsboro, North Carolina. They arrived there on Saturday, March 22, and set up camp a few miles outside the city at Camp Randolph. Unfortunately, they were once again plagued by disease.

Company Notes
March 4–17, 1862

Company A — Died: James F. Chavous
Company B — Died: Bennett Boler
Company C — Died: James H. Garner
Company D — Died: William H. Sibley

Camp Meadow

Around the middle of March, the Federal army began transporting men from Washington to Fort Monroe, Virginia. On March 18, 1862, orders were issued for the men to return from North Carolina to the Virginia peninsula and report for duty to Gen. Magruder. The cavalry was to march with the baggage wagons to Carter's Wharf and cross the James River to Jamestown Island. On Friday, April 4, the army of Union Gen. George B. McClellan advanced on Yorktown.

Cobb's Legion Cavalry moved to a place below Richmond called Camp Meadow to do vidette duty along the Chickahominy River. The men did not have tents, and trees were their only protection from the almost incessant rain. On April 22, Col. Thomas Cobb reported, "For two weeks my command have been exposed to severe weather in the trenches and not a pint of whiskey could be provided them nor a grain of coffee."[1]

On April 12, the Army of the Peninsula became a part of Gen. Joseph E. Johnston's command. Johnston, who was the commander of the Army of Northern Virginia, withdrew his troops from their lines in front of Manassas and sent them to reinforce Magruder's troops, who had built heavy earthworks, forts, and entrenchments from the York River on the east

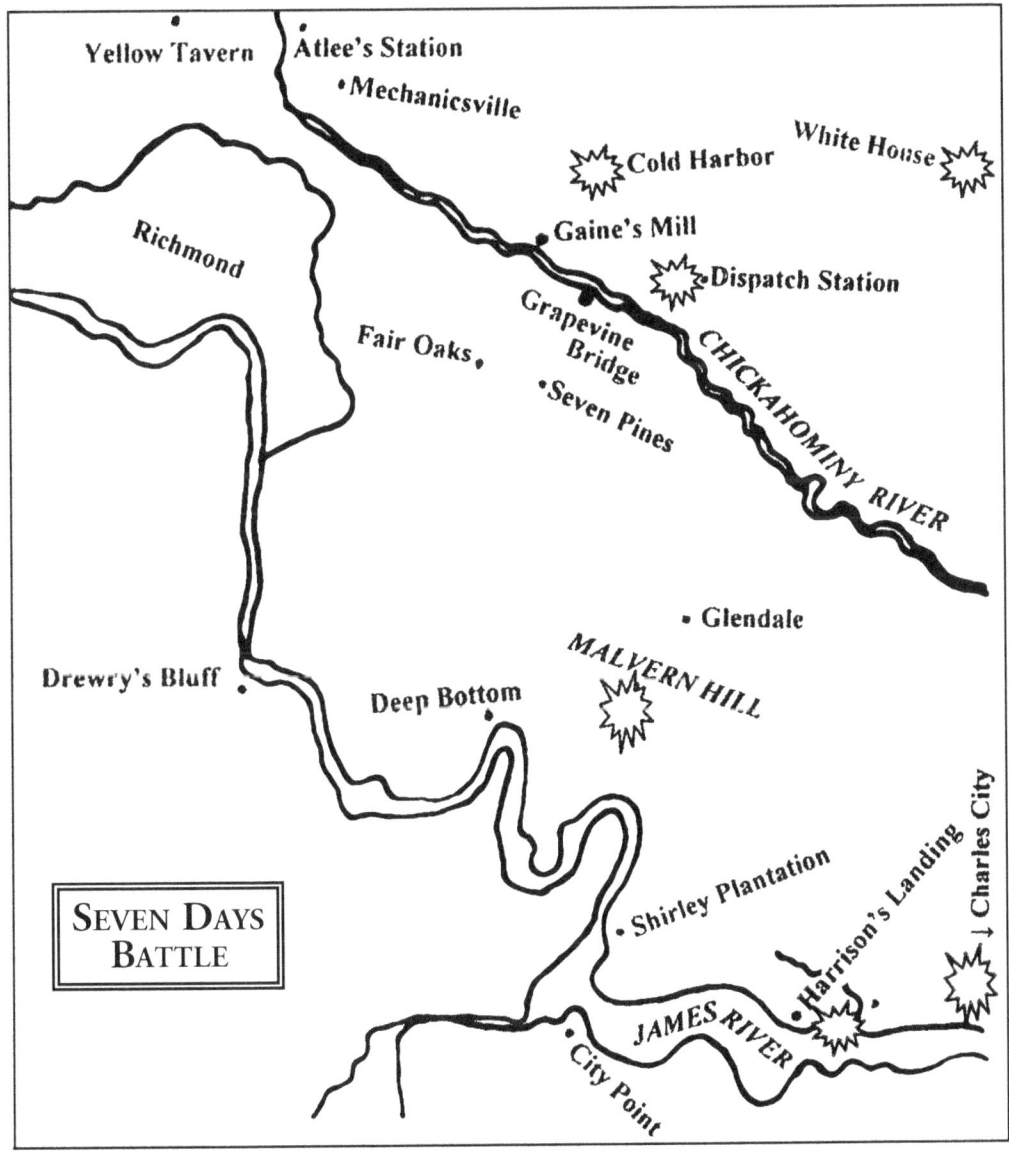

to the James River on the south and west. At that time, the Union army had its base of operations at Fort Monroe, Virginia. They were supported by a strong naval force in the adjoining waters and had the advantage of the best strategic position.

Johnston had no naval support. Since he was on a peninsula, both of his flanks were exposed to attack from the Federal warships, and he had a long line of communication to his base in Richmond. On Saturday, May 3, 1862, Johnston began an evacuation of Yorktown and retreated toward Richmond. A few days later Cobb's Legion Cavalry was sent to Guiney's (Guinea's) Station, while the infantry and artillery branches of the legion remained with Gen. Magruder, participating in the evacuation of Yorktown.

On May 28, 1862, Gen. Joseph Johnston separated the cavalry from the rest of Cobb's Legion, and they would never again serve together as a unit. He placed Cobb's Legion Cavalry in Gen. Wade Hampton's brigade, which was under the command of the flamboyant and brilliant cavalry commander, Gen. James Ewell Brown (J.E.B.) Stuart.

Sometime between May 28 and June 25, Cobb's Legion Cavalry returned to Camp Meadow. Both measles and typhoid fever plagued the troopers.

Company Notes
March 18–June 24, 1862

Company B — Died: William Harris (may have been in the infantry), James H. Todd
Company C — Died: Walton T. Barrett, Abel B.C. Densmore, Green B. Jackson
Company D — Wounded: William Bryson
Company E — Wounded: James A. Allbritten
Company F — Wounded: J.D. Huckabee (may have been in the infantry)
Company H — Died: William Boyd Tuck

Chapter 3

The Seven Days Campaign

Cold Harbor

On the evening of Wednesday, June 25, 1862, the day that the Seven Days Battles began, Cobb's Legion Cavalry was given an hour's notice to leave their camp and cross the Chickahominy River. The men had three days' rations in their haversacks and they traveled without baggage.

On the Brook Turnpike, they joined Gen. J.E.B. Stuart, along with the 1st, 4th, and 9th Virginia cavalries, and the Jeff Davis Legion, and then marched until they met Gen. Stonewall Jackson near Ashland, Virginia. Jackson, who was all covered with dust, was riding at the head of his troops. They had just arrived from the Shenandoah Valley. Jackson was

> mounted upon a dun [dull grayish-brown] cob [a short, thick-set breed of horse] of rather sorry appearance, though substantial in build, and was dressed in a threadbare, faded, semi-military suit, with a disreputable old Virginia Military Institute cap drawn down over his eyes, presenting a strong contrast to the dashing appearance and splendid mount of Stuart and his staff, all in full Confederate gray uniforms, cocked felt hats and long black plumes, and high cavalry boots.[1]

Jackson's men, who were attempting to flank McClellan, cheered enthusiastically when they saw Stuart. The cavalry took their position as advance guard to the front and left of Jackson and his troops, so they could keep Jackson informed of the enemy's movements. This put the cavalry between Jackson and the enemy as they moved toward Mechanicsville, Virginia. There was constant skirmishing with the Union cavalry along the route, and by 10:00 that night, the enemy was in full retreat. That night, the men slept on the field.

After moving from Ashland on Friday, June 27, to the battlefield at Gaines Mill, then to the battlefield at Cold Harbor, Cobb's Legion Cavalry had its first experience under fire. For two hours the men were mounted and drawn up in a battle line while waiting to charge the enemy. Unfortunately, they were exposed to the enemy's artillery fire. A trooper described the experience as follows:

> ...the bursting of shells and the occasional whizzing of minie balls about us, the terrific roar of musketry and booming of cannon to our right, the clouds of dust that noted the track of the moving combatants, the occasional sight of the wounded being taken back, and wild cheering of Jackson's men and others as they pressed back the serried ranks of the foe from one line of defense to another, the rapid riding of couriers and staff officers scurrying hither and thither with messages and orders to commanding officers.[2]

Shells were exploding over their heads and under their horses, so Col. Cobb moved them to the cover of a hill. Fortunately, no casualties occurred. The battery they were waiting to attack withdrew from the battlefield, making the charge unnecessary. Instead, until nightfall, the men pursued the retreating foe, skirmishing and taking prisoners in the process.

Company Notes
June 25–27, 1862

Company I — Died: Stephen F. Burnley

Dispatch Station

When night came, the legion had gone what seemed to them a long way, and they found themselves passing among the dead and wounded. They had their first experience of hearing the heartrending groans and cries of the wounded for "Help!" and "Water!" A countersign of "Tomlinson" was whispered from man to man, and they continued their slow march until very late that night. The troopers slept on the battlefield, surrounded by the dead and the wounded of the enemy. The whole night they could hear groaning and praying all around them.

After resting on their arms, the men arose early the next morning, Saturday, June 28, 1862, and rode about fifteen or sixteen miles with Stuart to the plantation called White House on the Pamunkey River near West Point, Virginia. (White House was the home of Robert E. Lee's son, William Henry Fitzhugh [Rooney] Lee.) McClellan had his main supply base at White House. They took a route parallel to Gen. Richard (Dick, Old Bald Head) Stoddert Ewell, and passed the head of his column near Dispatch Station. When they reached Dispatch Station, they found it defended by Federal cavalry.

Stuart ordered Maj. William G. Delony of Company C to lead Cobb's Legion Cavalry in a charge of the station and to clear it. This was the legion's first time to lead a charge, but it would not be their last. When they charged, the enemy fled, leaving the ground strewn with carbines and pistols. The troopers pursued them and found another company of enemy cavalry waiting in a battle line beyond the station which they charged and routed. After dispersing the enemy, the men captured three wagons along with their teams of horses and sent several prisoners to the rear. They tore up the railroad and cut the telegraph wires, breaking communication between the Union forces and their base. Sometime during the day, while skirmishing, Cobb's Legion Cavalry lost its first man killed in battle, after having lost twenty-one men to disease.

That night, Union soldiers set fire to their own supply base at White House, lighting up the sky for miles around as clouds of smoke rose hundreds of feet into the air.

Company Notes
June 28, 1862

Company A — Killed: Henry Hillens
Company B — Died: Henry N. Ash
Company C — Wounded: William H. Early, Fred W. Walter

White House

The next day, Sunday, June 29, 1862, only one of the enemy's gunboats remained. After exchanging a few shots, it steamed away. Although the enemy had destroyed most of its stores, vast quantities were left untouched, enough to supply all of the men and horses of Stuart's command. The Confederates found it curious to see, compared to their scant rations, the luxuries that the Union army enjoyed. They found the following:

> ...barrels of sugar, lemons by the millions, cases of wine, beer and other liquors of every description, confectionery, canned meats, and fruits and vegetables, and great quantities of ice, all in excellent condition. The eggs were packed in barrels of salt, and where they had been exposed to fire, the salt was fused into a solid cake with the eggs, deliciously roasted, distributed throughout the mass; it was only necessary to split off a block and then pick out the eggs, like the meat of a nut.[3]

Some of the men accompanied Col. Thomas Cobb to Tunstall Station, where they destroyed tracks and cars. That evening they rejoined the rest of the command at White House. On Monday, June 30, a squadron was left at the White House to complete the destruction there, with orders to preserve specific items and send them to Richmond. This squadron did not rejoin the others until Thursday, July 10.

When Cobb's Legion Cavalry left White House, the weather was dreadfully hot, without a breath of air stirring among the dismal pine forests of Virginia. The sweaty troopers rode to Forge Bridge, where they spent the night. At 3:30 the next morning, they moved out with orders to cross the Chickahominy at Grapevine Bridge in order to connect with Jackson. At Bottom's Bridge, they discovered that the army had moved to the south and that they would have to retrace their steps and cross at a lower ford to find Jackson. After backtracking, they forded the river at Forge Bridge and rode, past Nance's Shop, until they arrived at Malvern Hill, where a bloody battle had taken place. The next morning a dense fog hung over the battlefield and a drizzling rain was falling. They observed details of men busy at work collecting the dead and placing them in rows. The troopers left the ghastly scene to screen from the enemy the withdrawal of the Confederate troops.

Company Notes
June 29–July 10, 1862

Company B — Captured: John Howard Burr
Company E — Wounded: John P.M. Bird
Company H — Died: Aaron Brian, James Brian
Company I — Died: Joseph J. Kennedy; Captured: Michael Hanlon

Haxall's and Herring Creeks

On Thursday, July 3, 1862, Stuart ordered Cobb's Legion Cavalry to take a position near Shirley Plantation on the James River, in the rear of the enemy. There they found a rear guard of about 2,000 Federal infantry, one battery of artillery, and about 500 cavalry protecting a wagon train of 300 to 400 wagons, but they were unable to attack them without reinforcements. Unfortunately, the additional troops did not arrive in time. However, they captured numerous prisoners and collected a large number of small arms and other stores, while pursuing the retreating enemy on the river road.

They skirmished with the enemy at Haxall's Creek and Herring Creek (Harrison's Landing) on July 3 and 4, but they came under attack from a gunboat. Afterward, Francis Edgeworth Eve of Company A (later of Company K) quipped that "The gun boat's terrible firing forced us to believe that it would not do to charge ironclads, even on thoroughbreds."[4]

The Confederate army had withdrawn to a position nearer to Richmond, while the enemy held a strong position at Harrison's Landing. The two armies had a month of inactivity; however, the cavalry picketed on the Charles City front and frequently skirmished with the enemy, while the infantry rested.

**Company Notes
July 3–11, 1862**

Company A — Died: Alexander Hope
Company D — Captured: Dwight David Hays; Died: W. McDonald, J.J. Wise (may
   have been in the infantry)
Company E — Captured: James Buregard Chambers

Malvern Hill

Cobb's Legion Cavalry fell back to the vicinity of Malvern Hill, where they found that the country was stripped of the forage that they needed for their horses. For several weeks they did picket duty and skirmished with the enemy daily (and nightly). Eve reported: "[That was] our only way to drill new recruits."[5]

During the Seven Days Battle, according to official reports, Cobb's Legion Cavalry lost 1 killed, 2 wounded, and 1 missing. An examination of the men's service records shows that the casualties were a little higher.

Cavalry headquarters was established north of Richmond near Atlee's Station on Thursday, July 12. While they were there, the cavalry held its first brigade review, which was attended by the ladies from the surrounding countryside. Headquarters was moved to the Hanover Court House grounds on July 21, with the cavalry and horse artillery encamped around the village.

There was another reorganization of the army on July 28. Cobb's Legion Cavalry remained a part of Hampton's Brigade, Stuart's Corps, with Col. P.M.B. Young serving as its commanding officer. At this time, additional men were recruited into Cobb's Legion Cavalry until it was raised to regiment size.

The cavalry lines often extended over a front of forty or more miles, so it was necessary to keep couriers at headquarters to carry dispatches. The couriers were picked from the most reliable men with the best mounts. During the course of the war, those couriers from Cobb's Legion included J.T. Adams, S.D. Adams, Lewis Walton Barrett, Ethelbert Penn Bedell, Albert W.J. Carter, John William Clark, Robert T. Clingan, John Coston, William Macon Crumley, Elias Crockett Downs, Lewis R. Ford, Adolphus S. Gantt, Robert W. Gondelock, Nathan Goodman, Jasper B. Groves, Charles R.A. Harris, William O. Harrison, Thomas A. Holliday Paschal, William C. Houser, Elisha S. Howse, Martin V.B. Howse, Daniel J. Irby, John F. Isdal,

Chapter 3—The Seven Days Campaign

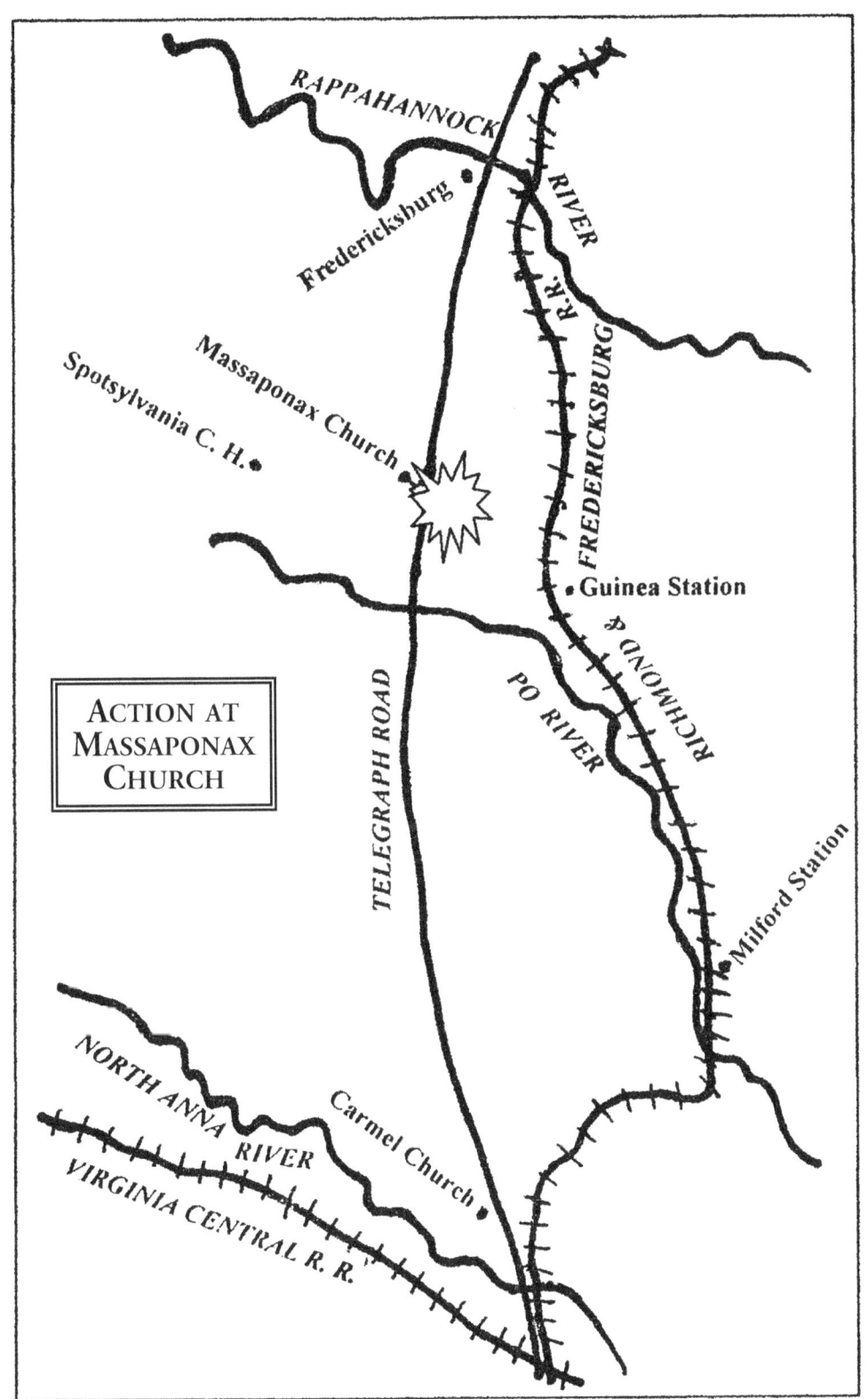

Thomas D. Johnson, Wiley M. Leatherwood, Henry M. McCroan, Lemuel S. Mead, Josiah Miller, Henry Alex Mitchell, Richard Moore, Moses Collins Murphey, James Rutherford Polk Nash, James Hamilton Nelson, A.B. Phelps, Henry N. Rhodes, Martin W. Riden, Andrew Jackson Rylee, Gustavus Schlesinger, Lewis Blackburn Scudder, Alexander P. Smith, Henry Strickland, Francis D. Tanner, J.R. Thomas, Calhoun H. Turner, Stephen Turner, James B. Waters, Frank R. Wilson, and Charles C. Winder.

The enemy attempted to reoccupy Malvern Hill on Saturday, August 2. Cobb's Legion Cavalry came under heavy artillery fire, and two men from Company C were captured and two were reported to be killed. Afterwards Gen. Lee wrote to "express to Lt. Col. Young my sense of the courage and efficiency which marked the conduct of himself, his officers and men, and of the success which attended his efforts against a superior force of the enemy."[6]

On July 25, Stuart was promoted to major-general and the cavalry was organized into two brigades, listed below:

1st Brigade, Gen. Wade Hampton, commanding:

Cobb's Legion Cavalry	Lt. Col. Pierce M.B. Young
1st NC Cavalry	Col. Laurence Simmons Baker
Jeff Davis Legion	Lt. Col. Wm. Thompson Martin
Hampton Legion	Maj. Matthew Calbraith Butler
10th VA Cavalry	Lt. Col. Z. S. Magruder

2nd Brigade, Gen. Fitzhugh Lee, commanding:

1st VA Cavalry	Col. L. Tiernan Brien
3rd VA Cavalry	Col. Thomas F. Goode
4th VA Cavalry	Col. Williams C. Wickham
5th VA Cavalry	Col. Thomas L. Rosser
9th VA Cavalry	Col. W.H.F. (Rooney) Lee

Company Notes
July 12–August 4, 1862

Company A — Wounded: Radford C. Rhodes

Company B — Died: James A. Harris, Coleman W. Marchman; Wounded: Charles N. Tank

Company D — Died: Carlos Williams (may have been in the infantry)

Company E — Died: Berrimon Woodruff

Company F — Wounded: Elisha S. Mallory

Company G — Died: Pickens Noble Calhoun

Company H — Died: O.M. Buffington, Ezekiel Francis Gilmer, James S. House

Chapter 4

The Second Manassas Campaign

Thornburg (Massaponax Church)

Cobb's Legion Cavalry marched north with the rest of Stuart's Cavalry in early August. They were leading an advance of Stonewall Jackson's army across the Rapidan River because Lee was preparing to encounter Union Gen. John Pope. During the intensely hot weather of Tuesday, August 5, 1862, the cavalry surprised Union forces at Thornburg, Virginia (Massaponax Church), fifteen miles from Fredericksburg. The Union troops were on an expedition down Telegraph Road (roughly current U.S. Route 1) from Fredericksburg to destroy the Virginia Central Railroad, which ran from Richmond to Gordonsville.

The Confederate cavalry used an alternate road, which ran through the woods parallel to Telegraph Road. When they came within sight of the enemy, they skirmished with the Union cavalry until they were fired upon by Union artillery. Being badly outnumbered, they withdrew but were successful in halting the enemy's advance. The Union forces, unaccustomed to such heat, were completely prostrated by it and unable to go any farther.

The next day the enemy brought up reinforcements from Fredericksburg, but the Confederate cavalry skirmished with them for two and a half hours, once again preventing their advance down Telegraph Road to the Virginia Central Railroad. Fifty-nine of the Yankees were taken as prisoners.

While at Massaponax Church, Francis Edgeworth Eve of Company A was sent out to scout the area. Neither he nor his horse had anything to eat during the thirty-six hours of scouting. After returning to camp and making his report, he went to get some food. When he discovered that there was nothing left for him, he said that his language was "neither chaste nor elegant." Just then he heard Maj. Delony say, "Come here, sir." He followed Delony into a tent, where he was ordered to sit down on a blanket. Delony threatened to make him carry a fence rail if he ever spoke of what was about to happen. Delony passed Eve his "historic flask" and then had his servant give Eve food from the major's haversack. Eve said, "I was ordered to eat my fill and make no more disturbance in camp or I would be sent to the guard house."[1]

While minor battles were being fought along the Rappahannock River, confirming Pope's location along the river, Lee ordered Jackson to swing around Pope and go through Thoroughfare Gap. This forced Pope to abandon his defensive line along the river. Meanwhile, James Longstreet's army moved north and then east through Thoroughfare Gap to join with Jackson's army, so together they could confront Pope.

Company Notes
August 5–28, 1862

Company A — Captured: Francis Marion Stovall
Company C — Captured: William P. Dearing; Died: John H. Cowen, William W. Smith
Company E — Captured: James A. Netherland
Company H — Captured: George W. McElhanon

Catlett's Station

Union troops had begun leaving Harrison's Landing on August 11, 1862, and had completed their evacuation by August 16. As the rest of the Confederate army moved into central Virginia, Hampton's cavalrymen were left to watch the Charles City and Fredericksburg front. Then on Friday, August 22, they crossed the Rapahannock at Waterloo Bridge and joined Stuart. After marching through Warrenton to Auburn, they arrived near Catlett's Station after dark. By then the rain was falling in torrents. Although they captured the enemy's pickets and were in the midst of the enemy's camps, they could not attack because it was so dark that they could not see anything.

Stuart, with other members of the cavalry, captured a number of Pope's staff officers, a large sum of money, and Pope's dispatch book, papers, personal baggage and other property. Before daylight Stuart's command withdrew and returned to Warrenton Springs, bringing with them more than three hundred prisoners.

Company Notes
August 11–29, 1862

Company C — Died: Aquilla Bruce

2nd Manassas (2nd Bull Run)

On Saturday August 30, 1862, Cobb's Legion Cavalry saw action in the Second Battle of Bull Run. They were positioned on Stonewall Jackson's right flank, at Groveton Heights near Dorkins Branch, where some of the most savage fighting took place; however, it was after 5:00 in the evening before they were brought into action. As Longstreet swept forward, pushing Pope back, they covered his right flank. Near Bull Run Creek, they encountered the enemy's cavalry, who for the first time showed them resistance. In the open fields the men fought with sabers. The battle continued until 10:00 that night, when the Southerners drove the enemy pell-mell across Bull Run, killing and capturing a large number of them.

Stuart wrote about the battle: "The fight was of remarkably short duration. The Lord of Hosts was plainly fighting on our side, and the solid walls of Federal infantry melted away before the straggling but determined onset of our infantry columns."[2]

Eve said, "[V]ictory of the 2nd Manassas put an end to Pope's vain glorious proclamations and boastings, but unfortunately made our own more sensible generals lose their heads,

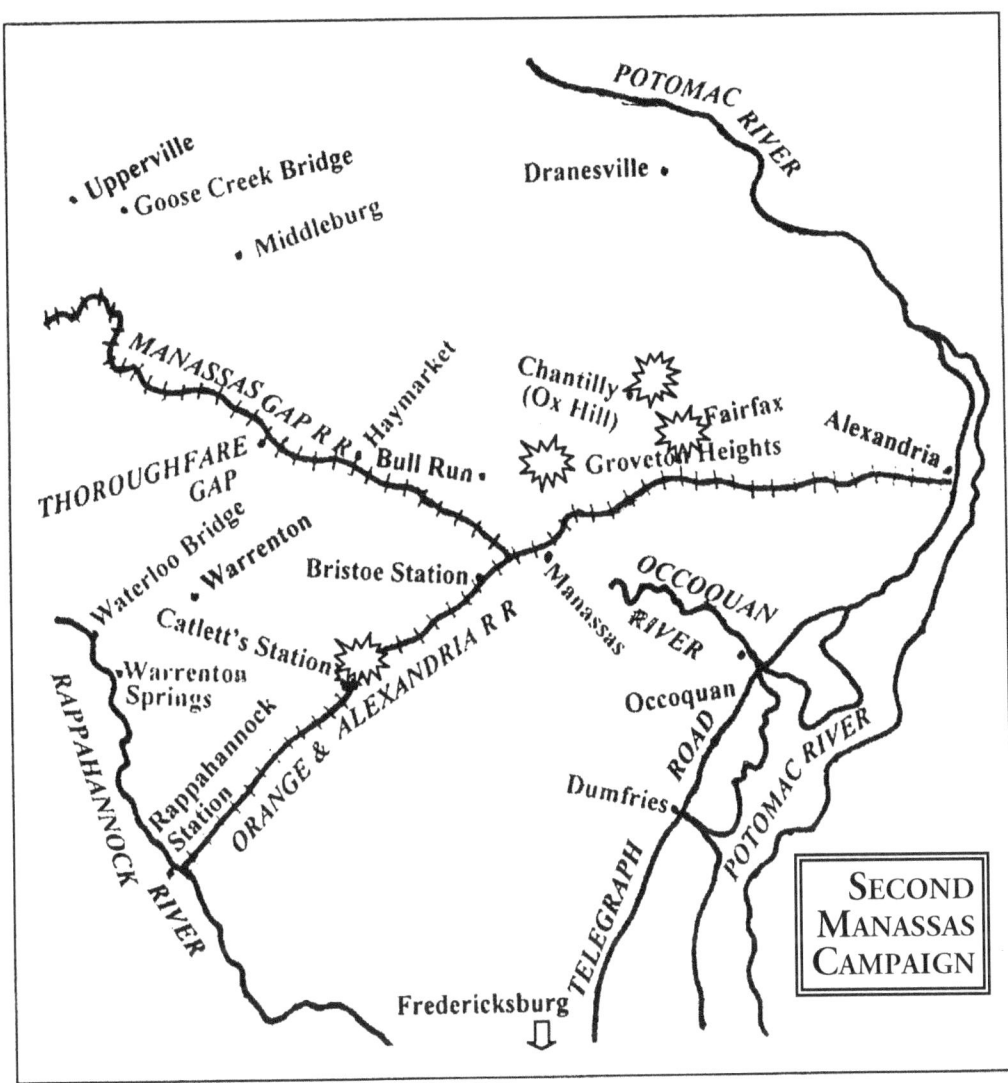

as they then believed the A.N.V. [Army of Northern Virginia] could whip anything on the planet, no matter how great the odds."[2]

**Company Notes
August 30, 1862**

Company H — Wounded: William J. King

Chantilly (Ox Hill)

After the battle of Manassas, the cavalry pursued Pope's army towards Washington and had "numerous tilts with the Yankee cavalry."[3] At 10:00 on the night of the battle, a heavy rainstorm began, impeding the movements of Lee's army but giving the enemy the opportunity to escape. The next afternoon it was still raining as the cavalry marched along a route parallel to the retreating enemy. The cavalry made camp at 10:00 that night near Chantilly Plantation.

The next afternoon, Monday, September 1, 1862, as the rain came down in torrents, Stuart's cavalry moved down the Little River Turnpike in front of Jackson's men, who were southeast of Chantilly at Ox Hill. The cavalry was ambushed by Pope's men, who were hidden in the woods around the turnpike. Fortunately, they sprang their ambush too soon, giving Jackson the opportunity to bring up several regiments to support the cavalry. The rainstorm was raging so violently during the battle that it drowned out the roar of the cannon.

If Jackson had been defeated, the Confederate cavalry would have been dangerously exposed, but, fortunately, after a hot engagement, Stuart's men found Pope's army moving toward Washington. Soon after dark, it became obvious that Pope's army was in full flight. That night the cavalry camped in a pine grove; they dried their clothing in front of roaring campfires that they kept lit all night.

The next morning, the cavalry followed a trail of burning houses and barns left by the Union army and skirmished with the enemy along the route, until they reached Fairfax, Virginia. When the Confederate cavalry rode into Fairfax, they planted their battle flag in the town square, where they were enthusiastically welcomed by the citizens of the town, who had endured the hardships of Union occupation for many months.

After leaving Fairfax, Stuart took the cavalry, which had more than doubled in size since the Seven Days Battle, to Dranesville, Virginia, where they made camp. Stuart declared September 4 to be a day of rest for his cavalrymen.

Company Notes
August 31–September 4, 1862

Company B — Wounded: William F. Lampkin

Chapter 5

The Maryland Campaign

Hyattstown, Maryland

On Friday, September 5, 1862, Stuart's Cavalry followed behind Lee's army to Leesburg, Virginia. That night, in the clear moonlight, Cobb's Legion Cavalry and the rest of the Confederate cavalrymen plunged across the Potomac River at White's Ford, where the banks of the river were sixty feet high and topped by towering vine-wrapped trees. The water reached to the saddles of the horses, and some of the smaller horses had to swim to make the crossing. As the horses climbed the bank on the opposite shore, the band played a stirring rendition of "Maryland, My Maryland." The cavalry rode for two or three miles in the moonlight until they reached the town of Poolesville, Maryland, where they were eagerly greeted by the townsfolk.

The next day, as Lee's army moved to Frederick City, Maryland, the cavalry units resumed their march on its right flank, with Hampton's brigade in the front. That night they halted at Urbana, Maryland. The next day, Stuart positioned his cavalry brigades so that they formed a twenty-mile long curtain of outposts east of Lee's army. Cobb's Legion Cavalry, with Hampton's brigade, was located near Hyattstown, Maryland, in the center of a line that spread from the Potomac River to the Baltimore & Ohio Railroad tracks, south of Frederick City, Maryland.

The plan was for the cavalry to skirmish with the enemy when they appeared, fending them off as long as possible and reporting back to Lee on the enemy's strength, location, and intentions. Their horses stood saddled day and night, and the men slept with their clothes, boots, and spurs on. Stuart reported that "Hampton's brigade became engaged in several skirmishes near Hyattstown, driving the enemy back on every occasion."[1]

Company Notes
September 5–10, 1862

Company C — Died: Berry T. Grindle, Samuel D. Means
Company G — Wounded: George Winship
Company Unknown — Died: Jasper Wells (may have been in the infantry)

Frederick City, Maryland

On Thursday, September 11, 1862, the left wing of the Federal army moved forward, forcing Col. Thomas T. Munford's 2nd Virginia Cavalry from Sugar Loaf Mountain. On the next

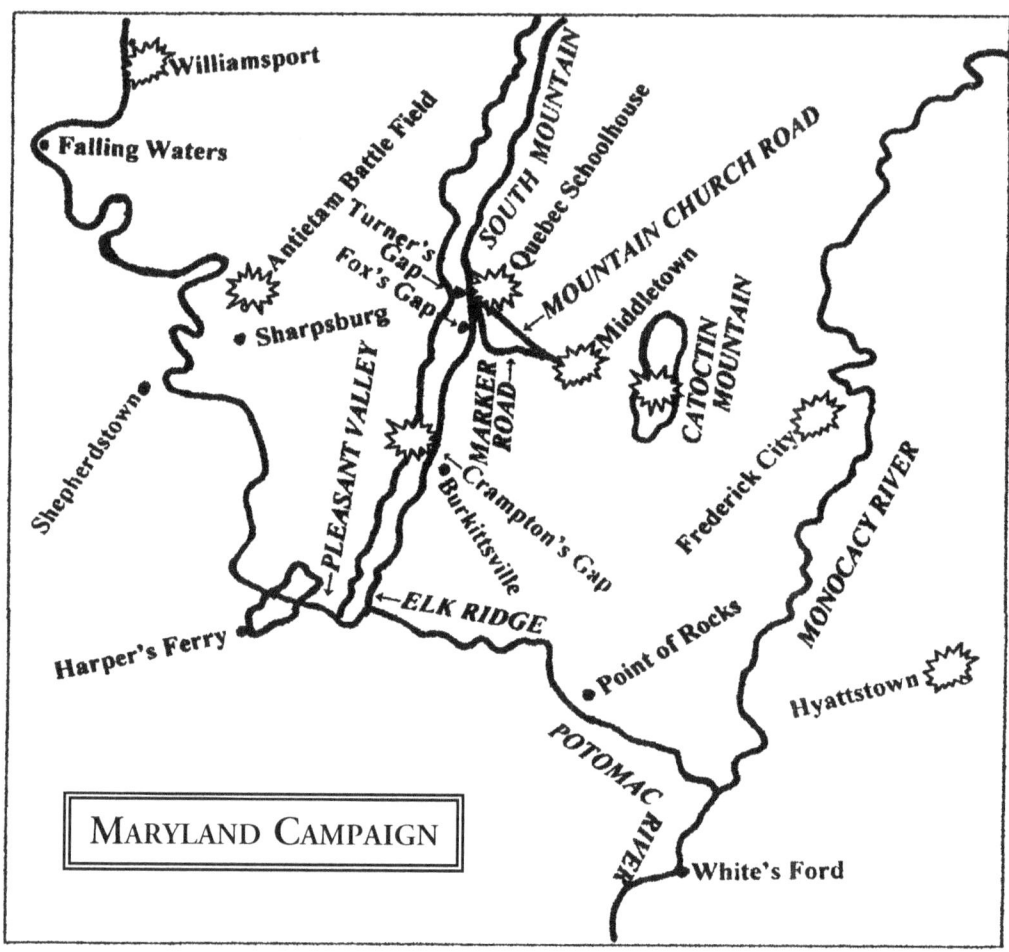

day, the whole line of the enemy began to advance, forcing all of Stuart's troopers to withdraw from their positions. Stuart directed Hampton's brigade to occupy Frederick City, Maryland, in the rear of Lee's army, which was moving toward Middletown, Maryland. Hampton placed pickets along the various roads that led to Frederick. Two companies from Cobb's Legion Cavalry were left on picket duty at the bridge over the Monocacy River, between Frederick City and Urbana.

Dan O'Connor and Wiley C. Howard were on advance picket duty on the National Road when they saw what looked like McClellan's whole army coming up the road. They exchanged shots with the advance guard and then fell back to their reserve, which consisted of fifteen men under Lt. Tom House. Howard told House that fifteen men could not hold off McClellan's whole army. House's reply was "By jaunties, give 'em h—l anyhow."[2]

It was imperative that the approach by the National Road be held until the companies left there could be withdrawn. Stuart added a rifle piece to the two guns already in position on the turnpike, and a squadron from Butler's 2nd SC Cavalry was sent to support the batteries. The enemy soon appeared and opened fire on the cavalry. When, the companies from the bridge were able to rejoin him, General Hampton slowly retired toward Frederick City, sending his artillery ahead of him to occupy high ground between the city and the mountain. It was about noon when the troopers entered Frederick City.

Both Union and Confederate banners were hanging from the balconies in the town, testifying to the divided loyalties of the people. Through some of the open windows, the men could hear women singing "Dixie" and "The Bonnie Blue Flag." The enemy moved forward, placed a gun in the suburbs, and then opened fire down the crowded streets of the city, showing no regard for the safety of the civilians. The 30th Ohio Infantry and two companies of enemy cavalry were supporting the gun. Not wanting to endanger the population with gunfire, Stuart ordered his men to charge the enemy, in order to protect Hampton's brigade as it retreated. During the course of the battle, Cobb's Legion Cavalry made a saber charge in the streets of Frederick City, scattering the enemy in all directions and capturing Col. August Moor of the 28th Ohio Infantry. After the enemy was repulsed, the brigade retired slowly, taking with them the prisoners they had captured. They bivouacked that night at Middletown, Maryland, leaving the Jeff Davis Legion to hold the gap in Catoctin Mountain.

Quebec Schoolhouse (Burkittsville), Maryland

Early the next morning, Saturday, September 13, 1862, Hampton began moving his brigade westward. They needed to cross two ridges of mountains. The first was Catoctin Mountain, and the next was the higher and more rugged South Mountain, which rose 1,300 feet.

By noon, Lee's legendary Special Order No. 191 had fallen into the hands of the enemy, revealing the march routes of each of Lee's divided elements of his army. In the meantime, Gen. Alfred Pleasonton, commander of McClellan's cavalry, was searching relentlessly for Lee. Pleasonton's most notable characteristic, according to another Union officer, was "systematic lying," a trait that irritated his own officers.

By chance, Pleasonton's main body of cavalry ran into Stuart's rear guard at Braddock's Gap on Catoctin Mountain on September 13. Hampton's troopers held the gap until 2:00 in the afternoon, when a division of enemy infantry advanced, compelling them to withdraw.

After withdrawing, the troopers made a desperate flight into the Middletown Valley. They were pursued by Col. John Farnsworth's 8th Illinois and 3rd Indiana cavalries. Hampton made a brief stand east of Middletown and again west of the town at the Catoctin Creek bridge. Next, he was directed by Stuart to turn his lathered horses toward South Mountain, where Gen. Daniel Harvey Hill's Confederate infantry was forming at Turner's Gap.

Farnsworth's troopers, although winded, were anxious to continue the fight and townsfolk at Middletown directed them to a side road that dropped suddenly away from Main Street to the southwest, where Stuart's baggage train had escaped just minutes before. The baggage, entrusted to Hampton, had been sent by an alternate route, so it would not hamper Stuart's flight with the rest of his cavalry to the mountains. The alternate route would take Hampton's troopers back to Burkittsville, five miles to the south near the southernmost pass in South Mountain, where they were to join forces with Munford's cavalry. As Hampton headed over the rolling valley landscape, he did not suspect that his move away from Stuart had been discovered.

Maj. William H. Medill took about 250 men from the 8th Illinois and 3rd Indiana and started out after Hampton. Finding Hampton was not easy. The rolling valley floor limited the view, while the wet roads from recent rains held down the dust from Hampton's cavalry. When Medill came to a fork in the road, he did not know which way to go. He chose the right fork, Mountain Church Road, which ascended into the South Mountain foothills. Hampton had chosen the left fork, Marker Road, a far easier road to travel with a burdensome wagon train. What neither officer realized was that Marker Road meandered briefly to the south, and then took a sharp turn to the west where it then joined Mountain Church Road. The two commanders were on a collision course.

Mountain Church Road was a longer, more difficult route. The small Federal force traveling on it kept their horses at a walk, but Hampton urgently hastened his troopers through the valley. Hampton arrived at the juncture of the road before Medill, but not soon enough to avoid discovery. Just before the intersection with Mountain Church Road was the small, country Quebec Schoolhouse. The Southerners observed the children in the schoolhouse peering apprehensively out of the windows at them.

By the time the last of his wagons were prodded onto Mountain Church Road, Hampton realized that he was being stalked. The unpaved road climbed steeply through rocks and underbrush then turned sharply south along the mountain wall. He hastily prodded the wagon train southward, but left Young to arrange an ambush with Cobb's Legion Cavalry.

The rigorous campaigning had reduced the size of Cobb's Legion Cavalry to only about 100 effective troopers. Young concealed his men in the only cover available, behind the tree line above Mountain Church Road. For the plan to work, the troopers had to keep their restless mounts quiet until the Yankees passed below them. They did not have to wait long before Medill's horsemen appeared, with their horses walking after the climb up the ridge. As they reached level ground, they picked up speed. Seeing the rear of Hampton's wagon train, Medill's troopers spurred their horses to a gallop. They did not notice the trees to their right where Cobb's Legion Cavalry anxiously waited.

William N. Pickerill of the 3rd Indiana, Company F later recorded the scene:

> Our pursuit of the wagon train was enthusiastic for a couple of miles, until we came in sight of it, slowly winding its way up a mountain road leading out from Burkittsville, the next hamlet below Middletown. In the rear of the train were six brass guns and cavalry enough to eat us up. We halted and formed in a meadow by the wayside and calmly viewed our retreating booty, and wisely decided to let it escape.
>
> From the meadow we again had a glorious vision of the beautiful Middletown Valley. We were in the midst of its most fertile farms. Fields of ripening, waving corn were on every hand. Orchards were the background of many a cottage with its shrubbery-bedecked lawn. Here and there herds of cattle grazed peacefully in the rich pastures or reposed under friendly shade trees, sheltered from the noonday sun.
>
> In the distance were the mountain crests, wreathed in the blue haze of a perfect Autumn day's loveliest sunshine. And two hundred yards away from where our column had halted, on the summit of a little ridge over-looking a rough country road leading to Middletown by a shorter route than we had come, stood an old-fashioned country, frame schoolhouse. It had one door opening in our direction and three windows were all open ... and school was in session. The noonday recess was over and pupils and teacher were apparently trying to give the attention to the things that pupils and teacher go to school for. But it did not seem to be a success. The teacher from the open door cast many a wistful look our way, and generally two or three of the little "tads" would follow him to the door and look out under his coat tail. Out of every window open in our direction were craned the necks of curious urchins.
>
> What a scene of peace was this sacred spot in the midst of war, and what memories did it bring to at least one-half of the writer's company, including himself, who had been a country school teacher and whose last work before entering the army had been to teach the district country school in just the same kind of an old-fashioned country schoolhouse. Although we were equipped for war, it seemed for the moment like old times, of friends

and the old schoolhouse of our far-off western homes again. For the moment we were on a furlough from the turmoil and anxieties of war, back in the old home schoolhouse, with its playgrounds and romping with the boys and girls who had been the playmates of our childhood.[3]

The Yankees were discouraged from following Hampton any further by the presence of those six brass guns and their large cavalry escort. They turned and started back down Mountain Church Road, but this time they choose the easier route by turning down Marker Road.

As Young "led Cobb's Legion Cavalry in a saber charge up the fence-bordered lane, he received a gunshot wound to the leg and several saber cuts to the face. He also lost several teeth when he was thrown from his dying horse. Capt. Gilbert "Gib" J. Wright of Company D was also wounded, while leading the charge. As Wright lay on the ground, he held up his wounded foot and shouted to the men, *"Give 'em hell boys! They've got me down!"*[4]

Cobb's Legion Cavalry dispersed the enemy, driving them nearly a mile and killing or wounding thirty men and taking five prisoners. In his report, Stuart said that Young and Wright "acted with remarkable gallantry."[4]

Pickerill of the Union remembered:

> The major commanding gave the command to about face and we filed off down the rocky ravine road, hemmed in on either side by a very crooked worm fence, on our return to Middletown and our regiments. The rear of our column had just entered this rocky, narrow way when a shot that seemed to come from behind the schoolhouse whizzed over our heads and left a white spot on the body of a little hickory ... to our right. We could not believe that innocent looking schoolhouse concealed our enemies, but two men from the forward end of the column filed out and passing through a pair of bars started up the winding road leading to the schoolhouse door. But they never reached their destination. When halfway up the hill, they, as well as we, heard a yell, and over the little ridge and down upon us leaped a body of Confederate cavalry apparently twice our numbers, with drawn swords, wild-eyed, cursing us furiously and demanding our surrender. This we did not do, but instead, at the sharp command of our officers, two hundred carbines cracked together and a good many men and horse of that wild, rushing mob went down, yet on they came, and for the next two minutes, in that rocky ravine road, there was a tussle for existence difficult to describe.
>
> The Confederate cavalry, which proved to be the Cobb Legion, dashed through the bars our men had laid down for them and slashed into our rear with their sabers, while a portion of their force fired into us from inside the fence, less than twenty feet away. It was an uneven fight until the advance of our column managed to tear down the fence on the side of the road that separated us from the children's playground surrounding the old schoolhouse that a few moments before had so enchanted us....
>
> The writer never knew our complete loss or the Confederate loss. It was one of those lively little cavalry battles whose details were probably never given, or perhaps forgotten in the larger events of the battle of South Mountain next day, or of Antietam, three days later. Yet it is doubtless still remembered by those who live to remember it.[5]

Young was worried about being separated from Hampton's main force, so he broke off contact with the enemy. His troopers galloped down Mountain Church Road to Burkittsville, leaving their dead and wounded behind.

The enemy lost 30 men killed or wounded in the battle and 5 men were taken prisoner. Cobb's Legion Cavalry lost 47 men killed and wounded in the battle.* Its total strength at that

---

According to McClellan, Hampton counted 4 killed, 9 wounded. A possible explanation is that Hampton's figures may have counted most of the losses from Quebec Schoolhouse with those lost at South Mountain.

time was 22 officers and 226 enlisted men. These figures show that the Yankees were not badly outnumbered as Pickerill remembered. Actually, since Cobb's Legion Cavalry had only about 100 effective, mounted troopers they were outnumbered by the Federals 2.5 to one, and they reportedly lost nearly half of those.

Company Notes
September 13, 1862

Staff—Wounded: Pierce M.B. Young
Company B—Captured: William E. Sutton
Company D—Killed: Green B. Barksdale, James F. Marshall; Wounded: Samuel D. Bostick, Gilbert Jefferson Wright
Company I—Wounded and Captured: E. McKnight
Company Unknown—Killed: Barksdale

Crampton's Gap (South Mountain)

There were three passes over South Mountain: Turner's Gap, Fox's Gap, and Crampton's Gap. Cobb's Legion Cavalry and the rest of Hampton's cavalry were sent to Crampton's Gap, which was the weakest point in the line. When they neared the gap, they were mistaken for a portion of the enemy's cavalry by the Confederate infantry already entrenched there. Munford ordered his 2nd Virginia Cavalry's artillery to fire on them. The gunners had their lanyards in hand and were waiting for the horsemen to come into effective range when Hampton became aware of the danger. He frantically fashioned a white flag and waved it. What could have been a serious disaster was averted.

That night, Saturday, September 13, 1862, as Hampton's men spread out along the ridge of South Mountain, they could see thousands of Federal campfires in the valley east of the mountain. The next morning, Stuart moved Hampton's brigade nearer to the Potomac at the south end of South Mountain to guard the road next to the river.

Sharpshooters from the Federal army swarmed along the base of South Mountain, and soon the enemy was pouring through Crampton's Gap. Cobb's Legion Cavalry had to fight from position to position until late that night, at which time they came through Crampton's Gap. Pickets were sent out on the roads toward Point of Rocks and Frederick City.

On the night of September 14, Lee withdrew from South Mountain toward Sharpsburg through mountainous country with half of his army, while McClellan followed him with 90,000 men. The cavalry's stand on South Mountain bought time for Lee's infantry so they could regroup at Sharpsburg, Maryland.

Hampton's troopers moved towards Harpers Ferry, where the Union army had a garrison of 11,000 men. It was necessary for Lee to send Stonewall Jackson to capture the garrison, as Lee could not move the rest of his army up the river with 11,000 men on his flank and 90,000 men in his rear. Lee's total force was about 30,000 men and he sent half of it to Harpers Ferry.

From Harpers Ferry northward there is a narrow depression between Elk Ridge and South Mountain called Pleasant Valley. The cavalry took possession of the valley and held the passes at Elk Ridge on the night of September 14. That night the enemy made a vigorous attack, gaining possession of the valley. This placed the cavalry in a critical position, caught between the enemy and the garrison at Harpers Ferry, with no outlet to the south.

The next morning, Jackson began bombarding Harpers Ferry. The cavalry could observe the enemy infantry in the valley below them, their lines reaching across the valley from mountain range to mountain range. Although they were badly outnumbered, Stuart was prepared to contest every foot of ground with them. The enemy had advanced until they were within two hundred yards of the cavalry, when suddenly Jackson's guns ceased. A silence fell over the scene, and the enemy stopped advancing. Then, from far away, rolling closer and closer, came the sounds of cheering. The cavalry realized that Harpers Ferry had fallen and began cheering also. After that, Stuart led his troops to the other side of the river.

Company Notes
September 13–16, 1862

Company A — Wounded, captured (and may have died): J.H. Rockman (may have been in the infantry)

Company B — Mortally wounded and captured: Seaborn W. Chisolm; Wounded: Charles Wallace; Wounded and captured: John N. Wood; Captured: H.B. Ashmand (may have been in the infantry)

Company D — Killed: J.F. Kennedy (may have been in the infantry); Mortally wounded and captured: James T. Broadway; Wounded and captured: H.M. Fowler, David P. Godfrey

Company E — Captured: James M. Evans, George W. Vaughan

Company F — Captured: Theodore Floyd Daniel

Company H — Captured: James S. Patterson, H.J. Stewarder

Company I — Captured: E. McKnight

Company Unknown (may have been in the infantry) — Wounded and captured: G. Doubleday, William R. Joie, J.C. Pemberton, J. Tredell, Otis S. Turner, and G. Wimperly

Sharpsburg (Antietam)

After observing the battle of Harpers Ferry from the Maryland side of the Potomac River on Maryland Heights, Wade Hampton's troopers crossed the Potomac River on pontoon bridges into the town. They paused there to feed their horses on captured Federal grain.

Leaving Harpers Ferry on Wednesday, September 17, 1862, they marched up the Virginia side of the Potomac until they were near Sharpsburg. The battle at Sharpsburg (Antietam) was in progress as they recrossed the river through deep water and emerged near the right end of the Confederate line. In order to support Stuart, who was engaged in fierce fighting on McClellan's flank, they worked their way to the left, where Cobb's Legion Cavalry was "subjected to some fierce and destructive cannonading, not to speak of the zip of the minies."[7]

The armies spent the next morning lying in wait and watching each other. In the afternoon, a truce was called to gather the dead and wounded. Late in the afternoon, Lee had a council meeting. When Stuart returned from the meeting, he sent his engineer, Capt. William W. Blackford, with orders to find a crossing of the Potomac for the cavalry near Shepherds-

The Potomac River ford where Cobb's Legion Cavalry crossed going into the Battle of Sharpsburg (Antietam). Photograph by Harry R. Mesic.

town, above the regular ford. He was instructed to ask no questions of civilians to take enough cavalrymen with him to leave some men at the crossing and station others two hundreds yards apart all the way back, and to return before sundown. Stuart wanted Blackford to be able to guide a column to the river crossing in the dark.

Williamsport, Maryland

That night, Thursday, September 18, 1862, was pitch black, and a cold, misting rain was falling. A dense fog enveloped the landscape, reducing the visibility to just a few feet. Stuart's cavalry set off on a diversionary maneuver to draw the enemy away from Lee's army so it could retreat across the Potomac on September 19. Two sections of artillery accompanied the troopers. Blackford led the cavalry to the Potomac crossing at an old blind ford between Falling Waters and Sharpsburg. The ford was below a fish trap, where a shallow dam of loose stones had been built, but water was pouring over the dam. For about ten or fifteen yards below the dam, the water was shallow enough for crossing, but then it became deeper, until it was past the saddle. The distance across the river at this point was considerable.

Maj. Heros Von Borcke, who rode to the river with Stuart, wrote in his journal: "I can safely say that the ride to the Potomac was one of the most disagreeable of my life. A fine rain,

Cobb's Legion Cavalry passed through the West Woods behind the Dunker Church, the white building in the background, to join J.E.B. Stuart in the Battle of Sharpsburg (Antietam). Photograph by Harry R. Mesic.

Cobb's Legion Cavalry camped in the pleasant countryside of Bunker Hill, [West] Virginia, after the Battle of Sharpsburg (Antietam). Photograph by Harry R. Mesic.

which had been falling all the evening, had rendered the roads so deep with mud and so slippery that it was difficult to make any progress at all."[6] Von Borcke's horse fell five times with him, and Stuart came close to being killed when his horse fell into the path of a heavy wagon.

It was a dangerous crossing for the troopers. Blackford led the head of the column across the river close to the dam, but no one thought to post men at the downstream edge of the crossing or to tell the men that they had to cross close to the dam. The fog was so thick that visibility was only a few horse lengths; consequently, no one could see the crisis as it arose. The first riders into the water tried to stay in the shallower water near the dam, but the current pushed them downstream during the crossing. The horses instinctively followed the ones in front of them. Before long the whole column had moved farther downstream, until the mounted men farther back in the column found themselves in water halfway up their legs one moment, then plunging neck deep in water with the horse's next step. At the rear of the column, the horses crossed in water so deep that they had to swim, and the men had difficulty saving themselves. A few horses and men were lost in the deep water, but most of them made it, cold and dripping wet, to the other side.

On the Virginia side of the river, the men dismounted and led their horses through the continuing rain and pitch-black dark until shortly before dawn, when they were allowed to halt. A trooper reminisced: "I remember sleeping a while before day on a rock pile in clothes soaking wet, and oh! How delicious to be thus allowed to sleep, wet and hungry, while I dreamed of a soft down feather bed away at home."[7] After about an hour, they were awakened by the buglers.

With the infantry safely across the river in Virginia, Lee sent Stuart's Cavalry back across the Potomac to harass Union Gen. McClellan, and prevent him from pursuing the Confederate army. For the next two days there were minor skirmishes near Williamsport, Maryland, until Stuart's men were nearly trapped by heavy columns of Federal infantry.

Defended by Jackson's artillery on the Virginia side of the Potomac, the cavalry, fighting step by step, escaped across the river on the dark cloudy night of September 20. Maj. Heros Von Borcke described the scene in his journal: "The whole landscape was lighted up with a lurid glare from the burning houses of Williamsport, which had been ignited by the enemy's shells. High over the heads of the crossing column and the dark waters of the river, the blazing bombs passed each other in parabolas of flame through the air, and the spectral trees showed their every limb and leaf against the red sky."[8]

The enemy pursued them across the river, but Jackson's men drove the Yankees back, seizing hundreds of prisoners. A number of the Federals were drowned in the waters of the Potomac. Stuart wrote in his report:

> During the Maryland campaign my command did not suffer on any one day as much as their comrades of other arms, but theirs was the sleepless watch and the harassing daily petite guerre in which the aggregate of casualties for the month sums up heavily. There was not a single day, from the time my command crossed the Potomac until it recrossed, that it was not engaged with the enemy, and at Sharpsburg was several times subjected to severe shelling. Their services were indispensable to every success attained.[9]

Company Notes
September 18–27, 1862

Company B — Wounded: Clement C. Green
Company D — Wounded: Samuel D. Bostick, Walter C. Reynolds
Company G — Killed: Robert T. Clingan

Chapter 6

Stuart's Raid into Pennsylvania

The Baltimore & Ohio Railroad

The cavalry occupied a line from Williamsport to Harpers Ferry for a few days, and then on Sunday, September 28, 1862, Cobb's Legion Cavalry moved to Bunker Hill, about eight miles south of Martinsburg, [West] Virginia, and between Winchester, Virginia, and Harpers Ferry, [West] Virginia. They stayed there for a few weeks, enjoying the warm days and cool nights. The leaves on the trees on the surrounding hills turned from green to blazing shades of color. Provisions were plentiful and life was pleasant. While there, the men were not completely idle. They assisted in tearing up the Baltimore & Ohio Railroad beyond Martinsburg as far as a little place called Funkstown, where some of the men were killed and wounded in "a hot little fight."[1]

The Baltimore & Ohio Railroad was Washington's direct link to western Maryland, western Virginia, and areas beyond. It was used to move Union troops, supplies, and coal. If its traffic were disrupted, all railroad traffic would have to detour through the mountains of western Pennsylvania. The disruption of the Baltimore & Ohio was an important objective of the South.

Although detached to serve under Stuart, Cobb's Legion Cavalry had not been officially separated from the infantry portion of the legion. In theory, they were still under the command of Thomas R.R. Cobb, who considered it his duty to visit their camp and check on the welfare of his men. While visiting Bunker Hill, Cobb wrote his wife that he and Delony "lay on the grass in the dim moonlight long after all the others were asleep, and talked about home and the dear ones there and the hopes of peace and our plans and wishes for a quiet life by our firesides."[2] Unfortunately, neither one would live to see those dreams come true.

Rooney Lee was commanding the brigade of his cousin, Fitz Lee, while Fitz Lee recovered from a mule kick. Rooney Lee had agreed to warn Hampton if his men observed the enemy approaching. Apparently, he forgot to do so, and Union Gen. Alfred Pleasonton took possession of Martinsburg on Wednesday, October 1, with a force of 700 troopers.

Stuart became angry when Union forces fired on him from the town. He called Rooney Lee and Hampton to a meeting and told them, "Gentlemen, this thing will not do; I will give you twenty minutes, within which time the town must be again in our possession."[3] Within the twenty-minute time limit, Hampton's and Rooney Lee's troopers were chasing Pleasonton's cavalry northward at a gallop. They pursued them all the way back to the Potomac River, having an engagement with them at Shepherdstown on the way. The enemy withdrew in a panic across the Potomac. Quite a number of the Federals were killed and many of them were captured.

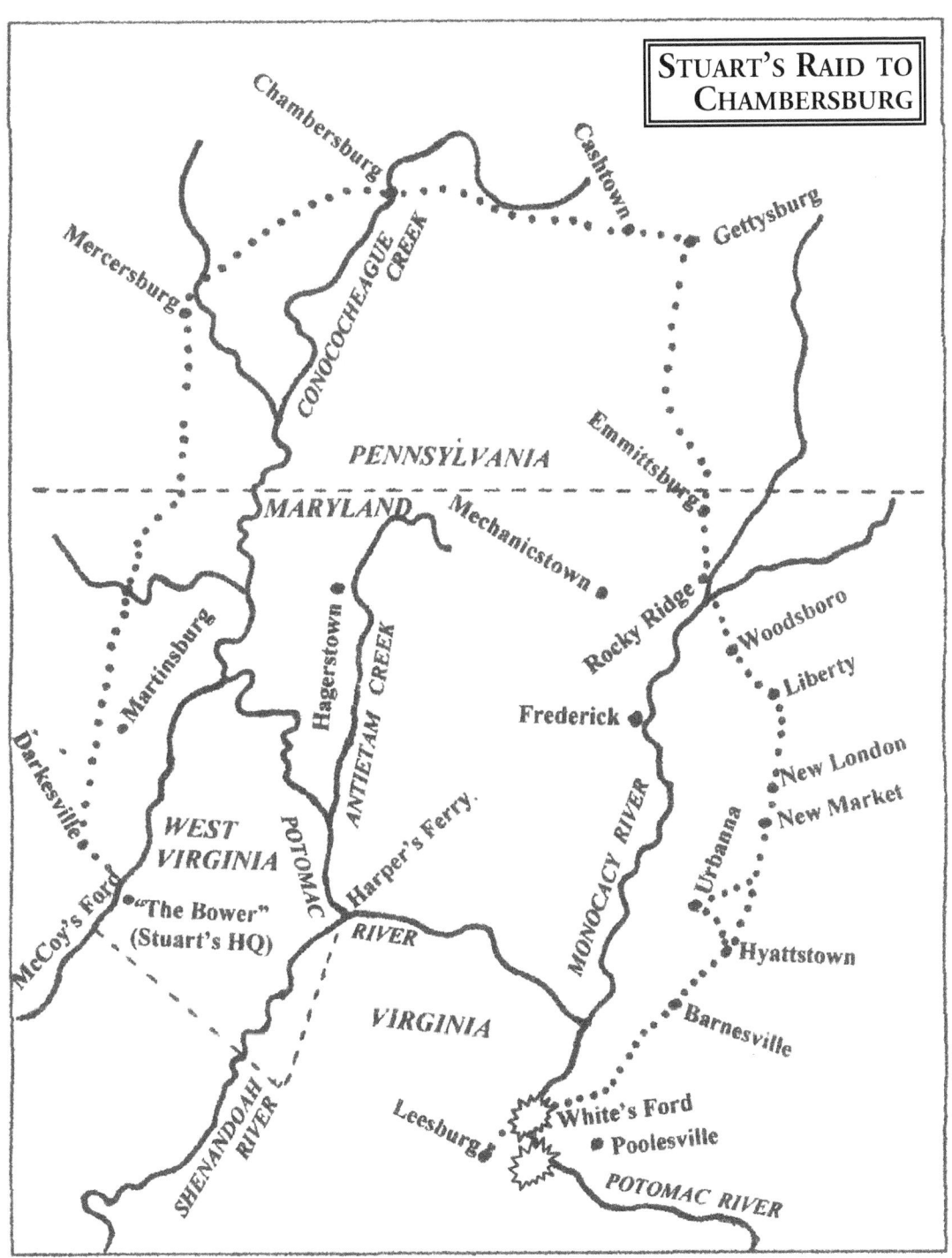

Company Notes
September 28–October 5, 1862

Company C — Captured: Thomas C. Gower
Company H — Died: Joseph W.M. Reidling

Stuart's Raid to Chambersburg, Pennsylvania

Riding a Raid
Author Unknown

'Tis old Stonewall, the Rebel, that leans on his sword,
And while we are mounting, prays to the Lord:
"Now each cavalier that loves honor and right,
Let him follow the feather of Stuart tonight."

(Chorus)
Come tighten your girth and slacken your rein;
Come buckle your blanket and holster again.
Try the click of your trigger and balance your blade.
For he must ride sure that goes Riding a Raid.

Now, gallop, now gallop, to swim or to ford!
Old Stonewall, still watching, prays to the Lord:
"Good-bye, dear old Rebel! The river's not wide,
And Maryland's lights in her window to guide."
(Chorus)

There's a man in the White House with blood on his mouth!
If there's knaves in the North, there are braves in the South.
We are three thousand horses, and not one afraid;
We are three thousand sabers and not a dull blade.
(Chorus)

Then gallop, then gallop, by ravines and rocks!
Who would bar us the way take his toll in hard knocks;
For with these points of steel, on the line of Penn,
We have made some fine strokes—and we'll make 'em again.
(Chorus)[4]

Fall came early for Virginia, and the Georgians grumbled about the frosty mornings, lack of forage for their horses, and the slowness of the mail. On Monday, October 6, 1862, Lee called Stuart and Jackson to his headquarters for a talk. One of the things they discussed was the possibility of Stuart going on a raid into Pennsylvania to gather information on the position, force, and probable intention of the enemy. It would be the most daring and brilliant expedition that the cavalry had attempted, and it would be executed by the cavalry alone.

Orders for the raid were issued by Lee on October 8. Stuart's destination would be Chambersburg, Pennsylvania, where he would attempt to destroy the Cumberland Valley Railroad bridge over Conococheague Creek. That would leave the Union with only one line, the Baltimore & Ohio Railroad, for the movement of men and supplies in that region. Stuart was also to inflict any other damage that he could upon the enemy and its means of transportation. Lee wanted Stuart to take hostages to exchange for Southern citizens who had been carried off by Union troops and were being held in despicable conditions in prisons such as the Old Capitol Prison in Washington, D.C., and the Fort Delaware Prison.* Stuart's hostages were,

---

*The author's great-great-grandfather, Lewis Wrenn, was at that time being held as a hostage in the Old Capitol Prison in Washington, D.C. After his release, he was once more taken as a hostage and held in the Fort Delaware Prison. His experiences are recounted in Beside the Stone Wall in Fredericksburg, Virginia, *by Harriet Bey Mesic, Heritage Publishing Co. (2005).*

of course, to be treated with all the respect and consideration that circumstances would admit. Stuart was to confiscate Pennsylvanian horses to replenish Lee's supply of cavalry, artillery, and draft animals. Lee suggested that Stuart take 1,200–1,500 troopers with him.

News quickly spread around the camp that the cavalry was going on a raid. The men did not know the destination of the raid or that they would be facing McClellan's army alone or that they would be crossing rivers, canals, railroads, and turnpikes in their trek. They did know that the intricate network of Federal telegraph lines would put them at risk of entrapment before they could safely return. Still, without questioning, the men were eager to go.

Stuart increased the number that Lee had suggested to 1,800 of his best troopers to take on the raid. Six hundred men were chosen from each of his three brigades. The ones selected were the most reliable men, the best riders, and the surest shots whose horses were in prime condition. They would be led by their brigade leaders, Wade Hampton, as second in command, Rooney Lee (who was still substituting for his cousin Fitz Lee, who had not recovered from his mule kick), and William E. (Grumble) Jones. Jones was a "rough hewn" man from Southwest Virginia who did not get along well with Stuart. His "Laurel Brigade" was formed from Turner Ashby's Shenandoah Valley Cavalry. Among the troopers chosen from Hampton's brigade were some of the men from Cobb's Legion Cavalry. Maj. John Pelham of the Stuart Horse Artillery was also a part of the expedition and brought four guns.

Before leaving on the raid, Stuart had his orders read to the men. He asked for "coolness, decision, and bravery" with "implicit obedience to orders" and "the strictest order and sobriety."[5] An order stipulating standards of conduct when dealing with enemy civilians and seizing property was distributed among the men. During the raid, one third of the men in each brigade would be detailed to seize horses and other property, while the rest of the brigade would be held in readiness for action. Receipts were to be given to noncombatants for every article taken from them so the civilians could apply for reimbursement from the Federal government. Individual plundering was forbidden. Public officials such as magistrates, postmasters, and sheriffs were to be taken as hostages so they could be exchanged for Southern citizens who had been arrested and imprisoned. While the troops were in Maryland, the seizure of property was forbidden.

The next afternoon Stuart and the others met Hampton and his troopers on the banks of the Potomac River north of Darkesville, [West] Virginia, some fifteen miles north of Winchester. The men spoke in whispers because a Federal signal station was hidden behind the trees on the other side of the river and Union pickets were nearby. The raid was to be a surprise, and they did not want the pickets to be alerted ahead of time.

They rode on to Hedgesville, [West] Virginia, arriving there after dark. While they slept that night in an open field, Hampton explored the area and selected McCoy's Ford as the place they should cross the Potomac. There was a heavy fog hanging over the landscape when they awoke at 4:00 in the morning and that fog would work to their advantage. Without building fires or eating breakfast, the men mounted their horses. Hampton's men were placed in front to clear the way for the others. Thirty men were selected to rush across the river and capture the Yankee pickets to prevent them from alerting the signal station that an attack was being made. When this was accomplished, the Confederates crossed the Potomac at McCoy's Ford and headed north. The Pennsylvania border was only eight miles away.

Matthew Calbraith Butler was in command of Hampton's advance. Butler was described as having "dashing courage" and "quick and intuitive instinct as to what was the best disposition of his troops as he went into action, the weak point of the enemy, and where to attack.

Added to this was the wonderful magnetism of the man himself, which seemed to give him complete control of his men, and to make them follow unhesitatingly wherever he chose to lead." His men were willing to ride "into the jaws of death" when Butler gave the order to "Charge!"[6]

The 12th Illinois was camped north of the place where the Confederates made their crossing. A civilian alerted the 12th that thousands of Rebels were crossing the river. The Union cavalry mounted their horses and formed a battle line, but they were too few in number to attack. As they watched, they estimated that 2,500 Confederate horsemen and eight pieces of artillery had crossed the river. Other reports estimated their numbers to be 3,000–4,000, 6,000, and 16,000.

Almost immediately, Union telegraphs notified dozens of posts from Washington, D.C., westward and reported each sighting of Stuart's men. Instead of taking the main road, Stuart's men were guided over a little known and seldom traveled road toward Mercersburg, Pennsylvania, by Capt. B.S. White of Stuart's staff. White was a Marylander from Poolesville who knew the terrain. At 10:00 in the morning, they reached the Pennsylvania state line and halted. Stuart galloped along the line, repeating his orders to the men. They were to impress horses for the army, never leave the ranks unless accompanied by an officer, and refrain from personal pillaging. He told them, "We are now in enemy country. Hold yourselves ready for attack or defense, and behave with no other thought than victory."[7]

The men cheered and then the march resumed. They were traveling on a northerly course "through a rocky, bleak, and almost barren region with here and there a lonely cabin to relieve the wild scenery."[8] The day was cloudy and dark, with intermittent showers throughout the day. A cold wind swirled around them and scattered the leaves falling from the trees. After a while, the mountains gave way to hills, which in turn gave way to flat fertile land.

In the middle division, parties of six to twelve men under an officer would dash to the right or left and bring in horses from the farms. The horses were tied three together by their halters and led by a trooper riding alongside. Although they were instructed not to pillage, Blackford reported seeing men with roasted turkeys, hams, and beef strapped to their saddles, and haversacks bulging with loaves of fresh bread, rolls of butter, and crocks of cream, which they shared with friends in the column.

They passed Mercersburg about noon, where the advance guard equipped themselves with new boots and shoes, for which they gave the merchant a receipt instead of money. The troopers halted five miles north of town to feed the horses on corn taken from the fields. At this time, the rain was falling in torrents. Their pace slowed by the rain, the column reached Chambersburg about 7:00 on the night of Friday, October 10. By then, it was pitch black and raining hard. They had traveled forty miles with scarcely any opposition.

Stuart did not want to attack the town, because it was full of women and children. Instead, he sent an officer and nine men from Hampton's brigade under a flag of truce into the town. They located some officials from the town and demanded their surrender. The local provost marshal managed to send a telegraph message of alarm to the governor before the telegraph wires were cut. Hampton's troopers, who were in the lead, were given the task of patrolling the place, and Hampton was named the "military governor" for the overnight stay. Grumble Jones and his men were given the task of destroying the railroad bridge over Conococheague Creek. Unfortunately, the trestle bridge was built of iron and they could not destroy it.

The men had an uncomfortable bivouac that night in what had begun as a drizzling rain that had turned into a steady downpour. The next morning, October 11, it was still raining.

The Confederate buglers blew "Boots and Saddles" at 4:00 in the morning, and the men gathered in the town. Hampton's men found stores of small arms, ammunition, and military clothing in the town. They confiscated what they wanted and destroyed what they could not carry. One Gettysburg newspaper correspondent described the scene: "The whole town was converted into one vast dressing room. On every hotel porch, at every corner, on the greater portion of the street doorsteps, might be seen Rebel cavalry donning Yankee uniforms, and throwing their own worn out and faded garments into the street. Each took as many coats, hats, and pairs of pants as he could conveniently handle."[9]

They also found railroad machine shops and loaded trains, which they destroyed. The town was rocked by explosions when they burned a warehouse full of ammunition. After relieving the banks and stores of their gold and greenbacks, they rounded up prominent citizens to take as hostages. McClellan issued orders for all of Stuart's men to be captured or killed, stating, "Not a man should be permitted to return to Virginia. Use any troops in Maryland or Pennsylvania against them."[10]

There was some anxiety among the Confederates that the rain would cause the Potomac to rise and impede their crossing to get home. It became a race to see which would reach the ford first, the cavalry or the swollen mountain streams. Stuart made the decision to ride around McClellan's army and left Chambersburg with his column sometime during the morning, heading east toward Gettysburg. Butler, who had led the advance to Chambersburg, now led the rear guard. It would be the longest march without a halt that the troopers had ever experienced. The only way the men were able to keep up with the march was by riding the captured horses as they rested their own mounts.

The direction they took was surprising, even to the troopers. For the greater part of the day they headed directly toward the enemy camps. Stuart concluded that the Yankees would expect him to take the shortest route back to Virginia and would be looking for him most aggressively to the west. The route Stuart selected was through open, rolling country, where the cavalry could operate to a better advantage on a road that led directly from Chambersburg to Gettysburg. After passing Catoctin Mountain in the Blue Ridge, they rode to within seven miles of Gettysburg, to the village of Cashtown. They stopped near Cashtown for a half hour to feed the horses and then turned back toward Hagerstown for a mile or so, to confuse any pursuers, and then headed south to Emmittsburg, Maryland. The day had turned sunny, but the ground was still moist from the rain of the previous day, which prevented clouds of dust from being raised by the riders. The lack of dust clouds helped to screen their location. The column was five miles long as it entered Maryland, and the troopers were growing weary. When they were in Maryland, they halted and the command was compactly closed up. Once again, the order was given that they were to stop seizing horses in the state of Maryland, and they were under strict orders not to use a firearm. If an enemy party appeared, they were to use sabers and the colonel of the regiment passing the enemy was to charge instantly and without further orders. Capt. B.S. White was placed at the head of the advance squadron as their guide.

When they entered Emmittsburg, Maryland, at 4:00 in the afternoon, they were thirty-one miles from Chambersburg. In Emmittsburg, they captured some troopers belonging to a detachment of Pennsylvania cavalry and were enthusiastically hailed by the inhabitants. Young girls snatched Confederate buttons for souvenirs. The townsfolk generously brought them food from their homes, which the men ate in their saddles before they pushed south at a trot in the twilight. The Potomac was still forty-five miles to the south of them.

Leaving Emmittsburg, they took the road toward Frederick. Six miles south of Emmittsburg, at the town of Rocky Ridge, they intercepted a Union courier and learned that there was a strong Federal force in Frederick. In addition, Union Gen. Pleasonton, with a large cavalry force, was heading for the village of Mechanicstown, just four miles west of their position. In order to escape, they had to ride all night. The head of the column was kept at a trot. The long, terrible march was "exquisite torture"[11] for the men. The constant, monotonous jingle and clatter of spurs, arms, and stirrups, and the monotonous tramp of hoofs made the troopers drowsy. " In order to keep awake, the men would dismount and walk for short distances. In spite of their efforts, some of the men fell asleep in their saddles, and their snores could be heard above the other sounds.

The artillery managed to keep up during the incredible march by changing horses three or four times during the night. As fast as one team of horses was broken down, it was turned out and others were substituted from the abundant supply of confiscated horses.

After crossing the Monocacy River, they continued the march through the dim moonlight through Woodsboro, Liberty, New London, New Market, and Monrovia on the Baltimore & Ohio Railroad, where they cut the telegraph wires and placed obstructions on the railroad tracks. At daylight on Sunday, October 12, they reached Hyattstown, having traveled sixty-five miles from Chambersburg in twenty hours. They still had twelve miles to travel before they would reach the Potomac River.

They then pushed on at a fast pace to Barnesville. A heavy fog hid the horsemen from the Union cavalry and lookouts, at the signal stations, who were trying to locate them. Learning that Union Gen. George Stoneman had between 4,000 and 5,000 troops at Poolesville guarding the river fords, Stuart avoided Poolesville by marching through a large tract of woods two or three miles to the west of the town, led once again by Capt. B.S. White. The trees enveloped the troopers and concealed their position from their pursuers. Within the woods, White led them to a long disused road, which they reopened by pulling down a few fences. Following that road they came to the junction of the road leading to the mouth of the Monocacy.

The night had been cold and the morning was chilly and damp, so the Confederates were still wearing the blue overcoats they had obtained in Chambersburg. The advance guard had just entered the road when Federal cavalry came into view. Noting the hesitation of the enemy, who did not know if they were friend of foe, Stuart restrained his men until they drew closer. When Stuart ordered a charge, the Federals fired only one volley before turning to run.

The Southerners arrived at White's Ford about 8:00 in the morning, where they were attacked by about 200 of Col. Edwin R. Biles' 99th Pennsylvania Infantry, who were positioned on the sixty-five foot tall cliffs above the ford. The 99th Pennsylvania was extended for four miles along the river from Conrad's Ferry on the left to three hundred yards above White's Ford on the right, with three companies in reserve at White's Ford. Stuart's troopers had to fight their way across the Potomac River, but the enemy retreated when Rooney Lee's men opened fire on them with two guns.

To cover the crossing of the cavalrymen, Butler and his rear guard skirmished with the enemy on the Maryland side of the river. Ahead of the cavalry, one piece of artillery was hurried down into the dry bed of the canal, up its steep bank and across the rough ford. It was quickly positioned on top of the bluff on the Virginia side. Another gun was positioned to sweep the towpath and other approaches to the ford while the troopers quickly made their crossing.

Traversing the long, rough ford to Virginia was difficult for the troopers. The river was swollen and moving fast from the rain of the day before, but it fortunately had not yet reached flood stage. The exhausted men were yelping in delight, but their horses, gaunt and heaving from their long ride without water, fought to drink as they crossed. Each company commander was given orders as he arrived at the ford that no man should halt to water his horse while crossing the river. In spite of everything the riders could do to stop them, some of the horses plunged their heads in the water up to their eyes to take deep swallows of water. The ford was so wide and the water so deep that most of the horses managed to drink all the water they wanted without stopping. When they reached the other side, the troopers were allowed to halt and water their horses.

As the last of the men were entering the water, Stuart rode up to Blackford with tears in his eyes and said, "Blackford, we are going to loose [sic] our rear guard.... I have sent four couriers to Butler to call him in, and he is not here, and you see the enemy is closing in upon us."[12] Blackford offered to go back and find Butler. As he rode up the bank on the Maryland side, Pelham was there with one gun, firing alternately up and down the river at masses of the enemy about one quarter of a mile away.

Blackford passed the four couriers who were on their way back because they had not been able to find Butler. Blackford located him several miles away and gave him the order to withdraw at a gallop, but Butler replied that he was afraid he could not save his gun. He was told to leave the gun, but he replied, "I don't want to lose it, but we will see what we can do."[12] The men could hear the boom of Pelham's gun in the distance and knew that as long as they could hear the gun, the way was still open. To everyone's surprise, Butler brought off his gun with every one of his men. As they galloped around the last bend in the road toward the ford amid the splatter of bullets, Stuart's troopers cheered them on. Butler's men rode with their swords drawn, in case they had to fight their way across the river, but Pelham had kept a gap open for them. They splashed into the water, with Pelham and his gun right behind them. Halfway across the river, the enemy swarmed on the bank behind them and opened fire, their bullets splashing into the water around Butler's men. Guns from the Virginia side fired back, and the last of Butler's troopers were soon on Virginia soil.

After riding two or three miles into Virginia, hundreds of exhausted men fell to the ground and quickly fell asleep for a couple of hours, worn out by two days and a night of continuous riding. When night came, it was accompanied by torrents of rain but the chase was over. The remainder of the march, which ended at Leesburg, Virginia, was without incident.

The 1,800 troopers had traveled 130 miles in three days. In the last thirty-six hours they had traveled nonstop and covered eighty miles. None of the Confederate troopers were killed on the mission and only a few suffered slight wounds. Two men were lost along the route and were presumed to be in the enemy's hands. The rest of the troopers had endured hardships without complaint and had spent seemingly endless hours in the saddle. During the raid, the men left behind about sixty horses that had become lame or were unable to keep up. However, the cavalrymen captured over 1,200 horses and had taken into custody around thirty prominent citizens as hostages who would be used in exchange for important prisoners being held in Northern prisons.

The effect on the Federal cavalry was described in Gen. McClellan's report. He said that it was necessary for him to use all of his cavalry against Stuart, and that "this exhausting service completely broke down nearly all of our cavalry horses and rendered a remount absolutely indispensable before we could advance on the enemy."[13]

The Chambersburg raid was memorable not only for its daring and success, but also for the magnificent discipline shown by the troopers. They had scrupulously shown respect for private property, had taken only what was necessary to subsist, and had impressed only horses. For the things which they took they had given official receipts to the owners, according to the practice of civilized armies. Thus, they had furnished vouchers with which the owners could make a claim for compensation to their own government.

Company Notes
October 6–15, 1862

Company H — Died: James H. Foster

Chapter 7

The Blue Ridge Campaign

Barbee's Cross Roads

Stuart's troopers had only two days of rest after their return from Chambersburg before, on Thursday, October 16, 1862, two columns of the enemy advanced from Shepherdstown, [West] Virginia, to Smithfield, [West] Virginia, and from Harpers Ferry, [West] Virginia, to Charlestown, [West] Virginia. Stuart opposed the forces advancing to Smithfield with Fitz Lee's brigade. The next day, Hampton's brigade joined them.

On Sunday, October 26, two divisions of the enemy crossed the Potomac below Harpers Ferry, east of the Blue Ridge Mountains, and moved to Warrenton, Virginia. Lee left Jackson's men in the Shenandoah Valley near Winchester, Virginia, but shifted Longstreet's men to counter the move of the enemy. His goal was to confront them on the Rappahannock, so he ordered Stuart to cover Longstreet's flank. Stuart's objectives were to keep the enemy from the Blue Ridge passes and to post a fifty-mile line of pickets between the two wings of the army. It was a daunting assignment, made more difficult by the fact that many of the horses were suffering from maladies described as "greased heel" and "sore tongue."

During a cold rain on the morning of October 29, Cobb's Legion Cavalry left the comfort of the camp at Bunker Hill and moved between Martinsburg, [West] Virginia, and the Potomac River with three of Hampton's other cavalry units. By afternoon the rain had stopped, the temperature had dropped to freezing, and a cold wind was blowing. They had orders to join Stuart near Upperville, Virginia, by Monday, November 3. Fearing that the enemy could interpose between his divided bodies of troopers, Stuart planned to consolidate his cavalry units in the Loudoun Valley.

On the morning of November 4, Stuart found Hampton's brigade west of Upperville at Millwood and ordered them to move south to join Rooney Lee's brigade at Markham. The enemy, however, had occupied Markham. When they reached Linden, due west of Markham, they were diverted by Stuart to Barbee's Cross Roads (now known as Hume), which is south of Markham. Late on the night of November 4, Hampton's brigade arrived at Barbee's Cross Roads. During the morning of November 5, with Rooney Lee's brigade on the right and Hampton's on the left, they faced the enemy. Stuart's artillery and sharpshooters were placed on the crest of the hill north of the town to rake the enemy's column when it moved down the road. Around 9:00 A.M., the enemy advanced toward them and an exchange of fire with the Confederate artillery and sharpshooters followed.

When several of Stuart's regiments refused to charge the overwhelming numbers of the enemy, who were advancing in full view, Maj. Delony of Company C galloped up to Stuart and called, "General! General! The Cobb Legion is not afraid! They will charge them, sir!"

Stuart answered, "Do you think they will charge, Major?"

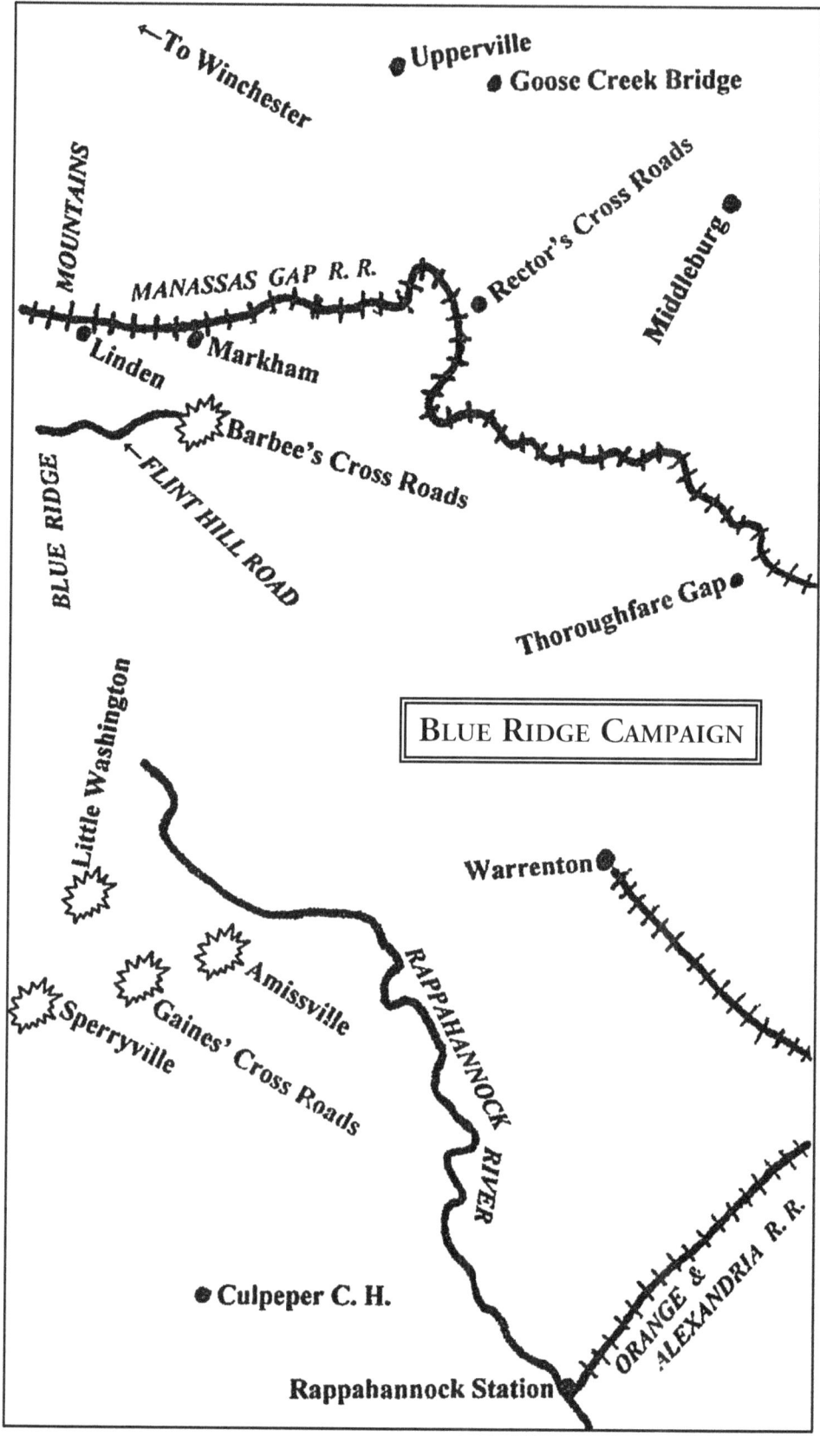

The Battle of Barbee's Cross Roads occurred in this peaceful rural setting. The Flint Hill Road is in the background. Photograph by Harry R. Mesic.

Delony answered him indignantly. "Charge, sir? Why they would charge so close to the gates of hell as to singe their mustaches and eyebrows off. We came here to charge, sir."[1]

After hours of intense action, during which they could make no headway, the enemy decided to utilize the cover of ravines and the forest to approach the Confederate cavalry stationed at the crossroads. Close-quarters combat with sabers and pistols soon followed. According to Union reports, thirty-seven Confederates were killed in the skirmishing. Hearing a rumor that evening that Federal troops were in their rear, Stuart ordered Hampton to withdraw his men westward along the Flint Hill Road.

Company Notes
October 16–November 5, 1862

Company A — Killed: Henry N. Rhodes
Company B — Captured: Michael J. Ivey, J.F. Noose
Company E — Killed: John E. Mitchell
Company F — Wounded: John Randolph Byne, William C. Palmer, Robert Augustus Reynolds
Company G — Captured: James E. Henry, Joseph L. Moore, Marcus V. Woods
Company H — Died: Isaac Sterling
Company I — Captured: Richard L. Mass, Merriman Winters

Little Washington

The next morning, Thursday, November 6, 1862, Hampton's brigade was sent to cover the front at Sperryville, with advance posts at Gaine's Cross Roads and Amissville. After a skirmish at Gaine's Cross Roads, where the Federals were beaten back by Cobb's Legion Cavalry, Stuart commended the troopers for behaving with gallantry and for routing the enemy. The same day, they resumed picket duty in front of Longstreet's Corps near Culpeper Court House, where afterward they skirmished with the enemy every day. In these skirmishes, they were badly outnumbered and often faced cavalry augmented by infantry. Each day they would fight and then fall back.

On November 7, Lincoln replaced McClellan with Gen. Ambrose E. Burnside. The new commander decided to move the Union army east to Fredericksburg by crossing the Rappahannock River on pontoon bridges and make a drive toward Richmond.

The next day, Cobb's Legion Cavalry was at Little Washington, Virginia, in a concealed position behind a hill by a road that was flanked by stone walls. Col. Delony of Company C was in command. The 5th U.S. Cavalry was advancing up the road in force. Delony left Maj. Zack Rice with the troopers while he rode forward to estimate the number of the enemy. Suddenly a group of about ten mounted Federals came cantering up the road and spied Delony, who had just turned his horse to return to his men. Delony wheeled his horse around and charged the Yankees, emptying his pistols at them and then drawing his saber. When he met them, they dashed around him, hacking his bridle hand and gashing his head and side. Delony was "fighting like a mad boar with a whole pack of curs about him."[2] His coat was cut, but his silver flask acted as a breastplate.

One of the more aggressive Yankees yelled for him to surrender, but Delony shouted, "I will never surrender!"

The Yankee answered, "Surrender! By God! I am the best man!"[3]

Rice had a hard time keeping all the men from dashing down the hill to Delony's aid. He finally let eight or ten of them go, and they "went like lightning"[4] to his rescue. When his rescuers arrived, Delony and one of his adversaries were leaning on their horses until their heads nearly touched. James Luke Clanton of Company C knocked the other Yankees out of the way and then plunged his saber into the side of Delony's antagonist. As the man fell forward, Delony drew his blade and cleaved his skull.

The fight was described as "Perhaps, one of the most desperate single-handed contests against fearful odds and one of the bloodiest little fights that the history of our great struggle for right and liberty will ever record."[5] Four troopers from Cobb's Legion Cavalry and more than that number of the Federals were wounded in the clash. The next day Delony displayed a small metallic flask he carried in his inside coat pocket near the region of his heart and lungs. A saber had been thrust clear through the metal and four deep indented cuts were on its side. Delony remarked that if he were killed in battle, he would not want his wife to know he carried the flask, but he thought it was a good idea for every man to carry one to protect a vulnerable spot.

On November 15, Burnside began moving his army toward Fredericksburg.

Company Notes
November 6–9, 1862

Company A — Wounded: Charles E. Bassford, William Finch, Patrick Gallaher, Andrew Jackson Thomas, Jonathan Pinckney Thomas

Company B — Killed: Jacob McCarty Scudder; Wounded: Lewis Alexander Juhan

Company E — Wounded: William Choice Dial

Company I — Wounded: Owen O'Connor

Chapter 8

Picketing the Rappahannock

Yellow Chapel (Hartwood Church)

There was another reorganization of the cavalry on November 10, 1862. Cobb's Legion was once again assigned to serve under Gen. Wade Hampton. Other members of their brigade were Phillip's Georgia Legion, the 1st and 2nd South Carolina and the 1st North Carolina regiments.

The cavalry had accomplished their objective, and their screening of the army was successful. Longstreet was able to march unopposed to Culpeper Court House. In his report, Stuart said, "In all these operations I deem it my duty to bear testimony to the gallantry and patient endurance of the cavalry, fighting every day most unequal conflicts, and successfully opposing for an extraordinary period the onward march of McClellan."[1]

Based on intelligence information furnished by Stuart, Lee shifted Longstreet's corps to Fredericksburg and ordered Jackson to move his men from the Shenandoah Valley to join him. Stuart moved his headquarters five miles south of Fredericksburg on Telegraph Road to a place he called "Camp No Camp." His men were spread out for fifty miles along the Rappahannock River, from thirty miles above to twenty miles below Fredericksburg. While Stuart and his staff were comfortably housed in people's homes and the Virginia brigades were quartered in ill-ventilated but cozy huts, Hampton's brigade guarded the fords along the Rappahannock above Fredericksburg, with his men camping in the woods. Cobb's Legion Cavalry was positioned near Kelly's Ford about twenty-five miles above Fredericksburg. Kelly's Ford was one of the more accessible points on that stretch of the river, and, therefore, the most vulnerable.

Hampton organized a detail of scouts from the coon hunters and deerstalkers in his command. These men habitually dressed in captured blue uniforms and operated behind enemy lines. They made friends with Southern sympathizers in Federal occupied territories, slept and ate in the homes of the sympathizers, and dated their daughters. They avoided battle, except in close quarters, where they blithely used pistols and shotguns with deadly accuracy. The Federal troops nicknamed them the "Iron Scouts" because they were so hard to kill and condemned to death any Confederate captured with buckshot in his pockets. When captured, they often escaped, even from pens and shackles. Among those who served in the Iron Scouts were James H. Brent, Charles L. Camback, B.L. Dickens, John Stapler Dozier, Francis Edgeworth Eve, Alexander C. Guedron, John Schley Haines, Charles R.A. Harris, James M. Hartsfield, John Jenkins, John H. Keogh, Artemus M. Lazenby, William N. Liverman, Lee M. Lyle, Henry Hugh McCall, W.H. McCullough, S. Marcus McCurry, Rufus B. Merchant, Owen O'Keefe, Thomas A. Holliday Paschal, Isaac Simmons, William D. Simmons, Isaac Simon, David E. Smith, James W. Stokes, Daniel F. Tanner, George A. Williams, and Charles C. Winder.

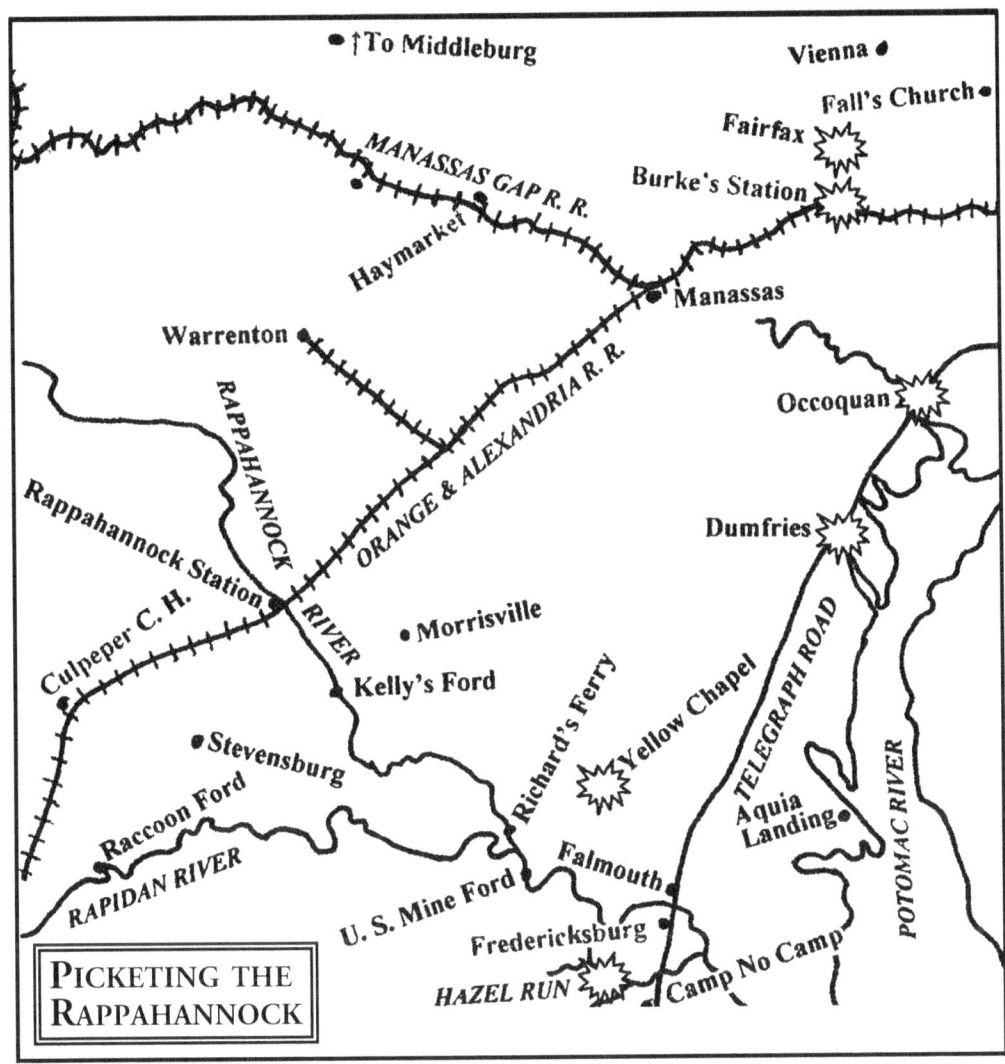

PICKETING THE RAPPAHANNOCK

On the blustery, cold morning of November 27, Hampton led a detachment of fifty men from Cobb's Legion Cavalry and 158 men from other cavalry units across the Rappahannock River at Kelly's Ford. They proceeded east over frost-covered ground through Morrisville, Virginia, across the country, and toward White Ridge Road. Their objective was to cut off the enemy at Richard's Ferry. Before reaching White Ridge Road, they learned that a regiment of the enemy was camped at Yellow Chapel, eight miles from Falmouth, Virginia.

Since they could not reach the enemy before night, they halted and camped in the woods two miles from the chapel. At 4:00 A.M., they moved out, going through the woods between White Ridge Road and Marsh Road. They came out of the woods on Marsh Road a half mile from the chapel and charged the enemy, dashing into their camp before they could form. Within a few minutes, they captured every man in the camp, and then they discovered that one squadron of the enemy was on picket duty on the two roads mentioned above. A detachment from Cobb's Legion Cavalry was sent to capture the pickets on White Ridge Road. When the detachment returned to the camp, they had with them seventeen prisoners. After sending the prisoners to the rear, the cavalry went up Marsh Road and captured the pickets there.

Hartwood Church, where the enemy were camped when Cobb's Legion Cavalry attacked them on a cold winter day in 1862. Photograph by Harry R. Mesic.

In all, eighty-seven men and noncommissioned officers, two captains, three lieutenants, two colors, about 100 horses, and about 100 carbines were taken. Five of the enemy's pickets escaped capture by leaving their horses and fleeing on foot through the woods.

Hampton's troopers were so reduced in number by the necessary guards for the prisoners that he had to abandon his plans to move on to Richard's Ferry. Four of the enemy were too severely wounded to move, but there were no casualties among Hampton's men. Afterwards, Stuart said, "General Hampton and his gallant command deserve the highest praise for this handsome affair, and are warmly commended."[2] Lee also praised them, saying, "The energy and courage displayed by General Hampton and the officers and men under his command, in my opinion, are deserving of high commendations."[3]

Hampton reported that his men "bore privations and fatigues on the march—three nights in the snow—without complaint."[4] Afterward, Cobb's Legion Cavalry camped for a time near Raccoon Ford and continued their picketing duty.

Company Notes
November 10–30, 1862

Company A — Wounded: Joseph W. Thurman

Kelly's Ford was used by both armies as a convenient place to cross the Rappahannock River. Many skirmishes took place here. Photograph by Harry R. Mesic.

Company D — Wounded and captured: David P. Godfrey
Company E — Captured: Isma W. Thomas, Andrew T. Baugh
Company G — Died: M. T. Donnan (may have been in the infantry)

Kelly's Ford

In late November 1862, Union Gen. Ambrose Burnside, who had shifted the huge Federal army eastward, came to a halt on the northern bank of the Rappahannock River opposite Fredericksburg, Virginia. The same day, Longstreet's men fortified the heights behind the town as Jackson's men were moving to join Longstreet. The weather was bitter cold.

A portion of Cobb's Legion Cavalry and some detachments of Virginia cavalry, with three guns of a Maryland battery under the command of Gen. P.M.B. Young, protected Lee's wagon train as it passed through Culpeper Court House and across Hazel Run into Fredericksburg, Virginia. At Kelly's Ford, two corps of enemy soldiers crossed the Rappahannock and moved rapidly toward the wagon train.

Lacking infantry and sufficient cavalry to prevent their progress, Young quickly and skillfully concealed his men (who numbered not over 500 troopers) in the woods and brought the artillery forward. Soon the men were engaged in a protracted duel with the enemy. Young ordered the men to yell "like hell and damnation"⁵ and ordered couriers and others to zigzag the edge of the woods to give the illusion of a concealed battle line. The enemy shelled the woods for two hours, until sunset. Young's deportment gave courage to his small band of cavalry as he sat on his iron-gray stallion, shouting orders and directing the gunners. He seemed "absolutely without fear or mistrust of his ability to successfully cope with the situation at hand,"[6] while "bursting shells ripped open horses and disabled men."[7] Although they knew they would not get any reinforcements, the badly outnumbered Confederates held their ground.

When night came, Young placed a band in front of the battery and had them play "Dixie." The men shouted the Rebel yell and lit bonfires along the supposed line of battle. The enemy, not wanting to be outdone, lit campfires and brought up their band, which played "Annie Laurie." Young's band then played "Way Down Upon the Swannee River." By this time, Lee's wagon train was safely over Hazel Run, and the next morning the Yankees had retreated to the other side of the Rappahannock.

**Company Notes
November 1862**

Company F — Died: John H. Hudson, James J. Kennedy

Hampton's Raid on Dumfries

Most of Burnside's supplies were shipped to Aquia Landing on the Potomac and then moved by rail over the peninsula to his base, located across the Rappahannock River from Fredericksburg. The approximately fifty miles of open country between Burnside's army and Washington, with its communications and overland supply routes used by the sutlers, were vulnerable to Confederate cavalry raids. Hampton's scouts had reported that the Dumfries and Occoquan areas had become assembly points for the wares of the sutlers. There were dozens, maybe hundreds, of wagons filled with all kinds of supplies waiting to be sent to Burnside's troops. Because the wagons and their merchandise were privately owned and operated, only a few troops had been detailed to guard them.

Before daylight, on the icy-cold morning of December 10, 1862, Hampton led a detachment of 520 men from their camp in Culpeper County on a daring raid across the Rappahannock River. With him were Cobb's Legion under Capt. Jerry E. Ritch of Company H, the 1st SC under Col. J.D. Twiggs, 2nd SC under Col. M.C. Butler, 1st NC under Col. James B. Gordon, and the Jeff Davis Legion under Col. W.T. Martin. Hampton had received a report from the Iron Scouts that there was a wagon train on Telegraph Road, which was a heavily patrolled Union supply route that ran almost parallel to the Potomac.

Although there were several inches of snow on the ground, and his men would be exposed to extreme weather conditions, Hampton had hopes of supplying his troops from the enemy's larder. They headed toward the Potomac River with the objective of capturing Dumfries, Virginia, then making a sweep up Telegraph Road to Occoquan.

Hampton divided his command on the morning of Friday, December 12, giving Col. Butler the Cobb's Legion Cavalry, the 1st North Carolina, and 2nd South Carolina, and giving Col. W. T. Martin the 1st South Carolina and the Jeff Davis Legion. After marching sixteen miles, they reached the town of Dumfries at dawn. Col. Butler's men moved into the town from the north side, completely surprising the small force of the enemy there. All fifty of the enemy were captured after only a few shots were fired. Also captured were twenty-four sutlers' wagons, a telegraph operator, and his battery. The troopers destroyed two of the

Chapter 8— Picketing the Rappahannock 51

The route to Dumfries was through snow-covered forests and over icy streams, making traveling on horseback difficult. Photograph by Harry R. Mesic.

wagons before leaving the town at 8:00 A.M. with their prisoners and captured wagons. After marching forty miles, they camped near Morrisville that night and safely crossed the river the next morning. By the time that they returned to base, they had spent three nights in the snow and had endured a long march and many privations, but they did not have any casualties. Following the raid, Cobb's Legion Cavalry made camp in an old pine field near Stevensburg, where they "shivered without tents" and picketed along the Rappahannock.

Stuart wrote to Lee that "Brigadier-General Hampton, with a command thinly clad and scantily fed, displayed, amid the rigors of winter and on the desert track of an invading host, an activity, gallantry, and cheerful endurance worthy of the highest praise and the nation's gratitude."[8]

While their raid was being executed, the Battle of Fredericksburg, a great victory for the South, had taken place a few miles to the south of them. Thomas Cobb, who organized Cobb's Legion and was the cavalry's first commander, was killed while leading Cobb's Legion Infantry. Cobb and his men repulsed repeated attacks by the enemy at the stone wall in Fredericksburg. A trooper recorded how Cobb's cavalrymen felt about him: "The Confederacy never lost a truer, abler or nobler defender.... Thank God [for] the life and character of our peerless Cobb.... Glorious Tom Cobb and his brave command will live forever in history among the brightest constellations that shine out in the annals of great achievements and military glory."[9]

Company Notes
December 10–16, 1862

Company B — Killed: Gustavus Schlesinger.

Hampton's Raid on Occoquan

On the cold wintry day of Wednesday, December 17, 1862, Hampton led another raid across the Rappahannock, with seventy-five men from Cobb's Legion Cavalry, commanded by Major Delony of Company C, and 365 cavalrymen from other units. The troopers crossed the Rappahannock River at the railroad bridge upstream from Kelly's Ford and rode to Cole's Store, where they camped for the night. The next morning at daylight they rode to Neabsco Creek and found a post of the enemy. They surrounded them and captured the whole party with their eight wagons, but only two of the wagons had stores in them.

After that, Gen. Hampton divided his forces into three columns and sent Cobb's Legion Cavalry by Telegraph Road to Occoquan, while the other two columns took different routes to the same place. Cobb's Legion Cavalry captured all the pickets on Telegraph Road, about twenty in number, along with two wagons, and then joined the rest of the cavalrymen in the town where a wagon train and their guards already had been captured.

There was just one small ferryboat to move all the wagons across the river. It was a slow undertaking because the approaches on both sides of the river were bad. Before the wagons could be moved, it was learned that about 2,500 Union cavalrymen had marched from Alexandria and planned to cross the river at Selectman's Ford, one and a half miles from Occoquan. Hampton ordered Capt. T.H. Clark of the 2nd South Carolina and forty sharpshooters to hold the ford at Occoquan until he could bring the wagons across the river. Twice the sharpshooters were attacked by enemy cavalrymen, but they were able to drive them off.

In the meantime, the larger force of the enemy had arrived at Selectman's Ford and was attempting to cross the river. If they succeeded, they would be in the rear of Hampton and his men. Knowing this, Hampton called in the rest of his men, abandoned the unmoved wagons, and withdrew with the wagons that were already across the river. The sharpshooters were left with orders to hold the ford for an hour longer. As soon as Capt. Clark withdrew his men, the enemy followed him across the river, but they withdrew when Capt. Clark and his men charged them. Hampton and the rest of the cavalry headed for Cole's Store, camping for the night at Tackett's Ford on Cedar Run.

When the men got back to base, they had not lost a man but had captured 150 prisoners (plus seven who had been paroled), twenty wagons with valuable stores in them, thirty stands of infantry arms, and one stand of colors. The men were delighted as they celebrated Christmas with the delicacies they had captured. One North Carolinian listed them as "Candies, syrups, pickled oysters, lobsters, smoked beef tongues, Westphalia hams, coffee, sugar, lemons, oranges, plums, nuts, and in fine a little of everything that a well assorted confectionery on Broadway would contain; and then — what is hardly thinkable —'Thomas and Jeremiah,' and brandies and wines of the most approved brands."[10]

One of the kegs, which had been labeled for delivery to Burnside, went to Hampton. Afterwards, Lee wrote:

> I take great pleasure in expressing my gratification at the conduct and result of General Wade Hampton's expeditions to Dumfries on the 11th instant, and to Occoquan on the 18th instant. The plan and execution of these expeditions were bold and admirable, and the results most satisfactory. Please express to General Hampton my high sense of his service, my just appreciation of the conduct of the officers and men of his command, and my congratulations on his complete success without the loss of a man.[11]

Stuart agreed that "General Hampton has again made a brilliant dash."[12]

Company Notes
December 17–28, 1862

Company C—Died: Elijah D. Cowen, Moses R. Hill, George W. Pierce
Company D—Died: Augustus Alford

Stuart's Raid on Occoquan and Dumfries

Not to be outdone by Hampton, Stuart led 1,800 cavalrymen from three of his brigades almost twenty miles to Kelly's Ford, where they crossed the Rappahannock River on the bracing cold morning of Friday, December 26, 1862. Their objective was to sweep Telegraph Road between the towns of Dumfries and Occoquan and to attack Union forces in those towns. They traveled ten miles north and bivouacked for the night near Morrisville.

The next morning, the troopers and artillerymen were awakened before dawn. Stuart divided his force for a three-pronged attack on the highway. Hampton led his men by way of Cole's Store on an attack against Occoquan, while Fitz Lee led his men ten miles to the south of Hampton to strike on Telegraph Road between Dumfries and Aquia Landing, and Rooney Lee took a road between the two other brigades directly to Dumfries. The nearest goal was twenty miles away.

With Hampton were 180 cavalrymen from Cobb's Legion Cavalry and 690 other cavalrymen from the 1st North Carolina, 1st South Carolina, Phillip's Legion, and Jeff Davis Legion. As they approached Cole's Store, the road was blocked by fifteen of the enemy pickets. Twenty of Hampton's men charged the pickets and captured four of them. The other eleven tried to escape but were captured by Rooney Lee's men.

Hampton sent Col. Martin of the 2nd South Carolina into Occoquan with the main body of men, while Hampton took Cobb's Legion Cavalry and the Jeff Davis Legion along River Road to cut off the enemy as it retreated. Before Hampton could reach his destination, Martin and his men dashed into the town, surprising several hundred of the enemy's cavalry. The Union cavalry broke and ran, with most of them escaping, since Hampton had not reached the point where he could cut them off. Nineteen of the enemy and eight wagons were captured. By this time it had become dark, so Hampton moved his men back toward Cole's Store, where they found the other two brigades. They spent a miserable night in the worsening weather.

The next morning before dawn, in the cold and dark, the march began. To keep from freezing to death in their saddles, the cavalrymen walked, leading their horses, for a considerable distance. As they moved toward the Occoquan River with the objective of crossing it to Occoquan, they became so exhausted that when they mounted their horses they dozed in their saddles. When they reached Greenwood Church, the Jeff Davis Legion was detached and sent to Bacon Race Church to cut off a detachment of the enemy. The rest of Hampton's troopers planned to join them there.

Fitz Lee's brigade, which was in front of Hampton's, routed a party of Union cavalry after they left Greenwood Church. Shortly following that, the sounds of artillery and musketry told them that the Jeff Davis Legion had engaged the enemy. Stuart ordered Hampton to cross the river, leaving the Jeff Davis Legion to follow if it could. Hampton took two detachments of his men to Selectman's Ford and crossed toward Occoquan. They met a small force of the enemy and drove them back, but since it was late they did not follow them very far. Much to their relief, the Jeff Davis Legion joined them there. Hampton's men caught up with Stuart's other two brigades and followed them during the march that night. When they reached Burke's Station on the Orange & Alexander Railroad, a mere fifteen miles from Washington, D.C., a telegraph operator was captured in the act of sending messages about Stuart's raid. Stuart had his own telegrapher send a message that has since become famous:

> Quartermaster-General Meigs
>
> United States Army:
>
> Quality of the mules lately furnished me very poor. Interferes seriously with movement of captured wagons.
>
> J.E.B. Stuart

After cutting the wires and burning a bridge, the men moved to Fairfax Court House, where they ran into an ambush. After building huge campfires, as though they planned to remain, Stuart led the men farther north to Falls Church and Vienna. Realizing their pursuers would be to the south, Stuart then headed west to Frying Pan, where they rested for a few hours in the frigid temperature. The next morning they traveled through hill passes to Middleburg and Warrenton and back to the Confederate lines at Culpeper. They arrived back at their camp on Thursday, January 1. During the expedition, Hampton's brigade captured thirty-three prisoners. The only casualties for Cobb's Legion Cavalry were a number of horses, broken down by the long march, and one man wounded. In his report, Stuart said, "The conduct of officers and men on this expedition deserves the highest praise, evincing patient endurance, heroic dash and unflinching courage."[13]

Hampton wrote to his sister, Mary Fisher Hampton, that he considered the expedition "a failure, inasmuch as but little was accomplished & many horses ruined. My men think Stuart came up here because my expeditions had been successful & he was jealous of my Brigade. On the scout he gave my men the hardest work to do, & cut them off from their chance of distinction."[14]

Company Notes
December 26–31, 1862

Company A — Wounded: Andrew J. Fish
Company E — Wounded: S. Thomas Ramsey, Isma W. Thomas

Plight of the Cavalrymen

Wade Hampton wrote his youngest sister, Mary Fisher Hampton, on November 22, 1862: "The country is exhausted, and I do not see how we are to live. General Stuart never thinks of that; at least as far as my Brigade is concerned. He has always given us the hardest work to perform and the worst places to camp at. My numbers are already greatly reduced by our hard service, and I fear there will be no chance to restore our horses [*sic*] condition."[15]

Hampton wrote her again on December 25, 1862: "My men are pretty well worn out, by the recent raids. This sort of work is very hard...."[16]

In mid–January he wrote her: "As long as the enemy are in my front, my Brigade will not be moved, even if all my horses starve to death. The other two Brigades are having a good time, whilst we are left out here to scuffle for ourselves. But we have the satisfaction of knowing that we have done more this winter than all the Va. Cavalry put together."[17]

Both the men and their horses were worn out. Some of those horses had been lost during the raids on Occoquan and Dumfries, but throughout the Southern cavalry hundreds of horses were dying of disease and lack of forage. The men were faring only a little better than the horses. Their rations had been reduced and scurvy was raging. Through necessity, the men were gathering roots, herbs, and tree buds to eat.

By the winter of 1863, major changes were made in the Union cavalry. Scattered cavalry regiments were consolidated, and there were new schools for riders and camps of instruction for grooms, hostlers, and troopers. Old, incompetent officers were replaced by aggressive young men. The morale of the Federal cavalry was stronger than it ever had been. The North had the numerical advantage of manpower, horseflesh, weaponry, ammunition, and equipment.

While the Union cavalry's system was improving, the shortcomings of the Confederate system were becoming apparent. The law that required them to furnish their own mounts was handicapping them. In theory, the government provided feed, shoes, and blacksmithing, and paid the owners forty cents a day for the use of their horses. The government was supposed to reimburse the men for horses killed in action, but if a trooper received any compensation, it was at a fixed value for the horse at the time of his enlistment and paid in depreciated currency, which amounted to only a small fraction of the value of the horse.

Maj. Henry B. McClellan said:

> The evil results of this system were soon apparent, and rapidly increased as the war progressed. Perhaps the least of these was the personal loss it entailed upon the men. Many a gallant fellow whose horse had been irrecoverably lamed for the want of a shoe, or ridden to death at the command of his officer, or abandoned in the enemy's country that his owner might escape capture, impoverished himself and his family in order that he might keep his place in the ranks of his comrades and neighbors. Nor should it be a cause for wonder if this property question affected the courage of many a rider; for experience soon proved that the horse as well as the man was in danger during the rough cavalry melee. If the horse were killed the owner was compensated; but a wounded horse was a bad investment.[18]

Troopers whose horses were captured, worn out, died of disease, or simply lost, had to furnish a new mount for themselves without compensation or transfer to an infantry unit. Often the cavalry lost good men who were unable to buy a fresh mount. Procuring a new mount from home took thirty to sixty days. At times, the cavalry was deprived of more than half of its men while the troopers were home on horse detail. Stuart nicknamed the useless, dismounted detail as "Company Q," while the men called the camp of cavalrymen without horses the "deadline." Many of the men were unable to buy a new mount in the time allotted on their "detail" orders. Those men were classified as "absent without leave." Since it would be an injustice to punish a man for circumstances beyond his control, discipline was relaxed on this point, but there were some men who abused the situation. This was especially apparent in Fitz Lee's brigade, which never should have had less than 2,500 mounted men, but had only 800 at Kelly's Ford and 1,500 at Chancellorsville.

The daily forage ordered to be issued for the horses was ten pounds (five and three-fourths quarts) of corn and ten pounds of long forage for each animal. In reality, that amount was never given out. Often only five pounds of corn and no long forage and, infrequently, only two and one-half pounds of corn were issued. Sometimes there was no corn and scant rations of hay or straw. The deprivation of grain was very bad for the animals, but the absence of long forage was worse. Without the long forage, the horses could not digest the grain. This produced a morbid appetite and the horses would swallow almost anything that would distend their stomachs: empty bags, scraps of paper, bark, and small trees.

Horseshoes and nails were scarce. An unshod horse represented the loss of a saber and rifle in a battle. Troopers were observed leading limping horses, "while from the saddle dangled the hoofs of a dead horse, which he had cut off for the sake of the sound shoes nailed to them."[19]

On November 28, 1862, Stuart approved Hampton's request to establish a camp south of the Rapidan River for the recuperation of the health of the brigade's horses, so that once they recovered the horses could return to duty. While the camp had a beneficial effect on Hampton's brigade, it also made it possible for large numbers of troopers to linger there waiting for their horses to recover—from glanders, grease-heel, and hoof-rot—miles from the fighting front. In early 1863, the camp for horses was "bursting at its seams." The horses still on duty were in danger of having to be sent to the camp due to the lack of forage. The working farms in middle Virginia had been denuded of their crops, while thousands of acres lay fallow because the owners had fled and the hired hands had gone to war.

Stuart seemed to confirm Hampton's complaints of preferential treatment being given to the Virginia brigades. In early January 1863, he sent Fitz Lee's brigade from Fredericksburg to King William County, where forage was more plentiful, and sent Rooney Lee's brigade away from the war zone to the farmlands of Essex County on Virginia's Middle Peninsula. Hampton's brigade, which had seen more service during the past three months than the other two brigades combined, was left to picket the Rappahannock River, where the nearby countryside was devoid of adequate supplies of forage.

Hampton wrote his sister, Mary Fisher Hampton, in late January:

> All my time and correspondence of late have been taken up in quarreling with Stuart, who keeps me here doing all the hard work, while the Virginia Brigades are quietly doing nothing. His partiality towards these Brigades is as marked as it is disgusting and it constantly makes me indignant. I do not object to the work, but I do object to seeing my command broken down by positive starvation. We cannot get forage, and in the course of a few weeks, my Brigade will be totally unfit for service. This is a hard case, but unless Genl. Lee, to whom I have appealed, interferes, Stuart will certainly have my Brigade out of the field before very long.[20]

Unfortunately, Lee did nothing to rectify the problem. It took a written complaint from Hampton to Jefferson Davis before anything was done.

The troopers also suffered from the want of proper arms and equipment. At the beginning of the war, the men furnished their own bridles and saddles, which were often the English round-tree saddle. The use of this saddle resulted in sore-backed horses, so the government ended up issuing an unsightly saddle that protected the horses' backs but completely disregarded the comfort of the riders. In addition, in the Southern cavalry, there were whole regiments that did not have pistols.

Winter of 1863, Union Mud March

Hampton's troopers continued to picket the Rappahannock in the severe weather of the winter of 1863. In late January, Burnside pulled his army out of Falmouth (across the Rappahannock from Fredericksburg) and moved them west toward the Confederate left and rear. For four days, as the Union movement continued, Hampton's men "were almost constantly in the saddle, keeping tabs on Burnside, sending word of his movements to army headquarters, and exchanging rifle and carbine fire with the cavalry in his vanguard."[21]

Fortunately for the Confederates, Burnside's men became bogged down in the frozen rain, sleet, and snow, in what became known as their "Mud March." After the Federals were compelled to return to their camp, Burnside was removed from command.

Company Notes
January 1–February 4, 1863

Company A — Wounded: William T. Cone; Captured: Joseph R. Wilson; Died: Thomas Adams
Company C — Died: John P. Hill
Company H — Died: David Glenn Blackwell

Rappahannock Bridge Action

After the Mud March, Hampton's Brigade continued to picket the Rappahannock River from the United States (or U.S. Mine) Ford above Fredericksburg to a point above the Orange & Alexandria Railroad bridge at Rappahannock Station, eighteen miles to the north. The bitter weather took its toll on the men as they began to die from exposure and disease.

There was a violent snowstorm during the day on February 5, 1863, with intermittent hail and rain throughout the day. During the storm, three brigades of enemy infantry with a force of cavalry moved up Marsh Road on the other side of the Rappahannock and camped near Grove Church. The next day, they attacked Hampton's pickets at the railroad bridge of the Orange & Alexandria Railroad. The enemy cavalry tried to destroy the bridge but were foiled by Hampton's men.

After nightfall, in the bitter cold, the enemy got under the bridge on the opposite side of the river. Hidden behind the abutments, they managed to cut a few posts and attempted to set the bridge on fire. To create a diversion during their attempted destruction of the bridge, they attacked the Confederate pickets. Hampton's men took cover in rifle-pits and held their ground. After several hours of fighting, the enemy withdrew from the bridge. At 2:00 A.M., the entire enemy force left the area, but Hampton's men could not pursue them because of the condition of their horses. During the action, six of the enemy were killed and twenty-five were taken prisoner. One of the Confederates was wounded.

Stuart finally withdrew Hampton's men from their picketing on the Rappahannock on February 12. Hampton wrote a friend: "My Brigade is at last ordered to rest after it is so broken down that it can do nothing more to keep the Va. Brigades off duty."[22] Hampton led his men south of the James River in Virginia, where provisions were plentiful. This area had not yet experienced the brunt of the war.

Company Notes
February 5–May 28, 1863

Company A — Died: John F. Isdal

Company C — Died: James J. Tuck
Company D — Died: R.J. Brown
Company E — Died: Henry J. Donor, A. John Freeman
Company F — Captured: Samuel Burchardt Haesler
Company G — Wounded: Leroy Isadore Couparle
Company H — Died: Thomas A. Smith, Henry Whisenant
Company I — Died: Martin O'Donohoe
Company K — Died: William L. Galaway

Battle of Chancellorsville

In the Union army, Gen. Joseph Hooker replaced Gen. Burnside, and Gen. George Stoneman was put in charge of the Union cavalry. In the South, Lee issued orders on March 9, 1863, officially separating Cobb's Legion's infantry and cavalry into distinct organizations, with the objective of raising each to regimental strength.

On the third of May, 8,000 Union cavalry and artillerymen under Stoneman crossed the Rappahannock on an expedition to cut Lee's communication lines. Simultaneously, on May 1–3, Hooker led the main army across the river into a battle at Chancellorsville, a few miles west of Fredericksburg. Stuart considered Stoneman's raid to be a nuisance expedition and sent only Rooney Lee's brigade to pursue him. Hampton's brigade was rushed to Culpeper Court House in an unproductive attempt to counter Hooker or Stoneman or both.

By remaining with Lee's army, Stuart helped to change the outcome of the battle. He found a route around Hooker's right flank in the Wilderness, which made it possible for Jackson to attack his flank and force the Union army back across the river. However, with the Confederate victory there was a shattering loss. On May 2, Gen. Stonewall Jackson was mortally wounded. On May 3, Stuart replaced Jackson in the battle, leading Jackson's men.

The official report of the Battle of Chancellorsville states that Cobb's Legion Cavalry was South of the James River "recruiting" when the battle took place. (When the records use the word recruiting, they usually mean recuperating, which was the case in this instance.) Most historians have assumed, therefore, that none of Cobb's Legion Cavalry were present at the Battle of Chancellorsville. However, this must not have been true for the whole regiment. Perhaps only those whose horses were unfit for service were recuperating south of the James. This is made clear in Wiley C. Howard's "Sketch of Cobb's Legion Cavalry." He said: "We had our share in the conflicts of the Wilderness and Gettysburg, Chancellorsville and Spotsylvania Court House.... We were with him [Stuart at Chancellorsville] on that last great and memorable flank movement of Jackson in Hooker's rear. The next day, when he [Stuart] passed us in command of Jackson's corps, we bared our heads and cheered our cavalry ideal hero, fearing that he would be taken from us for good."[23]

While they were at southside Virginia, the horses of Hampton's brigade devoured most of the available crops. After the danger had passed in the Culpeper Court House area, they moved their headquarters there. An account of the strength of Cobb's Legion Cavalry on May 25, 1863, reported the following:

Officers effective mounted	31
Men effective mounted	383
Officer non-effective	1

Men non-effective 109
Men absent 29

Company Notes
May 3–21, 1863

Company B — Died: Albert W.J. Carter
Company C — Mortally Wounded: H. Wade (may have been in the infantry)
Company K — Died: W.B. Holeman

Chapter 9

The Gettysburg Campaign

The Grand Reviews

Stuart had the largest number of men that had ever been assigned to him — 9,536 officers and troopers. On Friday, May 22, 1863, when the cavalrymen had drilled to his satisfaction, he held a grand review of the 4,000 troopers under three of his brigade commanders: Hampton, Rooney Lee, and Fitz Lee. The review was held northwest of Culpeper on an open plain near the Brandy Station depot of the Orange & Alexandria Railroad. The cavalrymen passed in front of Stuart in columns of squadrons, first at a walk and then at a charge. The guns of the artillery battalion were fired from a hill opposite the review stand, making the pageant seem like real warfare. Many of the local folks turned out to see the impressive display and to cheer for the men. This inspired Stuart to hold an even grander review.

On Friday, June 5, the performance was repeated for civilian and military officials from Richmond, well-to-do planters and their families, and other distinguished guests. When the mostly female guests arrived, they quickly filled the nearby private homes and the available accommodations in Culpeper. To provide a place for the overflow crowd to stay, tents were pitched near Stuart's headquarters. This time the brigades of Grumble Jones and Beverly Robertson joined the brigades of Hampton and the two Lees, and all 9,536 of Stuart's men participated. The troopers and artillerymen held mock battles, firing pistols, brandishing sabers, and discharging cannons with blank rounds, while shouting at the top of their lungs. The enthusiastic audience was awed by their performance. Unfortunately, the anticipated guest of honor, Robert E. Lee, was unable to attend, so Stuart staged a third performance for Lee on Monday, June 8. In spite of the pomp and ceremony, there were serious deficiencies in the cavalry — ragged uniforms, an inferior quality and quantity of equipment, and worn-out horses — when compared to their Northern counterparts.

By then, Ewell's infantry corps was on its way to the Shenandoah Valley with Longstreet's men at their rear. A.P. Hill's infantry corps was preparing to leave Fredericksburg. Stuart's men were to fall in with the main column the next day, to screen the infantry movements and protect their flank, as they proceeded north across the Blue Ridge Mountains.

That night, after the third review, the men were fatigued and slept soundly in their camp on the south bank of the Rappahannock River. Stuart had stationed his men along the fords of the Rappahannock and Hazel rivers. From west to east, Fitz Lee's brigade under Col. Thomas T. Munford was at Stark's Ford, Rooney Lee's brigade was at Wellford's Ford, and Robertson's brigade was at Beverly's Ford, with pickets stationed six miles farther to the east at Kelly's Ford. Maj. Robert F. Beckham's horse artillery was on the west side of the Beverly's Ford Road near St. James Church and in plain view of Fleetwood Hill, which was to their south. Stuart was encamped on the two and a half mile long Fleetwood Hill, which was located north of

Chapter 9—The Gettysburg Campaign

The rolling countryside of Brandy Station concealed the positions of the armies. Photograph by Harry R. Mesic.

Brandy Station. Grumble Jones' and Wade Hampton's brigades were camped between Brandy Station and Stevensburg. Cobb's Legion Cavalry was bedded down in the fields and meadows that surrounded Brandy Station.

Company Notes
June 1–June 8, 1863

Company K — Captured: John W. Hammond

Brandy Station

On the next morning, Tuesday, June 9, 1863, Cobb's Legion Cavalry was involved in the largest and most hotly contested cavalry battle ever fought in the Western Hemisphere. Of the 20,500 troops engaged in this battle, 17,000 were cavalrymen. One trooper described the battle as being the "greatest distinctive cavalry battle in our experience."[1]

Hooker had interpreted the Confederate presence south of the Rappahannock to mean they were planning a raid of his supply lines. He ordered the Union troops to disperse and destroy the Confederate forces. In the early hours of the morning on June 9, Gen. John Buford

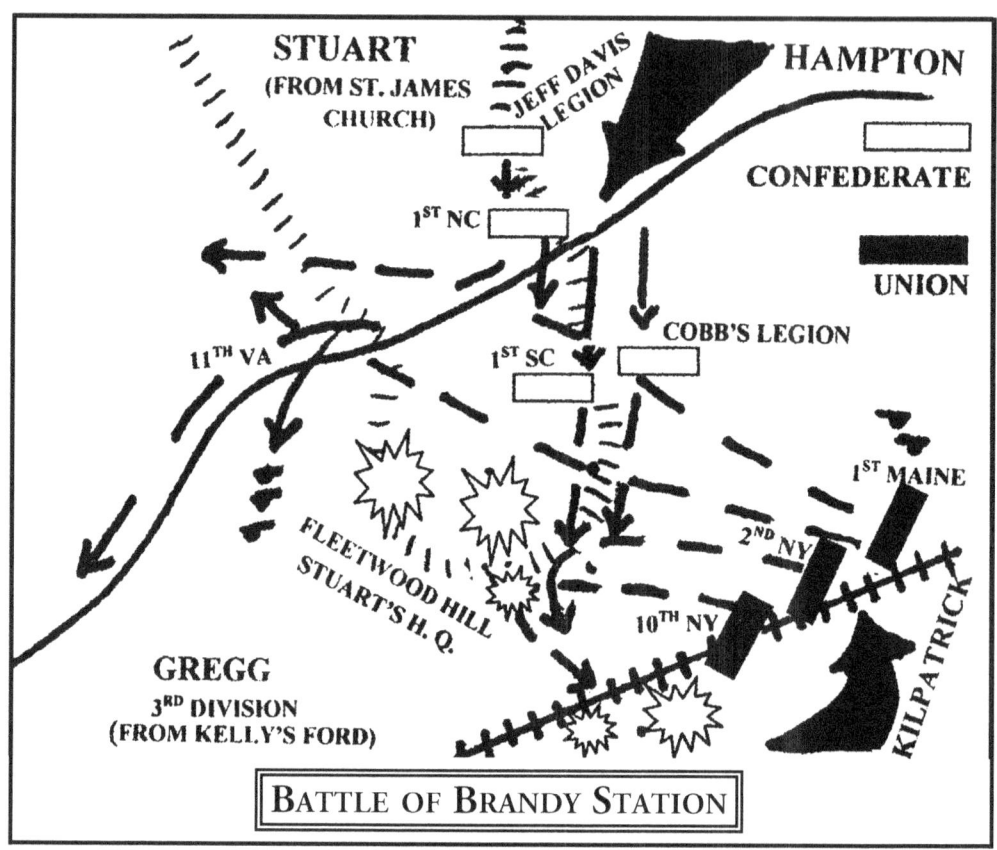

positioned a large column of Federal cavalry along the fog-shrouded north bank of the Rappahannock River. While the Confederate cavalry was still sleeping, two regiments of infantry and some cavalry under U.S. Gen. David McMurtrie Gregg stormed across the Rappahannock at Kelly's Ford. (Gregg was a native of Pennsylvania who got mounted experience early in his career fighting Indians on the frontier.) The 1st South Carolina regiment from Hampton's brigade was sent up Kelly's Ford Road to hold the enemy in check, until Robertson's brigade could relieve them.

Several miles away, around 4:30 in the morning, a large column of New York Cavalry under Col. Benjamin F. "Grimes" Davis began rushing across the foggy Rappahannock River at Beverly's Ford, surprising the Confederate pickets. In addition to Davis, the Union cavalry commanders included Cols. H. Judson Kilpatrick and Percy Wyndham, and Capts. Wesley Merritt, George Armstrong Custer, and Elon J. Farnsworth.

Kilpatrick was described as "a feisty little Celt from New Jersey, a man with a shrill voice, a long red beak, reddish side-whiskers, and scraggly, sandy-colored hair. He had graduated from West Point in May 1861 and thereafter had enjoyed an active career that fed his boundless ambition. He was brave and impetuous, but erratic and lacking in sound judgment."[2] In 1864, Sherman would call him "a hell of a damned fool."[3] Col. Joseph Frederick Waring of the Jeff Davis Legion said of him, "[T]hat fool Kilpatrick. Of all the Yankee humbugs he is the greatest."[4]

Custer was a native of Ohio and only twenty-one when the war began. He was described as being "a brash but capable young man regarded highly by his superiors and loved by his men, who were inspired by his bravery"[5]; "Custer had graduated from USMA in June 1861, a class behind Kilpatrick, and he very nearly didn't make it because of having acquired close to the limit in demerits. He was ... a very daring and unconventional young man."⁶ He was a classmate and best friend of P.M.B. Young.

Along with the U.S. Cavalry were two brigades of infantry under U.S. Gen. Alfred Pleasonton. There were about 5,500 men in all. After crossing Beverly's Ford, they moved through the woods to the west of Beverly's Ford Road. Their gunfire awakened Grumble Jones' men, who scrambled to their horses only partially dressed and with some riding bareback. Jones mounted barefooted, hatless, and coatless. His men hotly engaged the enemy near a bend in Beverly's Ford Road and temporarily checked its progress. In the fighting, Grimes Davis, with a saber in his hand, was killed on the road by a bullet wound to his head. Davis' men had been halted just short of where Beckham's Horse Artillery was camped.

Beckham's cannoneers swung a couple of their guns around and fired down the road at Buford's men, enabling the rest of the artillerymen to hastily hitch up and get into position at the Gee House and St. James Church. Those two buildings were located on knolls on either side of Beverly's Ford Road.

At 5:00 A.M., Young was ordered to move down the railroad with as little delay as possible. (The railway was south of Fleetwood Hill and ran east to west.) Cobb's Legion Cavalry moved about a mile beyond Fleetwood to where the 1st North Carolina had already engaged the enemy. Jones' brigade then moved to the left of Beckham's Horse Artillery. Robertson's men moved towards Kelly's Ford, while the rest of Hampton's men moved into position between the Kelly's Ford and Beverly's Ford roads. Col Thomas T. Munford, with Fitz Lee's brigade at Stark's Ford, moved east towards Beverly's Ford. All the wagons of Stuart's division were sent to the rear towards Culpeper Court House.

Rooney Lee's brigade formed a line facing east along a north-south ridge of Yew Hills to the left of Jones. He placed his artillery on a plateau beside Dr. Daniel Green's house and positioned dismounted cavalrymen behind a low stone wall several hundred feet beneath and to the east of the Green's house. Rooney Lee's brigade attacked the enemy's right flank, while Hampton's brigade deployed sharpshooters in the woods in the enemy's front and attacked their left flank. Being assaulted on three sides, the enemy withdrew.

Realizing that the direct route to Brandy Station was blocked by Confederate artillery, Buford moved most of his cavalry to the Cunningham farm, east of Rooney Lee's troopers, and assaulted the men behind the stone wall below the Green's house in an attempt to turn the Confederate left. Rooney Lee had the advantage of the best terrain, and his men held firm. It was only after sustaining heavy losses that Buford's men were able to wrestle the stone wall away from the Confederates. To their amazement, Rooney Lee pulled his men back.

Meanwhile, the enemy was still crossing at Kelly's Ford, and two regiments of their cavalry were moving towards Stevensburg. To stop them, Col. Butler's 2nd South Carolina was sent to Stevensburg, and Col. Wickham's 4th Virginia regiment was sent to his support along with one piece of artillery. Robertson, at Kelly's Ford, had enemy infantry at his front and enemy cavalry to his right. The entire Union cavalry force had crossed the river with a large portion of artillery and were supported by nine regiments of infantry on Kelly's Ford Road and seven on Beverly's Ford Road. Their orders were to proceed to Brandy Station, but they had not anticipated meeting such a large number of Confederate cavalrymen. Gregg discovered that a circuitous route to Brandy Station was unguarded, so he moved his men over that route and arrived there at 11:00 A.M.

Surveying the situation, Stuart decided to make the real stand on the ridge of Fleetwood

Hill. Because the field was so densely wooded and so extensive, with so many avenues of approach, he divided his command into detachments to guard all approaches and delay the enemy, while concentrating his forces near Fleetwood. Two regiments (the 12th and 35th Virginia Cavalry) of Jones' brigade were sent to hold the heights, while the rest of Jones' men were to keep the enemy occupied in his front. Hampton and Robertson were ordered to move their men to the ridge, and the rest of Jones' men were to follow. Rooney Lee was to join them on their left.

Hampton ordered a body of skirmishers to move forward. In conjunction with the skirmishers, 100 sharpshooters under Capt. Ritch of Company H dismounted and engaged the enemy for about two hours in the woods, causing heavy losses among the enemy and driving them back steadily. (Whenever the men fought dismounted, the order would be given to "Dismount to fight!" The first, second, and third man would dismount and attach together the bridle reins of their horses, while the fourth man remained mounted and would lead the horses to a sheltered spot.) Because the enemy force was so large, Hampton sent an additional 100 men in to support the dismounted sharpshooters.

The 12th and 35th Virginia Cavalry took the ridge about fifty yards in front of the enemy, and with one piece of artillery they were able to check the enemy's advance. The 12th Virginia charged the enemy but broke in confusion when the enemy's reserve came forward. The 35th Virginia's column, which was coming up to support the 12th Virginia, charged, but the enemy was too strong for them, also. For a time the Southern artillerymen were engaged in hand-to-hand combat, with a pistol in one hand and a saber in the other. The 6th Virginia Cavalry then attacked the flank, but was unable to stop the enemy.

Around noon, one of Stuart's aides brought Young the information that, while fighting a force in his front towards the river, the enemy somehow got into Stuart's rear. When his men faced about, they discovered the vast plain was swarming with mounted bluecoats vigorously coming toward them. Gregg had arrived from Kelly's Ford with his cavalry division of 2,200 men. They had taken a route through the village of Brandy Station and were approaching from the south in Stuart's rear. U.S. Col. Wyndham formed his men into a line and charged up the western slope of Fleetwood. As they neared the top, men from Jones' brigade, who were withdrawing from St. James Church, rode over the crest. Meanwhile, Kilpatrick's men swung south and attacked the southern and eastern slopes of Fleetwood, but they were met by Hampton's men. Knowing that he would be surrounded if the enemy took the hill, Hampton recalled his regiments singly, before recalling the sharpshooters. They fell back fighting.

At this critical point in the battle, Hampton made a brilliant charge upon the flank of the enemy, with Cobb's Legion Cavalry in the lead. Hampton threw off his coat to leave his sword-arm free, and flung the coat to his son Preston, who was his acting orderly. Preston held the coat for a few seconds, and then threw it on the ground, saying, "I came here to fight, not carry coats!"[7] He was soon galloping beside his father. The seasoned troopers who observed this incident smiled and said, "A chip off the old block!"[8]

Young moved Cobb's Legion Cavalry in the direction of Stuart's headquarters. Col. J.L. Black's 1st South Carolina Cavalry supported him. Hampton ordered them to move at a gallop and engage the enemy in the front and on the right. After riding for about a mile at almost a full gallop, they began to ascend a steep hill called the "Peach Orchard," where Stuart's headquarters was located. A second aide from Stuart brought the report that his headquarters were in possession of the enemy and Cobb's Legion Cavalry should clear the hill.

They discovered a line of enemy cavalrymen with drawn sabers and pistols on the hill, watching as a battery was being put into position. The enemy cavalry swung down the hill, charging the Southern troopers. Cobb's Legion Cavalry swung to the right into line within two hundred yards of the enemy. Young, in a clear ringing voice, commanded, "By squadron front into line, ho!" Just then, the Yankees came charging over the crest of the hill, firing as they came. Young ordered, "Forward charge!"

Delony had the foresight to see that the troops were about to mix. The dust and smoke from the battle were so thick that it was impossible at a distance, and difficult up close, to distinguish between comrades and enemy. In his deep voice, Delony commanded, "Sabers, boys, sabers, no pistols!"[7] As soon as they engaged the enemy, the dust was so dense and the fighting was so close that it would have been impossible to use either pistols or artillery without the risk of hitting friends instead of foes. Eve said that they had about one hundred twenty men with sabers, while the enemy had the 2nd and 10th New York, 1st Maryland, 1st Maine, plus a squadron of Washington, D.C., Cavalry under Kilpatrick.

In a letter to his wife, Delony wrote, "When Young ordered the charge — our men went in with a rousing cheer — I had the old Ga. Troopers and the old Richmond Hussars with me...."[8] They charged in close columns of squadrons up to the enemy's lines, which, at that point, were unbroken. The front rank of the enemy emptied their pistols at them, while the shining sabers of the enemy's rear rank glistened and flashed in their faces. The opposing forces 'mixed.' Soon the enemy's splendid line was all broken, and each man was fencing and fighting for a time with his individual foe. The blows fell fast, and the sabers slashed, while most of the enemy were heading for their rear, some mounted, some unhorsed, while others were pinned to the earth by a fallen steed.

A participant reported that "Thousands of flashing sabers streamed in the sunlight; the rattle of carbines and pistols mingled with the roar of cannon; armed men wearing the blue and the gray became mixed in promiscuous confusion; the surging ranks swayed up and down the sides of Fleetwood Hill, and dense clouds of smoke and dust rose as a curtain to cover the tumultuous and bloody scene."[9]

The battle was described as being "like what we read of in the days of chivalry, acres and acres of horsemen sparkling with sabers, and dotted with brilliant bits of color where their flags danced above them, hurled against each other at full speed and meeting with a shock that made the earth tremble."[10]

Wiley C. Howard reported that all sorts of experiences and incidents were happening all about him. After the first charge, his men deftly wheeled to the rear. He rushed to the aid of one of his comrades, who was tangled in the limbs of a peach tree and was being chopped over the head by his adversary. With a fortunate swing of the arm, Howard's blade touched the enemy's neck and the blood flowed, much to the relief of his friend. The friend dashed after his man, but Howard was swept along by his unruly mare amid the confused mass of jumbled-up, retreating Yankees. His horse never stopped until she ran up against a piece of artillery the Federals were trying to save. The drivers and others jumped down and ran for their lives.

As Howard got control of his steed and faced her about, he saw Delony, his former captain, smiting Yankees right and left as he charged along in advance. Delony sat grandly on his charger, his fine physique and full mahogany beard flowing, looking like a Titan war god, flushed with the exuberance and exhilaration of victory. Delony called to Howard to rally with others of his old company. He led them, pressing the retreating foe right down to a railroad cut, until they ran into cross fire from the enemy's dismounted men. The Federals had apparently organized there to stop the stampede of their own men who had been driven back, and if possible to stop the Confederate's progress.

Young, seeing the danger from his position, dashed rapidly down and ordered Delony to withdraw. Shaking his head and lion-like beard, Delony said, "Young, let's charge them!"[11] In two or three minutes five horses fell and a number of their men had been shot. By this time, however, the enemy's whole line was giving way, so on they went — those not unhorsed or crippled. So fierce and fast was the fighting they had no time to accept surrender offered by many of the Yankees. They just rode on and left them behind.

William L. Church of Company C was unhorsed and fighting with two mounted Yankees. While one of them was leaning over with his hand on Church's shoulder, Church succeeded in fatally wounding him with a thrust of his sword. As the Yankee fell off his horse, Church mounted it and galloped to the front of the others. Delony wrote to his wife: "In the midst of the charge Church's horse was wounded and quicker than thought he was mounted on a Yankee's horse and in the charge again — He behaved very gallantly and came out with a bloody saber."[12] Hampton reported that "the leading regiments [Cobb's Legion Cavalry and the 1st South Carolina] charged gallantly up the steep hill upon which the enemy were strongly posted, and swept them off in a perfect rout without a pause or a check."[13]

As their portion of the field was won, across the way on an elevation near a brick house Gen. Hampton was manning the guns of James F. Hart's Battery. Yankee cavalry suddenly appeared and were riding among the guns, chopping down the men. Hart's men were fighting them with rammers and swab sticks. They knocked two of the cavalrymen from their horses. Fitz Lee and his Virginia Cavalrymen charged the position and cleared it of Yankees in about three minutes' time. About this time, Stuart dashed up to where officers were reforming the men. He waved his hat with the black rooster feather above his head, and shouted, "Cobb's Legion, you've covered yourself with glory. Follow me!"[14]

When Stuart sent Jones and Hampton to save his headquarters, that left Rooney Lee dangerously unsupported. He pulled his men back through the Yew Hills toward the higher ground of Fleetwood. As he retreated, Buford followed him, fighting his rear guard all the way. Stuart ordered Rooney Lee to counterattack. When the Confederates crashed into Buford's men, they disengaged and retreated across Beverly's Ford.

The charges made by Hampton's men won Fleetwood Hill and the ground south of the railroad. Cobb's Legion Cavalry captured 60 of the enemy. Among the captured were several commissioned officers, including a lieutenant-colonel. In his report, Young stated that:

> [T]he officers and men of my command acted in a gallant and praiseworthy manner. All acted so well that it seems unfair to mention names of any particular individuals; but I cannot fail to mention the intrepid personal gallantry of my lieutenant-colonel, W.G. Delony. Among others whose distinguished conduct came under my personal observation, was my adjutant, Lieut. W.L. Church [of Company C]; Capt. J.E. Ritch [of Company H], commanding sharpshooters (who, I regret to say, while dismounted, was captured by a cavalry charge), and Lieutenant [James Luke] Clanton [of Company K]. Capt. [Barrington S.] King [of Company E] also deserves praise for the manner in which he commanded his sharpshooters. I desire also to mention the most distinguished gallantry of McCroan [probably Henry M. McCroan of Company F] and Landrum [probably Benjamin Landrum of Company H], who on foot, refused to surrender when surrounded by the enemy, but cut their way through safely.[15]

Hampton said in his report that "I have never seen any troops display greater coolness, bravery, and steadiness."[16]

Delony wrote to his wife:

> It is the first time we have ever met the enemy in an open field in a charge — Heretofore it has been in byways & roads & we succeeded as I have always told you we would succeed — with such a set of men to follow. I never have seen, nor do I ever again expect to see a field swept in such splendid style, as was that battle field by Hampton's Brigade.... But for Hampton I think the day would have been lost.... The highest compliment we have received ... came from Lt. Col. [James Byron] Gordon of the 1st N.C. Regt — He met me soon after our charge with the greeting — "Well Delony, Cobb's Legion have done *as usual*."[17]

At the end of the daylong battle, the casualties were: Confederacy — 515, Union — 868. During the fighting, Company K lost 22 men killed, wounded, or captured out of 27, and 13 horses killed.

Among the wounded was Col. M.C. Butler, who lost his foot. Among those killed in the battle was Wade Hampton's brother, Lt. Col. Frank Hampton of the 2nd South Carolina Regiment, who was mortally wounded because Wickham's men ran, leaving him unsupported. He died that night. Hampton would never fully recover from the death of his brother and would resent Wickham and hate the Yankees from then on.

Stuart ordered his staff to reestablish his camp exactly where it had been before the attack. The dead men and horses that covered the ground made the task impossible, so, in the end, that ground was abandoned to the flies and the buzzards. The Southerners were clearly the victors. They captured three cannons and five hundred prisoners and held the field. Although the Union cavalry lost the battle, they were in high spirits as they recrossed the Rappahannock. For the first time, they had engaged the Southern cavaliers and had offered a determined resistance. From then on, they would confront them with poise, power, and self-confidence. On the other hand, from that time on, the Confederate cavalry would have difficulty getting remounts, which would have a negative effect on the morale of the men and the strength of the cavalry. Although, they were willing to risk being shot themselves, they knew that they would be transferred into the infantry if their horses were killed and they could not replace them. The men were not willing to take the risks that they had taken before.

Company Notes
June 9–12, 1863

Company A — Wounded: William Joseph Wynne

Company C — Killed: James Dunahoo, Wounded: Wellington L. Bryant; Captured: Julius J. Fields

Company E — Captured: John N. Brooks, James A. Netherland

Company F — Killed: William Hardwick; Wounded: George Ira Barwick, Henry M. McCroan, Francis A. Sinquefield; Captured: Samuel J.L. Gordon, George William Hughes, Thomas J. Nasworthy, James L. Oates, Andrew B. Oats, William E. Penrow

Company H — Killed: Bennett H. Carter, Augustus F. Hardy, Nicholas C. Ware; Wounded: John B. O'Shields; Captured: Lewis W. Barrett, Thomas D. Brooks, John Hawkins Bulloch, Jeremiah E. Ritch, Moses Sylvanus Simmons; Missing: Tilman H. Brown

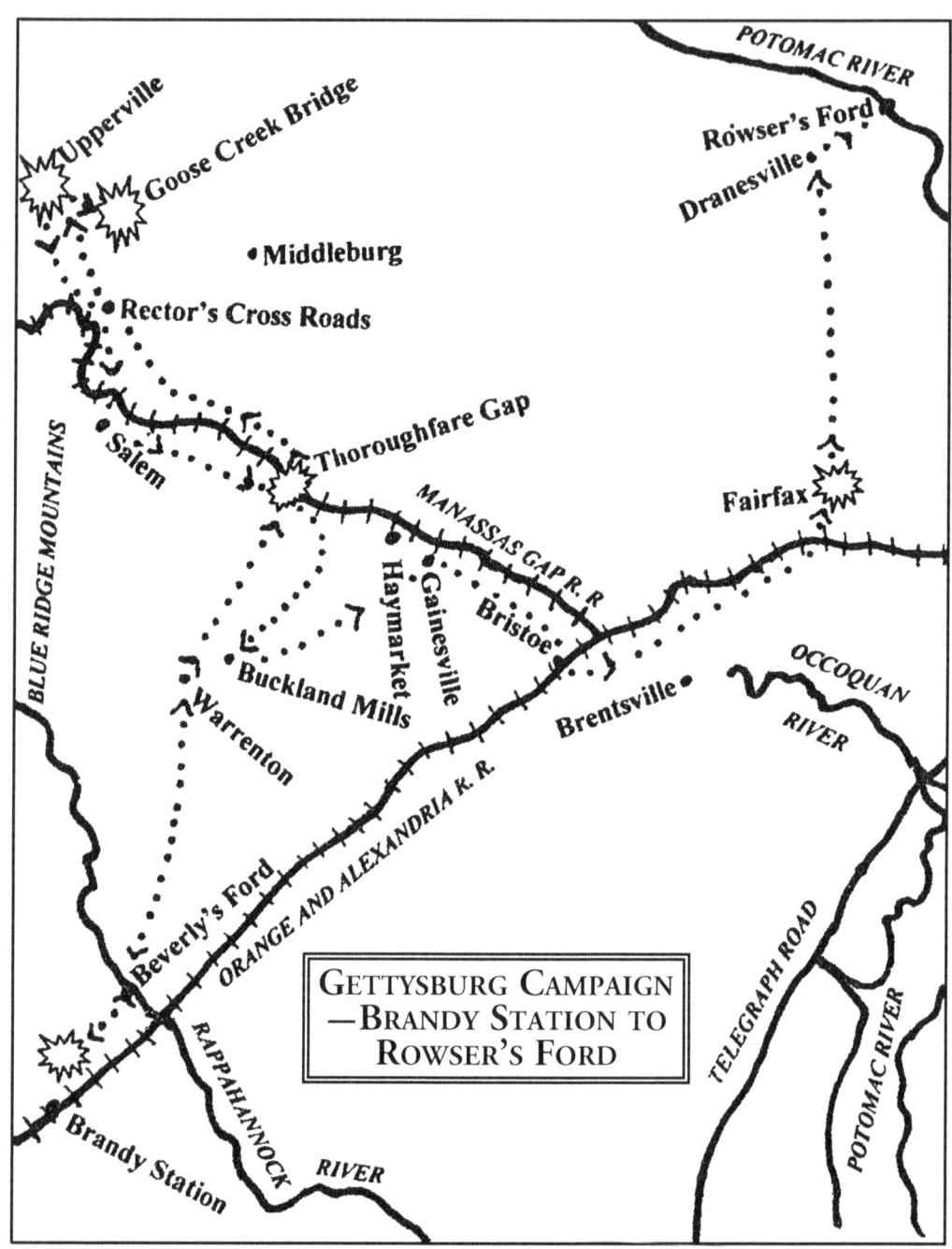

Company I — Wounded: James M. Cobb, Owen O'Connor; Captured: Josiah Miller
Company K — Mortally wounded: Dan Higgons; Wounded: B.A. Ball, James Luke Clanton, John T. Higdon, T.R. Laffew, J.F. Strickland
Company L — Killed: T.W. Cates, Richard Sconyers; Mortally Wounded: James Turner; Wounded: Daniel L. Burnett, William E. Goodwin, Jeremiah Berry Jones, James M. Thomas; Captured: Oscar L. Carter, Samuel L. Cowart

Goose Creek Bridge

Hampton's Brigade supervised the abandonment of the camp at Brandy Station, while the other cavalry brigades crossed the Rappahannock with Lee's advance units, screening the army as it marched north behind the shelter of the Blue Ridge Mountains. Hampton was under orders from Stuart to remain on the Rappahannock River until the last of Pleasonton's videttes left the north shore.

On Saturday, June 13, 1863, one hundred eighteen remounted "dead-liners" from the South Carolina units rejoined the brigade, bringing the total to about 1,400 officers and men. On June 17, after the Union videttes were gone, Hampton's troopers crossed the Rappahannock at Beverly's Ford. Those who lost their horses at Brandy Station but desired to continue in the campaign rode double, expecting to find a replacement horse along the way. This placed an additional strain on the horses. The brigade passed through Warrenton and camped that night outside of the town.

The next day, during an incessant rain, two regiments of cavalry from the defense forces of Washington rode down to the area that the brigade had evacuated. Hampton was unwilling to leave such a large body of the enemy in his rear, so he turned his men around and sparred with the Union troopers for several hours. When night came, Hampton's troopers returned through the pitch-black darkness to their camp outside of Warrenton. They spent a restless, uncomfortable night in the soggy downpour, concerned about the enemy in the area.

On Friday, June 19, they started north to join Stuart. Hampton led his men up the east side of the Bull Run Mountains, through Thoroughfare Gap and into the Loudoun Valley. The cavalry were engaged "in a number of skirmishes and hot little bouts near Thoroughfare Gap."[18] Late on June 20, they reached Stuart's headquarters at Rector's Cross Roads. That night, it rained continuously. The men were damp, tired, and hungry as they marched along the Upperville Turnpike the next day. They had been separated from their wagons for days, and the only rations they had were green corn and apples, which they gathered along the way. The horses had to get by with grazing whenever they had a chance.

Cobb's Legion Cavalry and the 1st South Carolina were on the north side of the road being led by Young. The 1st North Carolina and the Jeff Davis Legion were on the south side of the road under Col. Laurence Simmons Baker. The rain ceased and it turned into a beautiful day. After passing through Upperville and reaching Goose Creek (about two miles from Upperville and between Upperville and Middleburg), Gregg's cavalry attacked them. Kilpatrick's brigade of cavalry and Vincent's brigade of infantry were in front. Gregg was attempting to pierce the screen of Stuart's cavalry and had over 1,500 infantrymen with his cavalry — more than Hampton's entire brigade. Their original plan was for Kilpatrick to make a feint against Hampton while Buford attacked Col. John Randolph Chambliss and Beverly Robertson on Stuart's flank. Buford found Chambliss and Robertson so strong that the feint against Hampton became a serious attack involving Hampton's entire force. The fighting lasted for several hours, until the regiments under Baker were overpowered and forced to retreat. This left Young's regiments unprotected.

Over to their left the men could see the smoke of battle and hear cannon fire, so they knew that Robertson's and Jones' brigades were also engaged with the enemy on a parallel road. Hampton sent word to Young to fall back to the next crest, where Hampton planned to make a stand. As the Union cavalry advanced with the support of their horse artillery and dismounted troopers, Hampton spied an opening. Standing up in his stirrups with his saber lifted above his head, he bellowed to the nearest Confederates, "Follow me!" Then he galloped straight toward the enemy. With a cheer, the 1st North Carolina followed him. Behind them, the other units formed and charged.

The 1st North Carolina struck the enemy with sabers as Hampton yelled, "Give it to them!" Then they dropped back and the other units attacked in turn. After three assaults, Gregg was driven back. Many of the enemy were killed and wounded and eighty of them were taken as prisoners. Gregg had failed to meet his objective of piercing the Confederate cavalry screen. After the furious fighting, Stuart had them withdraw to a strong defensive position at Ashby Gap.

An unfortunate postscript to this battle is that Park Service signs are posted at the Goose Creek Bridge today, describing the battle as a great victory for Gregg.

Upperville

After grazing their horses, Hampton's brigade rode in the middle of Stuart's column, followed by two of Beverly Robertson's regiments. The enemy kept flanking Robertson, so Robertson ordered his men to return to Upperville. The Federal cavalry under Kilpatrick rode hard and arrived at Upperville first.

Stuart reported, "I was anxious on account of the women and children to avoid a conflict in the village, but the enemy, true to those reckless and inhuman instincts, sought to take advantage of this disinclination on our part, by attacking furiously our rear guard."[19] They chased Robertson's men through the streets of Upperville, inflicting numerous casualties. When Stuart saw what was happening, he ordered reinforcements for Robertson.

Hampton was the first to respond. He turned his men around and, with his saber in his hand, led the Jeff Davis Legion at a gallop in a charge of the enemy. The troopers gave a war whoop and hit the Union column so hard that they cut a swath through the middle of it, bringing it to a halt. A shooting and slashing conflict followed for several minutes, until the enemy, stunned by the savagery of the fight, broke and galloped off.

Both sides regrouped. Within minutes, Hampton led Cobb's Legion Cavalry, the Jeff Davis Legion, and the 1st North Carolina Cavalry through the town toward the head of the enlarged enemy column. The men fought hand to hand for a while before both sides retreated. Dozens of horses and riders were left piled in the streets.

During the battle, the color bearer for Cobb's Legion Cavalry was cut down and their battle flag was captured. William L. Church of Company C rescued the flag by thrusting his saber through the body of the Yankee carrying it and then tearing the flag from his hands. He brought the flag back to the Legion "amid a hail storm of bullets."[20]

When darkness fell, the battle ended. Hampton's troopers captured eighty prisoners. In his book, Henry B. McClellan said, "If victory in any passage at arms is to be claimed by either side, it must be accorded to Hampton's brigade, which at the close of the day relieved the pressure on Robertson's two regiments, drove back the forces opposed to it, regained more than half a mile of ground, and retired from the battle at a walk, and unmolested."[21]

As usual, Stuart had nothing but praise for Hampton's men, saying, "General Hampton's brigade participated ... in a brilliant manner."[22]

Stuart's losses for June 17–21 were: total killed, wounded or missing — 510. Federal losses for this same time period were: total killed, wounded or missing — 827. The significance of the five days of fighting around Upperville becomes apparent when the losses for both sides are compared to the losses at Brandy Station. They are virtually the same.

Company Notes
June 19–21, 1863

Company A — Captured: Joseph Smith
Company B — Wounded: Henry F. Williams
Company D — Wounded: George T. Gallaway
Company E — Wounded: Henry W. Smith
Company I — Captured: Solomon L. Bassford, James Walter Day, Bartholomew J. Murphy
Company K — Captured: B.A. Ball, D.R. Davis, Frank Hartford, Henry Marshall, Edward McGinness, William Young

Rector's Cross Roads

On Monday, June 22, 1863, the Union cavalry, along with their infantry support, withdrew to the east. Stuart followed them eastward and concentrated his men around Rector's Cross Roads. During the next five days, the troopers were refurbished and resupplied. On the night of June 23, a downpour drenched the land. Stuart ordered his blanket and oilcloths to be spread under a tree at the rear of a house. When his staff encouraged him to sleep inside, his reply was, "No! my men are exposed to this rain, and I will not fare any better than they."[23]

Lee's army was already advancing into Pennsylvania, and Stuart needed to find a way to lead his cavalry to the head of the army. He could not move along the eastern side of the Blue Ridge Mountains. All roads leading northward through the valley were clogged with trains of artillery and quartermaster, commissary, and ordnance wagons, in addition to infantry columns. The alternative route that Stuart suggested, and Lee approved, was for Stuart to pass through Hopewell Gap or some other gap in the Bull Run Mountains, sweep around the rear of Meade's army and make a dash northward between Meade and Washington. He would cut communication lines and damage railroads along the route. He would then cross the Potomac into Maryland, joining Lee's army north of the Potomac. Stuart planned to link with Ewell's infantry somewhere along the Susquehanna River. No date was set for his reunion with Ewell, and the plans were contingent on their being practical. The downside of the plan was that Stuart's men would have to ride nearly 150 miles in just a few days.

Until Meade moved, the mountain passes had to be protected in order to prevent Union cavalry from pouring through them and attacking Lee's rear. Lee requested that Stuart leave Hampton's brigade with Longstreet. Instead, Stuart left his two least experienced brigades, Jones' and Robertson's brigades, with Robertson in command — about 3,000 men — to hold the passes until their front was clear, and then to operate as Lee directed. Future events would show that this was a serious mistake. Afterwards, Longstreet complained that Stuart simply rid himself of the two brigades he did not like, and that he should have left behind someone reliable, like Hampton.

Stuart kept with him Hampton's, Fitz Lee's, and Rooney Lee's brigades, the latter under the command of Chambliss because Rooney Lee had not recovered from his wounds. On the

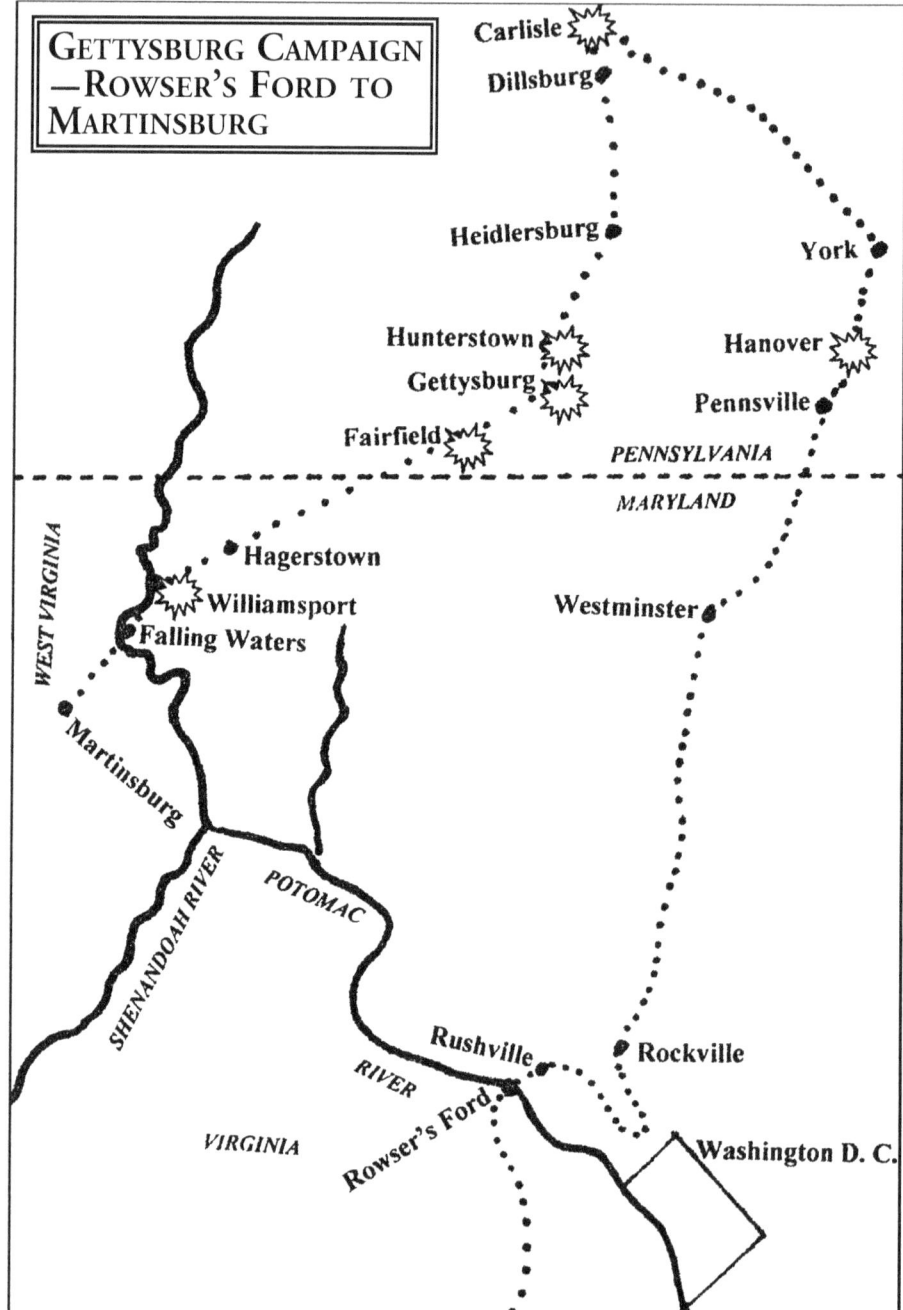

GETTYSBURG CAMPAIGN
—ROWSER'S FORD TO
MARTINSBURG

night of Wednesday, June 24, with six artillery pieces and three days' rations, they rendezvoused secretly near Salem Depot. It has been estimated that there were between 2,000 and 4,500 officers and men. At 1:00 A.M., the brigades very quietly moved out. This precaution was necessary because the enemy had possession of the Bull Run Mountains from which, in the daytime, they could observe all movements in that region. Since Union Gen. Winfield Scott Hancock's corps occupied Thoroughfare Gap, they moved to the right, passing through Glasscock's Gap, and marched toward Haymarket, Virginia.

Company Notes
June 22–24, 1863

Company A — Captured: John B. Hays
Company B — Wounded: John M. Clayton
Company I — Captured: John McCale

Haymarket

The cavalry started out a little after midnight on the morning of Thursday, June 25, 1863, with the men in high spirits. They had come to think of themselves, and their leaders, as being invincible because of their many successes in battle. Early in the day's march, as they neared Haymarket, they discovered that Hancock's corps was en route through Haymarket, going toward Gum Springs. His troops were blocking the road that Stuart needed to cross for many miles in each direction.

Stuart planned to raid the enemy's wagon train. Cobb's Legion Cavalry was at the head of the column with Delony in command as they moved toward the train. They were ready to pounce on it when they discovered infantrymen marching with fixed bayonets alongside of the train. Unfortunately, it was too late to avoid being spotted by the enemy, and Cobb's Legion Cavalry was subjected to cannonading by a nearby battery. The charge was cancelled and Cobb's Legion Cavalry was recalled, but Delony had wanted to attack, anyway, and protested the withdrawal.

Stuart chose a good position for his artillery and shelled the passing column for a while. Union men, wagons, and horses were scattered in wild confusion and some prisoners were captured. The troopers were delayed for most of the morning, until they were able to make a circuitous detour around the rear of Hancock's corps. They withdrew to Buckland Mills, then Gainesville, with the objective of crossing the Occoquan River at Wolf Run Shoals on June 26.

Rockville, Maryland

In a drizzling rain on Friday, June 26, 1863, Stuart took a southerly route through Bristoe Station and Brentsville before turning north through Fairfax Station, where the troopers encountered Major Remington leading "Scott's Nine Hundred" cavalry on their way to Centreville. Eighty of the enemy were captured.

After passing through Dranesville, it was discovered that the Potomac River was at a high water stage, and a suitable ford had to be found. Recent rains had swollen the river two feet higher than usual. The troopers paused for a rest and devoted the remainder of the day to grazing the horses, since that was the only forage available, while their scouts searched for a ford. It had taken the troopers ten days to travel from Brandy Station in Culpeper County, Virginia, to the Potomac River near Dranesville, Virginia, during which time they "were skirmishing with the enemy or pursuing them or being pursued by them every day."[24]

Early in the pleasant summer evening of June 27, Hampton's brigade managed to make a difficult crossing of the Potomac River at Rowser's Ford near Rushville, less than twenty miles

The width, depth and rapid current at Rowser's Ford, and the fact that the Potomac River was at flood stage, made the crossing difficult in June 1863. Photograph by James Edward Rowe.

from Washington, D.C. The ford was wide and deep, with a rapid current flowing over the pommels of the troopers' saddles. To keep their powder dry, Stuart had the artillery cartridges distributed among the men, who held them over their heads as they crossed the swollen river. Near midnight, Fitz Lee's and Rooney Lee's (Chambliss') brigades followed. As the guns and caissons crossed, they were completely submerged beneath the surface of the river, but the entire force crossed without the loss of an artillery piece or a man, in spite of the fact that it was a very dark night. There were no prominent objects to mark the entrance of the ford on either side of the river, but the horses followed the ones in front of them through nearly a mile of water that was so deep it often covered the saddles. When the strong current would cause the line to drift down the river past the ford, a rider on the other side would go into the river and correct the alignment. By 3:00 in the morning, all of the guns and caissons had been dragged through the river and up the steep, slippery bank, and the last of the dripping wet troopers were standing on the Maryland shore. It had been an arduous crossing and both men and animals were exhausted.

On the Maryland side of the river, the men discovered that the Chesapeake & Ohio Canal, which ran parallel to the river, would also have to be crossed. To expedite the crossing they captured canal boats as they traveled through the locks — forty of them before daylight. They turned the boats crosswise and used them as a bridge. The bulk of Robert E. Lee's Army was already deep into Pennsylvania, and the Union troops were between Stuart and Lee.

The Chesapeake and Ohio Canal offered an unanticipated obstacle for the cavalry on their way to Gettysburg. Photograph by James Edward Rowe.

With the first light of morning, the men could see that, after traveling for three days through a poor countryside completely stripped by war, they were now in an untouched land overflowing with plenty. Although pressed for time, it was necessary to stop and let the hungry horses graze on the ample supply of fine grass. The troopers followed a route that took them less than eight miles from Washington, D.C., which caused panic in the streets of that city. They were so close they could see the dome of the Capitol building,

Early on Sunday, June 28, Hampton's brigade was sent to Rockville, Maryland (which was nine or ten miles from Washington), by way of Darnestown, while the two other brigades took the direct route to the same place. Hampton's brigade encountered small parties of the enemy along the way, which they captured, along with a number of wagons and teams. Still, Hampton's worn out and hungry brigade reached Rockville before Stuart's main body. Fitz Lee and Chambliss had paused long enough to damage some locks of the canal by jamming barges into the locks and burning them, and then they tore up some tracks of the Baltimore & Ohio Railroad before going to Rockville. In Rockville, girls from a nearby academy gathered around to see the famous raiders.

It turned out that Rockville was on the direct supply line between Washington and Hooker's army, and a slow-moving wagon train was headed their way. The troopers waited, and then captured 125 brand new wagons, which were being pulled by superb teams of sleek, fat mules wearing new harnesses. Blackford wrote:

> Galloping full tilt into the head of the train, we captured a small guard and a lot of gaily dressed quartermasters and over half the wagons, before they could turn round; but then those beyond took the alarm, turned and fled as fast as their splendid mules could go. After them we flew, popping away with our pistols at such drivers as did not pull up, but the more we popped the faster those in front plied the whip; finally, coming to a sharp turn in the road, one upset and a dozen or two others piled up on top of it, until you could see nothing but the long ears and kicking legs of the mules sticking above bags of oats emptied from the wagons upon them.[25]

From bags of grain found in some of the wagons, the troopers were able to feed their hungry horses.

Company Notes
June 25–28, 1863

Company C — Died: H. Wade; Captured: Simeon William Hill
Company H — Captured: William H.B. Jay

Hanover, Pennsylvania

After much delay in Rockville, Stuart paroled 400 prisoners, who were slowing his progress. (Those paroles were not recognized by the Federal government, and all of the prisoners returned to duty with the Union army without waiting to be exchanged, a violation of the rules of civilized warfare.) The troopers tore up railroad tracks at Rockville, and then they finally got underway again on Monday, June 29, 1863. Stuart and his men reached Westminster, Maryland, about 5:00 in the evening and found abundant forage for the horses and food for the men.

The troopers spent the latter part of the night at the Shriver farm at Union Mills before Stuart led his three brigades into Pennsylvania on June 30. Cobb's Legion Cavalry, along with the rest of Hampton's brigade, was in the rear of the column with the captured wagons, the wagons separating them from the rest of Stuart's command. Chambliss, leading Rooney Lee's brigade, was in front. One squadron of Cobb's Legion Cavalry under a Capt. Crawford was detached and sent toward Gettysburg, Pennsylvania, on a foraging party.

Stuart's overnight stay near Westminster gave Kilpatrick's cavalry division time to begin looking for them. Farnsworth's brigade reached Hanover, fifteen miles east of Gettysburg, followed by the supply wagons of the 5th and 6th Michigan. He had a strong force of 3,500 troopers. At this point, he was between Stuart and the Confederate army. At about 10:00 A.M., when Chambliss came into Hanover from the ridge to the South, he could see the 18th Pennsylvania cavalry snaking through the little town of Pennsville, just southwest of Hanover. He charged the flank and rear of the Pennsylvanians, capturing the supply wagons and throwing the Yankees into confusion.

Farnsworth heard the conflict and dashed back from the head of his column. He turned the 5th New York Cavalry around and made a counterattack. A severe engagement fought at close range took place. The 2nd North Carolina was pushed back, but other troops from both sides were attracted to the scene. What started out as a series of small actions escalated into a full-blown battle that lasted most of the day. Stuart was in the thick of the battle and was only able to escape the enemy by jumping his mare over a wide ditch. He rallied the men and they were able to force the enemy out of the town.

When the fighting began, Cobb's Legion and the rest of Hampton's troopers were a long way behind, guarding the unwieldy wagon train in the rear of the column. In mid-afternoon, they worked their way to the front to support the other brigades in the battle. They moved to the right and used their sharpshooters to dislodge the enemy in that part of the town. Meanwhile, Fitz Lee was off on the flank fighting Col. Gray's 6th Michigan column. In the late afternoon, close to sundown, Hampton's troopers returned to the wagon train and escorted it under cover of darkness around the town. Once they cleared the town, Stuart and the two other brigades fell in behind them and they headed for the Susquehanna River, believing that they would meet Lee's army there.

**Company Notes
June 29, 1863**

Company A — Wounded: Jefferson Bassett

Hunterstown, Pennsylvania

In order to escape the Union cavalry to his west, Stuart left Hanover on the night of Tuesday, June 30, 1863, and turned east. He made a night march ten miles to Jefferson, where his troopers rested for a few hours. They had accumulated almost 400 more prisoners, who were a serious hindrance during the march, although some of them acted as drivers. The mules often became unmanageable because they were suffering from hunger and thirst. The drivers were so fatigued that some of them fell asleep, causing their teams to stop and delaying the march.

Leaving Jefferson, they marched north toward York. Stuart had found Pennsylvania newspapers in Hanover that reported Jubal Early was in York, Pennsylvania, and Stuart made plans to join him there. To reach York, the men made another grueling night march over a very dark road. Stuart afterwards said, "Whole regiments slept in the saddle, their faithful animals keeping the road unguided. In some instances they fell from their horses, overcome with physical fatigue and sleepiness."[28]

Kilpatrick had marched north on June 30, assuming that Stuart had gone to East Berlin, Pennsylvania. He had not bothered to maintain contact with Stuart by having him followed. Of course, he would not find Stuart at East Berlin, because Stuart was to the east of him. He also failed to detect that Early had passed through East Berlin the day before, on his way to join Ewell, although the farmers in the area must have remarked about the event.

On July 1, Stuart reached Dover, Pennsylvania, but could not find either army or any information about them. While the men had a short rest, staff officers hunted for Lee. Rations were short and the men and captured wagon teams went hungry. Leaving Dover in the afternoon, the troopers marched to Carlisle, where Ewell was reported to have moved. They were actually moving away from Gettysburg, the place where their presence was needed. When the sleep-deprived troopers arrived at Carlisle in the early evening, Stuart demanded the surrender of the town. When the townspeople refused, the Confederate horse artillery fired shells on the army barracks, but the men were too exhausted to attack. After dark, Stuart's staff officers returned with the news that Lee was passing through Cashtown Pass and was headed toward Gettysburg.

About 1:00 in the morning, Stuart turned his exhausted men around and led them southward on another all night march, this time towards Gettysburg. Hampton's men had halted at Dillsburg, southeast of Carlisle, for an essential rest. They were in the rear, giving them a shorter journey than the other brigades, when they reversed their march. However the men were already totally exhausted. The canopy of trees that lined the road to Gettysburg blocked out the sky. They slowly rode through the pitch-dark guided only by the horse in front. By dawn of Thursday, July 2, they were to the left of Lee's position, but the troopers were so weary they could hardly sit in their saddles. Since crossing the Potomac on the night of June 27, they had slept for only ten hours. The men were allowed to rest for a short period, but as the sun rose on the hot misty fields, they could hear the sounds of combat — the deep booming of artillery and the rolling popping sound of musketry.

About midmorning, Stuart's column reached York Springs (then called Petersburg). Near Heidlersburg, they turned off the pike and took a country road that leads to Gettysburg by way of Hunterstown, which is five miles to the northeast of Gettysburg. It is likely that Lee had specified that route, because it would bring the cavalry into the proper position to cover Ewell's flank. A little known fact is that the squadron of Cobb's Legion Cavalry under Capt. Crawford, on a foraging party, had reached Hunterstown on the evening of June 29, three days before Stuart arrived. This squadron of Cobb's Legion Cavalry seized an important crossroads in Hunterstown, where five roads came together. This crossroads was a key point in the protection of the northeast flank of both armies at Gettysburg.

Shortly after noon, Stuart's column came over the high ground to the north of Hunterstown. The long column of cavalry, artillery, and captured wagons took a couple of hours to pass through the town and out the Gettysburg road. About a mile south of Hunterstown, Hampton was sitting in his saddle, a little in front of his brigade, talking to his subordinates. Suddenly he heard the whicker of a bullet from a sniper. Locating the young sniper standing out in the open on a tree stump, Hampton, who was an expert marksman, exchanged shots with him. The sniper missed, but Hampton hit the tree stump. In the second exchange, Hampton felt the bullet rip his cavalry cape and graze his chest. The sniper signaled a temporary truce because his pistol had jammed. Hampton patiently waited for him to swab the bore of his carbine and reload. On the third exchange of shots, Hampton's bullet shattered the sniper's wrist, and the sniper dropped his carbine, jumped off the stump, and disappeared in the trees. The sniper was Frank Pearson, a 19-year-old trooper from the 6th Michigan Cavalry.

What Hampton did not realize was that while he was having a gentlemanly dual with the young sniper, a lieutenant from the 6th Michigan Cavalry was charging him from behind. The soft earth muffled the hoof beats. When the Yankee was within reach, he slashed the back of Hampton's head, opening a four inch gash with his saber. Hampton whirled his horse around, roaring with pain, and fired at his attacker, but his pistol jammed. The lieutenant raced away from the scene, fleeing for his life. Hampton chased him, pointing his gun and pulling the trigger several times, but every charge left in the cylinder failed to explode. After the lieutenant escaped through a break in a fence, Hampton returned to his own lines to have the cut on his scalp plastered shut. He suffered from an intense headache for the rest of the day but remained on duty.

The exchange with the Federal scouts warned Hampton that the enemy was approaching his rear. Hampton went to report this fact to Stuart. While the two were standing on a ridge and talking, they saw Union cavalry coming out of the woods east of Huntersrown. The Federals moved toward the town, pulled back, and then repeated the maneuver. This puzzled Stuart, until he received word that Crawford's squadron of Cobb's Legion Cavalry was being forced to withdraw. Hampton was ordered to return with his brigade to Huntersrown to protect the flank and rear of the Confederate army from the Yankee cavalry.

It was about 4:00 in the afternoon when Kilpatrick's cavalry division, with Custer at its head, moved toward the Confederate left. They rode through the streets of Huntersrown until they met the squadron of Cobb's Legion Cavalry, which had formed in the town square. The squadron delayed the enemy advance, but they were so badly outnumbered that it was suicidal. A lively saber fight with the enemy ended up in a dead end alley.

Before he could reach his brigade, Hampton met the squadron of Cobb's Legion Cavalry, which had been considerably cut up before being driven out of Huntersrown. Young placed Cobb's Legion Cavalry astride the road about three-fourths of a mile from town, to block the path of the Union cavalry. On the right of Cobb's Legion Cavalry, he placed Phillip's Legion, and on the left, the 2nd South Carolina. The rest of the brigade, which was closer to Gettysburg, countermarched to support the troopers.

Federal artillery was placed on the east and west sides of the Gettysburg road. Each battery was supported by cavalry, which was concealed to the north of the ridge. Dismounted Yankee sharpshooters were positioned at an angle in a waist-high wheat field with repeating carbines, so they could enfilade any countercharge by the Confederates. On the opposite side of the road, a regiment of the enemy was massed behind some red brick farm buildings. Custer's cavalry rode out of the south side of Huntersrown until they encountered the Southern cavalry. Custer deployed his men in attack formation and led a charge with no more than fifty officers and men. With sabers and pistols upraised, and shouting an imitation of the Rebel yell, they rode toward Hampton's men four abreast. Dismounted Georgians and South Carolinians fired at them. Union men and horses were shot down before they could reach the position of Cobb's Legion Cavalry. One of the Union cavalrymen, who lost his horse, was Custer. He escaped death when one of the few of his unhurt men took him to safety on the back of his horse. After a hacking contest that swirled around some farm buildings, those of Custer's men who were able scampered for the rear.

In spite of the fact that the road was blocked with downed horses, the wounded Hampton ordered a charge. It was a costly mistake. Young led Cobb's Legion Cavalry up the road, closely pursuing the Yankees while yelling and shooting. The sharpshooters in the wheat field stood up, and the troopers in Cobb's Legion Cavalry were hit with carbine fire and artillery shells. Young wheeled around to lead his men to safety and went "flying down the pike, hat in hand,"[26] with cavalrymen from the 6th Michigan close behind and firing at him constantly. His horse was shot and he went flying over the head of his dead horse.

When Delony, who was second in command, led a charge down a lane by Felty's barn, the Virginia cavalry cheered them, but the men were ambushed by enemy soldiers hiding in the barn. Within five minutes, four or five officers and fifteen men were killed or wounded. Bugler H.E. Jackson of Company C said that "Every door and window was a blaze of fire, and every man that was with me fell."[27]

Delony's prancing bay, Marion, was shot and fell on top of him. While he was trying to extricate himself from under the horse, his men passed by him, driving the enemy before them. Three Yankees saw his helpless position and dashed up to him, shooting and slashing him

Every window in Felty's barn blazed with gunfire when Cobb's Legion Cavalry rode into an ambush. Photograph by James Edward Rowe.

from their horses. Unwilling to surrender, Delony raised himself up on one knee and fenced with them, parrying their blows. Delony was struck over the right eye, near the temple, and fell paralyzed on the horse's neck. Bugler Jackson came to his aid and fenced with the assailants. Seeing that one of the men was about to kill Delony, he knocked the Yankee's saber up. He managed to thrust another one of the enemy through his side. The others escaped with the saber wounds they had received from Delony. Jackson's bugle, coat, and shirt were cut through by the enemy's sabers, and his sword had four or five distinct gashes along its edge. Delony was severely injured, having been shot and sabered at close quarters. The saber cut over his left eye came close to cutting his eye out. Afterwards he wrote his wife that "The charge did not last ten minutes, but it was desperate and Bloody.... The [Cobb] Legion did its duty as usual ... and we drove the enemy back in splendid style."[28]

As the Yankees whirled to retreat, for several paces they were mixed with Cobb's Legion Cavalry as the men knocked, cut, and shot each other. Afterwards, the troopers from Cobb's Legion Cavalry sought cover in some woods but came under heavy shelling from a battery of the enemy's artillery. Cobb's Legion Cavalry lost thirty-two men in the battle, nearly half their strength, including nearly every commissioned officer. Hampton ordered back the survivors of the charge while dismounted skirmishers continued the fight with the help of two 10-pound Parrott rifles loaned to them by Ewell. The battle was discontinued after dark. The next morning the area was free of Yankees, so Hampton moved his men toward Gettysburg. Hampton's brigade suffered about 100 casualties in the fighting in the town and along the Gettysburg road.

Stuart described the battle at Hunterstown as "a fierce engagement, in which Hampton's brigade performed gallant service."[29] He also said, "The gallant and spirited resistance offered by Hampton's brigade to a body of the enemy's cavalry, greatly superior in numbers ... deserves the highest commendation."[30]

Hampton wrote in his report, "The Cobb Legion, which led this gallant charge, suffered quite severely, Lieutenant-Colonel Delony and several other officers being wounded, while the regiment lost in killed and wounded quite a number of brave officers and men...."[31] Kilpatrick reported that Custer's brigade lost thirty-two men killed, wounded and missing. Hampton reoccupied Hunterstown on July 3 and placed his wounded in the Presbyterian church, Grass Hotel, King house, general store, and the Gilbert home.

Company Notes
June 30–July 2, 1863

- Company A — Mortally Wounded: John Weaver Cheesboro
- Company C — Killed: Thomas R. Barrett
- Company D — Captured: Othniel E. Cory
- Company E — Captured: Thomas S. Jenkins
- Company F — Missing: James A. Hatch
- Company G — Wounded: William S. Robertson
- Company H — Killed: Cicero C. Brooks, Charles Harrington
- Company I — Killed: Nathan S. Pugh; Wounded: Owen O'Connor; Captured: Francis M. Goss
- Company K — Captured: John T. Adams; Wounded: James Luke Clanton

Gettysburg

Although it rained during the night, the exhausted troopers were able to get a good night's sleep, probably because they were so exhausted. "Reveille" sounded at the customary hour of 4:00 A.M. At 4:30 "Boots and Saddles" sounded. Most of the men had left the saddles on their horses the night before, so they simply cinched the girths. "To Horse" sounded at 5:00 and the cavalry spent the early daylight hours of Friday, July 3, 1863, the last day of the Battle of Gettysburg, hunting for the Federal cavalry among the farms and country lanes to the north of the main battle. H.E. Jackson of Company C observed, "We found our [dead] lying here and there...."[32] They found them lying in the road, with Jackson's brother-in-law among them. His brother-in-law's pockets had been turned inside out and his watch, knife, and spurs were gone. His hat was lying beside him with two holes in it where a bullet had passed through his head. The burial detail took the men and placed them in the corner of a field under a big cherry tree. They halted in Hunterstown in front of the Grass Hotel, and details were formed to bury the dead and move the wounded of both armies into town.

Finally, orders came from Stuart. Leaving the captured supply train in the hands of Lee's quartermasters, Hampton led his column across the tracks of the Gettysburg & Hanover Railroad, then onto the turnpike to York. They turned left and followed Col. Chambliss's brigade northeast, marching for almost an hour in the increasing heat of the cloudless day as the sounds of the battle at Gettysburg grew fainter. About three and a half miles from Gettysburg, the column turned south off the turnpike. The troopers rode across farmland, removing fences to allow the horses and riders to pass. For Cobb's Legion Cavalry and the rest of

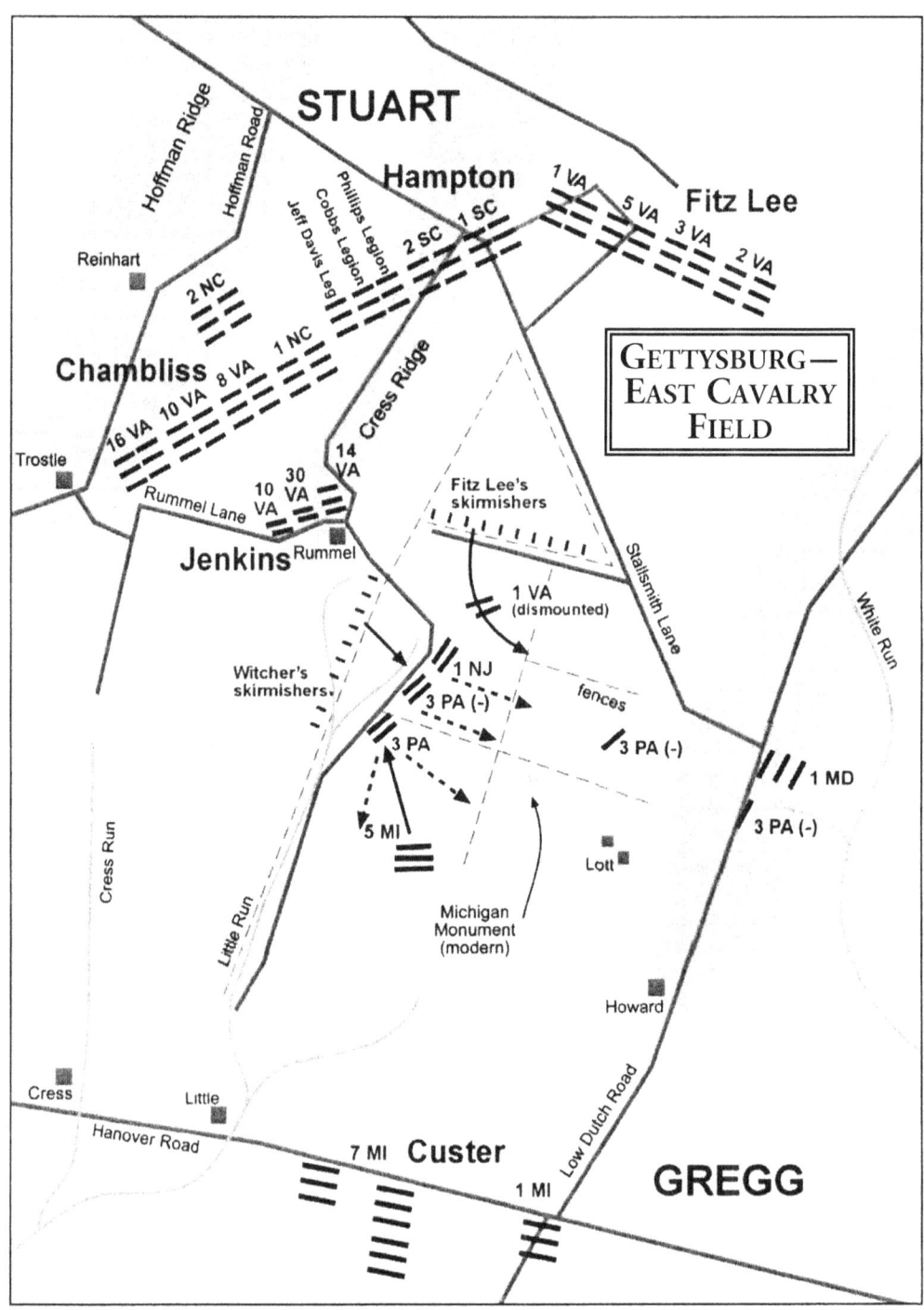

Hampton's brigade, the journey ended when Stuart's staff officers guided them onto some tree-fringed high ground known as Cress's Ridge.

The men dismounted and sharpshooters were thrown out to the south and east, while cannons were rolled into position on the ridge. Chambliss's brigade was on their right, and Fitz Lee's brigade on their left. Col. Milton J. Ferguson's brigade (Gen. Albert Gallatin Jenkins' brigade of western Virginians) held the far right of the line on the Rummel's farm. Jenkins, who was from mountainous Cabell County of [West] Virginia, had been wounded the day before by a shell fragment.

Soon after their arrival, a Parrott gun from Ferguson's brigade was fired from successive positions facing north, south, east, and west. There was no explanation for this event, but some of the officers thought that Stuart wanted to coordinate the timing of his attack on the Federal right with Lee's frontal attack and this was his signal to Lee that the cavalry was in position. The afternoon was sweltering, with the temperature climbing toward ninety degrees. About 2:00, the advance elements began to exchange shots, and Ferguson's men became heavily engaged with Custer's men. The Virginians, who had been issued only ten rounds per man, began to run out of ammunition for their Enfield rifles, so Chambliss sent some of his men, both mounted and on foot, to Ferguson's aid. Hampton kept Cobb's Legion Cavalry and the rest of his men in a sheltered spot under the trees at the base of Cress's Ridge.

Sometime between 3:30 P.M. and 4:30 P.M., Stuart sent for his two senior brigadiers, Hampton and Fitz Lee, to give them orders. Hampton, who was the senior brigadier, did not think it wise for both men to leave their units at the same time. He told Fitz Lee that he would go to Stuart first, and when he returned Fitz Lee could go. Unfortunately, Hampton could not find Stuart, so he returned to his brigade earlier than expected. He arrived in time to see that all his men, under orders from Fitz Lee, were riding out from the cover they held into a wide clearing in front of the Union position. He knew the Yankees had at least two batteries near the crossroads and feared his men would be the victims of a devastating cannonade, so he countermanded Fitz Lee's order. It was too late, because their position had already been exposed to the enemy.

A short time after that, one of Chambliss's officers reported to Hampton that he had asked for support from Fitz Lee but that Lee had replied that Hampton's brigade was the nearest and should be the one to support Chambliss. Hampton sent Phillip's Legion and the 1st North Carolina to support Chambliss. They drove the enemy back but followed them too far and encountered a reserve force large enough to assault them in the front and flank while also hitting them from the rear. Seeing what was happening, Hampton rode rapidly to the front to take charge of his two regiments and bring them back. As he did so, his assistant adjutant-general, Capt. Theodore G. Barker, misunderstood his action and thought he was ordering a charge of the whole brigade. Barker passed the word along for the men to charge. The men were more than willing, and Hampton's brigade went forward with their sabers drawn and up. Fitz Lee's brigade followed them and then Chambliss' brigade. With reinforcements, each of the armies' cavalry corps numbered about 6,000 men.

Row after row of the men galloped toward the enemy giving the Rebel yell, with their flags and guidons fluttering. As they approached, Gregg's artillery fired at them, and volley after volley of shots from the Yankee carbines ripped into the waves of riders. As men and horses fell, the troopers closed ranks and rode on without faltering. At this point, Custer led a counterattack. Columns drove into columns at a gallop. The sound of the impact was described as being like the crash of falling timbers. Arms, legs, and ribs were broken in the multiple collisions. Riders flew from their saddles and dozens of horses somersaulted head over heels, crushing their riders beneath them.

The men were now within saber length of one another. While Hampton's men dueled in front with the enemy, Gregg attacked the other Confederate brigades on their flank. The battle was desperate and went on for several hours. Men slashed each other with sabers and then clinched, rolled from their saddles together, and died while tearing at each other's throats. The burial parties that night had trouble dragging the bodies apart.

Even the commanders were involved in hand-to-hand combat. Fitz Lee's life was saved by a revolver shot from a staff member while he was fencing with a Yankee. Hampton had ridden to the head of a narrow lane where the fighting was the hottest to regain control of his charging men. He yelled, "Charge them, my brave boys, charge them!" His yell and his giant figure attracted the attention of a number of Yankees, who surrounded him. Hampton fought with his saber and his pistol, while two Mississippians tried to come to his aid, but they were sabered down before they could reach him. Hampton was surrounded and showered with saber cuts. Five of the six chambers of his revolver misfired, having been exposed to wet weather the night before. The head wound from the previous day was opened and the splashing blood blurred his vision, but he was able to fire the sixth shot. Hampton fought his way out and rode to the aid of one of his men, but was cut in the head again by one of the enemy. The next moment Hampton brought his sword down on the head of his adversary, cutting his skull in two to the chin. Covered in blood, he reeled in his saddle as more of the enemy surged around him. He was forced into a corner of a fence and was protecting himself with a saber against the attack of three Yankees when another Yankee rode up and shot him in the back. Hampton turned his head with his eyes flashing, and thundered, "You dastardly coward — shoot a man from the rear!"[33] and continued to fight his foes in front until he was rescued by men in his brigade. Two troopers came to Hampton's rescue, Nat Price of the 1st North Carolina, and a trooper named Jackson* from Georgia. Price begged, "General, general, they are too many for us. For God's sake, leap your horse over the fence; I'll die before they have you."[34] Injured, stunned, and almost blinded with blood, Hampton soared over the fence. At that moment, a piece of shrapnel hit him in his right hip and left him almost helpless. He was barely able to remain in the saddle and was forced to dismount.

As the badly wounded Hampton was carried from the field flat on his back, he ordered Col. Laurence Baker of the 1st North Carolina to take command and urged his men to continue fighting. The men fought to a standstill, both sides claiming victory. However, Stuart did not attain his objective of striking the rear of Meade's army, so from that viewpoint, he lost the battle. At almost the exact time as the cavalry's ill-fated charge, the greater battle of Gettysburg was being lost. Pickett's men were making their ill-fated charge toward Cemetery Hill. Of Hampton's twenty-three field officers, twenty-one became casualties during the ride to Gettysburg, the battle there, and the skirmishes back to Virginia.

After dark, Stuart moved his men from the battlefield to the York road, where they camped for the night. The main army withdrew during the night, but Stuart was not informed of their movement. The next morning Stuart's cavalry was in an exposed and isolated position, but he was able to successfully withdraw his troopers.

Company Notes
July 3, 1863

Company C — Killed: Noah C. Strickland; Died: Richard Moore (while serving with Troupe Artillery)

---

*Jackson was identified as being from Company B by Col. U.R. Brooks, "Memories of Battles," in Confederate Veteran, page 409, but there were no Jacksons in Company B of Cobb's Legion Cavalry.

Company E — Killed: Ebenezer F. Smith; Captured: Thomas J. Chatham, B. Newton (may have been in the infantry); Missing (perhaps killed): James M. Evans

Company I — Captured: James H. Manning

Williamsport

During the retreat from Gettysburg, Young's men took the rear-guard post of the train of over-crowded ambulance wagons as they drove over broken terrain through a wind-whipped, drenching rainstorm. Further damage was inflicted to their bloody, maimed cargo as the wagons jounced over the rutted roads all during the day and night of Saturday, July 4, 1863. The weak and feverish men were ill-bandaged, if they were bandaged at all. As the springless wagons, few of which had mattresses or straw, jolted along, the wounded men begged to be either left by the side of the road or shot. However, there was no time to stop, tend or comfort the wounded, or even give them water, as the drivers kept their mules moving at a trot. Hampton was in a semiconscious state due to his injuries and the opiates administered to dull the searing pain.

As the first wagons reached Williamsport, Maryland, at dawn on the fifth of July, 7,000 Union cavalry appeared with eighteen guns. The Potomac River was so swollen by the rain that the wagons could not cross it. They would have to wait for the water to go down or for pontoon bridges to be built. Meanwhile, Cobb's Legion Cavalry was skirmishing with the enemy in the rear at Fairfield, Pennsylvania.

The next day, July 6, Buford's Union cavalry attacked the ambulance train of the wounded, which was parked at the water's edge. The rear guard was out of reach, now fighting at Hagerstown. To augment the reduced guard that was at the front of the train, about 700 ambulance drivers were armed to resist the Yankees. Every staff office, orderly, courier, quartermaster, and even the walking wounded were pressed into service. There were probably less than 2,000 men.

Some of the seriously wounded crawled out of the wagons and joined in the fight. Col. Delony of Cobb's Legion Cavalry was in an ambulance, badly disabled with his head in bandages. When they were attacked, Delony mounted his horse and organized a small force of dismounted sick and disabled men. Using whatever arms and ammunition they could gather, the men were able to hold off two charges by the enemy until Young's troopers reached them, thus averting a stampede of the wagons.

For the next week, the wagon train was stranded beside the river, but they were now in the protective embrace of Lee's army. Lee's engineers constructed a floating bridge near Falling Waters, and they finally were able to cross into the safety of Virginia on the night of Monday, July 13. Longstreet's and Hill's corps crossed on the pontoon bridges, but Ewell's corps forded the river at Williamsport. Fires were lit on both sides of the river to illuminate the landscape:

> The ford was very wide and still almost past fording.... The water reached the armpits of the men and was very swift. By the bright lurid light the long line of heads and shoulders and the dim sparkling of the musket barrels could be traced across the watery space, dwindling away almost to a thread before it reached the further shore.
>
> The passage of the wagon trains was attended with some loss, for the current in some

The Confederate uniform jacket worn by P.M.B. Young is perforated with bullet holes. It is displayed at the Alexander H. Stephens Museum in Crawfordville, Georgia. Photograph by James Edward Rowe.

cases swept them down past the ford into deep water. It was curious to watch the behavior of the mules in these teams. As the water rose over their backs they began rearing and springing vertically upward, and as they went deeper and deeper the less would be seen of them before they made the spring which would bring their bodies half out of the water; then nothing would be seen but their ears above the water, until by a violent effort the poor brutes would again spring aloft; and indeed after the water had closed over them, occasionally one would appear in one last plunge high above the surface.[35]

Company Notes
July 4–10, 1863

Company B — Mortally Wounded: Richard P. Burtz
Company C — Wounded: James Riley Barrett
Company E — Wounded: Russell Smith; Wounded and captured: James B. Watson
Company G — Wounded and captured: James M. Harris; Wounded: Stephen Turner
Company H — Killed: James M. Glaze; Wounded: Page Jefferson Roark
Company I — Wounded and captured: Morris Harris; Captured: George C. Tanner
Company K — Wounded: Edward Kelley; Captured: James R. Lankford

The Retreat into Virginia

As soon as all of the infantry had crossed, the cavalry followed across the ford at Williamsport. After being exposed to ten days of rain following the Battle of Gettysburg, the troopers then had to endure the bone chilling effect of a cold dousing in the river in the middle of the night. They got almost as wet as Ewell's men did, and afterwards they were much worse off, as they had to sit in wet saddles without the benefit of the warming effect that walking gives a man.

Some of the wounded were put on railroad cars and sent to military hospitals in Charlottesville. Others were taken by wagon to Winchester, where hospitals were readied for them. On Thursday, July 23, Cobb's Legion Cavalry clashed with the enemy on Wapping Heights at Manassas Gap, and at Martinsburg, [West] Virginia.

A favorite saying among the infantry was, "Who has ever seen a dead cavalryman?" Gen. D.H. Hill was reputed to have said that he would pay $20,000 for every dead cavalryman who died with his spurs on. However, during the Gettysburg campaign, "There were more men killed and wounded (not captured), but killed and wounded, in the cavalry division than any infantry division in the Army of Northern Virginia."[36] The cavalry more than disproved the validity of Hill's assertions in June and July 1863.

Company Notes
July 11–24, 1863

Company A — Wounded: James Luke Clanton; Captured: George W. Parrish, William J. Tucker
Company B — Died: Richard P. Burtz
Company E — Captured: Dennis Hogan
Company G — Captured: Marcus V. Woods
Company H — Killed: Thomas W. Salter
Company I — Captured: Allen Chavous, James M. Cobb, John D.D. Harben, Josiah Middleton Seago, Allen R. Stanford
Company L — Wounded: J.N. Thomas

Chapter 10

Late Summer and Fall of 1863

2nd Battle of Brandy Station

After returning to Virginia, the infantry withdrew behind the Rapidan, while the cavalry occupied the line of the Rappahannock. Cobb's Legion Cavalry was involved in skirmishes at Kelly's Ford, Virginia, on Friday, July 31, and Saturday, August 1, 1863.

Hampton's brigade of scarcely 900 troopers fought at Brandy Station on August 1 on the same field as the battle of June 9. They were badly outnumbered and fought with sabers from early dawn to almost sundown, when A.P. Hill's infantry came to their support. It was a costly battle for the Confederate cavalry commanders. At the beginning of the battle, Col. Baker of the 1st North Carolina was in command because Hampton was still disabled from his wounds at Gettysburg. After Baker was wounded, Col. Young of Cobb's Legion became commander, but Young was shot in the chest. Then Col. John Logan Black of the 1st South Carolina took command, until he was wounded, and then Col. T.J. Lipscomb of the 2nd South Carolina took command. After Lipscomb was disabled and carried off the field, Col. Rich of the Phillip's Legion commanded for the remainder of the battle.

While participating in a desperate cavalry charge, the color bearer, Marcus DeLafayette Pittman of Company C, was severely wounded and disabled for life. His horse was shot from under him and he was wounded in the foot and ankle. Although his horse fell on top of him and the flagstaff shattered and pierced his boot, he held Cobb's Legion's tattered battle flag aloft until another comrade seized the flag and carried it to victory. The two armies fought to a bloody draw before the Southerners fell back to prepare defenses below the Rapidan.

Company Notes
July 25–September 2, 1863

Staff—Wounded: Pierce M.B. Young
Company B—Wounded: Robert Huntsinger
Company C—Wounded: Marcus De Lafayette Pittman; Captured: Thomas Rollins, James Overton Simmons
Company D—Captured: Martin J. Frie
Company F—Wounded: Thomas B. Wells; Captured: Andrew J. Graffan, George Woolley; Died: William R. Rountree
Company G—Wounded: George Winship
Company H—Wounded: Henry J. Simmons, Thomas B. F. Todd, Cornelius C. Turner
Company I—Killed: Thomas Reynolds; Captured: William D. Heffernan

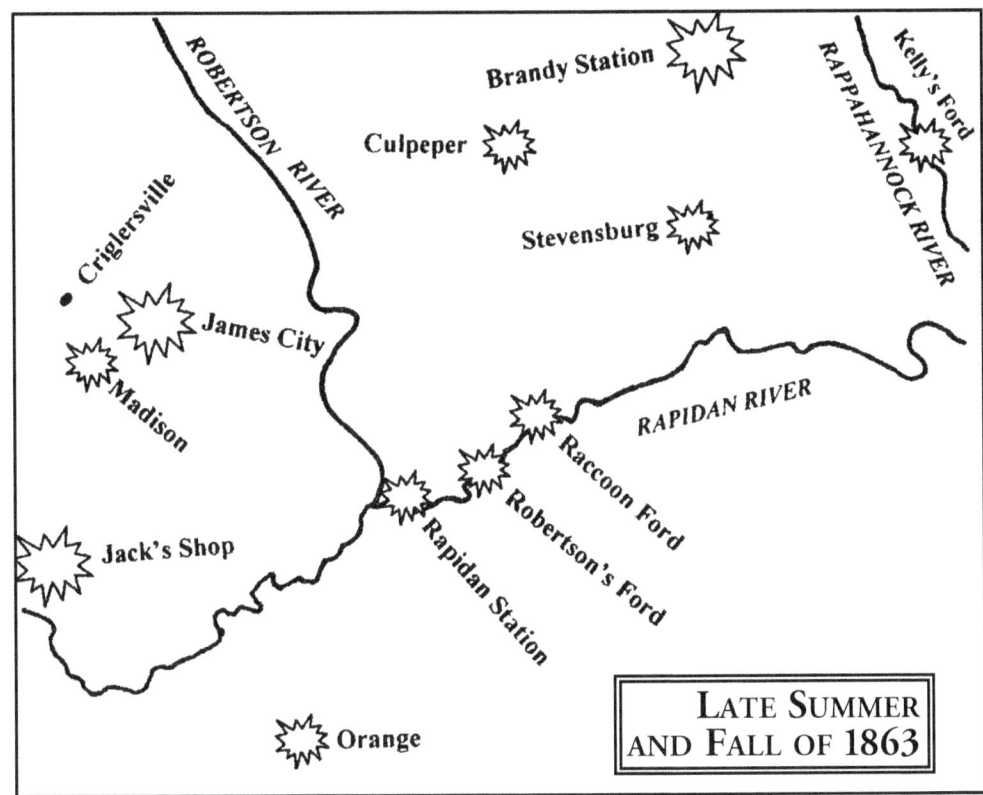

Reorganization

On Thursday, September 3, 1863, there was a reorganization of the army. Of all the cavalry brigadier generals who had been on parade at the Grand Review before the Battle of Brandy Station, only Stuart and Fitz Lee were present for duty. Rooney Lee, who had not recovered from his wounds, had been captured by the enemy. Hampton was convalescing in South Carolina. Laurence Baker of the 1st North Carolina Cavalry, Calbraith Butler of the 2nd South Carolina Cavalry, and Lunsford Lindsay Lomax, who were recovering from wounds, were promoted to brigadier generals. Hampton and Fitz Lee were promoted to major generals. P.M.B. Young and James Gordon were promoted to brigadier generals, along with Thomas Rosser, who had been one of Fitz Lee's colonels. The cavalry was divided into two divisions, with Hampton and Fitz Lee as the division commanders under the whole command of Stuart:

J.E.B. Stuart, Major General

WADE HAMPTON'S DIVISION

Butler's Brigade, Gen. M. Calbraith Butler (Col. P.M.B. Young temporarily commanding)

Cobb's Legion Cav.	Col. P.M.B. Young
2nd SC	Col. T.J. Lipscomb
Phillip's Legion GA	Lt. Col. W.W. Rich
(Col. W.G. Delony temporarily commanding)	
Jeff Davis Legion MS	Col. Joseph Frederick Waring

Baker's Brigade, Gen. Lawrence S. Baker
(Lt. Col. James B. Gordon temporarily commanding)

1st NC Cav.	Lt. Col. James Byron Gordon
2nd NC Cav.	Lt. Col. W.G. Robinson
4th NC Cav.	Col. Dennis D. Ferebee
5th NC Cav.	Col. Stephen B. Evans

Jones Brigade, Gen Wm. E. Jones

6th VA Cav.	Lt. Col. John Shac Green
7th VA Cav.	Col. R.H. Dulany
12th VA Cav.	Col. A.W. Harman
35th Batt. VA Cav.	Lt. Col. E.V. White

FITZHUGH LEE'S DIVISION

Wickham's Brigade, Gen. W.C. Wickham

1st VA Cav.	Col. R.W. Carter
2nd VA Cav.	Col. Thomas T. Munford
3rd VA Cav.	Col. Thomas H. Owen
4th VA Cav.	Lt. Col. William H. Payne

Lomax's Brigade, Gen. Lunsford Lindsay Lomax

5th VA Cav.	Col. Thomas L. Rosser
1st Batt. MD Cav.	Lt. Col. Ridgeley Brown
11th VA Cav.	Col. O.R. Funsten
15th VA Cav.	Col. William B. Ball

Lee's Brigade, Gen. W.H.F. [Rooney] Lee
(Col. John Randolph Chambliss temporarily commanding)

1st SC Cav.	Col. John L. Black
9th VA Cav.	Col. R.L.T. Beale
10th VA Cav.	Col. J. Lucius Davis
13th VA Cav.	Col. John R. Chambliss

Albert Gallatin Jenkins was detached to protect Richmond, but Grumble Jones and Beverly Robertson were transferred.

Other Skirmishes and Actions

In Hampton's absence, Stuart often led Hampton's division. The Union cavalry under Kilpatrick was getting better almost daily and skirmished with them constantly. Cobb's Legion Cavalry fought skirmishes at Stevensburg, Virginia, on September 10 and 11, 1863, and at Raccoon Ford on September 11.

James Longstreet's corps was sent to northern Georgia to reinforce Braxton Bragg's army. When Meade heard that Longstreet was no longer with Lee, he knew that he had the numerical advantage. At dawn on Sunday, September 13, two Federal divisions of cavalry with infantry and artillery support crossed the Rappahannock in order to exploit the circumstances. Cobb's Legion Cavalry was involved in an action at Culpeper Court House when the enemy advanced into Culpeper County. From September 14 to 16, they saw action at Raccoon Ford and Rapidan Station. Stuart had no choice except to fall back to the Rapidan River.

Cobb's Legion Cavalry had another skirmish at Robertson's Ford on September 15, and again at Raccoon Ford on September 17 and 19. On September 21, they had a skirmish at Madison Court House and White's Ford. They had another skirmish at White's Ford on September 22.

Company Notes
September 10–21, 1863

Company B — Wounded: William Hugh Mills
Company C — Wounded: Alexander S. Whelchel
Company D — Mortally Wounded: J.D. Ford, E.N. Wilson
Company K — Wounded: J.J. Karr, George W. Bennett

Jack's Shop

Hampton's cavalry had been marching and fighting almost daily since June 9, 1863. Their horses were starved and the men were worn out. On Tuesday, September 22, they reached a place called Jack's Shop near Liberty Mills, which is on the north branch of the Rapidan near Madison Court House, Virginia.

Some of the troopers from Cobb's Legion were lying on the ground, holding their horses by looping the reins around their feet—a favorite way with old cavalrymen—so that the horses could graze. They were smoking pipes in a hollow at the head of the column. The increasingly aggressive cavalrymen of Buford and Kilpatrick surprised and nearly surrounded them. When the battle began, Young took a line of dismounted skirmishers to the front and left Delony in charge of mounted troopers of Cobb's Legion Cavalry, who were in a battle line at the crest of a hill. They were unsupported by the other cavalry brigades, although Eve complained of passing through miles of Virginia cavalry "coming to our assistance" after he was wounded and the fight was lost.[1]

Bullets were whistling around the men on the horses, but they were used to that sound. Then they heard the thud of a ball hitting the flesh of one of the men at the head of the column. The man fell from his horse with a clean wound through the fleshy part of his arm. It was what the men called a "furlough wound," serious enough to get a furlough but not bad enough to maim or kill. Some of the men began to bewail the fact that they would like to get a furlough wound. Why, they would give a thousand dollars for one. Before this battle was over, those troopers were cured of wishing for furlough wounds.

Stuart's artillery was firing in both directions from the top of the hill, while, within sight of each other, the Confederate cavalry regiments were charging in opposite directions. Buford had been driving Young and his dismounted skirmishers back, causing Delony to fear that they would be captured. Eve was given permission to advance with mounted skirmishers to give Young and his dismounted men time to fall back to their horses. Within fifteen minutes,

Delony received a mortal wound and Eve was shot through the left breast and side. Several of the other mounted men were also wounded, but Young and his men were able to reach their mounts. As Eve turned, he saw Delony's horse lunge and then fall against a picket or clapboard fence which surrounded a garden at the rear of the shop. The fence was hurled to the ground in the horse's death struggle with Delony's leg being crushed between the horse and the fence.

The regiment was ordered back from the rear of the shop to form a line of battle in front of and beyond the shop. The Atlanta squadron of Lt. David H. Dougherty, Company B, came to reinforce the men, but Dougherty was shot almost immediately. Somehow, Cobb's Legion managed to break free of the encirclement and withdrew in good order, but not before Kilpatrick got into their rear.

After checking on some of his wounded men, Eve went to look for a surgeon, following the line of the wounded, which had been ordered to Liberty Mills. He overtook Delony, who was mounted on another horse. Delony said that none of his bones were broken and that the horse falling on him was more painful than his bleeding bullet wounds. He asked Eve to ride forward and get an ambulance for him, as he was feeling faint. Eve rode off and had an ambulance sent to Delony, not knowing that Delony would be captured and he would never see him again.

Kilpatrick attacked and then captured nearly all of the wounded, including Delony. Dr. Henry Stiles Bradley and Reuben Long Nash, both of Company C, chose to stay with Delony and share the horrors of his imprisonment because of their great devotion and respect for him. Unfortunately, the enemy separated the faithful friends from Delony almost immediately. Delony was carried to a hospital in Washington, D.C., where he was so neglected that gangrene set into the gunshot wound in his leg. He refused to allow it to be amputated and he died on Saturday, October 2, 1863. The next day, a magnificent metallic coffin was secretly left on the steps of the hospital with a note that said it was for the remains of Col. William G. Delony. After the war, Delony's wife tried in vain for years to learn who had furnished the coffin.

Eve said of Delony that he was the

> ...idol of the Cobb Legion, and our chevalier ... cut down in the midst of a most brilliant career, marked by bullet and saber cut, whose gallantry had been recognized by all the commanding officers under whom he had served, adored by his men who dreaded his displeasure even more than they feared Yankee bullets. I can picture that martial form even now, with red lined cape thrown back to give full play to sword arm, his soft brown eye changed to a fiery scintillating black, his face aglow with the glare of the battle dashing in front of us, one glance down the line and with a "Follow me, Cobb Legion" more inspiring than bugle blast, and how we would go.[2]

Wiley C. Howard said:

> Golden-hearted, brave, brainy DeLoney [sic], how his men loved him, and how he stood by them, contending always for their rights and looking after their comforts, when others would treat them indifferently! His heart and his purse were ever open to their needs.... He has been justly called the Henry of Navarre of our cavalry, a real hero above the most extravagant descriptive powers of the gifted novelist writing fiction. He deserved a Brigadier General's Commission, but never sought notoriety or promotion. I admired his character so much that I gave up a first Lieutenancy in an infantry company at Americus and begged a private's place in his company. He took me, though the ranks of his company were already full, and I am proud to have been considered worthy to ride and fight with him.... The

world never produced a better, braver soldier, truer patriot or grander hero than William G. DeLoney [sic].³

Both armies rested, reorganized their infantry, and trained new recruits on the rolling hills of Virginia between Madison Court House and Culpeper, while the cavalry continued to be involved in skirmishes and engagements. Hampton's division was reported to have 8,789 men, but fewer than 4,000 were present, mounted, and equipped for duty. On Wednesday, September 23, 1863, Cobb's Legion Cavalry had a skirmish at Raccoon Ford and another one at Orange Court House, and then they saw action at Robertson's Ford.

Company Notes
September 22–23, 1863

Company A — Mortally Wounded: John Ross; Wounded: John Stapler Dozier
Company B — Wounded: David H. Dougherty; Captured: George W. Slatern, Robert Stockton Morris
Company C — Mortally wounded and captured: William Gaston Delony; Wounded and captured: Daniel O'Connor; Captured: Henry Stiles, Bradley, William N. Bryant, Reuben Long Nash
Company E — Mortally wounded: Marcus L. McDermont; Wounded: Thomas J. Mitchell
Company F — Killed: Edward Preston Stone; Wounded: Samuel P. Fleming
Company H — Wounded: Elisha F. Morris
Company I — Killed: John L. Jowers
Company K — Wounded: Frances Edgeworth Eve
Company Unknown — Captured: O. Morris

Chapter 11

The Bristoe Campaign

James City

Cobb's Legion Cavalry's action in the Bristoe Campaign began on Friday, October 9, when Hampton's division advanced from the Rapidan River. Stuart was in command of the division because Hampton had not recovered from the wounds he suffered at Gettysburg. Their objective was to guard the right flank of the Army of Northern Virginia, which was advancing from Madison Court House so they could execute a flank movement on the enemy, which was at Culpeper.

On the evening of October 9, the cavalry bivouacked in the neighborhood of Madison Court House and Robertson's River. Pickets from Cobb's Legion were placed from the mouth of the river to Criglersville. Leaving the pickets along the river on October 10, Cobb's Legion Cavalry and Gordon's brigade crossed the river at Russell's Ford, moving towards James City. Their objective was to divert the enemy's attention while the infantry executed its flank movement.

After crossing the river, Stuart planned to attack the enemy's cavalry simultaneously in their front and on their right flank. He sent Gordon's brigade forward dismounted, while Cobb's Legion moved through the woods on the left to attack the enemy's right. The Federal forces were drawn up in a line of battle but broke and fled in confusion when they were attacked. Almost all of the enemy were either killed or captured. Those who were not captured scattered in every direction, using the mountains as a means of escape. Cobb's Legion took 87 prisoners and sent them to the rear.

Stuart's cavalry pursued the enemy to James City, where they found two brigades of Kilpatrick's cavalry, French's division of infantry, and six pieces of enemy artillery. The Federal troops quickly withdrew to a strong position on the hills overlooking Bethel Church. Stuart did not pursue them, as his objective was to take James City, which he had accomplished. Instead, he ordered demonstrations by Cobb's Legion Cavalry in the enemy's front and by Gordon's brigade on their right flank until nightfall.

Company Notes
September 23–October 11, 1863

Company C—Died: William Gaston Delony; Wounded: John A. Wimpy
Company D—Died: J.D. Ford, E.N. Wilson
Company H—Died: John James Alexander

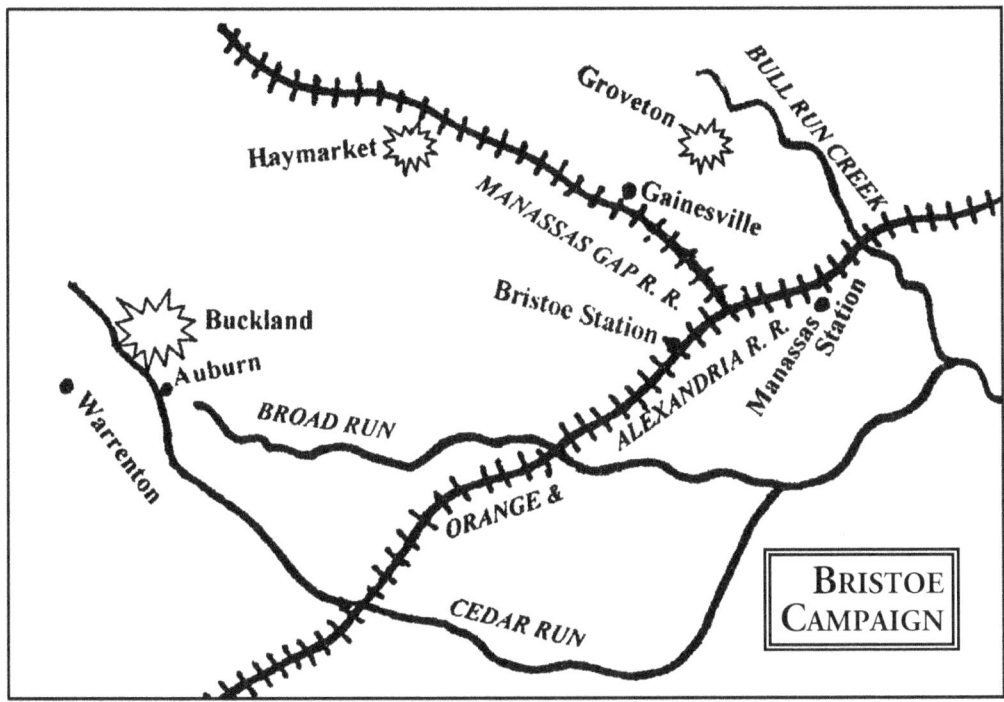

Slaughter's Hill

During the night, the enemy disappeared. The next morning Stuart left Cobb's Legion Cavalry to hold James City, while Gordon's brigade continued the march along the flank of Lee's army. On the morning of Monday, October 12, 1863, Stuart ordered Butler to move his brigade (including the pickets at Robertson's River) to Culpeper Court House to guard the quartermaster's and commissary stores being unloaded from the trains on their way to the Hazel River.

In the afternoon, a courier arrived and informed Young that a heavy force of the enemy's cavalry and infantry was advancing towards Rosser's 5th Virginia Cavalry at Fleetwood (Brandy Station), and was forcing them to fall back towards Culpeper.

Young hurried Cobb's Legion Cavalry to their assistance. About three-fourths of the men were deployed dismounted, with five pieces of artillery, along a wooded ridge known as Slaughter's Hill. They could see a strong line of the enemy's skirmishers in advance of a regiment of infantry, which was supported on the flanks by at least three brigades of cavalry. Large numbers of additional troops also could be seen moving toward Brandy Station.

The 5th Virginia Cavalry fell back until they reached Cobb's Legion's line, at which time the artillery and sharpshooters opened fire. The firing continued until dark, and then Young ordered the men to light campfires along the entire front and for the band to play music. The band was moved from point to point, giving the enemy the illusion that the Confederate force was much larger than it actually was. Before morning, the enemy, which was discovered to be a division of cavalry and an entire corps of infantry, withdrew and recrossed the Rappahannock. Young pursued them with a portion of Cobb's Legion Cavalry and captured about 30 prisoners. The next afternoon, October 14, the Battle of Bristoe Station took place between A.P. Hill's infantry division and Meade's army.

Company Notes
October 12–14, 1863

Company D — Wounded: James D. Scott
Company F — Captured: Thomas M. Murdock; Died: James Curran

Frying Pan Church

On the evening of Thursday, October 15, 1863, Young moved Cobb's Legion Cavalry to Manassas Station, where they rejoined Hampton's division. The division moved out on the morning of October 16 over muddy roads and through heavy rains toward Groveton (near Manassas). As they passed Groveton, their pickets skirmished with the enemy. That night they crossed Bull Run Creek, which was swollen from the rain, and bivouacked near Stone Castle.

When the division moved out on October 17, Cobb's Legion Cavalry was in front. After passing Gum Springs, they arrived at Frying Pan Church, where enemy pickets were posted. A squadron from Cobb's Legion charged and captured a number of the pickets. A brisk engagement followed with a regiment of the U.S. 6th Army Corps. The Confederates managed to gather information on the strength and location of the enemy, and other details. After sundown, they withdrew and Cobb's Legion Cavalry along with the rest of Hampton's division bivouacked near the Little River Turnpike.

Company Notes
October, 15–17, 1863

Company K — Wounded: James Moony

The Buckland Races (Chestnut Hill)

Stuart moved Hampton's division back to Gainesville on Sunday, October 18, 1863, and then, towards night, he moved them above Haymarket for forage and supplies. There was a terrible rainstorm that night. While they were encamped on the road, their pickets were attacked and driven in. Cobb's Legion Cavalry was ordered to saddle up during the storm and move to Haymarket to hold that point.

On October 19, the advance of the enemy cavalry began crossing to the south bank of Broad Run at the Buckland Ford. Fitz Lee's division was a few miles off at Auburn, but in supporting distance. Leading Hampton's division, Stuart retired slowly for about five miles, until they were within two and a half miles of Warrenton. Stuart concealed Hampton's troopers behind a low range of hills and had them wait for the sound of Fitz Lee's guns. The men were formed in two columns behind gaps in the ridge.

Kilpatrick thought Hampton's division was retreating, so he crossed Broad Run and followed them, not knowing that he was being drawn into a trap. He followed cautiously, but left Custer's brigade behind at Buckland Ford. Kilpatrick's splendidly equipped cavalry came marching toward the Confederates down the broad straight turnpike with their flags fluttering and their arms glittering in the bright autumn sunlight. The column stretched as far as the eye could see.

Meanwhile, Fitz Lee brought his men up from Auburn to attack the enemy in the flank and in the rear. The plan was a great success. When Fitz Lee's men arrived, they encountered Custer, and a stiff fight followed. Once Fitz Lee's guns were heard, Hampton's cavalry whirled around on their mounts and attacked vigorously in front. Gordon's brigade charged down the road, while Young, who was commanding Butler's brigade, had his men gallop through the woods on the right of the road and Rosser's troopers charged on the left of the road. Kilpatrick could hear the firing in his rear and knew that his men were being attacked on both sides and that they were trapped.

At first Hampton's men met stubborn resistance, but then the enemy broke and there was a rout. The enemy retreated in wild disorder, while Hampton's cavalry, making a final successful charge, pursued them at full gallop from within three miles of Warrenton to Buckland. It was "like a fox chase."[1] Custer could see the cloud of dust and hear the rumble of hoofbeats coming toward him, and he beat a hasty retreat across the ford before the stampede reached him.

Some of the fleeing Yankees drowned in their frantic attempt to cross the creek. Those who could not cross at the ford fled in a panic toward Haymarket. The Confederates captured about 250 prisoners, 8 wagons and ambulances, many arms, horses, equipment, Custer's headquarters wagon, and his baggage and official papers. Some racy letters from Custer to a female friend ended up being published in the Richmond papers.

Kilpatrick had to search for his men, who had not been captured. Many did not stop galloping until they reached the lines of the 1st U.S. Army Corps. This action became known in both the North and South by the derisive name of "The Buckland Races." The rout was described by Stuart as being "the most complete that any cavalry has ever suffered during the war." One of the Union writers described it as "the deplorable spectacle of 7,000 cavalry dashing riderless, hatless, and panic-stricken" through the ranks of their infantry.

Fitz Lee crossed at Buckland and pushed down the pike toward Gainesville, taking many prisoners from the 1st Army Corps. Meanwhile, Cobb's Legion Cavalry was sent around to the rear. That night by moonlight, Stuart attacked the enemy's pickets near Haymarket. Losses for the Confederates were 408 casualties, but most of them were only slightly wounded. The Federal cavalry casualties were 1,251; all but about 300 of them were killed or captured, and 600 infantrymen were taken prisoner. During this campaign, forage for the horses was in short supply. They were "operating in a country worn out in peace, but now more desolate in war."[2] Stuart said that the men willingly shared their "last crust" with their horses.[3]

The Confederate army leisurely recrossed the Rappahannock into Culpeper and placed pickets on the south bank of the river on October 20, 1863. Overall, the campaign was a Confederate success, in spite of the losses by the infantry at Bristoe Station. Meade was forced to withdraw sixty miles, from the Rapidan to beyond Bull Run.

Company Notes
October 18–November 2, 1863

Company A — Wounded: Patrick Wallace
Company B — Died: George Cicero Montgomery
Company E — May Have Died: B. Newton

CHAPTER 12

The Mine Run Campaign

Kelly's Ford and Rappahannock Station

Wade Hampton reported for duty at Richmond, Virginia, on November 3, 1863, and afterward took a train to the front. The two armies had been observing each other across the Rappahannock for three weeks, with Lee expecting Meade to attempt to drive him back to his former position south of the Rapidan. The enemy appeared in force about noon on Saturday, November 7, and advanced to Kelly's Ford and Rappahannock Station. In the late afternoon, the Union 5th Corps attacked the Confederates with bayonets. Cobb's Legion Cavalry was at Kelly's Ford, where the first attack occurred. Although they did not participate in the action, they stood "to horse" all day in case they were needed. After driving back the Southerners, the Federals laid down a pontoon bridge at Kelly's Ford, over which a considerable number of their force crossed. As a result, Lee retreated with his army to the Rapidan.

Company Notes
November 3–7, 1863

Company F — Died: William Boyd

Stevensburg

While the cavalry were fighting near Stevensburg on Sunday, November 8, 1863, Hampton rode onto the field. His men cheered so loudly that they almost drowned out the sound of the gunfire. Hampton led his men south to the army's new position near Orange Court House, where they joined Fitz Lee in protecting the army's flanks and rear. To protect the right flank, Cobb's Legion Cavalry was sent with the brigades of Young and Gordon to the North Anna River near Orange Springs, nine miles southeast of Lee's headquarters. A picket line was put out that ran north for twelve miles, as far as Raccoon Ford on the Rapidan.

About a week later, Hampton took a reconnaissance party on a seventy mile round-trip back across the Rapidan into enemy territory. As they neared Stevensburg, they discovered an enemy campsite. When Hampton gave the word, his men gave the Rebel yell and attacked. The enemy were startled awake and fled the area "as fast as their horses could carry them."[1] Hampton described the scene: "The officers ... ran off in their drawers and bare-footed, leaving all their clothes behind. The men were scattered all over the woods, and my men were chasing them about like rabbits. It will be a long time before that unfortunate Regt. can get organized again."[2]

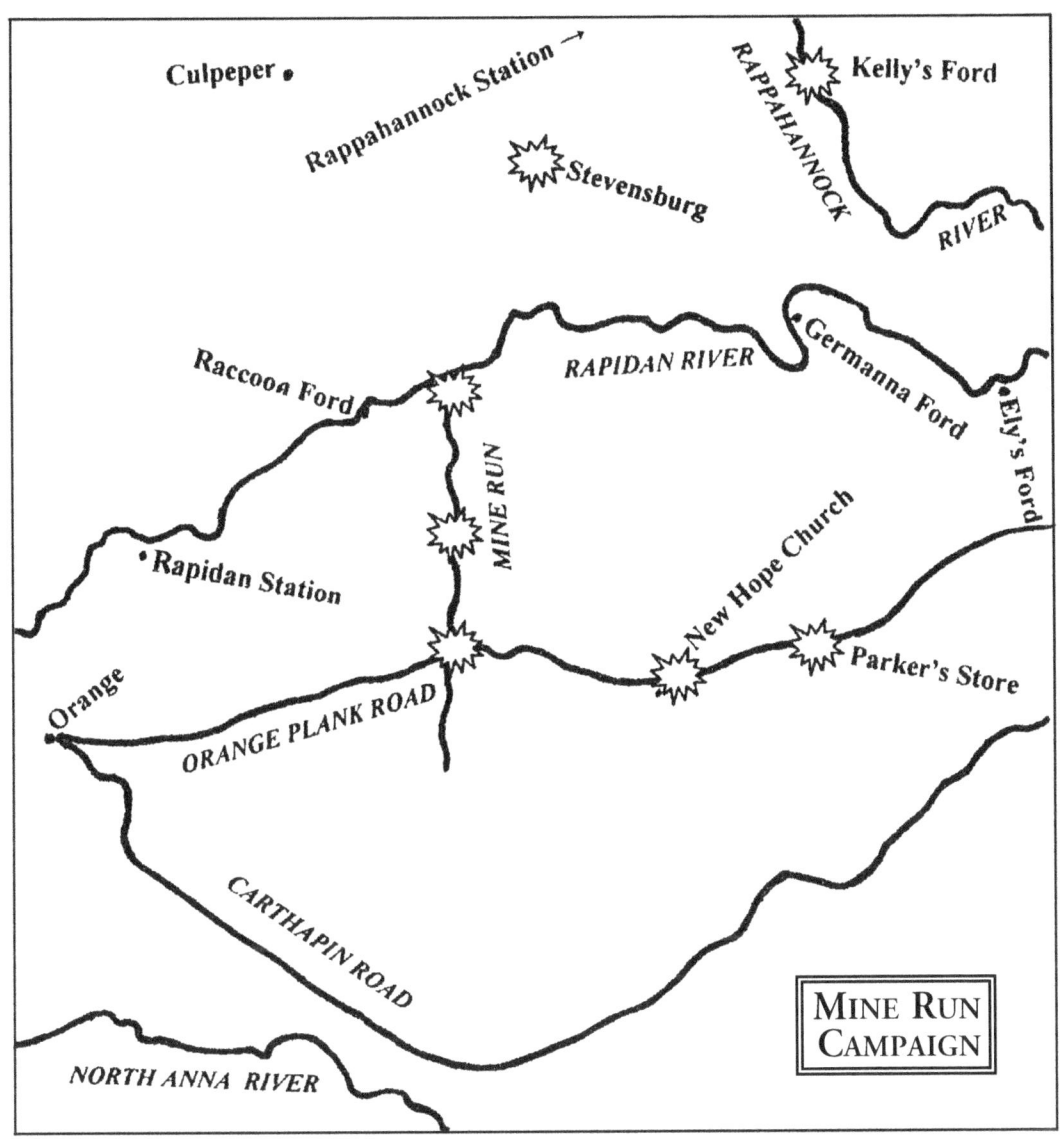

Company Notes
November 8–25, 1863

Company C — Captured: William H. Pass; Died: William N. Bryant
Company H — Killed: Tilman H. Brown
Company L — Captured: J.F. Mollere

New Hope Church

Stuart seemed reluctant to return to his administrative duties and persisted in leading Hampton's men, although Hampton was present. This caused dissatisfaction on the part of Hampton. The enemy crossed the Rapidan beyond Lee's right at Germanna and Ely's fords on Thursday, November 26, 1863. They moved up the river in the direction of Orange Court House with the intent of maneuvering Lee from his position to the west. Hampton's pickets alerted Lee of the Union troops' movement, and Lee prepared for a conflict with Meade's army. An engagement between Lee and Meade took place east of Mine Run, a little stream on Lee's right flank.

As the main army moved toward Mine Run, Stuart headed for New Hope Church on the Orange Plank Road. Hampton was supposed to meet him there that evening. For some reason, the advance element of Hampton's division, which was Gordon's brigade, did not arrive until the next morning, November 27. Without waiting for Hampton, Stuart led Gordon's brigade into a battle that brought the lower one of Meade's three columns to a halt. When Hampton arrived on the scene with 158 Georgians and Carolinians, he attacked dismounted with Young's brigade with such force that the enemy's left came apart and their offensive was halted east of Mine Run for several hours. The delay gave Lee the time he needed to bring up the main army to the threatened area.

Company Notes
November 26–27, 1863

Company B — Captured: Noah Allison
Company F — Wounded: James B. Dawson, John Kelly, Maurice Whalin
Company I — Wounded: Charles H. Rogers

Parker's Store

There was some skirmishing with the enemy along Mine Run on Saturday, November 28, 1863. The next morning, Stuart planned to meet Hampton on the Catharpin Road, south and roughly parallel to the Orange Plank Road. When Stuart arrived at the rendezvous point, only Rosser's Virginia brigade, but not Hampton, was there. Without waiting for Hampton, Stuart led Rosser's brigade cross-country to Parker's Store on the plank road. When he discovered a lightly defended camp of the enemy's cavalry deep in the woods, Stuart attacked with Rosser's men and captured a supply train. A large body of the enemy counterattacked, surrounding Stuart and his men.

Fortunately for Stuart, Hampton arrived in time to rescue him. Young's brigade was at the head of his column, followed by Gordon's brigade. They attacked and drove off the enemy. Hampton bragged about them in a letter to his sister: "My old Brigade ... did splendidly. No men could have behaved better and the movement made by them, which drove the enemy from the field, was executed in the finest style. Stuart, who saw it, said he had seen nothing finer, and I was proud of my brave old soldiers."[3] Later he complained that his position as division commander had been ignored by Stuart.

Meade stayed in position opposite Lee's flank until December 2, when he withdrew his army back across the river. The failure of the Mine Run Campaign would cost Meade his unsupervised command of the Union Army in the East. When Grant assumed the command of all the armies of the United States, Meade was left in command of the Army of the Potomac, but he had Grant overseeing his every move.

Company Notes
November 28–December 2, 1863

Company C — Wounded: Thomas Ransom Tuck
Company D — Wounded: George W. Mock
Company E — Died: Thomas J. Chatham
Company F — Wounded: Benjamin Brown Palmer
Company H — Wounded: Thomas J. Rives

Chapter 13

Winter of 1864

Fords Along the Rapidan

As winter set in, the cavalry corps became less active. Deprived of men and equipment, Stuart was not able to raid the Union army. Hampton's brigade camped near Guiney's (Guinea's) Station on the Richmond, Fredericksburg & Potomac Railroad and constantly picketed the Rapidan and its many tributaries. Young's and Gordon's brigades had almost forty miles of riverbank to patrol, with only minimal assistance from Fitz Lee's brigade. Unfortunately, the men not only lacked weapons, ammunition, and equipment, but they also lacked sufficient rations, clothing, and bedding.

Perhaps, the worst problem was that they lacked enough healthy horses to perform their duties. Col. John Logan Black wrote that the horses were "poorly foraged.... Our corn issues for nearly two months did not exceed 3 lbs. to the horse.... It was little better than actual starvation to our poor horses."[1]

On the cool, rainy day of February 6, the enemy crossed the Rapidan River and attacked the pickets at Morton's, Barnett's, and Raccoon fords. Orders were given to be ready to move on a moment's notice.

Company Notes
December 1, 1863–February 7, 1864

Company A — Captured: Henry Hugh McCall
Company B — Captured: Michael J. Ivey, Charles H. Nelson, Thomas Ozias Ozburn
Company D — Died: Moses W. McCollum
Company E — Captured: Henry Steen
Company F — Wounded: William Patterson Netherland, Cuthbert C. Torrance
Company H — Wounded: Alonzo A. Brooks; Died: Robert W. Wier
Company K — Wounded: John T. Higdon, J.J. Karr

Defense of Richmond

Despite the condition of the horses, Hampton's brigade was ordered to assist in the defense of Richmond. On Monday, February 8, 1864, in weather that was harsh enough to kill their mounts, the troopers started marching toward Bowling Green. They were attacked near Bottom's Bridge on the Chickahominy but repulsed the enemy. While they were still seven miles from the city, they learned that the commander at Richmond had stranded the

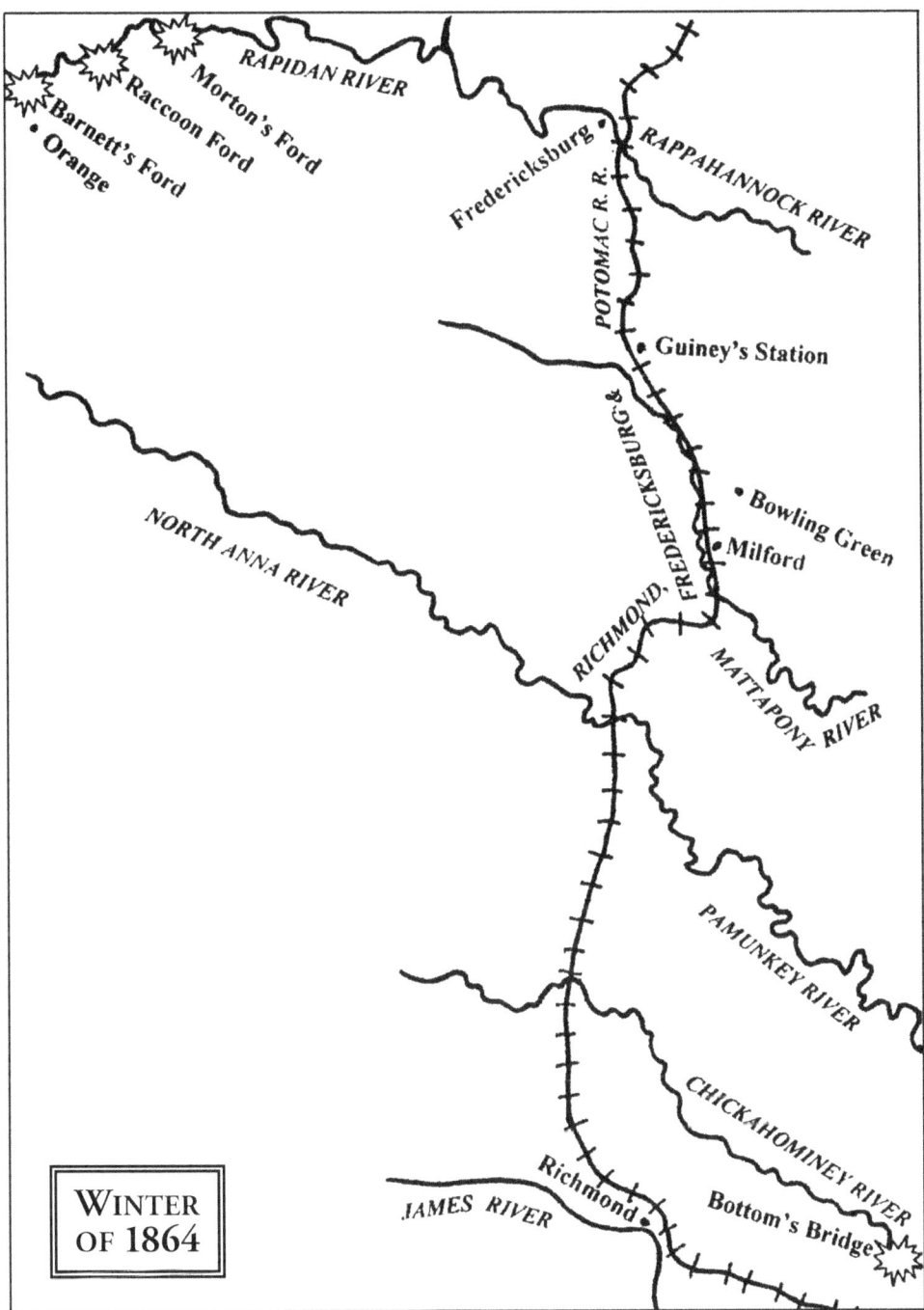

Winter of 1864

Yankees by simply removing the planking from the bridge at Bottom's Bridge. Hampton turned his men around and camped that night near Milford on the Mattapony River. The next day they had a very cold ride as they returned to the Rapidan. Some of the troopers arrived before sundown, but the wagons did not get back with their equipment until midnight. They were summoned to Richmond on another false alarm a week later. This time, Hampton refused to move his brigade without the assurance that an attack was imminent.

On February 28, Hampton's command, which at that time consisted of Young's and Gordon's brigades, numbered 719 men present for duty and with serviceable animals. (Rosser's brigade was detached to the Shenandoah Valley.) The next day, February 29, Hampton learned from one of his Iron Scouts that the Federal infantry was getting ready to move and that Kilpatrick's cavalry was in motion.

Company Notes
February 21–29, 1864

Company A — Captured: William B. Young
Company B — Captured and May Have Died: James H. Brent
Company C — Wounded: Francis Marion Whelchel; Captured: James C. Oliver
Company D — Died: James Holcomb Bailey
Company F — Died: John M. Lawson
Company H — Captured: Isham Humphrey Pittard
Company K — May Have Died: James R. Lankford

Hampton's Command Is Worn Down While the Union Calvary Improves

Union Gen. Ulysses S. Grant was appointed head of all the Union armies on March 9, 1864, and thirty-three year old Philip H. Sheridan, who had been an aggressive infantry commander, was made his new cavalry commander. Grant planned to use his superiority in numbers of men and supplies to crush the South. At that time, the Southern cavalry was seriously suffering from a lack of horses. Although captured horses by law became the property of the government, and not the men taking them, by this time an unwritten law overrode the written law. Captured horses became the property of their captors, replacing their dead or unserviceable animals. Rosser said, "I often went into battle or on a raid with one-third at least of my men dismounted, and generally succeeded in mounting them from captures."[2]

Hampton was faced with the fact that his men were hungry and weary. Lacking rations, they boiled their horses' corn in lye and ate it themselves in order to survive. The currency in which the men were paid was so devalued that $22 worth of Confederate money was equal to one dollar in silver. The lack of forage in war-torn Virginia took its toll on the horses. The ravenous animals were gnawing the bark from trees from the ground as high as they could reach. Smaller trees were being completely devoured and the horses were chewing empty bags and paper scraps. Of course, the condition of the horses affected the efficiency of the cavalry. But Stuart refused to let Hampton's division go south of the James to recuperate. Hampton appealed for relief for his men and horses to a fellow South Carolinian, James B. Chesnut, who was a staff colonel and political favorite in Richmond. He wrote:

> Will you do me the favor to speak to the Sec. or to Gen. Bragg for me on this matter? I propose that this Brigade should be relieved from duty here & placed near the city. Their horses are not in condition to do picket duty on my long line, but in case of an advance on Richmond they could answer to mount the majority of the command. The men who are dismtd. could do good service in the works. With rest & forage the Brigade would soon recruit [revitalize] & when the campaign opens, it can be put into the field...."

He went on to express his complaints about Stuart and Fitz Lee:

Fitz Lee disbanded two of his brigades, which have been idle for two months & which are just reassembling. Let one of Lee's Brigades take the place of Butler. His Regts. are very full & the duty will be light on them. I suppose however that some one of Fitzhugh Lee's Brigades will be kept at Richmond, as Stuart always manages to give them the lightest duty....[3]

With Chesnut's help, Hampton was given permission to obtain fresh regiments in South Carolina for Butler's badly used regiment. Butler by this time was ready to return to duty with a cork foot.

While the best men and horses of the South were being lost, the Union cavalry was improving steadily in command and training. The Federal cavalry by this time were primarily using breech-loading carbines, which were considered to be superior to the muzzle-loading muskets carried by Hampton's troopers. There were some advantages in the muzzle-loaders, though, since their range was greater and the minié balls they fired were heavier. In addition, Hampton's men were fine marksmen and skilled at loading their weapons.

Waring reported in his diary concerning an inspection of the Jeff Davis Legion that "The arms were in good order.... The horses were in deplorable condition; only 56 were in serviceable condition. The balance need recruiting [recuperation] sadly."[4] Most likely Waring's observation was typical of the rest of the division. On April 12, Gen. Stuart ordered Lt. William H. Payne of Company G to take sixty-four men from Cobb's Legion to Georgia to procure fresh horses. After 30 days, they were to reassemble and march back to Virginia to rejoin their brigade.

After enduring a very cold winter in the field, on May 2 Hampton reported that the effective force in his division was only 673 men. On May 5, Hampton's division was reorganized. Rooney Lee had come home in an exchange of prisoners and was promoted to major-general. To give him a division, Chambliss's brigade was taken from Fitz Lee's division and Gordon's brigade was taken from Hampton's division. This arrangement displeased Hampton. After that, Hampton's division consisted of Young's Georgia brigade (with Cobb's Legion Cavalry), Rosser's Virginia brigade, and Butler's South Carolina brigade.

Company Notes
March 1–May 3, 1864

Company A — Wounded: Lucas T. Penick; Captured: Charles L. Camback
Company B — Wounded: John H. Marchman
Company C — Captured: Charles R.A. Harris
Company D — Died: D.A. Powell
Company G — Wounded: John W. Spencer
Company I — Captured: Owen O'Keefe; Captured and May Have Died: J.D. Howell
Company K — Died: C.H. Barden
Company L — Wounded: Robert J. Parker

Chapter 14

The Overland Campaign

The Wilderness

The enemy began to cross the Rapidan on Wednesday, May 4, 1864, with the objective of once more trying to get around Lee's right. The Union army had spent its winter in camps north of the Rapidan, preparing, organizing, and drilling. It was the best army that money could create, and the soldiers were "better cared for, clothed, and fed than most of them had been when at home, and, in numbers and equipment, far surpassed any army that had ever been mustered on American soil."[1] There were 150,000 of them, including those detailed to the Quartermaster Department, and 50,000 reinforcements would join them in the next four weeks.

In advance of the Union army rode 16,000 troopers in handsome uniforms, better mounted, armed, and equipped than any cavalry force their army had possessed. Following them were the infantry, their rifle barrels flashing in the sunlight and hundreds of standards waving in the breeze. The wheels of their artillery wagons were so numerous they sounded like distant thunder, and behind them thousands of wagons in a single line stretched for over sixty miles in length, transporting ample rations. Behind them came swarms of camp followers of both sexes. They filled the roads and overflowed into the open spaces like a gigantic blue river.

They would be facing a "thin line of gray"—men who were underpaid, ill-fed, ragged, and out-numbered 5 to 2. These were the descendants of those who fought for freedom in the War for American Independence. Like their forefathers, they were fighting for their traditions, laws, and liberty. Yet, in spite of all their advantages, the Union army would lose sixty thousand men in the next thirty days—more than the total number in the thin line of gray.

This time the Union used a route across Ely's Ford and through the Wilderness area, well to the east of Mine Run. Grant was gambling on being able to move through the Wilderness area before Lee could respond. Stuart's scouts and Hampton's pickets detected the presence of the Union army and warned Lee, who blocked Meade's path and trapped him in the Wilderness. The battle that ensued on May 5–6 took place in an area so thick with undergrowth and tree cover that the armies could not see each other.

On May 4, Cobb's Legion Cavalry received one hundred remount horses. At that time Young's brigade had no more than 250 officers and men, and they were detained at Milford awaiting orders until the afternoon of May 7.

Company Notes
May 4–6, 1864

Company B — Died: William F. Lampkin
Company L — Missing: Thomas Gay

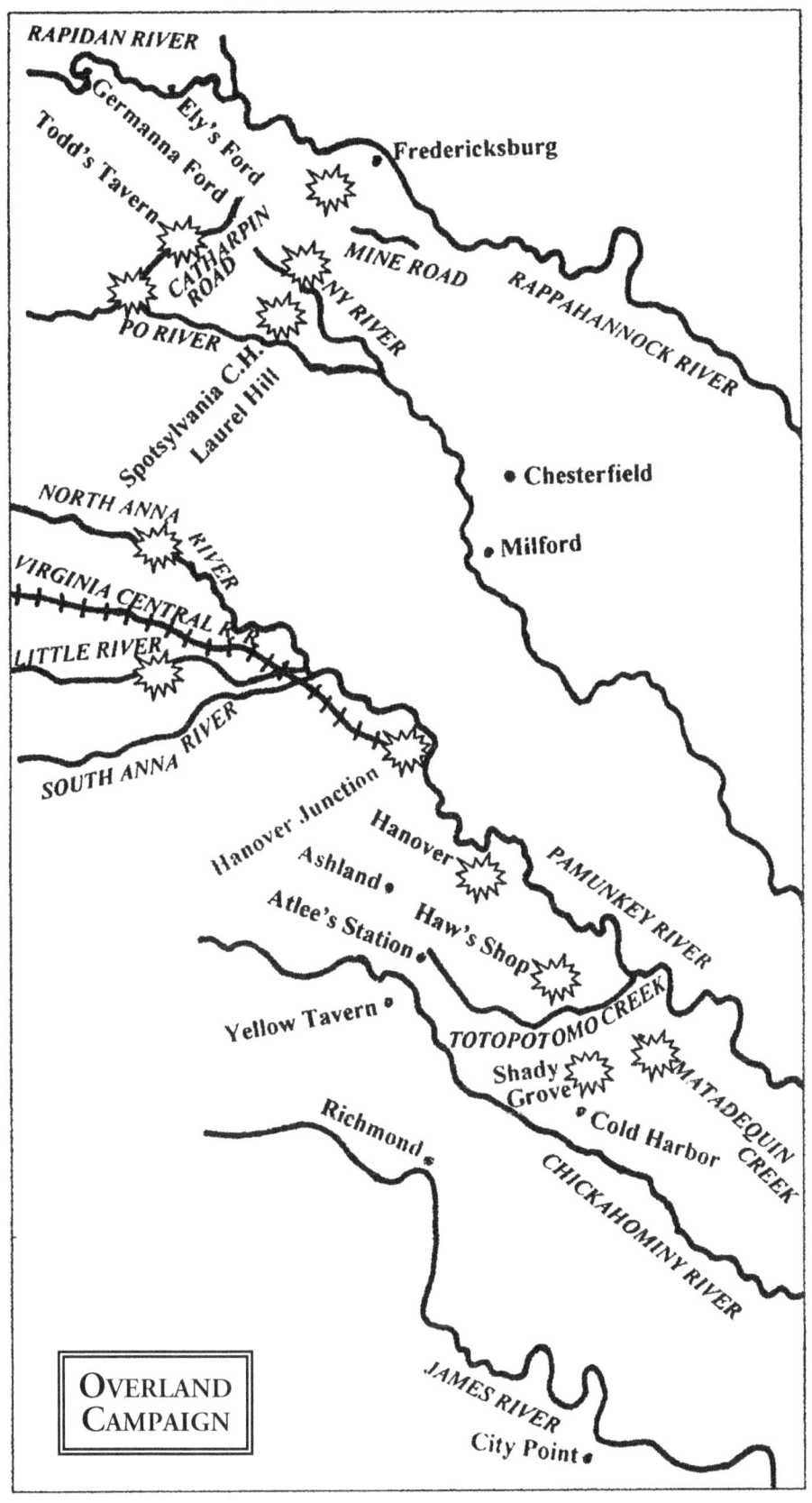

Todd's Tavern

Sheridan's cavalry tried to move to Spotsylvania Court House by way of Todd's Tavern on Saturday, May 7, 1864. They found the crossroads at Todd's Tavern blocked by dismounted troopers from Fitz Lee's division. In the fighting that ensued, Fitz Lee's troopers were overwhelmed and driven back from one line of breastworks to another. Late in the day, after finally getting orders to move from Milford, Hampton's men galloped to Fitz Lee's aid, approaching from the south. Shortly after passing Shady Grove, they learned that the Yankees were in their rear. Gordon's troopers attacked and drove them back with the aid of Cobb's Legion Cavalry. Rosser's brigade of Virginians was sent into action with their flanks protected by Young's small command, fighting dismounted. They were able to secure the road from Todd's Tavern to Spotsylvania Court House, thus slowing the progress of Grant and Meade.

On May 8, after suffering repulses for three days in the Wilderness, Grant began a rush to his left toward Spotsylvania Court House in order to turn Lee's right flank. It was vital that Lee arrive at the point of attack and prepare before Grant arrived. The Federal cavalry tried to keep the roads clear for their infantry, while it was the task of the Southern cavalry to delay the Union movement as much as possible. The road below Todd's Tavern was clogged with Union infantry and Sheridan's dismounted cavalrymen. Fitz Lee's troopers slowed their progress by using fight-and-fall-back tactics. Hampton's men remained in position west of Todd's Tavern. Around noon, Young's and Rosser's brigades were sent to attack the front and right flank of the enemy while Jubal Early's infantry division attacked their left. Hampton reported, "Both movements were executed handsomely & vigorously, the enemy falling back rapidly and leaving us in possession of his camp."[2] That afternoon Hampton moved south along with Early to be closer to the fighting in Spotsylvania. At that time, he held a position on the Confederate left. After May 9, Hampton's troopers guarded both flanks of the army.

Company Notes
May 7, 1864

Company B — Killed: Oliver Hazard Perry Juhan; Wounded: J.K.P. Ridling
Company H — Wounded: Richard D. Harris

Yellow Tavern and the Death of Jeb Stuart

Cobb's Legion Cavalry fought at Spotsylvania Court House, Laurel Hill, the Ny River, and on the Fredericksburg Road on May 8 and 9, 1864, during the Battle of the Wilderness.

Sheridan, who had orders to draw Stuart's cavalry away from the Army of Northern Virginia (Lee's army) and destroy it, took 10,000 cavalrymen with him on his mission. On May 9, he made a detour around Lee's right flank and began a raid toward Richmond. Along with him were seven batteries of horse artillery. Stuart left Hampton with Lee's Army, and took Fitz Lee's division and part of Rooney Lee's division, about one-third of the number of Sheridan's men, and set out to head off the raiders.

Cobb's Legion Cavalry grazed their horses near Shady Grove before they moved to the lower fords of the Po River with the Jeff Davis Legion. Shortly after they arrived, Yankee skirmishers crossed the fords. The Southern troopers deployed skirmishers and waited for further developments. Late in the afternoon, a heavy force of the enemy crossed the Po River and drove the troopers off the Catharpin Road, so they retreated to Mine Road. It was 10:30 P.M. before they camped with orders to move at 2:30 A.M. There was no corn for the horses or food for the men. Rations did not arrive until the next day.

On May 11, the Federals again crossed the Po and tried to take the Catharpin Road. Hampton's cavalry captured a number of the enemy, who were described as being "mere boys."[3] On the same day, by riding hard, Stuart got between Sheridan and Richmond at Yellow Tavern, nine miles from Richmond and a scant three miles north of the capital's outer defenses. During the fierce battle that ensued, the far greater numbers of Federal cavalry broke Stuart's line. Stuart was shot in the abdomen by a dismounted Yankee. He was carried to a house in Richmond, where he died the next morning. His last words were "God's will be done."

Stuart's death was quite a shock to his men. They had thought that he was invincible. He habitually rode with the advance guard, was always present at the point of greatest danger, and, until he was killed, he had never even been wounded.

Cavalryman Edward L. Wells said of Stuart:

> Thus fell a gallant, devoted soldier and a lovable man. His personal dash was splendid and his handling of mounted cavalry spirited. The daring raids and adventurous expeditions conducted by him are captivating to the imagination and surround his memory with romantic association.[4]

Wiley C. Howard said:

> Stuart was a superb man and magnetic leader of men, a born commander, with all the geniality of a jolly comrade, absolutely without fear — like Jackson, a man of destiny — and when he fell fighting, all hearts were melted with sadness over our great loss. I have seen him in the midst of whizzing bullets and hurtling shell humming some favorite ditty, as for instance, "Old Joe Hooker, come out of the Wilderness." We were with him on that last great and memorable flank movement of Jackson in Hooker's rear. The next day, when he passed us in command of Jackson's corps, we bared our heads and cheered our cavalry ideal hero, fearing that he would be taken from us for good.[5]

Waring wrote: "Gen. J.E.B. Stuart is dead. A more gallant spirit never breathed the breath of life."[6]

Gen. James Byron Gordon of the 1st North Carolina was also mortally wounded, fighting courageously at the front in this unequal battle. He was carried to Richmond and died six days later. He had been an excellent officer, and his death was a great loss to the cavalry.

With Stuart's death, Wade Hampton became Lee's ranking cavalry commander. He was forty-six years old, but in excellent physical condition. He was not immediately confirmed as chief of cavalry, but when there were joint actions involving Fitz Lee or Rooney Lee, he was in command. He was aware that Fitz Lee disliked him and that Rooney Lee was at the most just neutral. This meant that he had to depend heavily on his own division, which had only 673 officers and men at the beginning of the Wilderness campaign. The entire cavalry corps never exceeded 7,000 men with serviceable horses during the entire campaign — less than half of the Federal cavalry corps. The force underwent constant reductions by broken down horses as well as casualties, while new recruits were few. Hampton did have three loyal brigadiers, Pierce Young, Calbraith Butler, and Tom Rosser, whom he could depend upon.

Stuart had repeatedly taken risky chances against the odds, but Hampton believed in concentrating his forces and using his strength at the proper place and moment. He was more modest in dress than Stuart was and a fiercer fighter. He was one of the most (if not the most) successful hand-to-hand combatants among all the general officers in American history. Where Stuart preferred mounted actions, under Wade Hampton the troopers doubled as infantry and fought both mounted and dismounted. By rushing his men mounted to desirable points, dismounting them, and hurrying them into battle, and then, if necessary, quickly withdrawing them to attack another weaker position, he was able to multiply the effectiveness of each of his men. The enemy often thought they were fighting a much larger force, or that they were fighting infantry when they encountered Hampton.

Although the men had loved Stuart, they adored Hampton. Wiley C. Howard said:

> When ... Stuart was killed near Richmond, Hampton, our own beloved, brave and skillful, unselfish Wade Hampton, who knew by name almost all the men of his old brigade, and delighted to recognize the humblest private just the same as the highest officer — took command of all the cavalry of Northern Virginia, and with such magnificent Division and Brigade commanders as Fitz Lee, Rosser, Mat Butler, Wicham [sic], Young, Lomax, Munford, and others, he managed it masterfully and gloriously, until called to the Carolinas to help beat back William Tecumseh Sherman.[7]

After a fruitless attack on the mostly citizen soldiers in the defenses at Richmond, Sheridan returned to his infantry. He had lost 650 men. Although Stuart had been killed, Sheridan's raid was a failure from a military point of view. He had accomplished nothing of value for the Union Army.

Company Notes
May, 8–11, 1864

Company E — Wounded: John W.S. Mahaffy; Captured: John A. Johnson, John D. Lowe
Company H — Wounded: Marcus L. Lay
Company L — Wounded: Jeremiah Berry Jones

Spotsylvania Court House and the North Anna

At daybreak on Thursday, May 12, 1864, the battle of Spotsylvania Court House began in earnest. Gib Wright counted 49 cannon discharges within one minute's time. Troopers were sent out in every direction on details, but by 4:00 P.M. the heaviest fighting was over. Every day, from the beginning of the campaign until the battle of Cold Harbor, Cobb's Legion Cavalry was engaged with the enemy, trying to delay his forward march. They were always forced to fall back, due to the overwhelming numbers of the Yankees.

When they received orders to be ready at 2:30 A.M. on May 13, one of the officers wrote in his diary, "My heart sank within me, for I conjectured we were going to retreat, & that the Cavalry were to take the place of the Infantry."[8] Edward L. Wells of the Charleston Light Dragoons said that this sort of service was the hardest on the men, because they knew full well each morning that the struggle was hopeless, and yet they had to endure it day after day, always being forced back but disputing every inch of ground.

It was cool and rainy when Cobb's Legion Cavalry moved east of the Po, to the left of the Jeff Davis Legion and the infantry. The enemy was massing on the right. It was not until May 15 that the troopers began to learn the full extent of the numbers of the enemy's dead. Grant had sacrificed wave after wave of his men, and their losses were ghastly. Waring reported:

> The enemy's dead lay in all conceivable positions along their entire line of battle. I counted one hundred and forty six bodies rotting above ground, & got tired of counting. I must have seen three hundred Yankees lying dead. I saw but four Confederate graves, I saw too about two hundred Yankee graves. If the slaughter along the whole line is like what I have seen, the enemy's dead must be numerous indeed. I hear that the slaughter on our right is greater still.[9]

After Grant lost the battle of Spotsylvania Court House, he moved toward the North Anna River, trying to mask the movements of his infantry in order to turn the Confederate flank. Hampton kept unmasking his movements and reporting them to Lee, while at the same time concealing the movements of the Army of Northern Virginia, and protecting its flanks.

Rosser's troopers made a daring reconnaissance in the direction of Fredericksburg in the rain on May 15, discovering the position of Grant's right flank. Cobb's Legion Cavalry left camp at 5:00 on the morning of May 16 and scouted toward Germanna Ford. They found the road strewn with thick, new blankets, overcoats, and the like that had been thrown away by the Yankees in their march. After returning to camp, James Bolling of Company B arrived with some corn for the men to eat.

Grant ordered that all of his pontoons be removed from the Rappahannock River. He intended to stay in the South and was sending a message to his men that no escape route was being left open. On May 19, Hampton received a telegraph from Fitz Lee saying that Sheridan was on his way back to join Grant. Ewell was ordered by Lee to make a reconnaissance and to utilize the cavalry to shield him. Cobb's Legion Cavalry was sent out to scout. The next day, May 21, was clear and hot. Grant moved toward Hanover Junction at 7:00 A.M., and the southern troopers began marching. By evening, they caught up with the enemy near Milford. After camping at Milford, the brigade moved back toward Chesterfield during the heat of the next day. After crossing Pole Cat Creek, the troopers were issued three days' rations of corn and allowed to rest, while their horses grazed on clover until they could eat no more. About sundown, they moved back to the North Anna and camped on the north side. The next morning, May 23, the horses were saddled but allowed to graze. By 6:00 A.M., the pickets were driven in and the troopers skirmished with Union infantry. Late in the afternoon, the Confederates marched into camp on the South Anna.

On May 23 the troopers left camp before daylight. As they rode toward Little River, they found the Confederate infantry in a line of battle and throwing up entrenchments. As they approached Little River, a line of Yankee skirmishers appeared on a hill on the opposite bank. In the afternoon, the enemy's infantry attempted to cross the river, but the Southern skirmishers and artillery drove them back. As the armies clashed along the North Anna, Hampton's men were involved in action mainly against Union infantry. The Union army withdrew from the North Anna on May 26 and began moving to the southeast toward the Pamunkey River. When, on May 27, Lee moved his headquarters to Atlee's Station on the Virginia Central Railroad, Hampton's men brought up the rear of the army. At Atlee's Station, Hampton received orders to ascertain if the Federal infantry had crossed to the south side of the Pamunkey River. The men learned that the Yankees were burning all the homes that they found deserted.

Company Notes
May 12–26, 1864

Company B — Captured: Richard Nathaniel Juhan, William H. McDaniel, B. F. Saunders, John N. Warwick
Company C — Mortally wounded: Elisha S. Howse
Company D — Captured: Jesse C. Gibson, Isaac T. Smith
Company E — Captured: Samuel D. Paden
Company F — Captured: John P. Peel
Company G — Mortally wounded: James H. Johnson; Wounded: Osborne A. Seay; Captured: James W. Stokes
Company I — Captured: James A. Bryan, Edward Wyatt Collier, William Capers Dickson
Company K — Wounded: Frances Edgeworth Eve
Company L — Wounded: Leonidas D. Johnson

Haw's Shop

Sheridan's cavalry crossed to the South bank of the Pamunkey River on Friday, May 27, 1864, and the Union infantry crossed on the following day. It became necessary for Hampton to drive back Sheridan's cavalry in order to establish whether the Federal infantry had crossed in force. Lee needed this information to determine if he should move further to the left or cross the river. The troopers camped that night on the north bank of the South Anna River.

The cavalry went on a reconnaissance on the hot day of May 28, crossing the South Anna and marching to Ashland, to determine the movement plans of the Union Army. It happened that, at the same time, Sheridan was in motion trying to learn the position of the Confederate infantry. Hampton's men headed for the Hanovertown Ferry. After crossing Totopotomoy Creek, they turned east. Wells said, "There were no bands nor gorgeous uniforms; none of the artificial 'frills' of war. There was no need for these, for here, magnificent in simplicity, ragged, battle-stained, and gaunt, but confident and cheery, marched the victors of the Wilderness and Spotsylvania."[10]

Two miles beyond Haw's Shop, they encountered pickets of David Gregg's Union division. Wickham's Virginia brigade, which was in front, attacked them, and scattered their pickets. After the pickets fled, Sheridan and Custer appeared in their front and dug in, while Gregg brought up horse artillery to sweep the road. Hampton ordered his new South Carolina regiments to dismount and form as infantry in the woods. The new men stood their ground, even when their horses stampeded. The topography, which was covered with thick woods and dense undercover, worked to the Confederates' advantage. They could hide behind trees and logs and use their superior marksmanship skills. The South Carolinians' proficiency with their long Enfield rifled muskets shocked Sheridan and Custer.

Wickham's and Rosser's brigades attacked vigorously, and then Hampton placed Wickham's men in the center, with Cobb's Legion Cavalry and the rest of Butler's men on Wickham's right. Rosser's men were placed on Wickham's left. Rooney Lee's men were sent down a road to the left with the expectation of being able to turn the enemy's left, but that proved to be impractical, so Lee used his artillery to cover Rosser's left. The hottest part of the battle was on the Confederate right, where Cobb's Legion Cavalry was located. A trooper reported, "We coped with Sheridan in a number of conflicts ... with hard brushes at Nances [sic] and Hawe [sic] Shops."[11]

The enemy held their ground and the battle lasted for seven hours, until Sheridan was heavily reinforced. Hampton had his troopers to withdraw, but the order was not passed to the new recruits, so Hampton found it necessary to go in himself to withdraw the South Carolinians. They did not want to fall back, although a number of the new recruits lost their lives in the battle, and their Col. Millen was killed while leading his mounted men, enabling his unmounted men to retire.

Hampton had accomplished his objective. Captured infantry prisoners revealed that the Union army had crossed to the south bank of the Pamunkey River but were in supporting distance of their cavalry. Their army was headed toward Cold Harbor. Both Hampton and Sheridan considered this little known battle at Haw's Shop to be the most severe that the cavalry had ever been engaged in. Among Union casualties that day was John A. Huff of the 5th Michigan Cavalry, the reputed killer of J.E.B. Stuart.

Afterwards, the Virginia mountaineer Capt. Frank M. Myers, of Rosser's brigade, noted:

> Up to this time the Cavalry Corps had not learned the style of their new commander, but now they discovered a vast difference between the old and the new, for while General Stuart would attempt his work with whatever force he had at hand, and often seemed to try to accomplish a given result with the smallest possible number of men, Gen. Hampton always endeavored to carry every available man to his point of operation, and the larger his force, the better he liked it.
>
> The advantage of this style of generalship was soon apparent, for while under Stuart stampedes were frequent, with Hampton they were unknown, and the men of his corps soon had the same unwavering confidence in him that the "Stonewall Brigade" entertained for their general.[12]

Late in the afternoon, after the bloody battle of Haw's Shop, the troopers crossed the Chickahominy River and camped near Atlee's Station on the Virginia Central Railroad in a clover field where their horses could graze. The cavalry then saw action every day as Grant continued his Overland Campaign moving from the Wilderness and going toward Richmond.

Company Notes
May 27–30, 1864

Company C — Killed: Williamson F. Early; Captured: John M. Anderson, John White David

Matadequin Creek

On Sunday, May 29, 1864, after the battle of Haw's Shop, Young's and Butler's brigades were positioned to block a move of the Federals around Lee's right at the junction of the Matadequin and Totomoi creeks. When they were fired upon by Yankee artillery, Butler had no guns with which to respond. Some of the Georgian cavalry deployed against them but were driven back. It turned out that they were facing the extreme left of the Union army.

Cobb's Legion Cavalry joined the fray, and then the infantry came to help them. The Yankees were situated behind a farmhouse and some outbuildings. The Confederates had to cross an open wheat field as they attacked the enemy. They then took cover behind a fence that they tore down. The enemy made a strong resistance but was driven from its position.

The fence behind which the Southerners were positioned ran along a road, where on the left a dense mass of blue appeared, covering the road from side to side. Butler's new recruits with their Enfield rifles could not resist such a tempting target, where each shot produced results. The problem was that the target shot back, and the rail fence did not offer much protection. The Yankees deployed and the rail fence was soon enfiladed. In withdrawing, the Confederates had to recross the open field, where the wheat was being mowed down by Yankee bullets as they crossed. Wells said, "It was a plucky fight, but to have been successful it would have been necessary to beat the left wing of Grant's army, a feat which would have eclipsed David's exploit against Goliath."[13] The cavalry had determined the position of Grant's army, which was their objective.

On the night of May 30, Cobb's Legion Cavalry crossed a run and was deployed as skirmishers near Hanover Court House. The numbers of the enemy were too great, and they had to fall back to the run. Confederate artillery was brought up and the enemy stopped pursuing them. On June 2, Young was wounded while leading a North Carolina brigade. The ball struck him on the left breast and came out near his left shoulder, passing under his arm. No bones were broken, so it was a wound from which he could recover.

Lee used the intelligence gathered by the cavalry to arrive at Cold Harbor first and fortify before Meade arrived. In the battle of Cold Harbor that ensued on Friday, June 3, about five Yankees were killed for every Confederate soldier who lost his life. The stench emanating from the dead, rotting bodies of the Yankees piled in front of Lee's men was described as being "fearful."[14]

Grant's army numbered nearly 113,000 men, of whom 13,000 were killed in the space of about an hour's time at Cold Harbor. In the previous month, Grants losses of 60,000 men almost equaled the entire number of troops with which Lee had begun the campaign. Lee lost 20,000 men during that time. After losing the battle of Cold Harbor, Grant then marched around the Confederates to City Point on the James River below Richmond, a place he could have reached with ships without the loss of a single man.

Company Notes
May 31–June 6, 1864

Staff—Wounded: Pierce M. B. Young
Company A—Wounded: George W. Roberts
Company C—Died: Joseph Robert Howard
Company D—Wounded: John S. Thrash; Captured: B.L. Dickens, E. D. High
Company E—Killed: A.M. Quarles (while serving with infantry)
Company F—Captured: George W. Vaughan
Company H—Captured: Thomas B.F. Todd
Company I—Wounded: James Franklin Seago
Company K—Captured: L. Rigand

Chapter 15

The Trevilian Campaign

Sheridan's Raid on the Virginia Central Railroad

Phil Sheridan set out with the largest cavalry force ever taken on a raid on Tuesday, June 7, 1864. He took with him hand picked men from Albert T.A. Torbert's and Gregg's divisions, such as the 1st and 5th United States Regulars, Custer's brigade and the 1st New Jersey. There were 8,000 cavalrymen, each carrying 100 rounds of ammunition, two days' feed for his horse, and three days' rations for himself. Along with the troopers were 125 wagons, four batteries of four guns each, and another 2,000 men.

Sheridan's raid was part of a larger strategic plan. He was supposed to draw the Confederate cavalry away from Grant so Grant could slip across the James River and capture Petersburg, which would then cut off Lee from his supplies from the Deep South. Sheridan was supposed to destroy the Virginia Central Railroad (today called the Chesapeake & Ohio Railroad) at Charlottesville, Lynchburg, and Gordonsville. The Virginia Central was essential to the Confederacy because it was Lee's connection to the Shenandoah Valley, the "Breadbasket of the Confederacy." Next, Sheridan was supposed to link up with Gen. David Hunter, who had just defeated Grumble Jones' small force at Piedmont, Virginia. Sheridan and Hunter were to capture and burn Lynchburg and then to return to Grant's army, destroying more stretches of railroad and the James River Canal along the way. If the plan worked, Lee would be hemmed in on three sides without supplies. The only part of Grant's grand plan that actually worked was that Grant slipped across the James River.

On the morning of June 8, Hampton's Iron Scouts discovered that Sheridan had crossed the Pamunkey River on pontoon bridges at New Castle with his Union cavalry, had moved north for about ten miles, and then had turned a little to the northwest. He was following a course nearly parallel with the north bank of the North Anna River, a branch of the Pamunkey River, and Custer had camped for the night on Pole Cat Creek near Chesterfield (now Bowling Green).

Hampton's cavalry was mustered at dawn on June 9. They slung their horse corn and three days' rations over their saddles. Some of the men grumbled about having to carry the extra weight of three days' forage for their horses. Each trooper had one and a half pounds of hardtack and a half-pound of bacon, which had to be eaten raw in the saddle as the men were only allowed to stop long enough to graze their horses twice each day. Food had been scarce and some of the men were so hungry that they ate all their rations at once. Hampton's force did not exceed 4,700 men, and for eight days and nights they did not have time to unsaddle.

Cobb's Legion Cavalry, with the rest of Young's brigade, was led by Col. Gilbert J. Wright because Pierce Young had been seriously wounded in fighting on June 1 while he was leading Gordon's old brigade.

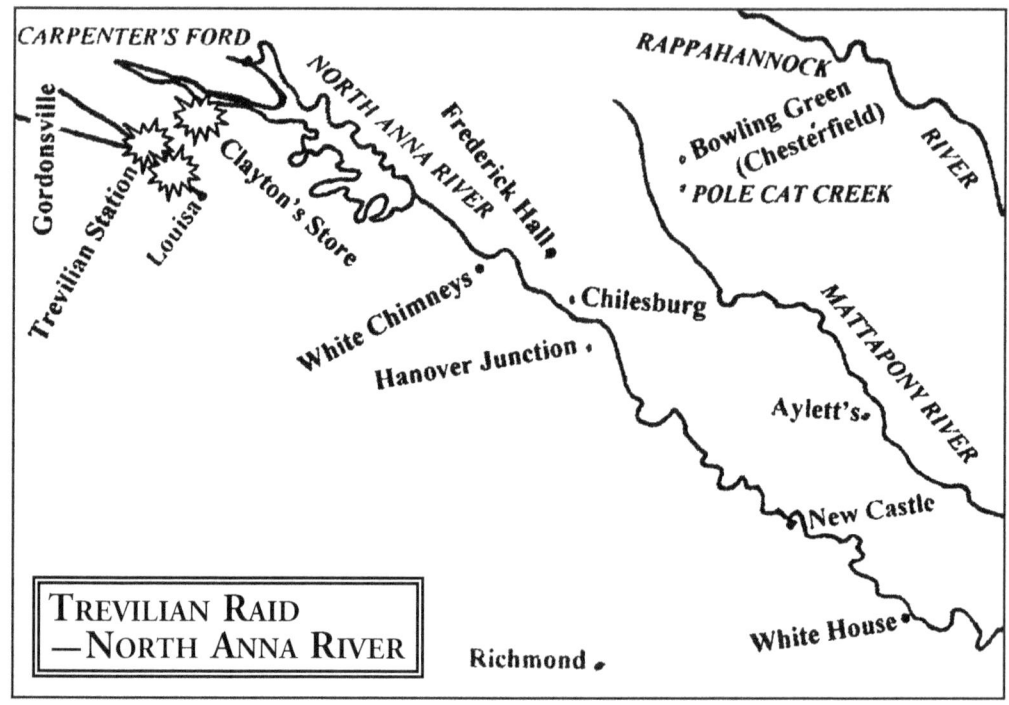

TREVILIAN RAID
—NORTH ANNA RIVER

Wright's brigade was in the front, and Fitz Lee was in the rear, with two batteries of horse artillery of four guns each under Maj. James Hart and Lt. James W. Thompson. The total number of troopers and artillery was less than half of Sheridan's. Considering that the Yankees were carrying breechloaders and magazine rifles, their effective advantage should have been closer to at least three to one. Rooney Lee's third division remained with the army at Atlee's Station.

The men rode all through the hot and dusty morning, then paused for two hours at noon to rest and graze the horses. After their break, the men climbed back in their saddles and rode until midnight. They bivouacked halfway between Richmond and Trevilian Station but got very little sleep. They rested on the ground holding their horses, expecting to get marching orders at any minute.

The march resumed at 2:00 A.M. The next morning was hot, and it grew hotter in the afternoon as the troopers continued their trek. Virginia was having an unusually severe drought. Clouds of stifling dust blinded and choked the men, but the only water available was from the small streams through which they slogged. After being churned up by thousands of hoofs, it was undrinkable. They marched all day long, not stopping to water their horses until they reached Louisa Court House at 3:00 P.M. By nightfall of June 10, Hampton reached Green Spring Valley, three miles west of Trevilian Station, where he bivouacked for the night. Butler's men camped east of Trevilian Station. Gib Wright's men were at Trevilian Station, Rosser's men were beyond Trevilian Station on the Gordonsville Road, and Fitz Lee was in the rear at Louisa Court House, four or five miles away but also on the railroad.

The hard riding had paid off. Hampton learned from his Iron Scouts that, by taking a shorter route and using all possible speed, his troopers were in front of Sheridan. At the beginning of the march, the men, and even the brigade commanders, were ignorant of where Hampton was leading them or what his objective was. By this time, the men pretty much knew that Hampton was seeking Sheridan and a battle was imminent.

That night, those of Hampton's men who still had some ate the last of their rations. It is not known at what point the men got sick, but their service records reveal that a large number of the troopers from Cobb's Legion Cavalry were hospitalized with chronic diarrhea after the campaign. Perhaps storing raw pork in a haversack for three days in hot weather had caused it to spoil, or perhaps they were ill from drinking polluted water.

As the Southerners ate, Sheridan crossed the North Anna at Carpenter's Ford, about sixty-five miles from his starting point, and headed for the vicinity of Trevilian Station. When Torbert's division, which was in advance, was going into camp, ten or twelve men dashed toward the head of his column, fired their pistols, and galloped off. Torbert mistook the men for some countrymen or home guards. They were, in fact, Hampton's Iron Scouts, and the incident should have been a warning that Hampton was nearby. That night Sheridan's men slept peacefully under the starry sky, thinking that the Confederate cavalry was miles away.

Trevilian Station, First Day

Before dawn on Saturday, June 11, 1864, those who were the nearest to the approaching Federals could hear the enemy's bugles. In the Confederate camps, no bugles were used, in order to prevent betraying the presence of the troops. Wells noted that "The air was crisp and bracing with the smell of clover, and the foot-hills of the Blue Ridge looked cool and refreshing after all the dust and heat of the previous day."[1] Cobb's Legion Cavalry was mounted and ready to move at dawn. As they waited with Wright's other regiments (the Phillip's Legion, the Jeff Davis Legion, and the 7th Georgia), Rosser rode up to Butler and asked, "What is Hampton going to do here today?"

Butler replied, "Damned if I know. We have been up mounted since daylight and my men and horses are being worsted by nonaction."[2]

As the two turned their horses toward Hampton's headquarters to inquire about the plans for the day, their troopers dismounted and stood by their horses and waited. Hampton's plans were to take a road that ran northerly from Trevilian Station toward Carpenter's Ford, where Sheridan had been located. There was a fork in the road that the Yankees would be taking, with a wedge shaped tract of woods in the center, at a place called Clayton's Store. The surrounding countryside was thickly wooded, and would provide good cover for Hampton's men, so they could use their superior marksmanship skills, thus neutralizing the Yankees' advantage of numbers.

From Clayton's Store, one of the roads at the fork ran to Louisa, so Hampton sent word for Fitz Lee to take that road and meet him at Clayton's Store. Hampton planned to strike the Yankees head-on with Butler's and Wright's brigades while Fitz Lee came against their flank. The enemy would be hemmed in, with a river in their rear. Rosser's men would guard the Confederate left and rear west of Trevilian Station on the road to Gordonsville.

About 5:00 A.M., Hampton led Wright's and Butler's brigades north up the road toward Clayton's Store. Fitz Lee reported that his men were moving out as ordered. After going about two miles, Hampton encountered Torbert's Union division. Hampton ordered Wright's and Butler's troopers forward, but the Federals counterattacked. Butler's and Wright's brigades dismounted and advanced through the woods on each side of the road. They struck the enemy and pressed him back. A battle which lasted for several hours followed, with troopers taking cover behind trees, fences, and thick underbrush. Hampton sent a series of staff officers to get

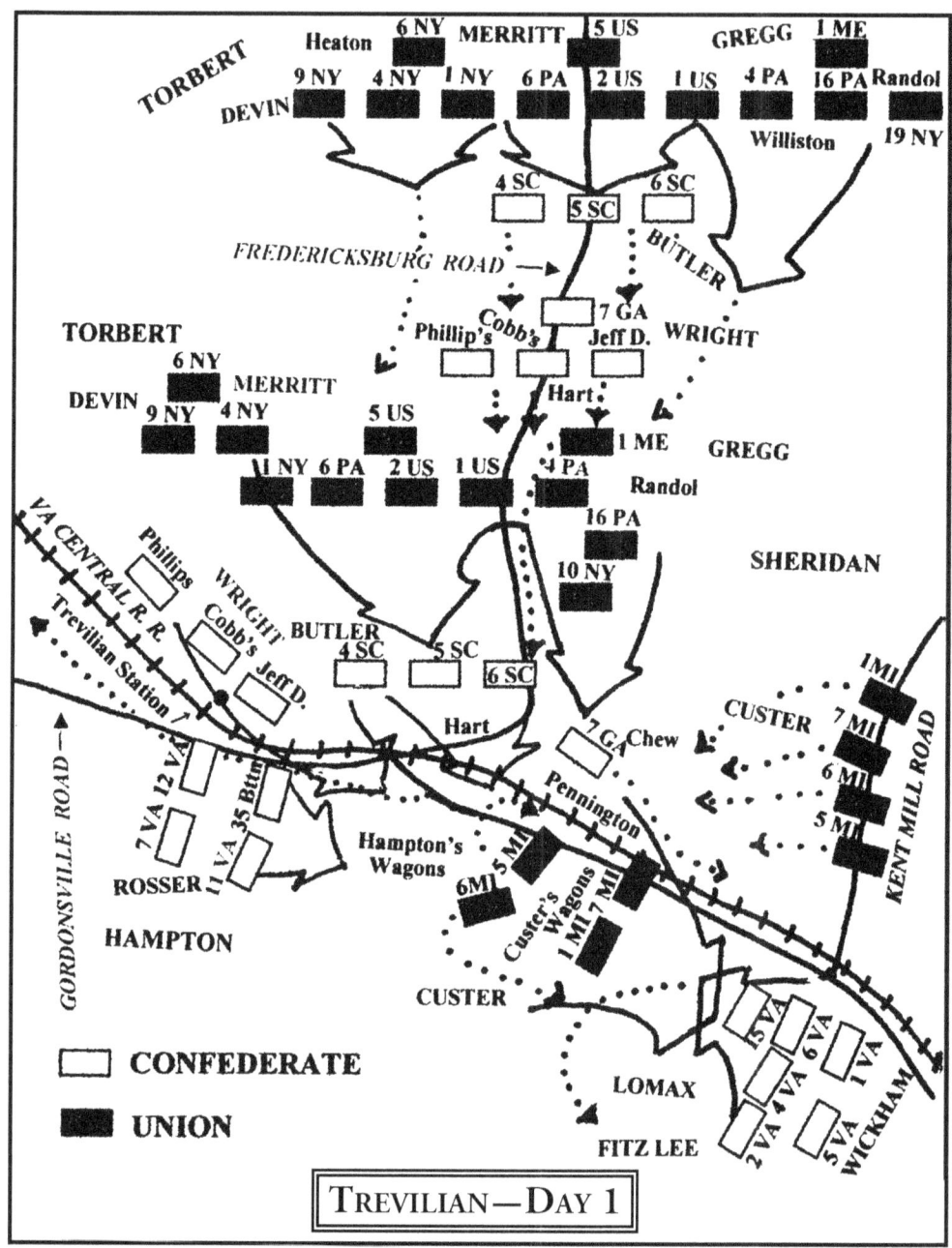

Trevilian — Day 1

Fitz Lee to reinforce him. However, either the officers could not locate Lee or they were captured, and Fitz Lee failed to bring his men up to support Butler and Wright.

Custer briefly engaged Fitz Lee's Virginians above Louisa Court House. The skirmish was so feebly conducted by Fitz Lee's men that Custer drew off and found a side road through the woods between Fitz Lee and Hampton. He traveled almost to Trevilian Station with no opposition and arrived at a point below the depot in the Confederate rear. There he discovered Hampton's unprotected wagons and ambulances and about 800 horses of Butler's dismounted men.

Chapter 15—The Trevilian Campaign

Custer seized the horses, but before he could lead them away, his position was overrun by retreating Confederates. Wiley C. Howard had been left with the horses because he was ill with a sore throat. In the confusion that followed, Howard was chased for a mile by fifty or more Yankees before he jumped his horse over a pile of shells that had fallen from a caisson. While descending a slope, his horse stumbled and fell. Howard put his hands forward to catch himself as he fell from his horse. One of his hands was ripped open, exposing the tendons. He jumped up and ran while a Yankee shot at him and shouted for him to surrender. Howard did not stop but scrambled over a fence. He heard a bullet hit the rail behind him as he began running across a field. The Yankees behind him practiced target-shooting on him, but they all missed. Howard finally reached the safety of some woods. Pushing on, he encountered an elderly citizen who was hiding his favorite mare from the Yankees. Next, he ran into William W. Hopkins of the Jeff Davis Legion, Company D, who had just experienced a similar incident. Together they hid in a thick clump of alder bushes by an old pond near a stream. The Yankees soon surrounded the area, cursing as they looked for Howard. Howard's sore throat was getting worse, and he could not suppress a cough. Hopkins would force his canteen into Howard's mouth as each spasm of coughing came on. After the Yankees left, the two troopers stealthily crept down the stream and back toward their own lines. When they spied their provost guard, Lt. Mike Simmons, corralling a large group of Yankee prisoners, they scrambled over a fence and ran the last mile back to their own lines.

Meanwhile, Hampton heard of the threat from Custer and turned Rosser's men around to go after him. He called up the nearest body of horsemen, Butler's 6th South Carolina, and ordered them to charge. This regiment included a company of young cadets from the South Carolina Military Academy (now known as the Citadel). Hampton led the students through a clearing south of the depot, and their charge scattered the Yankees, preventing them from reaching the horse artillery. Rosser's Laurel Brigade came clattering up in a cloud of dust and attacked Custer's flanks. Unfortunately, Rosser was wounded in the charge. Wright's and Butler's brigades overran Custer's position and, after a hard battle, recaptured most of the horses, several caissons, limbers, and ambulances that the Yankees were about to carry off.

Sometime during the afternoon, Hampton sent Howard, who was wearing a sling on his arm to protect his wounded hand, to deliver a message to Rosser. Howard found Rosser's brigade hotly engaged dismounted. After Howard delivered the message, Rosser said, "Give the general my compliments and tell him we are giving 'em hell."[3] Howard swiftly rode away, because the fighting was too hot and uncomfortable to linger in that vicinity. Wright's brigade, with Cobb's Legion in the center, was located on Rosser's flank.

Hampton sent a messenger to Butler (on Wright's left) with an order to withdraw his men to the railroad west of the station and form a line so he could protect the ambulances and the wounded. Butler's reply was "Say to General Hampton that it is hell to hold on and hell to let go."[4] He mounted his men a regiment at a time and had them withdraw while his dismounted troopers covered their movement with rifle fire. A strong line was formed along the railroad embankment and the road leading to Gordonsville, which ran parallel to the railroad. From west to east were Wright's brigade (Phillip's Legion, Cobb's Legion Cavalry, and the Jeff Davis Legion in that order, with the 7th Georgia in reserve), and then Butler's brigade (the 4th, 5th, and 6th South Carolina in that order).

Custer, who was facing west, continued the conflict, but he was soon assaulted from the east, also, as Fitz Lee belatedly arrived from Louisa Court House. For the next hour, Custer fought against encirclement and sunstroke, losing about 400 of his men.

At the end of the day Custer held the ground at Trevilian Station with Lee on the east and Hampton on the west of the station. Late in the afternoon, Custer was rescued by Yankees who broke through to him. Each side then retreated to the positions they held before the battle. Custer abandoned his spoils and lost four of his caissons and some of his own wagons, including his headquarters wagon with brigade reports and private correspondence.

Both sides spent much of the night constructing temporary defenses using rails, logs, brush, and dirt. Although it was less than a year before the end of the war, all but one of the men from Cobb's Legion Cavalry who were captured on this day would die at Elmira Prison in New York. It is possible that some of them were already sick when they were captured and may not have received medical care.

Company Notes
June 11, 1864

Company C — Mortally Wounded, Captured and Died: Daniel C. Baxter; Captured: M. Rufus McCurry, Samuel S. Parks
Company F — Killed: Jethro W. Rogers
Company H — Captured: John A. Moore, James C. Wilborn
Company I — Killed: Thomas Jefferson Colvin; Wounded: George A. Williams

Trevilian Station, Second Day

The next morning, Sunday, June 12, 1864, Custer's men demolished 100 feet or so of track on each side of the station* as Hampton dug in across the road to Charlottesville, barring Sheridan's access to Mallory's Ford. Fitz Lee took his men in a wide circle around Custer, and rejoined Hampton by noon. At that time, Hampton turned his division over to Butler and assumed command of all of the forces.

Sheridan was in a situation where he had to attack or admit defeat and retreat, because Hampton was blocking the roads to Gordonsville and Charlottesville and the Virginia Central Railroad, which were his objectives. Between 1:00 and 2:00 that afternoon, Sheridan formed his men along the railroad track and advanced toward Butler.

Butler's brigade (4th, 5th, and 6th SC) had formed behind the railroad embankment, where they had thrown up extra earth for protection. Fitz Lee was ordered to form to Butler's left with one of his brigades (1st, 2nd, 3rd, and 4th VA), make a circle to the left with his other brigade (5th, 6th, and 15th VA) and strike the enemy on his right flank. Hart's battery was to the right and Thompson's to the left of Butler. The men in the line along the railroad (Butler's and Lee's men) were protected by the embankment, but the part of the line down the wagon road leading to Gordonsville, where Rosser's (7th, 11th, 12th, and 35th VA) and Wright's (Cobb's Legion, Phillip's Legion, Jeff Davis Legion, 7th and 20th GA) troopers were located, was protected only by a few fence rails and a little earth that had been thrown up by the men digging with tin plates, cups, and their hands. These "fortifications" and "rifle-pits," as the Federal generals later called them, were inadequate to protect the men from bullets, much less from artillery.

*This is according to Wells, who was present (page 203). Others have said several miles, which seems impossible. Custer's men would have been too strung out and easy prey for the Confederates.

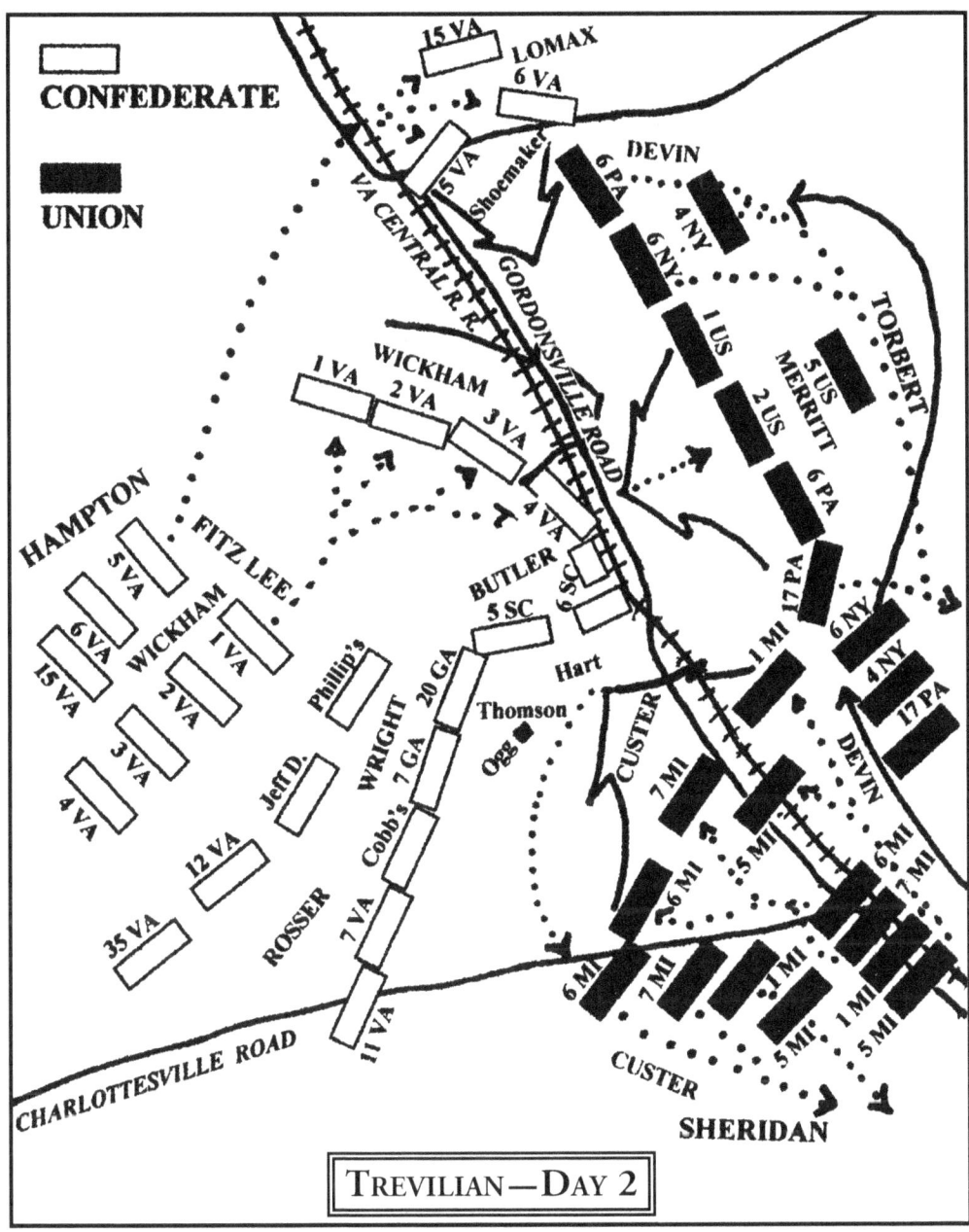

Trevilian—Day 2

Sheridan ordered his dismounted men to charge. His men knew that the success or failure of their expedition depended on this fight, so they eagerly attacked, firing with their magazine rifles as they charged. They were quickly repulsed by the expert Southern marksmen, who fired at will with muzzle-loaders. The field was rapidly strewn with the enemy's dead and wounded.

The Federal artillery had a clear advantage on the field, as they outnumbered the Southern guns two to one. Cobb's Legion Cavalry and the rest of Wright's and Rosser's men, who were in the unprotected line along the wagon road to Gordonsville, suffered the most from the enemy's artillery.

Most accounts report that the Confederates repulsed five assaults. M.W. Wellman reported there were six assaults, but Hampton and Edward Wells, both of whom were present, reported seven. The lines were so close together that the Confederates could hear the enemy's bugle calls and see the Yankees bracing themselves by swigging from flasks of whiskey. This angered the thirsty Southerners.

As sunset approached, the Confederates' ammunition for their rifles was almost gone. While being fired upon with shell and grape, the exhausted troopers collected cartridges from the dead and wounded. Meanwhile, the Federals were forming for another attack. At almost the last moment, the ordnance man came up from the rear, his horses at full gallop, with a wagonload of cartridge boxes. A man in the rear of his wagon frantically tossed them at his comrades as Yankee bullets struck the wagon repeatedly, but the two men escaped unhurt. The troopers eagerly caught the cartridge boxes and prepared for the onslaught.

Hart's guns shelled the Ogg House, where Sheridan had snipers posted, and Thompson's guns answered the enemy's batteries in the dimming light. Just as the sun was setting, Sheridan's men charged forward in close order, firing carbines from their hips. They advanced almost to the fence rails that topped the makeshift earthworks along the Gordonsville wagon road before they were driven back by point-blank sheets of bullets.

At this point in the battle, as the sun set, flashes from Fitz Lee's rifles announced that he had finally brought his men into the fight on the enemy's flank. At the same time, a Federal caisson was blown up by a Confederate shell, and, as if by prearranged signal, Cobb's Legion Cavalry and the rest of Wright's and Rosser's men sprang up and leaped over their breastworks. They charged down the embankment giving the Rebel yell. Sheridan's men put up a stout fight before being swept back into a rapid retreat. They were said to be "good fighters as well as runners."[5]

By the time the enemy's works were stormed, it was 10:00 P.M. Sheridan's entire column abandoned their dead and wounded on the field, retreated rapidly towards Carpenter's Ford, and continued moving all night without halting. Fitz Lee's men intercepted a portion of Sheridan's force that was in charge of captured prisoners and horses and recaptured them.

Afterwards, Butler said, "Pursuit by my command was out of the question. We had been engaged in this bloody encounter from the beginning without food or rest for either men or horses, in the broiling sun of a hot June day, and recuperation was absolutely necessary. As it was, I was not relieved and did not withdraw from my lines until 2 o'clock on the morning of the 13th, and in the meantime had to care for the wounded and bury the dead."[6]

Rosser related that "It was a spirited infantry-style attack and a stubborn infantry resistance. Sheridan displayed no skill in maneuvering; it was simply a square stand up fight, man to man, and Hampton whipped him — defeated his purpose and turned him back."[7]

Sheridan's casualties for the day were over 250 men in addition to his 700 or more casualties from the previous day. When Hampton's men climbed out of their works, they found the field in front of them covered with dead and wounded Yankees. Hampton wrote to his family that "The cavalry has never had harder fights or achieved greater success than on this expedition & I am very much gratified that they have done so well under me."[8] In a letter to Robert E. Lee, Hampton wrote, "Butler's brigade held their ground against seven desperate charges under as heavy fire — artillery and musketry — as troops are often subjected to, without even giving way a foot."[9]

At dawn, Hampton sent Fitz Lee, whose two brigades had not fought or suffered very much during the battle, to cut off Sheridan's retreat. True to his character, Fitz Lee was too slow to prevent Sheridan from using pontoons to escape across the river. As the Southern troops passed through Sheridan's campsite, they gathered a harvest of abandoned weapons. They buried the dead and bandaged the wounded before moving north, where they discovered the carcasses of horses shot by Sheridan's men to prevent them from being captured by the Confederates. Sheridan's men had remounted on fresh horses they plundered from the farmers along their path. One of the Union officers remembered that "the weather was hot and the roads were heavy with dust, causing the weaker horses to drop out; in all cases where this occurred the disabled animals were shot by the rear-guard."[10] In one day's time, they slaughtered about 2,000 of their own horses.

The Southerners, who loved horses, were shocked and angry. Afterward, Hampton's courier, U.R. Brooks, wrote, "It really seems that the little general should have been punished for cruelty to animals. Yes, we had several hundred horses unfit for service after the Trevilian fight, but I don't recall that we shot any of them. Such cruelty was never our practice."[10]

After the battle, both sides claimed victory. However, the facts show that Sheridan had been forced to retreat. He had been prevented from joining Gen. David Hunter in the Shenandoah Valley or achieving any of his objectives. Even worse, his losses were far heavier than Hampton's were. He had accomplished nothing of value for Grant.

Trevilian Station was the largest and bloodiest all-cavalry battle of the Civil War. There were over 15,000 horsemen engaged. The campaign had been brutal on the Southern horses. Hundreds of troopers were sent to the dead-line camps. Lt. Robert Aldrich of the 6th South Carolina organized three companies of these dismounted troopers into what the men called the Stud Horse Battalion. For the rest of the month those men laboriously marched on foot to keep up with the mounted troopers in other engagements.

Hampton's losses were: killed, wounded or captured — 612. Fitz Lee's losses were: killed, wounded, or captured — 201. Fitz Lee's losses were very small when compared to Hampton's. If he had carried out his orders, Sheridan's entire force could have been destroyed on the first day. Both Butler and Rosser urged Hampton to court-martial him, but Hampton refused, perhaps out of respect for Robert E. Lee, since Fitz Lee was his nephew.

Sheridan's losses were: killed, wounded or captured —1,387. He had 375 seriously wounded men to transport and nearly 300 Confederate prisoners, which necessitated a slow retreat. Sheridan later said, "I have met Butler and his cavalry, and I hope to God I never meet them again."[11]

The Confederates carried the wounded from both sides to the railroad, if they were fit enough to be moved, and shipped them to a hospital in Gordonsville. Unfortunately, they had to use whatever cars were available, and some of them were construction cars without springs and open to the weather. While the wounded waited at the station for transportation, the women in the area brought them what little food they could find. Most of the citizenry's food had been eaten, plundered, or destroyed by the Federals. Yet, they shared the little they had equally with both the wounded Confederates and Yankees. Wiley C. Howard, whose hand was badly wounded, said, "[W]hile I saw much of war and human suffering there, I also witnessed the devotion and heroism of those angels of mercy and loving kindness, the lovely women — mothers and daughters of that far famed Green Spring neighborhood — to our boys and our holy cause."[12]

Adjutant Frank Jones of Cobb's Legion Cavalry had been mortally wounded as he stormed the enemy's works; he died on June 13. A piece of shell tore away his side, exposing his heart and lungs. Earlier that day, as he ate his lunch, he ironically had remarked, "Eat, drink, and be merry, for to-morrow you may die."¹³ He died the next day with a faint smile on his face. Howard described him as being "among the purest, gentlest, knightliest gentlemen whose wealth and blood were spent and poured out, a willing libation on the altar of Southern liberty."¹⁴ Waring said, "He was a good officer, a gallant soldier, & a very fine fellow."¹⁵

While the cavalry was still at Trevilian Station, Grant abandoned his position at Cold Harbor on June 12 and began to move his army south of the James River, where for ten weary months he would conduct a siege on Petersburg.

Company Notes
June 12, 1864

Staff— Mortally Wounded: Henry Francis Jones
Company C — Wounded: Wiley Chandler Howard
Company D — Killed: H.M. Fowler; Mortally Wounded: C.J. Blundell; Wounded: James W. Hanlon
Company I — Wounded: James H. Goff
Company L — Wounded: John A. W. Fleming

White House

When Hampton left Trevilian Station, his men returned along the route by which they had come, along the south side of the Virginia Central Railroad on the south bank of the North Anna River. On the cool night of Monday, June 13, 1864, they camped six miles from Frederick Hall. Their horses had nothing to eat until the next day and then it was only clover. On June 16, the troopers left at sunrise and crossed the North Anna at DeJarnette's Ford. They marched through Chilesburg and Centreville and camped at Cane's Farm, where their horses grazed in a clover field. Wagons brought the men their rations and corn for the horses.

News reached the men that the Yankees were threatening Lynchburg. The men were appalled by the Yankees' treatment of civilians. When in enemy territory, the Southerners had followed the rules of civilized warfare, sparing the women, children, elderly, and disabled, and paying for necessary supplies. Waring sarcastically wrote in his diary that "Hunter has played the devil with the non-combatants in the Valley. What manly sport, to starve women & children."¹⁶ Later he wrote: "To starve women and children is the height of Yankee ambition."¹⁷ Another entry in his diary said, "North of the Anna is a wilderness. From Swift Run Gap near Green County to the Potomac at Mathias Point, there is nothing to eat for man or beast. How the women & children manage to live is a miracle. Some families, I have heard, have lived for days together on wild onions & berries."¹⁸

On the hot day of June 16, the troopers left camp after sunrise and marched to Pole Cat Creek, near Chesterfield Station. After getting their own rations and corn for the horses and resting for several hours, they moved toward White Chimneys. They found that the Yankees on their way to Trevilian Station had ravaged the countryside and laid waste to every farm. Scarcely a Negro, horse, or cow was seen along the route. The dust was the worst that they had ever seen. The men did enjoy a rare treat on this day. They found "first rate" cherries along the road. That night they camped at Boot Swamp. The next day was clear and hot. The troopers left camp about 7:00 A.M. and marched to the Mattapony River, where they ate and

Chapter 15—The Trevilian Campaign

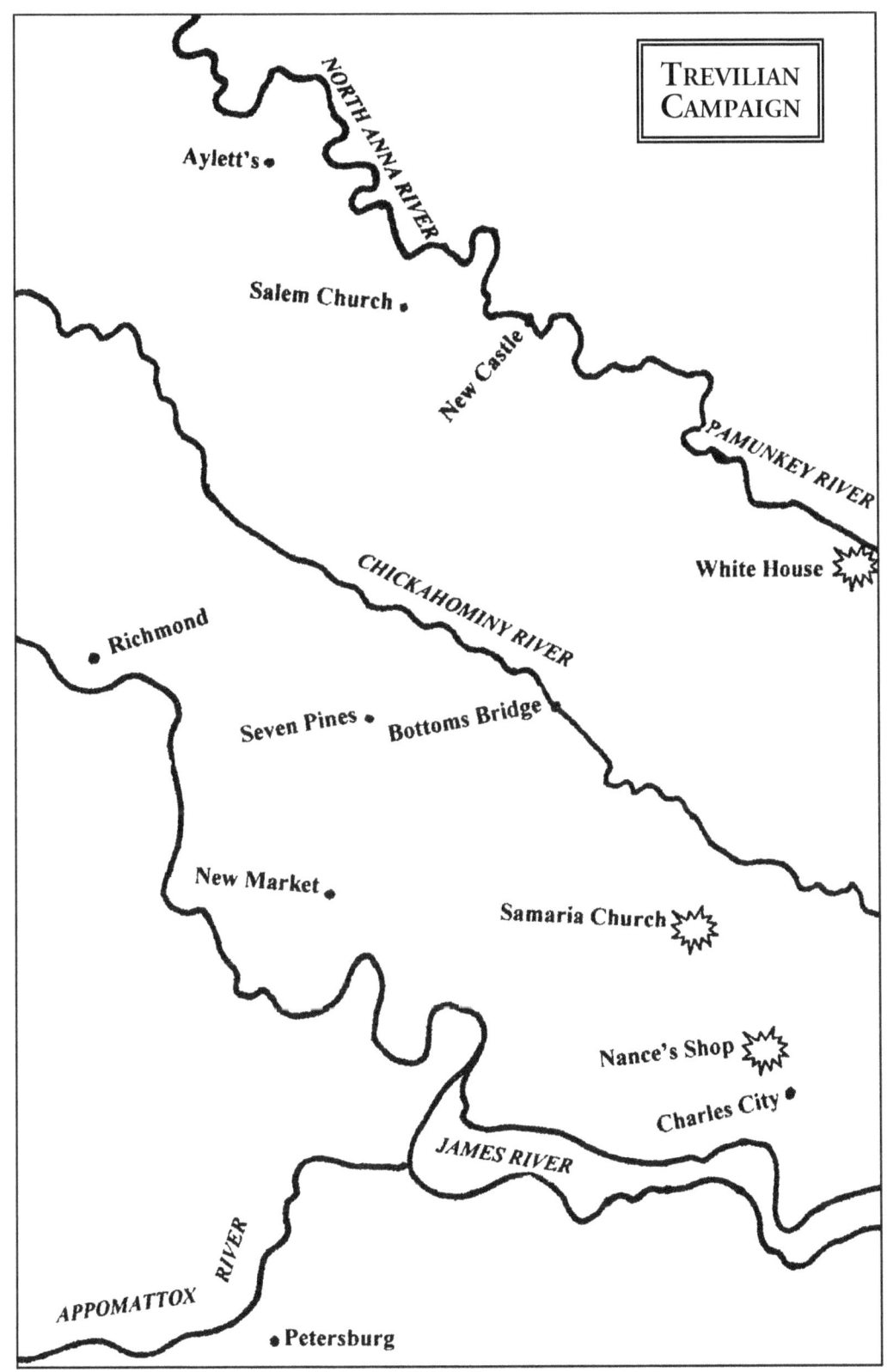

grazed their horses before resuming their march. It was 2:00 A.M. before they went into camp by the Mattapony, but they were not allowed to unsaddle, because Sheridan was on the other side of the Mattapony. The next morning, June 18, they were up at daylight. After marching a mile to some woods, they halted to wait for orders. After waiting until 3:00 P.M., they marched through King William County, choking on the heavy dust, until they arrived at Wickham's Farm.

At sunrise on June 19, the troopers left Wickham's Farm and marched through country that had been ravaged by Grant's men, and then to Ruffin's Farm, where they found plenty of clover on which to graze their horses. After a short rest, they resumed their trek, marching toward White House until 11:30 that night. Although the men were exhausted, they had orders to be ready to move again at 2:00 A.M.

Fitz Lee's division had taken the upper route via Chilesburg, New Market, and Aylett's, following the route Sheridan had taken to Trevilian Station. Because Sheridan used a more roundabout route, and was delayed while forwarding his wounded to Washington at the York River, both Hampton and Fitz Lee arrived at White House on Monday, June 20, 1864, twenty-four hours before Sheridan arrived there.

When Hampton's division neared White House, Butler sent out a squadron of his men, who captured almost the entire party of enemy pickets. Hampton arrived before Fitz Lee and placed his artillery on the high ground to the west of the Union supply base. He began shelling the garrison, wharves, warehouses, and the train of 900 wagons. The troopers were dismounted and put into a line of battle. When orders came for them to move forward and assault the enemy's works, Butler objected. He advised Hampton not to assault them unless the sacrifice of life could be justified by sufficient gain. Fitz Lee arrived and argued against the attack, also. Hampton acquiesced and canceled the assault. The men were halted, and they waited in line until dark.

The next morning, the pickets reported that the enemy had evacuated White House, but, shortly after that, the troopers were fired upon and the order was given for them to mount. Both Wright and Col. William W. Rich were sick, so Col. Joseph F. Waring was in command of Wright's brigade. The enemy was sighted on a hill opposite the run, but they fled when the line of Southerners moved forward. The troopers pursued them for a short distance until Hampton ordered them to halt. Later the enemy tried to flank them, but Cobb's Legion Cavalry and the Jeff Davis Legion easily repelled and captured a number of them. At sundown, the troopers moved to Bottom's Bridge, crossed the Chickahominy, and went into camp at 1:00 A.M. on the Williamsburg Road near Seven Pines. It was a long and tedious march, but the next day the troopers were able to rest and enjoy full rations for the first time since leaving on the Trevilian raid. The men had plenty of coffee and made "Hopping John" by boiling rice, peas, and bacon together.

In his report Hampton wrote:

> The enemy in his retreat crossed the river at Carpenter's Ford and kept down on the north bank of the stream. As he had a pontoon train with him which enabled him to cross the river at any point, I was forced to keep on the south of the river, so as to interpose my command between him and Grant's army, which he was seeking to rejoin. During several days while we marched on parallel lines I constantly offered battle, which he studiously declined, and he followed the northern bank of the Mattapony and the Pamunkey until he gained the shelter of his gun-boats on the latter at the White House, where he crossed during the night.[19]

Company Notes
June 13–22, 1864

Company C — Wounded: Alfred R. Thompson; Died: Elisha S. Howse
Company E — Wounded: William M. Shaw

Samaria Church/Nance's Shop

Sheridan rested his men for forty-eight hours before leaving the area of White House on Thursday, June 23, 1864, and heading for the Chickahominy River and then Charles City Court House and the James River. This time a brigade of infantry accompanied him, and his column was greatly lengthened by the addition of Meade's 800 supply wagons. The train of wagons was strung out for ten miles as it snaked across the countryside, making it a tempting target. Hampton's men left camp before daylight and attacked the enemy's wagons every chance they got, but they were repulsed each time. Hampton had been reinforced with Chambliss' brigade from Rooney Lee's division and an unattached brigade under Gen. Martin W. Gary. Chambliss clashed briefly with the enemy near Nance's Shop on June 23, reinforced by Lomax's brigade.

The troopers went into camp at Salem Church near the river road at 11:00 P.M., but they were ordered out again after an hour. Hampton wanted to make a night attack but changed his mind, so the men spent the night holding their horses in readiness to move. At daylight, the troopers were allowed to go into camp and sleep for a couple of hours.

Hampton planned to attack the Yankees at 8:00 in the morning on Friday, June 24, with six full brigades of cavalry. After Torbert's men crossed the Chickahominy, Hampton attacked Sheridan's rear guard of Gregg's men, who were raiding along the James River. The enemy was driven back to Samaria (St. Mary's) Church, about seven miles northwest of Charles City Court House and three and one-half miles south of Long Bridge over the Chickahominy River. The area around Samaria Church is mostly flat, with gentle undulations in the terrain. The weather was uncomfortably hot and dry. Sheridan ordered Gregg to hold, at all hazards, his position near Samaria Church, until the wagon train could reach a place of safety. Gregg fortified his position and made preparations to carry out his orders. His men and horses had been rested, well fed, and amply supplied with rations at White House, and he had been reinforced with new recruits. In spite of this, one of Gregg's troopers humorously wrote: "Since starting on the Trevilian Raid, June 7, we had been living chiefly on horse hair, dust, and hotness, and while we didn't complain of it as food to fight upon, we did not consider it as composed of material which would produce corpulency, and most of the men had buttoned the front lapel of their pantaloons around onto their back suspender buttons, as a necessary precaution against falling through them when they dismounted."[20]

On the other hand, Hampton's men, with the exception of the new reinforcements, had been marching and fighting continuously for the past sixteen days. Their food was scarce. Wells wrote that "Often the hungry fellows, as they watched their animals browsing on grass, or, in its absence, on any green thing, could not avoid envy, wishing they, too, could graze."[21] At the beginning of the campaign, Hampton's men were outnumbered two to one. At this point, his number of effective troops had been greatly reduced by casualties and exhaustion.

The Confederates formed on a low ridge with a north-south axis, anchored on the north by Nance's Shop and on the south by Salem Church, one and a half miles to the southwest of Samaria Church. Wright (with Cobb's Legion Cavalry), Butler, Dulany, and Wickham held the southern end of the line. At 4:00 P.M. in the steamy, hot afternoon, Gary's brigade dismounted and took a position near Nance's Shop on the enemy's flank. Chambliss' brigade went forward and connected with Gary's line. A heavy growth of pine trees separated the shop from Gregg's line, so the Southerners were able to move into position, unobserved by the Yankees. The two brigades gave the Rebel yell, rushed forward and attacked the exposed right flank of the enemy. Then the whole front line under the command of Fitz Lee rushed on the enemy's fortifications, with Wickham's brigade connecting with Gary's.

Gregg's men had formed behind hastily constructed works in a line that faced west, parallel to Hampton's. They strongly resisted the Southerners with their breechloaders and artillery. The battle raged at such close quarters that the men could make out each other's facial features. After Gary's men became engaged with the enemy, Col. Richard H. Dulany's Laurel Brigade attacked the extreme left flank. The Southerners shattered Gregg's initial position and his men were routed and forced to retreat. At this point Hampton brought up the Phillips and Jeff Davis legions, who charged with sabers. As he watched the Southerners approaching, Giles Taylor of the 1st Massachusetts was reported to have remarked:

> I wish I had enlisted in the infantry ... because the doughboys don't have to stay up all night doctoring sick horses, and then fight on foot, and have their horses led off so far that if they get whipped they can't use them to run away with. Here's the whole Southern Confederacy coming down on our one little division, and the general has had our horses taken so far to the rear that we never can reach them if we are obliged to get out of this. This is going to be a worse place than the Wilderness.... I'd rather be killed in an open field, on horseback, than sabred to death behind a fence.[22]

The Confederates charged three times before the Yankees were routed from the field by the ferocity of the Southern attack. Hampton's men seemed to forget their fatigue and hunger as they pursued the enemy for three miles, until 10:00 that night. For some reason, the noise of the battle did not reach Sheridan's headquarters, and he was ignorant of the intense fight going on a few miles away. One hundred fifty-seven prisoners were captured, including one colonel and twelve commissioned officers. As the enemy retreated, they left their wounded lying on the ground where they fell. Although Hampton failed to cut Gregg off from Sheridan, he hurt him badly. Gregg had 400 casualties, while Hampton had about 330 casualties.

Wiley C. Howard noted that they had a "hard brush" at Nance's Shop.[23] This was the last battle of the Trevilian Campaign. Hampton had captured 852 prisoners, not counting the wounded that fell into his hands. Sheridan captured about 300, including the nurses he carried off. The Trevilian Campaign is of special interest because only cavalry were involved, with no infantry in supporting distance.

Lee wrote to Hampton: "I am rejoiced at your success. I thank you and the officers and men of your command for the gallantry and determination with which they have assaulted Sheridan's forces and caused his expedition to end in defeat."[24]

Company Notes
June 23–24, 1864

Company B — Killed: Robert A. Lampkin
Company C — Wounded: William E. Anderson
Company I — Captured: John McCale
Company L — Mortally wounded: James A. Parker

Chapter 16

The Siege of Petersburg

Wilson's Raid: Sappony Church

Gregg escaped to join Torbert, while Hampton moved in the opposite direction on a new assignment. His men camped near Ladd's Store on the night of June 24, 1864, and then moved toward Richmond the next day. The troopers found the march to be very oppressive because of the dust and heat. When they crossed Malvern Hill, they avoided the road so they would not raise a cloud of dust. They did not want the Yankees on the gunboats in the James River to see the dust and shell them. They camped at New Market that night. After dark, no campfires were allowed because the gunboats would have seen the light from the fires and bombarded them.

There were three railroads that went south from Petersburg. The Weldon Railroad ran nearly due south, but its seizure would not be fatal to the Confederacy if the other two lines were preserved. The Southside Railroad from Petersburg and the Danville Railroad from Richmond had a junction at Burkeville and were protected by the right flank of the Confederate army. Grant by this time realized the futility of attacking Lee's fortified positions, so he turned his attention to the Weldon Railroad. He began to swing to his left to strike the railroad on June 21, but in two days of fighting he lost an appalling number of men killed and wounded plus 2,200 men captured.

James H. Wilson and August V. Kautz started on an expedition on June 21, with 6,714 effective mounted troopers. Their objective was to permanently disable both the Southside and Danville railroads near their junction at Burkeville. Their orders came from Meade and were based on the supposition that Sheridan would detain Hampton long enough for them to accomplish their mission. Wilson had expressed the opinion that he could accomplish his objective only if he were not followed by Hampton, and he operated under the assumption that these arrangements had been made. He was also under the supposition that the railroad at Ream's Station would be occupied by Federal forces.

Wilson and Kautz passed around the right flank of the Confederate line near Ream's Station on June 22. Rooney Lee's men pursued them and harassed their movements but were unable to stop them. The Yankees penetrated to the Southside Railroad and did a considerable amount of damage to the tracks and destroyed supplies all the way to the Burkeville junction. Next, they attempted to destroy the Staunton River bridge. If they had succeeded, this would have had serious consequences for Lee, as the Staunton River was wide and unfordable. They were foiled in their efforts by local militiamen, so Wilson turned back with his men and tried to reach his lines.

After being in the saddle for about two weeks, and fighting nearly every day, Hampton's troopers were exhausted and their horses were worn out. In spite of this, they crossed to the

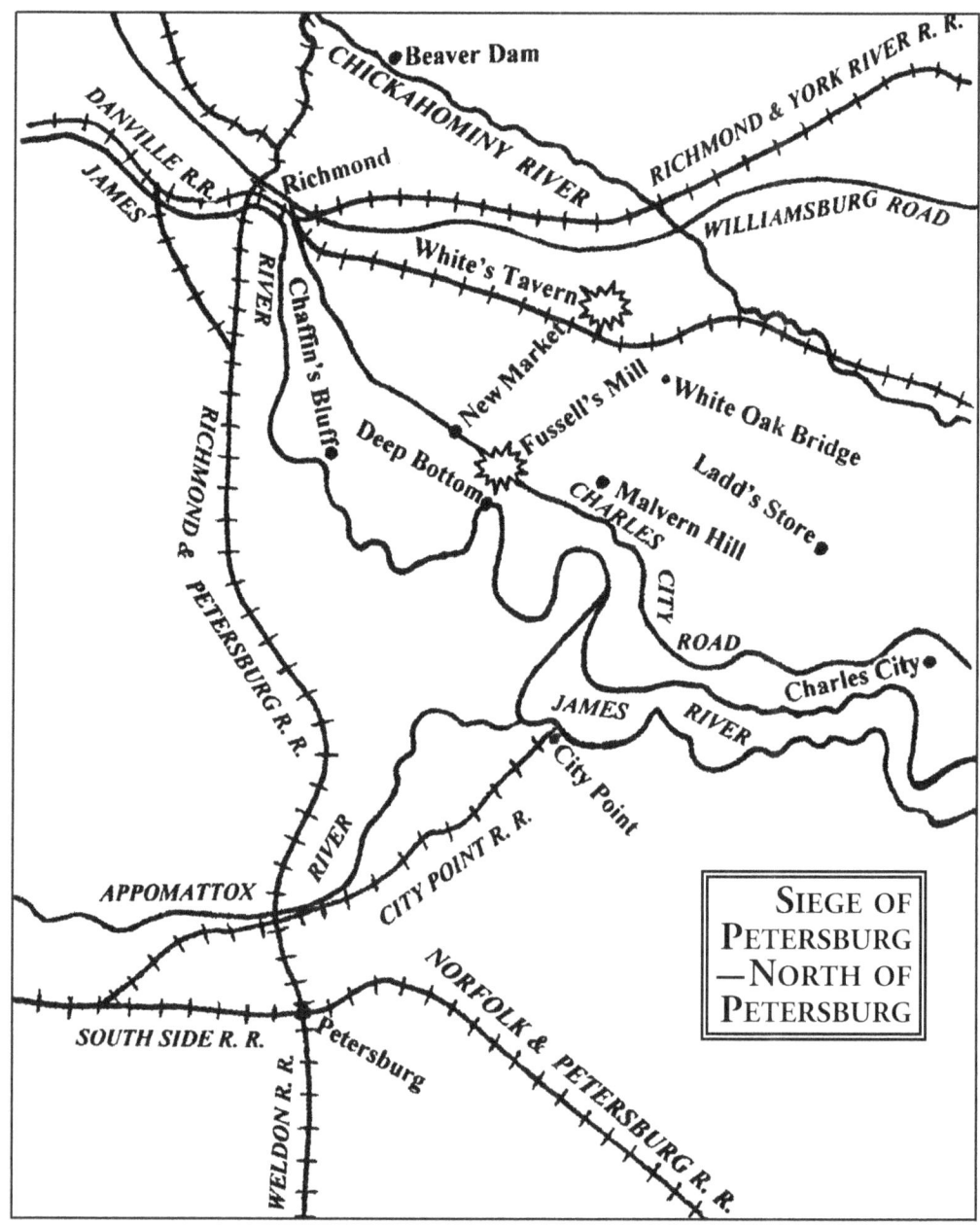

south side of the James River on a pontoon bridge near Chaffin's Bluff, five miles south of Richmond, on Sunday, June 26. The next day, they headed toward the Stony Creek Station on the Petersburg & Weldon Railroad, which was located south and west of Petersburg, about ten miles south of Ream's Station. Their objective was to intercept Wilson's cavalry. Fitz Lee was left behind on the north side of the James River.

The next day, June 28, Hampton's Iron Scouts encountered Wilson's column of 3,300 men at Sappony Church, just west of the depot. Hampton at once planned a surprise attack. He sent word to Lee to send infantry and Fitz Lee to Ream's Station, with instructions to keep in contact with him. Hampton took his men to Sappony Creek, a few miles westward.

He sent forward Chambliss' brigade of Rooney Lee's division. They had orders to charge vigorously as soon as Wilson's column was met. The Yankees were driven back to Sappony Church, where they dismounted and took up a strong position. Chambliss' men also dismounted. They were attacked but held their ground and were reinforced by 200 infantrymen. Wilson tried to break through, but he was not successful. The battle spilled over into the fields and woods on all sides of Sappony Church and lasted for the rest of the day and into the night. While Hampton attacked Wilson from the east with Cobb's Legion Cavalry and the rest of his men, Rooney Lee attacked him from the west.

Wiley C. Howard reported that "We ... fought all night at Sapponia [sic] Church."[1] Although the fighting was heavy, the battle was inconclusive. Thinking that Federal infantry had possession of Ream's Station, Wilson made preparations during the night to move in that direction.

Company Notes
June 24–28, 1864

Company A — Wounded: Thomas B. Archer
Company G — Wounded: John N. Ash

Ream's Station, Stony Creek Station, and Rowanty Creek

The last of Sheridan's force crossed the James River on the morning of June 29, 1864. Before dawn on that day, Hampton's Iron Scouts discovered that Wilson had sent Kautz's cavalry up the Weldon Railroad to Ream's Station, seven miles south of Petersburg. Hampton sent Butler's and Rosser's brigades around the enemy's left flank to pursue Kautz and engage him in battle before Wilson could move from Sappony Church to support him. Butler found a Virginian who lived near Stony Creek who was able to lead him and one hundred hand-picked men through an almost impenetrable swamp to Wilson's rear. He dismounted his men, and attacked.

Hampton's troopers opened fire on the enemy at dawn. By then, Hampton had been reinforced by William Mahone's foot soldiers, and the Southerners virtually encircled both Kautz and Wilson. After being hammered for hours, the Union line broke and the Yankees fled for their lives in various directions and in great disorder. They left their dead and wounded behind. One group of the fleeing soldiers broke through the line in front of a hill on which Hampton had his field headquarters. Hampton recalled that "I was writing an order to [Fitz] Lee, when a company of fugitives nearly ran over me & my staff."[2] Hampton threw the letter aside, mounted his horse, and led the aides, couriers, and orderlies, who were near him, down the hill to attack the enemy. More than 200 of the demoralized Yankees surrendered to him.

A large number of the fleeing Yankees headed in the direction of Ream's Station. Hampton knew that Fitz Lee's division was waiting there with infantry support and expected him to capture them. The enemy, on the other hand, expected to find their own men there. To their surprise, they found hostile infantry and cavalry. At first, Wilson and Kautz did not know the size of the force that they were facing, and they tried to cut their way through. When they realized what they were up against, in their haste to escape, Wilson and Kautz

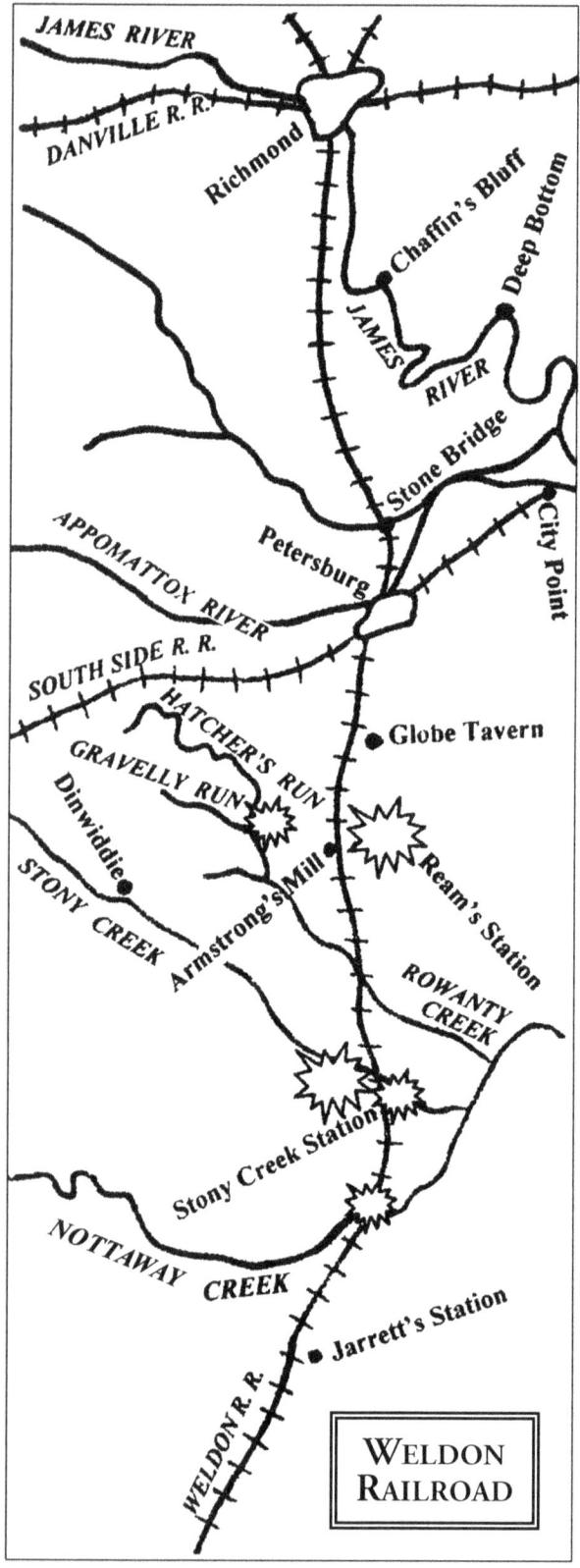

abandoned all of their artillery, most of their forage wagons and ambulances, hundreds of runaway slaves, and a huge amount of plunder, including the communion service from St. John's Church in Lunenburg County. Without preserving any organization, they retreated at a gallop through the woods and byroads. Wilson's exhausted troopers rode all night to get back to their army.

Cobb's Legion Cavalry, with the rest of Hampton's troopers, pursued the enemy for a couple of miles, taking many prisoners. Then Hampton ordered them to fall back toward Stony Creek Station to prevent the Yankees from getting away by crossing between the two stations. Two Federal detachments that had become separated from the main body appeared. The mounted Confederates charged them and most of them were captured. Another detachment was run down and captured near the Rowanty Creek Bridge. Although most of the Yankees made it back to Petersburg, dozens of them were captured during their flight. When night came, Hampton's troopers rested near the Stony Creek Station. This position was chosen because it was between Ream's Station to the north and Jarratt Station to the south. If the enemy attempted to cross at either of those points, the Southerners were in striking distance.

During the evening, Sheridan moved towards Ream's Station to assist Wilson, but he arrived too late. Hampton waited anxiously all night to hear from Fitz Lee concerning what Fitz Lee had done, what direction the enemy had taken, and if Fitz Lee had captured all of them. He never heard from Fitz Lee. When dawn came, Hampton's men were rested and ready to resume the fight, but they did not know where Fitz Lee was. Finally, at 9:00 A.M. on June 30, a note arrived saying that Fitz Lee was "still pursuing the enemy, capturing prisoners, etc.," and he was five miles away from the Nottoway River on the Hicksford Road. He thought that "the enemy, after crossing the river, will try to cross the railroad at Jarratt depot," and he wanted "all the available force sent to that point to intercept their march, until he got up."[3] Hampton immediately moved his men in the direction of Jarratt Station. When they were within five miles of their destination, the Iron Scouts reported to Hampton that the enemy had passed there at daylight. The troopers were taken on a rapid march to catch up with the enemy, but it was too late. Hampton had hoped that Fitz Lee would trap Kautz at Ream's Station, but, true to his character, Fitz Lee failed to do so.

In the two days of fighting, 1,306 prisoners were captured. A large number of the enemy were killed and wounded, then abandoned on the field. The Union troops probably lost one-fourth of their men. Federal reports stated that they had taken 5,000 horses from the local farmers. Fortunately, all of the horses were recovered along with household furniture, vehicles, and personal articles, after Wilson and Kautz fled for their lives. The pillaging had been so bad that the Federal headquarters conducted an investigation. The explanation they received was that Kautz's division had previously served under Benjamin F. Butler, who did not discourage pillaging.

Hampton's losses were considered to be insignificant: killed, wounded or captured — 22. Losses in the other Southern divisions were also small.

Wilson's division was so reduced in numbers and so badly demoralized by their means of escape that it took a long time for his division to recover. Kautz's division never recovered. The railroads were rapidly repaired, so, even according to Federal authorities, the results were not compensated for by the losses. On the other hand, the morale among Hampton's men had never been higher. They appreciated Hampton's gallantry and skill in leading them and his concern for their well-being. He shared their privations and fatigue, as well as their victories, and inspired his men by being in the front during a battle, leading by example. He seemed to know every private by name and face, and it was said that he knew every horse. He would often notice if a man were riding a different horse other than his own, and he would ask him the reason. The men felt the utmost loyalty and devotion to Hampton.

Company Notes
June 29–30, 1864

Company A — Killed: John Smith
Company C — Wounded: Henry E. Jackson
Company E — Missing: James A. Cox

Rest and Reward

Hampton's men had been fighting nearly every day for the last six weeks, and they were exhausted. They had marched 400 miles and had repeatedly won against the superior numbers of the Yankees. They had taken more than 2,000 prisoners, while losing 719 men, killed, wounded and missing. Among the wounded were Young and Rosser. The trooper's horses suffered also. For example, in Butler's well-mounted brigade, some 1,600 men went to the dead-line camps. "Losses in Fitz Lee's division were so small as not to swell the aggregate number materially."[4] Hampton praised his men liberally and received praise himself for their accomplishments.

Both Butler and Rosser thought that Fitz Lee had deliberately sabotaged Hampton's plans at both Trevilian Station and Ream's Station in hopes of making Hampton look bad so Fitz Lee would be promoted as Stuart's successor instead of Hampton. They urged Hampton to have him court-martialed, but Hampton refused to do so. Instead, after that, Hampton simply used Fitz Lee as little as possible in his campaigns.

Gen. Lee ordered Hampton's troopers to go into camp south of Petersburg and get some rest. During this period, their duties were few but included scouting, picketing, and skirmishing. Wells recorded that during this period there were "two somewhat sharp brushes, but the Federal cavalry did not venture much beyond their infantry." He also reported that the cavalry disliked picketing more than fighting, because in picketing, "Not only are there hardships and loneliness on post, but annoyances and dangers without excitement, or credit to be gained."[5]

Robert E. Lee wrote to Davis on July 2: "You know the high opinion I entertain of Gen Hampton and my appreciation of his character and services. In his late expedition he has displayed both energy and good conduct.... I request authority to place him in command."[6] On July 11, there was a reorganization of the cavalry. The eleventh company of Cobb's Legion Cavalry, Company K, was detached and transferred to Phillip's Georgia Legion.

At 4:49 A.M. on July 30, the Yankees exploded a mine at Petersburg and began an assault. The cannonading lasted until 10:00 A.M. Five hundred troopers from Young's brigade were ordered to saddle up and move out. It was 10:00 P.M. before they returned. Early the next day, news arrived that the enemy was advancing on Ream's Station. Hampton was ill with dysentery, so he turned the command over to Butler, who marched the troopers to Ream's Station and kept them there until 4:00 P.M.

Sheridan was relieved of his command of the cavalry in the Army of the Potomac and ordered to the Shenandoah Valley on August 2, 1864. In April, he had taken command of a body of cavalry that was, in numbers and equipment, absurdly out of proportion to Hampton's force. His strategy in battle had proved to be so poor that anything he accomplished was by the weight of his greatly superior numbers. His losses during that period had been about equal to Hampton's entire force. When Sheridan was sent to the Shenandoah Valley, Torbert accompanied him, and on August 17 Wilson was also sent there.

By August 2, the Southern troopers were finding their camp quite intolerable from the odor of dead horses and an invasion of flies. The next day they left at sunrise and moved to a better location. It had not rained for a couple of weeks, and the dust, even in the new camp, was becoming unbearable. On hot August days, the men found bathing in the warm water of the Nottoway River a pleasant way to cool off.

Wade Hampton's appointment as chief of cavalry of the Army of Northern Virginia was officially confirmed on August 11. Hampton's division was turned over to Butler, and Fitz Lee's division was sent to the Shenandoah Valley. Hampton did not exult over his new position. He wrote home that "We gain successes but after every fight there come to me an ominous paper, marked 'Casualties,' 'killed' and 'wounded.' Sad words which carry anguish to so many hearts. And we have scarcely time to bury the dead as we press on in the same deadly strife. I pray for peace. I would not give peace for all the military glory won by Bonaparte."[7]

The Army of Northern Virginia was trapped at Petersburg by Grant's superior forces. If they moved, they would not be able to protect Richmond or the lower South. It became the job of the cavalry to scout and delay repeated thrusts at the army from all directions.

Company Notes
July–August 10, 1864

Company B — Wounded: Henry North
Company C — Wounded: William E. Anderson

White's Tavern

On Thursday, August 11, 1864, Lee ordered Hampton to go to Culpeper Court House and make a demonstration while reinforcements were being sent to Early and Fitz Lee in the Valley. Hampton took Cobb's Legion Cavalry along with the rest of Butler's division with him, and left at 8:00 A.M., crossing the Nottoway and marching toward Petersburg. The temperature was a stifling 95 degrees. The next day, it was 99 degrees as the troopers passed through Petersburg and camped for the night near Stone Bridge. The extreme heat continued the next day as they marched through Richmond. That night, they camped near the South Anna River. The next day, the thermometer climbed to 100 degrees. After leaving at sunrise, the men marched to Beaverdam Station, where they received orders to return to Richmond.

Grant had the ability to quickly and easily transfer his troops, both cavalry and infantry, from one bank of the James River to the other with his pontoon bridges and steamers. Because of that, the Federals had gained a foothold at Deep Bottom on the north bank of the James. Their objective was to see if the Confederate works near Chaffin's Bluff were weak enough for them to attack Richmond. Butler's division reached that area on August 16.

Hampton led Butler's division toward the sound of heavy fire, across the White Oak Bridge, up the Williamsburg Road, then across open fields until they reached the road from Charles City. By 10:00 in the morning, they had reached White's Tavern on the Charles City Road, eight miles below Richmond. There they found Rooney Lee's division fighting Gregg's cavalry. Rooney Lee was being hard pressed by a much larger force, chiefly infantry. His men had been driven back somewhat, and Gen. John Randolph Chambliss had been wounded while gallantly rallying his men. He died in enemy hands. He had been an excellent officer and his death was a great loss to the cavalry.

It was at this point that Butler's division came on the scene. Butler's men dismounted and moved to the right and rear of Gregg's men. Hampton led them in an attack on Gregg's rear, while Rooney Lee's division and Gary's brigade attacked his front. Once Hampton joined the assault, the enemy hastily withdrew, and some prisoners, mostly infantry, were taken.

The next day, the Confederates attacked again. Once more Rooney Lee was in front, while Butler's men attacked and turned the enemy's right flank. The enemy was driven back, and their breastworks were taken. The Southerners captured 167 prisoners. Waring noted in his diary that "The Yankees were thoroughly whipped yesterday & lost heavily. The negroes [*sic*] suffered particularly. They were put in front in every assault."[8] During the night, the enemy retreated, and Hampton took his men to the south side of the James.

Lee wrote to Hampton that "I desire to express the gratification I have derived from the conduct of the cavalry during its late operations north of the James River.... Please express to the officers and men my thanks for their gallant and valuable services."[9]

Company Notes
August 11–17, 1864

Company A — Wounded: Lucas T. Penick
Company C — Wounded: William C. Orr
Company F — Killed: William L. Stone
Company H — Died: George W. McElhanon
Company I — Mortally Wounded: William H. Byrd
Company K — Wounded: Marshall N. Seay
Company L — Died: Byrd Park; Wounded: Oscar L. Carter

Fussell's Mill

The men were not able to get much rest after the battle at White's Tavern. The next day, Thursday, August 18, 1864, Robert E. Lee ordered an attack on the Federal 2nd Corps at Fussell's Mill, which was about three miles north of Deep Bottom. The troopers moved out at 6:00 A.M. Hampton's cavalry and Gen. Charles William Field's infantry attacked the enemy's breastworks, which were manned by foot soldiers. Butler's and Rooney Lee's troopers attacked the right flank, while Field's men struck the enemy's front. The Southerners drove the Yankees from their defenses and then pursued them for two miles, capturing 167 of them. As a result of this action, the Federals abandoned their line. That night the Yankees retreated, and Hampton returned to his former position on the south side of the James. The enemy had learned that the defensive lines below Richmond had not been depleted, so two nights later they crossed the James. Hampton bragged about his men in a letter to Mary Fisher Hampton saying, "They charge Infty. and take breast-works, and they are as steady in a fight as our best troops."[10]

Monck's Neck Bridge

Before Hampton could return from the north side of the James, the enemy obtained a foothold on the Weldon Railroad, holding the tracks from near Petersburg down to Ream's Station. On Thursday, August 18, 1864, Gouverneur K. Warren's 5th Corps began wrecking tracks south of Globe Tavern. Confederate forces from Petersburg that included James Dearing's cavalry and A.P. Hill's infantry drove them back to Globe Tavern.

When the Federal cavalry crossed to the south side of the James on August 20, 1864, most of them headed for the Weldon Railroad, where they resumed their work of demolishing tracks. Over the next four days, they tore up tracks to a point three miles south of Ream's Station. At daybreak on August 22, Butler's division marched to Armstrong's Mill, opposite Ream's Station. When they got there, they found nothing for the horses to eat, as the forage train did not arrive. The next day, they encountered the enemy at Monck's Neck Bridge on Rowanty Creek, about two miles west of Ream's Station. There they attacked a division of enemy infantry and, after a stiff fight, drove them back into their breastworks at Ream's Station. In the fighting, the enemy lost 136 men, killed, wounded, or missing.

After that, the Yankees established a picket line at Ream's Station. The next day, the

Southerners marched to a camp on the Vaughn Road, four miles from Dinwiddie Court House, arriving at dusk. Their horses needed rest and food. The Confederate action had been so skillfully and gallantly carried out that Hampton became convinced that Ream's Station could be captured.

Company Notes
August 18–23, 1864

Company A — Wounded: John C. Allen, Milton B. Young
Company B — Died: Josiah N. Clayton
Company L — Wounded: Alpheus M. Rodgers

Ream's Station

On the morning of Wednesday, August 24, 1864, Lee sent Hampton's cavalry to stop the Yankees. Hampton's men consisted of Butler's and Rooney Lee's divisions, along with A.P. Hill, who had Henry Heth's division of infantry with him. Rooney Lee's division was temporarily under Gen. Rufus Barringer. Gen. John Dunovant was leading Butler's old brigade, and, although he had not completely recovered from his wound received at Trevilian Station, Rosser was at the head of his Laurel Brigade. The cavalry moved out at 5:00 A.M. and quietly led Hill's infantry through the countryside to the Monck's Neck Bridge, where they halted for the night.

Hill attacked at noon, driving in Gregg's and Kautz's videttes, and then struck Hancock's defenses astride the railroad. The enemy savagely repulsed their attack. The New Yorkers formed a battle line in an open field, where they fought with the Confederates for an hour. Hampton's troopers were on Hill's right, and they pretended to retire. Hampton took Dunovant's and Barringer's divisions and slipped around Hancock's left. At 3:00 P.M., Cobb's Legion Cavalry and the rest of the troopers formed in the woods near Ream's Station, less than 300 feet from the enemy. Then the Southerners moved up both sides of the railroad tracks. Barringer's division moved up the Halifax Road toward Malone's Crossing. Chambliss' brigade, under command of Colonel J. Lucius Davis, moved up Malone's Road and across Malone's Bridge to the same point. Davis' brigade was supported by Cobb's Legion Cavalry and the rest of Young's and Rosser's brigades. Young's brigade was commanded by Butler, in Young's absence.

They met Gregg's advance pickets a short distance beyond the bridge west of the tracks. After a mounted charge, the enemy's pickets were driven in. Davis immediately engaged their main body with a dismounted portion of his brigade. After a sharp fight, the enemy gave way, falling back toward Malone's Crossing. The Confederates rapidly and vigorously pursued Gregg, forcing him to retreat toward Ream's Station, leaving his dead and wounded on the ground. Gregg's men were driven into their works near Ream's Station. Once they were behind their breastworks, the enemy brought in their infantry to replace their cavalry and attempted to turn both of Hampton's flanks. In this they were thwarted, as the Southern troopers held their ground. Hampton's men instinctively followed the directions that Butler once gave to a colonel who complained he was being flanked and wanted reinforcements. Butler had replied, "Well! Flank them back, then!"[11]

Throughout the afternoon wave after wave of Hampton's troopers attacked the Union infantry. At about 4:00 P.M., Hampton's men charged Hancock's defenses and scrambled over his inadequate breastworks, which were made of cane stalks. Hancock's flank crumbled, and his men were driven back into other fortifications nearer Ream's Station. Hampton notified Hill of the progress he had made and suggested that Hill attack. Hill requested that Hampton fall back as if he were retiring, so the enemy would follow him down the railroad, and then Hill would attack his rear. Hampton drew back about 400 yards, but the Yankees were very cautious about following him. Perhaps they had fallen for that trick once too often.

At 5:00 P.M., Hill's artillery opened fire, announcing his advance, and Hampton at once ordered a charge by his whole line, which had formed across the railroad to the west. At about 7:00 P.M., Hampton saw that General Hill was forcing the enemy back from the west side of the railroad into their works around the station, so he withdrew all of his forces from that side of the road. He formed his troopers into a line, with Butler's brigade on the right, the North Carolina brigade in the center, and Davis' brigade on the left. Rosser formed a second line to support the first. Most of the men were dismounted as they went forward.

The ground over which Cobb's Legion Cavalry advanced was very difficult to traverse, as the enemy had cut down the timber, leaving the felled trees and other impediments. In spite of this, Hampton's line advanced steadily under heavy artillery fire and musketry, driving the enemy from several outer works that they had fortified, through an open field of corn or sorghum cane, and into their works at Ream's Station.

For a time some of the troopers in Cobb's Legion Cavalry were subjected to destructive cannonading from their own artillery positioned near the railroad station, as the artillery had not been advised of their successful advance. They were forced to lie prone between the corn or sorghum rows, while shells burst around them, until they could fall back to the cover of the woods. Gib Wright, who did not comprehend what had happened, came to their part of the line and "indulged in uncomplimentary and uncalled for strictures."[12] Lt. Thomas J. Dunnahoo of Company H resented his comments and was insulted by the remarks. He offered to take Wright on in a personal combat. The next day, Gib Wright made a public apology, admitting his mistake and improper conduct. In spite of the altercation, the men respected Wright. Wiley C. Howard said of him, "Daring and fearless old Gib Wright, with scars of the Mexican war and our own upon him, he was a rusher in any sort of a fight, and despite his faults, commanded the confidence and admiration of the men under him; for he hesitated not to lead into the jaws of death with all the furious ferocity of a maddened tiger."[13]

The enemy put up a stubborn fight until around 10:30 P.M., when the Southern cavalry gave the Rebel yell and rushed over the breastworks. The Yankees ran from their breastworks and those who were not captured joined their main column on the Danville Railroad. The fighting had lasted for twelve hours. Afterwards, General Hill directed Hampton to put his command in the trenches to cover the withdrawal of the infantry. This was done, and seven regiments of cavalry remained at the Ream's Station until 6:30 the next morning. At sunup, they discovered that the enemy had completely withdrawn, and Butler's men were left to remove the wounded and to collect arms. They buried one hundred and forty-three of the enemy.

In the battle, Butler's division lost:

Killed	6
Wounded	25
Missing or captured	2

Hampton lost:
- Killed — 16
- Wounded — 78
- Missing or captured — 2

The enemy lost:
- Killed — 143
- Wounded and captured — 66
- Captured — 2,150

The cavalry had captured 781 men. Also captured by the Southerners were 7 flags, 9 guns, and 3,150 small arms. Lee sent Hampton a note, saying, "I am very much gratified with the success of yesterday's operations. The conduct of the cavalry is worthy of all praise."[14] Lee wrote to Governor Zebulon B. Vance of North Carolina that the men "advanced through a thick abatis of felled trees under a heavy fire of musketry and artillery and carried the enemy's works with a steady courage, which elicited the warm commendations of their corps and division commanders and the admiration of the army.... The operations of the cavalry were not less distinguished for boldness and efficiency than those of the infantry."[14]

Hampton wrote in his report that "Here he [the enemy] made a stubborn stand, and for a few moments checked our advance, but the spirit of the men was so fine that they charged the breastworks with the utmost gallantry, carried them, and captured the force holding them. This ended the fighting of the day, my men having been engaged for twelve hours."[15]

Hill wrote that "The saber and the bayonet have shaken hands on the enemy's captured breastworks."[16] Hancock, who commanded the Federal troops at Ream's Station, was reported to have told friends that he would rather have died than have witnessed his corps in such a rout.

Wiley C. Howard said, "Our participation in the Ream's Station fight contributed largely to the turning of the tide and causing the enemy to give up their position and abandon their purpose to turn Lee's left and destroy the railroad."[17] The Confederates had to use wagons to transport supplies from the Stony Creek Station, due to the fact that the enemy with their overwhelming numbers had a permanent lodgment on the Weldon Railroad, but the victory at Ream's Station bought extra time for Lee.

Company Notes
August 24–26, 1864

Company A — Killed: George B. White
Company C — Wounded: Thomas C. Williams
Company D — Captured: W.H. Lippitt; Died: Napoleon B. Algers
Company F — Wounded: Emanuel Aiman, John H. Sharpe
Company G — Killed: Andrew J. Smith
Company H — Wounded: Benjamin J. Davis; Captured: Cornelius C. Turner
Company I — Wounded: Henry C. Reese

Rest and Recuperation

Hampton received an order from Lee on Saturday, August 27, 1864, stating, "I wish you now to rest the two divisions as much as practicable, and to take such position as would enable you most speedily to intercept and punish any party which they might send out against our communication. It would be well to let Dearing's brigade do all the picketing if practicable, so as to give the rest of the cavalry a good period of repose for refreshing their horses."[18]

In fulfilling the order, Hampton moved his men into the country about ten miles south of Petersburg, where there was plenty of good water. For two weeks, the men and their horses were able to rest and recuperate. The men were tired and dirty but lacked soap with which to bathe. The government was unable to supply them with this basic necessity, so Butler canvassed his brigade until he found twenty-five farm boys who knew how to make soap. They stripped oak and hickory bark to burn for lye, which they mixed with bacon drippings and fat cut from mules and horses that had been killed in battle. It was not long before they were making 150 pounds of soap a day—enough for the cavalry and the nearby infantry.

The monthly return of August 31 showed the number of men in Hampton's corps as 5,344, but many of them were either without horses or without serviceable horses. In addition, a number of men from Cobb's Legion Cavalry were suffering from diarrhea and dysentery, probably as a result of eating raw pork from their haversacks and drinking polluted water during the Trevilian Campaign.

Company Notes
August 27–September 4, 1864

Company E — Captured: John A. Voss

The Great Cattle Raid: Sycamore Church and Coggin's Point

Lee's whole army had been short of food since Sheridan's Yellow Tavern raid had forced them to burn vast ration dumps. On Monday, September 5, 1864, George B. Shadburne of the Iron Scouts reported to Hampton that, while the supply wagons at City Point were well guarded by the Federals, they had 3,000 head of beef that were less well guarded at Coggin's Point on the James River, eight miles east of City Point. City Point was the headquarters and base of the Army of the Potomac. Hampton asked the scout to learn when Grant would visit either Washington or Sheridan in the valley. The Iron Scouts captured a courier with papers revealing that Grant would leave on the 14th to visit Sheridan.

With Lee's approval, Hampton assembled his raiders south of Petersburg in the predawn darkness of Wednesday, September 14, as Grant was leaving City Point to visit Sheridan. Hampton's force numbered 2,700 men and included 100 men picked from Cobb's Legion Cavalry. The other troopers were from the rest of Young's and Butler's brigades, Rooney Lee's division, and Rosser's and Dearing's brigades, but only the Iron Scouts and Hampton knew the purpose of their mission. At that time, Lee had enough meat to last just fifteen days.

The distance to the cattle pens at Coggin's Point was about thirty-five miles, but Hampton did not take a direct route. He headed south on a swift march, down the Boydton Plank Road south of Petersburg, swung around and along Rowanty Creek to Wilkinson's Bridge, and camped there for the night. The men were well behind Federal lines. At dawn on September 15, he swiftly moved his men north until they reached Cook's Bridge, which he knew had been dismantled. He knew that the Yankees would not be looking for an attack from this direction. The bridge crossed the sluggish but deep Blackwater River. This detour took the men around the left flank of the enemy. They were nearly due south of Coggin's Point and the picket guards.

The column halted, and forty engineers with tools strapped to their saddles were ordered forward to repair the bridge. While they worked, pickets were strung out to stop anyone from coming into the vicinity and the other men dug sweet potatoes from the adjoining fields. Since they were forbidden to light fires, or to do anything that would alert the Federals to their presence, they ate the sweet potatoes raw. During this period, the horses were rested and fed. It was nightfall when Hampton's chief engineer pronounced that the bridge was safe for use, but Hampton delayed his men from crossing until midnight. They were about ten miles from Coggin's Point. The artillery gun wheels were muffled with grain sacks, and the few unruly men who broke into song were immediately hushed mid-syllable. The raiders moved slowly and as silently as they could, until Hampton ordered them to halt about 3:30 A.M. on September 16. The road was dark from the canopy of tall trees, and whippoorwills could be heard singing above them. The men were weary, so some of them slipped out of their saddles and napped on the ground with their horses' reins in the crooks of their elbows.

The largest detachment of the enemy was at Sycamore Church and the cattle were two miles beyond. Smaller bodies of Federals were to the right and left. When they moved again, Rooney Lee was sent to the left on Lawyer Road to hold the road between the herds and Federal headquarters and drive away any opposition from that direction. Dearing's brigade was sent to the right on Hine's Road toward Cook's Mill. When he heard the firing, his men were to dash into and demolish a post about three miles from Fort Powhatan on the James River and hold the road leading from the fort. Hampton, with Cobb's Legion Cavalry and the rest of Young's brigade, Butler's brigade under Gen. John Dunovant, and Rosser's troopers, advanced in the center, guided by the Iron Scouts toward Sycamore Church and the cattle. Everyone was in position before sunup.

Rosser led the men in an attack at 5:00 A.M. and drove off the videttes of the 1st District of Columbia Cavalry, who were at Sycamore Church. The Southerners pursued the videttes into their camp, yelling for the main body to surrender. "Come and get us if you want us,"[19] the Yankees yelled back, as they rallied behind barricades. The Confederates rode over them, scattering in every direction those that they did not kill, wound, or capture, and confiscated their sixteen shot Henry rifles. Hampton was given one of the prized rifles, and he carved his name into the stock and carried it throughout the rest of the war. The enemy's casualties were 219 of their 250 men. Next, Hampton proceeded to the James River, without any opposition en route.

The civilian drovers detected their approach and tried to stampede the cattle. This tactic failed because the raiders approached the herd from several directions, boxing it in. They overpowered the cattle guards, about 120 men, and began to drive out the 2,486 big, well-fed animals. The Federal herders willingly helped the Confederates. The Southerners also captured a number of horses, eleven wagons, and three flags. Three camps were burned and valuable stores, including blankets, were carried away. Many of the prisoners had been taken from their pup tents half-dressed. They were mounted on the captured horses and led away.

When Rooney Lee and Dearing heard the firing, they struck the units in front of them, riding down and dispersing the enemy and holding the roads. By 8:00 A.M., they converged with Hampton, who was retiring with the herd, and the whole column started back at a trot with the artillery covering them. Such a large herd of cattle would have been difficult to keep together, so they were broken up into smaller groups with intervals between them.

In conjunction with Hampton's cattle raid, Lee's infantry demonstrated strongly against the enemy at Petersburg, driving in their pickets west of the Jerusalem Plank Road and moving bodies of troops about, as though they were going to attack. At the same time, Butler, with the rest of his other brigades, made it unpleasant for the Federals in their vicinity. The Federals were in confusion and did not realize what had happened until their cattle were spirited away.

The Great Cattle Raid: Belches Mill

Hampton retired toward the Blackwater River, where the separated units of his men were united, then quietly crossed the river. He then divided his men again to confuse their pursuers. Rosser was sent two miles north of Hampton's route to hold the Jerusalem Plank Road at a point thirteen miles south of Petersburg and east of the Weldon Railroad. Union Gen. Henry E. Davies, with the cavalry of Gregg and Kautz, caught up with Rosser at Ebenezer Church on the Jerusalem Plank Road. They drove Rosser's troopers about three miles south to Belches Mill. Rosser made a stand there, but he was so hard pressed that he had to be reinforced, first with Dearing's brigade, then with Rooney Lee's entire division. The men fought until after dark, while Hampton made off with the cattle. By the next morning Davies realized that he had been delayed too long to overtake and recapture the herd, so he broke off his pursuit of Hampton's men.

Gregg and Kautz brought a sizable force to Freeman's Ford, where the cattle were being driven across a dam over the Nottoway River. The cattle were turned over to Hampton's staff, while his main column fought off the pursuers. While driving the enemy back with gunfire, Hampton's troopers taunted them by bellowing like bulls. By 9:00 the next morning, all of the cattle had crossed the dam, and Dunovant's men escorted the raiders back to camp.

Hampton's losses were: killed—10, wounded—47, missing—4. During the three-day raid, the men had marched more than a hundred miles in the enemy's rear and captured 304 prisoners. A South Carolina trooper wrote his family that, after the raid, "Anytime the yankees [sic] Genls [sic] would order a charge & bring their men up toward our lines one of our boys would bellow tremendously very much to the annoyances of the yankees [sic] no doubt. Much as to say to them we have gotten your beeves."[21]

This raid was more profitable than Stuart's raid on Chambersburg. The men brought in almost 2,000,000 pounds of beef, which, at a pound per man, would feed 10,000 men for 200 days. In addition to the steaks, the raiders supplemented their diet with sardines, other canned foods, and pickles that they had picked up in the burned enemy camps. These were luxury foods for men who had eaten nothing but scant rations of bacon and flour for months. The information provided by the Iron Scouts and their aid during the raid was vital to the success of the expedition. One scout was killed and three were wounded during the fighting.

Lee wrote to Hampton:

> I have received your report of the result of your operations, and beg to express my high appreciation of the skill and boldness you have displayed, and my gratification at your handsome and valuable success. You will please convey to the officers and men of your command my thanks for the courage and energy with which they have executed your orders, by which they have added another to the list of important services rendered by the cavalry during the present campaign.[20]

Richard E. Roberts, of Company A, wrote to his family that the group of raiders included dismounted troopers who had lost their horses. They were given a furlough to go home and get new horses as a reward for their action in the raid. On September 20, 1864, the largest number of men on horse detail, ever, from Cobb's Legion Cavalry were sent with Capt. Bostick of Company D to Georgia to buy horses. Unfortunately for many of the men, this was their last record, because the service records for 1865 were burned to prevent them from falling into the hands of the enemy. The exception is for those who were at Greensboro for the surrender. Some of these men were captured before they could return to their regiment, but it is unknown what happened to the other men. On September 27, Rosser's Laurel Brigade was sent to the Shenandoah Valley.

**Company Notes
September 8–26, 1864**

Company C — Died: William H. Pass, Thomas Rollins
Company E — Captured: James M. Head
Company F — Died: SeaBorn H. Peterson
Company H — Killed: William Nabers (while serving in the infantry)
Company K — Died: John L. McCune

Vaughn Road

Grant simultaneously renewed his maneuvers on both the north and south of the James River. His objective on the south was to push toward the Southside Railroad. North of the James, he hoped for a surprise attack on Richmond, or at least to create a diversion. Ben Butler, reputed to be the most incompetent of the many incompetent Union generals, was in command on the North side.

Dismounted members of Hampton's command were sent to occupy Lee's main line of entrenchments. On Sunday, September 27, 1864, Butler's division was attacked on the Vaughn Road west of the Weldon Railroad. Elements of the Union 5th Corps infantry charged the breastworks held by Dearing's brigade, which was attached to Butler's division, and commanded by Joel R. Griffin. The defenders abandoned their positions and began to run.

Pierce Young, who was at the firing line, was not used to seeing his men run. For years, he had led the intrepid men of Cobb's Legion Cavalry, who were legendary for holding their ground and fighting, and they had never once turned and run. Rushing after the fugitives, he roared so loud that his voice carried for a mile, "Hold your ground down there, you damned scoundrels!"[21] Butler managed to halt some of the fleeing men at the point of his pistol, but Griffin's men lost their works. The enemy drove Griffin's men back to Hatcher's Run.

On September 28, a partial second line was formed to block the enemy advance. Cobb's Legion Cavalry and the rest of Butler's division were positioned along Vaughn Road, and Rooney Lee's men were along Squirrel Level Road. The men fought dismounted in trenches until evening, and the battle seemed to favor the Southerners. The Yankees were driven back, and some prisoners taken, but at dawn the next day, the enemy began to make more vigorous assaults.

Hampton hurried to the scene, and on September 30 he assisted in driving back the enemy to Wyatt's farm and recovering the lost ground, but he was unable to recapture the works from which Griffin's men had run. Heth's division of infantry attacked in front, while Hampton's troopers struck the left flank. While the enemy was preoccupied bringing up reinforcements, Rooney Lee quietly led the dismounted troopers forward in line of battle, until they were at close range. The men began firing as they continued to advance. The enemy was completely routed and about 900 prisoners were taken along with 10 flags. During the two days of fighting, nearly 1,000 prisoners, including a very large number of commissioned officers, were captured. The Federals had been unsuccessful in moving toward the Southside Railroad, but they still held ground that they had attained.

Company Notes
September 27–30, 1864

Company C — Died: John H. Abercrombie
Company E — Captured: Isaac G. Allbritten
Company F — Wounded: Thomas J. Nasworthy

Arthur's Swamp

The Yankees again struck Butler's position on the morning of Saturday, October 1, 1864. Young rode out with an aide down the road in front of where Cobb's Legion Cavalry was fighting, in order to observe the enemy through his field glasses. When he looked back, he saw that a group of Yankee officers had positioned themselves between him and his men. He spurred his horse and rode at full speed toward the officers, hoping to pass by them. When he neared them, they pointed their pistols at him and demanded that he surrender, but he did not slow down. They began firing at him as he continued to gallop toward them. As he passed one officer, the man again demanded his surrender. Young's answer was, "Surrender, hell!"[22] and he cut the man across his face with his riding whip, the only weapon he had. He was soon safely back within his own lines.

Hampton responded by attacking the Federal rear with two of Rooney Lee's regiments while Butler attacked from the front. The strategy worked, and the Federals fell back. Hampton withdrew at dusk, after having driven the enemy some distance and capturing 30 or 40 prisoners. Waring described the fight as "an 'all day' affair & a stubborn fight."[23] Unfortunately, Gen. Dunovant was shot while leading Butler's old brigade in the fight at McDowell's farm below Petersburg. As he fell, his foot became caught in the stirrup and he was dragged until the saddle turned, releasing his foot. By then he was dead. Butler described him as a gallant and distinguished officer. Col. Hugh H. Aiken succeeded Dunovant.

Company Notes
October 1–12, 1864

Staff — Captured: Capt. Jones, Young's A.D.C.
Company C — Died: M. Rufus McCurry

Hatcher's Run (Boydton Plank Road, Burgess Mill)

The troopers had a couple of weeks of quiet. The biggest complaint they had was the lack of hardwood for their campfires. Throughout the countryside, traces of old campsites could be seen where Rosser's men had bivouacked in the past and had harvested the oak trees for their campfires. The only wood available now was pine, which burned too quickly. Without action, the men became bored. To amuse themselves, they held horse races and footraces and played cards. They were eating beef a couple of times a day from the cattle they had captured from the Yankees. Waring wrote in his diary: "Yankee beef for breakfast and dinner. Really we have eaten so much beef, that I am getting tired of it."[24]

On the raw windy day of Thursday, October 13, 1864, Cobb's Legion Cavalry had an engagement on Darbytown Road. Then, on the dark and rainy morning of Thursday, October 27, Grant made his last serious attempt in 1864 to get around and turn Lee's lower flank at Petersburg. The Yankees had learned that they could not take the Petersburg fortifications by assault, and Ben Butler had not made any progress toward Richmond on the north side of the James River. Grant's plans were to extend the Federal lines to the left (west), seize the Southside Railroad, sever Lee's communications, force an evacuation of Petersburg, and move Lee away from Richmond. Grant correctly believed that Lee's extreme right on Hatcher's Run was not strongly fortified. What he did not realize was that, even without fortifications, the Confederate line was powerful, and the Jeff Davis Legion had already moved its headquarters to Hatcher's Run. To implement his plans, Grant had been urging Secretary of War Edward McMasters Stanton during September to send him at least 40,000 new recruits. These had gradually been received. The attackers included part of the 2nd, 5th, and 9th corps with 5,471 cavalry under Gregg. The time of the attack was planned to occur before the November 5 presidential and congressional elections in the North. In addition, the attack needed to take place before bad weather set in and produced the bad roads that were typical of a November in Virginia. Each of the enemy was given four days' rations.

As the maneuver began, Ben Butler was ordered to make a strong diversion on the north side of the river to draw troops away from Lee. At 3:30 A.M., Hancock headed across the Boydton Plank Road to seize the Southside Railroad. Although the troops on his right were unable to keep up with him, Hancock, with Gregg's cavalry division leading the advance, fought his way down Vaughn Road. They arrived at the south side of Hatcher's Run, the extreme Confederate right, by noon. The other two Union corps, on the right of Hancock, were not heavily engaged in the battle and did not accomplish anything of consequence.

The Confederate cavalry immediately mounted their horses without "attending to the niceties of the toilette, or to breakfast, which was postponed by unanimous consent until about eight o'clock that evening."[25] Dismounted Southern troopers swore as they were forced to vacate the camp in unseemly haste, while their mounted comrades poked fun at them.

Gregg's cavalry made numerous attempts to cross to the Petersburg side of Hatcher's Run, but they met strong resistance from the defenders. Butler reinforced his pickets, but they became heavily engaged with Hancock's infantry and were driven from Armstrong's Mill to the Monck's Neck Bridge, a distance of about two miles.

Hancock's men reached the Boydton Plank Road below Burgess Mill, and then moved to White Oak Road, which was even closer to the railroad, but they needed to cross the boggy little stream called Gravelly Run that joined Hatcher's Run near the Monck's Neck Bridge. However, Hart held the opposite bank with one battery of guns. When Hampton was informed by the Iron Scouts of the Yankees' movement, he ordered Hart to "Hold the bridge at all hazards until I can support you."[26] The artillerymen and dismounted cavalry prevented the Yankees from fording Gravelly Run as Hampton rushed Cobb's Legion Cavalry and the rest of Butler's troopers west across muddy fields. Hill's foot soldiers under Henry Heth and William Mahone followed them.

Sixty men from the wagon trains were sent into the conflict with muskets to support Hart, who was soon wounded and carried off the field. His leg was so badly smashed that it had to be amputated. At that crucial moment, Cobb's Legion Cavalry, with the rest of Young's brigade, arrived on the scene and held the bridge.

Hampton realized that if the gap between Butler's left and Hatcher's Run were not filled, the enemy would proceed up the run toward Burgess Mill where the Boydton Plank Road crossed the stream. He sent staff member A. Reid Venable to order Dearing's brigade from the works on the north side of the run to fill this gap. Hill, who was in command, answered Hampton's order with a message saying that he did not think Dearing's men could be spared from their position. However, Venable was captured on his way back to Hampton, so Hampton was left with the impression that Dearing's brigade would fill the gap.

Hancock took advantage of the gap and proceeded up the stream. Hampton was notified that the enemy was advancing from the Vaughn Road, down the Quaker Road, toward its junction with the Boydton Plank Road. Hampton took a position at the Quaker meeting house and ordered Rooney Lee to move up Military Road and strike the enemy in the rear. It was at this point that Hampton discovered that the gap had not been filled and the enemy was getting in his rear. To counteract the enemy's move, Butler's men did an about-face and galloped over to White Oak Road to stop the advance in that direction. At White Oak Road, Butler formed his men in a line across the road, with his left at Burgess Mill. His troopers dismounted and threw up fieldworks. They had just completed their task when Hancock's vanguard appeared and put forth a limited attack. Rooney Lee was ordered to attack at the Boydton Plank Road, which his men did with great spirit.

After inconclusive skirmishing until 4:00 P.M., with the Southern cavalry alone holding back both Federal cavalry and infantry, Hill planned a full-scale attack. Heth's infantry division crossed the run and went forward in concert with Hampton's troopers. Cobb's Legion Cavalry and the rest of Butler's men had fought so often on foot that they could easily function as infantry. When they heard musketry, they knew that the infantry was engaged. Butler led his division in a dismounted saber charge across an open field.

Hampton rode almost to the front of the charge with his son, Wade IV, who was on leave from Johnston's Army of Tennessee. Hampton's other son, Preston, impetuously joined the charge near the head of Butler's column instead of staying with the staff officers. When Hampton saw this, he sent Wade IV to stop him and followed with his staff officers, but they were too late. Seeing Butler's younger brother, Nat, Preston waved his hat and called, "Hurray, Nat!"[27] His gesture must have attracted the attention of an expert shooter from the enemy, because in the next instant he fell from his saddle, shot through the groin.

Col. Zimmerman Davis of the 5th South Carolina recalled, "I saw a staff officer, who appeared to be riding to meet me, fall from his horse. I galloped up to see who he was and to render assistance, when General Hampton and his staff rode up. We all dismounted and General Hampton stooped over the prostrate form, gently raised his head and kissed him, saying, 'My son, my son.'"[28]

Preston's eyes rolled into his head and he lost consciousness. Just then, a minié ball thudded into the back of Wade IV and he fell almost on top of his brother. A wintry rain had begun to fall and the raindrops mingled with the tears running down Wade Hampton's face. By the time a surgeon and a wagon arrived to remove the brothers from the field, Preston had died, and three other staff members had been shot.

Hampton mounted his horse and rode off to direct Hart's battery, since Hart had been severely wounded and removed from the field. Col. Zimmerman Davis was amazed by the accuracy of the battery's fire, which he attributed to Hampton's supervision. He said it was "an ennobling and inspiring sight to see this grand hero, with the kiss from the lips of his dead son still warm upon his own, while the other son was being born from the field severely wounded, thus subordinating parental affection to duty to his country."[29]

Meanwhile, Cobb's Legion Cavalry and the rest of Butler's division cleared White Oak Road of the enemy and drove them towards Boydton Plank Road, where Rooney Lee's dismounted men attacked them. Butler's right united with Rooney Lee's left, and the enemy was enveloped on three sides. Hancock's men were driven from their positions on the roads into the fields east of the Boydton Plank Road, where they were isolated from the support of the other corps and defeated. That evening, Hampton turned over the command to Rooney Lee so he could spend the night by the side of his dead child.

Under the cover of the gathering darkness and chilling, pelting rain, the enemy withdrew to avoid being entirely cut off on the next day. They retreated to their previous lines, leaving their dead and dying behind. On the other side of the James, Ben Butler had accomplished nothing of consequence. Meanwhile, the Confederate cavalry line maintained its position, ready to fight the next day. Mounted videttes were thrown out, while the rest of the men dismounted in the downpour and ate their meager breakfast, which had been postponed from that morning. The next morning when the sun rose, they discovered that the Yankees were gone. The cavalry attempted to follow the enemy, but the only ones they overtook were stragglers. During the fighting, the cavalry captured 239 prisoners. Altogether, 1,365 prisoners were delivered to Richmond. The Yankees left behind them several caissons and many small arms and accoutrements. This ended the most severe threat to Petersburg and Richmond up until that time.

Company Notes
October 13–29, 1864

Company A — Captured: Fred Hogrefe, Henry A. Watkins
Company B — Wounded: John Howard Burr, James T. Lamkin
Company C — Died: John M. Anderson, Edward W. Cowen
Company G — Wounded: George Winship
Company H — Wounded: Jasper Evans
Company I — Wounded: John McAuliffe
Company Unknown — Captured: James M. White (may have been in the infantry)

Union Reconnaissance to Stony Creek

The inspection report of October 30, 1864, showed that the total strength of the cavalry had fallen to fewer than 5,000 men. On the south side of the James River, Gregg's cavalry was inactive. Gregg reported they were too weak in numbers to attempt any movements, but his November returns showed that he had 6,189 men, more than Hampton's entire force.

In preparation for the winter, the men began building winter quarters. Young was concerned about the horses as well as the men and managed to acquire clapboard so stables could be built. In late November, freezing rains and floods began to plague the troopers while they cut down trees and built entrenchments near Gravelly Run. On November 24, Young received orders to go to Augusta, Georgia, in command of the dismounted men of his brigade. He left the next morning.

In the freezing weather of Thursday, December 1, 1864, Gregg reconnoitered the Stony Creek district south of Ream's Station on the Weldon Railroad. He surprised a small number of dismounted men from the dead-line (those without horses) who were guarding a few supplies and were on the construction squad. The 6,189 men with Gregg captured all 170 of the men. The Federals returned to Ream's Station where a congratulatory order was issued to the troops for this very minor, easy achievement, especially considering that the Southerners were outnumbered 6,189 to 170.

When Butler heard about the raid, he routed his men out of their blankets and into the saddle in order to overtake Gregg. It was the first really cold night of the winter, and the men's diaries reveal they were not very cheerful about having to leave their warm covers. The seasoned troopers were accustomed to joking about almost everything in their daily lives, and the men were soon laughing about a strange sight among them. One of the troopers had lost one of his eyes and had replaced it with a glass eye. At night, he would remove his glass eye and place it in a glass of water. When he was awakened that morning, he discovered that his glass eye was entombed in ice, and he did not have time to defrost it over a fire. He put the glass with the frozen eye in his pocket and put an old sock over his face to hide the empty eye socket. He rode off, swearing at his glass eye, while his comrades shared a hearty laugh at his unusual appearance.

Butler's troopers pursued Gregg, but they were too late, as Gregg had escaped.

Company Notes
October 30–December 6, 1864

Staff—Wounded: James T. Norris
Company A—Captured: H. H. Walkin
Company C—Wounded: Thomas C. Williams; Captured: George M. D. Moon, N. C. Parker, Harvey Calhoun Parks
Company G—Wounded: William M. Williams; Captured: Joseph N. Hill
Company I—Wounded: Walter H. Chavous

Warren's Raid to Hicksford, Virginia

Encouraged by Gregg's "successful raid" on the small supply base, and thinking that the Weldon Railroad was guarded by only a small force, Grant decided to attempt to destroy the Weldon Railroad as far south as Hicksford. Although the Federals held Ream's Station, supplies were still getting to Lee from the South on trains to Stony Creek Station, and then by wagon to Petersburg. Hicksford was located on the Meherrin River about twenty miles south of Stony Creek Station, and taking Hicksford would cut off the Stony Creek Station.

When Warren started out on the raid with his 5th Corps and five batteries of guns, unknown to him someone rode along with him who had not enlisted in the Union army. It was George Shadburne, Hampton's legendary Iron Scout, dressed in a captured Federal blue uniform. He rode among the troops as they marched along, without pausing long enough to arouse suspicion. Sneaking back to Hampton, he reported 34,000 Yankees heading toward the Weldon Railroad south of Petersburg. (There were 22,000 infantry, 4,000 cavalry, and five batteries under Warren, plus 8,000 additional troops.) At that time, Hampton had about 5,000 mounted men, including Dearing's brigade, which was temporarily attached to him. Hill, who joined him in stopping Warren, had 15,000 infantry. However, Lee's right flank could not spare all of the men, so in reality only about 16,000 Confederates went to face Warren's 34,000 men.

Along with Warren's raid, there were to be four other attacks at the same time. Five armies, each almost the size of Lee's whole force, would be making the five assaults. Nelson A. Miles was sent to Hatcher's Run on the Confederate right to determine which troops had been detached to pursue Warren, and see if he could create a diversion. With him were a large column of Federals. When he confronted the Confederate works along the run, he did a little skirmishing and nothing more. Ben Butler, on the north side of the James River, was to assume a threatening attitude, while Wilmington, North Carolina, was to be attacked with pyrotechnics, and Petersburg was to be attacked, and, if possible, captured.

The Confederate pickets around Stony Creek, who originally had been sent out with four days' rations, were spread thin. They could not be relieved because their comrades saddled up and rode off to pursue Warren. One of the pickets complained that instead of getting rations, he "got" to take up many holes in his sword belt.

Hampton's small force rode out on the extremely cold and sleety night of Wednesday, December 7, 1864, to harass Warren as best they could. The cavalry could not remember a colder or more terrible night. Five of Hampton's ill-clad and weary pickets froze to death, while the others rode all night. Butler's division was involved in some serious skirmishing along the way. They reached the Nottoway River around 1:00 A.M. and it took the rest of the night to get everything across the river. At daybreak the men began their march toward Hicksford. They encountered the enemy on the road that ran from Sussex Court House to the railroad bridge, and had a slight skirmish with them before Hampton drew his troopers off. They continued their march to the Double Bridge, where they camped from 7:00 P.M. until 3:00 A.M., and then resumed their march toward Hicksford. The next day, December 8, the forces with Warren captured 851 of their own men who were trying to desert. The desertion rate had become so bad in the Union army that a general order had been issued promising a twenty-day furlough to any man who shot a comrade in the act of deserting.

The Confederates' cavalry arrived at Hicksford at daylight on the very cold morning of December 9 and made preparations to defend the place and protect the bridge over the Meherrin River. The cavalry skirmished with Warren all day, interfering as much as possible with their destruction of the tracks, but before the Southerners could concentrate against the Yankees, Warren's men tore up twenty miles of track. Hill's corps was sent from the Petersburg trenches to assist in stopping Warren. His barefooted men suffered great hardship during the march, leaving bloody footprints in the sleet covered roads. Hill and his men arrived on the scene sometime during the day.

The next day, December 10, there was a sleet storm, but when Warren's forces appeared at 3:00 P.M., the Confederates attacked. "Well, boys," Butler growled, as he hunched his shoulders in the icy storm, "if we survive this weather and this night, we need not fear the Yankees."[30]

Warren's troops were repulsed after Hart's and Maj. William McGregor's guns fired on them. The firing continued until dark, at which time Hampton and Hill made plans to strike Warren from two directions in the morning again. The men slept on the ground in an icy rain. At 2:30 A.M. it was raining hard as the troopers saddled their horses. They were prevented from carrying out their leaders' plan of battle because Warren was cold and tired himself, so he drew his men off and retreated. Hampton followed him until he crossed the Nottaway, inflicting as much punishment as possible. About 300 prisoners and many arms were captured by Hampton's troopers. The damage inflicted by the Yankees on the Weldon Railroad was small when compared to their preparations and the size of their force.

The war took an ugly turn when stragglers from Warren's corps began looting and burning homes in the area and assaulting the men, women and children who inhabited them. The North Carolinians were enraged by the inhumanity of stragglers who would assault civilians and then burn their homes, leaving them without shelter in the freezing cold. They took the stagglers they captured and threw them alive into the fires they had set.

Butler's men were given the task of repairing the railroad tracks. With the help of three hundred blacks impressed from nearby estates, the trains were soon running again. Except for Dearing's brigade, the cavalry was moved into camp near Belfield. It had been a long, dreary, cold march, but at Belfield forage for the horses was available. The men repaired the tracks and then got some rest. The condition of their horses improved, and their numbers increased as previously wounded men returned to active duty.

The Federals made no serious movements for the rest of the month. Waring noted in his diary that "The Yankees made sad havoc on this trip. On every side chimneys were alone standing, where once were stately mansions. The track of the enemy can be easily known."[31]

Hampton and his troopers were given marching orders on December 21, and on the next day they started for Gordonsville along with Rooney Lee's Division. On December 31, 1864, the monthly return shows that the number of Hampton's men had increased to 7,063. Besides these, there were about 1,000 men absent on horse-furloughs.

Company Notes
December 7, 1864–January 19, 1865

Staff— Wounded: James T. Norris
Company B — Died: John Howard Burr
Company C — Died: Samuel S. Parks
Company E — Died: J. Harvey Fraser
Company F — Wounded: Augustus Drake
Company G — Wounded: J.T.M. Wharton; Captured: James J. Turner
Company H — Died: John A. Moore
Company I — Wounded: Walter H. Chavous, Michael Hanlon; Died: William H. Bird
Company K — Wounded: S.J. Bunch
Company L — Captured: John J. Moran

Chapter 17

The Campaign of the Carolinas

Augusta, Georgia

In November 1864, dismounted troopers in Young's brigade, with Young in command, were sent to Georgia to remount, recruit, and assist Maj. Gen. Joseph Wheeler's small cavalry division of the Army of Tennessee, which was opposing Sherman's "March to the Sea." Shortly afterwards, an article signed, "Wade Hampton" in the Augusta, Georgia, newspaper instructed the cavalrymen to rendezvous in Augusta. This article caused some confusion for Grant, who did not know if all, or just some, of Wade Hampton's men had departed from Virginia. In fact, Hampton left the divisions of the two Lees in Virginia, while he, with Butler's division, followed Young to the Carolinas on November 19. The mounted troopers of Cobb's Legion, who were still in Virginia at that time, left with him. In sending Hampton to South Carolina, Lee wrote Davis that "I think Hampton will be of service in mounting his men and arousing the spirit and strength of the State and otherwise do good, I therefore send him."[1] Hampton's cavalrymen were expected to return to Virginia in the spring.

When the Southern cavalry arrived in Columbia, South Carolina, the citizens welcomed them as their deliverers. Young's brigade had been recalled from Georgia, and the men paraded through the city to the cheers of the populace. Confederate flags hung from the balconies and windows along the way. The cavalry crossed the bridge over the Congaree River and camped west of town.

Hampton's command consisted of Butler's old brigade of 940 men, now under Hugh Aiken, Young's 586 Georgians, Wheeler's cavalry, and several unattached regiments and companies. Altogether, there were about 7,600 men, but the effective force was probably only about 6,100. Getting fresh horses was a problem for these reduced forces. Hampton met with Gen. Pierre Gustave Toutant Beauregard, Gov. Andrew C. McGrath, and others to urge them to abandon Charleston and concentrate their forces. If the garrison of William Hardee's 15,000 men at Charleston would join Hampton's and Wheeler's men, they would have a force of about 30,000 — enough, perhaps, to stop Sherman and his 60,000 men. Beauregard agreed with him and Charleston was abandoned.

William Tecumseh Sherman had burned Atlanta and cut a path of destruction across Georgia to Savannah. His 60,000 well-supplied, well-fed troops subsisted off the countryside, plundering, burning, and destroying everything they could not use. Leaving Savannah after New Year's Day, he fought his way north across South Carolina against a feeble resistance that could delay him no more than a few hours.

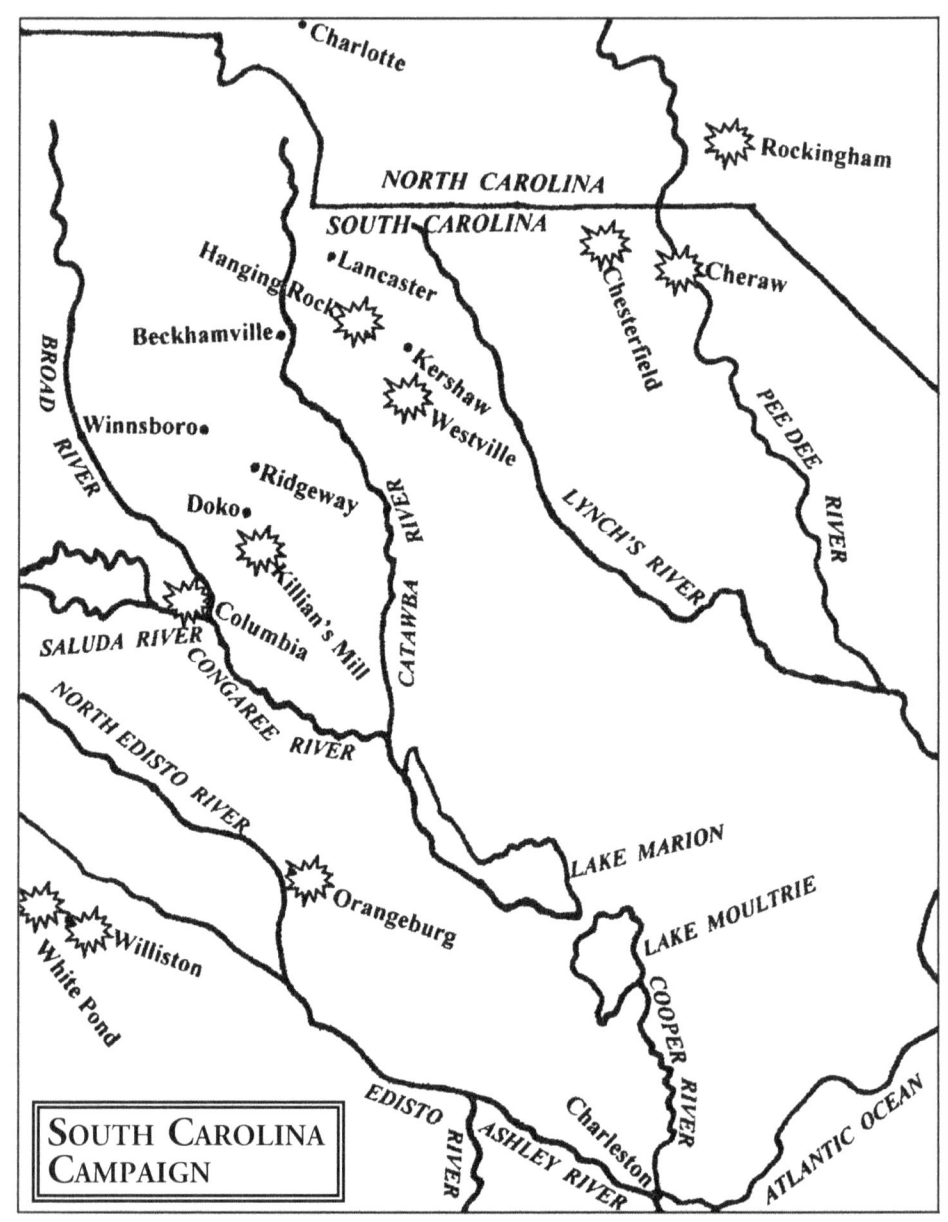

**Company Notes
January 19–February 3, 1865**

Company G — Died: James J. Turner
Company H — Mortally Wounded: E.J. Wilson

Angley's Post Office

On Saturday, February 4, 1865, a division of the enemy under Manning F. Force attacked Cobb's Legion Cavalry while they were posted at the bridge across Whippy Swamp at Angley's

Post Office. The enemy approached from their camp on the opposite bank. The troopers blocked the enemy from crossing the bridge, so the Yankees tried to push a line across the stream. The enemy soon found themselves in murky water up to their necks. After retreating to safety on their side of the stream, they attacked Cobb's Legion Cavalry with sharpshooters, musket fire, and two artillery guns. Confronted by the superior force, the troopers were forced to abandon their camp to the enemy.

Company Notes
February 1–7, 1865

Company C — Wounded: Francis Reeves Howard

Williston and White Post

Cobb's Legion Cavalry had a skirmish at Williston and then White Post, South Carolina, on Wednesday, February 8, 1865, against the 5th Ohio Cavalry, 5th Wisconsin Cavalry, and 10th Battery Light Artillery. The enemy reported that the Union losses were 25 killed, wounded, and missing, and that 8 or 10 Confederates were captured.

On February 10, Gen. Beauregard arrived in Columbia and put Hampton in charge of all troops in the vicinity of the South Carolina capital. They included Gen. Carter L. Stevenson's infantry division. In mid–February, Hardee's troops arrived from Charleston, and what remained of John Bell Hood's Army, about 5,000 demoralized men, were on their way to South Carolina. Later a few thousand troops under Gen. Braxton Bragg and Gen. Robert F. Hoke would join them.

Orangeburg and the North Edisto River

Cobb's Legion Cavalry had skirmishes at Orangeburg on February 11, 12 and 13, 1865, and the North Edisto River on February 13 and 14. John T. Wood of Company A described the action: "I well know that we had to skeedadle [sic] from the enemy at Orangeburg, S.C. [We] were fortified at a bridge on the Edisto River, having a wide swamp and a good position, if [only] we could have had force enough to hold them…. The enemy was too strong & flanked us the second day by wading the water, though we killed several…. While marching out, two men were wounded in front of me (about two feet). We were then marched to a station some fifteen miles distant. From morn until dark, [we took] the cars for Columbia, where we built fortifications."[2] (Punctuation was added for clarity.)

Company Notes
February 11–14, 1865

Company A — Captured: John H. Keogh
Company D — Died: Isaac T. Smith
Company K — Killed: John W. Hammond

Columbia

Columbia did not have any fortifications or natural defenses, other than the barriers provided by rivers, so a successful stand could not be made without first building fortifications. One trooper wrote his father that after arriving in Columbia, "We built fortifications, but done no fighting, yet were under a little fire from the enemy."[3] (Punctuation was added for clarity.)

Refugees were streaming out of the city. On Monday, February 13, 1865, Beauregard went to Charleston, leaving Hampton in command. On February 15, Wade Hampton was promoted to lieutenant general. This made him the highest ranking cavalry commander thus far in the war. Later, Nathan Bedford Forrest would also attain that rank.

When Sherman's troops reached the south bank of the Congaree River on February 16, they began shelling Columbia without any notice to the civilians or a demand of surrender. Hampton had already had the bridges burned that spanned the Congaree, Broad, and Saluda rivers. Butler's division put up a stubborn fight, slowing the Yankees' advance. Cobb's Legion Cavalry lay in line of battle all day on the river bank, but the enemy made no attempt to cross. Meanwhile, Wheeler's cavalry left Columbia without firing a shot or doing anything to defend the city. They did pause long enough to loot as many stores and homes as they could. When Hampton tried to stop them, several of the pillagers aimed pistols and carbines at him and threatened to shoot him if he intervened. Mary Boykin Chesnut recorded the incident in her diary:

> Either [Wheeler's men] did not know Hampton, or they were drunk, and angry at his being put over Wheeler's head. Hampton was sitting on his horse, alone, and beset by about twenty of them. He called out to my husband: "Chesnut, these fellows have drawn their pistols on me!" He is a cool hand, our Wade. General Chesnut galloped up. "Fall in there! Fall in!" By instinct the half-drunken creatures obeyed. Then Chesnut saw a squad of infantry, and brought them up swiftly, and the drunken cavalry rode off.[4]

A trooper wrote his father:

> After remaining [in Columbia] for two or three days, most [of the time] in the works, Gen. Hampton took us late at night & silently crept to the arsenal near the river. The bridge [had] been burnt, and Yankee pickets [were] on the opposite bank. We equipped our command, after which we went up in the city. The stores were opened & we loaded ourselves with sugar & everything, and wasted any quantity of sugar, coffee, etc. The night being well spent we moved out a mile or so.[5] [Punctuation was added for clarity.]

When the Yankees began crossing the river on the Friday, February 17, Cobb's Legion Cavalry saddled up around 1:00 A.M., although they had slept but little. They rode through the city with their sabers drawn and formed a line to charge the enemy. They were under orders to use only sabers if they were attacked. Hearing that the mayor had surrendered the city, Gen. Hampton led his men quietly in a retreat from the south side of Columbia and through the streets of the city at about 9:00 A.M. Hampton retired with Young's brigade, which was commanded by Gib Wright, along the Winnsboro Road, while Butler went with Butler's brigade, which was commanded by Col. B.H. Rutledge, along the Camden Road.

Sherman had promised the mayor of Columbia that if the Confederates withdrew without resistance the city would have immunity from assault and violence. Believing Sherman's promises, Butler's troopers acted as rear guard of Beauregard's retiring army and saw to it that Sherman's incoming troops had no excuse for the violation of their agreement. However, the

Yankees soon dishonored the agreement. Cobb's Legion Cavalry watched the city go up in flames as they stood by a train that had stalled, ready to defend it if necessary. The train was filled with terrified women and children refugees. There were no Confederate soldiers in Columbia when the city was engulfed in walls of flame.

Butler said:

> The burning of Columbia by Sherman was among the last acts of the great tragedy of 1861–65. This act was wholly unnecessary and a clear, flagrant violation of all rules of civilized warfare, but the city had been marked as the capital of the "Cradle of Secession," and fell a victim to venom and hatred of her enemies.... The compact was strictly carried out on our part, let the charred remnants of this beautiful, disarmed, and helpless city speak for the good faith and honorable conduct of the other side.[6]

John T. Wood wrote that when Columbia was burned it was, "the only time I ever saw [Hampton] look sad, for it was his native home, & a beautiful place too."[7]

An ugly footnote to the burning of Columbia is the fact that Sherman tried to shift the blame to Wade Hampton, saying that Hampton, "in anticipation of our capture of Columbia, ordered that all cotton, public and private, should be moved into the streets and fired.... The smouldering [sic] fires, set by Hampton's order, were rekindled by the wind, and communicated to the buildings around."[8] However, Sherman revealed that it was a lie when he continued his narrative by saying, "Having utterly ruined Columbia, the right wing began its march northward."[9]

Henry W. Slocum, commanding Sherman's left wing, admitted that drunken Yankees burned Columbia, saying, "A drunken soldier with a musket in one hand and a match in the other is not a pleasant visitor to have about the house on a dark windy night."[10] The Yankees considered South Carolina to be "the hell-hole of secession," so their pillage and destruction in this state was far more severe than in Georgia. Their march north toward North Carolina was characterized by wholesale thefts of food, livestock, and personal property from the helpless civilians of the Palmetto State.

On February 20, 1865, the size of Cobb's Legion Cavalry was:

Officers   14
Enlisted men   232 (10 dismounted)
Total   246

Company Notes
February 15–17, 1865

Company B — Wounded: Thomas Leach
Company I — Captured: John Dorris

Killian's Mill

Cobb's Legion Cavalry marched eight miles from Columbia to Killian's Mill, where they were joined by Butler's brigade, and then they camped for the night. The men were exhausted from the anxiety and loss of sleep during the two previous days. Sherman's army began to move northeast toward their next objective, Goldsboro, North Carolina, after looting, vandalizing, and burning the stores and homes in Columbia and committing acts of rape and violence against the populace. The Georgian and Carolinian troopers were enraged over the devastation of their homes and their states, and, as a result, their fighting became more savage.

On Saturday, February 18, 1865, the Union 17th Regiment, Blair's corps, marched along the Charlotte & Columbia Railroad and appeared on the other side of Killian's millpond and creek. During a sharp encounter with them, Butler ordered his men to cut the dam and flood the low ground where Blair's men were located. The Confederates deployed along the ridge in front of the train station and fought until dark. The Confederates captured some prisoners, but lost two men killed and several wounded. The next morning they marched through Doko (now called Blythewood) and Ridgeway and arrived at the outskirts of Winnsboro at 1:00 A.M.

Company Notes
February 18–20, 1865

Company B — Captured: James G. Ringgold

Wateree River

Supposing that Sherman would go to Charlotte, North Carolina, next, Butler's division moved through Winnsboro on Tuesday, February 21, 1865. They marched to Gladden's Grove to get forage for their horses and to watch Sherman's right flank. Hood's army, with Wheeler's cavalry, continued up the railroad. Hampton ordered Butler to send his artillery and wagons to Charlotte and then move with his cavalry around Sherman's right flank to join him at Land's Ferry.

Early in the morning of February 22, Butler moved his men toward Columbia so they could pass between Columbia and Sherman. They had not gone far before they ran into Sherman's 15th Corps. The 15th and 17th corps were on Sherman's right flank, while the 14th and 20th corps were on his left flank. During a sharp fight, Butler determined that he was too badly outnumbered to overcome the enemy. He moved his men to the left to get to the river road, which was the only road left open between his column and the Wateree River, but he discovered that the enemy had occupied this road in force.

Butler determined from information gained from a prisoner that Sherman was not headed for Charlotte, but for Cheraw, South Carolina. He sent a dispatch to Hampton and then moved his men through Beckhamville, intending to cross the Wateree higher up. At Beckhamville, a Dr. Cloud provided feed for all the horses from his well-stocked barns. After leaving Beckhamville, the men moved to Fishing Creek and camped for the night at Anderson's Mill. All day long, the men had seen houses burning. When darkness fell, Sherman's position could easily be determined by the glare of incendiary fires lighting up the horizon for miles above and below the troopers.

Hanging Rock

Joseph Johnston was put in command of the western theater, including what remained of the Army of Tennessee, Braxton Bragg's and Robert Frederick Hoke's infantry from North

Carolina, Pierre Gustave Toutant Beauregard's command, William Joseph Hardee's cavalry from Charleston, and Wade Hampton's cavalry corps on Saturday, February 22, 1865. All together, there were no more than 25,000 troops. Many of the men were poorly clad and equipped, and others, especially Hardee's men, were inexperienced in field campaigning. Sherman's men outnumbered Johnston's more than two to one, and if John M. Schofield's and Alfred H. Terry's corps, who were marching from the North Carolina coast, linked up with Sherman, Johnston would be facing 100,000 men. Johnston's objective was to overtake and stop Sherman before he reached Goldsboro.

While the rest of Johnston's command moved from their various locations to amass at Charlotte, North Carolina, Hampton followed the enemy. On February 23, Butler moved his division from Fishing Creek toward Gouche's Ferry, on the Catawba River. It was necessary to get to the other side of the Catawba because the 20th and 14th corps were closing in above them, while the 15th and 17th were closing in below. They were unable to find a place where they could ford the river, so Butler decided to move the men and equipment over on the ferryboat and have the horses swim the river.

One squadron unsaddled their horses and a man on a strong horse started across the river. The loose horses followed. They were almost to the other side when, for some unknown reason, the loose horses turned around and swam back. The horses drifted in the current down the river and struck a steep, muddy bank below the landing. It was only by prompt, hard work that the horses were recovered. Men were sent up and down the river to search for a crossing. After finding one below Gouche's Ferry at Wades, all the troopers mounted and headed there, where they crossed in the late afternoon. After passing through Lancaster Court House, they turned east, because Sherman had changed his line of march and was moving southward and eastward. When they came to the old Hanging Rock battleground of the Revolutionary War, Cobb's Legion Cavalry met a regiment of Sherman's bummers. (Bummer was a name given to plunderers, thieves, house burners, and rapists.) They drove the bummers pell-mell for some distance, killing and capturing quite a number of them. They camped that night in the rain within sight of the enemy's campfires.

The next day they moved toward Camden, South Carolina, and encountered the enemy's foraging parties numerous times. They captured men from the 15th, 17th and 20th corps. When they came to a crossroad, where a large number of wagons had passed, they pursued the wagon train but were unable to overcome it before night fell. It was raining hard when they camped for the night, and once again they were within sight of the enemy's campfires.

**Company Notes
February 22–24, 1865**

Company G — Captured: William Givens

Cantey's Plantation

While marching toward Lynch's Creek in Kershaw County on Tuesday, February 25, 1865, Cobb's Legion had a skirmish as West's Cross Roads. That evening, Butler planned a night march in order to attack the 15th Corps at daylight. When night fell, a terrific storm came up. Butler later said, "The night was the darkest and the rain the hardest that I have ever known before or since."[11] The attack was cancelled.

When they arrived at Cantey's Plantation at about 9:00 on the morning of February 26, they discovered about 200 of the enemy loading eight or ten wagons with goods stolen from Cantey's barns. The 4th South Carolina charged the Yankees, killing most of them, and captured the wagons, along with several prisoners. Butler hurried his troopers, the wagons, and prisoners to a bridge over Little Lynch's Creek. When the Confederates reached the other side of the bridge, the swampy ground was covered with water. In some places, it was up to the saddle skirts, causing the troopers to move at a slow pace. Just as the Jeff Davis Legion, which was in the rear, cleared the bridge, Federal infantry appeared and opened fire. Seventeen bummers followed them across the bridge and fired on their rear. The Jeff Davis Legion spun around and fired back, killing, wounding, or capturing all of the bummers. The troopers also had a skirmish near Stroud's Mills on February 26.

Company Notes
February 25–27, 1865

Company C — Captured: Julius J. Fields

Yankees More Savage Than Indians

The enemy invaders speedily made their way toward the North Carolina border. On their route, the Yankees encountered much resistance from Hampton's cavalry, especially from Butler's division. Hampton, who was in advance of Sherman, kept up a series of rear-guard actions to slow down Sherman's progress. Every day, Butler attacked the head and flanks of both of the enemy's columns. Sometimes Wheeler's men also attacked, and, at times, the enemy had to slow their march to a crawl, and sometimes they had to halt.

Detachments of Kilpatrick's division led Sherman's advance, and most of Hampton's encounters were with them. In Kilpatrick's wake, Yankee bummers terrorized the populace. Rather than disciplining them, Sherman seemed amused at the thefts and arsons. In defense of the bummers, Sherman wrote to Hampton: "You cannot question my right to 'forage on the country.' It is a right as old as history.... I have no doubt that this is the occasion of much misbehavior on the part of our men, but I cannot permit an enemy to judge or punish [them]."[12] Sherman seemed to be rejecting any idea of punishing his own men.

Hampton replied to him: "Your line of march can be traced by the lurid light of burning houses, and in more than one household there is now an agony more bitter than that of death. The Indian scalped his victim regardless of age or sex, but with all his barbarity he always respected the persons of his female captives. Your soldiers, more savage than the Indian, insult those whose natural protectors are absent."[12] Hampton was referring to the Southern women being raped by Sherman's men. Mary Chesnut recorded in her diary an episode where seven of Sherman's bummers raped a young girl to death in front of her mother, who had first been tied up by the Yankees.[13]

Cheraw

Satisfied that Sherman was moving toward Cheraw, Hampton started in that direction with his troopers at 2:00 in the morning on Tuesday, February 28, 1865. Waring described the march as the hardest he ever made. They moved at a gallop until daylight, at which time they stopped to eat. After breakfast, they marched leisurely until they were near Cheraw, South Carolina. Cheraw was a pleasant little town that had become a haven for wealthy refugees from Charleston and a storage place for both civilian valuables and military supplies. It was just before sunset when they arrived. Blair's corps of 17,000–20,000 Federals arrived the same evening, about twelve hours ahead of the other Federal corps. Sherman's troops were gathering in Cheraw for their push into North Carolina.

Hardee ordered Butler to have some of his command to picket Thompson's Creek, four miles from Cheraw, and for him to go in person to Chesterfield Court House with part of his command to watch for movements of the enemy from that direction. Butler reported, "We retired, fighting at every point, from Chesterfield C. H. toward Kershaw."[14] Cobb's Legion Cavalry skirmished with the enemy near Big Black Creek, Blakeny, and Himsborough, South Carolina, and then galloped back toward Cheraw.

On February 28, the chiefs of quartermaster, ordnance, and subsistence departments began moving their trains away from Cheraw. By daylight the next morning, the infantry, artillery, and wagon trains had departed from the town. Butler's division was left to bring up the rear of the army, after first destroying what public stores were abandoned and burning the covered bridge over the Pee Dee River.

Company Notes
February 28, 1865

Company H — Captured: Augustus C. Baker

Kellytown

After moving through a pine woods, the troopers came to Big Lynch's Creek (now called Lynch's River), crossed the water at Pierce's Bridge, and then turned downstream to Kellytown, a little village near Tiller's Ferry. The men halted for two days at Kellytown while Hampton tried to determine Sherman's plans. Butler sent Aiken with a strong detachment from Butler's (old) brigade down the river on a reconnoitering expedition, and he sent Maj. Brown (perhaps Milton A. Brown) with troopers from Cobb's Legion Cavalry up the river on a similar expedition. On the second day, Wednesday, March 1, 1865, Brown reported that the 17th had crossed at Pierce's Bridge and were on the Old Stage Road seventeen miles from Cheraw. Aiken's troopers reported that the enemy had crossed below them, and that Col. Aiken had been killed the night before by a detachment from Sherman's army near Mt. Eron Church.

At dusk on that day the troopers drew rations from the commissary for the first time since they had left Winnsboro and were ordered to be ready to march at nightfall. As Butler's men moved up the Chesterfield Road toward the bridge, the enemy appeared on the Camden Road. Cobb's Legion galloped into sight as the enemy reached the suburbs of Cheraw, so a Georgia battalion of infantry was positioned at the fork of the two roads to hold back the enemy until Cobb's Legion could get onto the Chesterfield Road. Forty-six men from Cobb's Legion Cavalry were cut off by the enemy, but they managed to escape and cross the river higher up. At the covered bridge, as Cobb's Legion passed out the east end, the enemy entered the bridge from the west end. Cobb's Legion's rear guard was commanded by Capt.

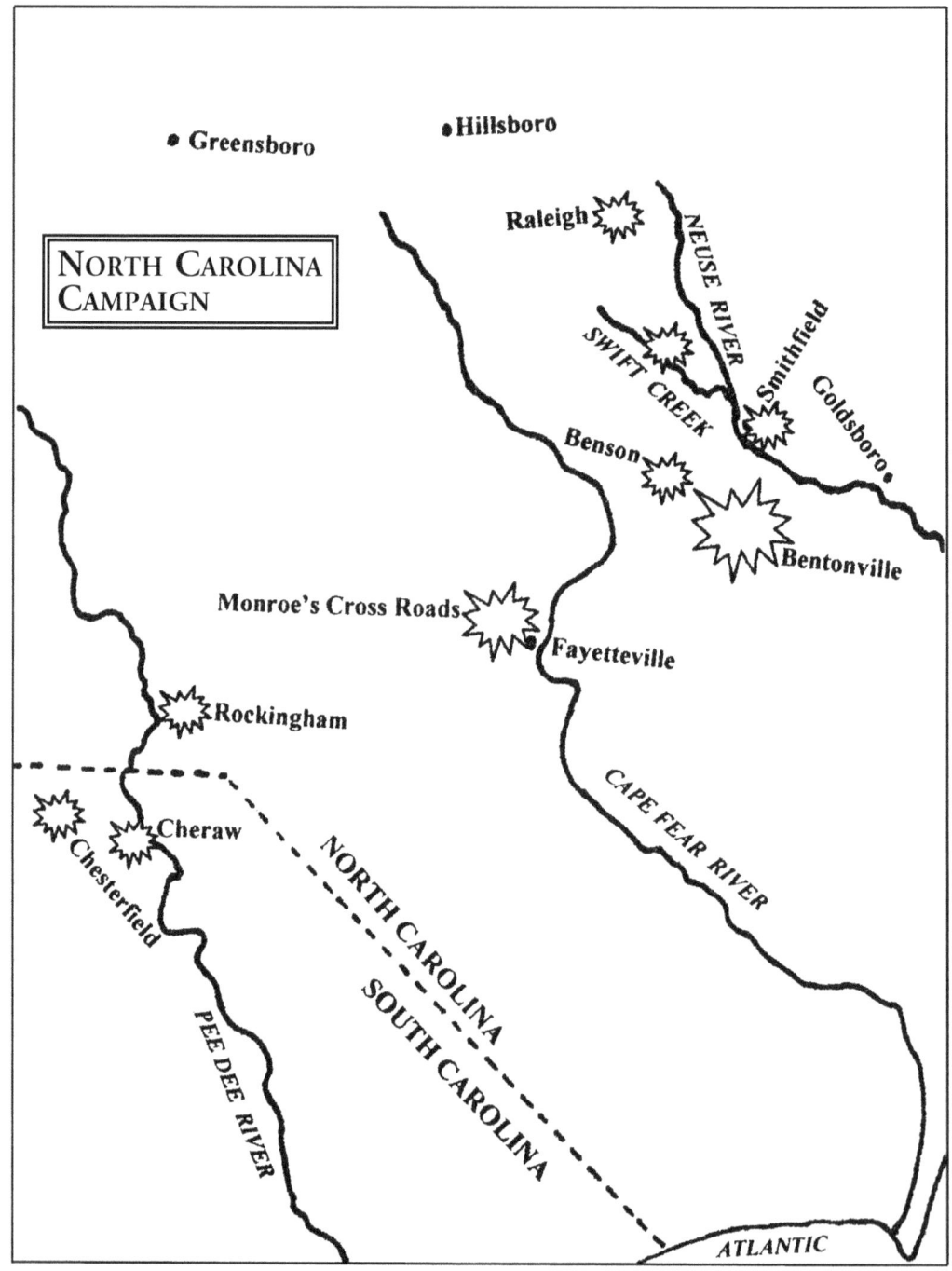

Andrew T. Baugh, of Company E, who directed his men to dismount, send the horses behind the abutment of the bridge, drive the enemy from the bridge, and then burn it. The troopers drove the enemy off the covered bridge and then set fire to the piles of rosin that Hardee's engineers had deposited at intervals along the floor of the bridge.

The troopers then marched to Chesterfield, arriving at daylight on March 2. The enemy advanced on Chesterfield that afternoon, so the cavalry retired across the creek. The next day,

March 3, the enemy started slowly advancing. The following day, a brigade of the Yankees crossed the Pee Dee River. Skirmishers were deployed to annoy them, which they did until the evening, when the enemy brought artillery over a pontoon bridge. The Southerners blew up their ordnance stores and burned commissary stores before retiring to the Fayetteville Road, where they camped for the night.

Company Notes
March 1–4, 1865

Company D — Wounded: John Dougherty Houston
Company I — Captured: Thomas Lyons, Joseph Syler

Love's Bridge

On Sunday, March 5, 1865, the enemy began advancing again. After the Southern pickets were driven in, the troopers marched to Rockingham, although a shortage in horseshoes made the march difficult. It soon became clear that Sherman was moving in the direction of Fayetteville, North Carolina, so Hampton moved in that direction, too. Miles from him, Hardee also was moving toward Fayetteville.

The next day a scouting party of the enemy got behind Hampton's pickets and charged them on the river road. On March 7, a portion of Kilpatrick's men managed to get between Hampton and Fayetteville without realizing that they were also between Hampton and Hardee. At 12:50 P.M., the pickets were charged, and the enemy tried to surprise the camp, but the Southerners were prepared and repulsed them. At 9:00 in the evening, the enemy advanced on Rockingham, and Hampton's troopers moved to the fairgrounds. Kilpatrick blocked the roads to Fayetteville, where the converging Confederates would have to cross the Cape Fear River. Kilpatrick then divided his command, keeping half of it with him, as he set up his headquarters at Monroe's Cross Roads, about fourteen miles northwest of Fayetteville.

It was raining as Cobb's Legion Cavalry moved out of camp on Wednesday, March 8. They marched down the Fayetteville Plank Road to the 47-mile post. At Love's Bridge they charged a party of Kilpatrick's cavalry, and afterward they camped near a mineral spring.

Company Notes
March 5–8, 1865

Company F — Captured: John C. Swan

Monroe's Crossroads

It had been raining all day and when night came, it was very dark, with cloudy skies and no moon or starlight. At 2:30 in the morning on Thursday, March 9, 1865, Gen. Butler and Lt. Tom Dunnahoo of Company H rode forward. Escorting them in column of fours were several men and a few scouts. The ground had turned to mud, which worked to their advantage, as it deadened their horses' hoofbeats. Butler stopped and signaled for Dunnahoo to do the same. Whispers were passed down the line for all the men to halt. Butler could hear the mud-dulled hoofs of others approaching them.

"Halt! Who goes there?" Butler called out in a clear, calm voice.

Thinking he had met friends, the leader answered that he commanded a patrol of the 5th Ohio Cavalry on picket duty for Kilpatrick. "March on!" Butler quietly and coolly ordered. The Ohioans separated into columns of twos and passed on either side of Butler's men. When they had marched far enough to be trapped, Butler spoke in a calm ordinary voice, "Halt there! You are prisoners!"[15]

Each of Butler's men laid a hand on the Yankee next him, while holding a pistol in the other hand. They captured the whole picket force of forty men without firing a shot or making any noise. One of the Confederates was a new recruit who rode a pony not over thirteen hands high, and his only weapon was a borrowed pistol. He had to stand in his stirrups and stretch to reach the shoulder of the Yankee next to him, who was over six feet tall. After the capture, the recruit was allowed to keep the mount and arms of his prisoner.

After a captured officer divulged the location of the home in which Kilpatrick was staying, Hampton's scouts dismounted and felt their way down the road in the direction from which the pickets had come. They reported to Hampton that there were no pickets between Hampton and Kilpatrick's camp, as they had all been captured, and no pickets by the swamp on the west side of his camp. Hampton called in his detachments and planned a surprise attack. During the night, Hampton's scouts lurked close to the Federal camp to capture anyone visiting the picket-post. Without firing a shot, they captured fifteen or twenty bummers who were caught outside of Kilpatrick's camp.

Hampton carefully observed the enemy during the night of March 9, while keeping his men in a battle line. In the woods on either side of the road, about a half mile from the enemy's camp, Hampton's cavalry waited in the cold driving rain, which was now falling in streams. Their horses remained saddled, but some of the men sat on the ground with the bridle reins in their hands or under their legs, ready to mount at a moment's notice. Others remained in their saddles. Before daylight, Hampton ordered Butler forward. His men noiselessly formed down the road in columns of fours. They advanced almost to the entrance of the camp, leaving a good interval between each man. This would give the men in back time to dismount in case of a counterattack. Visibility was low due to a dense fog which hung above the ground.

A third side of Kilpatrick's cavalry camp was bordered by a swamp, and beyond the fourth side lay camps of sleeping Union infantry. Hampton sent orders for Wheeler to advance from the right at an angle to Butler when he heard firing. His orders were to drive in the pickets, and then break through and assist Butler. Cobb's Legion Cavalry circled around the swamp so they could attack from the north. Col. Barrington S. King was in command, and Col. Gib Wright was commanding the brigade. They waited in a column, with the Fulton Dragoons, Company B, of Cobb's Legion Cavalry in front.

At the first light of dawn, the time came to attack. Butler rode to the front of his men and led them some distance into Kilpatrick's camp. They would have surrounded his headquarters had it not been for a number of captured Confederates prisoners who recognized them and gave the Rebel yell. Realizing they had been exposed, Butler removed his hat and waved it above his head, calling, "Troops from Virginia! Follow me! Forward, march!" and then he called out, "Charge!"[16] As usual, Butler could be seen by his men in the midst of the storm of bullets. He carried a silver-mounted riding-whip with which he would point out to those around him what needed to be done.

In the meantime, Cobb's Legion Cavalry rode pell-mell into the enemy's camp, finding many of them still asleep, while just a few were up and preparing their breakfasts. When they were sighted, the enemy called out asking what command they were with. The attackers answered, "Rebels," gave the Rebel yell, and began slashing the enemy with their sabers. Undressed, unarmed, and awakened from a deep sleep, the barely clad enemy took flight, running in all directions and leaving their accoutrements behind. The Confederates struck with such speed that they captured or put to flight all of the surprised Yankees around Kilpatrick's headquarters. Cobb's Legion dashed along the road in front of the house where Kilpatrick was sleeping. Many of the legion's men were on foot, because their horses had been left at Charlotte.

Awakened from his sleep by the commotion, Kilpatrick jumped out of bed, leaving his mistress behind, and ran outside bareheaded, wearing only a shirt over his long drawers and a pair of slippers. Capt. Bostick of Company D mistook him for a common soldier, pointed a pistol in his face, and demanded to know where the general was. Kilpatrick pointed to a Yankee riding by and said, "There he goes on that black horse!"[17] The cavalry galloped off, chasing the rider for a half of a mile, until he got away by jumping over a fence. One of the men captured Kilpatrick's spotted horse, which he rode until the end of the war.* In the meantime, Kilpatrick did not wait for a pair of trousers. He mounted the nearest horse, which was tethered nearby, and fled for the safety of the nearby woods. Wiley C. Howard reported riding past J.A. Shed from Gwinnett County, who had been shot through the ear. Howard struck Shed's Yankee antagonist on the back of the head, stopping the attack.

Instead of pursuing the attack, Wheeler's men stopped to loot the camp that Butler's men had cleared, allowing Kilpatrick time to reach his troops, rally them, and counterattack. The Yankees formed a line dismounted, four deep, with seven-shooter Spencer rifles, and advanced towards the Confederates. Cobb's Legion led the cavalry charge against the well-armed foe, which also had artillery support. When they got to within fifteen or twenty paces of the front line, men and horses were falling fast. Col. Barrington King was mortally wounded leading the charge when an artery in his thigh was severed. Numerous hand-to-hand conflicts followed. Kilpatrick soon had infantry support, and Hampton's men were driven back. Teams from the captured artillery and supply wagons had stampeded, so the Southerners smashed the wheels as they retreated.

Now that the fighting was all but over, Wheeler arrived to cover their retirement. Over 400 half-dressed prisoners and a number of horses had been captured, along with a large amount of arms and accoutrements, clothes, and some wagons. The enemy's artillery could not be hauled away, because Wheeler had not succeeded in carrying out his part of the action, but 173 jubilant Confederate prisoners, most of whom were half-naked, were released. The Confederate prisoners reported that they had been treated "very badly"[19] by the Yankees. Edward L. Wells, who was on hand for the battle, put the number of enemy wounded at over 300 and the number of captured at over 500, making their casualties almost 1,000, which was more than Butler's whole force. Wheeler's command numbered about 3,000, but they had been ineffectual in the battle. In the action, the Confederates were outnumbered five to one.

This action temporarily halted Kilpatrick and allowed Hampton to gain possession of the approaches to Fayetteville. However, little was accomplished by the action, other than the humiliation of Kilpatrick in what became known in both the North and South by the derisive term, "Kilpatrick's Shirttail Skedaddle." After the war, Kilpatrick said that while he "was

---

Kilpatrick recognized his horse during the armistice and gave the trooper two good horses for it.

making his escape, with his command scattering in every direction, he thought, 'Well! I have been working hard these four years for a major-general's commission and now in five minutes I have lost it all.'"[18] In his report, Kilpatrick said, "Hampton led the centre division [Butler's], and in less than a minute had driven back my people and taken possession of my headquarters, captured the artillery, and the whole command was flying before the most formidable cavalry charge I ever have witnessed."[19]

John T. Wood of Company A, wrote his father:

> I was carrying out 5 prisoners [that] I captured & made a Yankee exchange his fine hat ... for mine. [I] could have taken money, which some did, but my conscience would not allow me to search and plunder. [We] lost our Lt. Colonel Comary & several wounded. Good soldiers were killed after long service, by Yankees who had surrendered, but [took] advantage of the boys who told them [to] go to the rear. I ordered several to the rear & it was a wonder I did not meet the same fate.[20] [Punctuation has been added for clarity.]

Company Notes
March 9–10, 1865

Company B — Wounded: Edward Jones Appling
Company C — Killed: Barrington Simeral King
Company E — Wounded: J.A. Shed
Company G — Killed: James Russell Jack

The Goldsboro Road and the Black River

After the battle at Monroe's Crossing, Hampton led his men toward Fayetteville as far as the Cape Fear River, while Johnston's scattered infantry and artillery were also concentrating in that direction. Some of the enemy's infantry was crossing to the other side of the Cape Fear River as Hampton's men camped for the night.

The next day they crossed the river and burned the bridge. On Sunday, March 12, 1865, they moved down the river. Butler's horse was shot in the head while Butler was reconnoitering the enemy, who had constructed a pontoon bridge and crossed the river. Four Yankee bummers were captured in the act of plundering a house. On March 14, the troopers moved toward the Black River in order to hold its bridges. Cobb's Legion Cavalry encountered a group of the enemy on reconnaissance from Fayetteville on the Goldsboro Road. After skirmishing with them, the troopers made a detour through the woods, to the Black River. The bridges were prepared to be destroyed.

Company Notes
March 11–14, 1865

Company D — Captured: E.W. Scammell

Benton's Cross Roads

During a downpour, the enemy arrived at the bridges on Wednesday, March 15, 1865. At first, they were driven into the mud, but when they brought up their artillery the Southerners had to retire. The next day, the troopers made a difficult crossing over a ford on the Little Cohary River and then went into camp. On March 17, they moved toward Goldsboro. The next morning, they encountered advance units of the enemy, and Cobb's Legion Cavalry had a sharp skirmish near Benton's Cross Roads.

Johnston's little army consisted of 14,000 infantry plus Hampton's cavalry, an effective force of no more than 20,000 men. They were outnumbered by Sherman three to one, but Johnston was undaunted. He searched for a suitable location to battle against Sherman. On Hampton's advice, he chose to make his stand at Bentonville, where the surrounding countryside was heavily wooded and had few passable roads. The Yankees could advance toward the Southerners only on the Hillsboro Road. Sherman was marching toward them with Slocum's 14th Corps in advance, while his 20th Corps came behind them. They were separated by some miles from his 15th and 17th corps, who were one a parallel road and would have trouble joining him.

After the skirmish near Benton's Cross Roads, Hampton fell back to occupy the crest of a wooded hill, which was above open country. It would be a good position for a fight. His cavalry dismounted at the edge of the woods, and the artillery was positioned on the left the road that Sherman had to take. Hampton was determined to hold the position all night, until Johnston's infantry could catch up with him. If Sherman arrived before the Confederate infantry, Hampton's artillery would be lost to the enemy.

It was close to sunset when the enemy arrived. They made a feeble demonstration, then withdrew out of sight for the night. They had seen Hampton's strong position but did not know how inadequately it was held. During the night, Johnston arrived with most of his infantry, except Hardee's Corps, which had farther to travel than the rest and were camped some miles away.

Johnston was unable to examine the battlefield in the dark, but said he would approve Hampton's plan of action. It was decided that the cavalry would continue to hold their position and the infantry would form behind them. Bragg's Corps would straddle the main road with Hoke's men in the center. Hardee would be at an angle to Bragg's right, and Alexander P. Stewart at an angle to the right of Hardee. Hardee and Stewart would be in concealed positions in the woods to the northwest, virtually parallel to the road. When the infantry was in place, the cavalry would filter through Bragg's men, then mount, ride to the rear, and take a position on the extreme right. The enemy would see only Hoke's men. After they attacked him, Hampton and Stewart would deliver a blow to the enemy's flank, and Hardee would join in as the flank gave way.

Company Notes
March 15–18, 1865

Company F — Wounded: Augustus Drake

Bentonville, Day 1

At dawn on Sunday, March 19, 1865, the Confederates began to move into position, but the dense thickets on the ground to the right hampered the infantry's progress. Slocum had been told of the Confederates' plans and numbers by a Confederate deserter, but Hampton's men put up such a determined fight when Slocum arrived on the scene that he believed he had encountered only cavalry supported by a few cannon. Slocum sent word to Sherman that he would not need reinforcing. He would very shortly discover that he had made a serious mistake.

Cobb's Legion Cavalry along with the rest of Hampton's troopers withdrew at 10:00 A.M., drawing the enemy into an ambush. Hardee had not reached his post in the center, so Hampton sent two batteries of his horse artillery to hold the place where Hardee was supposed to be. Hoke's men were struck hard by Slocum's men just as Hampton's men cleared their rear. They fired on the Yankees from behind defenses, but when Slocum realized he was facing infantry, he pulled back. At this point Stewart and Hampton were supposed to attack Slocum's flank, but Hardee had not reached his assigned position. The proposed turning movement was weakened further when, at Bragg's insistence, Johnston sent troops to reinforce Hoke. Hampton disapproved the change in plans, and Johnston later admitted that it was a mistake to weaken his center.

It was another ninety minutes before Hardee moved into position, so the counterattack was delayed. When Hardee and Stewart finally attacked at 3:00, they forced the Yankees into a retreat. Unfortunately, by that time, the Federal reinforcements that Slocum sent for had arrived, and the Yankees with their overwhelming numbers were able to repel three more attacks by the Confederates. Johnston's men were worn down by excessive casualties during the past six months, and, although they fought desperately, they could not generate the power needed to carry the battle. The fighting continued for the rest of the day and into the evening, and then Johnston recalled everyone to their pre-attack positions. When darkness fell, Johnston held substantially his original infantry line. Both sides had fought hard and had lost heavily.

Bentonville, Days 2 and 3

During the night, Sherman arrived with Gen. Oliver O. Howard's column, and more of Slocum's men arrived on the field. They moved to Johnston's left and were in a position to threaten his rear. Cobb's Legion Cavalry with the rest of Hampton's men shifted to the left on the morning of Monday, March 20, 1865, to counteract the danger from the Yankees. By noon, Johnston's little army was fighting Sherman's whole army. They repulsed several attacks by the Federals, who left their dead and wounded on the field. When night came, there was another lull in the fighting.

On the morning of the twenty-first, Sherman again tried to flank Johnston's left along Mill Creek, where only some cavalry were patrolling. If Sherman could gain the bridge over Mill Creek, he would be able to cut off Johnston's line of retreat. Hampton reported the danger to Johnston and then rode out to the threatened bridge. He found that Sherman had sent Joseph A. Mower's division to drive back the Confederate cavalry pickets and take the approach to the bridge. Hampton summoned a small Georgia infantry brigade under Col. R. J. Henderson, no more than 250 men, and ordered them into action. He also sent in a nearby battery of artillery and about sixty to eighty troopers from the 4th Tennessee and 8th Texas cavalry regiments. After he formed them into a line facing the enemy, who were only a few hundred feet away, Hardee joined them. There were perhaps 300 men altogether in the charge. Among the troopers was Hardee's sixteen year old son, who had joined the 8th Texas cavalry about two hours before.

The suddenness of their charge made up for their weakness in numbers, and Mower's men were hurled back. Sherman later wrote that he ordered them back. When Hampton read Sherman's memoirs, he commented, "If this statement is true, the order was obeyed with wonderful promptness and alacrity."[21] Heroic efforts by Hampton's and Hardee's troops kept the escape route open. The bridge was held, so Johnston could safely withdraw. Hardee afterwards commented to Hampton, "That was nip and tuck, and for a while I thought tuck had it."[22] It was remarkable that Hardee was able to joke about it, because his beloved son had been killed in the charge.

Johnston withdrew his men across Mill Creek and camped about two miles beyond the bridge. Johnston's casualties for the battle were 2,600 men compared to Sherman's loss of 1,650 men. Throughout the past four days, Hampton's cavalry had fought both mounted and on foot. They had fought behind barricades and in hand-to-hand combat. They lost heavily, but they had come remarkably close to success, considering so few men were facing so many. The next morning, the cavalry repulsed Sherman's advance guard at the bridge, and then the Confederates moved toward Goldsboro in order to make it difficult for Sherman to link up with Grant. Afterward Butler said, "With scarce twenty eight thousand men he [Johnston] met Sherman's eighty thousand or ninety thousand at Bentonville and fought one of the fiercest battles of the war."[23]

Company Notes
March 21–23, 1865

Company E — Mortally Wounded: J.A. Shed

Hannah's Creek and Moccasin Creek

The best that Johnston could hope to do after the battle of Bentonville was to slow Sherman's inevitable march to Virginia, where he planned to join Grant. In a delaying action, Cobb's Legion Cavalry had a skirmish at Hannah's Creek on Wednesday, March 22, 1865. Sherman continued his march to Goldsboro, where he joined Gen. John M. Schofield and Gen. Alfred H. Terry on Thursday, March 23.

On March 24, the Southerners cautiously crossed Moccasin Creek. Hampton's men drove the enemy back for two or three miles into their entrenchments. These Yankees proved to be black soldiers, who abandoned their muskets in their haste to get away. For the next two days, the troopers rested, and then, the next day, they moved back across Moccasin Creek and camped near Crew's Bridge.

Company Notes
March 24–28, 1865

Company C — Wounded: William F. K. Garvin

Gulley's

Pickets were sent out before daylight on Wednesday, March 29, 1865, to a place where forage had been located near the enemy. Wright sent Cobb's Legion Cavalry to escort the wagons that were collecting the forage. Although the forage was within sound of the enemy's camp, the troopers were not interrupted.

On the same day, John T. Wood of Company A wrote his father, saying:

> I have not time to write more, as I am very dirty [and] must put on clean clothes. [I] have worn those I have had on for a month.... Since we are resting this morning, [I have] drawn a pair of shoes, drawers, and socks. [I] must clean up, [as I] lost my clothes.
>
> In this campaign, I have waded deep waters & rock for hundreds of yards, & sometimes over the horses' backs. But, thanks to Kind Providence, I am still alive, and [I have] escaped dangers seemingly incredible. [I am] mounted on a mule.... I was cut off from the command. A [illegible word] rode my horse down, [until] he dropped on the road....We are camped in ten miles of Goldsboro, N.C., on the Raleigh R.R.[24] [Punctuation was added for clarity.]

On March 31, an enemy foraging party drove in the Southern pickets, but they were out of luck. The Southerners had already made a clean sweep of the country, so they did not get anything. Cobb's Legion Cavalry skirmished with them at Gulley's, North Carolina.

Raleigh

At 6:30 in the morning on Sunday, April 2, 1865, Hampton's troopers left camp, marched almost to Smithfield, North Carolina, and then halted. The next day, they marched almost to Raleigh. The following day they marched into the city of Raleigh and halted in the streets. On April 10, they heard for the first time the distressing news that both Petersburg and Richmond had fallen. When members of the Charleston Light Dragoons met a party of horsemen headed south, the strangers said they were parolees from the Army of Northern Virginia. The Charlestonians called them liars and deserters. Hampton gathered his men in a square hollow north of Raleigh and told the troopers that the news of the surrender was a rumor he did not believe. He told them that he would lead everyone willing to go with him to the Trans-Mississippi (Texas), where the Confederacy still had territory, men, and equipment, and they would continue the fight.

Believing that Sherman would immediately attempt to join Grant, Johnston ordered Hampton to destroy the railroad outside of Goldsboro. Sherman left Goldsboro at 4:00 A.M. on Monday, April 10, but he headed for Raleigh, not Virginia. The enemy very rapidly advanced on the Smithfield Road, and Cobb's Legion Cavalry skirmished with them at Moccasin Creek. While the Jeff Davis Legion fought the enemy dismounted in Smithfield, Hampton's mounted troopers, after skirmishing with the enemy, crossed the Neuse River. They encamped about six miles from the river. Hampton's troopers challenged the oncoming enemy at several points and fought up to the eastern outskirts of Raleigh. The men "fell sullenly back to Raleigh, being constantly under fire and the baptism of blood."[25]

Company Notes
April 1–10, 1865

Company B — Captured: James T. Lamkin
Company E — Captured: James A. Allbritten
Company F — Captured: Theodore Floyd Daniel
Company I — Killed: William N. Liverman; Wounded: George A. Williams, Henry M. Williams; Captured: Thomas Lander

Swift Creek

Hampton ordered Wheeler to burn Battle's Bridge over Swift Creek to deny Sherman access to Raleigh. Meanwhile, Johnston's troops were retreating through the streets of the city. On Wednesday, April 12, 1865, it was discovered that Kilpatrick had moved from Mt. Olive and was camping between Hampton's troopers and Raleigh. While the rest of the brigade moved, Cobb's Legion Cavalry, with Lt. Wiley C. Howard in command, and the Jeff Davis Legion, with Adj. James T. Norris in command, were left as a rear guard to protect an important crossing at Swift Creek. They left camp at 3:00 in the morning and marched beyond the bridge. The troopers of Cobb's Legion Cavalry were mounted at the edge of the woods near the road protecting the flank of the Jeff Davis Legion, which was dismounted and entrenched in rifle pits and breastworks above the creek. Kilpatrick's cavalry arrived at Swift Creek at 10:30 A.M. and a battle broke out between them and the Jeff Davis Legion. The Yankees dismounted and plunged into the stream, cheering loudly as they crossed. Their cheering had been prompted by the news that Lee had surrendered at Appomattox Court House on April 9, 1865.

The enemy in great numbers rushed the position of the Jeff Davis Legion. "Bullets rained like hail,"[26] but the men held their position until Adj. J.T. Norris ordered a retreat. As the Confederates moved rapidly up the North Carolina Railroad, Lts. Jeffries and Norris of the Jeff Davis Legion, and Howard and Dunnahoo of Cobb's Legion Cavalry were the last to leave. When they descended into the road Howard said, "It was like plunging into the jaws of death under the concentrated fire of the enemy, now rushing along close to us."[27] Jeffries and Dunnahoo went down the road, while Norris and Howard dashed across the road and clung to the bushes for several hundred yards. Both Jeffries and Dunnahoo were shot, but their horses carried them quite a distance before they fell. Howard rushed up to Dunnahoo, halted and leaped off his horse. He raised Dunnahoo's head just as Dunnahoo gasped his last breath. The blood flowing from his chest wound had spattered on the picture of his little motherless daughter that he always carried. With the assistance of Humphries of the Phillip's Legion, Howard put Dunnahoo's body across his saddle. Humphries held his body on while Howard mounted his horse and led Dunnahoo's horse. The advancing enemy fired on them, but Howard and Humphries managed to get Dunnahoo to the ambulance that was carrying Jeffries' body. The bodies of Dunnahoo and Jeffries were taken to Raleigh and buried in the same grave late that evening. No coffins were available, but a lady in Raleigh furnished a blanket in which the bodies were wrapped. Howard said that he would always cherish Dunnahoo's memory and that he loved him as a brother. Once, when they were retreating over rough ground, Howard, who at the time was still the size of a small boy, became exhausted. Dunnahoo picked Howard up on his stout shoulders and literally carried him to safety.

A soldier in the 92nd Illinois wrote, "Oh, the price we paid. I never felt so sad in battle before, as I did then, when I looked upon the poor boys who there, after the great war was in fact over ... received marching orders to report to Heaven."[28]

The fighting did not end with the deaths of Dunnahoo and Jeffries. Cobb's Legion Cavalry continued fighting and falling back from place to place until late that night. While getting his men into line and preparing for the next onslaught, Howard dashed into a clump of blackjack oaks. A limb struck him in the face and a blackjack bud became stuck in his only good eye, leaving him unable to see. He called to William C. Orr of Company C to lead him to the rear. Orr had lost an eye in action below Richmond the year before. While they were leaving, someone wryly quipped, "The blind leading the blind."[29]

Howard soon met Gib Wright, who was commanding the brigade and wanted to know what had happened. Wright told them that the enemy was placing a battery on the hill and would soon be raking the road with shell. They would need to travel more than a mile straight down the road before they could reach a bend and the cover of the woods, so they had better hurry. Howard reported:

> Shortly after, as we jogged along, on came a screaming shell which bursted [sic] near by and another and another quickly followed. I cannot picture the demoralizing effect of the situation, stone blind and suffering while I was retreating, subjected to this horrible cannonading from the rear. It remains to-day amid all my experiences a living, vivid memory beyond my descriptive powers. It was my last experience under fire and was received with all the force of dread which my introduction to shell and shot produced at Cold Harbor.[30]

Sherman's men came up behind Kilpatrick and soon had full possession of the city of Raleigh.

Company Notes
April 12, 1865

Company B — Captured: William W. Dunn
Company H — Killed: Thomas Jordan Dunnahoo

Petition for Peace

The next day, Wednesday, April 13, 1865, Cobb's Legion Cavalry marched until they reached Old Hillsboro. They rested a little ways outside the town. In those last days of the war, they were still in Young's brigade, as they had been throughout the war, and Gib Wright, who recently had been promoted to general, was commanding the brigade. The brigade included Cobb's Legion Cavalry, the Jeff Davis Legion, the Phillip's Legion, and the 10th Georgia Cavalry.

On the night of April 13, Johnston met with President Jefferson Davis, who had fled from Richmond to Charlotte, North Carolina, and recommended that they seek a peace agreement with Sherman. That night a message was sent to Hampton's headquarters near Hillsboro requesting that a trusted officer of the cavalry staff deliver a letter through the lines. Johnston did not reveal to Hampton that he was asking for an interview to discuss terms of surrender. Hampton woke up his staff officer, Capt. Rawlins Lowndes, and sent him with the letter toward Sherman's pickets. Lowndes took the letter to the headquarters of Kilpatrick, who forwarded it to Sherman. He had to wait eight hours for a reply. During that time, Lowndes conversed with Kilpatrick, who was none too amiable. Kilpatrick complained that the attack on his camp below Fayetteville reflected unfairly on him. He suggested that another battle with his bluecoats in fighting order would have a different outcome.

Lowndes answered him by saying:

> Well, General, I will make you the following proposition, and I will pledge myself that General Hampton will carry it out in every respect. You, with your staff, take fifteen hundred men, and General Hampton, with his staff, will meet you with a thousand men, all to be armed with the saber alone. The two parties will be drawn up mounted in regimental formations, opposite to each other, and at a signal to be agreed upon will charge. That will settle the question which are the best men.[31]

Kilpatrick thanked Lowndes but declined the offer. The last thing Lowndes did before he left was to repeat the offer.

On April 14, the men marched along the railroad all day, undisturbed by enemy fire, and they found plenty of forage for their horses. Waring wrote in his diary: "Lots of rumours [sic] about Gen: Lee. The Yankees say, Lee has capitulated. All bosh. Lee is really tho' south of the Dan River."[32] The next day, the men marched to Hillsboro and waited in the town all day. Waring recorded in his diary that "Paroled prisoners from Virginia say, that Gen: Lee has surrendered his army. Only 8000 muskets were left. One of them brought out Gen: Lee's farewell address to his Army. He says that the army was overpowered 'by superior numbers and resources.' God help the cause."[33]

The letter from Johnston that Lowndes had delivered produced a meeting at the Bennett House near Durham Station on April 16. Sherman began the meeting by showing a dispatch that told of the assassination of Lincoln. The Confederates were deeply shocked. It was not until the next day that Sherman offered his surrender terms. On April 16, Waring wrote in his diary: "I fear that the War is over & that all our sacrifices are in vain. We shall be betrayed by our own leaders."[34]

During this period, a rumor circulated around Cobb's Legion Cavalry's camp that the troopers had been surrendered unconditionally as prisoners of war. Many of the men made preparations to slip away from camp and go home. When Gib Wright heard that his men were getting ready to leave, he went to the camp as fast as his horse could carry him and had the men assemble so he could talk to them. He promised that they would not be surrendered without their consent. (This was a promise he was not able to keep.) He also reminded them that he had more authority over them than anyone else. He told them that they should not bring disgrace to the brigade by going off that way, and the only way they could leave was over his dead body. Charles Hansell of the 10th Georgia Cavalry said that "the whole brigade was more afraid of him [Gib Wright] than of the Yankees."[35] The men who had saddled their horses quietly took their saddles off.

Hampton did not like the surrender plan. Wells wrote that "He had seen his homeland laid waste; men of his command in Sherman's hands had been threatened with execution for deeds they had not done; and he himself had not yet been beaten in the field to anything like his own satisfaction."[36] Hampton wrote to Jefferson Davis on April 17, stating:

> If I had 20,000 mounted men here I could force Sherman to retreat in twenty days. Give me a good force of cavalry and I will take them across the Mississippi — and if you desire to go in that direction it will give me great pleasure to escort you. My own mind is made up. As to my course I shall fight as long as my government remains in existence, for I shall

never take the "oath of allegiance." I am sorry that we paused to negotiate, for to my apprehension, no evil can equal that of a return to the Union.[37]

Wade Hampton knew that his troopers would follow him to Texas, or anywhere else. While he was in Charlotte conferring with Davis on April 26, Johnston signed the surrender agreement. Hampton argued that he was not included in the surrender, because he had not been present. Johnston agreed with him but insisted that the cavalry who had remained in camp had been surrendered and sworn out of service.

Late in the afternoon of April 27, Gib Wright ordered the troopers to get ready to move. As they moved through the town of Hillsboro, the town clock was striking eleven. After riding hard all night, they came to the little town of Company Shops as the sun was rising. Company Shops is twenty-two miles from Hillsboro on the road to Greensboro. After arriving, Gib Wright had the men to dismount and gather around him. He told them that they had a thirty mile start on "Mr. Kilpatrick's critter company"[38] and that he had the wagons loaded and everything was ready. He told them if they wanted to go to the Trans-Mississippi, he would go with them, either as their commander or as a private. He directed the company commanders to get together with their men and let each man decide for himself.

Before the troopers had a chance to make a decision, Wade Hampton galloped into the camp and ordered that the men be formed. He marched them toward Greensboro for a short distance and had them go into camp. Then he had the men to assemble around him. He reminded them of the very high reputation the brigade had won for itself. He told them that he had worked hard to have the cavalry excepted from the terms of the surrender and he was ready to go anywhere with them, but, if they were included in the surrender agreement, it was their duty to surrender, and he knew they would do their duty. He was able to persuade them to do the honorable thing and go to Greensboro to participate in the surrender ceremony. There was hardly a dry eye in the crowd, and many of the men sobbed like children.

The troopers were then marched to Greensboro, and, by the time they arrived on April 28, many of the men were so sleep deprived that they were in a fog. They had marched a distance of forty-four miles from Hillsboro. There was no grain for the horses in the Greensboro area, and the horses were starving. On May 2, 1865, at 11:00 in the morning, Lt. Jefferson Bassett of Company A and Lt. George A. Williams of Company I of Cobb's Legion Cavalry rode fifteen miles to High Point to get the troopers' paroles. After a delay of four hours, the Yankees started paroling the men. It was 6:30 in the evening before Bassett and Williams started back to Greensboro.

The bullet-riddled and shredded battle flag of Cobb's Legion Cavalry. Photograph courtesy Augusta Museum of History.

Each of the men was handed a parole. All the regiments of the Confederate army were ordered to surrender their flags, but William L. Church of Company C concealed Cobb's Legion Cavalry's battle flag under his shirt. He swore that no foeman's hand would ever desecrate the flag. He hid it in spite of orders that there would be a search for Confederate property. When he returned to Georgia, he turned the flag over to the Cavalry Survivors Association of Augusta, and it is now in the possession of the Augusta Museum.

Before they left Greensboro, Gen. Johnston directed that $17,000 in silver be divided among the officers and men. Butler, who distributed the money, received $1.75, which amounted to all of his worldly assets with which he had to begin life anew. Butler said:

> We separated about the first day of May 1865, and marched to our homes with the full consciousness of duty well performed. We made no apologies, and have made none since. The only regrets felt or expressed were that we had not triumphed in our cause and won the final victory, after so much hard fighting and so many sacrifices.... A few years more and there will be nothing left except the sacred memories of their lives and the lofty example of their unselfish patriotism.[39]

Company Notes
April 13–June 11, 1888

Company A — Died: John Ross, Johnathan Pinckney Thomas; Wounded: Robert Augustus Reynolds (exact date unknown)
Company C — Captured: William F. K. Garvin, John J. Nash
Company E — Died: John D. Lowe
Company K — Captured: C.W. Orrison

Afterword

The troopers of Cobb's Legion Cavalry had ridden off to war as brave and dashing young cavaliers, willing to defend their homeland and fight for its freedom, shed their blood, and sacrifice their lives. Their letters to the *Confederate Veterans Magazine* reveal that surrender was a humiliating, bitter pill for them to swallow. Most of them had been willing to continue fighting for their cause as long as there was breath left in them.

They returned home, some riding and some on foot, to their beloved Georgia, South Carolina, North Carolina, Virginia, Maryland, Alabama, Mississippi and Louisiana. They stayed together as long as possible on the homeward trek, and then they each turned toward his own home. They returned to poverty, hunger, and want. A few of them would gain financial comfort, but many of them had a pauper's grave waiting for them. The men had sacrificed almost everything for their cause, but they had the abiding satisfaction of knowing that their honor had never been sacrificed.

To demonstrate how many of these men returned home to poverty and hardship, Confederate pension information is included with the men's biographies. In order to qualify for a pension, a man not only had to serve his country honorably, but he also had to be completely disabled and unable to work, or living in poverty. Capt. Francis Edgeworth Eve said:

Sgt. William David Wiggins of Company A lost his horse before the surrender at Greensboro, North Carolina, and had to walk home to Augusta, Georgia. Photograph courtesy Sandra Bey Jaconetta.

> We fought for what we believed were our rights. We believed it as conscientiously as men can believe anything on this earth, and the bloody records of that war prove it. We believed that we were fighting for God and our fatherland and as Gen. Hampton said "the man that

would not fight for his country ought to be damned...." What could a Confederate soldier tell who had served four years in the A.N.V. [Army of Northern Virginia]? The recollections of those days rush vividly to one's brain. The blood goes tingling through their veins, the moisture unhidden dims the eye sight as we recall the forms and faces of those true comrades, ever responsive to the call of duty. Battling for what they then believed and died believing, that their cause was just, and that God would, at length, sanction it.[1]

After the war, Gen. Robert E. Lee wrote to Gen. Wade Hampton: "You cannot regret as much as I do that you were not present at the final struggle, for had you been present with all of your cavalry the disaster would not have happened."[1]

Pvt. John Stapler Dozier of Company A posed for this photograph at Brandy Station, Virginia. He served as a scout and was wounded at Jack's Shop, Virginia. Photograph courtesy Georgia Archives, Small Print Collection, RG 48-2-1.

Appendix A

Commanding Officers

Pierce Manning Butler Young

Pierce Manning Butler Young was born on November 15, 1836, in Spartanburg, South Carolina, the son of a country doctor. When he was two years old, his family moved to Cartersville, Georgia.

At the age of fifteen (thirteen by some accounts), he enrolled in the Georgia Military Academy. While there, he received an appointment to the U.S. Military Academy at West Point, where his closest friend was his classmate — George Armstrong Custer.

He resigned from West Point in 1861, three months before his graduation, in order to return south, when the Confederacy was organizing. He was commissioned as a lieutenant of the Georgia militia in an artillery unit on March 16, 1861, at Fort Pillow, Tennessee, and then transferred to the Confederate Regular Army. After serving under Brig. Gen. Braxton Bragg at Pensacola, Florida, for several weeks, he went to Richmond, Virginia, in early 1862, where he became the commander of Cobb's Legion Cavalry with the rank of major. He quickly earned a reputation for reckless bravery and of being a strong officer in Wade Hampton's cavalry brigade.

He was wounded twice in 1862 during the greater battle of South Mountain, first at Burkittsville, Maryland, on September 13, 1862, and then at Middletown, Maryland, where he sustained a chest wound. He was promoted to colonel on November 1, 1862. In June of 1863, he led the right advance of Hampton's command at the Battle of Brandy Station before fighting in the Gettysburg Campaign in July 1863.

He received a gunshot wound to the chest on August 1, 1863, during the Second Battle of Brandy Station. After he recovered, he returned to the cavalry brigade. On September 28, 1863, he was promoted to the rank of brigadier-general. He was wounded again in the chest at Ashland, Virginia, on June 2, 1864. When he returned to duty from that wound, he participated in the Great Cattle Raid.

In November 1864, he was sent to Augusta, Georgia, to secure remounts, recruit troops, and help defend Augusta and Savannah against Maj. Gen. William T. Sherman's forces. On December 30, 1864, he was promoted to the temporary rank of major general and became a division leader under Major General Wade Hampton. He spent the last months of the war commanding a cavalry division of the Army of Tennessee, fighting in the Campaign of the Carolinas.

After the war, he returned to Georgia and became a planter. He was elected to the U.S. House of Representatives for four terms (1868–1875), served as consul-general at St. Petersburg, Russia (1885–1887), and was the U.S. minister to Guatemala and Honduras (1893–1896). He died at the age of fifty-nine on July 6, 1896, in New York, New York.

Gilbert Jefferson Wright

Gilbert (Gib) Jefferson Wright was born in Gwinnett County, Georgia, on February 18, 1825. He was a lawyer, judge, and the mayor of Albany, Dougherty County, Georgia, and married Dorothy Chandler on February 19, 1850, in Carroll County, Georgia. He served in the Mexican War as a private and was wounded.

When Cobb's Legion Cavalry, Company D, was organized, he enlisted as a lieutenant on August 10, 1861. His horses were valued at $200 and $350 and his horse equipment at $30 and $25. In 1862, he was promoted to captain. He was promoted to major on June 9, 1863, at the First Battle of Brandy Station.

At the Battle of Quebec Schoolhouse (during the greater Battle of South Mountain, Maryland), he was wounded in the foot. He was admitted to C.S.A. General Hospital, Charlottesville, Virginia, on August 3, 1863, with another gunshot wound.

On October 9, 1863, he was promoted to colonel and led Cobb's Legion Cavalry from then until they were surrendered by Gen. Joseph E. Johnston on April 26, 1865. He had promised his men that they would not be surrendered against their will, but that was a promise he was unable to keep.

P.M.B. Young said about him that "This officer has proved his gallantry on many fields."* J.E.B. Stuart called him "a most competent officer" and commended "his gallant conduct in Maryland where he was wounded."†

He died at Forsyth, Georgia, on June 3, 1895, and was buried in Oakland Cemetery.

Matthew Calbraith Butler

Matthew Calbraith Butler was born near Greenville, South Carolina, in the foothills of the Blue Ridge Mountains on March 8, 1836. He was descended from a long line of soldiers and statesmen who settled first in Prince William County, Virginia, and then moved to Edgefield County, South Carolina.

He enrolled in South Carolina College in 1854 but left after his junior year to study law with his uncle, Judge A.P. Butler, a member of the United States Senate. He began his profession as a lawyer in Edgefield, South Carolina. He married Maria Calhoun Pickens, the daughter of a future governor of South Carolina. He served one term in the state legislature before the War Between the States began.

Butler enlisted as a captain in the Edgefield Hussars. On June 6, 1861, the Edgefield Hussars were sent to Columbia to join the Hampton Legion. Next, they were sent to Virginia. During the desperate fighting at Brandy Station on June 9, 1863, he lost his foot. He was twenty-seven years old at the time. He returned to his command as quickly as possible with a cork foot and was promoted to brigadier-general and soon after that to major-general. In nearly every fight that Butler led his men into, his horse was shot from under him. To his merit, it was said of him that he never ordered a soldier to go where he would not go himself.

After the war, he returned home to desolation and poverty, with only the $1.75 that he collected at Greensboro, to begin the practice of law. During the years of Reconstruction, he fought against the cruelties perpetrated against Southerners. In 1876, he was instrumental in having Wade Hampton elected as the governor of South Carolina. Butler was elected to the South Carolina legislature, and then to the Senate of the United States. On May 28, 1898, Butler was commissioned as a major-general in the United States Army, commanding the Second Army Corps. He died April 14, 1909.

Wade Hampton

Wade Hampton was born on Hassel Street in Charleston, South Carolina, on March 28, 1818. His great-grandfather came to South Carolina from Virginia before the Revolutionary War and settled in the Spartanburg district. There he and most of his family were murdered by the Indians in 1775. His grandfather, also named Wade Hampton, was away from home at the time and escaped the massacre. This Wade Hampton became the first in a dynasty of warriors. He served as a colonel in the Revolutionary Army in the cavalry commanded by George Washington. During the war of 1812, he served as a general and fought along the northern frontier. After the war, he amassed a fortune growing cotton.

---

*Letter from P.M.B. Young included in the CSR of G.J. Wright.
†Letter from J.E.B. Stuart included in the CSR of G.J. Wright.

His son, Col. Wade Hampton, was a planter who owned a large estate. He served on the staff of Gen. Jackson at the battle of New Orleans.

Lt. Gen. Wade Hampton owned land in both South Carolina and Mississippi, where he had a winter home. When war came, his allegiance was to South Carolina and the South. He was a graduate of the South Carolina College in Columbia, South Carolina, but had no formal military training. This fact worked against him in the beginning of the war, until practical experience in the field helped him to develop his natural abilities. He raised the Hampton Legion, which he commanded at the first battle of Manassas (Bull Run), where he received a head wound. The legion consisted of six companies of infantry, four troops of cavalry, and one battery of artillery. As was discovered with Cobb's Legion, the three arms did not function well together, and they were separated.

On July 28, 1862, Hampton was transferred as a brigadier-general to the cavalry of the Army of Northern Virginia. His command consisted of Cobb's Legion Cavalry, the Hampton Legion Cavalry (which became the 2nd South Carolina), the Jeff Davis Legion, the 1st North Carolina, and the 10th Virginia Cavalry.

In January 1865, Hampton was sent to the Carolinas with part of his cavalry to fight Sherman. He was promoted to lieutenant general on February 15, 1865. He was one of three civilians without formal military training who attained the rank of lieutenant general in the Confederacy. The others were Nathan Bedford Forrest and Richard Taylor. During the final year of the war, Hampton proved to be one of Lee's best officers. Butler said of him, "He never lost his head and rarely lost his temper.... He never seemed to realize what fatigue was."*

After the war, he was an outspoken opponent of Radical Reconstruction, and he was elected governor of South Carolina in 1876 and 1878. He served as a U.S. Senator from 1879 to 1891 and then became commissioner of the Pacific Railway.

Hampton died on April 11, 1902, in Columbia, South Carolina and was buried there.

John T. Wood of Company A said of him, "Gen. Hampton is loved like a father by his whole command.... While in front of enemy, his presence is cheering to us who know him, [and] have the utmost confidence in even his presence. He has never been whipped, & Gen. Kilpatrick, the Yankee Cavalry General, can certify to that...."† [Punctuation was added for clarity.]

Capt. Edgeworth Eve said that Hampton never ordered his men to go where he would not lead: "His history we have a right to feel that we helped to make and naturally glory in the honors accorded him. We believe him to be the greatest, grandest, purest, no stain upon his escutcheon."

Wiley Howard said, "God bless Wade Hampton and may he linger long among us who love him for all his glorious past and the grandeur of his aged life and unspotted character. As a soldier and a noble man, he is the peer of any man living, and after death worthy to join the brilliant galaxy of those knightly spirits of comrades, officers and privates, who have passed 'over the river and rest under the shade of the trees.' The memory of his deeds and fame shall go sounding down the corrodors [sic] of Time, inspiring generations that shall follow in the ages to come to lofty manhood, noble daring and self-sacrifice on the altar of truth and human liberty."§

Lt. John S. Wise of Robert E. Lee's staff said, "The fighting morale of Stuart's cavalry was nowise impaired under the dashing leadership of Hampton. He was as dauntless as Stuart, and if anything, a more distinguished-looking man. Thoroughly inured to fatigue by a lifetime spent in the saddle or in the field, his reputation as a sportsman was second only to his fame as a cavalryman. A born aristocrat, his breeding showed itself in every feature, word and look. Yet his manners and bearing with the troops were so thoroughly democratic, and his fearlessness in action so conspicuous, that no man ever excited more enthusiasm. He rode like a centaur, and possessed a face and form so noble that men vied with women in admiration of General Hampton."**

John Andrew Rice in his book, *I Came Out of the Eighteenth Century*, wrote about Hampton: "Heroes were to be found at every crossroad, but the greatest of them all was at Columbia."

---

*Matthew C. Butler's tribute to Wade Hampton, August 1902 (Butler Family Scrapbook, South Carolina Library).
†John T. Wood, CSR, letter to his father.
§Howard, page 8.
**The End of an Era *by John S. Wise, page 133.*

Thomas Reade Rootes Cobb

Thomas Reade Rootes Cobb was born on April 10, 1823, at Cherry Hill Plantation in Jefferson County, Georgia. He graduated from Franklin College in Athens, Georgia, in 1841 after earning the highest grades in the history of the school and was admitted to the bar as a lawyer in 1842. He was a deeply religious man and a leader in his community devoted to the service of others. He married Marion Lumpkin on January 9, 1844, and they had six children, two of whom died in infancy and a daughter who died at the age of thirteen.

Tom Cobb hated politics, but was opposed to the election of Abraham Lincoln. On election night, he gathered his family around an altar in his home and prayed for the preservation of the Union and the defeat of Lincoln. After his family went to bed, he remained on his knees for most of the night. The next morning when he heard the election results, a voice came to him saying, "Be free! Be free!" He interpreted that as a call to help liberate his people.

He strongly favored secession and served as a delegate to the convention of seceding states in Montgomery, Alabama, in February 1861. He was commissioned a colonel in Cobb's Legion on August 28, 1861, and promoted to brigadier general on November 1, 1862. His men adored him, as he was always looking out for their comfort and needs.

He was killed in the Battle of Fredericksburg, Virginia, on December 13, 1862, and died within sight of his grandparents' home, where he had played as a child. Wiley C. Howard said of Tom Cobb, "Peace to his ashes. The Confederacy never lost a truer, abler or nobler defender.... Thank God [for] the life and character of our peerless Cobb.... His brigade won world-wide fame resisting the most persistent and furious onslaughts of a determined foe until their slain bodies almost made a pyramid rivaling in height the memorable stone wall which witnessed the holocaust of death and destruction. Glorious Tom Cobb and his brave command will live forever in history among the brightest constellations that shine out in the annals of great achievements and military glory."*

---

*Howard, pages 5–6.

Appendix B

Roster

Introduction

The roster of Cobb's Legion Cavalry was assembled from several sources: *Compiled Service Records of Confederate Soldiers Who Served in Organizations from the State of Georgia*, National Archives Microfilm; The Muster Roll Commission's Roster, Georgia State Archives, Atlanta, Georgia; Confederate Pension Applications for the State of Georgia; Marriage and Cemetery Records; Research Files of Glen Spurloc and James Edward Rowe; *These Men She Gave: The Civil War Diary of Athens, Georgia*, by John F. Stegeman; *Civil War Soldiers and Sailors System*; and *History of Dougherty County Georgia* by Thronateeska Chapter, DAR.

There are men on the roster who do not have a substantial official record, or who have no official record at all. Those who enlisted after October/November 1864, and who were *not* at the surrender, do not have a service record. The reader must bear in mind that if a man has no service records in Cobb's Legion, that does not necessarily mean that he did not serve in Cobb's Legion. In addition, many of the military records end inconclusively, without indicating whether the soldier died, was discharged, captured, transferred, or paroled.

For many of the men, their last records are in the fall of 1864, when a large number of them were sent to Georgia to replace their horses that had died or had been killed in battle. Some of the gaps in the records were explained in the Confederate Pension Applications. If a man received a Confederate pension, then he was able to prove that he was where he was supposed to be when the war ended. One example of this is the records of John H. Keogh of Company A. His last official record shows that on September 20, 1864, he was on horse detail. On his application for a Confederate Pension, he states that he was captured nine miles from Orangeburg, South Carolina, and sent to a prison in Savannah, Georgia, from which he escaped, and that he had never been paroled. Since he was granted a pension, his story must have been corroborated.

Another explanation for inconclusive records is that military records for Cobb's Legion Cavalry were burned when Gen. Sherman approached, in order to prevent Union troops from confiscating them and then using them to bring "war criminal" charges against the Southern men. The entry "last record" has been used to indicate those military records that end inconclusively. Sometimes a post-war record will follow the "last record." One example is the records of James Russell Jack. His last record states that he went on horse detail on September 20, 1864. However, Wiley Howard said in his *Sketch of Cobb's Legion Cavalry* that James Russell Jack was killed in action at Monroe's Crossroads. That battle took place on March 9, 1865.

In other Confederate military units in 1861, many of the men enlisted for one year, expecting the war to be over quickly. Some of those men transferred to Cobb's Legion Cavalry after serving one year in another regiment. All of the men in Cobb's Legion Cavalry enlisted for three years or for the duration of the war.

The rank of lieutenant and the ranks of noncommissioned officers were broken into several grades. Sergeants, for instance, ranked from 5th Sergeant up to 1st Sergeant. For the purpose of this book, the gradations are not traced, but the rank of sergeant and lieutenant are used.

The terms "recruiting camp" and "infirmary camp" are used interchangeably in the men's records. The terms refer to a camp where men were sent with sick or injured horses, so the horses could be cared for until they recovered. "Recruiting" does not mean signing up new men. The word "mustering" was used for that purpose. A man was not sent to infirmary camp for his health, but for his horse's health, although there were a few instances of men becoming ill and dying at the infirmary camp. An example of that is C.H. Barden of Company K. When a soldier is listed as absent on "detail," he is absent from the company, but not necessarily from his regiment.

Most of the men who were admitted to a hospital were sent first to a Receiving and Wayside Hospital for evaluation before being sent (usually the next day) to a hospital that specialized in their kinds of cases. For instance, patients with smallpox were usually sent to Howard's Grove Hospital in Richmond, Virginia. (Toward the end of the war, Howard's Grove also accepted other types of patients.) The men's passage through the Receiving and Wayside Hospital is not included in their biographical sketches.

When a man was not where he was supposed to be at the time he was supposed to be there, he was listed as "absent without leave" or "deserted." Sometimes, a later service record indicated that he had been captured, killed in action, or severely wounded in battle and was in a hospital. When further service records were not available, an effort was made to locate all of the "deserters" on the 1870 or later census and through other sources. The men who could not be located may have given their lives for their beloved Southland and were buried in the graves of "unknown soldiers." Only those who truly seemed to be deserters were listed as such in this book.

When a man was sent home to procure a horse but did not return within the allotted time, his record states that he deserted. However, later records may show he returned to his unit. Since there were so many variables in how quickly a man could go home, procure a horse, and return, the legion did not prosecute a trooper for being unavoidably late.

When a man was said to take the Oath, it was the Oath of Allegiance to the government of the United States.

Important features of the records have been included in this book, but not all of the less important minutiae.

The muster roll records usually cover a two months' period. Users of these records should be aware that an entry on a record, such as "absent sick," indicates the circumstances on the last day of the period. A soldier could be absent sick for several weeks, but if he were present on the last day of the period, the record will *not* indicate that he had been sick. On the other hand, if he were present every day except the last day, the record will indicate that he is "absent." Unfortunately, some of the records on the microfilm were unreadable.

The age given is the age at enlistment in Cobb's Legion Cavalry, even if the man served in another unit before enlisting in Cobb's Legion Cavalry. If a man has no service records, it is assumed that he enlisted between October 1864 and April 1865. The date of January 1, 1865, is used as his estimated enlistment date for estimating his age. Unless his age is given on his enlistment muster roll, ages for the men are estimated mainly from these sources:

- Discharge papers due to disability
- Prisoner of war paroles
- Widows' applications for Confederate pensions
- Census records, primarily the one for 1860.

When the service record gives an age that does not mesh with the known birth date of the man, he may have lied about his age in order to enlist underage, or the enlisting officer may have recorded it wrong.

Alternate spellings of names in the service records are in brackets. Details are included about the men's horses, because, as cavalrymen, their horses were essential to them.

The Roster

1. Abercrombie, Andrew Jackson: 17-year-old farmer from Lumpkin County, Georgia. Born on 06/08/1846 in Lumpkin County, Georgia. Brother of John H. Abercrombie and William Wiley Abercrombie. Enlisted as a private in Company C on 07/15/1863 at Stevensburg, Virginia. Sent home to get a horse under Special Order No. 36 from corps headquarters on 04/01/1864. Sent to Georgia to get a horse with Capt. Bostick on 09/20/1864. Was surrendered by Gen. Joseph E. Johnston on 04/26/1865. Paroled at Greensboro, North Carolina, on 05/01/1865. After the war, became a farmer in Lincoln and Mitchell counties, Kansas, and then Dewey and Custer counties, Oklahoma. Married Nancy Emaline Pierce on 03/10/1866 in Hall County, Georgia, and they had at least thirteen children. Died on 12/14/1920 in Blaine County, Oklahoma.

2. Abercrombie, Clement: Enlisted as a private in Company K on 05/21/1864 at Macon, Georgia. Absent without leave beginning 07/27/1864. Last record, sent to Georgia to get a horse with Capt. Bostick on 09/20/1864.

3. Abercrombie [Abercrumbie], John H.: 39-

year-old from Georgia. Born on 12/22/1822 in Lumpkin County, Georgia. Brother of Andrew Jackson Abercrombie and William Wiley Abercrombie. Enlisted as a private in Company H on 03/03/1862 at Athens, Clarke County, Georgia. Transferred to Company C on 01/01/1863. On furlough of indulgence beginning 02/18/1864. Last record, sent to Georgia to get a horse with Capt. Bostick on 09/20/1864. Other records indicate he was wounded during the war and died in a hospital in Richmond, Virginia, on 09/30/1864. Married Mary Catherine Peck on 10/08/1846 in Lake City, Columbia County, Florida, and they had eight children.

4. Abercrombie, William H.: 29-year-old farmer. Enlisted as a private in Company C on 09/28/1861 at Athens, Clarke County, Georgia. Admitted to Institute Hospital, Richmond, Virginia, on 09/22/1862 with chronic bronchitis. Furloughed to Georgia beginning 10/01/1862. Given a medical discharge for chronic pulmonary disease on 09/20/1863. Described as having a dark complexion, dark hair, gray eyes, and being 6 feet tall.

5. Abercrombie [Abercrumbie], William Wiley.: 17-year-old from Georgia. Born on 04/16/1846 in Lumpkin County, Georgia. Brother of Andrew Jackson Abercrombie and John H. Abercrombie. Enlisted as a private in Company C on 01/16/1864 at Hamilton's Crossing, Virginia. Sent to Georgia to get a horse with Lt. Sinquefield under Special Order No. 27 from corps headquarters on 02/23/1864. On furlough of indulgence beginning 09/02/1864. Last record, sent to Georgia to get a horse with Capt. Bostick on 09/20/1864. Married Elizabeth Armon Brookshire on 08/28/1861 in Lumpkin County and they had eleven children. After the war, became a merchant in Leavenworth County, Kansas, and then a farmer in Mitchell and Payne counties, Oklahoma.

6. Adams, C.H.: Enlisted as a private in Company K on 02/23/1862 at Camp Maynard, Georgia. Admitted to C.S.A. General Hospital in Charlottesville, Virginia, with debility on 03/04/1863. Returned to duty on 03/05/1863 without being discharged from the hospital. Buried in Fairlawn Cemetery in Payne County, Oklahoma, on 03/01/1908.

7. Adams, J.T. [J.Y.]: Born in Madison County, Alabama. Enlisted as a private in Company A on 08/17/1861 at Augusta, Georgia. Value of horse $200 and horse equipment $25. Courier to General Magruder in November/December 1861. Last record, detailed as an orderly for Gen. Magruder in 12/1861.

8. Adams, James: Born ca. 1829 in Georgia. Enlisted as a private in Company B on 04/28/1862 at Atlanta, Georgia. Value of horse $175. Furloughed to Georgia for 30 days beginning 12/20/1863. Returned to duty on 01/16/1864. Sent to infirmary/recruiting camp on 03/10/1864. Was surrendered by Gen. Joseph E. Johnston on 04/26/1865. Paroled at Greensboro, North Carolina, on 05/01/1865.

9. Adams [Adam], John T.: 37-year-old. Enlisted as a sergeant in Company K on 02/02/1862 at Camp Maynard, Georgia. Captured on 07/02/1863 at Gettysburg and sent to Fort Delaware Prison. Deserted to the Union army on 08/30/1863. Joined the 3rd Maryland Cavalry on 09/22/1863.

10. Adams [Aidans], S.D.: Farmer from Georgia. Enlisted as a private in Company D on 08/10/1861 at Albany, Georgia. Value of horse $200 and horse equipment $25. Detailed as a courier in 01/1862. Sent home to get a horse in March/April 1863. Sent to infirmary/recruiting camp for horses on 12/08/1863. Sent to Georgia to get a horse with Capt. Bostick on 09/20/1864. Was surrendered by Gen. Joseph E. Johnston on 04/26/1865. Paroled at Greensboro, North Carolina on 05/01/1865.

11. Adams [Adam], Thomas: 20-year-old. Born on 10/20/1841 in Georgia. Enlisted as a private in Company A on 08/17/1861 at Augusta, Georgia. Value of horse $175, and horse equipment $25. Last record dated 09/04/1861. Other records indicate that he died on 01/21/1863.

12. Adams, W.H.: Enlisted as a private in Company D on 08/10/1861 at Albany, Georgia. Value of horse $150 and horse equipment $15, bridle furnished by State of Georgia. Present but convalescent in November/December 1861. Sent to infirmary/recruiting camp for horses on 02/23/1864. Sent to Georgia to get a horse with Capt. Bostick on 09/20/1864. Was surrendered by Gen. Joseph E. Johnston on 04/26/1865. Paroled at Greensboro, North Carolina, on 05/01/1865.

13. Adams, William: Enlisted as a private in Company L on 05/02/1864 at Decatur, Georgia. Last record, absent without leave beginning 05/12/1864.

14. Adcock, J.D.: 30-year-old. Enlisted as a private in Company K on 02/09/1862 at Camp Maynard, Georgia. Last record, returned to his regiment on 02/02/1863.

15. Agerton, Thomas Jefferson: 31-year-old overseer from Waynesboro, Burke County, Georgia. Born on 07/05/1830 in Burke County, Georgia. Enlisted as a private in Company F on 03/25/

1862 at Burke County, Georgia. Value of horse $135. Admitted to C.S.A. General Hospital No. 4, Wilmington, North Carolina, on 05/16/1862 with rubella. Returned to duty on 06/01/1862. Detailed to attend horses at the infirmary/recruiting camp on 08/01/1863. No horse in 04/1864. Admitted to Jackson Hospital, Richmond, Virginia, on 08/17/1864 with chronic diarrhea. Returned to duty on 08/29/1864. Sent to Georgia to get a horse with Capt. Bostick on 09/20/1864. Was surrendered by Gen. Joseph E. Johnston on 04/26/1865. Paroled at Greensboro, North Carolina, on 05/01/1865. After the war, became a farmer in Bethany, Jefferson County, Georgia, and then a general merchandise clerk in Burke County, Georgia. Married Rebecca Elizabeth Ponder ca. 1859 and they had at least eight children. Received a Confederate pension in Burke County, Georgia. Died on 07/18/1915. Buried in the Blythe Methodist Cemetery in Richmond County, Georgia.

16. Ahern, Frank J. [F.L., T.J.]: 18-year-old from Baltimore, Maryland. Enlisted as a private in Company A on 11/01/1862 at Bunker Hill, [West] Virginia. Detailed as a teamster at brigade headquarters 11/15/1863. Was surrendered by Gen. Joseph E. Johnston on 04/26/1865. Paroled at Greensboro, North Carolina, on 05/01/1865. After the war, worked as a brick manufacturer in Baltimore, Maryland. Was married and the father of at least one child.

17. Aiken [Aikin], Francis M.C.: Brick mason from Fulton County, Georgia. Born ca. 1840 in Tennessee. Enlisted as private in Company B on 08/14/1861 at Atlanta, Georgia. Value of horse $200, and horse equipment $5, saddle furnished by State of Georgia. Promoted to Corporal on 03/27/1863. Sent to infirmary/recruiting camp on 08/06/1863. Was surrendered by Gen. Joseph E. Johnston on 04/26/1865. Paroled at Greensboro, North Carolina, on 05/01/1865. After the war, worked as a brick mason in Fulton County, Georgia. He and his wife, Mary, had at least three children.

18. Aiman, Emanuel: 39-year-old carpenter from Holcombe, Burke County, Georgia. Born in 09/1825, possibly in Philadelphia, Pennsylvania. Enlisted as corporal in Company F on 03/25/1862 at Atlanta, Burke County, Georgia. Horse, valued at $600, was killed at Jack's Store (Jack's Shop), Virginia, on 09/22/1863. Received a gunshot wound in the right leg on 08/25/1864 at Ream's Station, Virginia, and sent to a hospital at Weldon, North Carolina. Admitted to Pettigrew General Hospital No. 13 in Raleigh, North Carolina, on 08/28/1864. Furloughed for 60 days beginning 09/05/1864. Was surrendered by Gen. Joseph E. Johnston on 04/26/1865. Paroled at Greensboro, North Carolina, on 05/01/1865. After the war, became a farmer in Montgomery County, Pennsylvania. Married to Jennie. Died after 1910.

19. Alexander, David J.: 27-year-old lawyer from Jefferson County, Georgia. Enlisted as a private in Company F on 03/25/1862 at Burke County, Georgia. Value of horse $150. On sick furlough in Jefferson County, Georgia, September through December 1862. Found medically unfit for service due to tuberculosis. Discharged on 12/16/1862. Described as having a fair complexion, gray eyes, dark hair, and being 6'1½" tall. After the war, became an attorney-at-law in Jefferson County, Georgia. He and his wife, Julia, had at least three children. Died on 09/13/1890. Buried in the Lowery Cemetery in Jefferson County, Georgia.

20. Alexander, D.L.: Enlisted as a lieutenant in Company L. Resigned on 06/03/1863.

21. Alexander, John James: 29-year-old farmer from Jackson County, Georgia. Born on 02/16/1833 in Georgia. Brother-in-law of Jeremiah E. Ritch. Enlisted as a private in Company H on 05/19/1862 at Athens, Clarke County, Georgia. Admitted to hospital 04/01/1863 in Petersburg, Virginia, with pneumonia. Died 10/01/1863 at General Receiving Hospital (also known as Charity Hospital, formerly the Exchange Hotel), Gordonsville, Virginia, of blood poisoning. He and his wife, Ridley, had four children.

22. Alford, Augustus: Overseer from Dougherty County, Georgia. Born ca. 1832 in Hancock County, Georgia. Enlisted as a sergeant in Company D on 08/10/1861 at Albany, Georgia. Value of horse $150 and horse equipment $30. On furlough in November 1862. Died in Hancock County, Georgia, on 12/17/1862. Married Mary E. Thompson in Dougherty County, Georgia, on 04/25/1861.

23. Algers [Alger], Napoleon B.: Farm laborer from Colquitt County, Georgia. Born ca. 1844 in Georgia. Enlisted as a private in Company D on 03/21/1863 at Brownsburg, Virginia. Absent with dismounted men March/April 1863. Admitted to C.S.A. General Hospital, Danville, Virginia, on 04/24/1863 with smallpox. Returned to duty on 05/08/1863. Admitted to Jackson Hospital in Richmond, Virginia, on 08/17/1864. Died on 08/26/1864 from intermittent fever (probably malaria).

24. Allbritten, Isaac G.: 42-year-old farmer from Cobb County, Georgia. Born on 10/04/1820 in Franklin County, Georgia. Enlisted as a farrier* in Company E on 03/22/1862 at Roswell, Georgia. Value of horse $100. Admitted to Winder Hospital, Richmond, Virginia, with rheumatism on 07/22/1862. Listed as a private from January/February 1863. Sent to the infirmary/recruiting camp in March/April 1863. Lost horse and absent without leave beginning 07/08/1863. Last service record September/October 1864, still absent without leave. Other records indicate he was captured in 09/1864 and remained in prison in Ohio until the close of the war. After the war, became a farmer in Blount County, Alabama. Married (1) Juda L. Sewell on 11/25/1841 in Franklin County, Georgia, and they had at least five children (2) Florence Adeline on 09/27/1891 and they had at least two children. Received a Confederate pension from Blount County, Alabama. Died after 1891.

25. Allbritten, James [John] A. [G.A.]: 21-year-old from Newton County, Georgia. Born in 09/1840 in Georgia. Brother of Pleasant and William Allbritten. Enlisted as a private in Company E on 3/22/1862 at Roswell, Georgia. Sent home to get a horse in March/April 1863. Sent to Georgia to get a horse with Lt. Sinquefield under Special Order No. 27 from corps headquarters on 02/23/1864. Admitted to Jackson Hospital, Richmond, Virginia, on 05/23/1864 with a gunshot wound in his thigh. Transferred to Columbia, South Carolina, on 05/27/1864. Sent to Georgia to get a horse with Capt. Bostick on 09/20/1864. Captured and sent to New Bern, North Carolina, on 04/10/1865. Transferred to Hart's Island, New York Harbor. Released on 06/15/1865. Described as having a fair complexion, light hair, blue eyes and being 5'8" tall. After the war, became a farmer in Morgan and Blount counties, Alabama. He and his wife, Emma, had nine children.

26. Allbritten, Pleasant Griffin: 19-year-old from Georgia. Born in 05/1842 in Georgia. Brother of James and William Allbritten. Enlisted as a private in Company E on 03/22/1862 at Roswell, Georgia. Value of horse $175. Admitted to Winder Hospital, Richmond, Virginia, on 07/22/1862 with debility. Returned to duty 07/24/1862. Sent home to get a horse with Lt. Sinquefield under Special Order No. 27 from corps headquarters on 02/23/1864. Last record September/October 1864, sent to Georgia to get a horse with Capt. Bostick on 09/20/1864. After the war, worked as a farm laborer in Cobb County, Georgia, and then as a farmer in Cullman County, Alabama. He and his wife, Missouri (or Manervia), had at least five children. Received a Confederate pension from Cullman County, Alabama. Died in 05/1930.

27. Allbritten, William A.: 19-year-old from Georgia. Brother of John and Pleasant Allbritten. Enlisted as a private in Company E on 03/22/1862 at Roswell, Georgia. Value of horse $150. Admitted to Winder Hospital, Richmond, Virginia, with typhoid fever on 07/22/1862. Returned to duty on 09/04/1862. Lost horse in 09/1862. Listed as corporal beginning January/February 1863. Reduced in rank by court-martial and fined one month's pay on 04/22/1863. Sent home to get a horse on 11/12/1863. Sent to Georgia to get a horse on 03/12/1864 by Special Order No. 36. Last record September/October 1864, sent to Georgia to get a horse with Capt. Bostick on 09/20/1864. After the war, lived in Jefferson County, Alabama. Received a Confederate pension from Jefferson County, Alabama.

28. Allen, Charles H.: Farmer from Clarke County, Georgia. Born ca. 1837 in Oglethorpe County, Georgia. Enlisted as a private in Company H on 02/27/1862 at Athens, Clarke County, Georgia. Sent to Georgia to get a horse with Lt. Sinquefield under Special Order No. 27 from corps headquarters on 02/23/1864. On sick furlough in Georgia beginning 09/12/1864. Was surrendered by Gen. Joseph E. Johnston on 04/26/1865. Paroled at Greensboro, North Carolina, on 05/01/1865. After the war, became a farm laborer in Clarke County, Georgia. Died after 1880.

29. Allen, Ira: Saddler from Richmond County, Georgia. Born ca. 1835 in New Jersey. Enlisted as a corporal in Company A on 08/17/1861 at Augusta, Georgia. Value of horse $250, and horse equipment $40. Appointed sergeant 05/01/1862, but was listed as a private after March 1863. Home on special furlough beginning 11/01/1863. Sent to infirmary/recruiting camp on 01/20/1864 and 08/01/1864 Was surrendered by Gen. Joseph E. Johnston on 04/26/1865. Paroled at Greensboro, North Carolina, on 05/01/1865.

30. Allen, John [Jack] C.: From Richmond County, Georgia. Born ca. 1845 in Georgia. Enlisted as a private in Company A on 06/10/1863 at Augusta, Georgia. Sent to infirmary/recruiting camp on 11/13/1863. Wounded in action at Ream's Station, Virginia, on 08/23/1864 and sent to hospital. Was surrendered by Gen. Joseph E. Johnston on 04/26/1865. Paroled at Greensboro, North Carolina, on 05/01/1865. After the war, worked as a butcher in Augusta, Georgia. Died after 1880. Was

---

*A farrier was the one who put the horse shoes on the horses.

married to Matilda and was the father of at least seven children.

31. Allexander, Jo. Newton: 18-year-old student from Gwinnett County, Georgia. Born on 07/26/1844 in Gwinnett County, Georgia. Enlisted as a private in Company E on 03/17/1863 at Brownsburg, Virginia. Sent home to get a horse with Lt. Sinquefield under Special Order No. 27 from corps headquarters on 02/23/1864. Admitted to Confederate States Hospital, Petersburg, Virginia, on 06/01/1864. Transferred to Raleigh, North Carolina, on 06/14/1864. Last record September/October 1864, sent to Georgia to get a horse with Capt. Bostick on 09/20/1864. After the war, became a farmer in McLennan County, Texas. Married Mary Elizabeth Patterson, possibly in Gwinnett County, Georgia (or Eagle Springs, Texas), and they had at least six children. Died on 12/03/1931. His widow applied for a Confederate pension in McLennan County, Texas.

32. Allison, Noah: 24-year-old farmer from Frogtown District, Lumpkin County, Georgia. Born on 11/29/1838 in Habersham County, Georgia. Enlisted as a private in Company B on 04/28/1862 at Atlanta, Georgia. Transferred to Company G in May/June 1862. Captured at Mine Run while on picket duty on 11/26/1863. Sent to the Old Capitol Prison, Washington, D.C. Transferred to Point Lookout, Maryland, on 12/03/1863. Exchanged on 02/24/1865. After the war, became a farmer in White County, Georgia. Married (1) Elizabeth after 1860 and (2) Mary L. O'Kelley on 10/19/1880. Was the father of at least four children and one stepchild. Applied for a Confederate pension in White County, Georgia. Died on 04/20/1924 in White County, Georgia.

33. Anderson, Edward A.: Miller from Hall County, Georgia. Born ca. 1844 in Georgia. Brother of Milus W. Anderson. Enlisted as a private in Company C on 08/01/1861 at Athens, Clarke County, Georgia. Died of disease in a hospital at Camp Marion, Yorktown, Virginia, on 02/17/1862. His father, A.C. Anderson, received his back pay, as he was not survived by a wife or children.

34. Anderson, John M.: From Lumpkin County, Georgia. Born ca. 1840 in Georgia. Enlisted as a private in Company C on 08/01/61 at Athens, Clarke County, Georgia. Sent home to get a horse with Lt. Sinquefield under Special Order No. 27 from corps headquarters on 02/23/1864. Captured at Hanover Court House, Virginia, on 05/29/1864. Sent to White House, Virginia, and then transferred to Elmira Prison, New York, on 07/12/1864. Died of remittent fever (probably malaria) at Elmira Prison on 10/17/1864. Buried in the Woodlawn Cemetery at Elmira, New York.

35. Anderson, Miles A. [Milus W.]: Carpenter from Hall County, Georgia. Born ca. 1837 in North Carolina. Brother of Edward A. Anderson. Enlisted as a private in Company C on 08/01/1861 at Athens, Clarke County, Georgia. Died on 09/16/1861 at Yorktown, Virginia. Married Martha Jane Johnson on 05/04/1859 and they had two children.

36. Anderson, Nicholas M.: From Georgia. Born ca. 1840. Enlisted as a private in Company C on 08/01/1861 at Athens, Clarke County, Georgia. Furloughed for 25 days beginning 07/1862. Sent home to get a horse on 11/10/1863. Returned to duty on 01/30/1864. Detailed as a teamster for Capt. Lumpkin beginning 07/10/1864. Sent to Georgia to get a horse with Capt. Bostick on 09/20/1864. Was surrendered by Gen. Joseph E. Johnston on 04/26/1865. Paroled at Greensboro, North Carolina, on 05/01/1865.

37. Anderson, Robert Branch: 35-year-old physician from Cobb County, Georgia. Born on 07/27/1826 in Virginia. Enlisted as a private in Company E on 03/15/1862 at Roswell, Georgia. Value of horse $175. Absent, sick in March/April 1862. Transferred from Lynchburg to General Hospital, Farmville, Virginia, on 07/30/1862. Returned to duty on 08/05/1862. Admitted to Winder Hospital, Richmond, Virginia, on 09/10/1862 with chronic rheumatism. Furloughed for 30 days beginning 10/08/1862. Lost horse and absent without leave beginning 07/08/1863. Last record September/October 1864, sent to Georgia to get a horse with Capt. Bostick on 09/20/1864. After the war, became a physician in Cobb County, Georgia. Married Sara Jane Frazen before 1860 and they had eight children. Died on 11/29/1904 in Alabama.

38. Anderson, William E. [B.]: 19-year-old from Lumpkin County, Georgia. Born on 11/12/1841 in Georgia. Enlisted as a private in Company C on 08/01/1861 at Athens, Clarke County, Georgia. Detailed as a teamster for Capt. Lumpkin beginning in 08/1862. Sent to infirmary/recruiting camp in November/December 1863. On furlough of indulgence beginning 02/18/1864. Wounded when a minié ball struck the back of his right hand, which caused the loss of his little finger and ring finger on 06/23/1864. Admitted to Jackson Hospital, Richmond, Virginia, on 06/23/1864. Transferred to Huguenot Springs Hospital on 07/08/1864. Wounded on 07/22/1864. Admitted to hospital in Richmond, Virginia, on 07/23/1864. Last record September/October 1864, on wounded furlough since 07/21/1864. After the war, became a farmer in

Lumpkin County, Georgia. Married ca. 1865. He and his wife, Mary, had fourteen children. Received a Confederate pension in Lumpkin County, Georgia, until 1907.

39. Anderson, Young J. [Wise J.]: Attorney, born in Savannah, Georgia ca. 1830. Enlisted as a private in Company A on 08/17/1861 at Augusta, Georgia. Value of horse $350, and horse equipment $49. Appointed captain and acting quartermaster in 09/1861. Resigned 05/07/1863. Died before end of war and was buried in the Memory Hill Cemetery in Baldwin County, Georgia.

40. Andrews, Thomas: Born ca. 1840. Enlisted as a private in Company F on 05/09/1862 at Burke County, Georgia. Had no horse. Transferred to Capt. Wilcox's 20th Georgia Infantry 09/1862.

41. Angle, Valentine: 17-year-old. Enlisted as a private in Company K on 01/24/1863 at Camp Maynard, Georgia. Deserted on 03/06/1863. Deserted again during an engagement at Culpeper Court House on 09/13/1863. Took the Oath at Bermuda Hundred, Virginia, on 10/22/1863. Sent to Philadelphia.

42. Anthony, Walter H: Druggist clerk from Augusta, Georgia. Born ca. 1842. Enlisted as a private in Company A on 08/17/1861 at Augusta, Georgia. Value of horse $150, and horse equipment $20. Furloughed for 25 days beginning 02/10/1862. No horse in March/April 1863. Admitted to Jackson Hospital, Richmond, Virginia, on 08/21/1863 with debilities. Furloughed for 30 days beginning 09/02/1863. Admitted to Winder Hospital in Richmond, Virginia, on 10/08/1863 with acute rheumatism. Transferred to Jackson Hospital, Richmond, Virginia, on 01/21/1864 with hepatitis. Furloughed for 40 days beginning 01/29/1864. Had no horse in 04/1864. Admitted to Jackson Hospital, Richmond, Virginia, on 05/27/1864 with stricture of the urethra. Admitted to Jackson Hospital, Richmond, Virginia, on 07/31/1864 with stricture of the urethra. Returned to duty on 09/13/1864. Sent to Georgia to get a horse with Capt. Bostick on 09/20/1864. Admitted to Jackson Hospital, Richmond, Virginia, on 11/16/1864. Last record, returned to duty on 12/04/1864.

43. Appling [Apling], Edward Jones: 26-year-old farmer from Cobb County, Georgia. Born on 11/08/1834 in Georgia. Enlisted as a private in Company B on 08/14/1861 at Atlanta, Georgia. Value of horse $175, and horse equipment $4, saddle furnished by State of Georgia. Promoted to sergeant on 03/15/1862. Sent home to get a horse on 03/06/1863. Lost horse on 11/13/1863. Sent to Georgia to get horses on 11/16/1863. Sent to Georgia to get a horse with Lt. Sinquefield under Special Order No. 27 from corps headquarters on 02/23/1864. Last record September/October 1864, sent to Georgia to get a horse with Capt. Bostick on 09/20/1864. Other records indicate he was shot through the neck at Fayetteville, North Carolina, and was paralyzed on the right side of his body from the wound. After the war, became a merchant at Atlanta, Fulton County, Georgia. Applied for a Confederate pension in Fulton County, Georgia, in 1907. Died after 1910.

44. Archer, John H: Merchant clerk from Augusta, Georgia. Born in South Carolina ca. 1841. Brother of Thomas B. Archer. Enlisted as a private in Company A on 04/17/1864 at Decatur, Georgia. Last record September/October 1864, sent to Georgia to get a horse with Capt. Bostick on 09/20/1864. After the war, worked in a livery stable in Fulton, County, Georgia, and was married to Jenny.

45. Archer, Thomas B: Livery worker from Augusta, Georgia. Born in South Carolina ca. 1837. Brother of John H. Archer. Enlisted as a lieutenant in Company A on 08/17/1861 at Augusta, Georgia. Value of horses, $300 and $200. Value of horse equipment $40 and $25. Furloughed beginning 01/20/1862. Promoted to captain on 05/26/1862. Admitted to General Hospital No. 4, Richmond, Virginia, on 10/23/1863 with remittent fever (probably malaria). Absent on sick leave on 04/01/1864. Wounded on 06/24/1864. Admitted to General Hospital No. 4, Richmond, Virginia, on 07/02/1864 with a gunshot wound to the left thigh involving the sciatic nerve. Furloughed for 60 days beginning 06/27/1864. Absent without leave beginning 08/27/1864. Paroled 05/27/1865 at Augusta, Georgia. After the war, owned a livery business in Fulton County, Georgia. Was married to Laura.

46. Armistead [Armisted, Armstead], David A.: Carpenter from Fulton, County, Georgia. Born ca. 1830. Enlisted as a private in Company B on 08/14/1861 at Atlanta, Georgia. Value of horse $200 and horse equipment $4, saddle furnished by the State of Georgia. Detailed as a teamster beginning 07/01/1862. Without a horse in January/February/1863 until 03/15/1863. Sent to infirmary/recruiting camp on 12/01/1863. Sent to Georgia to get a horse with Capt. Bostick on 09/20/1864. Was surrendered by Gen. Joseph E. Johnston on 04/26/1865. Paroled at Goldsboro 05/01/1865. After the war, worked as a carpenter and a farmer in Fulton County, Georgia. Was married to Margaret and was the father of at least one child. Applied for a

Confederate pension in Cobb County, Georgia. Died after 1900.

47. Arnold, Charles M.: Enlisted as a corporal in Company B on 08/14/1861 at Atlanta, Georgia. Value of horse $225 and horse equipment $11, saddle furnished by the State of Georgia. Furloughed for 25 days beginning 01/20/1862. Transferred to Company D on 05/01/1862. Sent home to get a horse in January/February 1863. Furnished C.J. Blundell as a substitute and was discharged on 05/10/1863.

48. Arnold, Givens W.: Merchant from Alpharetta, Milton County, Georgia. Born ca. 1826 in Georgia. Enlisted as a lieutenant in Company E on 03/22/1862 at Roswell, Georgia. Value of horses $250 and $225. Resigned 07/14/1862 due to total inability to endure camp life. He and his wife, Jane E., had at least five children.

49. Arnold, Stephen T. B.: Farm laborer from Jackson County, Georgia. Born ca. 1841 in Georgia. Enlisted as a private in Company H on 03/04/1862 at Athens, Clarke County, Georgia. Discharged 08/22/1862.

50. Arrington, Owen H.: Farmer from Jefferson County, Georgia. Born ca. 1836 in Jefferson County, Georgia. Enlisted as a private in Company F on 05/06/1862 at Burke County, Georgia. Value of horse $250. On sick furlough in Jefferson County, Georgia, in September/December 1862. Detailed to sub-enrolling office in Savannah, Georgia, due to disability on 02/04/1863. Admitted to Winder Hospital, Richmond, Virginia, on 10/11/1863. Sent to Georgia on horse detail with Capt. Bostick on 09/20/1864. Was surrendered by Gen. Joseph E. Johnston on 04/26/1865. Paroled at Greensboro 05/01/1865.

51. Asbury [Asberry, Asburry], Jesse: 28-year-old farmer from Worth County, Georgia. Born on 04/14/1833 in Taliaferro County, Georgia. Enlisted as a private in Company D on 08/10/1861 at Albany, Georgia. Detailed to pack hay beginning 02/26/1864. Detailed as a guard on 04/15/1864. Sent to Georgia to get a horse with Capt. Bostick on 09/20/1864. Was surrendered by Gen. Joseph E. Johnston on 04/26/1865. Paroled at Greensboro 05/01/1865. After the war, became a farmer in Dougherty and Taliaferro counties, Georgia. After that, became a landlord in Taliaferro County, Georgia. Married Sarah Frances Watson ca. 1856 and they had nine children. Died in 1905.

52. Ash, Henry N.: Born ca. 1839 in Georgia. Brother of John N. Ash and Thomas J. Ash. Enlisted as a private in Company B on 04/28/1862 at Atlanta, Georgia. Died at Camp Meadow near Richmond, Virginia, on 06/28/1862 of typhoid fever.

53. Ash, John N.: 21-year-old farmer from White County, Georgia. Born on 03/04/1841 in Georgia. Brother of Henry N. Ash and Thomas J. Ash. Enlisted as a private in Company G on 06/12/1862 at Atlanta, Georgia. Received a gunshot wound in his right thigh from a minié ball on 06/25/1864. Admitted to Jackson Hospital in Richmond, Virginia, on 06/26/164. Last record, furloughed for 30 days from Jackson Hospital to go to Walhalla, South Carolina, beginning 09/09/1864. After the war, became a farmer in White County, Georgia. Married Sarah Salvina McAfee on 12/02/1866 and they had at least two children. Died on 11/14/1880.

54. Ash [Ashe], Thomas J.: 23-year-old from White County, Georgia. Born in 12/1838 in Georgia. Brother of Henry N. Ash and John N. Ash. Enlisted as a private in Company H on 03/19/1862 at Athens, Clarke County, Georgia. Admitted to General Hospital No. 16, Richmond, Virginia, on 10/31/1862. Returned to duty on 11/10/1862. Deserted and took the Oath on 03/22/1864 at Chattanooga, Tennessee. Described as having a light complexion, brown hair, hazel eyes, and being 6'1" tall. After the war, became a farmer in Cleveland, White County, Georgia. He and his wife, Elizabeth, had eight children. Died after 1910.

55. Ashe [Ash], N.D.: Enlisted as a private in Company L on 04/19/1864 at Decatur, Georgia. Absent without leave beginning 05/12/1864. Last record September/October 1864, still absent without leave.

56. Ashfield, J.M.: House carpenter from Fort Gaines, Clay County, Georgia. Born ca. 1841 in Georgia. Enlisted as a private in Company D on 08/10/1861 at Albany, Dougherty County, Georgia. Value of horse $150, and horse equipment $25. Convalescent, sick in November/December 1861. Admitted to General Hospital, Petersburg, Virginia, on 03/08/1862 with chronic rheumatism. Returned to duty on 04/03/1863. Given a medical discharge on 04/25/1863.

57. Atterberry [Atteberry, Atterbeury, Atterbury], Darling C.: Overseer from Burke County, Georgia. Born ca. 1841 in Georgia. Enlisted as a private in Company F on 03/25/1862 at Burke County, Georgia. Value of horse $115. Promoted to corporal before July/August 1862. Promoted to sergeant in March/April 1864. Detailed as a provost guard on 03/15/1864 at Hanover Junction, Virginia. Lost horse ca. last of July 1864. Last record September/October 1864, sent to Georgia to get a horse with Capt. Bostick on 09/20/1864. Married Julia Tabb Mullis on 09/12/1861 in Burke County, Georgia.

58. Atterberry, James D.: 51-year-old overseer from Burke County, Georgia. Born 09/25/1814 in South Carolina. Listed on a roster of Company F published in *Roster of the Confederate Soldiers of Georgia, 1861–1865.* No service records in Cobb's Legion. After the war, lived in Screven County, Georgia. He and his wife, Eliza, had at least one child. Died 07/10/1871. Buried in the Brock Methodist Church Cemetery in Screven County, Georgia.

59. Autry [Awtry], H.S.: Resident of Georgia. Enlisted as a private in Company H on 02/16/1862 at Lynchburg, Virginia. Sent to Georgia to get a horse with Lt. Sinquefield under Special Order No. 27 from corps headquarters on 02/23/1864. Deserted and dropped from the rolls in March/April 1864.

60. Avera, Thomas: Resident of Georgia. Enlisted as a private in Company H on 04/03/1862 at Atlanta, Georgia. Sent to Georgia to get a horse with Lt. Sinquefield under Special Order No. 27 from corps headquarters on 02/23/1864. Admitted to Jackson Hospital, Richmond, Virginia, on 08/13/1864 with fever and diarrhea. Last record, furloughed to Quitman, Georgia, from Jackson Hospital, Richmond, Virginia, for 30 days beginning 08/15/1864.

61. Averell, Alfred M.: 23-year-old printer from Richmond County, Georgia. Born in 1838 in Georgia. Enlisted as a private in 1st Georgia Infantry, Company D, on 03/18/1861. Discharged at Warrington, Florida, in 1861. Enlisted as a sergeant in Cobb's Legion Cavalry, Company I on 02/27/1862 in Augusta, Richmond County, Georgia. Value of horse $240. Given a medical discharge on 09/16/1862 due to carditis. Described as being 23 years of age, having a fair complexion, hazel eyes, light hair, and being 5' 8" tall. After the war, worked as a printer in Richmond County, Georgia. Married Adelaide A. Ingalls on 06/22/1863 in Richmond County, Georgia.

62. Avery, Archer: From Columbia County. Born ca. 1845 in Columbia County, Georgia. Enlisted as a private in Company A on 10/01/1864 at Augusta. Served previously as a private for six months in the State Guards, Company A, 10th Georgia Calvary. Was surrendered by Gen. Joseph E. Johnston on 04/26/1865. Paroled at Greensboro 05/01/1865. After the war, became a druggist at Atlanta, Georgia. Died before 1880.

63. Avery, John: Listed on a roster of Company C in *These Men She Gave: The Civil War Diary of Athens, Georgia.* No service records in Cobb's Legion.

64. Avery, Thomas: Listed on a roster of Company C in *These Men She Gave: The Civil War Diary of Athens, Georgia.* No service records in Cobb's Legion.

65. Badger, Ralph Bostwick.: 26-year-old dentist from Atlanta, Fulton County, Georgia. Born on 02/02/1836 in DeKalb County, Georgia. Enlisted as a private in Company B on 04/19/1862 at Atlanta, Georgia. Value of horse $160 and horse equipment $7. Sent to General Hospital No. 14 in Richmond, Virginia, 09/1862 due to sickness. Furloughed to go to Atlanta, Georgia, beginning 10/17/1862. No horse since January 1, 1863. Detailed to duty with the Navy Department at Atlanta, Georgia, on 10/15/1863 by order of the secretary of war. Last record September/October 1864, absent without leave since July 1864; however his pension application stated he served until the end of the war. He married (1) Helen M. Pettis on 07/08/1861 in Fulton County, Georgia. After the war, moved to Orange County, Florida. He married ca. 1877 (2) Fannie and they had at least two children. Received a Confederate pension in Leesburg, Lake County, Florida, in 1907. Died in 1908, and is buried in the Lone Oak Cemetery in Leesburg, Florida.

66. Bailey, James [John] H.: 20-year-old from Georgia. Enlisted as a private in Company B on 03/31/1862 at Atlanta, Georgia. Value of horse $150. Detailed as teamster beginning 05/27/1862. Was present on last record, September/October 1864.

67. Bailey, James Holcomb.: Student from Dougherty County, Georgia. Born ca. 1844 in South Carolina. Enlisted as a private in Company D on 08/10/1861 at Albany, Georgia. Value of horse $225 and horse equipment $25, furnished by State of Georgia. Listed as a corporal in November/December 1861. Listed as a private in May/June 1862. Sent home to get a horse in March/April 1863. Lost horse on 08/13/1863. Admitted to Henningsen Hospital, Richmond, Virginia, on 10/27/1863 due to debility and anemia of two months duration from intermittent fever (probably malaria). Furloughed to Augusta, Georgia, for 30 days beginning 11/23/1863. Sent to Jackson Hospital, Richmond, Virginia, on 01/15/1864 with pneumonia. Died on 02/17/1864 of typhoid fever at Jackson Hospital, Richmond, Virginia.

68. Bailey, Oscar W.: 29-year-old farmer from Oglethorpe County, Georgia. Born on 11/01/1832 in Fairfax County, Virginia. Enlisted as a private in Company A on 08/17/1861 at Augusta, Georgia. On horse detail to Georgia in November/December 1863. Sent to infirmary/recruiting camp on 08/27/1864. Was still at infirmary/recruiting camp on last record, September/October 1864. Married (1) Mary Octavia Louisa Young on 06/03/1857 in Virginia. Married (2) Amelia Eloise Wesson on 05/30/1896 in Columbia County, Georgia. After the war, worked on a farm in Bartow, Hamilton County, Florida, and was the father of at least five children. Was the adjutant of the Stewart Camp, No. 155, United Confederate Veterans in Jasper County, Florida. Received a Confederate pension from Hamilton County, Florida. Died on 10/24/1917 in Hamilton County, Florida.

69. **Bailey, Samuel W.:** Student from Clarke County, Georgia. Born ca. 1841 in Georgia. Enlisted as a private in Company C on 08/01/1861 at Athens, Clarke County, Georgia. Promoted to corporal in November/December 1863. Sent to infirmary/recruiting camp on 12/01/1863. Was surrendered by Gen. Joseph E. Johnston on 04/26/1865. Paroled at Greensboro, North Carolina, on 05/01/1865. After the war, became a dairyman in Clarke County, Georgia. He and his second wife, Lou, had at least two children.

70. **Bailey, William H.:** 21-year-old. Born ca. 1841. Enlisted as a private in Company I on 04/19/1862 at Atlanta, Georgia. Discharged on 05/27/1862.

71. **Baker, Augustus C.:** Merchant from Hall County, Georgia. Born ca. 1835 in Georgia. Enlisted as a private in Company H on 02/25/1862 at Athens, Clarke County, Georgia. Listed as a sergeant in May/June 1862. Sent to Georgia to get a horse with Lt. Sinquefield under Special Order No. 27 from corps headquarters on 02/23/1864. Sent to Georgia to get a horse with Capt. Bostick on 09/20/1864. Captured near Cheraw, South Carolina, probably on 03/01/0865. Paroled, but not exchanged, at Cheraw, South Carolina, on 03/05/1865. Married Amanda E. Reeves in Lumpkin County, Georgia, on 01/13/1860 and they had at least two children. Died before 1870. His widow applied for a Confederate pension in White County, Georgia.

72. **Bale [Bail], James A.:** Clerk from Fulton County, Georgia. Born ca. 1829 in South Carolina or Georgia. Enlisted as a private in Company B on 08/14/1861 at Atlanta, Georgia. Value of horse $225 and horse equipment $30. Promoted to sergeant on 04/15/1862. Promoted to lieutenant in Smith's Legion Cavalry on 02/01/1863. After the war, became a general merchandiser and then a grocer and lived in Floyd County, Georgia. He and his wife, Naome, had at least two children. Possibly died on 12/15/1900.

73. **Ball, B.A.:** 19-year-old. Enlisted as a private in Company K 02/06/1862 at Camp Maynard, Georgia. Captured at Upperville, Loudoun County, Virginia, 06/21/1863 and sent to the Old Capitol Prison in Washington, D.C. Deserted and took the Oath. Paroled and sent to Philadelphia on 06/25/1863.

74. **Ball, J.C.:** Resident of Madison, Morgan County, Georgia. Enlisted as a private in Company G. Admitted to C.S.A. General Hospital, Farmville, Virginia, on 06/11/1863 with an ulceration of his left arm, resulting from blistering. Last record, furloughed from hospital for 60 days beginning 08/06/1863.

75. **Barber, Matthew S.:** Farmer from Newton County, Georgia. Born ca. 1840 in Georgia. Enlisted as a private in Company B on 05/02/1862 at Atlanta, Georgia. Value of horse $285. Given a medical discharge 07/13/1862. He became a farmer in Indian Springs, Butts County, Georgia. He and his wife, Ugene, had at least three children.

76. **Barden, C.H.:** Enlisted as a private in Company K on 02/08/1862 at Camp Maynard, Georgia. Sent to infirmary/recruiting camp on 01/17/1864. Died 03/09/1864.

77. **Barker, Elijah Henry Washington:** 33-year-old farmer. Born on 06/01/1830 in Walton County, Georgia. Enlisted as a private in Company B on 02/26/1864 at Hamilton's Crossing, Virginia. Sent to infirmary/recruiting camp on 06/08/1864. Lost horse on 07/01/1864. Still at infirmary/recruiting camp on last record, September/October 1864. After the war, became a farmer in Monroe County, Georgia, and then in Buncombe, Walton County, Georgia. Married Elizabeth Ann Hayes on 08/22/1858 and they had at least six children. Applied for a Confederate pension in Walton County, Georgia. Died on April 15, 1910, in Walton County, Georgia.

78. **Barksdale:** About 80 years old, with grandsons in Cobb's Legion Cavalry. Mentioned by Capt. Francis Edgeworth Eve's "Address to the Ladies Memorial Association," Athens, Georgia, April 26, 1893, Hargrett Library, University of Georgia. Killed in battle on 09/13/1862 at Middletown (Quebec Schoolhouse), Maryland. No service records in Cobb's Legion.

79. **Barksdale, Green B.:** Planter from Dougherty County, Georgia. Born ca. 1815 in Hancock, Georgia. Enlisted as a corporal in Company D on 08/10/1861 at Albany, Georgia. Value

of horse $150 and horse equipment $35. Promoted to sergeant before 05/07/1862. Killed in battle and horse killed in battle on 09/13/1862 at Middletown (Quebec Schoolhouse), Maryland. His wife, Cecilia, received his back pay. Married Celia Connell on 10/24/1839 in Greene County, Georgia, and they had at least one child.

80. **Barksdale, Samuel B.:** On a roster of Company D compiled by Glen Spurlock. No service records in Cobb's Legion.

81. **Barnwell, Thomas E.:** Blacksmith. Born ca. 1822 in Georgia. Enlisted as a private in Company B on 08/10/1861 at Atlanta, Georgia. Given a medical discharged on 09/03/1861. He married Catherine Jemima before 1850 and they had at least eight children.

82. **Barrett, James Riley:** Farmer from Lumpkin County, Georgia. Born ca. 1841. Enlisted as a private in Company C on 08/01/1861 at Athens, Clarke County, Georgia. Admitted to Institute Hospital, Richmond, Virginia, on 07/22/1862 with typhoid fever. Furloughed to Athens, Georgia, on 10/01/1862. Sent to infirmary/recruiting camp in 09/1863. Admitted to C.S.A. General Hospital, Charlottesville, Virginia, on 07/05/1863 with a gunshot wound. Returned to duty on 08/15/1863. Listed in Company H from November/December 1863. Sent to Georgia to get a horse with Capt. Bostick on 09/20/1864. Was surrendered by Gen. Joseph E. Johnston on 04/26/1865. Paroled at Greensboro, North Carolina, on 05/01/1865. After the war, became a farmer in Lumpkin County, Georgia. He and his wife, Betsy, had at least five children.

83. **Barrett, Lewis Walton [H.]:** Farmer from Lumpkin County, Georgia. Born ca. 1842 in South Carolina. Brother of Thomas R. Barrett. Enlisted as a private in Company H on 03/03/1862 at Athens, Clarke County, Georgia. Captured at Beverly's Ford, Virginia, on 06/09/1863 and sent to the Old Capitol Prison in Washington, D.C. Patient at Winder Hospital, Richmond, Virginia, in 07/1863. Detailed as a courier in 10/1863. Sent to Georgia to get a horse with Lt. Sinquefield under Special Order No. 27 from corps headquarters on 02/23/1864. Absent with leave beginning 08/01/1864. Deserted and took the Oath at Military Prison, Louisville, Kentucky, on 08/29/1864. Described as having a light complexion, dark hair, blue eyes, and being 5'11" tall. Sent north of the Ohio River. After the war, became a farmer in Lumpkin County, Georgia. He and his wife, Amanda, had at least five children. Died after 1870. His widow applied for a Confederate pension in Fulton County, Georgia.

84. **Barrett, Thomas R. [Richard T.]:** Born ca. 1841 in South Carolina. Brother of Lewis W. Barrett. Enlisted as a private in Company C on 08/01/1861 (or 09/28/1861) at Athens, Clarke County, Georgia. No horse in March/April 1863. Killed at Hunterstown, Pennsylvania, on 07/02/1863. Buried at the National Cemetery in Gettysburg, Pennsylvania. His widow, Elizabeth, received his back pay.

85. **Barrett, Walton [Walter] T.:** Student from Lumpkin County, Georgia. Born ca. 1845 in South Carolina. Enlisted as a private in Company C on 08/01/1861 at Athens, Clarke County, Georgia. Died on 04/22/1862 at Suffolk, Virginia.

86. **Barwick, George Ira:** 19-year-old student/farmer from Emanuel County, Georgia. Born on 04/1/1843 in Emanuel County, Georgia. Enlisted as a private in Company F on 05/09/1862 at Burke County, Georgia. Value of horse $190. Sent home on sick furlough for 60 days in September/October 1862. Received a gunshot wound to chest and left lung at Brandy Station, Virginia, on 06/09/1863. Admitted to Chimborazo Hospital, Richmond, Virginia, on 06/16/1863. Furloughed for 60 days beginning 06/25/1863. Absent without leave beginning 12/01/1863. Declared unfit for duty in January/February 1864. Returned to duty in March/April 1864. On sick furlough for 60 days beginning 09/01/1864. Was surrendered by Gen. Joseph E. Johnston on 04/26/1865. Paroled at Greensboro, North Carolina, on 05/01/1865. After the war, became a farmer in Emanuel County, Georgia. Member of the state legislature from Emanuel County, Georgia, in 1898. Married Jane Rountree on 11/16/1865 in Emanuel County, Georgia, and they had at least seven children. Stricken with paralysis at Atlanta, Georgia, and died on 12/19/1898. Buried at the Canochoee Primitive Baptist Church Cemetery in Emanuel County, Georgia. His widow applied for a Confederate pension in Emanuel County, Georgia.

87. **Bassett, Jefferson:** Enlisted as a private in Company A on 09/01/1861 at Richmond, Virginia. Value of horse $160, and horse equipment $20. Appointed sergeant on 05/01/1862. Promoted to lieutenant on 11/23/1862. Admitted to C.S.A. General Hospital in Charlottesville, Virginia, with a gunshot wound on 06/29/1863. Returned to duty on 08/14/1863 without a hospital discharge. Absent on detached service beginning 11/12/1863. Sent to infirmary/recruiting camp in 04/1864. Was surrendered by Gen. Joseph E. Johnston on 04/26/1865. Paroled at Greensboro, North Carolina, on 05/01/1865.

88. **Bassford, Charles E.:** From Augusta, Geor-

gia. Brother of Solomon Lambert Bassford. Born ca. 1842 in Georgia. Enlisted as a private in Company A on 08/17/1861 at Augusta. Value of horse $200, and horse equipment $40. Wounded at Little Washington, Virginia, on 11/12/62. Admitted to General Hospital No. 4, Richmond, Virginia, on 11/12/1862 and furloughed for 30 days beginning 11/18/1862. Sent to infirmary/recruiting camp in 08/1864. Sent to Georgia to get a horse with Capt. Bostick on 09/20/1864. Was surrendered by Gen. Joseph E. Johnston on 04/26/1865. Paroled at Greensboro, North Carolina, on 05/01/1865. After the war, worked as a brick-maker at Augusta, Georgia. Married Laura King on 01/17/1869 in Cobb County, Georgia, and they had at least five children. Died on 03/14/1884 in Richmond County, Georgia.

89. Bassford [Basford], Solomon L.: 22-year-old from Georgia. Born in Georgia on 11/20/1839. Brother of Charles Edward Bassford. Enlisted as a private in Company I on 02/27/1862 at Augusta, Georgia. Value of horse $200. Horse killed in action at Little Washington, Virginia, 11/08/1862. Captured at Upperville, Virginia, on 06/21/1863 and sent to Old Capitol Prison, Washington, D.C. Paroled on 06/25/1863. Sent to infirmary/recruiting camp on 12/20/1863. Surrendered by Gen. Joseph E. Johnston on 04/26/1865. Paroled at Greensboro, North Carolina, on 05/01/1865. After the war, became a farmer in Columbia County, Georgia. Married Cordelia Tippie Knox on 12/21/1860 in Columbia County, Georgia, and they had seven children. Died in 11/1875. His widow, Cordelia, applied for a Confederate pension in McDuffie County, Georgia.

90. Bates, A.J.: 20-year-old from Mississippi. Enlisted as a sergeant in Company K on 02/06/1863 at Camp Maynard, Georgia. Last record September/October 1864, sent to Georgia to get a horse with Capt. Bostick on 09/20/1864.

91. Bates, James: Enlisted as a private in Company K on 02/17/1863 at Camp Maynard, Georgia. Admitted to Episcopal Church Hospital, Williamsburg, Virginia, on 10/25/1861 with intermittent fever (probably malaria). Returned to duty on 11/16/1861. (The hospital date is before Company K was organized. Perhaps the hospital date is wrong.) Deserted on 03/23/1863.

92. Bates, William N.: Born ca. 1839. Enlisted as a private in Company H on 07/09/1864 at Stony Creek, Virginia. Last record September/October 1864, sent to Georgia to get a horse with Capt. Bostick on 09/20/1864.

93. Baugh, Andrew T.: Born ca. 1842 in Georgia. Brother of Reuben T. and Scott L. Baugh. Enlisted as a private in Company E on 04/09/1862 at Lawrenceville, Georgia. Value of horse $200 and horse equipment $30. Paroled at City Point, Virginia, on 11/16/1862 but date and place of capture not stated. Sent home to get a horse in March/April 1863. Promoted to lieutenant on 10/09/1863. Sent to Georgia to get a horse with Capt. Bostick on 09/20/1864. Last record, a requisition for forage dated 11/20/1864. Other records indicate that he was a captain by March 1865. After the war, worked as a farm laborer and then a store clerk in Gwinnett County, Georgia.

94. Baugh, Reuben P.: From Georgia. Born ca. 1839 in Georgia. Brother of Andrew T. Baugh and Scott L. Baugh. Enlisted as a private in Company E on 04/09/1862 at Lawrenceville, Georgia. Value of horse $225 and horse equipment $30. Horse killed in action at Stevensburg, Virginia, on 02/17/1863. Sent to Georgia to get a horse with Lt. Sinquefield under Special Order No. 27 from corps headquarters on 02/23/1864. Last record, on furlough beginning 09/02/1864. After the war, became a farmer in Gwinnett County, Georgia. Married Evaline Strickland before 1870 and they had at least one child. Died in Dallas, Texas.

95. Baugh, Scott L.: Born ca. 1843 in Georgia. Brother of Andrew T. Baugh and Reuben P. Baugh. On a roster of Company E compiled by Glen Spurlock. No service records in Cobb's Legion. After the war, worked as a farm laborer in Gwinnett County, Georgia, and then as a farmer in Walton County, Georgia. Married (1) Martha (2) Phidella M. and was the father of at least four children.

96. Baxter, Daniel C.: 22-year-old clerk from Fulton County, Georgia. Born on 03/02/1839 in Gwinnett County, Georgia. Enlisted as a private in Company B on 08/14/1861 at Atlanta, Georgia. Value of horse $175 and horse equipment $6, saddle furnished by the State of Georgia. Detailed as hospital orderly beginning 06/01/1862. Sent to infirmary/recruiting camp on 10/20/1863. Lost horse on 05/10/1864. Last record, captured at Trevilian Station, Virginia, on 06/11/1864. Died in 1864 in Virginia. Buried in the Suwanee Methodist Church Cemetery in Gwinnett County, Georgia.

97. Bedell, Ethelbert Penn: Clerk from Floyd County, Georgia. Born ca. 1831 in Georgia. Enlisted as a private in Company C on 08/01/1861 at Athens, Clarke County, Georgia. Detailed as a courier on 10/15/1861. Sent home on furlough in 12/1861. Discharged on 08/19/1862. He and his wife, Mary E., had at least four children. Died before 1870.

98. Bell, M.C.: 24-year-old. Enlisted as a corporal in Company K on 01/16/1862 at Camp Maynard, Georgia. Returned to his regiment on 02/17/1863.

99. Bell, Madison M.: Born on 06/25/1836. Enlisted as a private in Company C on 08/01/1861 at Athens, Clarke County, Georgia. Home on sick furlough beginning 12/01/1861. Last record, 01/1862 on sick furlough. After the war, became state comptroller general in Fulton County, Georgia, and then a lawyer in Fulton County, Georgia. Married Mary C. Cox on 05/13/1869 in Banks County, Georgia, and they had at least four children. Died on 08/19/1896 at Atlanta, Georgia. Buried in Oakland Cemetery.

100. Bell, Marlin [Mahlon] M.: 32-year-old miner from Lumpkin County, Georgia. Born on 03/16/1827 in Wilkes County, Georgia. Enlisted as a private in Company C on 08/15/1861 at Athens, Clarke County, Georgia. Detailed as a teamster beginning 06/10/1861. Lost horse on 03/20/1863. Last record, on horse detail to Georgia with Capt. Bostick beginning 09/20/1864. After the war, became a farmer in Lumpkin County, Georgia. Married (1) Huldah Early before 1850 and they had at least two children. Married (2) Huldah Dover on 08/21/1881 in Lumpkin County, Georgia, and they had at least eight children. Died on 02/28/1905 in Forsyth County, Georgia. His widow applied for a Confederate pension in Forsyth County, Georgia.

101. Bennett, Daniel: Farmer from Emanuel County, Georgia. Enlisted as a private in Company L on 12/15/1862 at Burke County, Georgia. Sent to Georgia to get a horse with Lt. Sinquefield under Special Order No. 27 from corps headquarters on 02/23/1864. Last record September/October 1864, sent to Georgia to get a horse with Capt. Bostick on 09/20/1864.

102. Bennett, George W.: Resident of Virginia. Enlisted as a private in Company K on 02/08/1862 at Camp Maynard, Georgia. Admitted to Winder Hospital, Richmond, Virginia, on 09/13/1863 with a gunshot wound. Returned to duty 10/05/1863. Horse valued at $400 killed in battle at Culpeper, Virginia, on 10/13/1863. Sent to Georgia to get a horse with Lt. Sinquefield under Special Order No. 27 from corps headquarters on 02/23/1864. Last record, appointed sergeant on 10/27/1864.

103. Bennett, James A.: 36-year-old. Enlisted as a lieutenant in Company A on 09/01/1861 at Augusta, Georgia. Value of horse $150 and horse equipment $24. Transferred to Company B before May/June 1862. Furloughed from hospital in Richmond, Virginia, for 30 days beginning 12/12/1862. Transferred to Company I before January/February 1863. Sent to infirmary/recruiting camp on 12/09/1863. Was surrendered by Gen. Joseph E. Johnston on 04/26/1865. Paroled at Greensboro, North Carolina, on 05/01/1865.

104. Bennett, John W. [J.H.]: 24-year-old. Born in 1837 in Georgia. Enlisted as a private in Company A on 09/01/1861 at Augusta, Georgia. Only service record dated November/December 1861. Died before 1880.

105. Beverly, Joseph J.: Planter from Dougherty County, Georgia. Born ca. 1820 in North Carolina. Listed on a roster of Cobb's Legion Cavalry, Company D, published in *The History of Dougherty County*, but not with the *Civil War Soldiers and Sailors System*. Service records are for the 15th Battalion, Georgia Cavalry (State Guards). No service records in Cobb's Legion. Married Roseann Cochran before 1846 and they had at least six children.

106. Bird [Byrd], John P.M.: Resident of Georgia. Enlisted as a private in Company E on 03/22/1862 at Roswell, Georgia. Value of horse $125. Wounded on 07/10/1862. Lost horse on 04/10/1863. Last record September/October 1864, states he was absent wounded since 07/10/1862.

107. Bird, William H: Born ca. 1841. Enlisted as a private in Company C on 03/27/1862 at Roswell, Georgia. Transferred to Company I. Died in 1864.

108. Bishop, John J.: Teacher from Hall County, Georgia. Born ca. 1835 in Georgia. Enlisted as a private in Company C on 08/01/1861 at Athens, Clarke County, Georgia. Discharged on 07/27/1862 at Richmond, Virginia. After the war, became a schoolteacher in Dawson County, Georgia. Married (1) Misiner and they had two children. Married (2) Lucindy and they had six children. Applied for a Confederate pension in Dawson County, Georgia. Died before 1900.

109. Blackburn, Josiah [Joseph] E.: 20-year-old student from Hall County, Georgia. Born in 05/1842 in Georgia. Enlisted as a private in Company C on 08/01/1861 at Athens, Clarke County, Georgia. Transferred to Company H after March/April 1863. Sent to infirmary/recruiting camp on 08/01/1863. Admitted to General Hospital, Scottsville, Virginia, on 07/11/1863. Last record, September/October 1864, on sick furlough in Georgia since 08/30/1864. After the war, worked as a farm laborer and then as a painter in Lumpkin County, Georgia. Married Nancy Hall prior to 1866 and they had eight children. Applied for a Confederate pension in Nimblewill, Lumpkin County, Georgia. Died ca. 1914. His widow applied for a Confederate pension in Lumpkin County, Georgia.

110. Blackwell, David Glenn: Farmer from Hall County, Georgia. Born ca. 1821 in Spartanburg, South Carolina. Enlisted as a private in Company H on 02/25/1862 at Athens, Clarke County, Georgia. Admitted to General Hospital, Liberty, Virginia, in 01/1863. Died on 01/31/1863 of chronic diarrhea. He and his wife, Mary, had seven children. His widow applied for a Confederate pension in Milton, Cherokee, and White counties, Georgia.

111. Blackwell, James M.: Policeman from Fulton County, Georgia. Enlisted as a private in Company G on 03/16/1864 at Atlanta, Georgia. Furloughed to go to Georgia beginning 09/28/1864. Last record, admitted to C.S.A. General Hospital No. 3, Greensboro, North Carolina, in 04/1865. He and his wife, E.C., had at least one child.

112. Blackwell, Josiah Sanford [A.S.]: Farmer from Lumpkin County, Georgia. Born ca. 1840 in Georgia. Enlisted as a private in Company C on 08/01/1861 at Athens, Clarke County, Georgia. Sent to infirmary/recruiting camp on 12/24/1863. Furloughed for 25 days beginning 01/18/1864. Promoted to sergeant in September/October 1864. Last record September/October 1864, on horse detail to Georgia with Capt. Bostick beginning 09/20/1864. After the war, became a farmer in Hall County, Georgia. Married Sara Elizabeth Stephens on 01/24/1860 and they had at least six children. Died after 1880.

113. Blanchard, Uriah: 23-year-old from Columbia County, Georgia. Enlisted as a private in Company A on 08/17/1861 at Augusta, Georgia. Value of horse $190, and horse equipment $25. Sent to a hospital in Williamsburg, Virginia, from Yorktown, Virginia, and died there on 12/08/1861. His mother, Rebecca Blanchard, received his back pay, as he was not survived by his father, a wife, or children.

114. Blount, A.H.: Student from Burke County, Georgia. Born ca. 1842 in Georgia. Enlisted as a private the 2nd Georgia Infantry, Company D at Waynesboro, Georgia, on 04/19/1861. Enlisted in Cobb's Legion Cavalry, Company L, on 04/19/1862 at Yorktown, Virginia. (His record says "in exchange of W.A. Blount," but both men have records in Cobb's Legion Cavalry after that date.) Admitted to General Hospital No. 9, Richmond, Virginia, on 02/04/1864. Returned to duty on 02/15/1864. Appointed corporal on 06/01/1864. Last record September/October 1864, sent to Georgia to get a horse with Capt. Bostick on 09/20/1864.

115. Blount, William Augustus: Student from Burke County, Georgia. Born on 10/24/1841 in Jefferson County, Georgia. Enlisted as a private in 2nd Georgia Infantry, Company D, on 04/19/1861 at Waynesboro, Georgia. Enlisted in Cobb's Legion Cavalry, Company L, on 08/18/1863 at Waynesboro, Georgia. (His record says "in exchange of A.H. Blount," but both men have records in Cobb's Legion Cavalry after that date.) Was surrendered by Gen. Joseph E. Johnston on 04/26/1865. Paroled at Greensboro, North Carolina, on 05/01/1865. After the war, became a farmer in Burke County, Georgia. Married Georgia Cates on 11/08/1866 and they had at least five children. Died on 04/29/1904 in Burke County, Georgia. Buried in the Waynesboro Magnolia Cemetery in Burke County, Georgia.

116. Blundell, C.J.: Resident of Virginia. Enlisted as a private in Company D on 05/01/1863 at Buckingham, Virginia, as a substitute for Charles M. Arnold. Sent to Georgia to get a horse with Lt. Sinquefield under Special Order No. 27 from corps headquarters on 02/23/1864. Mortally wounded in action at Trevilian Station 06/12/1864. Admitted to C.S.A. General Hospital, Charlottesville, Virginia, 06/15/1864 with a gunshot wound in right thigh. Ball was not extracted. Died at hospital 06/25/1864. Buried at the University of Virginia Confederate Cemetery at Charlottesville, Virginia.

117. Boatright, Reuben: 31-year-old farmer from Bryan County, Georgia. Born on 12/28/1830 in Emanuel County, Georgia. Enlisted as a private in Company F on 03/25/1862 at Burke County, Georgia. Discharged on 07/18/1862. After the war, became a farmer and then a spectacle peddler in Emanuel County, Georgia. Married (1) Julia Ann Sconyers in Emanuel County, Georgia, on 01/06/1850 and (2) Sarah. Was the father of at least six children. Died on 09/15/1913 in Emanuel County, Georgia.

118. Boggs, Aaron H.: Farmer from Pickens County, South Carolina. Born ca. 1832 in South Carolina. Enlisted as a private in Company H on 03/03/1862 at Athens, Clarke County, Georgia. Provided Burwell G. Rives as a substitute on 03/01/1863. After the war, became a farmer in Loudon County, Tennessee. He and his wife, Sarah E., had at least eight children.

119. Boggs, Milton Alonza: Farmer from Jackson County, Georgia. Born in 05/1839 in Jackson County, Georgia. Enlisted as a private in the Troup Artillery on 05/12/1862. Transferred to Cobb's Legion Cavalry, Company C, on 03/19/1862 at Athens, Clarke County, Georgia. Sent to infirmary/recruiting camp in November/December 1863. Sent home to get a horse with Lt. Sinquefield under Special Order No. 27 from corps headquarters on

02/23/1864. Sent to Georgia with Capt. Bostick to get a horse on 09/20/1864. Was surrendered by Gen. Joseph E. Johnston on 04/26/1865. Paroled at Greensboro, North Carolina, on 05/01/1865. After the war, became a farmer in Jackson County, Georgia. Married Julianne Cash on 10/21/1859 in Jackson County, Georgia. Died prior to 1870. Believed to be buried in the Stone Family Cemetery, Hwy. 334, near Center, Jackson County, Georgia.

120. Boler, Bennett: Enlisted as a private in Company B on 08/14/1861 at Atlanta, Georgia. Value of horse $140. Died at Suffolk, Virginia, on 03/28/1862. Married Nancy Harris on 11/20/1830 in Elbert County, Georgia.

121. Bolling, James: Born ca. 1838. Enlisted as a private in Company B on 05/06/1862 at Atlanta, Georgia. Value of horse $190. Detailed to Quarter Master Department beginning July/August 1862 as acting quartermaster sergeant. Furloughed for 30 days beginning 02/21/1863 to go to Ringold, Georgia. Last record, pay voucher dated 06/04/1864.

122. Bonds, Flavius A.: 25-year-old from Monroe, Walton County, Georgia. Born on 09/22/1836. Enlisted as a private in Company E on 04/09/1862 at Lawrenceville, Georgia. Value of horse $150. Last record dated 04/22/1862. After the war, became a farmer in Gwinnett County, Georgia. Married Martha Cranford in Walton County, Georgia, and they had at least ten children. Died on 11/27/1912 at Godwinsville, Dodge County, Georgia. Buried at Woodlawn Cemetery, Eastman, Dodge County, Georgia.

123. Bone, Joseph H.: Painter from Jackson County, Georgia. Born ca. 1841 in Georgia. Brother of Willis C. Bone. Enlisted as a private in Company E on 04/09/1862 at Lawrenceville, Georgia. Value of horse $150. Last record dated 04/22/1862.

124. Bone, Willis C.: 17-year-old in Georgia. Born in 07/1843 in Madison County, Georgia. Brother of Joseph H. Bone. Enlisted as a private in Company C on 08/01/1861 at Athens, Clarke County, Georgia. Present, but convalescent and unable to perform duty for a long time in November/December 1861. Detailed to the Quarter Master Department at Milford Station, Virginia, beginning 02/01/1864. On sick furlough beginning 07/01/1864. Detailed on guard duty in 12/1864. Was surrendered by Gen. Joseph E. Johnston on 04/26/1865. Paroled at Greensboro, North Carolina, on 05/01/1865. After the war, became a painter in Jefferson County, Kentucky, and then a resident of the Confederate Soldiers Home in Oldham County, Kentucky. Married twice. (2) Cassandra. Was the father of at least two children.

125. Booker, F.: 18-year-old. Enlisted as a private in Company K on 01/23/1862 at Camp Maynard, Georgia. Deserted 03/14/1862.

126. Born, Daniel M.: 25-year-old from Georgia. Born on 03/15/1837 in Georgia. Enlisted as a private in Company E on 04/09/1862 at Lawrenceville, Georgia. Value of horse $225 and bridle $7. Elected lieutenant on 08/01/1864. Was surrendered by Gen. Joseph E. Johnston on 04/26/1865. Paroled at Greensboro, North Carolina, on 05/01/1865. After the war, worked as a farm laborer in Gwinnett County, Georgia, and then as a dry goods merchant in Suwanee, Gwinnett County, Georgia. Married Florence Cloudon on 06/18/1859 in Gwinnett County, Georgia, and they had at least nine children. Died on 06/15/1891. Buried at the Suwanee Cemetery in Gwinnett County, Georgia.

127. Bostick, Samuel D.: Farm laborer from Dougherty County, Georgia. Born ca. 1840 in Jefferson County, Georgia. Enlisted as a corporal in Company D on 08/01/1861 at Albany, Georgia. Value of horse $150 and horse equipment $25, furnished by State of Georgia. Listed as a corporal in November/December 1861, as a sergeant on 05/07/1862, and as a lieutenant in November/December 1862. On sick furlough in Georgia beginning 02/21/1862. Horse killed in battle on 09/13/1862 at Middletown (Quebec Schoolhouse), Maryland. Admitted to C.S.A. General Hospital in Charlottesville, Virginia, with a wound to the hip on 09/23/1862. Transferred to Winder Hospital, Richmond, Virginia, on 10/10/1862. Promoted to captain on 01/01/1864. On leave for 24 days in 04/1864. Admitted to Winder Hospital, Richmond, Virginia, on 08/16/1864 with a diagnosis of diarrhea. Returned to duty on 09/15/1864. Led detachment to procure fresh horses from Georgia for the command by order of Gen. Lee on 09/20/1864. Was surrendered by Gen. Joseph E. Johnston on 04/30/1865. Paroled at Greensboro, North Carolina, on 05/01/1865. After the war, became a farmer in Worth County, Georgia, and then a schoolteacher in Dougherty County, Georgia. Married Mary Ann Claudia Wilder on 04/12/1866 and they had at least three children.

128. Boston, Jerome M.: 26-year-old. Enlisted as a sergeant in Company E on 03/15/1862 at Roswell, Georgia. Transferred as a private to Phillips Legion on 11/01/1863.

129. Bothwell S.W.: From Dooly, Georgia. Born ca. 1843 in Georgia. Enlisted as a private in Company A on 04/17/1864 at Decatur, Georgia. Sent to hospital at Kittrell Springs, North Carolina, on 08/25/1864. Last service record September/October 1864, lists him as absent without leave since 10/25/1864. There is no record of his being captured. After the war, became a grocer in Augusta, Georgia. Died ca. 1883.

130. Bowen, Isaac: Resident of Georgia. Enlisted as a private in Company H on 09/16/1863 at Culpeper, Virginia. Sent to Georgia to get a horse with Lt. Sinquefield under Special Order No. 27 from corps headquarters on 02/23/1864. Listed in April/September 1864 as a corporal. Last record September/October 1863, sent to Georgia to get a horse with Capt. Bostick on 09/20/1864.

131. Bowen, James R: 23-year-old musician. Born in Macon, Mississippi. Enlisted as a bugler in Company A on 08/17/1861 at Augusta, Georgia. Discharged from Company A when elected 1st lieutenant of Company H on 02/10/1863. His discharge describes him as having a fair complexion, dark eyes, black hair, and being 5'7" tall. Enlisted as a lieutenant in Company H on 02/15/1863 at Camp Maynard, Georgia. Admitted to the Confederate States Hospital in Petersburg, Virginia, on 09/24/1863. Sent to C.S.A. General Hospital in Charlottesville, Virginia, on 10/28/1863 with a fistula. Transferred to Hospital No. 4 in Richmond on 11/03/1863 due to attacks of mental derangement. Resigned on 11/24/1863 due to the fistula and mental derangement. After the war, lived in Mississippi and was the father of at least four children.

132. Bowers, Charles E.: Enlisted as a private in Company L on 09/14/1863 at Waynesboro, Virginia. On last record, September/October 1864, was listed as absent without leave since 09/15/1863.

133. Bowie, Charles Lee: Farmer from Cobb County, Georgia. Born in 08/1837 in South Carolina. Brother of John W. and William H.H. Bowie. Enlisted as a private in Company B on 08/14/1861 at Atlanta, Georgia. Value of horse $180 and horse equipment $4, saddle furnished by the State of Georgia. Promoted to sergeant in November/December 1862. Sent to Georgia to get a horse with Lt. James H. Johnson on 04/14/1863. Horse killed in action at Upperville, Virginia, on 06/21/1863. Sent to Georgia to get a horse with Lt. Sinquefield under Special Order No. 27 from corps headquarters on 02/23/1864. Admitted to hospital in Wilson, North Carolina, on 07/30/1864. Was surrendered by Gen. Joseph E. Johnston on 04/26/1865. Paroled at Greensboro, North Carolina, on 05/01/1865. After the war, worked as a traveling salesman and lived in Walton and Fulton counties, Georgia. Married Nancy F. Mobley on 01/17/1871 in Walton County, Georgia, and they had at least fourteen children. His widow applied for a Confederate pension in Fulton County, Georgia.

134. Bowie, John W.: Farmer from Cobb County, Georgia. Born ca. 1836 in South Carolina. Brother of Charles Lee and William H.H. Bowie. Enlisted as a corporal in Company B on 08/14/1861 at Atlanta, Georgia. Value of horse $160 and horse equipment $7.50, saddle furnished by the State of Georgia. On sick furlough beginning 01/20/1862. Returned to duty on 04/10/1862. Promoted to sergeant in November/December 1863. Lost horse on 11/11/1863. Sent to Georgia to get a horse on 11/13/1863. Sent to infirmary/recruiting camp on 05/26/1864. Last record, he received pay for his horse at Lynchburg, Virginia, on 12/22/1864. After the war, became a farmer in Newton and then Whitfield County, Georgia. Married Sarah A. Hamilton on 08/18/1868 in Newton County, Georgia, and they had at least one child. Applied for a Confederate pension in Whitfield County, Georgia.

135. Bowie, William H.H.: Student from Cobb County, Georgia. Born ca. 1844 in South Carolina. Brother of Charles Lee and John W. Bowie. Enlisted as a private in Company B on 05/01/1862 at Atlanta, Georgia. Value of horse $165. Admitted to C.S.A. General Hospital at Danville, Virginia, with measles on 05/16/1862. Returned to duty on 05/28/1862. Detailed at infirmary/recruiting camp on 02/23/1864. Sent to Georgia to get a horse with Capt. Bostick on 09/20/1864. Was surrendered by Gen. Joseph E. Johnston on 04/26/1865. Paroled at Greensboro, North Carolina, on 05/01/1865. After the war, became a student and then a druggist in Collins County, Texas. He and his wife, Mary, had at least one child.

136. Bowman, George Grover: 21-year-old from Hall County, Georgia. Born on 10/21/1838 in Gwinnett County, Georgia. Enlisted as a private in Company B on 08/01/1861 at Athens, Clarke County, Georgia. Sent to infirmary/recruiting camp on 02/23/1864. Sent to Georgia to get a horse with Capt. Bostick on 09/20/1864. Was surrendered by Gen. Joseph E. Johnston on 04/26/1865. Paroled at Greensboro, North Carolina, on 05/01/1865. After the war, became a farmer in Sugar Hill, Gwinnett County, Georgia. Married Rose Ann Light in Georgia in the late 1860s and they had ten children. Applied for a Confederate pension in Gwinnett County, Georgia. Died on 10/02/1918. Buried at the New Prospect Cemetery in Gwinnett County, Georgia.

137. Boyd, James William Walter: 22-year-old. Born on 11/08/1839 in Wilkes County, Georgia. Enlisted as a private in Company A on 05/01/1862 at Augusta, Georgia. Last service record dated 01/02/1863. Furnished Edward Pearce Morris as a substitute on 02/01/1863. After the war, worked as a farmer in Wilkes County, Georgia. Married Annie Elizabeth Fortson on 04/05/1865 in Wilkes County, Georgia, and they had at least five children. Died after 1910. His widow applied for a pension in Wilkes County, Georgia.

138. Boyd, Robert J.: 21-year-old student from Jefferson County, Georgia. Born on 11/25/1840 in Jefferson County, Georgia. Enlisted as a sergeant in Company F on 03/25/1863 at Burke County, Georgia. Value of horse $150. Sent to infirmary/recruiting camp on 10/27/1863. Was present on last record, September/October 1864. After the war, became a farmer and then an editor in Jefferson County, Georgia. Married Lavica Jordan on 10/25/1866 in Jefferson County, Georgia. Died on 10/30/1882. Buried in the Louisville Cemetery in Burke County, Georgia

139. Boyd, William: Clerk from Jefferson County, Georgia. Born ca. 1829. Enlisted as a lieutenant in Company F on 03/25/1863 at Burke County, Georgia. Value of horses $250 and $200 and horse equipment $70. Admitted to Wayside Hospital, Richmond, Virginia, on 08/16/1863. Died on 11/04/1863 near Stevensburg, Virginia.

140. Bradford, J.A.: On a roster of Company A compiled by the Muster Roll Commission. Enlisted November 7, 1861. No service records in Cobb's Legion.

141. Bradley, Henry Stiles.: Physician from Madison County, Georgia. Born ca. 1836 in Georgia. Enlisted as a private in Company C on 08/01/1861 at Athens, Clarke County, Georgia. Appointed assistant surgeon on 06/02/1862. Captured at Madison County (Jack's Shop), Virginia, on 09/22/1863 while attending to the wounded on the field. Continued to minister to the wounded after captured until sent to the Old Capitol Prison in Washington, D.C., and then transferred to Fort McHenry, Maryland, on 11/16/1863. Sent to City Point on 11/22/1863. Last record, signed receipt for pay on 07/18/1864. After the war, became a physician in Tadmore, Hall County, Georgia, and then a minister in Gainesville, Hall County, Georgia. Married Susan Celina Jackson on 05/16/1858 or 05/23/1858 in Jackson County, Georgia, and they had at least four children. Died on 10/18/1895 in Wilkes County, Georgia. His widow received a Confederate pension in Barrow County, Georgia, in 1919.

142. Brady, George W.: Farm laborer from Thompson District, Hall County, Georgia. Born in Georgia ca. 1820. Enlisted as a private in Company C on 09/03/1862 at Bunker Hill, [West] Virginia, as a substitute for Reuben J. Pierce. Sent to infirmary/recruiting camp on 10/27/1863. Was surrendered by Gen. Joseph E. Johnston on 04/26/1865. Paroled at Greensboro, North Carolina, on 05/01/1865. After the war, worked as a farm laborer in Thompson District, Hall County, and then a farmer in Hall County, Georgia. Married (1) Mary (2) Martha (3) Sarah. Was the father of at least four children. Applied for a Confederate pension in Hall County, Georgia.

143. Brent, James H.: 20-year-old clerk from Atlanta, Georgia. Born in Tennessee. Enlisted as a corporal in Company B on 08/14/1861 at Atlanta, Georgia. Value of horse $200, and horse equipment $25. Promoted to sergeant in November/December 1862. Lost horse on 03/15/1863. Detailed as scout 11/13/1863. Lost horse and captured at Stafford County, Virginia 02/27/1864. Sent to Old Capitol Prison in Washington, D.C., 03/05/1864. Admitted to hospital at Old Capitol Prison from 03/22/1864 until 04/06/1864 with erysipelas (an acute, infectious, streptococcus disease which causes inflammation of the skin). Transferred to Fort Delaware Prison on 06/17/1864. There is no record of his taking the Oath or being released from Fort Delaware. Since he could not be identified on a later U.S. census, it is presumed that he may have died at Fort Delaware.

144. Brian, Aaron: Student from Hall County, Georgia. Born in Hall County, Georgia, in 1845. Brother of Ezekiel, James, and William Burr Brian. Enlisted as a private in Company H on 03/03/1862 at Athens, Clarke County, Georgia. Died at Camp Meadow, Virginia, 07/12/1862.

145. Brian, Ezekiel: 21-year-old student from Hall County, Georgia. Born on 12/07/1840 in Georgia. Brother of Aaron, James, and William Burr Brian. Enlisted as a private in Company H on 03/03/1862 at Athens, Clarke County, Georgia. Last record, May/June 1862. Married Rachel L. Simpson on 10/21/1886. Died on 11/21/1918 in Hall County, Georgia.

146. Brian, James: Student from Hall County, Georgia. Born ca. 1844 in Georgia. Brother of Aaron, Ezekiel, and William Burr Brian. Enlisted as a private in Company H on 03/03/1862 at Athens, Clarke County, Georgia. Died at Camp Meadow, Virginia, 07/08/1862.

147. Brian, William Burr: 25-year-old from Hall County, Georgia. Born in Georgia on 01/1/1837. Brother of Aaron, Ezekiel, and James Brian. Enlisted as a private in Company H on 03/03/1862

at Athens, Clarke County, Georgia. Sent to Georgia to get a horse in 11/1863. Last record September/October 1864, sent to Georgia to get a horse with Capt. Bostick on 09/20/1864. After the war, worked as an agent and then as a farmer in Hall County, Georgia. Died in Hall County, Georgia, on 06/27/1905.

148. Brinson, N.M.: 37-year-old farmer from Emanuel County, Georgia. Born on 10/8/1825 in Emanuel County, Georgia. Enlisted as a lieutenant in Company B. Transferred to Company L. Resigned on 06/10/1863 due to bad health. After the war, worked as a farmer in Emanuel County, Georgia. Married Elizabeth Durden on 01/11/1849 in Emanuel County, Georgia, and they had at least eight children. Died on 04/02/1878 in Emanuel County, Georgia.

149. Broadway, James T.: Resident of Georgia. Enlisted as a private in Company D on 08/10/1861 at Albany, Georgia. Value of horse $175 and horse equipment $25. Wounded in battle and captured at Crampton's Pass on 09/13/1862. Paroled 09/14/1862. Died in 09/1862. His back pay and bounty of $50 was paid to his father, William Broadway.

150. Broadway, William A.: Possibly a physician from Mitchell County, Georgia. Enlisted as a private in Company D on 08/10/1861 at Albany, Georgia. Value of horse $175 and horse equipment $25. Sent to Georgia to get a horse with Lt. Sinquefield under Special Order No. 27 from corps headquarters on 02/23/1864. Admitted to Pettigrew Hospital, Raleigh, North Carolina, on 09/17/1864 due to sickness. Returned to duty on 10/08/1864. Was surrendered by Gen. Joseph E. Johnston on 04/26/1865. Paroled at Greensboro, North Carolina, on 05/01/1865.

151. Bromley, George W.: On a roster of Company I compiled by Glen Spurlock. No service records in Cobb's Legion Cavalry.

152. Brooks, Alonzo A.: Student from Jackson County, Georgia. Born in Jackson County, Georgia, in 1841. Brother of Cicero and Thomas Brooks. Enlisted as a private in Company H on 03/28/1862 at Athens, Clarke County, Georgia. Admitted to Jackson Hospital, Richmond, Virginia, with wounds on 12/10/1863. Diagnosed with typhoid fever on 12/15/1863. Furloughed for 30 days from beginning 01/06/1864. Last record September/October 1864, sent to Georgia to get a horse with Capt. Bostick on 09/20/1864. After the war, became a farmer in Jackson County, Georgia, and then an Atlanta City policeman in Fulton County, Georgia. Married Laura Louisa Simmons in 1860, possibly in Hall County, Georgia, and they had at least five children. His widow applied for a Confederate pension in Fulton County, Georgia.

153. Brooks, Cicero C.: 34-year-old farmer from Jackson County, Georgia. Born on 10/10/1827 in Jackson County, Georgia. Brother of Alonzo and Thomas Brooks. Enlisted as a sergeant in Company H on 03/03/1862 at Athens, Clarke County, Georgia. Elected lieutenant on 06/18/1862. Killed in action on 07/02/1863 (his tombstone says 07/03/1863) at Hunterstown, Pennsylvania, during a countercharge against Gen. George Armstrong Custer and his troops. Buried in the National Cemetery, Gettysburg, Pennsylvania, and reinterred on 08/21/1871 at Laurel Grove Cemetery, Gettysburg Section, Lot 853, Savannah, Georgia. Married on 08/24/1848 in Jackson County, Georgia, to Sarah Ann King and they had two children. His widow, Sarah Ann Brooks, received his back pay. She applied for a Confederate pension in Jackson County, Georgia.

154. Brooks, John N.: Born ca. 1845 in Monroe County, Georgia. Enlisted as a corporal in Company E on 03/15/1862 at Roswell, Georgia. Value of horse $175. Listed as a private beginning January/February 1863. Captured at Beverly's Ford, Virginia, on 06/09/1863. Sent to the Old Capitol Prison in Washington, D.C. Paroled on 06/25/1863 and sent to Camp Lee Hospital near Richmond, Virginia. Exchanged before 08/04/1863. Sent to Georgia to get a horse with Lt. Sinquefield under Special Order No. 27 from corps headquarters on 02/23/1864. Last record September/October 1864, sent to Georgia to get a horse with Capt. Bostick on 09/20/1864. After the war, became a schoolteacher in Coweta County, Georgia. Married ca. 1867 to Rosa Lee Parks and they had at least six children. Died in 10/1899 in Pike County, Georgia.

155. Brooks, Thomas D.: 27-year-old farmer from Jackson County, Georgia. Born in Jackson County, Georgia, on 03/12/1835. Brother of Alonzo and Cicero Brooks. Enlisted as a private in Company H on 03/28/1862 at Athens, Clarke County, Georgia. Captured at Beverly's Ford, Virginia, 06/09/1863. Sent to the Old Capitol Prison in Washington, D.C. Paroled 06/25/1863. Sent to infirmary/recruiting camp on 12/10/1863. Listed as corporal in 09/1864. Was surrendered by Gen. Joseph E. Johnston on 04/26/1865. Paroled at Greensboro, North Carolina, on 05/01/1865. After the war, became a farmer in Jackson County, Georgia. Married (1) Augusta Ann Simmons on 01/31/1861 in Hall County, Georgia (2) Martha C. Long on 12/30/1866. Was the father of at least ten children. Applied for a Confederate pension in Jackson County, Georgia. Died on 01/01/1916. Buried at the Pendergrass Baptist Cemetery in Jackson County, Georgia.

156. Brookshear, Green W.: Born ca. 1847 in Georgia. Enlisted as a private in Company C on 04/01/1864 at Chesterfield, Georgia. Last record September/October 1864, sent to Georgia to get a horse with Capt. Bostick on 09/20/1864. After the war, worked as a farm laborer in Lumpkin County, Georgia, then as a farmer in Gaddistown, Union County, Georgia, and then as a farmer in Grant County, Oklahoma. Married (1) Fanny Montgomery in Lumpkin County, Georgia, prior to 1868 and they had at least five children. Married (2) Virginia. Died after 1920.

157. Broom, James: Merchant from Richmond County, Georgia. On a roster of Company I compiled by Glen Spurlock. No service records in Cobb's Legion Cavalry. He and his wife, Helen, had at least one child.

158. Broome, Joseph: Resident of Georgia. Enlisted as a private in 1st Georgia Infantry, Company I, on 03/18/1861. Transferred as a private to Cobb's Legion Cavalry, Company I, on 02/13/1862 at Winchester, Virginia. Value of horse $200. Sent to infirmary/recruiting camp in November/December 1863. Admitted sick to hospital in Powhatan County, Virginia, on 06/15/1864. Was surrendered by Gen. Joseph E. Johnston on 04/26/1865. Paroled at Greensboro, North Carolina, on 05/01/1865.

159. Brown, Allen: Enlisted as a private in Company L on 12/15/1862 at Burke County, Georgia. Last record, absent without leave beginning 02/01/1863.

160. Brown, Henry: 23-year-old day laborer from Richmond County, Georgia. Enlisted as a private in Company F on 03/25/1862 at Burke County, Georgia. On sick furlough in Burke County, Georgia, in September/October 1862. Detailed as a teamster in March/April 1863. Discharged on 05/17/1863.

161. Brown, James F.: Enlisted as a private in Company L on 12/15/1862 at Burke County, Georgia. Last record, absent without leave from 02/01/1863.

162. Brown, Jesse T.: 28-year-old from Georgia. Enlisted as a private in Company B on 03/26/1862 at Atlanta, Georgia. Value of horse $140. Detailed as a teamster beginning 05/26/1862. Lost horse on 11/20/1862. Sent to Georgia to get a horse on 02/21/1863. Listed in Company G from November/December 1863. Sent to Georgia to get a horse with Lt. Sinquefield under Special Order No. 27 from corps headquarters on 02/23/1864. Last record September/October 1864, sent to Georgia to get a horse with Capt. Bostick on 09/20/1864.

163. Brown, Matthew L.: 30-year-old farmer from Emanuel County, Georgia. Born in Emanuel County, Georgia, in 1831. Enlisted as a private in Company F on 05/09/1862 at Burke County, Georgia. Value of horse $225. Sick, on furlough of indulgence for 24 days beginning 02/19/1864. Sent to Georgia to get a horse with Capt. Bostick on 09/20/1864. Was surrendered by Gen. Joseph E. Johnston on 04/26/1865. Paroled at Greensboro, North Carolina, on 05/01/1865. After the war, became a farmer in Emanuel County, Georgia. Married Mary Jane Cowart in Emanuel County, Georgia, on 12/18/1860 and they had nine children. Died after 1910.

164. Brown, R.J.: Enlisted as a private in Company D on 08/10/1861 at Albany, Georgia. Value of horse $175 and horse equipment $25. Detailed as carpenter building houses in 12/1861. Died at Buchanan, Virginia, on 04/12/1863.

165. Brown, Tilman H.: Born ca. 1846 in Georgia. Enlisted as a private in Company H on 04/02/1862 at Athens, Clarke County, Georgia. Reported as missing on 06/09/1863 after the cavalry battle at Brandy Station, Virginia. Killed near Stevensburg, Virginia, on 11/09/1863.

166. Bruce, Aquilla: Farmer from Lumpkin County, Georgia. Born in Habersham County, Georgia, ca. 1833. Enlisted as a private in Company C on 08/01/1861 at Athens, Clarke County, Georgia. On furlough for 25 days beginning 01/20/1862. Died at Hanover Court House, Virginia, 08/24/1862. Married Parthena A.E. Bryan on either 09/06/1855 (or 09/16/1855) in Lumpkin County, Georgia, and they had at least three children.

167. Brumley, George W.: Resident of Georgia. Transferred from 1st Maryland Battery. Enlisted as a private in Company H on 10/13/1862 at Bunker Hill, Virginia. Rode a government horse. Sent to infirmary/recruiting camp on 08/27/1864. Detailed from his command and serving at army headquarters when he was surrendered by Gen. Joseph E. Johnston on 04/26/1865. Paroled at Greensboro, North Carolina, on 05/01/1865.

168. Bryan, G.W.: Listed on a Roster of Company D published in *The History of Dougherty County* but not with the *Civil War Soldiers and Sailors System*. His service records are for the 12th Regiment, Georgia Cavalry. No service records in Cobb's Legion. Possibly married to Madeline.

169. Bryan, James A.: Painter from Richmond County, Georgia. Born ca. 1834 in Georgia. Enlisted as a sergeant in Company I on 02/27/1862 at

Augusta, Georgia. Value of horse $250. Captured at Bowling Green, Stafford County, Virginia, 05/16/1864. Paroled at Point Lookout, Maryland, 02/13/1865. Last record, exchanged at Camp Lee near Richmond, Virginia. After the war, worked as a journeyman printer and then as a city sexton in Richmond County, Georgia. Married (1) Martha (2) Ann and was the father of at least six children. Died after 1880.

170. **Bryan, Matthew L.:** Farmer from Houston County, Georgia. Born ca. 1833 in Georgia. Enlisted as a sergeant in Company B on 08/14/1861 at Atlanta, Georgia. Value of horse $225 and horse equipment $27. Elected lieutenant on 12/17/1861. Resigned commission on 08/22/1862 at Hanover Court House, Virginia. Last record, admitted to Stuart Hospital, Richmond, Virginia, on 11/26/1864. After the war, became a farmer in Houston County, Georgia. His wife's name was Mary J.

171. **Bryant, Burrell:** Resident of Hall County, Georgia. Listed on a roster of Company C in *These Men She Gave: The Civil War Diary of Athens, Georgia*. No service records in Cobb's Legion.

172. **Bryant, Wellington L.:** Farmer from Jackson County, Georgia. Born ca. 1832 in Georgia. Enlisted as a private in Company C on 03/04/1862 at Athens, Clarke County, Georgia. Admitted to C.S.A. General Hospital, Charlottesville, Virginia, with a saber wound on 06/10/1863. Returned to duty on 07/09/1863. Sent home to get a horse on 11/10/1863. Last record September/October 1864, sent to Georgia to get a horse with Capt. Bostick on 09/20/1864. After the war, became a farmer in Jackson County, Georgia. Married Susan A. and they had at least five children. Died after 1870.

173. **Bryant, William N.:** Enlisted as a private in Company C on 03/01/1863 at Brownsville, Virginia. Value of horse $500. Horse killed in action at Brandy Station on 06/09/1863. Captured at Jack's Shop on 09/22/1863. Sent to the Old Capitol Prison, Washington, D.C., on 09/24/1863. Transferred to Point Lookout, Maryland, on 09/26/1863. Admitted to U.S.A. Smallpox Hospital on 11/17/1863 and died of smallpox on 11/17/1863.

174. **Bryce, George B.:** Enlisted as a private in Company B on 08/14/1861 at Atlanta, Georgia. Value of horse $250, and horse equipment $5, saddle furnished by State of Georgia. Discharged on 11/21/1861.

175. **Bryson, William:** 20-year-old merchant clerk from Richmond County, Georgia. Born in Georgia in 03/1842. Enlisted as a private in 1st Georgia Infantry, Company D on 03/18/1861. Mustered out at Augusta, Georgia, on 03/18/1862. Enlisted as a private in Company I on 04/15/1862 at Augusta, Georgia. Wounded at Hanover, Virginia, on 05/27/1862. Medical examining board ordered him to return to regiment on 02/27/1863. Last record, March/April 1863 did not state if he was present. After the war, worked as a cotton merchant, farmer, and then as a landlord in Richmond County, Georgia. Married Ella in 1863 and they had ten children. Died after 1900.

176. **Buckingame, L.:** 27-year-old. Enlisted as a private in Company K on 02/08/1863 at Camp Maynard, Georgia. Returned to his regiment on 02/21/1863.

177. **Buffington, O.M.:** Farmer from Hall County, Georgia. Born ca. 1842 in Georgia. Enlisted as a private in Company H on 05/04/1862 at Athens, Clarke County, Georgia. Died at Richmond, Virginia, on 07/18/1862. Buried at Hollywood Cemetery in Richmond, Virginia.

178. **Bulloch, John Hawkins:** 21-year-old overseer from Clarke County, Georgia. Born in Madison County, Georgia, on 10/18/1838. Enlisted as a private in Company H on 03/04/1862 at Athens, Clarke County, Georgia. Captured at Beverly's Ford, Virginia, on 06/09/1863. Sent to the Old Capitol Prison in Washington, D.C., and paroled on 06/25/1863. Sent to infirmary/recruiting camp on 02/23/1864. Detailed as a teamster for the A.Q.M. beginning September/October 1864. Was surrendered by Gen. Joseph E. Johnston on 04/26/1865. Paroled at Greensboro, North Carolina, on 05/01/1865. After the war, became a farmer in Madison County, Georgia. Married Mildred Louise Pass on 11/16/1865 in Madison County, Georgia, and they had six children. Applied for a Confederate pension in Madison County, Georgia. Died on 06/05/1925 in Madison County, Georgia.

179. **Bunch, Hill:** Born ca. 1830 in Georgia. Enlisted as a private in Company A on 08/17/1861 at Augusta, Georgia. Value of horse $150, and horse equipment $25. Elected lieutenant on 06/04/1862. Horse killed while making a charge at Malvern Hill on 07/10/1862. Transferred to Company K before 09/01/1863. Another horse, valued at $800, was killed near Culpeper C.H. on 09/10/1863. Bunch court-martialed on 03/26/1863. Sent to infirmary/recruiting camp on 11/15/1863, with rank reduced to private. Admitted sick to General Hospital No. 8, Raleigh, North Carolina, on 07/08/1864. Last service record September/October 1864, at the hospital since 07/20/1864.

180. **Bunch, S.J.:** Enlisted as a private in Company K on 07/01/1864 at Decatur, Georgia. Admitted to C.S.A. General Hospital, Charlottesville,

Virginia, with a wound on 01/19/1865. Last record, released to another hospital on 01/22/1865.

181. Burford, Drewry: 24-year-old. Born on 10/20/1836 in Forsyth County, Georgia. Enlisted as a private in Company B on 08/14/1861 at Atlanta, Georgia. Value of horse $200 and horse equipment $8, saddle furnished by State of Georgia. Detailed as assistant wagon master in the Quartermasters Department on 01/15/1863. Detailed to issue forage to disabled horses of brigade at infirmary/recruiting Camp on 06/16/1864. Admitted to Jackson Hospital, Richmond, Virginia, on 06/16/1864. Last record, returned to duty on 06/20/1864. After the war, worked as a dry goods merchant in Anderson County, South Carolina, and then as a retail merchant of farm tools in Abbeville County, South Carolina. Married Margaret (Maggie) Elizabeth Shirley on 11/14/1866 and they had ten children. Died on 06/30/1913 at Calhoun Falls, South Carolina. His widow applied for a Confederate pension on 04/08/1915 in Calhoun Falls, Abbeville County, South Carolina.

182. Burgess, R.U.: Enlisted as an assistant surgeon to the Cavalry Regiment on 01/19/1864. Date of enlistment or commission is unknown. Was a medical officer at Chesterfield Station, Virginia, on 04/12/1864 and 07/22/1864.

183. Burkhalter [Berkhalter], David C.N.: 20-year-old college student from Marion County, Georgia. Born on 12/08/1840. Resident of Georgia. Enlisted as a private in Company B on 08/14/1861 at Atlanta, Georgia. Value of horse $200 and horse equipment $6, saddle furnished by State of Georgia. Transferred to Company D. Promoted to sergeant in Company B on 12/27/1861. On furlough for 23 days beginning 01/20/1862. Declined serving as a sergeant on 03/15/1862. Transferred back to Company D on 05/01/1862. Sent home to get a horse in March/April 1863. Last record September/October 1864, sent to Georgia to get a horse with Capt. Bostick on 09/20/1864. After the war, worked as a laborer in Sumter County, Georgia. Married (1) Rebecca Alberta Brown on 02/06/1868 in Sumter County, Georgia. Married (2) Lula Hooks and they had at least three children. Died on 07/08/1910 in Sumter County, Georgia, and is buried in the Oak Grove City Cemetery in Americus, Sumter County, Georgia.

184. Burnett, Causby D.: 22-year-old from Georgia. Enlisted as a private in Company B on 04/29/1862 at Atlanta, Georgia. Value of horse $185. Sent to Georgia to get a horse with Lt. James H. Johnson on 04/14/1863 and 11/10/1863. Transferred to Company G before end of November/December 1863. Sent to Georgia to get a horse with Capt. Bostick on 09/20/1864. Was surrendered by Gen. Joseph E. Johnston on 04/26/1865. Paroled at Greensboro, North Carolina, on 05/01/1865.

185. Burnett, Daniel L.: Enlisted as a private in Company L, details unknown. Wounded at Battle of Brandy Station on 06/09/1863. His only record shows he was admitted to C.S.A. General Hospital, Charlottesville, Virginia, on 06/25/1863 with a wound. Furloughed for 30 days beginning 06/25/1863.

186. Burnley, Stephen Franklin: 22-year-old. Born in Warren County, Georgia, on 03/28/1840. Enlisted as a private in Company I on 03/15/1862 at Augusta, Georgia. Value of horse $135. Died on 06/26/1862. Described as being 6 feet tall and having dark hair, dark eyes, and a sallow complexion. His widow, Martha J. Burnley, received his back pay and bounty money.

187. Burr, John Howard: Tinner from Fulton County, Georgia. Born ca. 1835 in Spalding County, Georgia. Enlisted as a private in Company B on 08/14/1861 at Atlanta, Georgia. Value of horse $200 and horse equipment $26. Captured near Harrison's Landing (Carter's Farm), Virginia, on 07/07/1862 and sent to Fort Monroe, Virginia. Transferred to Fort Delaware Prison on 07/11/1862. Described as being 6 feet tall and having dark brown hair, dark blue eyes, and a light complexion. Exchanged at Aiken's Landing, Virginia, on 08/05/1862 from the steamer *Katskill*. Furloughed to Georgia for 25 days beginning 08/09/1862. Promoted to lieutenant on 10/02/1862. Promoted to captain on 05/09/1864. Wounded on 10/27/1864. Admitted to General Hospital, Petersburg, Virginia, with a wound to left ankle on 10/29/1864. Died of blood poisoning on 01/01/1865. Married Mariah Winship on 05/24/1859 in Spalding County, Georgia, and they had at least one child.

188. Burton, Robert H.: 18-year-old student from Burke County, Georgia. Born on 12/22/1844. Enlisted as a private in Company L on 12/15/1862 at Burke County, Georgia. Sent to infirmary/recruiting camp on 04/01/1864. Admitted to C.S.A. General Hospital, Farmville, Virginia, with intermittent fever (probably malaria) on 07/29/1864. Returned to duty on 08/18/1864. Was surrendered by Gen. Joseph E. Johnston on 04/26/1865. Paroled at Greensboro, North Carolina, on 05/01/1865. After the war, became a farmer and a landlord in Burke County, Georgia. Married (1) Fannie E. Malone on 02/27/1873 in Burke County, Georgia, and they had one child. Married (2) Hattie. Died on 08/25/1909.

189. **Burtz, Richard P.:** 19-year-old. Enlisted as a private in Company B on 04/28/1862 at Atlanta, Georgia. Value of horse $175. Sent to Georgia to get a horse with Lt. James H. Johnson on 04/14/1863. Wounded at Funkstown, Maryland, on 07/10/1863 and sent to hospital in Williamsport, Maryland. Died on 07/12/1863.

190. **Butler, J.J.:** Farmer from Worth County, Georgia. Enlisted as a private in Company D on 08/10/1861 at Albany, Georgia. Value of horse $200, and horse equipment $25, furnished by State of Georgia. Last record, November/December 1861, present but sick.

191. **Butler, Robert:** 18-year-old. Enlisted as a private in Company K on 01/24/1863 at Camp Maynard, Georgia. Last record, March/April 1863, returned to his regiment on 02/18/1863.

192. **Byne, John Randolph:** 21-year-old student from Jefferson County, Georgia. Born on 06/14/1840 in Richmond County, Georgia. Enlisted as a private in Company F on 03/15/1862 at Burke County, Georgia. Value of horse $175. On furlough in Jefferson, Georgia, recovering from injury received from a fall a horse in 10/1862. Detached to attend horses at infirmary/recruiting camp on 01/16/1864. Sent to Georgia with Capt. Bostick to get a horse on 09/20/1864. Was surrendered by Gen. Joseph E. Johnston on 04/26/1865. Paroled at Greensboro, North Carolina, on 05/01/1865. After the war, became a planter from Richmond County, Georgia. Married Harriet (or Hattie) Rhodes on 12/13/1867 in Richmond County, Georgia, and they had at least three children. Killed in a hunting accident on 01/17/1875. Buried at the Hopeful Cemetery in Burke County, Georgia. His widow, Hattie Byne Murrow, applied for a Confederate pension in Richmond County, Georgia.

193. **Byrd, John P.M.:** 25-year-old. Born in 12/1839 in Cass County, Georgia. On a roster of Company E compiled by Glen Spurlock. No service records in Cobb's Legion Cavalry. After the war, became a farmer in Cherokee County and then in Floyd County, Georgia. Later worked as a cotton buyer in Floyd County, Georgia. Married Margaret Glenn in 1860 and they had eight children. Applied for a Confederate pension in Floyd County, Georgia.

194. **Byrd, William H.:** Bookkeeper. Resident of New York for 12 months prior to the war. Born ca. 1840 in Georgia. Enlisted as a private in Company F on 03/05/1862 at Augusta, Georgia. Value of horse $230. Horse permanently disabled in battle on 07/07/1862 at Shirley Plantation below Malvern Hill during a severe skirmish with the enemy. Received a medical furlough beginning 12/12/1862. Admitted to General Hospital No. 16, Richmond, Virginia, on 03/02/1863. Returned to duty 03/09/1863. Transferred to Company I on 04/18/1863. Received wound to left foot on the road to Charles City, Virginia, on 08/17/1864. Admitted to Jackson Hospital, Richmond, Virginia, on 08/17/1864 and furloughed to Georgia for 30 days beginning 08/22/1864. His last known rank was that of a sergeant. Died in Augusta, Georgia, on 09/07/1864 from wounds. Described as being 5'10" tall and having hazel eyes, dark hair, and fair complexion. His widow, Mrs. Emma D. Byrd, received his back pay. Was the father of two children.

195. **Calaway, Jesse:** 34-year-old from Georgia. Born on 06/29/1828. Enlisted as a private in Company G on 06/18/1862 at Atlanta, Georgia. Lost his horse on 04/14/1863. Detailed to infirmary/recruiting camp in charge of horses in 08/1863. Admitted to C.S.A. General Hospital No. 4, Wilmington, North Carolina, on 08/02/1864 with colitis. Released from hospital on 09/08/1864 and furloughed until 11/15/1864 by medical examining board. Was surrendered by Gen. Joseph E. Johnston on 04/26/1865. Paroled at Greensboro, North Carolina, on 05/01/1865.

196. **Calaway, Joseph Woodson Brown:** 28-year-old from Walton County, Georgia. Born on 12/23/1834 in Wilkes County, Georgia. Enlisted as a private in Company B on 04/22/1862 at Atlanta, Georgia. Value of horse $200. Listed as a corporal in Company G beginning May/June 1862. Listed as a sergeant beginning March/April 1863. Sent to Georgia to get a horse with Lt. James H. Johnson on 04/14/1863. Sent home to get a horse on 11/10/1863. Sent to Georgia to get a horse with Capt. Bostick on 09/20/1864. Was surrendered by Gen. Joseph E. Johnston on 04/26/1865. Paroled at Greensboro, North Carolina, on 05/01/1865. After the war, became a farmer in Walton County Georgia, and then in Dallas County, Texas. Married Martha Celia Terrell in 1865 and they had at least ten children. Died on 12/13/1894 at Ft. Chadbourne, Coke County, Texas.

197. **Calhoun, Edward Livingston:** Physician from Fulton County, Georgia. Born ca. 1837 in DeKalb County, Georgia. Brother of Pickens Noble Calhoun. Enlisted as a private in Company B on 04/22/1862 at Atlanta, Georgia. Value of horse $150. Transferred to Company G as a company bugler in May/June 1862. Lost horse on 01/01/1863. Admitted to hospital in Gordonsville, Virginia, on 02/21/1863. No horse on 05/01/1863. Sent to Atlanta, Georgia, to get a horse on 06/09/1863.

Listed as a private beginning 11/01/1863. Detailed as an ambulance driver in March/April 1864. Last record September/October 1864, sent to Georgia to get a horse with Capt. Bostick on 09/20/1864. After the war, became a physician in Henry County, Georgia.

198. Calhoun, Pickens Noble: Clerk from Fulton County, Georgia. Born about 1840 in DeKalb County, Georgia. Brother of Edward Livingston Calhoun. Enlisted as a private in Company B on 04/18/1862 at Atlanta, Georgia. Value of horse $210. Transferred to Company G as a sergeant in May/June 1862. Died of typhoid fever at Mr. Merriwether's near Richmond, Virginia, on 08/09/1862. Buried in Hollywood Cemetery, Richmond, Virginia. His father, Eziekiel N. Calhoun, of Fulton County, Georgia, received his back pay as he was not survived by a wife or children.

199. Calloway, J.M.: Enlisted as a private in Company K on 06/06/1864 at Macon, Georgia. Last record, absent without leave 06/16/1864.

200. Camback, Charles L.: Resident of Fredericksburg, Virginia. Enlisted as a private in Company A on 01/28/1864 at Hamilton Crossing, Virginia. Detailed as a scout by order of Gen. Hampton, no horse, 01/28/1864. Captured at Fauquier County, Virginia, on 03/01/1864. Sent to Old Capitol Prison, Washington D.C., on 03/05/1864. Transferred to Fort Warren, Massachusetts, on 09/23/1864. Paroled at Fort Warren, Boston Harbor, Massachusetts, on 06/12/1865. Described as being 5'10 1/2" tall and having a dark complexion, brown hair, and gray eyes.

201. Camfield, Caleb Halstead: 27-year-old bookkeeper from Dougherty County, Georgia. Born on 07/15/1834 in Augusta, Richmond County, Georgia. Enlisted as a sergeant in 4th Georgia Infantry on 04/28/1861. Transferred as a private to Cobb's Legion Cavalry, Company D, on 08/10/1861 at Albany, Georgia. Value of horse $200 and horse equipment $45. Promoted to sergeant before November/December 1861. Elected lieutenant on 12/31/1861. On furlough beginning 10/01/1862. Listed as a captain in November/December 1863. Promoted to major in Hood's Georgia Infantry Regiment on 04/01/1864. Paroled at Albany, Georgia, in 05/1865. After the war, worked as a bookkeeper in Dougherty County, Georgia. Married (1) Sarah Harvey Talbot on 12/13/1855 and they had at least two children. Married (2) Julia F. Spicer on 08/08/1886. Died on 09/04/1904. Buried in Oakview Cemetery in Dougherty County, Georgia.

202. Camp, Dilmus McPherson: 21-year-old student from Jackson County, Georgia. Born in 03/1841 in Georgia. Enlisted as a private in Company C on 03/04/1862 at Athens, Clarke County, Georgia. Sent to infirmary/recruiting camp on 12/01/1863. Last record September/October 1864, sent to Georgia to get a horse with Capt. Bostick on 09/20/1864. After the war, became a farmer in Jackson County, Georgia. Married (1) Louisa Graige ca. 1886 (2) Sarah L. Died after 1910.

203. Campbell, John L.: Apprentice blacksmith from Cobb County, Georgia. Born ca. 1837 in Georgia. Enlisted as a blacksmith in Company E on 03/05/1865 at Roswell, Georgia. Value of horse $225. Last record, April 1862. He and his wife, Mary A., had at least one child. Died before 1870. His widow applied for a Confederate pension in Cobb and Milton counties, Georgia.

204. Cannon, John: 25-year-old. Born in Ireland. Enlisted as a private in Company I on 04/24/1862 at Augusta, Georgia. Admitted to Winder Hospital, Richmond, Virginia, on 09/25/1862. Given a medical discharge on 04/25/1863. Described as being 5'7" tall and having a florid complexion, brown eyes, and light hair.

205. Cantrell, Alfred Webb: Resident of Lumpkin County, Georgia. Brother of John H. and Starlin B. Cantrell. Enlisted as a private in Company H on 02/25/1862 at Athens, Clarke County, Georgia. Sent to Georgia to get a horse with Lt. Sinquefield under Special Order No. 27 from corps headquarters on 02/23/1864. Sent to Georgia to get a horse with Capt. Bostick on 09/20/1864. Was surrendered by Gen. Joseph E. Johnston on 04/26/1865. Paroled at Greensboro, North Carolina, on 05/01/1865. Married Elizabeth Lucinda Whelchel on 08/30/1858 in White County, Georgia.

206. Cantrell, John H. [C.]: Resident of Georgia. Brother of Alfred Webb Cantrell and Starlin B. Cantrell. Enlisted as a private in Phillip's Legion, Company C, on 06/11/1861 at Camp McDonald, Georgia. Transferred to Cobb's Legion Cavalry, Company H, on 11/12/1863. On provost duty on 01/26/1864. Last record September/October 1864, sent to Georgia to get a horse with Capt. Bostick on 09/20/1864.

207. Cantrell, Starlin [Starling] Blackwell: Farmer from Lumpkin County, Georgia. Born ca. 1829 in Georgia. Brother of Alfred Webb and John H. Cantrell. Enlisted as a private in Company H on 02/25/1862 at Athens, Clarke County, Georgia. Sent to Georgia to get a horse on 11/11/1863. Elected tax receiver in Georgia on 01/1864. Last record, September/October 1864, states he was absent without leave since 01/18/1864. (He may have been excused from service due to his government position.) After the war, became a farmer in Reno, Leavenworth County, Kansas. Married (1) Narcessa E. Bell in either Hall County or White County, Georgia, on 11/27/1859 and they had one child (2) Nancy Jane Hulsey on 04/23/1909 in Hall County, Georgia. Died on 07/14/1906.

208. Carey, Silas Jennings: 17-year-old merchant clerk from Richmond County, Georgia. Born in Augusta, Richmond County, Georgia, on 12/23/1845. Enlisted as a private in Company I on 02/27/1862 at Augusta, Georgia. Value of horse $200. Admitted to General Hospital No. 19, Richmond, Virginia, on 10/31/1862. Detailed to take up railroad iron at Fredericksburg, Virginia, on 04/01/1864. Sent to Georgia with Capt. Bostick to get a horse on 09/20/1864. Was surrendered by Gen. Joseph E. Johnston on 04/26/1865. Paroled at Greensboro, North Carolina, on 05/01/1865. Married Annie Parker on 04/1/1869 or 12/21/1870 and they had at least two children. Died on 11/07/1875 in Augusta, Richmond County, Georgia.

209. Carley, W.W.: Listed on a roster for Company D in *The History of Dougherty County*, but not with the *Civil War Soldiers and Sailors System*. No service records in Cobb's Legion.

210. Carpenter, J.P.: Resident of Georgia. Enlisted as a private in Company D on 08/10/1861 at Albany, Georgia. Value of horse $200 and horse equipment $25, furnished by State of Georgia. Detailed as a teamster in January/February 1862. Last record dated April/October 1864 stated that he had no horse and was sent to the infirmary/recruiting camp in September 1863.

211. Carroll, J.: Overseer from Dougherty County, Georgia. Listed on a roster of Company D published in *The History of Dougherty County*, but not with the *Civil War Soldiers and Sailors System*. No service records in Cobb's Legion.

212. Carroll, Robert C.: Clerk from Augusta, Georgia, born in Ireland ca. 1835. Enlisted as a private in Company A on 08/17/1861 at Augusta, Georgia. Value of horse $200, and horse equipment $25. Admitted to General Hospital No. 14, Richmond, Virginia, in 12/1862 and General Hospital No. 16, Richmond, Virginia, in January/February 1863. On sick furlough in March/April 1863. Admitted to Winder, Hospital Richmond, Virginia, in 08/1863 and on 10/08/1863 with rheumatism. On furlough in November/December 1863. Admitted to Jackson Hospital, Richmond, Virginia, in February/March 1864 with lumbago and carditis. Returned to duty on 03/11/1864. Discharged from the service on 03/19/1864. After the war, worked for the railroad. He died ca. 1882– 1883 and is buried in Magnolia Cemetery at Augusta.

213. Carter, Albert W.J.: Enlisted as a private in Company B on 08/14/1861 at Atlanta, Georgia. Value of horse $200 and horse equipment $8, saddle furnished by the State of Georgia. Courier for Gen. Raines at Yorktown in November/December 1861. Died at Gordonsville, Virginia, on 05/28/1863, leaving neither father, wife, nor child. His mother, Sarah L. Carter, received his back pay.

214. Carter, Bennett H.: Enlisted as a private in Company H 03/01/1862 at Athens, Clarke County, Georgia. Killed on 06/09/1863 during the cavalry battle at Brandy Station, Virginia. He and his wife, Lucy Ann, had at least two children. His widow applied for a Confederate pension in Hall County, Georgia.

215. Carter, Oscar L.: 37-year-old. Born in Ireland. Enlisted as a private in Company L on 12/15/1862 at Burke, Georgia. Captured at Beverly's Ford, Virginia, 06/09/1863 and sent to Old Capitol Prison, Washington, D.C. Furloughed from Jackson General Hospital, Richmond, Virginia, in December 1863. Admitted to Winder Hospital, Richmond, Virginia, with pneumonia on 01/18/1864 and then transferred to Jackson Hospital. Furloughed for 30 days beginning 01/27/1864. Admitted to Jackson General Hospital, wounded on 08/17/1864. Sent to Georgia with Capt. Bostick to get a horse on 09/20/1864. Was surrendered by Gen. Joseph E. Johnston on 04/26/1865. Paroled at Greensboro, North Carolina, on 05/01/1865 Described as having blue eyes and dark hair.

216. Casey, Michael G.: 23-year-old from Georgia. Enlisted as a private in Company B on 03/20/1862 at Atlanta, Georgia. Value of horse $135. Transferred to Company G during May/June 1862. Sent to infirmary/recruiting camp on 02/23/1864. Last record, sent to Georgia to get a horse with Capt. Bostick on 09/20/1864.

217. Cash, Noah B.: 24-year-old county surveyor. Resident of Jackson County, Georgia. Born on 01/07/1838 in Jackson County, Georgia. Enlisted as a private in Company C on 08/1/1861 at Athens, Clarke County, Georgia. Sent to infirmary/recruiting camp on 10/27/1863. Last record, September/October 1864, sent to Georgia to get a horse with Capt. Bostick on 09/20/1864. After the war, became a physician and then a farmer in Jackson County, Georgia. Married Samantha Adelaide Johnson on 11/18/1868 in Jackson County, Georgia, and they had at least three children. Died on 12/15/1912 in Fulton County, Georgia.

218. Cassell, E.T.: Resident of Georgia. Enlisted as a private in Company E on 04/19/1864 at Atlanta, Georgia. Last record September/October 1864, sent to Georgia to get a horse with Capt. Bostick on 09/20/1864.

219. Cates, John: Native of Georgia. Enlisted as a private in Company F on 12/04/1862 at Burke County, Georgia. Admitted to hospital on 06/01/1864. Last record, discharged from the service on 10/08/1864 near Dinwiddie Court House, Virginia.

220. Cates, John: Enlisted as a private in Company L on 12/15/1862 at Burke County, Georgia. Admitted sick to Winder, Hospital, Richmond, Virginia, on 06/30/1863 and on 07/22/1863. Furnished John Moore as a substitute. Discharged on 12/17/1863.

221. Cates, John J.: Planter from Burke County, Georgia. Enlisted as a private in 20th Georgia Regiment on 05/16/1862 at Savannah, Georgia. Transferred to Cobb's Legion Cavalry, Company F, on 10/12/1862. Sent to infirmary/recruiting camp to attend horses in 08/21/1862. Admitted to General Hospital, Liberty, Virginia, on 04/08/1863. Sent to Georgia with Capt. Bostick to get a horse on 09/20/1864. Was surrendered by Gen. Joseph E. Johnston on 04/26/1865. Paroled at Greensboro, North Carolina, on 05/01/1865 and also paroled at Augusta, Georgia, on 05/18/1865. He and his wife, Parmelia or Nancy, had at least two children.

222. Cates, T.W.: On a list of those in Company K who were killed at Brandy Station, Virginia, on 06/09/1863. No service records in Cobb's Legion.

223. Cates, Thomas: Enlisted as a private in Company L on 12/15/1862 at Burke County, Georgia. Appointed corporal on 06/01/1864. Sent to Georgia with Capt. Bostick to get a horse on 09/20/1864. Was surrendered by Gen. Joseph E. Johnston on 04/26/1865. Paroled at Greensboro, North Carolina, on 05/01/1865.

224. Cavanaugh, William F.: Grocer born in Ireland ca. 1835. Enlisted as a private in Company A on 08/17/1861 at Augusta, Georgia. Value of horse $200, and horse equipment $25. Given a 30 days' medical furlough beginning 01/08/1863. No horse on 02/01/1863. Sent to Georgia on sick furlough in 02/1863. Discharged in 11/1863.

225. Chambers, James Buregard: 35-year-old farmer from Milton County, Georgia. Born on 02/06/1827 in Georgia. Enlisted as a private in Company E on 03/22/1862 at Roswell, Georgia. Captured 07/11/1862 near Malvern Hill, Virginia. Sent to Ft. Wood Prison on 08/26/1862. Absent, sick, March/April 1863. Absent without leave beginning 06/03/1863. Last record, sent to Georgia to get a horse with Capt. Bostick on 09/20/1864.

After the war, worked as a carpenter and then as a merchant in McLennan County, Texas. Married Martha Rebecca Stewart on 04/09/1848 and they had fourteen children. Died before 1910.

226. Chandler, Frank: 35-year-old grocer from Jackson County, Georgia. Enlisted as a private in Company C on 08/01/1861 at Athens, Clarke County, Georgia. No other service records.

227. Chandler, Green W.W. [M.]: 25-year-old overseer from Jackson County, Georgia. Born on 02/23/1837 in Georgia. Enlisted as a private in Company C on 03/04/1862 at Jackson County, Georgia. Transferred to Company H. Discharged on 07/17/1862. After the war, became a farmer in Jackson and then Gwinnett counties, Georgia. Married on 02/01 or 03 or 04/1875 to Frances Edwards Maddox and they had at least eleven children. Applied for a Confederate pension in Gwinnett County, Georgia. Died on 07/07/1901 in Auburn, Gwinnett County, Georgia. Buried at the Harmony Grove Methodist Church Cemetery in Barrow County, Georgia. His widow applied for a Confederate pension in Barrow County, Georgia, in 1920.

228. Chandler, Robert: Transferred from 2nd Georgia Regiment, Company A, in exchange for T.J. McCrackin. Enlisted as a private in Company L on 05/17/1862 at Richmond, Virginia. Admitted to Jackson Hospital, Richmond, Virginia, on 01/28/1864 with intermittent fever (probably malaria). Sent home to get a horse with Lt. Sinquefield under Special Order No. 27 from corps headquarters on 02/23/1864. Admitted to Jackson Hospital, Richmond, Virginia, on 02/24/1864. Sent to Georgia with Capt. Bostick to get a horse on 09/20/1864. Was surrendered by Gen. Joseph E. Johnston on 04/26/1865. Paroled at Augusta, Georgia, on 05/19/1865.

229. Chastain, Anderson: 24-year-old. Enlisted as a private in Company K on 02/08/1863 at Camp Maynard, Georgia. Last record, returned to his regiment on 02/21/1863.

230. Chatham, J.W.: Resident of Georgia. Enlisted as a private in Company E on 07/09/1863 at Roswell, Georgia. Sent to infirmary/recruiting camp on 11/28/1863. Last record, sent to Georgia to get a horse with Capt. Bostick on 09/20/1864.

231. Chatham, Thomas J.: Student from Forsyth County, Georgia. Born ca. 1846 in Georgia. Enlisted as a private in Company E on 03/15/1862 at Roswell, Georgia. Value of horse $125. Captured at Hunterstown, Pennsylvania, on 07/03/1863. Admitted to U.S.A. Smallpox Hospital, Point Lookout, Maryland, on 11/28/1863. Died 12/02/1863.

232. Chatham, William C.: 22-year-old from Georgia. Enlisted as a private in Company E on 03/15/1862 at Roswell, Georgia. Value of horse $150. Sent to infirmary/recruiting camp on 11/08/1863. Admitted to C.S.A. General Hospital, Farmville, Virginia, on 07/29/1864. Last record, returned to duty on 09/29/1864.

233. Chavous, Allen: Farmer from Richmond County, Georgia. Born ca. 1832 in the Barnwell District, South Carolina. Brother of James, John, and Walter Chavous. Enlisted as a private in Company A on 03/03/1862 at Augusta, Georgia. Value of horse $150. Transferred to Company I before February 1863. Captured near Martinsburg, Virginia [West Virginia], on 07/18/1863. Sent to Military Prison at Wheeling, Virginia [West Virginia], on 07/21/1864. Transferred to Prison at Camp Chase, Ohio, on 07/24/1863. Described as having a dark complexion, brown eyes, dark hair, and being 5'10¼" tall. Paroled at Augusta, Georgia, on 05/24/1865. After the war, became a farmer in Richmond County, Georgia. Married Sarah McElmurray ca. 1859 and they had eleven children. Died on 08/30/1908.

234. Chavous, James F.: Teacher from Richmond County, Georgia. Born ca. 1836. Brother of Allen, John, and Walter Chavous. Enlisted as a private in Company A on 08/17/1861 at Augusta, Georgia. Value of horse $150, and horse equipment $25. He died near Goldsboro, North Carolina, in 1862 (probably in March), leaving a young widow.

235. Chavous, John L.: Farmer from Richmond County, Georgia. Born ca. 1834. Brother of Allen, James, and Walter Chavous. Enlisted as a private in Company I on 03/3/1862 at Augusta, Georgia. Sent home to get a horse with Lt. Sinquefield under Special Order No. 27 from corps headquarters on 02/23/1864. Sent to Georgia with Capt. Bostick to get a horse on 09/20/1864. Surrendered and paroled on 05/29/1865 at Augusta, Georgia. He and his wife, Amelia, had at least one child.

236. Chavous, Walter [Wyatt] H.: 21-year-old student from Richmond County, Georgia. Born on 09/4/1842. Brother of Allen, James, and John Chavous. Enlisted as a private in Company I on 09/15/1863, at Culpepper County Courthouse, Virginia. Sent home to get a horse with Lt. Sinquefield under Special Order No. 27 from corps headquarters on 02/23/1864. Sent to Georgia with Capt. Bostick to get a horse on 09/20/1864. Admitted to Pettigrew Hospital, Raleigh, North Carolina, on 12/07/1864 with a wound in the left thigh. Was surrendered by Gen. Joseph E. Johnston on 04/26/1865. Paroled at Greensboro, North Carolina, on 05/01/1865. After the war, became a farmer in Richmond County, Georgia. Married Emma Gertrude Beall before 1880 and they had at least five children. Died on 08/15/1926. Buried in the Union Road Cemetery in Richmond County, Georgia.

237. Cheesboro [Cheeseboro, Cheesborough], John Weaver: Merchant from Richmond County, Georgia. Born ca. 1837 in Florida. Enlisted as a private in Company A on 08/17/1861 at Augusta, Georgia. Value of horse $250, and horse equipment $25. Furloughed for 25 days beginning 01/02/1862. Elected lieutenant 02/10/1863. Mortally wounded at Hunterstown, Pennsylvania, on 07/02/1863, and died in the Grass Hotel in Hunterstown. (His tombstone says 07/01/1863.) Buried in the National Cemetery, Gettysburg, Pennsylvania, and reinterred on 08/21/1871 at Laurel Grove Cemetery, Gettysburg Section, Lot 853, Savannah, Georgia.

238. Cherry, John P.: Born ca. 1830. Enlisted as a private in Company C on 08/01/1861 at Athens, Clarke County, Georgia. Accidentally shot two fingers off his left hand on 12/08/1861. Discharged due to disability on 07/08/1862.

239. Childers, Thomas M.: Carpenter from White County, Georgia. Enlisted as a private in Company H on 03/15/1862 at Athens, Clarke County, Georgia. Sent to Georgia to get a horse on 11/11/1863. Last record September/October 1864, absent without since leave 09/05/1864. He and his wife, Martha, had at least one child.

240. Chisolm, Seaborn W.: Student from Polk County, Georgia. Born in Cedartown, Georgia in 1841. Enlisted as a private in Company B on 10/01/1861 at Yorktown, Virginia. Wounded and captured at Crampton's Pass, Maryland, on 09/14/1862. Died in 1862 from wounds received in action.

241. Christian, James E.: 22-year-old. Born in 12/1844 in Georgia. Enlisted as a corporal in Company I on 03/19/1862 at Atlanta, Georgia. Value of horse $210. Admitted to Floyd House and Ocmulgee Hospital in Macon, Georgia, on 01/01/1864. Sent to Georgia with Capt. Bostick to get a horse on 09/20/1864. Was surrendered by Gen. Joseph E. Johnston on 04/26/1865. Paroled at Greensboro, North Carolina, on 05/01/1865. After the war, worked as a printer and then as a watchman at Atlanta, Fulton County, Georgia. Was married to Carrie. Applied for a Confederate pension in Fulton County, Georgia. Died after 1910. His widow applied for a Confederate pension in Fulton County, Georgia.

242. Christman, John: 20-year-old. Born in New York in 08/1844. Enlisted as a private in Company A on 08/01/1862 at Augusta, Georgia. Substitute for Ephraim Tweedy. Absent without leave beginning 03/16/1864. On furlough of indulgence beginning 07/21/1864. Last record, sent to Georgia to get a horse with Capt. Bostick on 09/20/1864. After the war, worked as a grave digger and a gardener. Married Amanda McKinney on 01/21/1867 in Richmond County, Georgia, and they had at least six children. Died on 07/26/1902. His widow applied for a Confederate pension in Richmond County, Georgia. On her application, she said that he was with his command when they surrendered.

243. Church, William Lee: 18-year-old. Born on 04/21/1843. Enlisted as a corporal Company C on 08/01/1861 at Athens, Clarke County, Georgia. Promoted to sergeant in November/December 1861. Appointed captain and A.A.G. on 12/04/1862. Colonel P.M.B. Young's report of the 06/09/1863 engagement at Brandy Station mentioned that "Among others whose distinguished conduct came under my personal observation, was my adjutant, Lieut. W. L. Church...." Col. Delony wrote to his wife about Brandy Station: "In the midst of the charge Church's horse was wounded and quicker than thought he was mounted on a Yankee's horse and in the charge again — He behaved very gallantly and came out with a bloody saber." Wiley Howard said about Brandy Station that "Wm. L. Church ... was unhorsed while contending with two men mounted. He finally succeeded in fatally thrusting one through, who was leaning over and had his hand on him, and as he tumbled off, Church mounted his adversary's horse and galloped to the front with us. He was indeed a gallant, dashing fighter and though often struck (twenty-five times) by spent balls, escaped serious wounds."* Died on 03/31/1871. Buried in Oconee Hill Cemetery, Clarke County, Georgia.

244. Clanton, James Luke: Student from Augusta, Georgia. Born ca. 1844 in Georgia. Enlisted as a private in Company A on 08/17/1861 at Augusta, Georgia. Value of horse $200, and horse equipment $35. Furloughed by the medical director in Richmond, Virginia, for 30 days beginning 11/17/1862. Promoted to lieutenant of Company K on 02/10/1863. Absent with leave from Camp Maynard 02/15/1863. Colonel P.M.B. Young's report of the 06/09/1863 engagement at Brandy Station mentioned that "Among others whose distinguished conduct came under my personal observation, was ... Lieutenant Clanton...."† Suffered an injury to his shoulder joint when he fell from his horse during fighting at Hunterstown, Pennsylvania, 07/02/1863. Admitted to General Hospital No.4 in Richmond, Virginia, 07/22/1863. Furloughed for 60 days beginning 07/26/1863. Listed as being absent, wounded, on last service record dated 10/31/1864. After the war, worked as a farmer from Columbia County, Georgia. Married to Mary Elizabeth Walton on 12/19/1868 in Columbia County. They had at least one child. Died on 04/05/1892 at Harlem, Columbia County, Georgia. His widow applied for a Confederate pension in Columbia County, Georgia. On her application, she stated that he was with his command when they surrendered, and a witness from another company of the same brigade also swore that he was present at the surrender.

245. Clark, James I.: On a roster of Company G compiled by Glen Spurlock. Listed in Cobb's Legion with the *Civil War Soldiers and Sailors System*. No service records in Cobb's Legion.

246. Clark, James Thomas [J.F.]: 26-year-old from Hall County, Georgia. Born in South Carolina in 05/1838. Enlisted as a private in Company K on 06/20/1864 at Decatur, Georgia. Admitted to hospital on 07/27/1864. Last record in Cobb's Legion Cavalry September/October 1864, sent to Georgia to get a horse with Capt. Bostick on 09/20/1864. Transferred in the fall of 1864 to Phillip's Legion, Company F. Was surrendered by Gen. Joseph E. Johnston on 04/26/1865. Paroled at Greensboro, North Carolina, on 05/01/1865. After the war, became a farmer in Hall County, Georgia. Married Maran Antoinnette Blackstock on 03/02/1862 and they had twelve children. Applied for a Confederate pension in Hall County, Georgia, from 1920 to 1928. Died on 04/14/1928.

247. Clark, John William: 17-year-old from Augusta. Born in Edgefield County, South Carolina, on 04/26/1844. Enlisted as a private in Company A on 08/17/1861. Value of horse $275, and horse equipment $35. Orderly for Col. Cobb in 11/1861. Courier for Col. Cobb 02/1862. Gen. McLaws wrote that during the battle of Fredericksburg, about 1:00 P.M., Gen. Cobb reported that he was short of ammunition: "I sent his own very intelligent and brave courier, little Johnny Clark from Augusta, Georgia, to bring up his ordnance supplies." Detailed by Gen. McLaws to the Medical

*Howard, page 7.
†OR, Series 1, Vol. 27, pt. 2, pages 732–733.

Department beginning 09/20/1863. Had no horse in March/April 1864. Detailed in Medical Department at Augusta, Georgia, beginning 10/1863. Last service record dated September/October 1864. Another record dated 03/21/1865 showed him as an aide to Col. William M. Browne, who recommended him for a commission, stating that Col. Browne "considers him in every way worthy." On his application for a Confederate pension, he stated that he was captured by Gen. Stoneman at Athens, Clarke County, Georgia, with Gen. William M. Browne on 04/01/1865. Was paroled at Athens, Clarke County, Georgia, and returned home to Augusta, Georgia. After the war, worked as a wholesale grocer. Married (1) Emma Thursby on 04/15/1869 and they had at least one child. Married (2) Annie. In 1894, President Cleveland sent him to Wyoming to allot land to the Shoshone and Arapaho Indians. He returned to Augusta, Georgia, in 1897 and went to work for the railroad. In the fall of 1898, he took a job with the Georgia Chemical Company and worked there until he was elected sheriff in 1903. Died on 10/18/1929.

248. **Clark, L.:** 21-year-old. Enlisted as a private in Company K on 01/30/1863 at Camp Maynard, Georgia. No other records.

249. **Clark, T.:** On a roster of Company K compiled by Glen Spurlock. No service records in Cobb's Legion Cavalry.

250. **Clark, Thomas Simmons:** 18-year-old student from Burke County, Georgia. Born on 09/14/1844 in Burke County, Georgia. Enlisted as a private in Company L on 12/15/1862 at Burke County, Georgia. Was surrendered by Gen. Joseph E. Johnston on 04/26/1865. He has two parole records. Paroled at Greensboro, North Carolina, on 05/01/1865 and at Augusta, Georgia, on 05/20/1865.

251. **Clark, W.H.:** On a roster of Company D compiled by Glen Spurlock. No service records in Cobb's Legion Cavalry.

252. **Clarkson, William O.[C.]:** Resident of Georgia. Enlisted in the 1st Georgia Infantry, Company I, as private on 03/18/1861. Mustered out at Augusta, Georgia, on 03/18/1862. Enlisted as a private in Cobb's Legion Cavalry, Company I, on 04/10/1862. Value of horse $185. Admitted to Episcopal Church Hospital, Williamsburg, Virginia, on 06/25/1862. Last record, sent to infirmary/recruiting camp in November/December 1863.

253. **Clayton, John M.:** From Fulton County, Georgia. Born ca. 1830 in Butts County, Georgia. Enlisted as a private in Company B on 04/19/1862 at Atlanta, Georgia. Value of horse $125. Wounded in right arm on 06/23/1863. Admitted to Jackson Hospital, Richmond, Virginia, on 07/03/1863. No horse from 07/21/1863 until 11/13/1863. Admitted to C.S.A. General Hospital, Charlottesville, Virginia, on 12/12/1863. Admitted to Jackson Hospital, Richmond, Virginia, on 05/28/1864 and on 07/30/1864. Retired on 09/01/1864. Died ca. 1903.

254. **Clayton, Josiah N.:** 24-year-old house carpenter from Henry County, Georgia. Native of Georgia. Enlisted as a private in Company B on 04/29/1862 at Atlanta, Georgia. Sent to Georgia to get a horse on 11/13/1863. Detailed to fish the Rappahannock for the regiment on 02/25/1864. Died on 08/18/1864 at Wilson Station Hospital, North Carolina, of diarrhea. Married Nancy E. Daniel in Clayton County, Georgia, on 05/05/1861.

255. **Clingan, Robert T.:** 22-year-old. Enlisted as a private in Company B on 04/14/1862 at Atlanta, Georgia. Value of horse $200. Transferred to Company G. Killed ca. 09/1862 during the Maryland campaign. Mentioned in the report of Gen. J.E.B. Stuart on 09/2–20/1862: "Private T. Clingan, Company G, Cobb's Georgia Legion, one of my couriers, was killed while behaving with the most conspicuous bravery, having borrowed a horse to ride to the field. He had been sent to post a battery of artillery from his native State."*

256. **Clitt, George:** Enlisted as a private in Company A. Was surrendered by Gen. Joseph E. Johnston on 04/26/1865. Paroled at Augusta, Georgia, on 06/02/1865. His single record does not indicate if he was in the infantry or the cavalry, but the fact that he was surrendered by Gen. Johnston at Greensboro, North Carolina (and not by Gen. Lee at Appomattox), and was paroled at Augusta, Georgia, indicates that he was most likely in the cavalry. A number of cavalrymen had gone to Georgia to procure horses and were ordered to rendezvous at Augusta. The war ended before some of them returned to their units.

257. **Cobb, James M.:** 19-year-old farmer from Georgia. Born on 03/2/1843 in Aiken County, South Carolina. Enlisted as a sergeant in Company I on 03/03/1863 at Augusta, Georgia. Value of horse $225. Captured near Martinsburg, [West] Virginia, on 07/18/1863. Imprisoned at Atheneum Military Prison, Wheeling, [West] Virginia. Described as having a florid complexion, dark eyes, black hair, and being 5'11½" tall. Sent to Camp

*OR, *Series 1, Vol. 19, Part 1, page 821.*

Chase Prison on 07/30/1863. Transferred to Fort Delaware Prison. Exchanged on 03/07/1865. Released and discharged at City Point, Virginia, on 04/01/1865. Other records indicate he received two wounds during the war, a saber cut on the hand or head, and a gunshot wound in the shoulder. One of the wounds was received at Brandy Station, Virginia, on 06/09/1863. After the war, lived in Aiken County, South Carolina. Applied for a Confederate pension in Aiken County, South Carolina, on 04/28/1919. Died after 04/28/1919.

258. Cochran, J.S.: Enlisted as a private in Company D on 05/26/1864 at Atlanta, Georgia. Was surrendered by Gen. Joseph E. Johnston on 04/26/1865. Paroled at Greensboro, North Carolina, on 05/01/1865.

259. Cochran, J.T.: Overseer from Dougherty County, Georgia. Born ca. 1837 in Georgia or Abbeville, South Carolina. Enlisted as a sergeant in Company D on 08/10/1861 at Albany, Georgia. Value of horse $150 and horse equipment $25. Absent sick at Richmond, Virginia, in November/December 1861. Listed as a private in November/December 1861. Promoted to corporal on 04/01/1862. Listed as a sergeant in January/February 1863. Given a 30-day sick furlough in February 1863. Extended 30 days and then listed as absent without leave. Admitted sick to hospital in Raleigh, North Carolina, on 07/28/1864. Paroled on 05/08/1865 at Athens, Clarke County, Georgia. Described as having hazel eyes, dark hair, dark eyes and being 5' 9" tall.

260. Cochran, John N.: Farmer from Dougherty County, Georgia. Born ca. 1835. On a roster of Company D compiled by Glen Spurlock. Not listed in the *Civil War Soldiers and Sailors System*. No service records in Cobb's Legion. He and his wife, H.M., had at least one child.

261. Cochran, William B.: Enlisted as a private in Company D on 08/10/1861 at Albany, Georgia. Value of horse $200 and horse equipment $25. Died of disease on 02/02/1862. His mother, Martha Cochran, a resident of Baker County, Georgia, received his back pay.

262. Cole, J.P.: 22-year-old. Enlisted as a private in Company K on 02/08/1863 at Camp Maynard, Georgia. Returned to his regiment on 02/21/1863.

263. Coleman, Hosey [Hosea] W.: Farmer from Milton County, Georgia. Born about 1844 in Alabama or Georgia. Enlisted as a private in Company E on 03/15/1862 at Roswell, Georgia. Value of horse $160. Furloughed for 60 days beginning 11/13/1862. Sent home to get a horse with Lt. Sinquefield under Special Order No. 27 from corps headquarters on 02/23/1864. Last record, September/October 1864 shows him present. After the war, became a farmer in Milton County, Georgia. He and his wife, Francis, had twelve children. Died after 1910. His widow applied for a Confederate pension in Milton County, Georgia.

264. Coleman, James Augustus: 22-year-old farmer from Emanuel County, Georgia. Native of Georgia. Enlisted as a private in Company F on 05/09/1862 at Burke County, Georgia. Value of horse $175. Detailed as a butcher beginning in March/April 1863. Was surrendered by Gen. Joseph E. Johnston on 04/26/1865. Paroled at Greensboro, North Carolina, on 05/01/1865. Was married.

265. Coleman, Phil Newton: 24-year-old from Georgia. Enlisted as a private in Company E on 03/15/1862 at Roswell, Georgia. Value of horse $175. Sent to infirmary/camp in March/April 1863. Admitted to C.S.A. General Hospital, Charlottesville, Virginia, on 11/14/1863. Sent to infirmary/recruiting camp on 12/12/1863. Detailed as a wagon driver beginning 05/26/1864. Last record, September/October 1864 shows him present. After the war, lived in Fulton County, Georgia, and was married to Sarah E. Applied for a Confederate pension in Fulton County, Georgia. His widow applied for a Confederate pension in Fulton County, Georgia.

266. Coleman, Pleasant: Clerk from Milton County, Georgia. Born ca. 1822 in Georgia. Enlisted as a sergeant in Company E on 03/15/1862 at Roswell, Georgia. Value of horse $165. On sick furlough beginning 12/20/1863. Sent home to get a horse on 04/20/1864. Was surrendered by Gen. Joseph E. Johnston on 04/26/1865. Paroled at Greensboro, North Carolina, on 05/01/1865. After the war, worked as a constable in Cobb County, Georgia. He and his wife, Sarah, may have had at least four children.

267. Coleman, Welcome Lafayette: 33-year-old farmer from Emanuel County, Georgia. Born in Georgia on 08/10/1828. Enlisted as a private in Company F on 05/09/1862 at Burke County, Georgia. Value of horse $175. Discharged on 07/18/1862. After the war, became a farmer in Emanuel County, Georgia. Married (1) Sabrina on 03/14/1850 in Emanuel County, Georgia (2) Georgia Ann Scott on 06/17/1858. Was the father of at least five children. Died on 11/04/1890.

268. Coleman, William: Enlisted as a private in Company L on 12/15/1862 at Burke County, Georgia. Sent to Georgia with Capt. Bostick to get a horse on 09/20/1864. Was surrendered by Gen. Joseph E. Johnston on 04/26/1865. Paroled at Greensboro, North Carolina, on 05/01/1865.

269. Collier, Edward Wyatt: 17-year-old from South Carolina. Born in Columbia County, Georgia, on 05/7/1845. Enlisted as a private in Company I on 03/05/1862 at Augusta, Georgia. Value of horse $175. Horse killed in action at the Chickahominy River on 06/10/1862. Admitted to General Hospital, Farmville, Virginia, on 06/11/1862 with typhoid fever. Returned to duty on 07/29/1862. Sent to infirmary/recruiting camp in November/December 1863. Captured at Stafford, Virginia, on 05/15/1864. Imprisoned at the Old Capitol Prison, Washington, D.C. Transferred to Fort Delaware Prison on 06/17/1864. Paroled at Ft. Delaware, Delaware, in 02/1865. After the war, became a farmer in Edgefield County, South Carolina, and then a cotton mill worker in Greenville County, South Carolina. Later, lived in Laurens County, South Carolina. Married Mary W. Mims ca. 1866 in Columbia County, Georgia, and they had at least five children. Applied for a Confederate pension in Laurens County, South Carolina, on 09/13/1919. Died in 1934.

270. Collins, William J: Farmer from Jackson County, Georgia. Enlisted as a private in Company C on 03/04/1862 in Jackson County, Georgia. Transferred to Company H in March/April 1862. Listed as a sergeant in May/June 1862. Listed as a farrier in September/October 1862. Sent to infirmary/recruiting camp on 12/23/1863. Sent to Georgia with Capt. Bostick to get a horse on 09/20/1864. Was surrendered by Gen. Joseph E. Johnston on 04/26/1865. Paroled at Greensboro, North Carolina, on 05/01/1865. After the war, lived in Jackson County, Georgia, and was married. Died after 1910.

271. Colvin, Thomas Jefferson: Butcher from Richmond County, Georgia. Born ca. 1829 in Georgia. Enlisted as a lieutenant in Company I on 03/04/1862 at Augusta, Georgia. Value of horse $280. Furloughed for 30 days beginning 12/26/1862. Killed at Trevilian Station, Virginia, on 06/11/1864. He and his wife, Estella or Esteller, had at least four children. His widow applied for a Confederate pension in Richmond County, Georgia.

272. Cone, William T.: Moulder from Augusta, Georgia. Born ca. 1838. Enlisted as a private in Company A on 08/17/1861 at Augusta, Georgia. Value of horse $150 and horse equipment $25. Last service record dated May/June 1862. Married Catherine on 04/12/1863 at Augusta, Georgia, and was the father of at least five children. He died on 09/15/1895. His widow applied for a Confederate pension in Richmond County, Georgia. On her application, she stated that he left his command because he was wounded and unfit for active duty, so he went to work in government shops at Augusta, Georgia. Her witness stated that William Cone was wounded at Hanover C.H., Virginia, about 01/1863. The pension was denied because she did not prove when and where he was wounded, how wounded, and in what way the wounds affected him to keep him out of the service, and when he was detailed to work in Government Shops.

273. Connelly, William Curran: 38-year-old lawyer from Dougherty County, Georgia. Born on 02/23/1823 in New York. Enlisted as a private in Company D on 08/10/1861 at Albany, Georgia. Value of horse $175 and horse equipment $25. Served on Thomas R.R. Cobb's brigade staff and then on Matthew C. Butler's staff. Married Ann Hora on 03/27/1860 in Dougherty County, Georgia. Applied for a Confederate pension in Douglas County, Georgia.

274. Cook, George W.D.: Boss of workshop in Fulton County, Georgia. Born ca. 1827 in Georgia. Enlisted as a lieutenant in Company B on 08/14/1861 at Atlanta, Georgia. Value of horses $250 and $225, and horse equipment $30 and $25. Furloughed to Georgia for 30 days beginning 01/20/1862. Extended 30 days. Resigned 11/06/1862. After the war, became a contractor in Fulton County, Georgia. Married Mary Winship on 12/24/1850 in Jones County, Georgia, and they had at least four children.

275. Cook, Joshua C. [J.D.]: Miller from Fulton County, Georgia. Born ca. 1835 in Georgia. Enlisted as a private in Company B on 08/14/1861 at Atlanta, Georgia. Value of horse $175 and horse equipment $5. Saddle furnished by the State of Georgia. Furloughed for 25 days beginning 01/20/1862. Furloughed for 30 days beginning 10/23/1863. Discharged at Camp Page on 02/18/1863. Married Mary M. Collier on 06/07/1860 in Fulton County, Georgia.

276. Cooley, John: Farmer from Cobb County, Georgia. Born ca. 1818 in Anderson, South Carolina. Enlisted as a private in Company E on 03/22/1862 at Roswell, Georgia. Value of horse $150. Discharged at Camp Marion, Yorktown, Virginia, on 07/23/1862 because of kidney stones. Described as having a fair complexion, sandy hair, blue eyes and being 5'7" tall. Was married and the father of at least three children.

277. Cooper, Fred L.: 17-year-old deputy county clerk from Richmond County, Georgia. Born in 03/1843 in Georgia. Enlisted as a private in Company I on 02/27/1862 at Augusta, Georgia. Value of horse $187. Promoted to lieutenant in an Alabama regiment. Discharged from Cobb's Legion Cavalry on 11/20/1863. After the war, worked as a department clerk in Richmond County, Georgia, and then as an insurance agent in Chatham County, Georgia. He and his wife, Theodosia, had six children. Died after 1900.

278. **Cooper, John M.:** 26-year-old from Hall County, Georgia. Born on 10/25/1835 in Gwinnett County, Georgia. Enlisted as a private Company C on 08/01/1861 at Athens, Clarke County, Georgia. Detailed building officers' quarters from 12/30/1861 until 01/14/1862. Detailed as a teamster beginning 11/01/1862. Sent to infirmary/recruiting camp in November/December 1863. Detailed as a teamster beginning 04/16/1864. Transferred to Company H on 08/01/1864. Was surrendered by Gen. Joseph E. Johnston on 04/26/1865. Paroled at Greensboro, North Carolina, on 05/01/1865. After the war, lived in Hall and Walton counties, Georgia. He and his wife, Elizabeth, had at least two children. Applied for a Confederate pension in Walton County, Georgia. Died after 1910.

279. **Cooper, R.E.:** Enlisted as a chaplain in Company F on 04/08/1861. Furloughed from General Hospital No. 9, Richmond, Virginia, on 01/24/1863. Appointed to staff on 03/06/1864. Last record, a pay voucher dated 06/20/1864.

280. **Copeland, Wiley R.:** Overseer from Greene County, Georgia. Born ca. 1840 in Georgia. Enlisted as a private in Company L on 05/02/1864 at Decatur, Georgia. Sent to Georgia with Capt. Bostick to get a horse on 09/20/1864. Was surrendered by Gen. Joseph E. Johnston on 04/26/1865. Paroled at Greensboro, North Carolina, on 05/01/1865. After the war, lived in Greene County, Georgia. He and his wife, Antonette, had at least two children. Died after 1880.

281. **Corlew, Thomas:** 26-year-old. Born in 03/1836 in Georgia. Enlisted as a private in Company D on 03/04/1862 at Dougherty County, Georgia. Value of horse $300 and horse equipment $40. After the war, worked as a retail grocer in Dougherty County, Georgia, and then as a farmer in McLennan County, Texas. Was married three times and was the father of at least two children. Among his wives were Alice and Jane. Died after 1910.

282. **Corley, M.:** Listed on a roster of Company D published in *The History of Dougherty County*, but not with the *Civil War Soldiers and Sailors System*. No service records in Cobb's Legion.

283. **Cory, Othniel E.:** Native of Watertown, New York. Enlisted as a private in Troup Artillery on 07/17/1861 at Albany, Georgia. Transferred to Cobb's Legion Cavalry, Company D, on 11/01/1862. Captured at Brookville, Maryland, on 06/30/1863 and sent to the Old Capitol Prison in Washington, D.C. Admitted to prison hospital. Released from hospital on 11/13/1863. Deserted and took the Oath in Washington, D.C., on 12/13/1863. Described as having a light complexion, light hair, blue eyes, and being 5' 8¾" tall.

284. **Cosnahan, Thomas J.:** 27-year-old planter from Burke County, Georgia. Born on 01/04/1835 in Georgia. Enlisted as a private in Company F on 03/25/1862 at Burke County, Georgia. Value of horse $225. On sick furlough in September/October 1862. Detailed as a teamster beginning 02/25/1863. Sent to Georgia to get a horse with Lt. Sinquefield under Special Order No. 27 from corps headquarters on 02/23/1864. Sent to Georgia with Capt. Bostick to get a horse on 09/20/1864. Was surrendered by Gen. Joseph E. Johnston on 04/26/1865. Paroled at Greensboro, North Carolina, on 05/01/1865. After the war, became a farmer in Burke County, Georgia. Married Susannah D. on 01/01/1857 and they had ten children. Died on 01/20/1903. His widow, Susannah D. Cosnahan, received a Confederate pension in Burke County, Georgia, from 1903 to 1907.

285. **Costello, Charles H.:** Enlisted as a private in Company B on 08/14/1861 at Atlanta, Georgia. Value of horse $225 and horse equipment $125, saddle furnished by the State of Georgia. Listed as a musician in November/December 1861. Discharged and paid off on 05/20/1862.

286. **Coston, John:** Born ca. 1841 in Georgia. Enlisted as a private in Company D on 08/10/1861 at Albany, Georgia. Sent to infirmary/recruiting camp at Camp Stephens on 05/07/1862. Detailed as a courier to Col. Wright on 11/22/1863. Sent to Georgia with Capt. Bostick to get a horse on 09/20/1864. Was surrendered by Gen. Joseph E. Johnston on 04/26/1865. Paroled at Greensboro, North Carolina, on 05/01/1865. After the war, became a farmer, and then did odd jobs in Lee County, Georgia. He and his wife, Amelia, had at least two children. Applied for a Confederate pension in Lee County, Georgia. Died after 1920.

287. **Cotter, Isaac:** 38-year-old overseer from Burke County, Georgia. Born in 1815 in Georgia. Enlisted as a private in Company F on 03/25/1862 at Burke County, Georgia. Value of horse $165. Detailed as a nurse at Winder Hospital beginning 08/15/1862. No horse in January/February 1864. Paroled at Augusta, Georgia, on 05/19/1865. Married Margaret Manson on 12/30/1846, in Jefferson County, Georgia, and they had at least one child.

288. Couch. B.H.: Transferred from Phillips Legion, Company D, to Cobb's Legion Cavalry, Company L, as a private on 08/02/1864 in exchange for Byrd Park. Last record, sent to infirmary/recruiting camp on 10/08/1864.

289. Couparle, Leroy Isadore: Teacher. Native of Georgia. Enlisted as a private in Cobb's Legion Infantry, Company G, on 08/25/1861 at Madison, Georgia. Transferred to Cobb's Legion Cavalry, Company F, as a private on 09/01/1862. Admitted to General Hospital No. 9, Richmond, Virginia, on 04/24/1863 for accidental gunshot wound in foot at Kelly's Ford, Virginia. Three toes were amputated. Transferred to Chimborazo Hospital, Richmond, Virginia, on 05/14/1863. Furloughed for 40 days beginning 06/04/1863. Last record, admitted to a hospital in Columbia, South Carolina, in September/October 1863.

290. Cowart, Samuel L.: Farm laborer from Jefferson County, Georgia. Born in Georgia on 10/7/1824. Enlisted as a private in Company L on 12/15/1862 at Burke County, Georgia. Captured 06/09/1863 at Beverly's Ford, Virginia. Imprisoned at the Old Capitol Prison, Washington, D.C. Paroled on 06/25/1863. Sent home to get a horse with Lt. Sinquefield under Special Order No. 27 from corps headquarters on 02/23/1864. Sent to Georgia with Capt. Bostick to get a horse on 09/20/1864. Was surrendered by Gen. Joseph E. Johnston on 04/26/1865. Paroled at Greensboro, North Carolina, on 05/01/1865. After the war, became a farmer in Jefferson County, Georgia. Married (1) Catharine Stephens in Jefferson County, Georgia, on 01/18/1849 and they had at least five children (2) Hattie. Applied for a Confederate pension in Jefferson County, Georgia. Died on 04/20/1900. Buried in the Oak Grove Methodist Church Cemetery in Jefferson County, Georgia.

291. Cowen, Edward W.: Laborer from Jackson County, Georgia. Born in Georgia ca. 1835. Brother of Elijah D., John H., and Stephen Cowen. Enlisted as a private in Company C on 06/10/1862 at Athens, Clarke County, Georgia. Sent home to get a horse with Lt. Sinquefield under Special Order No. 27 from corps headquarters on 02/23/1864. On furlough of indulgence beginning 09/02/1864. Sent to Georgia with Capt. Bostick to get a horse on 09/20/1864. Died at Weldon Navy Hospital, Weldon, North Carolina, from enteritis mucosa on 10/19/1864.

292. Cowen, Elijah D.: Born ca. 1837 in Georgia. Brother of Edward W., John H., and Stephen Cowen. Enlisted as a corporal in Company C on 08/14/1861 at Athens, Clarke County, Georgia. Elected lieutenant on 06/02/1862. Last record, November/December 1862. Died before 12/28/1862. (See John A. Wimpy.)

293. Cowen, John H.: Laborer from Jackson County, Georgia. Born in Georgia ca. 1837. Brother of Edward W., Elijah D., and Stephen Cowen. Enlisted as a private Company C on 08/01/1861 at Athens, Clarke County, Georgia. Died 08/22/1862 at Richmond, Virginia.

294. Cowen, Stephen D.: From Jackson County, Georgia. Brother of Edward W., Elijah D., and John H. Cowen. Born in Georgia ca. 1846. Enlisted as a private Company C on 04/01/1864 at Chesterfield, Georgia. Sent to Georgia with Capt. Bostick to get a horse on 09/20/1864. Was surrendered by Gen. Joseph E. Johnston on 04/26/1865. Paroled at Greensboro, North Carolina, on 05/01/1865.

295. Cox, James A: Resident of Georgia. Enlisted as a private in Company E on 06/01/1861 at Atlanta, Georgia. (Date may be an error and possibly should be 06/01/1862, but the June 1861 date is on all of his records. The June 1861 date is before Cobb's Legion Cavalry was organized.) Sent home to get a horse 11/12/1863. Promoted to corporal on 05/01/1864. Missing on 07/01/1864 after the battle at Ream's Station, Virginia. Last record, listed as absent without leave, September/October 1864. There is no record of his being captured or deserting, making the AWOL designation suspect, considering he went missing during a battle.

296. Craby, Pat: Born ca. 1834 in Ireland or Dougherty County, Georgia. Listed on a roster of Company D published in *The History of Dougherty County*, but not with the *Civil War Soldiers and Sailors System*. No service records in Cobb's Legion Cavalry.

297. Crawley, Joshua: Farmer from Morgan County, Georgia. Born ca. 1834 in Georgia. Enlisted as a private in Company B on 04/22/1862 at Atlanta, Georgia. Value of horse $220. No horse for 60 days in January/February 1863. In charge of horses at infirmary/recruiting camp in August 1863. Transferred to Company G in November/December 1863. Was surrendered by Gen. Joseph E. Johnston on 04/26/1865. Paroled at Greensboro, North Carolina, on 05/01/1865. After the war, became a farmer in Walton County, Georgia. Married Frances Elizabeth Higginbotham in Walton County, Georgia, on 12/25/1865. Died after 1870.

298. Cross, Rufus: 34-year-old from Burke County, Georgia. Born on 11/03/1828. Enlisted as a private in Company L on 12/15/1862 at Burke County, Georgia. Sent home to get a horse with

Lt. Sinquefield under Special Order No. 27 from corps headquarters on 02/23/1864. Sent to Georgia with Capt. Bostick to get a horse on 09/20/1864. Was surrendered by Gen. Joseph E. Johnston on 04/26/1865. Paroled at Greensboro, North Carolina, on 05/01/1865. After the war, became a farmer and then a landlord in Burke County, Georgia. Married (1) Sarah and they had at least seven children (2) Susan. Died on 04/20/1901. Buried in the Cross Family Cemetery in Burke County, Georgia.

299. Crumley, William Macon: 18-year-old from Fulton County, Georgia. Born possibly in Henry County, Georgia, on 04/07/1847. Enlisted as a private in Company I on 03/01/1862 at Augusta, Georgia. Value of horse $200. Detailed as a courier to Gen. Kershaw on 05/29/1862. Last record, March/April 1863. After the war, worked as a hardware merchant in Fulton County, Georgia. Married Carrie Mabrie Berry on 02/24/1875 in either Henry County or Fulton County, Georgia, and they had at least two children. Applied for a Confederate pension in Fulton County, Georgia. Died on 01/04/1921.

300. Curran, James: 34-year-old ditcher in Burke County, Georgia. Born in Ireland. Enlisted as a private in Company F on 03/25/1862 at Burke County, Georgia. Value of horse $225. Died in Georgia on 10/13/1863 from a "personal difficulty" with a railroad conductor. Cause of death is listed as "stabbed." Buried in the Magnolia Cemetery in Augusta, Richmond County, Georgia.

301. Cutter, Joseph S.: Clerk from Augusta, Georgia. Born in New Jersey ca. 1841. Enlisted as a sergeant in Company A on 08/17/1861 at Augusta, Georgia. Value of horse $225, and horse equipment $30. His service record for May/June 1862 shows his rank reduced to a private. Last service record states that he was discharged on 08/17/1862. He hired Irvine as a substitute, but Irvine deserted the same day he enlisted. The Muster Roll Commission lists Cutter as a deserter in 1864. Other records show that he joined the Union army on 08/30/1862 in New Jersey. After the war, lived in Plainfield, Union County, New Jersey. Was married and the father of at least three children.

302. Dagnell, Elisha J.: 25-year-old from Georgia. Born in 06/1832 in South Carolina. Enlisted as a private in Company I on 03/18/1862 at Augusta, Georgia. Value of horse $200. Sent to infirmary/recruiting camp in November/December 1863. Detailed at Fredericksburg to take up railroad iron on 04/01/1864. Sent to Georgia with Capt. Bostick to get a horse on 09/20/1864. Was surrendered by Gen. Joseph E. Johnston on 04/26/1865. Paroled at Greensboro, North Carolina, on 05/01/1865. After the war, was an inmate at the Georgia Lunatic Asylum. After that, he was paralyzed and lived with his wife. Later, he worked as a cemetery cleaner. He and his wife, Nancy, had six children. Applied for a Confederate pension in Richmond County, Georgia. Died before 1910. His widow, Nancy Ann Dagnell, applied for a Confederate pension in Richmond County, Georgia.

303. Dalvigny, Charles F. S.: Farmer from Fulton County, Georgia. Born ca. 1844 in South Carolina. Enlisted as a private in Company B on 04/18/1862 at Atlanta, Georgia. Value of horse $160. Detailed to Commissary Department in July/August 1862. Transferred to Company G in November/December 1863. Sent to infirmary/recruiting camp in January/February 1864. Was surrendered by Gen. Joseph E. Johnston on 04/26/1865. Paroled at Greensboro, North Carolina, on 05/01/1865. After the war, became a farmer in Black Hall, Fulton County, Georgia, and then moved to Greenville County, South Carolina. He and his wife, Elizabeth, had at least three children. Applied for a Confederate pension in Fulton County, Georgia. Died after 1920.

304. Daniel, Julius Foster: 15-year-old* student from Jackson County, Georgia. Born ca. 1845. Enlisted as a private in Company C on 04/01/1864 at Chesterfield, Georgia. On sick furlough beginning 09/15/1864. Was surrendered by Gen. Joseph E. Johnston on 04/26/1865. Paroled at Greensboro, North Carolina, on 05/01/1865. Died in 1896.

305. Daniel, Theodore Floyd: 21-year-old farmer from Burke County, Georgia. Born on 05/24/1840 in Richmond County, Georgia. Enlisted as a sergeant in Company F on 08/01/1861 at Waynesboro, Georgia. Admitted to Winder Hospital, Richmond, Virginia, on 01/10/1862 and on 10/29/1862. Captured at South Mountain on 09/14/1862. Sent to Fort Delaware Prison. Exchanged at Aiken's Landing, Virginia, on 11/10/1862. Elected lieutenant on 07/05/1863. Admitted to General Hospital No. 3 at Lynchburg, Virginia, on 05/07/1864. Promoted to lieutenant on 08/16/1864. Captured at Sailor's Creek, Virginia, on 04/06/1865. Sent to Johnson Island, Ohio, prison on 04/17/1865. Released on 06/17/1865. Described as having a fair complexion, dark hair, blue eyes and being 5'11" tall. After the war, became a farmer in

Howard, page 19.

Burke County, Georgia. Married Mary Emeline Miller on 08/10/1865 and they had five children. Applied for a Confederate pension in Burke County, Georgia, in 1920. Died on 02/14/1928.

306. Daniel, W.C.: Enlisted as a private in Company B as a private on 04/22/1864 at Atlanta, Georgia. No horse until 08/16/1864. Was listed as present on last record, September/October 1864.

307. Davenport. Joseph T.: From Georgia. Born ca. 1830 in Virginia. Enlisted as a private in Company I on 03/04/1862 at Augusta, Georgia. Sent to infirmary/recruiting camp on 12/20/1863. Was surrendered by Gen. Joseph E. Johnston on 04/26/1865. Paroled at Greensboro, North Carolina, on 05/01/1865. After the war, became a farmer in Richmond County, Georgia. He and his wife, Mary, had at least six children. Died after 1870.

308. David, John White: Farm laborer from Jackson County, Georgia. Born ca. 1838 in Georgia. Enlisted as a private in Company C on 08/01/1861 at Athens, Clarke County, Georgia. Detailed building winter quarters in November/December 1861. Horse killed in action at Hunterstown, Pennsylvania, on 07/02/1863. Sent to infirmary/recruiting camp on 12/01/1863. Captured 05/29/1864 at Hanover Court House, Virginia. Sent to White House, Virginia, on 06/11/1864. Transferred to Elmira Prison, New York, on 07/12/1864. Died of typhoid fever at Elmira Prison Camp, New York, on 02/16/1865. Buried at the Woodlawn Cemetery in Elmira, New York, grave 2158.

309. Davis, Benjamin: Born ca. 1840. Enlisted as a private in Company H on 03/03/1862 at Athens, Clarke County, Georgia. Discharged from service and paid off on 07/17/1862. After the war, became a farmer in White County, Georgia. He and his wife, Mattie or Medda, had at least two children. His widow applied for a Confederate pension in White County, Georgia.

310. Davis, Benjamin J.: Farmer from Lumpkin County, Georgia. Born in Georgia ca. 1840. Enlisted as a private in the 1st Georgia Infantry, Company H, on 03/18/1861. Appointed corporal on 12/01/1861. Appointed sergeant on 02/09/1862. Mustered out at Augusta, Georgia, on 03/18/1862. Enlisted as a sergeant in Cobb's Legion Cavalry, Company G, on 04/18/1862. Value of horse $185. Furloughed to Georgia for 30 days beginning 02/21/1863. Sent to Georgia to get a horse on 11/10/1863. Sent to Georgia to get a horse with Lt. William H. Payne under orders from Gen. Stuart in 04/1864. Admitted to Chimborazo Hospital No. 6, Richmond, Virginia, on 07/05/1864. Transferred to a hospital at Lynchburg, Virginia, on 07/10/1864. Wounded at Ream's Station, Virginia, on 08/25/1864. Admitted to Pettigrew General Hospital No. 12, Raleigh, North Carolina, on 08/25/1864, where right leg was amputated at the thigh. Last record, furloughed to Georgia for 60 days beginning 11/24/1864. After the war, became a planter in Fulton County, Georgia. Married Delilah or Lila J. Davis on 11/05/1873 in Lumpkin County. Applied for a Confederate pension in Lumpkin County, Georgia. Died after 1873. His widow, Lila J. Davis, applied for a Confederate pension in Fulton County, Georgia.

311. Davis, Cyrus C.: Clerk from New York. Born ca. 1840 in Nova Scotia. Enlisted as a private in Company D on 08/10/1861 at Albany, Georgia. On sick furlough beginning 07/29/1862. Admitted to Winder Hospital, Richmond, Virginia, on 10/31/1863. On furlough to Georgia for 60 days beginning 11/20/1863. Furlough extended. Sent to Blind Asylum Hospital, Macon, Georgia, on 01/15/1864. On furlough from Winder Hospital, Richmond, Virginia, to Georgia for 30 days in 04/1864. Furlough extended. No horse on 08/04/1864. Admitted to Floyd House and Ocmulgee Hospital, Macon, Georgia, on 09/04/1864. Given discharge due to chronic diarrhea and debility for more than 12 months. Described as having a light complexion, blue eyes, dark hair and being 5' 8" tall. After the war, became a retail merchant in Mitchell County, Georgia. Married Hannah McGee on 10/07/1876 in Mitchell County, Georgia.

312. Davis, D.R.: 16-year-old from Mississippi. Enlisted as a private in Company K on 01/18/1863 at Camp Maynard, Georgia. Captured at Upperville, Virginia, on 06/21/1863. Paroled at the Old Capitol Prison, Washington D.C., on 06/25/1863. Sent home to get a horse 08/23/1863. Absent without leave on 10/22/1863. Last record, still absent without leave March/April 1864.

313. Davis, Daniel: Resident of Lumpkin County, Georgia. Enlisted as a private in Company C on 03/18/1863 at Brownsburg, Virginia. Value of horse $350. Horse killed in action at Brandy Station, Virginia, on 06/09/1863. Admitted to Jackson Hospital, Richmond, Virginia, on 05/23/1864. Returned to duty on 06/01/1864. Sent to Georgia with Capt. Bostick to get a horse on 09/20/1864. Wiley Howard wrote of him that "I saw ... [at Ream's Station] my friend Dan Davis, of Lumpkin county, with the cool courage and utter disregard of danger which the one-quarter Indian blood in his veins nourishes, had his gun stock splintered in his hands while preparing to shoot, and another minié ball at the same instant cut his hat band in two, still holding his shattered gun and with an oath said, 'Lieutenant, they broke my gun and nearly knocked my hat off before I could get another crack at 'em, Lend me your gun and I'll kill some more.'"*

314. Davis, L.B.: Enlisted as a private in Company D on 08/10/1861 at Albany, Georgia. Value of horse $250 and horse equipment $25, saddle furnished by the State of Georgia. Sent home on sick furlough from 11/28/1861 to 12/24/1861. Was absent on last record, November/December 1861.

315. Davis, R.G.: Resident of Georgia. Enlisted as a private in Company E on 05/08/1863 at Atlanta, Georgia. Sent to infirmary/recruiting camp on 11/20/1863. Sent home to get a horse with Lt. Sinquefield under Special Order No. 27 from corps headquarters on 02/23/1864. Absent sick on 03/23/1864. No horse on 08/01/1864. Last record, September/October 1864, lists him as absent without leave since 08/01/1864.

316. Davis, William L.: Enlisted as a private in Company H on 07/15/1864 in Madison, Georgia. Sent to Georgia with Capt. Bostick to get a horse on 09/20/1864. Was surrendered by Gen. Joseph E. Johnston on 04/26/1865. Paroled at Greensboro, North Carolina, on 05/01/1865. Applied for a Confederate pension in Fulton County, Georgia.

317. Davis, William S.: Enlisted as a private in Company F on 04/15/1864 at Greensboro, Georgia. Sent to Georgia with Capt. Bostick to get a horse on 09/20/1864. Was surrendered by Gen. Joseph E. Johnston on 04/26/1865. Paroled at Greensboro, North Carolina, on 05/01/1865.

318. Davis, William W.: Resident of Georgia. Enlisted as a private in Company H on 03/25/1862 at Athens, Clarke County, Georgia. Fined $12 by order of court-martial on 02/1863. Sent to Georgia with Capt. Bostick to get a horse on 09/20/1864. Was surrendered by Gen. Joseph E. Johnston on 04/26/1865. Paroled at Greensboro, North Carolina, on 05/01/1865. Applied for a Confederate pension in Jackson County, Georgia. He later applied for a transfer of his pension to Clarke County, Georgia.

319. Dawson, James B.: 22-year-old from Burke County, Georgia. Born in 06/1840 in Georgia. Enlisted as a corporal in Company F on 03/25/1862 at Burke County. Value of horse $140. Wounded in left arm and side by a minié ball on 11/27/1863 at Mine Run, Virginia. Admitted to Jackson Hospital, Richmond, Virginia, on 11/29/1863. On furlough to Georgia in November/December 1863. Admitted to hospital at Weldon, North Carolina, on 09/01/1864. Last record September/October 1864, on furlough for 60 days beginning 09/20/1864. After the war, became a farmer in Burke County, Georgia. Married Sarah Eliza J. Causey on 07/15/1873 in Jefferson County, Georgia, and they had five children. Died ca. 1905. Buried in the Lowery Cemetery in Burke County, Georgia. His widow, Eliza Dawson, applied for a Confederate pension in Jefferson County, Georgia.

320. Day, James Walter: 18-year-old from Georgia. Enlisted as a private in Company I on 03/01/1862 at Augusta, Georgia. Value of horse $240. Became a bugler in January/February 1863. Admitted to General Hospital, Staunton, Virginia, on 03/17/1863 with chills. Captured at Upperville, Virginia, on 06/21/1863. Paroled at the Old Capitol Prison, Washington D.C., on 06/25/1863. Exchanged at City Point, Virginia, on 06/30/1863. Admitted to Winder Hospital, Richmond, Virginia, on 07/14/1863. Admitted to Jackson Hospital, Richmond, Virginia, on 08/1863. Returned to duty on 09/10/1863. Absent without leave on 01/01/1864. Last record, listed as present in September/October 1864.

321. Dearing, William P.: 18-year-old from Richmond County, Georgia. Born in 07/1843 in Georgia. Enlisted as a private Company C on 05/03/1862 at Athens, Clarke County, Georgia. Captured at Malvern Hill on 08/05/1862. Paroled at Fort Wool, Virginia, on 08/26/1862. Admitted to General Hospital No. 16, Richmond, Virginia, on 10/28/1862. Returned to duty on 11/05/1862. Transferred to Troup Artillery on 11/13/1862. After the war, worked as a coal dealer in Richmond County, Georgia, and then as the manager of the Neely Institute in Fulton County, Georgia. Married Emma Kennon on 03/21/1867 in Newton County, Georgia, and they had at least four children. Died after 1900.

322. Delony, William Gaston: 34-year-old attorney in Clarke County, Georgia. Born on 09/08/1826 in Camden County, Georgia. Graduated from the University of Georgia in 1846. Enlisted as a captain in Company C on 08/01/1861 at Athens, Georgia. Furloughed for 25 days in 12/1861. Extended to 50 days. Promoted to major on 05/22/1862. Promoted to colonel on 11/01/1862. P.M.B. Young mentioned him in his report of the Battle Brandy Station on 06/10/1863: "I cannot fail to

*Howard, page 12.

mention the intrepid personal gallantry of my lieutenant-colonel, W.G. Delony." Wounded and captured at Jack's Shop, Virginia, on 09/22/1863. Horse killed at Jack's Shop, Virginia, on 09/22/1863. Died on 10/02/1863 at Stanton U.S. General Hospital in Washington, D.C., from gunshot wound to left leg. Buried at Oconee Hill Cemetery at Athens, Clarke County, Georgia. Married Rosa Eugenia Huguenin on 05/16/1854 in either Chatham County or Clarke County, Georgia, and they had two children. His widow applied for a Confederate pension in Clarke County, Georgia.

323. Dempsey, Harrington E.: Farmer from DeKalb County, Georgia. Born ca. 1828 in Georgia. Enlisted as a private in Company G on 12/31/1862 at Camp Randolph, DeKalb County, Georgia. Sent to Georgia to get a horse with Lt. Sinquefield under Special Order No. 27 from corps headquarters on 02/23/1864. On furlough to Georgia for 24 days beginning 08/12/1864. Absent without leave on 09/15/1864. Last record, still absent without leave in September/October 1864. After the war, became a farmer in DeKalb County, Georgia. He and his wife, Harriet, had at least seven children. Died after 1880.

324. Densmore, Abel B.C.: Farmer from Lumpkin County, Georgia. Born ca. 1840 in Georgia. Enlisted as a private in Company C on 08/01/1861 at Athens, Clarke County, Georgia. Died on 04/17/1862 at Garysburg, North Carolina. His father, Samuel P. Densmore, received his back pay, as he was not survived by a wife or children.

325. Dent, Albert F.: Enlisted as a private in Company C on 03/19/1862 at Clark County, Georgia. Last record, receipt for pay dated 07/04/1864.

326. Dent, Alexander F.[T.][P.]: 20-year-old student from Clarke County, Georgia. Born on 01/13/1842 in Clarke County, Georgia. Brother of Stephen P. Dent. Enlisted as a private in Company H on 03/27/1862 at Athens, Clarke County, Georgia. Listed in May/June 1862 as a corporal. Elected lieutenant on 08/01/1864. Was the only officer left in the company after the death of Lt. Dunnahoo on 04/12/1865. Was surrendered by Gen. Joseph E. Johnston on 04/26/1865. Paroled at Greensboro, North Carolina, on 05/01/1865.

327. Dent, Stephen P.[T.]: Student from Clarke County, Georgia. Born ca. 1845 in Georgia. Brother of Alexander F. Dent. Enlisted as a private in Company H on 03/27/1862 at Athens, Clarke County, Georgia. Admitted to Jackson Hospital, Richmond, Virginia, on 08/01/1863. Sent to Georgia to get a horse on 11/11/1863. Appointed cadet in the Confederate States Army on 12/22/1863. Ordered to report for assignment and duty to Maj. Gen. Wade Hampton on 03/19/1864. Assigned to duty with Maj. Henry S. Farley commanding the Cavalry Sharpshooters by Maj. Gen. Hampton on 01/08/1865.

328. Deriso, J.D.: Resident of Georgia. Enlisted as a private in Company D on 08/10/1861 at Albany, Georgia. Value of horse $125 and horse equipment $15, bridle furnished by the State of Georgia. Sent to infirmary/recruiting camp on 12/20/1863. Sent to Georgia with Capt. Bostick to get a horse on 09/20/1864. Was surrendered by Gen. Joseph E. Johnston on 04/26/1865. Paroled at Greensboro, North Carolina, on 05/01/1865.

329. Deriso, James M.: Born ca. 1828 in Georgia. Enlisted as a private in Company L on 12/15/1862 at Burke County, Georgia. Absent without leave beginning 04/01/1864. Rejoined the command on 07/01/1864. Sent to Georgia with Capt. Bostick to get a horse on 09/20/1864. Was surrendered by Gen. Joseph E. Johnston on 04/26/1865. Paroled at Augusta, Georgia, on 05/18/1865. After the war, became a farmer in Jefferson County, Georgia. Married Elizabeth J. ca. 1850 and they had at least 11 children. Died after 1880. His widow applied for a Confederate pension in Jefferson County, Georgia.

330. Dial, Tully John: 28-year-old farmer from Cherokee County, Georgia. Born on 01/25/1834 in Georgia. Enlisted as a sergeant in Company E on 03/22/1862 at Roswell, Georgia. Value of horse $185. Listed as a lieutenant in January/February 1863. Resigned on 03/18/1863. Married Frances Pitts ca. 1858 and they had at least three children. Died on 01/03/1865, possibly in Woodstock, Cherokee County, Georgia.

331. Dial, William Choice: 36-year-old farmer from Cherokee County, Georgia. Born on 04/11/1826 in South Carolina. Enlisted as a lieutenant in Company E on 03/22/1862 at Roswell, Georgia. Value of horse $200. Wounded at Barbee's Crossroads on 11/08/1862. Sent on a 60 day furlough beginning 11/13/1862. Admitted to General Hospital No. 10, Richmond, Virginia, on 02/20/1863. Promoted to captain on 10/09/1863. Still absent from wounds received at Barbee's Crossroads, September/October 1864. Retired 01/16/1865. After the war, became a farmer in Cherokee County, Georgia. Married Sarah Foster on 10/9/1855 in Cherokee County, Georgia, and they had six children. Applied for a Confederate pension in Cherokee County, Georgia. Died after 1900.

332. Dickens, B.L.: Resident of Georgia. Enlisted as a private in Company D on 08/10/1861 at Albany, Georgia. Value of horse $225 and horse equipment $5. Listed as sergeant on 05/07/1862. Elected lieutenant on 06/02/1862. Detailed as a scout with Lt. Shiver on 01/14/1864. Captured at Hanover Court House on 05/31/1864. Transferred to Elmira Prison, New York, on 07/12/1864. Last record, exchanged on 10/29/1864.

333. Dickerson, Augustus C.: 37-year-old from Georgia. Enlisted as a private in Company E on 03/22/1862 at Roswell, Georgia. Value of horse $160. Sent home to get a horse in March/April 1862. No horse on 08/12/1863. Sent home to get a horse on 11/12/1863. Absent sick on 01/17/1864. Absent without leave on 02/17/1864. Last record September/October 1864, sent to Georgia to get a horse with Capt. Bostick on 09/20/1864.

334. Dickinson, Walter M.: 35-year-old carpenter from Bibb County, Georgia. Born in 02/1826 in Massachusetts. Enlisted as a private in Company D on 08/10/1861 at Albany, Georgia. Value of horse $200 and horse equipment $25, saddle furnished by the State of Georgia. Detailed as a master carpenter in November/December 1861. Detailed to Commissary Department in September/October 1862. Detailed to work on S.W.R.R on 01/14/1864. Last record 11/01/1864, still on detail work on the S.W.R.R. After the war, became a carpenter in Bibb County, Georgia. He married (1) Margaret and (2) Elizabeth and was the father of at least two children. Applied for a Confederate pension in Bibb County, Georgia. Died after 1900.

335. Dickson, William Capers: Student from Newton County, Georgia. Born on 06/14/1845 in Newton County, Georgia. Enlisted as a private in Company I on 10/08/1862 at Bunker Hill, [West] Virginia. Detailed at Fredericksburg to fish on 04/01/1864. Captured at Stafford County, Virginia, on 05/15/1864. Imprisoned at the Old Capitol Prison, Washington, D.C. Transferred to Fort Delaware Prison on 06/17/1864. Last record, sent to General Hospital No. 9, Richmond, Virginia, on 03/05/1865. After the war, read law and then became a lawyer in Newton County, Georgia. Died on 06/11/1914. Buried in the Oxford Historical Cemetery, Newton County, Georgia.

336. Dill, James S.: Born ca. 1835 in Georgia. Enlisted as a private in Company A at Decatur, Georgia, on 04/17/1864. Admitted to Jackson Hospital, Richmond, Virginia, with dysentery on 08/15/1864. Discharged from hospital on 08/29/1864. Sent to Georgia to get a horse with Capt. Bostick on 09/20/1864. Last record, a receipt for clothing dated 11/26/1864. After the war, worked as a clerk in a textile warehouse in Richmond County, Georgia. Married Anna and was the father of at least four children.

337. Dixon, James A.: 34-year-old grocery merchant from Burke County, Georgia. Born in 1828 in Georgia or New York. Enlisted as a private in Company F on 05/09/1862 at Burke County, Georgia. Value of horse $300 and horse equipment $30. Transferred to Company L on 03/01/1863. Appointed sergeant on 09/01/1863. Sent to Georgia with Capt. Bostick to get a horse on 09/20/1864. Was surrendered by Gen. Joseph E. Johnston on 04/26/1865. Paroled at Greensboro, North Carolina, on 05/01/1865. Married Mary J. Frailey on 09/25/1851 and they had at least three children. Died on 01/20/1872. His widow, Mary J. Dixon, received a Confederate pension in Burke County, Georgia, in 1904 and 1905.

338. Dodgen, James Anison: 17-year-old from Cobb County, Georgia. Born on 05/17/1844 in Georgia. Enlisted in 7th Georgia Infantry, Company H, as a private on 03/30/1862. Discharged as being underage on 12/26/1862. Enlisted as a private in Cobb's Legion Cavalry, Company E, on 07/04/1863. No horse on 09/01/1863. Sent home to get a horse on 11/12/1863. No horse, detailed as a guard on railroad on 02/15/1864. Was surrendered by Gen. Joseph E. Johnston on 04/26/1865. Paroled at Greensboro, North Carolina, on 05/01/1865. After the war, lived in Fulton County, Georgia. Married Harriett ca. 1872 and they had at least four children. Applied for a Confederate pension in Fulton County, Georgia.

339. Dodgen, John W.: Enlisted as a private in Company B on 04/25/1864 at Atlanta, Georgia. No horse. Sent to Georgia with Capt. Bostick to get a horse on 09/20/1864. Was surrendered by Gen. Joseph E. Johnston on 04/26/1865. Paroled at Greensboro, North Carolina, on 05/01/1865.

340. Donohue, Martin: 20-year-old laborer from Richmond County, Georgia. Born in Ireland. Enlisted as a private in Company F on 03/25/1862 at Burke County, Georgia. Value of horse $250. Sent to infirmary/recruiting camp on 10/27/1863 to attend horses. Detailed to ambulance corps on 05/01/1864. Detailed to carry horses to infirmary/recruiting camp on 09/01/1864. Was surrendered by Gen. Joseph E. Johnston on 04/26/1865. Paroled at Greensboro, North Carolina, on 05/01/1865.

341. Donor [Donough], J. Henry: 21-year-old. Enlisted as a private in Company E on 03/22/1862 at Roswell, Georgia. Value of horse $200. Admitted to Winder Hospital, Richmond, Virginia, on 09/25/1862. Returned to duty on 09/29/1862. Admitted to Charity Hospital, Gordonsville, Virginia. Died 03/14/1863 of typhoid fever.

342. Doris, Bernard: From Georgia. Born ca. 1833 in Ireland. Enlisted as a sergeant in Company I on 03/01/1862 at Augusta, Georgia. Value of horse $275. Sent to infirmary/recruiting camp on 11/13/1863. Sent to Georgia with Capt. Bostick to get a horse on 09/20/1864. Was paroled at Savannah, Georgia, on 05/06/1865. Described as having gray eyes, brown hair, dark complexion and being 5'11" tall. Note said, "Wished to go home." After the war, became a retail grocer in Richmond County, Georgia. Was married to Ellen.

343. Dorris, John: Resident of Richmond County, Georgia. Enlisted as a private in Company I. Captured at Columbia, South Carolina, on 02/17/1865. Sent to New Bern, North Carolina. Transferred to Hart's Island, New York Harbor, on 04/10/1865. Released on 06/15/1865. Described as having fair complexion, light hair, blue eyes, and being 5'6" tall.

344. Dosier, J.S.: Resident of Georgia. Enlisted as a private in Company D on 08/10/1861 at Albany, Georgia. Value of horse $150 and horse equipment $25, furnished by the State of Georgia. Sick in November/December 1861. Absent with dismounted men, in March/April 1863. Was surrendered by Gen. Joseph E. Johnston on 04/26/1865. Paroled at Greensboro, North Carolina, on 05/01/1865.

345. Dougherty, David H.: 18-year-old. Born in Tennessee in 05/1843. Enlisted as a private in Company B on 03/06/1862 at Atlanta, Georgia. Value of horse $200 and horse equipment $33. Elected lieutenant on 02/15/1863. Transferred to Company G. Furloughed to Georgia for 30 days beginning 02/21/1863. Horse killed in action near Culpeper Court House on 09/13/1863. Wounded in left hand at Jack's Shop, Virginia, on 09/22/1863 and sent to Richmond, Virginia. Furloughed to Georgia beginning 10/14/1863. Detailed to commissary department at Atlanta, Georgia, in 04/1864 due to disability. Was surrendered by Gen. Joseph E. Johnston on 04/26/1865. Paroled at Atlanta, Georgia, on 05/01/1865. After the war, became a dry goods merchant in Fulton County, Georgia. He and his wife, Mary, had three children. Applied for a Confederate pension in Fulton County, Georgia. Died after 1900.

346. Dougherty, Henry R.: Resident of Georgia. Enlisted as a private in Company H on 03/19/1862 at Athens, Clarke County, Georgia. Transferred to Company G on 06/01/1862. Detailed to Commissary Department in July/August 1862. Sent home to get a horse with Lt. Sinquefield under Special Order No. 27 from corps headquarters on 02/23/1864. Was surrendered by Gen. Joseph E. Johnston on 04/26/1865. Paroled at Greensboro, North Carolina, on 05/01/1865.

347. Dougherty, John: 18-year-old. Enlisted as a private in Company K on 02/01/1863 at Camp Maynard, Georgia. Deserted 04/25/1865 and confined to penitentiary.

348. Douglas, G.C.[B.]: Student from Dougherty County, Georgia, enlisted under the age of 16. Born ca. 1846. Enlisted as a private in Company D on 08/10/1861 at Albany, Georgia. Value of horse $300 and horse equipment $25, saddle furnished by the State of Georgia. Furloughed for 60 days beginning 02/10/1862. Discharged on 05/16/1862 for being a minor. Recommended for cadetship.

349. Dover, Augustus: 24-year-old from Georgia. Enlisted as a private in Company B on 04/28/1862 at Atlanta, Georgia. Transferred to Company G. Sent to infirmary/recruiting camp in November/December 1863. Admitted to hospital May/September 1864. Was surrendered by Gen. Joseph E. Johnston on 04/26/1865. Paroled at Greensboro, North Carolina, on 05/01/1865.

350. Downs, Elias Crockett: 22-year-old barkeeper from Fulton County, Georgia. Born on 12/10/1840 in Walton County, Georgia. Enlisted as a private in Company G on 04/18/1863 at Camp Randolph, Georgia. Detailed as a courier to Maj. Rice on 04/18/1863. Sent home to get a horse with Lt. Sinquefield under Special Order No. 27 from corps headquarters on 02/23/1864. Sent to Georgia with Capt. Bostick to get a horse on 09/20/1864. Was surrendered by Gen. Joseph E. Johnston on 04/26/1865. Paroled at Greensboro, North Carolina, on 05/01/1865. After the war, worked as a real estate agent in Colbert County, Alabama. He and his wife, Mary, had two children. Died after 1920.

351. Downs, Lindsey Warren: 21-year-old carpenter from Richmond County, Georgia. Born in Georgia in 05/1839 or 05/30/1840. Brother of William W. Downs. Enlisted as a private in Company I on 03/03/1862 at Augusta, Georgia. Value of horse $155. Sick at Lynchburg, Virginia, on 10/07/1863. Absent without leave on 02/13/1864. Sick in hospital in Powhatan County on 06/15/1864. Last record, name appears on a receipt for clothing on 10/12/1864. After the war, became a farmer in Clarke and Oconee counties, Georgia. Married (1) Nancy Smith on 04/14/1859 (2) Sarah Hinton Daniel on 05/18/1865 in Oglethorpe

County, Georgia. Was the father of at least twelve children. Applied for a Confederate pension in Oconee County, Georgia. Died on 09/15/1913. His widow, Sarah H. Downs, applied for a Confederate pension in Oconee County, Georgia.

352. **Downs, William W.:** Laborer from Richmond County, Georgia. Born ca. 1838 in Georgia. Brother of Lindsey Warren Downs. Enlisted in 48th Georgia Infantry, Company K, as a private in 03/4/1862. Transferred to Cobb's Legion Cavalry, Company I, on 10/20/1862. Enlistment date in Company I was 03/04/1862 at Augusta, Georgia. Admitted to Jackson Hospital, Richmond, Virginia, on 01/02/1864. Deserted from hospital on 01/11/1864. After the war, became a carpenter in Richmond County, Georgia. Married Lucy ca. 1872 and they had at least four children. Died on 05/24/1912 in Fulton County, Georgia.

353. **Dozier [Dosier], John Stapler:** 18-year-old from Columbia County, Georgia. Enlisted as a private in Company A on 05/01/1862 at Augusta, Georgia. Detailed on a scouting party with Lt. Shivers of the 2nd South Carolina Cavalry in Culpeper County, Virginia, from 12/15/1863 until 12/17/1863. Sent to infirmary/recruiting camp on 02/23/1864. Sent to hospital in March/April 1864. Admitted to Kittrell Springs Hospital on 08/23/1864. Wounded at Jack's Shop, Virginia, on 09/23/64. Detailed with Gen. P.M.B. Young in December 1864 until close of war. Was in South Carolina with Gen. Young at the time of the surrender. After the war, lived at Atlanta, Georgia. Applied for a Confederate pension in Fulton County, Georgia. Died after 11/1919.

354. **Dozier, William L.:** 29-year-old native of Georgia. Enlisted as a private in Company F on 05/05/1862 at Burke County, Georgia. Value of horse $200. Admitted to Winder Hospital, Richmond, Virginia, on 10/31/1863. On furlough for 30 days beginning 12/04/1863. Absent without leave beginning 01/01/1864. Became sick on return from furlough to Georgia and was sent to hospital on 01/17/1864. Admitted to Jackson Hospital, Richmond, Virginia, on 01/26/1864 with scabies. Returned to duty on 03/04/1864. Was present on last record, September/October 1864.

355. **Drake, Augustus:** From Burke County, Georgia. Born in Georgia ca. 1842. Enlisted as a private in Company F on 03/25/1862 at Burke County. Value of horse $200. Admitted to U.S.A. General Military Hospital No. 4, Wilmington, North Carolina, on 05/17/1862. Returned to duty on 05/21/1862. On sick furlough to Georgia in September/October 1862. Admitted to hospital at Liberty, Bedford County, Virginia, on 04/08/1863 with pneumonia. Admitted to Winder Hospital, Richmond, Virginia, on 12/04/1863. Returned to duty on 12/23/1863. Admitted to Jackson Hospital, Richmond, Virginia, 01/25/1864 with wound to right arm. Returned to duty on 02/09/1864. Sent home to get a horse with Lt. Sinquefield under Special Order No. 27 from corps headquarters on 02/23/1864. Admitted to Jackson Hospital, Richmond, Virginia, on 03/06/1864 with fracture to right arm. Last record, returned to duty on 03/14/1864.

356. **Drake, James Madison:** Brick mason from Cobb County, Georgia. Born ca. 1832 in Georgia. Enlisted as a private in Company E on 03/22/1862 at Roswell, Georgia. Value of horse $160. Sent to infirmary/recruiting camp on 08/20/1863. Sent to Georgia with Capt. Bostick to get a horse on 09/20/1864. After the war, became a farmer in Milton County, Georgia. Married Elizabeth Stancil ca. 1853 and they had nine children. Applied for a Confederate pension in Milton County, Georgia. Died in Milton County, Georgia, in 11/1918.

357. **Drinkwater, John W.:** Brick mason from Dougherty County, Georgia. Born ca. 1838 in Randolph County, Georgia. Enlisted as a private in Company D on 08/10/1861 at Albany, Georgia. Value of horse $175 and horse equipment $25, furnished by State of Georgia. Absent with dismounted men March/April 1863. Sent to infirmary/recruiting camp 03/07/1864. Sent to Georgia with Capt. Bostick to get a horse on 09/20/1864. Was surrendered by Gen. Joseph E. Johnston on 04/26/1865. Paroled at Greensboro, North Carolina, on 05/01/1865. After the war, worked as a butcher in Dougherty County, Georgia. Married Mary P. Roby on 10/04/1866 in Dougherty County, Georgia.

358. **Duckett, Berry [Liberry] T.:** From Dahlonega, Georgia. Born ca. 1834 in Georgia. Enlisted as a private in Company C on 01/18/1863 at Athens, Clarke County, Georgia. Admitted to hospital in Richmond, Virginia, on 11/03/1863 with typhoid fever and severe pneumonia. On sick furlough to Georgia for 60 days beginning 11/30/1863. Sent to Georgia with Capt. Bostick to get a horse on 09/20/1864. Was surrendered by Gen. Joseph E. Johnston on 04/26/1865. Paroled at Greensboro, North Carolina, on 05/01/1865. After the war, became a farm laborer in Banks County, Georgia. He and his wife, Martha, had at least one child.

359. **Duke, James H.:** Overseer from Burke County, Georgia. Listed in Cobb's Legion Infantry,

Company F, in 11/1862. Enlisted as a private in Cobb's Legion Cavalry, Company L, on 12/15/1862 at Burke County, Georgia. Admitted to a hospital at Liberty, Bedford County, Virginia, on 04/08/1863 Sent to infirmary/recruiting camp before 04/01/1864. Admitted to Pettigrew General Hospital No. 12, Raleigh, North Carolina, on 03/20/1865. Returned to duty on 03/27/1865. Was surrendered by Gen. Joseph E. Johnston on 04/26/1865. Paroled at Greensboro, North Carolina, on 05/01/1865.

360. Dunn, William W.: Resident of Fulton County, Georgia. Enlisted as a bugler in Company B on 10/01/1861 at Yorktown, Virginia. Listed as a private in November/December 1863. Sent to Georgia to get a horse on 11/13/1863. Detailed in ambulance corps on 04/20/1864. Admitted to Ocmulgee Hospital, Macon, Georgia, on 05/11/1864. Returned to duty on 05/23/1864. Captured at Salisbury, North Carolina, on 04/12/1865. Imprisoned at Military Prison, Louisville, Kentucky, on 05/01/1865. Transferred to Camp Chase, Ohio, on 05/02/1865. Paroled on 06/13/1865. Described as having a fair complexion, dark hair, blue eyes, and being 5' 4" tall and 33-years-old.

361. Dunahoo, James: From Jackson County, Georgia. Enlisted in Company C. No service records in Cobb's Legion. Other records indicate he was killed at the Battle of Brandy Station, Virginia, on 06/09/1863. (May have been misidentified and was Augustus Hardy.)

362. Dunnahoo, Thomas Jordan: Enlisted as a private in Company H on 03/03/1862 at Athens, Clarke County, Georgia. Elected lieutenant on 09/01/1863. On 01/29/1864 was sent with a detail of thirty men to Port Royal, Virginia, to patrol the country around Port Royal and picket the Rappahannock River until receipt of further orders, by special order of Brig. Gen. P.M.B. Young. Ordered to Georgia with Gen. P.M.B. Young on 11/19/1864. Killed while trying to escape the enemy on horseback during the action at Swift Creek near Raleigh, North Carolina, on 04/12/1865. Buried in Oakwood Cemetery, Raleigh, North Carolina. Howard described his death and said, "I gladly pay just tribute to the memory of my warm friend, the brave and fearless Lieutenant Tom Donahoo [sic] of Company H. We had been much together and I saw much of him in camp and in numerous encounters with the enemy, and I loved him as a brother. On one occasion while retreating over ugly ground afoot when I was exhausted he took me on his stout shoulders and literally bore me to a place of safety.... I shall ever cherish his memory."*

363. Durden, Berrien Walter: Farmer from Emanuel County, Georgia. Born on 06/07/1838 or 06/17/1839. Enlisted as a private in Company L on 12/15/1862 at Burke County, Georgia. Sent home to get a horse with Lt. Sinquefield under Special Order No. 27 from corps headquarters on 02/23/1864. Sent to Georgia with Capt. Bostick to get a horse on 09/20/1864. Was surrendered by Gen. Joseph E. Johnston on 04/26/1865. Paroled at Greensboro, North Carolina, on 05/01/1865. After the war, became a farmer in Emanuel County, Georgia. Married Elizabeth Jane Roundtree on 03/03/1859 in Emanuel County, Georgia, and they had nine children. Died on 06/17/1922. Buried at Antioch Primitive Baptist Church Cemetery in Emanuel County, Georgia.

364. Dyes, John: 35-year-old. Enlisted as a private in Company K on 02/08/1863 at Camp Maynard, Georgia. Returned to his regiment on 02/21/1863.

365. Early, Alfred [Alford] W.: Born ca. 1841 in Georgia. Brother of Joseph, Lemuel, William H. and Williamson F. Early. Enlisted as a private in Company C on 08/01/1861 at Athens, Clarke County, Georgia. Sent to infirmary/recruiting camp in November/December 1863. Sent home to get a horse with Lt. Sinquefield under Special Order No. 27 from corps headquarters on 02/23/1864. Was surrendered by Gen. Joseph E. Johnston on 04/26/1865. Paroled at Greensboro, North Carolina, on 05/01/1865. After the war, worked as a farm laborer in Lumpkin County, Georgia.

366. Early, Joseph G.: Born ca. 1842 in Georgia. Brother of Alfred, Lemuel, William H. and Williamson F. Early. Enlisted as a private in Company C on 09/15/1863 at Orange Court House, Virginia. Sent to infirmary/recruiting camp on 02/01/1864. Was surrendered by Gen. Joseph E. Johnston on 04/26/1865. Paroled at Greensboro, North Carolina, on 05/01/1865. After the war, worked as a farm laborer in Dahlonega, Lumpkin County, Georgia.

367. Early, Lemuel: Born ca. 1843 in Georgia. Brother of Alfred, Joseph, William H. and Williamson F. Early. Listed on a roster of Company C published in *These Men She Gave*. No service records in Cobb's Legion Cavalry. After the war, worked as a photographer in Lumpkin County, Georgia.

368. Early, William H.: 25-year-old. Born ca.

*Howard, pages 18–19.

1833 in South Carolina. Brother of Alfred, Joseph, Lemuel, and Williamson F. Early. Enlisted as a private on 07/15/1861 in Dahlonega, Georgia. Sent to Athens where he joined what would become Company C on 08/01/1861. Promoted to lieutenant on 05/26/1862. Wounded in the arm at Dispatch Station, Virginia, on 06/28/1862. Sent to Georgia with Capt. Bostick to get a horse on 09/20/1864. Elected captain. Was surrendered by Gen. Joseph E. Johnston on 04/26/1865. Paroled at Greensboro, North Carolina, on 05/01/1865. After the war, became a farmer in Lumpkin County, Georgia. Married Francis Neisler in Lumpkin County, Georgia, on 02/03/1869. Applied for a Confederate pension in Lumpkin County, Georgia.

369. **Early, Williamson F.:** From Georgia. Born ca. 1836. Enlisted as a private Company C on 08/01/1861 at Athens, Clarke County, Georgia. Sick in November/December 1861. Promoted to sergeant in November/December 1863. Killed in action on 05/29/1864 at Hanover Court House, Virginia.

370. **Eason, Augustus:** Farmer from Bowdon, Carroll County, Georgia. Listed on a roster of Cobb's Legion Cavalry, Company B, in the 1910 souvenir-historical publication of the Annie Wheeler Chapter. No service records in Cobb's Legion Cavalry.

371. **Eaton, Robert H.:** Resident of Georgia. Enlisted as a private in Company H on 04/03/1862 at Atlanta, Georgia. Lost horse due to lack of forage on 07/10/1863 near Martinsburg, [West] Virginia, during the retreat from Pennsylvania. Sent to Georgia to get a horse on 11/11/1863. Absent without leave beginning 01/11/1864. Admitted to General Hospital No. 4 in Richmond, Virginia, on 04/17/1864 with a kidney stone. Admitted to Episcopal Church Hospital in Williamsburg, Virginia, on 04/29/1864 with a kidney stone. Last record, admitted to C.S.A. General Hospital in Danville, Virginia, on 12/06/1864 with a kidney stone.

372. **Eckles, Joel D.:** Born in Gwinnett County, Georgia, on 10/30/1843. Listed on a roster of Company I. No service records in Cobb's Legion. After the war, became a farmer in Rockdale County, Georgia. Married Susan Jane Lucas on 12/06/1863 in Gwinnett County and they had at least five children. Died after 1870.

373. **Edward, Samuel:** 25-year-old farm laborer from Orange County, North Carolina. Brother of William Edward. Enlisted as a private in Company A on 04/01/1865 at Booneville, North Carolina. Was surrendered by Gen. Joseph E. Johnston on 04/26/1865. Paroled at Greensboro, North Carolina, on 05/01/1865.

374. **Edward, William:** 23-year-old farm laborer from Orange County, North Carolina. Brother of Samuel Edward. Enlisted as a private in Company A on 04/01/1865 at Booneville, North Carolina. Was surrendered by Gen. Joseph E. Johnston on 04/26/1865. Paroled at Greensboro, North Carolina, on 05/01/1865.

375. **Edwards, Edward H.:** Enlisted as a private in Company B on 08/14/1861 at Atlanta, Georgia. Value of horse $200 and horse equipment $1.75, saddle furnished by the State of Georgia. Last record, November/December 1861.

376. **Edwards, J.F.:** Enlisted as a private in Company K on 07/01/1864 at Decatur, Georgia. Last record, on horse detail to Georgia with Capt. Bostick beginning 09/20/1864.

377. **Emanuel, Columbus:** Enlisted as a private in Company L on 04/01/1864 at Decatur, Georgia. Admitted to a hospital in Lynchburg, Virginia, in 07/1864. Was surrendered by Gen. Joseph E. Johnston on 04/26/1865. Paroled at Greensboro, North Carolina, on 05/01/1865.

378. **Epps, Joseph [S.]A.:** From Clarke County, Georgia. Born ca. 1844 in Georgia. Enlisted as a private in Company H on 03/04/1862 at Athens, Clarke County, Georgia. Sent home to get a horse with Lt. Sinquefield under Special Order No. 27 from corps headquarters on 02/23/1864. On sick furlough to Georgia beginning 06/12/1864. Was surrendered by Gen. Joseph E. Johnston on 04/26/1865. Paroled at Greensboro, North Carolina, on 05/01/1865. Other records indicate he was wounded in service. After the war, became a farmer in Clarke County, Georgia. Married Martha Fields on 12/1/1897 in Jasper County, Georgia. Applied for a Confederate pension in Clarke County, Georgia. Died after 1920. His widow, Martha A. Todd, applied for a Confederate pension in Clarke County, Georgia.

379. **Evans, James M.:** 26-year-old from Georgia. Enlisted as a private in Company E on 03/22/1862 at Roswell, Georgia. Value of horse $200. Captured at South Mountain, Maryland, on 09/15/1862. Imprisoned at Fort Delaware Prison. Exchanged at Aiken's Landing, Virginia, on 11/10/1862. On furlough for 20 days beginning 11/10/1862. No horse on 07/03/1863. Last record, September/October 1864, missing since 07/03/1863.

380. **Evans, Jasper:** From Hall County, Georgia. Born ca. 1844 in Georgia. Enlisted as a private in Company H on 03/03/1862 at Athens, Clarke County, Georgia. Sent to infirmary/recruiting camp on 08/04/1863. Last record, wounded and sent to a hospital on 10/27/1864.

381. **Evans [Evins], Justinian:** 18-year-old

farmer/student from Fulton County, Georgia. Born in DeKalb County, Georgia, on 10/15/1843. Enlisted as a private in Company B on 04/15/1862 at Atlanta, Georgia. Value of horse $140. Transferred to Company G in November/December 1863. Detailed as a teamster in November/December 1863. Was surrendered by Gen. Joseph E. Johnston on 04/26/1865. Paroled at Greensboro, North Carolina, on 05/01/1865. After the war, became a farmer in DeKalb County, Georgia, and then Buckhead, Fulton County, Georgia. Married Martha Cunningham Polk on 05/14/1867 and they had at least eight children. Died on June 9, 1930.

382. Evans, Richard Jones: 27-year-old from Jefferson County, Georgia. Born on 03/28/1834. Enlisted as a private in Company F on 04/18/1862 in Burke County, Georgia. Value of horse $200. On sick furlough in Georgia in September/October 1862. Sent to Georgia with Capt. Bostick to get a horse on 09/20/1864. Was surrendered by Gen. Joseph E. Johnston on 04/26/1865. Paroled at Greensboro, North Carolina, on 05/01/1865. He and his wife, George Ann (or Georgia V.) had at least four children. His widow, Georgia V. Evans, applied for a Confederate pension in Richmond County, Georgia.

383. Eve, Frances Edgeworth: 17-year-old farm worker from Augusta, Georgia. (He told the enlisting officer that he was 21.) Born 08/15/1844 in Augusta, Georgia. Enlisted as a lieutenant in the 5th North Carolina Infantry prior to enlisting as a private in Company A on 05/01/1862 at Augusta, Georgia. Elected Captain in Company K on 02/10/1863. On his discharge from Company A, was described having a dark complexion, grey eyes, light hair, and being 6'½'" tall. Furloughed on 02/15/1863. Returned to duty on 06/23/1863. Wounded 09/23/1863 at Jack's Shop (Liberty Mills) near Culpeper C.H., Virginia. Admitted to General Hospital No. 4 in Richmond, Virginia, on 04/18/1864. Returned to duty on 05/01/1864. Absent sick on 05/10/1864. Admitted to Jackson Hospital, Richmond, Virginia, with a wound to the left thigh 05/21/1864. Furloughed in 05/1864. Transferred from Jackson Hospital, Richmond, Virginia, to Augusta, Georgia, on 06/06/1864. Transferred to Phillips' Legion, Company K, as a captain in 11/1864. After the war, had a large plantation 10 miles southwest of Augusta. In 1877 became junior partner in the law firm of Jones & Eve. Married (1) Mary Elizabeth Lamkin of Columbia County on 11/20/1866. Married (2) Katherine Remsen Tutt (or Ewing) on 05/12/1897. He had no children. Died on 05/10/1908 in Augusta, Georgia, and is buried in Magnolia Cemetery.

384. Everett, J.B.: Resident of Georgia. Enlisted as a private in Company D on 08/10/1861 at Albany, Georgia. Value of horse $175 and horse equipment $25. Sent home to get a horse March/April 1863. Sent to Georgia with Capt. Bostick to get a horse on 09/20/1864. Was surrendered by Gen. Joseph E. Johnston on 04/26/1865. Paroled at Greensboro, North Carolina, on 05/01/1865.

385. Everett, John G.: Farmer from Gwinnett County, Georgia. Born in Georgia ca. 1825. Enlisted as a bugler in Company E on 04/09/1862 at Lawrenceville, Georgia. Value of horse $150. Admitted to Chimborazo Hospital No. 6, Richmond, Virginia, on 11/23/1862 with dropsy. Transferred to C.S.A. General Hospital, Danville, Virginia, on 12/19/1862 with rheumatism. Returned to duty on 01/17/1863. Released from Charity Hospital, Gordonsville, Virginia, on 03/03/1863 after being treated for edema. Listed as a private in January/February 1863. Given a medical discharge on 02/25/1862. After the war, worked as a book agent in Cobb County, Georgia. He and his wife, Adaline, had at least five children. Died after 1880.

386. Ezzard, John F.: Clothier in Fulton County, Georgia. Born ca. 1831 in Georgia. Enlisted as a private in Company B on 04/18/1862 at Atlanta, Georgia. Elected lieutenant on 05/30/1862. May have transferred to Company G. Admitted to a hospital in Richmond, Virginia, in 12/1862. Given a medical furlough beginning 12/30/1862. Resigned 02/21/1863. Married his wife, Fannie, in 1859 in Fulton County, Georgia.

387. Fanning, William P.: 20-year-old. Born in 1844. Enlisted as a private in Company K on 06/21/1864 at Decatur, Georgia. Admitted to Jackson Hospital, Richmond, Virginia, on 08/24/1864 with chronic diarrhea. Returned to duty on 09/03/1864. Last record September/October 1864, sent to Georgia to get a horse with Capt. Bostick on 09/20/1864. May have transferred to the Irwin Artillery after being in the legion for about ten months. After the war, lived in Wilkes County, Georgia. Married Laura B. Wooten on 12/02/1869 in Wilkes County, Georgia. Applied for a Confederate pension in Wilkes County, Georgia, in 1897. Died after 1897.

388. Farr, John Hayes: 32-year-old farm worker from Fayette County, Georgia. Born in Jackson County, Georgia, on 11/27/1829. Enlisted as a private in Company B on 05/06/1862 at Atlanta, Georgia. Value of horse $175. Admitted to C.S.A. General Hospital, Danville, Virginia, on 05/16/1862 with rubeola. Returned to duty on 05/28/1862. Detailed to go with disabled horses to the infirmary/recruiting camp in Lynchburg, Virginia, on 08/28/1864. Was surrendered by Gen. Joseph E. Johnston on 04/26/1865. Paroled at Greensboro, North Carolina, on 05/01/1865. After the war, became a farmer in Fayette County, Georgia. He and his wife, Mary A., had nine children. Applied for a Confederate pension in Fayette County, Georgia. Died on 04/20/1923.

389. Farrow, Alfred A.: 26-year-old farmer from Burke County, Georgia. Born on 12/15/1836. Enlisted as a private in Company F on 03/25/1862 at Burke County, Georgia. Value of horse $175. Sent to Georgia on sick furlough in September/October 1862. Admitted to Henningsen Hospital, Richmond, Virginia, on 11/02/1862 with rheumatism. Given a medical discharge on 11/10/1862. Described as having a florid complexion, blue eyes, sandy hair, and being 5'8" tall. After the war, worked as a farm laborer in Burke County, Georgia. Married (1) Elizabeth Strain on 09/16/1858 in Jefferson County, Georgia (2) Delia. Was the father of at least four children. Died on 08/15/1903. Buried at Bark Camp Baptist Church Cemetery, Burke County, Georgia.

390. Fenn, E.: Enlisted as a private in Company D before 09/03/1861. Value of horse $200 and horse equipment $20, furnished by State of Georgia. Only record, 09/03/1861, does not state if he was present.

391. Ferguson [Fergerson, Furgerson], Lorenzo D.: Carpenter from Walton County, Georgia. Born ca. 1835 in Georgia. Enlisted as a private in Company H on 04/01/1862 at Athens, Clarke County, Georgia. Lost horse on 06/19/1863 when ordered by P.M.B. Young to abandon his horse behind enemy lines. Without a horse for four months December 1863/January 1864. Last record September/October 1864, sent to Georgia with Capt. Bostick to get a horse on 09/20/1864. After the war, became a carpenter in Morgan County, Georgia. He and his wife, Margaret, had at least two children. Died after 1870.

392. Fesler [Fessler], Daniel: Resident of Georgia. Enlisted as a private in the 3rd Georgia Infantry, Company K, on 06/10/1861. Transferred into Cobb's Legion Cavalry, Company H, on 01/30/1863 at Athens, Clarke County, Georgia. Sent to infirmary/recruiting camp in November/December 1863. Sent to Georgia with Capt. Bostick to get a horse on 09/20/1864. Was surrendered by Gen. Joseph E. Johnston on 04/26/1865. Paroled at Greensboro, North Carolina, on 05/01/1865.

393. Fesler [Fessler], Jacob: Enlisted as a private in Company H on 03/03/1862 at Athens, Clarke County, Georgia. Was surrendered by Gen. Joseph E. Johnston on 04/26/1865. Paroled at Greensboro, North Carolina, on 05/01/1865.

394. Fesler [Fessler], John: Resident of Georgia. Enlisted as a private in Company H on 02/27/1862 at Athens, Clarke County, Georgia. Listed in May/June 1862 as corporal. Sent to infirmary/recruiting camp in 06/1864. Listed in May/September 1864 as a sergeant. Sent to infirmary/recruiting camp on 09/03/1864. Was surrendered by Gen. Joseph E. Johnston on 04/26/1865. Paroled at Greensboro, North Carolina, on 05/01/1865.

395. Few, Marcus C.: 28-year-old from Georgia. Born on 07/01/1833 in Jackson County, Georgia. Enlisted as a private in Company C on 08/01/1861. Detailed to commissary department on 06/01/1862. On sick furlough beginning 08/09/1864. Was surrendered by Gen. Joseph E. Johnston on 04/26/1865. Paroled at Greensboro, North Carolina, on 05/01/1865. After the war, may have become a dentist in Clarke County, Georgia, and then lived in the Confederate Soldiers Home in Fulton County, Georgia. Married Martha Weir on 11/25/1875. Applied for a Confederate pension in Clarke County, Georgia. Died on 05/08/1915.

396. Fields, Julius J.: Farmer/student from Lumpkin County, Georgia. Born ca. 1843 in Georgia. Enlisted as a private in Company C on 08/01/1861 at Athens, Clarke County, Georgia. Absent sick in Madison County, Virginia, on 02/24/1863. Returned to duty on 03/29/1863. Captured on 06/09/1863 at Beverly's Ford on the Rappahannock River during the cavalry battle at Brandy Station, Virginia. Sent to the Old Capitol Prison, Washington D.C. Paroled on 06/25/1863. Exchanged on 07/07/1863. Transferred to Company H. Sent home to get a horse with Lt. Sinquefield under Special Order No. 27 from corps headquarters on 02/23/1864. Sent to Georgia with Capt. Bostick to get a horse on 09/20/1864. Captured at Lynches Creek, South Carolina, on 02/25/1865. Sent to New Bern, North Carolina, and transferred to Hart Island, New York Harbor. Paroled on 06/18/1865. Described as having a dark complexion, brown hair, gray eyes and being 5'10" tall. After the war, worked as a farm laborer in White County, Georgia, and then Murray County, Georgia. Married (1) Martha and (2) Jane. Was the father of at least four children. Died after 1880.

397. Fields, Levi C.: 21-year-old farmer from Milton County, Georgia. Born on 06/08/1840. Enlisted as a private in Company B 08/14/1861 at Atlanta, Georgia. Value of horse $175 and horse equipment $20. No horse on 03/12/1863. Sent home to get a horse with Lt. James H. Johnson on

04/14/1863. Sent home to get a horse with Lt. Sinquefield under Special Order No. 27 from corps headquarters on 02/23/1864. Sent to Georgia with Capt. Bostick to get a horse on 09/20/1864. Was surrendered by Gen. Joseph E. Johnston on 04/26/1865. Paroled at Greensboro, North Carolina, on 05/01/1865. After the war, worked as a farm laborer. Married Polly (or Mollie) Fuller on 02/09/1870 in Gordon County, Georgia, and they had three children. Applied for a Confederate pension in Gordon County, Georgia. Died on 04/05/1924. Buried in Gordon County, Georgia.

398. Fields, Richard J.: Farmer from Milton County, Georgia. Born ca. 1834 in Georgia. Enlisted as a private in Company B on 08/14/1861 at Atlanta, Georgia. Value of horse $225 and horse equipment $7.25, saddle furnished by the State of Georgia. On sick furlough for 20 days beginning 04/29/1862. Furlough extended 15 days. Listed as sergeant in March/April 1862. Promoted to lieutenant on 11/21/1862. Detailed on extra duty on 08/20/1863. On furlough to Georgia for 24 days beginning 02/18/1864. Detailed as an AQM beginning 01/1864. Last rank was captain. Was surrendered by Gen. Joseph E. Johnston on 04/26/1865. Paroled at Greensboro, North Carolina, on 05/01/1865. Was married to Francis.

399. Fife, Robert A.: 20-year-old clerk from Fulton County, Georgia. Enlisted in 1st Georgia Infantry, Company F, as a private on 03/18/1861. Discharged due to disability on 08/25/1861. Enlisted as a private in Cobb's Legion Cavalry, Company B, on 04/03/1862 at Atlanta, Georgia. Value of horse $175. Furloughed for 30 days beginning 04/13/1863. Appointed corporal in Company G on 11/01/1863. Admitted to Jackson Hospital, Richmond, Virginia, 06/02/1864 with dysentery. Returned to duty on 06/04/1864. Admitted to Jackson Hospital, Richmond, Virginia, on 06/21/1864. Using a public horse beginning 07/01/1864. Was surrendered by Gen. Joseph E. Johnston on 04/26/1865. Paroled at Greensboro, North Carolina, on 05/01/1865. After the war, worked as a dry goods clerk in Harris County, Texas. He and his wife, Jane, had at least four children. Died before 1900.

400. Finch, William: Cabinet maker from Augusta, Georgia. Born in Fairfield District, South Carolina, ca. 1831. Enlisted as a private in Company A on 08/17/1861 at Augusta, Georgia. Value of horse $224, and horse equipment $25. Appointed corporal on 05/01/1862. Wounded at Little Washington, Virginia, on 11/08/1862. Admitted to General Hospital No. 11, Richmond, Virginia, on 11/12/1862. Furloughed for 30 days beginning 11/17/1862. No horse on 01/01/1863. Listed as a sergeant on 01/01/1863. Absent on furlough in January/February 1863. Given a surgical discharge on 04/26/1863. Described as being 5'9" tall, and having a fair complexion, blue eyes, light hair and by profession a mechanic. After the war, worked as a carpenter, then a foreman at a planing mill. Married (1) Caroline and was the father of at least three children. His wife and one of his daughters died before 1870. Married (2) Mary J. and was the father of at least two children by his second wife.

401. Fish, Andrew J.: Clerk at livery stable in Augusta, Georgia. Born in Kentucky ca. 1838. Enlisted as a private in Company A on 08/17/1861 at Augusta, Georgia. Value of horse $200 and horse equipment $30. No horse on 01/01/63. Admitted to hospital on 01/01/63. Detailed as a teamster beginning March/April 1863. Detailed at division headquarters as forage master on 11/20/1863. On detached service on 12/20/1863. Sent to Georgia with Capt. Bostick to get a horse on 09/20/1864. Was surrendered by Gen. Joseph E. Johnston on 04/26/1865. Paroled at Greensboro, North Carolina, on 05/01/1865.

402. Fitzjerrald, James: Laborer from Richmond County, Georgia. Enlisted as a private in Company K on 02/24/1863 at Camp Maynard, Georgia. Horse killed in action at Brandy Station on 06/09/1863. Absent without leave on 06/29/1863. Last record, reimbursed on 09/18/1863 for horse killed in battle. After the war, worked as a carpenter and then a train hand in Columbia County, Georgia. Married (1) Levinia and they had at least six children. Married (2) Gertrude and they had nine children. Died after 1910.

403. Fleming, James A.: 38-year-old farmer from Jefferson County, Georgia. Born on 07/12/1827 in Georgia. Not listed with Cobb's Legion in the *Civil War Soldiers and Sailors System*. Listed on a roster of Company C compiled by Glen Spurlock, but not in *These Men She Gave*. No service records in Cobb's Legion. After the war, became a farmer in Jefferson County, Georgia. Married Mary L. Marshall on 03/09/1852 in Jefferson County, Georgia, and they had at least four children. Died on 11/27/1910. Buried in the Ebenezer ARP Church Cemetery in Jefferson County, Georgia.

404. Fleming [Flemming], John A.W.: Farmer from DeKalb County, Georgia. Born ca. 1839 in Georgia. Enlisted as a private in Cobb's Legion Infantry, Company C, on 03/10/1862 at Decatur, Georgia. Transferred to Cobb's Legion Cavalry, Company L, on 12/15/1862 at Burke, Georgia. Sent home to get a horse with Lt. Sinquefield under Special Order No. 27 from corps headquarters on 02/23/1864. Appointed sergeant on 06/01/1864. Wounded and on furlough in May/June 1864. Sent to Georgia with Capt. Bostick to get a horse on 09/20/1864. Was surrendered by Gen. Joseph E. Johnston on 04/26/1865. Paroled at Greensboro, North Carolina, on 05/01/1865. After the war, became a farmer in DeKalb County, Georgia. He and his wife, Martha, had at least six children. Applied for a Confederate pension in Fulton County, Georgia, and DeKalb County, Georgia.

405. Fleming [Flemming], Samuel P.: 27-year-old farmer from Jefferson County, Georgia. Born on 05/22/1835 in Jefferson County, Georgia. Enlisted as a private in Company F on 05/05/1862 in Burke County, Georgia. Value of horse $225. Detailed as commissary beginning 08/25/1862. Lost horse and wounded on 09/22/1863 at Jack's Shop, Virginia. Admitted to Winder Hospital, Richmond, Virginia, on 09/25/1863. Furloughed to Georgia. Admitted to Ocmulgee Hospital, Macon, Georgia, on 01/08/1864. On furlough for 60 days beginning 04/05/1864. Sent to Georgia with Capt. Bostick to get a horse on 09/20/1864. Was surrendered by Gen. Joseph E. Johnston on 04/26/1865. Paroled at Greensboro, North Carolina, on 05/01/1865. After the war, became a farmer in Jefferson County, Georgia. Married (1) Mary Thompson on 08/16/1860 in Jefferson County, Georgia (2) Ganzada S. Jordan in Jefferson County, Georgia, on 04/03/1872 (3) Margaret A. Thompson on 12/30/1884 in Jefferson County, Georgia, and (4) Ela. Was the father of at least three children. Died on 05/08/1910. Buried in Ebenezer ARP Church Cemetery, Jefferson County, Georgia.

406. Fleming [Flemming], William W.: 37-year-old farmer from Louisville, Jefferson County, Georgia. Born on 02/2/1825 in Georgia. Enlisted as a private in Company L on 12/15/1862 at Burke County, Georgia. Admitted to Chimborazo Hospital No. 6, Richmond, Virginia, on 04/19/1863. Transferred to C.S.A. General Hospital, Danville, Virginia, on 04/21/1863 with debility. Sent home to get a horse with Lt. Sinquefield under Special Order No. 27 from corps headquarters on 02/23/1864. Sent to Georgia with Capt. Bostick to get a horse on 09/20/1864. Admitted to Pettigrew General Hospital No. 12, Raleigh, North Carolina, on 03/15/1865. Returned to duty on 03/18/1865. Was surrendered by Gen. Joseph E. Johnston on 04/26/1865. Paroled at Greensboro, North Carolina, on 05/01/1865. After the war, became a farmer in Jefferson County, Georgia. Married Martha I. Manson on 11/16/1848 in Jefferson County, Georgia, and they had five children. Died on 07/09/1904. Buried at Ebenezer ARP Church Cemetery, Jefferson County, Georgia. His widow, Martha Fleming, applied for a Confederate pension in Jefferson County, Georgia.

407. Ford, J.D. [J.H.]: Enlisted as a private in Company D on 08/10/1861 at Albany, Georgia. Value of horse $250 and horse equipment $25. Detailed as teamster in 12/1861. Furloughed to Georgia for 30 days beginning 02/27/1862. Wounded on 09/13/1863 and sent to hospital in Gordonsville, Virginia. Note on his record says he was "supposed to be dead." Admitted to Samaritan Hospital, Richmond, Virginia, on 09/21/1863. Died on 10/08/1863 at Samaritan Hospital, Richmond, Virginia. Buried at Hollywood Cemetery in Richmond, Virginia, on 10/11/1863.

408. Ford, Lewis R. [Bird, J.R.]: 17-year-old from Augusta, Georgia. Born 11/22/1843 in Burke County, Georgia. Enlisted as a private in Company A on 08/17/1861 at Augusta, Georgia. Value of horse $250 and horse equipment $25. Courier to Gen. Rains in November/December 1861. Orderly for Gen. Johnson in 12/1861. Courier for Col. Johnson in January/February 1862. Promoted to corporal in March/April 1863. Promoted to sergeant in November/December 1863. Sent home to get a horse under Special Order No. 36 Corps Headquarters on 04/01/1864. Was surrendered by Gen. Joseph E. Johnston on 04/26/1865. Paroled at Greensboro, North Carolina, on 05/01/1865. After the war, became a physician and lived in Augusta, then Waynesboro, Georgia. Married Fannie S. Blount on 11/18/1873 in Waynesboro, Burke County, Georgia. They had at least one child. Died on 06/26/1903. His widow applied for a Confederate pension in 1920.

409. Ford, Thomas: 22-year-old from Georgia. Enlisted as a private in Company G on 03/06/1862 at Augusta, Georgia. Value of horse $175. Admitted to Floyd House and Ocmulgee Hospital, Macon, Georgia, on 12/13/1863 with rheumatism. Admitted to a hospital in Powhatan County, Virginia, on 06/15/1864 due to sickness. Last record, September/October 1864, still sick at hospital in Powhatan County, Virginia.

410. Fortson, Richard Eaton: 39-year-old farmer from Madison County, Georgia. Born on 11/20/1824 in Elbert County, Georgia. Enlisted as a private in Company L on 04/22/1864 at Decatur, Georgia. In hospital sick on 05/01/1864. Last record September/October 1864, sent to Georgia with Capt. Bostick to get a horse on 09/20/1864. After the war, became a farmer in Hart County, Georgia.

Married Lucie Jane Campbell on 12/23/1841 and they had at least eight children. Died on 02/18/1896 (or 1897). Buried in the Presbyterian church cemetery in Madison County, Georgia.

411. **Foster, Felix Walker:** Student from Cherokee County, Georgia. Born ca. 1845 in South Carolina. Enlisted as a private in Company E on 01/09/1863 at Cherokee County, Georgia. At infirmary/recruiting camp with a public horse on 11/28/1863. No horse until 01/01/1864. Sent to Georgia with Capt. Bostick to get a horse on 09/20/1864. Was surrendered by Gen. Joseph E. Johnston on 04/26/1865. Paroled at Greensboro, North Carolina, on 05/01/1865. After the war, became a farmer in Cherokee County, Georgia. Married Emma Evans on 08/10/1865 and they had at least seven children. Died 11/20/1926.

412. **Foster, James H.:** Student from Richmond County, Georgia. Born ca. 1843 in Georgia. Enlisted as a private in Company H on 03/03/1862 at Athens, Clarke County, Georgia. Died on 10/07/1862 at General Hospital in Staunton, Virginia, of chronic diarrhea. Buried in Thornrose Cemetery in Staunton, Virginia.

413. **Foster, Robert Thomas [B.]:** 21-year-old student from Cherokee County, Georgia. Born on 01/09/1839 in Union County, South Carolina. Enlisted as a blacksmith in Company E on 06/15/1862 at Camp McDonald, Georgia. Sent home to get a horse in March/April 1863. Sent home to get a horse with Lt. Sinquefield under Special Order No. 27 from corps headquarters on 02/23/1864. Absent sick on 05/05/1864. Admitted to Jackson Hospital, Richmond, Virginia, on 05/10/1864. Admitted to Jackson Hospital, Richmond, Virginia, on 05/20/1864. Transferred to C.S.A. General Hospital, Danville, Virginia, on 05/22/1864. Released from hospital on 06/02/1864. Last record, September/October 1864, absent sick since 05/05/1864. After the war, became a farmer in Oglethorpe County, Georgia. Married (1) Louise Oliver about 1864 (2) Mary Caroline Westmoreland on 10/09/1872 in Stephens County, Georgia, and was the father of at least ten children. Died on 11/30/1909 in Nevada County, Arkansas.

414. **Foust, William:** 24-year-old student from Oglethorpe County, Georgia. Enlisted as a private in Company K on 02/07/1863 at Camp Maynard, Georgia. Returned to his regiment on 02/21/1863. After the war, became a farmer in Oglethorpe County, Georgia. He and his wife, Harriet, had two children. Died before 1910.

415. **Fowler, H.M.:** Enlisted as a private in Company D on 08/10/1861 at Albany, Georgia. Value of horse $175. Horse killed in action on 06/26/1862 at Mechanicsville, Virginia. Wounded in battle and captured on 09/13/1862 at Crampton's Gap, Maryland. Paroled on 09/14/1862. Sent to Baltimore, Maryland, and then Fort McHenry, Maryland. Exchanged at Aiken's Landing, Virginia, on 10/25/1862. Promoted to corporal on 11/01/1862. Furloughed for 30 days beginning 11/06/1862 from General Hospital No. 1 in Richmond, Virginia. Sent to infirmary/recruiting camp on 12/08/1863. Killed in action at Trevilian Station on 06/12/1864. His last rank was listed as a sergeant.

416. **Francisco, John:** Resident of Tennessee. Enlisted as a private in Company H on 03/13/1864 at Atlanta, Georgia. On extra duty on 04/1864. No horse, so transferred to C.S. Navy on 04/25/1864.

417. **Fraser, J. Harvey:** Student from Cobb County, Georgia. Enlisted as a private in Company E on 04/09/1862 at Lawrenceville, Georgia. Value of horse $160. Died on 12/29/1864. Buried at Liberty, Bedford County, Virginia.

418. **Freeman, A. John:** Farmer from Gwinnett County, Georgia. Born ca. 1837 in Georgia. Enlisted as a private in Company E on 04/09/1862 at Lawrenceville, Georgia. Value of horse $150 and bridle $8. Died before 03/30/1863, the date a family member filed for a settlement from his death. He and his wife, Frances, had at least two children. His widow applied for a Confederate pension in Gwinnett County, Georgia.

419. **Frie [Fry], Martin J.:** Native of Switzerland. Enlisted as a private in Company D on 03/10/1862 at Albany, Georgia. Captured at Culpeper, Virginia, on 08/25/1863 and sent to the Old Capitol Prison in Washington, D.C. Deserted and took the Oath on 09/02/1863. Sent to Philadelphia, Pennsylvania, on 09/28/1863. Described as having a dark complexion, brown hair, hazel eyes and being 6'1¼" tall.

420. **Friedenthal, Morris:** 19-year-old from Fulton County, Georgia. Enlisted in 1st Georgia Infantry, Company F, as a private on 03/18/1861. Mustered out on 03/18/1862 at Augusta, Georgia. Enlisted as a private in Company B, Cobb's Legion Cavalry, on 04/30/1862. Value of horse $170. Detailed to Q.M. Department on 04/18/1863. Transferred to Company G in November/December 1863. Sent to Georgia to get a horse on 11/10/1863. Sent home to get a horse with Lt. Sinquefield under Special Order No. 27 from corps headquarters on 02/23/1864. Absent without leave beginning 05/28/1864. Admitted to Floyd House and Ocmulgee Hospital, Macon, Georgia, on 10/22/1864. Returned to duty on 11/12/1864. Was surrendered by

Gen. Joseph E. Johnston on 04/26/1865. Paroled at Greensboro, North Carolina, on 05/01/1865.

421. Frix [Fix], Julius Michael: 18-year-old farm laborer/student from Gordon County, Georgia. Born in 1843 in Cass County, Georgia. Enlisted as a private in Company B on 08/14/1861 at Atlanta, Georgia. Value of horse $160 and horse equipment $50, saddle furnished by State of Georgia. Sent to Chimborazo Hospital No. 2 in Richmond, Virginia, on 12/11/1861 with diarrhea. Died from disease of the heart on 02/01/1862.

422. Fulcher, William: Enlisted as a private in Company L on 04/08/1864 at Decatur, Georgia. Sent to Georgia with Capt. Bostick to get a horse on 09/20/1864. Was surrendered by Gen. Joseph E. Johnston on 04/26/1865. Paroled at Greensboro, North Carolina, on 05/01/1865.

423. Gabbett, William: Enlisted as a private in Company B on 08/14/1861 at Atlanta, Georgia. Value of horse $250 and horse equipment $37. Discharged on 12/17/1861 at Yorktown, Virginia, due to tuberculosis. Described as being 31 years old, 5' 9½" tall, with a fair complexion, gray eyes and sandy hair. He became the superintendent at the C.S. Department of Nitre Mining in District 9 and was listed as a captain in October 1863. After the war, became a farmer in Fulton County, Georgia. Was married to Martha, and they had at least two children.

424. Galaway [Gallaway, Galloway], William L. [J.T.]: Enlisted as a private in Company K on 01/20/1862 at Camp Maynard, Georgia. Admitted to Howard's Grove Hospital, Richmond, Virginia, on 02/25/1863 with smallpox. Died on 03/10/1863.

425. Gallaher, Patrick: 40-year-old merchant from Augusta, Georgia. Born in Ireland. Enlisted as a sergeant in Company A on 08/17/1861 at Augusta, Georgia. Value of horse $200 and horse equipment $35. Severely wounded at Little Washington, Virginia. Admitted to General Hospital No. 11 on 11/12/1862 and furloughed on November 17, 1862. On furlough for 25 days beginning 02/08/1863. Discharged due to disability on 07/31/1863. Was described as being 6 feet tall, and having a fair complexion, blue eyes, and dark hair. After the war, worked as a retail dry goods merchant. Was married and the father of at least two children.

426. Gallaway, George T. [E.T.]: Born ca. 1844 in Georgia. Enlisted as a private in Company D on 05/04/1862 at Albany, Georgia. Value of horse $175 and horse equipment $10. Wounded in the right arm on 06/21/1863 at Upperville, Virginia, and lost his horse. The severity of the wound necessitated the amputation of the arm. Furloughed indefinitely. After the war, became a farmer in Baker County, Georgia. He and his wife, Francis (or Frances), had at least one child. Received a Confederate pension in Baker County, Georgia. The pension was for the purchase of an artificial arm.

427. Gallaway, W.L.: Resident of Georgia. Enlisted as a private in Company D on 08/10/1861 at Albany, Georgia. Value of horse $150 and horse equipment $25, furnished by State of Georgia. Sent home to get a horse in March/April 1863. Admitted to Winder Hospital, Richmond, Virginia, on 12/04/1863 with neuralgia. Returned to duty on 12/18/1863. Sent to Georgia with Capt. Bostick to get a horse on 09/20/1864. Was surrendered by Gen. Joseph E. Johnston on 04/26/1865. Paroled at Greensboro, North Carolina, on 05/01/1865.

428. Gamblin [Gambling], John L. [S.]: Born ca. 1841 in Georgia. Enlisted as a private in Company H on 03/12/1862 at Athens, Clarke County, Georgia. Horse killed in action at Barbee's Cross Roads (Wild Cat Mountain), Virginia, on 11/05/1862. Sent home to get a horse with Lt. Sinquefield under Special Order No. 27 from corps headquarters on 02/23/1864. Detailed as wagon driver in September/October 1864. Was surrendered by Gen. Joseph E. Johnston on 04/26/1865. Paroled at Greensboro, North Carolina, on 05/01/1865. After the war, worked as a farm laborer in Lumpkin County, Georgia. Married Melinda Turner on 09/3/1865 in Lumpkin County, Georgia, and they had at least six children. Applied for a Confederate pension in Lumpkin County, Georgia.

429. Gantt, Adolphus S.: 19-year-old farmer from Fulton County, Georgia. Born on 12/18/1842 at Athens, Clarke County, Georgia. Enlisted as a private in Company B on 04/16/1862 at Atlanta, Georgia. Value of horse $175. Last record, detailed as a courier for Gen. McLaws on 08/24/1862. Transferred to Cobb's Legion Infantry, Company G. After the war, worked as a painter in Fulton County, Georgia, and then as a real estate agent in Bexar County, Texas. Married (1) Amelia Popkins. Married (2) Maroah Jane Walker on 11/08/1876 and they had two children. Died on 05/06/1937 in Bexar, Texas. Buried in Mission Park Cemetery, Bexar County, Texas.

430. Gardner, Nathaniel Edward [G.]: 43-year-old coach maker from Fulton County, Georgia. Born on 01/18/1817 in New Jersey. Enlisted as a sergeant in Company B on 08/14/1861. Value of horse $225 and horse equipment $25, equipment furnished by company. On sick furlough beginning 11/21/1861. Last record, furlough extended 30 days on 12/21/1861. He and his wife, Elizabeth, had one child. Died at Atlanta, Georgia.

431. **Garner, James H.[N.]:** 22-year-old. Enlisted as a private in Company C on 08/01/1861 at Athens, Clarke County, Georgia. Died on 03/15/1862 at Camp Marion, Yorktown, Virginia.

432. **Garron, John S.:** Enlisted as private in Company B on 08/14/1861 at Atlanta, Georgia. Value of horse $200 and horse equipment $1.75, saddle furnished by the State of Georgia. Last record March/April 1863, states he was without a horse from 02/01/1863 until 03/20/1863.

433. **Garvin, William F.K.:** Resident of Gainesville, Hall County, Georgia. Enlisted as a private in Company C on 03/17/1863 at Athens, Clarke County, Georgia. Sent to Georgia with Capt. Bostick to get a horse on 09/20/1864. Admitted to Pettigrew General Hospital No. 13, Raleigh, North Carolina, on 03/24/1865 with a wound in his left foot from a shell. Captured at Raleigh, North Carolina, when the city fell to the enemy on 04/13/1865. No further record.

434. **Gay, Thomas:** Enlisted as a private in Company L on 09/14/1863 at Sawdust, Georgia. Admitted to Jackson Hospital, Richmond, Virginia, on 01/03/1864 with debility. Returned to duty on 02/10/1864. Sent home to get a horse with Lt. Sinquefield under Special Order No. 27 from corps headquarters on 02/23/1864. Absent without leave beginning 05/05/1864 at the time of the Battle of the Wilderness in Virginia. Last record, still absent without leave in September/October 1864. There is no record of his being captured or deserting to the enemy.

435. **Gibson, C.[G.]:** Enlisted as a private in Company D. Value of horse $200 and horse equipment $25, saddle worth $20 furnished by the State of Georgia. Transferred to infantry. Surrendered by Gen. Sam Jones in Tallahassee, Florida, on 05/10/1865. Paroled at Albany, Georgia, on 05/20/1865.

436. **Gibson, James E.:** 29-year-old. Born on 04/19/1835 in Greenwood County, South Carolina. No service records, but according to South Carolina Confederate Pension Records, he enlisted as a private in Company F in 10/1864, and was surrendered at Greensboro, North Carolina, on 04/26/1865. (Service records from the time that he enlisted until the end of the war were burned.) After the war, lived in South Carolina. Applied for a South Carolina Confederate Pension on 02/07/1923. Died after 02/07/1923.

437. **Gibson, Jesse C.:** Farm laborer from Worth County, Georgia. Born ca. 1827 in Georgia. Enlisted as a private in Company D on 08/10/1861 at Albany, Georgia. Absent with dismounted men in March/April 1863. Admitted to C.S.A. General Hospital, Danville, Virginia, on 04/24/1863 with smallpox. Returned to duty on 05/08/1863. Captured on 05/14/1864 in King George County, Virginia. Sent to the Old Capitol Prison in Washington, D.C., on 05/17/1864. Transferred to Fort Delaware Prison on 06/17/1864. Paroled at Fort Delaware in 02/1865.

438. **Gilbert, Jasper Norman:** 27-year-old farmer from Lumpkin County, Georgia. Born on 10/23/1834 in South Carolina. Enlisted as a private in Company H on 02/25/1862 at Athens, Clarke County, Georgia. Without a horse for 1 month and 23 days in January/February 1864. On extra duty in 04/1864. Admitted to Jackson Hospital, Richmond, Virginia, on 06/01/1864 with acute diarrhea. Returned to duty on 06/14/1864. Admitted to Jackson Hospital, Richmond, Virginia, on 06/22/1864. Sent to Georgia with Capt. Bostick to get a horse on 09/20/1864. Was surrendered by Gen. Joseph E. Johnston on 04/26/1865. Paroled at Greensboro, North Carolina, on 05/01/1865. After the war, worked as a day laborer in DeKalb County, Georgia, and then as a farmer in Gwinnett and Fulton counties, Georgia. He and his wife, Hannah, had at least eleven children. Died on 09/30/1901 in DeKalb County, Georgia. Buried at Pleasant Hill Baptist Cemetery in DeKalb County, Georgia. His widow applied for a Confederate pension in Fulton County, Georgia.

439. **Gillespie, Milton William:** 17-year-old student from Banks County, Georgia. Born on 09/18/1845 in Franklin County, Georgia. Brother of William P. Gillespie. Enlisted as a private in Company H on 07/12/1863 at Homer, Georgia. Sent to Georgia on sick furlough beginning 05/15/1864. Last record September/October 1864, still on sick leave. Surrendered at Washington, Wilkes County, Georgia. After the war, became a farmer in Banks and Jackson counties, Georgia. Married Mary Elizabeth Patterson on 09/29/1867 in Banks County, Georgia, and they had at least five children. Received a Confederate pension in Banks County, Georgia. Died on 03/08/1930.

440. **Gillespie, William P.:** 24-year-old. Born on 05/18/1837 in Franklin County, Georgia. Brother of Milton William Gillespie. Enlisted as a private in Company H on 03/03/1862 at Athens, Clarke County, Georgia. Sent to infirmary/recruiting camp on 11/10/1863. Last record September/October 1864, sent to Georgia to get a horse with Capt. Bostick on 09/20/1864. After the war, became a farmer in Lumpkin County, Georgia. He and his wife, Mary, had at least seven children. Died after 1910.

441. Gilmer [Gilmore], Albert C.: Farmer from Hall County, Georgia. Born ca. 1829 in Georgia. Brother of Ezekiel Francis Gilmer. Enlisted as a private in Company H on 02/28/1862 at Athens, Clarke County, Georgia. Elected lieutenant on 05/26/1862. Resigned on 06/18/1862 due to poor health. He and his wife, Jane, had at least three children.

442. Gilmer [Gilmore], Ezekiel Francis: 25-year-old farmer from Hall County, Georgia. Born in Hall County, Georgia, on 06/25/1836. Brother of Albert C. Gilmer. Enlisted as a private in Company H on 02/28/1862 at Athens, Clarke County, Georgia. Died on 07/25/1862 at General Hospital No. 14 in Richmond, Virginia. He and his wife, Susan, had at least one child.

443. Gilstrap, Benjamin D. [Josiah]: 33-year-old farmer from Forsyth County, Georgia. Born on 09/09/1828 in Pickens County, South Carolina. Enlisted as a private in Company B on 05/02/1862 at Atlanta, Georgia. Value of horse $200. Admitted to Winder Hospital in Richmond, Virginia, on 07/15/1862 due to sickness. Horse killed in action on 11/05/1862 at Barbee's Cross Roads, Virginia. Sent to Georgia to get a horse on 06/08/1863. Absent without leave beginning 08/16/1863. Last record, still absent without leave in September/October 1864. Married Mary Ann Mears ca. 1853 in Greenville, South Carolina, and they had at least nine children. After the war, became a farmer in Milton County, Georgia. Applied for a Confederate pension in Milton County, Georgia. Died on 05/01/1911 in Alpharetta, Milton County, Georgia.

444. Givens, George W.: Born ca. 1846 in DeKalb County, Georgia. Son of William Givens. Enlisted as a private in Company B on 04/22/1862 at Atlanta, Georgia. Value of horse $125. Sent home to get a horse on 11/10/1863. Transferred to Company G in November/December 1863. Was surrendered by Gen. Joseph E. Johnston on 04/26/1865. Paroled at Greensboro, North Carolina, on 05/01/1865. Married Augusta S. Holmes in 1865.

445. Givens, William: 37-year-old carriage maker from DeKalb County, Georgia. Born in 09/1824 in South Carolina. Father of George W. Givens. Enlisted as a private in Company B on 04/09/1862 at Atlanta, Georgia. Value of horse $170. Furloughed to Stone Mountain, Georgia, beginning 02/14/1863. Sent home to get a horse on 08/12/1863. Transferred to Company G in November/December 1863. Absent without leave beginning 10/12/1863. Sent to Georgia with Capt. Bostick to get a horse on 09/20/1864. Captured at Waynesboro, North Carolina, on 02/22/1865. Sent to New Bern, North Carolina, and transferred to Point Lookout, Maryland, on 03/30/1865. Released on 06/27/1865. Described as having a light complexion, light hair, blue eyes, and being 5' 6 1/2" tall. After the war, became a wagon maker in Walton County, Georgia, and then a farmer from Gwinnett County, Georgia. Married (1) Katherine, and they had five children. Married (2) Amanda Brand on 06/17/1866 (or 1867) in Gwinnett County, Georgia. They had twelve children. Died before 1910.

446. Glaze, Jacob Harris: 29-year-old from Georgia. Born on 03/24/1833 in Lumpkin County, Georgia, or in South Carolina. Enlisted as a private in Company H on 03/03/1862 at Athens, Clarke County, Georgia. Sent home to get a horse with Lt. Sinquefield under Special Order No. 27 from corps headquarters on 02/23/1864. Admitted to Jackson Hospital, Richmond, Virginia, on 06/21/1864 with a fever. Returned to duty on 07/06/1864. Last record, September/October 1864, sent to Georgia with Capt. Bostick to get a horse on 09/20/1864. After the war, became a farmer in Murray County, Georgia. Married Mary A.F. Barker on 09/22/1853 in Lumpkin County, Georgia, and they had at least seven children. Received a Confederate pension for infirmity and poverty in Hall County, Georgia, in 1908.

447. Glaze, James M.: 25-year-old from Lumpkin County, Georgia. Born in 01/1837 in Lumpkin County, Georgia. Brother of John H. Glaze. Enlisted as a private in Company H on 03/03/1862 at Athens, Clarke County, Georgia. Killed in action ca. 07/10/1863 in Maryland. His mother, Martha J. Evans Glaze, received his back pay, as he was not survived by his father, a wife, or children.

448. Glaze, John H. [M.]: 21-year-old. Born on 04/12/1840 in Georgia. Brother of James M. Glaze. Enlisted as a private in Company H on 03/03/1862 at Athens, Clarke County, Georgia. Without a horse and absent without leave on 01/01/1864. Last record, 09/01/1864, in Georgia on sick furlough since 07/16/1864. After the war, worked as a farm laborer in Polksville and Quillians, Hall County, Georgia. Married Nancy Caroline Wofford on 08/22/1861 in Hall County, Georgia, and they had at least seven children. Applied for a Confederate pension in Hall County, Georgia. Died on 12/06/1918 in Waco, Texas.

449. Gleaton, Dudley C.: 19-year-old farm laborer from Worth County, Georgia. Born on 09/19/1842 in Dooly County, Georgia. Enlisted as a private in Company D on 03/04/1862 at Albany, Georgia. Value of horse $150 and horse equipment

$35. Sent to infirmary/recruiting camp on 10/20/1863. Sent to Georgia to get a horse with Capt. Bostick on 09/20/1864. Was surrendered by Gen. Joseph E. Johnston on 04/26/1865. Paroled at Greensboro, North Carolina, on 05/01/1865. After the war, became a farmer in Worth County, Georgia. He and his wife, Catherine, had five children. Died on 10/18/1885 in Worth County, Georgia.

450. Glenn, James R.: Enlisted as a sergeant in Company B on 08/14/1861 at Atlanta, Georgia. Value of horse $225 and horse equipment $30. Furnished Lawson V. White as a substitute on 01/07/1862.

451. Glenn, Joseph T.: 16-year-old from Georgia. Enlisted as a private in Company C on 08/01/1861 at Athens, Clarke County, Georgia. In November/December 1861, was convalescing, but unable to perform duty. Sent to Georgia to get a horse on 11/10/1863. Returned 02/29/1864. Was present on his last record, September/October 1864.

452. Godbee, William T.: 18-year-old student from Burke County, Georgia. Born 1846 in Burke County, Georgia. Enlisted as a private in Company L on 04/29/1864 at Waynesboro, Georgia. Last record, September/October 1864, sent to Georgia to get a horse with Capt. Bostick on 09/20/1864. After the war, became a farmer and then a merchant in Burke County, Georgia. Married Sarah Jane Wynn on 10/06/1869 in Richmond County, Georgia. Applied for a Confederate pension in Burke County, Georgia, in 1905. Died after 1905.

453. Godfrey, David P.[G.]: Farmer from Thomas County, Georgia. Born in South Carolina. Enlisted as a private in Company D on 08/10/1861 at Albany, Georgia. Value of horse $175 and horse equipment $25, furnished by the State of Georgia. Wounded and captured at Crampton's Gap, Maryland, on 09/13/1862. Paroled on 09/14/1862. Captured at Burkettsville and admitted to General Hospital, Baltimore, Maryland, on 11/13/1862. Sent to Fort McHenry, Maryland, on 11/17/1862. Admitted to General Hospital, Petersburg, Virginia, on 11/21/1862, where his left arm was amputated. Discharged on 11/30/1862. Described as being 21 years old, 5'10" tall, and having a fair complexion, blue eyes and dark hair. After the war, became a retail merchant in Thomas County, Georgia, and then lived in Taylor County, Georgia. His wife's name was Margaret. Applied for a Confederate pension in Taylor County, Georgia.

454. Goff, James H.: 19-year-old farm hand from Richmond County, Georgia. Born in South Carolina on 09/22/1842. Twin of William Henry Goff. Enlisted as a private in Company I on 05/08/1862 at Augusta, Georgia. Detailed as an ambulance driver on 02/23/1864. Horse killed in action at Trevilian Station, Virginia, on 06/11/1864. Admitted to C.S.A. General Hospital in Charlottesville, Virginia, on 06/13/1864 with wounds in the face and head received at Trevilian Station. Returned to duty on 07/07/1864. Last record, September/October 1864, sent to Georgia to get a horse with Capt. Bostick on 09/20/1864. After the war, became a farmer from Burke County, Georgia. His wife's name was Lucy. Died before 1880.

455. Goff, William Henry: 19-year-old farm hand from Richmond County, Georgia. Born in South Carolina on 09/22/1842. Twin of James H. Goff. Enlisted as a private in Company I on 03/04/1862 at Augusta, Georgia. Value of horse $225. Horse killed in action at Malvern Hill, Virginia, on 07/16/1862. Goff detailed as an ambulance driver on 11/12/1863. Last record, September/October 1864, sent to Georgia to get a horse with Capt. Bostick on 09/20/1864. After the war, became a farmer in Burke County, Georgia. Married Emma Perkins ca. 1877 and they had eight children. Died on 03/17/1902.

456. Gondelock, Robert W.: 20-year-old from Georgia. Enlisted as a private in Company C on 08/01/1861 at Athens, Clarke County, Georgia. On courier duty for Gen. Hampton on 10/27/1862. On furlough for 25 days beginning 01/20/1862. Last record, September/October 1864, still on detail to corps headquarters.

457. Goodman, Nathan: Native of Georgia. Enlisted as a private in Company B on 08/14/1861 at Atlanta, Georgia. Value of horse $225 and horse equipment $10, saddle furnished by State of Georgia. Detailed as a courier for Col. Soulowski in 12/1861. Detailed as a courier for Gen. Howard Cobb on 01/15/1862. Captured at Macon, Georgia, on 4/20 (21)/1865.

458. Goodwin, Jacob: Farmer from Richmond County, Georgia. Born in South Carolina ca. 1842. Enlisted as a private in Company I on 03/04/1862 at Augusta, Georgia. Value of horse $200. Discharged on 08/25/1862. After the war, worked as a teamster in Columbia County, Georgia, and then a laborer in Richmond County, Georgia. He and his wife, Elizabeth, had at least two children. Died after 1880.

459. Goodwin, William E.: Enlisted as a private in Company L on 12/15/1862 at Burke County, Georgia. Admitted to C.S.A. General Hospital in Charlottesville, Virginia, on 06/10/1863 with a wound. Furloughed for 30 days beginning 06/29/1863. Admitted to Jackson Hospital in Richmond,

Virginia, on 01/14/1864 with pneumonia. Returned to duty on 02/09/1864. Sent to Georgia with Capt. Bostick to get a horse on 09/20/1864. Was surrendered by Gen. Joseph E. Johnston on 04/26/1865. Paroled at Greensboro, North Carolina, on 05/01/1865.

460. Gordon, Elijah A.: Farmer from Burke County, Georgia. Born ca. 1834 in Burke County, Georgia. Enlisted as a private in Company F on 05/09/1862 at Burke County, Georgia. Value of horse $200. Admitted to a hospital in Lynchburg, Virginia, and then transferred to C.S.A. General Hospital, Danville, Virginia, on 08/20/1862 with hepatitis. Returned to duty on 08/22/1862. Discharged on 09/02/1862. Described as being 5'8" tall, with a dark complexion, brown eyes, and dark hair. After the war, became a farmer in Burke County, Georgia. Married Emily J. White on 02/14/1856 in Jefferson County, Georgia. Died after 1880.

461. Gordon, James: 33-year-old native of Georgia. Enlisted as a sergeant in Company F on 03/25/1862 at Burke County, Georgia. Value of horse $175. Admitted to Winder Hospital, Richmond, Virginia, on 12/04/1863. Furloughed for 30 days beginning 12/24/1863. Sent to Georgia with Capt. Bostick to get a horse on 09/20/1864. Was surrendered by Gen. Joseph E. Johnston on 04/26/1865. Paroled at Greensboro, North Carolina, on 05/01/1865.

462. Gordon, James A.: 25-year-old from Winterville, Georgia, native of Georgia. Enlisted as a private in Company F on 03/25/1862 at Burke County, Georgia. Value of horse $125. Admitted to C.S.A. General Hospital No. 4 in Wilmington, North Carolina, on 05/16/1862. Returned to duty on 05/17/1862. Admitted to C.S.A. General Hospital in Danville, Virginia, on 08/20/1862 with debility. Returned to duty on 08/22/1862. No horse for 3 months in November/December 1863. Detailed to attend horses at infirmary/recruiting camp on 02/22/1864. On provost duty at Hanover Court House on 03/15/1864. Was surrendered by Gen. Joseph E. Johnston on 04/26/1865. Paroled at Greensboro, North Carolina, on 05/01/1865.

463. Gordon, Samuel J. L.: 28-year old. Born in Georgia in 07/1833. Enlisted as a private in Company F on 03/25/1862 at Burke County, Georgia. Value of horse $140. Captured at Beverly's Ford, Virginia, on 06/09/1863 and sent to the Old Capitol Prison in Washington, D.C. Paroled on 06/25/1863. Admitted to Winder Hospital in Richmond, Virginia, on 12/23/1863 and then transferred to Jackson Hospital in Richmond, Virginia, on 01/21/1864 with spinal disease. Returned to duty 03/15/1864. Detailed as teamster on 08/12/1864. Sent to Georgia with Capt. Bostick to get a horse on 09/20/1864. Was surrendered by Gen. Joseph E. Johnston on 04/26/1865. Paroled at Greensboro, North Carolina, on 05/01/1865. After the war, became a farm laborer and then a manager in Jefferson County, Georgia. Applied for a Confederate pension in Jefferson County, Georgia. Died after 1910.

464. Goss, Francis M.: 27-year-old. Enlisted as a private in Company I on 03/26/1862 at Augusta, Georgia. Value of horse $175. Captured at Gettysburg, Pennsylvania, on 07/02/1863 and sent to Fort McHenry, Maryland, on 07/06/1863, and then transferred to Fort Delaware Prison. Deserted and took the Oath as a prisoner of war. Discharged on 08/25/1863.

465. Goswick, W.H.: 20-year-old. Enlisted as a private in Company K on 02/09/1863 at Camp Maynard, Georgia. Returned to his regiment on 02/21/1863.

466. Gough, Joseph Simeon: Farm hand from Burke County, Georgia. Born on 08/10/1842 or 1843 in Georgia. Enlisted as a private in Company F on 05/09/1862 at Burke County, Georgia. Value of horse $250. Sent to infirmary/recruiting camp on 01/10/1864. Sent to Georgia with Capt. Bostick to get a horse on 09/20/1864. Was surrendered by Gen. Joseph E. Johnston on 04/26/1865. Paroled at Greensboro, North Carolina, on 05/01/1865. After the war, became a farmer in Burke County, Georgia. Died on 03/10/1918. Buried in the Gough Family Cemetery in Burke County, Georgia.

467. Gower, Thomas C. [J.C.]: 20-year-old. Born in 06/1841 in South Carolina. Enlisted as a private in Company C on 08/01/1861 at Athens, Clarke County, Georgia. Listed as corporal in November/December 1861. Captured on 09/29/1862 at Warrenton, Virginia, but listed as present in September/October 1862. Provided Job Smith as a substitute on 04/06/1863.

468. Graffan [Graffin, Graffis], Andrew J.: 23-year-old from Burke County, Georgia. Enlisted as a private in Company F on 05/09/1862 at Burke County, Georgia. No horse beginning 05/09/1862. Captured on 07/25/1863 and sent to Fort Mifflin, Pennsylvania, on 07/27/1863. Deserted and took the Oath. Transferred from Harrisburg, Pennsylvania, to Philadelphia, Pennsylvania, on 08/08/1863. Released on 10/28/1863.

469. Graham, James S.: 18-year-old from Georgia. Enlisted as a private in Company B on 05/02/1862 at Atlanta, Georgia. Transferred to Company G in May/June 1862. Sent on horse detail on 11/10/1863. Sent home to get a horse with Lt. Sinquefield under Special Order No. 27 from corps headquarters on 02/23/1864. Last record September/October 1864, absent without leave since 05/01/1864.

470. **Gramling, John R.:** From Georgia. Born ca. 1842 in North Carolina. Enlisted as a private in Company B 04/28/1862 at Atlanta, Georgia. Value of horse $200. Transferred to Company G in May/June 1862. Sent home to get a horse with Lt. Sinquefield under Special Order No. 27 from corps headquarters on 02/23/1864. Was surrendered by Gen. Joseph E. Johnston on 04/26/1865. Paroled at Greensboro, North Carolina, on 05/01/1865. After the war, worked as a clerk and then as a wholesale shoe merchant in Fulton County, Georgia. He and his wife, Annie, had five children. Died before 1900.

471. **Graham, J.W.:** Enlisted as a private in Company B on 03/29/1863 at Staunton, Virginia, in exchange for J.A. Perkins. Transferred to 1st Maryland Cavalry on 02/09/1864.

472. **Gray, Joseph:** Resident of Georgia. Born in South Carolina. Enlisted as a private in Company K. Deserted to the enemy and took the Oath on 03/05/1865. Described as 25 years old, having a dark complexion, dark hair, dark eyes, and being 5'8" tall.

473. **Gray, William M.D.:** Native of Georgia. Enlisted as a private in Company F on 03/25/1862 at Burke County, Georgia. Value of horse $225. Detailed to attend horses at infirmary/recruiting camp on 12/11/1863. Lost horse on 06/11/1864. Sent to Georgia with Capt. Bostick to get a horse on 09/20/1864. Was surrendered by Gen. Joseph E. Johnston on 04/26/1865. Paroled at Greensboro, North Carolina, on 05/01/1865.

474. **Green, Clement C.:** 33-year-old farmer from Fulton County, Georgia. Enlisted as a private in Company B on 04/18/1862 at Atlanta, Georgia. Transferred to Company G in May 1862. Elected lieutenant on 05/30/1862. Furloughed to Georgia for 30 days in 07/1862. Was found to be unfit for service due to a gunshot wound in his left hand, which left him unable to manage a horse, on 09/24/1862. After the war became a farmer in Fulton County, Georgia. Married (1) Mary and they had at five children. Married (2) Louisa J. and they had three children. Died before 1900.

475. **Green, G.C.:** Resident of Georgia. Enlisted as a private in Company A on 04/01/1863 at Dogtown, Virginia. Last record, 04/01/1864, sent to infirmary/recruiting camp on 12/20/1863.

476. **Green, G.M.:** Overseer from Carroll County, Georgia. Born ca. 1828 in Georgia. Enlisted in 6th Georgia Infantry (State Guards). Listed on a roster of Company D published in *The History of Dougherty County*, but not with the *Civil War Soldiers and Sailors System*. No service records in Cobb's Legion.

477. **Green, James:** 24-year-old. Enlisted as a private in Company E on 04/03/1862 at Roswell, Georgia. Only service record dated 04/22/1862.

478. **Green, Jesse P.:** 23-year-old planter from Burke County, Georgia. Born on 04/11/1839. Enlisted as a private in Company F on 03/25/1862 at Burke County. Value of horse $350 and horse equipment $70. Provided John Milledge McCoy as a substitute on 08/04/1862. He and his wife, Mary, had one child. Died on 04/13/1864 in Florida. Buried in the Green Cemetery in Burke County, Georgia.

479. **Green, Lucius R. [J.R.]:** Overseer from Burke County, Georgia. Born ca. 1833 in Columbia County, Georgia. Enlisted as a private in Company F on 05/09/1862 at Burke County, Georgia. Value of horse $175. On sick furlough in September/October 1862. No horse on 02/22/1864. Detailed as a wagon driver on 02/22/1864. Admitted sick to General Hospital No. 7, Raleigh, North Carolina, on 08/01/1864. Admitted to. General Military Hospital No. 4 in Wilmington, North Carolina, on 09/12/1864 with chronic diarrhea. An undated note from the hospital in Raleigh stated that he was sent to the Wilmington hospital for assignment as a fisherman. Last record, returned to duty on 12/09/1864. After the war, worked as an overseer in Dougherty County, Georgia. Married (1) Josephine Rosetta Denham on 04/3/1853 in Columbia County, Georgia (2) Mary Ann (or Mollie) Brinson on 02/10/1870 in Decatur County, Georgia. Was the father of at least four children. Died after 1870.

480. **Green, Sanders:** Enlisted as a private in Company K on 02/23/1863 at Camp Maynard, Georgia. Last record, returned to his regiment on 03/23/1863.

481. **Green, T.G.:** 25-year-old from Cobb County, Georgia. Enlisted in the 7th South Carolina on 04/15/1861 at Charleston, South Carolina. Transferred as a private in Company A on 11/12/1862 at Dog Town, Culpeper County, Virginia. No horse on 01/01/1863. Promoted to corporal sometime between April 1863 and November 1863. Last record, was listed as present in September/October 1864.

482. **Greer [Grier], Henry N.:** Farmer/student from DeKalb County, Georgia. Born ca. 1843.

Brother of Robert Simeon and William A. Greer. Enlisted as a private in Company B on 05/06/1862 at Atlanta, Georgia. Value of horse $130. Transferred to Company G in May/June 1862. Sent to Georgia to get a horse with Lt. James H. Johnson on 04/14/1863 and again on 11/10/1863. Sent home to get a horse with Lt. Sinquefield under Special Order No. 27 from corps headquarters on 02/23/1864. Last record September/October 1864, sent to Georgia to get a horse with Capt. Bostick on 09/20/1864.

483. Greer [Grier], Robert Simeon: 21-year-old student from DeKalb County, Georgia. Born on 11/11/1840 in DeKalb County, Georgia. Brother of Henry N. and William A. Greer. Enlisted as a private in Company B on 05/05/1862 at Atlanta, Georgia. Value of horse $225. Transferred to Company G in May 1862. Admitted to Winder Hospital, Richmond, Virginia, on 07/22/1862 with diarrhea. Returned to duty on 07/24/1862. Horse killed in action at Upperville, Virginia, on 06/21/1863. Sent to Georgia to get a horse on 11/10/1863. Sent to infirmary/recruiting camp in January/February 1864. Last record September/October 1864, sent to Georgia to get a horse with Capt. Bostick on 09/20/1864. After the war, became a farmer and then an owner of a slaughter pen, in Fulton County, Georgia. Married Samantha Emaline Buchanan in 1863 and they had at least nine children. Died on 06/03/1910. His widow applied for a Confederate pension in Fulton County, Georgia.

484. Greer [Grier], William A.: 30-year-old farmer from Gwinnett County, Georgia. Born in 09/1831 in Georgia. Brother of Henry N. and Robert Simeon Greer. Enlisted as a private in Company B on 04/29/1862 at Atlanta, Georgia. Transferred to Company G in May/June 1862. Sent to Georgia to get a horse on 02/21/1862. No horse on 10/27/1862. Sent home to get a horse on 11/10/1863. Sent home to get a horse with Lt. Sinquefield under Special Order No. 27 from corps headquarters on 02/23/1864. Sent to Georgia with Capt. Bostick to get a horse on 09/20/1864. After the war, became a farmer in Gwinnett County, Georgia. He and his wife, Mary, had at least eleven children. Died after 1900.

485. Gregory, John Jefferson: 25-year-old medical student from Jefferson County, Georgia. Born on 06/02/1835 in Jefferson County, Georgia. Enlisted as a private in Company F on 03/25/1862 at Burke County, Georgia. Value of horse $175. No horse on 01/26/1864. Sent home to get a horse with Lt. Sinquefield under Special Order No. 27 from corps headquarters on 03/31/1864. Last record September/October 1864, sent to Georgia to get a horse with Capt. Bostick on 09/20/1864. After the war, became a physician in Bell County, Texas, and then a physician and dentist in Nueces County, Texas. Married (1) Laura Lucas Hunt in 1857 (2) Annie McCampbell on 12/09/1880 in Corpus Christi, Nueces County, Texas. Was the father of at least five children. Died on 03/28/1882 in Corpus Christi, Nueces County, Texas. Buried in the Old Bayview Cemetery, Corpus Christi, Texas.

486. Griffeth [Griffith], David Alexander: 27-year-old farmer from Clarke County, Georgia. Born in Georgia in 05/1835. Enlisted as a private in Company H on 04/30/1862 at Atlanta, Georgia. A card in his compiled service record states that he died on 06/26/1862 at Camp Meadow near Richmond, Virginia. Unless there were two D.A. Griffeths in Company H, this is in error, because another document in his compiled service record lists him as being discharged from service and paid off on 08/23/1862. After the war, became a farmer in Clarke and Oconee counties, Georgia. Married Emaline Fambra on 02/13/1859 in Morgan County, Georgia, and they had at least six children. His widow, Mrs. Rosella E. Griffeth, applied for a Confederate pension in Oconee County, Georgia. Died after 1900.

487. Griffin, Eli: Enlisted as a private in Company B on 08/14/1861 at Atlanta, Georgia. Value of horse $175 and horse equipment $7, saddle furnished by the State of Georgia. Detailed to work as an assistant surgeon in hospital at college in Williamsburg, Virginia, in November/December 1861. Discharged and paid off at Landing Tavern, Virginia, on 08/02/1862.

488. Grimes, Allen T.: Student from Milton County, Georgia. Born ca. 1836 in Georgia. Brother of Newton J. Grimes. Enlisted as a private in Company E on 10/05/1862 at Bunker Hill, [West] Virginia. Sent to Georgia to get a horse on 11/12/1863. Lost horse on 01/01/1864. Absent sick on 01/17/1864. On provost duty detail on 09/20/1864. Was surrendered by Gen. Joseph E. Johnston on 04/26/1865. Paroled at Greensboro, North Carolina, on 05/01/1865. After the war, became a farmer in Milton County, Georgia. Died after 1900.

489. Grimes, Newton J.: 23-year-old farmer from Milton County, Georgia. Born on 03/22/1833 in Georgia. Brother of Allen T. Grimes. Enlisted as a private in Company E on 03/15/1662 at Roswell, Georgia. Value of horse $160. Last record, September/October 1864, at infirmary/recruiting camp since 12/15/1863. After the war, became a farmer in Milton County, Georgia. Married (1) Dicey and (2) Eliza, and was the father of at least one child. Applied for a Confederate pension in Milton County, Georgia. Died on 12/18/1914. Buried at the Roswell Methodist Church Cemetery in Fulton County, Georgia.

490. Grindle, Berry T.[F.]: Farm laborer from Clarke County, Georgia. Born ca. 1842 in Dawson County, Georgia. Son of Daniel Grindle. Enlisted as a private in Company C on 08/01/1861 at Athens, Clarke County, Georgia. Detailed as a teamster in December 1861. Died on 09/07/1862 at Richmond, Virginia, from severe burns.

491. Grindle, Daniel: 41-year-old. Born in 04/1820 in Georgia. Father of Berry T. Grindle. Enlisted as a private in Company C on 08/01/1861 at Athens, Clarke County, Georgia. Was sick in November/December 1861. Detailed as a teamster in 12/1861. Discharged on 10/23/1862. After the war, became a farm worker in Pickens County, Georgia, and then moved to Lumpkin County, Georgia. He and his wife, Mary, had at least six children. Applied for a Confederate pension in Lumpkin County, Georgia. Died after 1900.

492. Groves, Jasper B.: Resident of Georgia. Enlisted as a private in Company G on 10/01/1862 at Atlanta, Georgia. Detailed as a courier in McLaw's infantry division on 10/01/1862. No horse in March/April 1863. Courier to Gen. Young in November/December 1863. Absent sick 05/01–09–01/1864. Last record, September/October 1864, sent to Georgia to get a horse with Capt. Bostick on 09/20/1864.

493. Grubbs, James, Jr.: Overseer from Burke County, Georgia. Born ca. 1836 in Georgia. Enlisted as a private in Company F on 05/09/1862 at Burke County, Georgia. Detailed to attend horses at infirmary/recruiting camp on 12/10/1863. Sent to Georgia to get a horse with Capt. Bostick on 09/20/1864. Was surrendered by Gen. Joseph E. Johnston on 04/26/1865. Paroled at Greensboro, North Carolina, on 05/01/1865. After the war, became a farmer in Burke County, Georgia. His wife's name was Jane. Died after 1880.

494. Guard [Guarde], David S.: From Georgia. Born ca. 1835 in Georgia or Virginia. Enlisted in 1st Georgia Infantry, Company F, as a private on 03/18/1861. Mustered out at Augusta, Georgia, on 03/18/1862. Enlisted as a private in Cobb's Legion Cavalry, Company B, on 04/16/1862 at Atlanta, Georgia. Value of horse $230. Transferred to Company G as a blacksmith in May/June 1862. Appointed corporal in January/February 1863. Sent home to get a horse on 11/10/1863. Listed as present on last record, September/October 1864. After the war, worked as a carpenter in Fulton County, Georgia. He and his wife, Oregon, had at least ten children. Died after 1900.

495. Guedron, Alexander C.: From Georgia. Born ca. 1846 in Kentucky. Enlisted as a private in Company A on 08/17/1861 at Augusta, Georgia. Value of horse $150 and horse equipment $25. Lost his horse on 01/01/1863. Sent to Georgia with Capt. Bostick to get a horse on 09/20/1864. Was surrendered by Gen. Joseph E. Johnston on 04/26/1865. Paroled at Greensboro, North Carolina, on 05/01/1865. Francis Edgeworth Eve described an escape they made in a canoe, using a clapboard as an oar, while scouting. He said of Alexander Guedron, "All honor to the Confederate soldier who, like 'Sandy' Guedron, always did his duty."* After the war, worked as a butcher in Richmond County, Georgia. Was married on 05/12/1869 and was the father of at least two children. Died on 04/29/1894 at Augusta, Georgia.

496. Guedron [Guidrant, Guidron], John C.: Resident of Richmond County, Georgia. Enlisted as a private in Company A on 08/17/1861 at Augusta, Georgia. Value of horse $175 and horse equipment $25. Last service record dated January 1862 states that he was on furlough for 25 days. Other records show that he enlisted as a corporal 04/10/1862 in the 12th Georgia Battalion Heavy Artillery, Company A. He received a disability discharge from the 63rd Georgia Infantry, Company A.

497. Gulick [Guelick], Joseph H.: Enlisted as a private in Company A on 05/01/1862 at Augusta, Georgia. Last record dated November/December 1863 states that he had no horse and was absent without leave. The Muster Roll Commission listed him as a deserter.

498. Gunby [Gomby, Gumby], William T.: From Fulton County, Georgia. Born ca. 1831 in Georgia. Enlisted as a private in Company B on 08/14/1861 at Atlanta, Georgia. Value of horse $275 and horse equipment $6, saddle furnished by State of Georgia. On special furlough to Georgia for 25 days beginning 02/10/1862. Promoted to sergeant in November/December 1862. Detailed to be in charge of horses at infirmary/recruiting camp on 08/15/1864. Was surrendered by Gen. Joseph E. Johnston on 04/26/1865. Paroled at Greensboro, North Carolina, on 05/01/1865. He and his wife, Elizabeth, had at least two children.

499. Guthrie, William M.R.: 35-year-old. Enlisted as a private in Company B at Atlanta, Geor-

---

*Confederate Veteran Magazine, *Vol. II (1894) page 143.*

gia, on 05/06/1862. Value of horse $190. Sent on sick furlough to Ringgold, Georgia, for 30 days in July/August 1862. Transferred to 11th Georgia, Company G, on 05/14/1863.

500. Haesler [Haeseler, Hasler, Hassler], Samuel Burchardt: 22-year-old native of Germany. Born on 11/03/1829 in Prussia. Enlisted as a private in Company A on 08/17/1861 at Augusta, Georgia. Value of horse $160 and horse equipment $25. Transferred to Company F on 07/01/1862. Captured at Waterloo, Virginia, 04/18/1863. Sent to Old Capitol Prison, Washington, D.C., on 04/23/1863 and paroled from there on 05/10/1863. Detailed 07/01/1864 as a courier for regiment headquarters. Sent to Georgia to get a horse under Capt. Bostick beginning 09/20/1864. Was surrendered by Gen. Joseph E. Johnston on 04/26/1865. Paroled at Greensboro, North Carolina, on 05/01/1865. After the war, worked as a sheriff in Waynesboro, Burke County, Georgia. Married (1) Francis M. Lawes of Burke County, Georgia, on 04/04/1867 (2) Sarah Ann Chance Reese on 08/17/1884 in Burke County, Georgia, and was the father of at least four children. Died on 07/19/1895. Buried in the Waynesboro Confederate Cemetery in Burke County, Georgia.

501. Haines [Hains], John Schley [C.]: Resident of Georgia. Enlisted as a private in Company A on 08/17/1861 at Augusta, Georgia. Value of horse $150 and horse equipment $25. Sent to Georgia to get a horse in November/December 1863. Detailed in Signal Corps at division headquarters in 04/1864. On last service record September/October 1864, was still detailed to Signal Corps. Applied for a Confederate Pension from Macon, Bibb County, Georgia. Testified that he was scouting within Gen. Sherman's lines at the time of the surrender.

502. Ham, John Dalton: 37-year-old miller from Burke County, Georgia. Native of Georgia. Enlisted as a private in Company F on 03/25/1862 at Burke County, Georgia. Value of horse $200. On sick furlough in Georgia in September/October 1862. Detailed in Burke County to make shoes in March/April 1863. Admitted to Jackson Hospital, Richmond, Virginia, on 05/25/1864 with rheumatism. Returned to duty on 06/12/1864. Sent to Georgia with Capt. Bostick to get a horse on 09/20/1864. Was surrendered by Gen. Joseph E. Johnston on 04/26/1865. Paroled at Greensboro, North Carolina, on 05/01/1865. He and his wife, Charity, had at least one child.

503. Hamby, John: 23-year-old. Enlisted as a private in Company K on 01/29/1863 at Camp Maynard, Georgia. Returned to his regiment on 02/21/1863.

504. Hamilton, Archibald N.: 25-year-old from Georgia. Enlisted as a private in Company G on 04/29/1862 at Atlanta, Georgia. Value of horse $200. Admitted to Winder Hospital in Richmond, Virginia, on 07/22/1862 with debility. Returned to duty on 07/24/1862. Sent home to get a horse on 06/09/1863. Absent without leave beginning 08/09/1863. Last record September/October 1864, sent to Georgia to get a horse with Capt. Bostick on 09/20/1864.

505. Hamilton, George W.: 24-year-old from Georgia. Enlisted as a private in Company E on 04/09/1862 at Lawrenceville, Georgia. Value of horse $200. Sent home to get a horse in March/April 1863. Sent home to get a horse with Lt. Sinquefield under Special Order No. 27 from corps headquarters on 02/23/1864. Last record September/October 1864, detailed to infirmary/recruiting camp since 06/20/1864.

506. Hamilton, Jacob W.: Overseer. Born in Edgefield, South Carolina. Enlisted as a private in Company A on 08/17/1861 at Augusta, Georgia. Detailed as a carpenter at Yorktown, Virginia, in 12/1861. Given a medical discharge on 09/16/1862. Described as having a fair complexion, gray eyes, dark hair, and being 42 years of age and 6 feet tall.

507. Hammond, John W.: 19-year-old from Virginia. Enlisted as a private in Company K on 02/01/1863 at Camp Maynard, Georgia. Captured at Brandy Station, Virginia, on 06/07/1863. Exchanged and sent home to procure a horse. Horse valued at $250 killed in action at Jack's Shop, Madison County, Virginia, on 09/22/1863. Killed at Orangeburg, South Carolina.

508. Hampton, D.B.: Listed on a roster of Company D published in *The History of Dougherty County*, but not with the *Civil War Soldiers and Sailors System*. No service records in Cobb's Legion.

509. Hampton, J.R.: Farmer from Dougherty County, Georgia. Born in Laurens County, Georgia. Enlisted in Nelson's Independent Company, Georgia Cavalry. Listed on a roster of Company D published in *The History of Dougherty County*, but not with the *Civil War Soldiers and Sailors System*. No service records in Cobb's Legion. He and his wife, W.J., had at least one child.

510. Hancock, Robert Jackson: 22-year-old farm laborer from Jackson County, Georgia. Born on 02/09/1839. Enlisted as a private in Company C on 08/01/1861 at Athens, Clarke County, Georgia. Sent to recruiting/infirmary camp on 08/05/1863. Last record, September/October 1864, sent to Georgia to get a horse with Capt. Bostick on 09/20/1864. After the war, became a retail merchant in Jackson County, Georgia. Married Sarah Sophia Pendergrass on 01/15/1868 in Jackson County, Georgia. Died on 07/06/1877. Buried in the Woodbine Cemetery in Jackson County, Georgia.

511. Hancock, William Dawson: Farmer from Whitfield County, Georgia. Born ca. 1822 in Georgia or South Carolina. Enlisted as a private in Company B on 08/14/1861 at Atlanta, Georgia. Value of horse $200 and horse equipment $9.50, saddle furnished by State of Georgia. On furlough for 25 days beginning 11/29/1861. Transferred to the 2nd Georgia Infantry on 08/01/1862. After the war, kept water and wood at a railroad station in Whitfield County, Georgia. He and his wife, Frances T., had at least four children. Applied for a Confederate pension in Whitfield County, Georgia. Died before 1910.

512. Hanlon [Hanlin], James W.: 15-year-old farm laborer from Dougherty County, Georgia. Born in Ireland in 06/1846. Enlisted as a private in Company D on 08/10/1861 at Albany, Georgia. Value of horse $200 and horse equipment $25; $20 saddle furnished by State of Georgia. On furlough of indulgence to Georgia for 24 days beginning 01/25/1864. Admitted to C.S.A. General Hospital in Charlottesville, Virginia, on 06/14/1864 with a wound in the right shoulder. Furloughed from the hospital for 50 days beginning 06/22/1864. Sent to Georgia with Capt. Bostick to get a horse on 09/20/1864. Was surrendered by Gen. Joseph E. Johnston on 04/26/1865. Paroled at Greensboro, North Carolina, on 05/01/1865. After the war, worked as a printer in Irwin County, Georgia. Was married and the father of at least three children. Died after 1900.

513. Hanlon, Michael: 18-year-old day laborer and mason from Sumter County, Georgia. Born ca. 1834 in Ireland. Enlisted as a private in Company I on 03/26/1862 at Augusta, Georgia. Value of horse $225. Captured near Harrison's Landing, Virginia, on 07/10/1862 and sent to Fort Monroe, Virginia. Date of release not given. Described as having a fair complexion, blue eyes, and brown hair and being 5'6" tall. Admitted to General Hospital, Staunton, Virginia, with diarrhea on 03/13/1863. Received a flesh wound to the left leg at Funkstown, Maryland, on 07/06/1863 (or 08/1863). Admitted to Chimborazo Hospital in Richmond, Virginia, on 07/17/1863. Furloughed for 35 days beginning 08/02/1863. Admitted to C.S.A. General Hospital No. 11 in Charlotte, North Carolina, on 01/19/1865 with a wound to his lower left leg. Transferred to another hospital on 04/14/1865. After the war, worked as a railroad laborer in Richmond County, Georgia. Married Johanna Murphy on 06/18/1868 in Richmond County, Georgia, and they had three children. Died after 1880.

514. Harben [Harbin], John D.D.: 17-year-old from Richmond County, Georgia. Enlisted as a private in Company I on 03/03/1862 at Augusta, Georgia. Value of horse $230. Captured near Martinsburg, Berkeley County, [West] Virginia, on 07/17 (or 18)/1863 and sent to Fort Chase, Ohio, on 07/30/1863. Transferred to Fort Delaware Prison on 03/04/1864. Paroled 06/16/1865. Described as having a dark complexion, dark hair, blue eyes and being 5'11" tall. Married (1) Susan Bevens in Richmond County, Georgia, on 01/28/1866 and (2) Jane Cannon on 09/18/1872 in Richmond County, Georgia. Was the father of at least one child. Died after 1880.

515. Hardford, F.: Enlisted as a private in Company K on 02/25/1863 at Camp Maynard, Georgia. Was present on his only record, February 15–March 1, 1863.

516. Hardwick, George Washington: 20-year-old merchant clerk from Augusta, Georgia. Born on 03/11/1841 in Georgia. Enlisted as a private in Company A on 08/17/1861 at Augusta, Georgia. Value of horse $150 and horse equipment $25. On sick furlough in March/April 1863. Detailed with Quartermaster Department in Augusta, Georgia, beginning 12/1863 due to bad health. Had no horse in March/April 1864. Last record September/October 1864, still detailed with Quartermaster Department in Augusta, Georgia. After the war, worked in a cotton factory in Summerville, Georgia. Was married and the father of at least four children. Died on 12/05/1906. Buried in Summerville Cemetery, Augusta, Georgia.

517. Hardwick, William: Enlisted as a private in Company F on 01/29/1863 at Burke County, Georgia. Killed in battle at Brandy Station, Virginia, on 06/09/1863. His back pay was given to his widow, Caroline Hardwick.

518. Hardy, Augustus F.: 22-year-old student from Jackson County, Georgia. Born in 1841 in Georgia. Enlisted as a private in Company H on 02/28/1862 at Athens, Clarke County, Georgia. Killed on 06/09/1863 during the cavalry battle at Brandy Station, Virginia.

519. Hardyman, B.L.: 24-year-old. Enlisted as a private in Company K on 02/09/1863 at Camp Maynard, Georgia. Returned to his regiment on 02/21/1863.

520. Harman, T. Moore: Enlisted as a private in Company L on 04/19/1864 at Decatur, Georgia. Transferred from Camp Randolph, Georgia, on 05/12/1864 but was absent without leave. Last record, September/October 1864 still absent without leave.

521. Harper, Anselin [Anselm] L.: 22-year-old farmer from Clarke County, Georgia. Born on 07/05/1839 in Clarke County, Georgia. Possibly brother of George Harper. Enlisted as a private in Company C on 08/15/1861 at Athens, Clarke County, Georgia. Sent to recruiting/infirmary camp on 08/05/1863. Sent to Georgia with Capt. Bostick to get a horse on 09/20/1864. Was surrendered by Gen. Joseph E. Johnston on 04/26/1865. Paroled at Greensboro, North Carolina, on 05/01/1865. After the war, became a farmer in Oconee County, Georgia. Married (1) Martha and they had at least two children. Married (2) Susan America Malcom Butler on 09/15/1881 in Clarke County, Georgia, and they had seven children. Died 01/25/1911, in Clarke County, Georgia.

522. Harper, George: Native American from Clarke County, Georgia. Possibly brother of Anselin Harper. Enlisted as a private in Company H on 03/01/1862 at Athens, Clarke County, Georgia. Discharged from service and paid off on 08/20/1862. After the war, worked as a laborer in Richmond County, Georgia. Married Maggie E. Foster in Clarke County, or Walton County, Georgia, on 02/08/1872. Died on 04/13/1883. His widow applied for a Confederate pension in Richmond County, Georgia.

523. Harper, William: 18-year-old. Enlisted as a private in Company K on 02/08/1863 at Camp Maynard, Georgia. Returned to his regiment on 02/21/1863.

524. Harrington, Charles: Enlisted as a private in Company H on 01/01/1863 at Stevensburg, Virginia. Killed during the Gettysburg campaign, probably at Hunterstown, Pennsylvania, on 07/02/1863. His widow, Jane Harrington, received his back pay.

525. Harris, Charles R.A.: 27-year-old from Georgia. Enlisted as a private in Company C on 08/01/1861 at Athens, Clarke County, Georgia. Detailed as a courier in 12/1861. On furlough for 25 days beginning 01/20/1862. Detailed as a scout on 01/14/1864. Captured at Fauquier County, Virginia, on 03/15/1864. Sent to the Old Capitol Prison, Washington, D.C., on 04/12/1864. Transferred to Fort Delaware Prison on 06/17/1864. Paroled at Fort Delaware Prison in 02/1864. Admitted to Jackson Hospital, Richmond, Virginia, on 03/11/1865 with chronic diarrhea. Last record, furloughed for 60 days beginning 03/23/1865. After the war, lived in Fulton County, Georgia. Married Eugenia M. Applied for a Confederate pension in Fulton County, Georgia. His widow applied for a Confederate pension in Fulton County, Georgia.

526. Harris, George W: Native of Georgia. Enlisted as a private in 24th Georgia Infantry on 08/27/1861 at Lawrenceville, Georgia. Transferred to Cobb's Legion Cavalry, Company B, on 04/19/1862. Without a horse in 03/1863. Sent to Georgia to get a horse on 04/12/1863. Sent to recruiting/infirmary camp on 12/20/1863. Sent to Georgia to get a horse on 04/21/1864. Last record September/October 1864, sent to Georgia to get a horse with Capt. Bostick on 09/20/1864.

527. Harris, Henry S.: Native of Georgia. Enlisted as a private in Company B on 08/14/1861 at Atlanta, Georgia. Value of horse $150 and horse equipment $3, saddle furnished by State of Georgia. Sent on sick furlough to Georgia for 30 days in 02/1862. Admitted to Winder Hospital in Richmond, Virginia, on 07/22/1862. Lost horse on 03/15/1863. Sent to Georgia to get a horse with Lt. James H. Johnson on 04/14/1863. Detailed as a teamster beginning 11/20/1863. Last record September/October 1864, sent to Georgia to get a horse with Capt. Bostick on 09/20/1864.

528. Harris, James A.: 30-year-old from Gwinnett County, Georgia. Enlisted as a private in Company B on 05/06/1862 at Atlanta, Georgia. Value of horse $125. Died of disease at a hospital in Richmond, Virginia, on 07/25/1862.

529. Harris, James M.: 35-year-old from Georgia. Enlisted as a private in Company G on 03/06/1862 at Atlanta, Georgia. Value of horse $185. Listed as corporal in November/December 1862. Captured at Williamsport, Maryland (probably between 07/04/1863 and 07/10/1863), and admitted to Seminary Hospital, Hagerstown, Maryland, in August 1863. Promoted to sergeant on 11/01/1863. Sent home to get a horse with Lt. Sinquefield under Special Order No. 27 from corps headquarters on 02/23/1864. Last record September/October 1864, sent to Georgia to get a horse with Capt. Bostick on 09/20/1864.

530. Harris, Morris: From Georgia. Born ca. 1838 in Prussia. Enlisted as a bugler in Company I on 02/27/1862 at Augusta, Georgia. Value of horse $225. Admitted to Winder Hospital, Richmond, Virginia, on 09/25/1862. Returned to duty on 10/05/1862. Admitted to Winder Hospital in Richmond, Virginia, on 02/09/1863. Captured near Williamsport, Maryland, on 07/10/1863. Admitted to U.S.A. General Hospital, Frederick, Maryland, on 08/14/1863 with wounds to his left thigh and penis. Sent to Fort McHenry, Maryland, on 08/28/1863 and transferred to Point Lookout, Maryland, on 09/15/1863. Paroled and exchanged at Camp Lee near Richmond, Virginia, on 02/28/1865. Last known rank was private. After the war, worked as a dry goods merchant in Richmond County, Georgia. Married Ella Myers on 10/12/1869 in Richmond County, Georgia. Died after 1870.

531. Harris, P.S.: Listed on a roster of Company D published in *The History of Dougherty County*, but not with the *Civil War Soldiers and Sailors System*. No service records in Cobb's Legion.

532. Harris, Richard D.: Resident of Georgia. Enlisted as a private in Company H on 04/03/1862 at Atlanta, Georgia. Sent home to get a horse with Lt. Sinquefield under Special Order No. 27 from corps headquarters on 02/23/1864. Admitted to Jackson Hospital in Richmond, Virginia, on 05/09/1864 with a wound from a minié ball in the left shoulder. Sent to Georgia for 60 days on wounded furlough on 05/28/1864. Sent to Georgia with Capt. Bostick to get a horse on 09/20/1864. Admitted to C.S.A. General Hospital No. 11 in Charlotte, North Carolina, on 11/25/1864 for neuralgia. Returned to duty on 11/28/1864. Paroled on 05/18/1865 at Thomasville, Georgia.

533. Harris, Tira [Ira, Tyra] L.: Farmer from Gwinnett County, Georgia. Born ca. 1835 in Georgia. Enlisted as a private in 24th Georgia Infantry on 08/27/1861 at Lawrenceville, Georgia. Transferred to Cobb's Legion Cavalry, Company B, on 04/19/1862. Promoted to corporal on 06/15/1862. Lost horse on 04/03/1863. Sent to Georgia to get a horse with Lt. James H. Johnson on 04/14/1863. Sent to recruiting/infirmary camp on 10/20/1863. Was surrendered by Gen. Joseph E. Johnston on 04/26/1865. Paroled at Greensboro, North Carolina, on 05/01/1865. He and his wife, Nancy Catherine, had at least four children. After the war, became a farmer in Gwinnett County, Georgia. Applied for a Confederate pension in Gwinnett County, Georgia. Died after 1910.

534. Harrison, William O.: 18-year-old student from Jackson County, Georgia. Born in 02/1845 in Georgia. Enlisted as a private in Company C on 01/18/1863 at Athens, Clarke County, Georgia. Detailed as an orderly for Col. Wright beginning 06/09/1863. Detailed as a courier on 10/11/1863. Sent home to get a horse with Lt. Sinquefield under Special Order No. 27 from corps headquarters on 02/23/1864. Was surrendered by Gen. Joseph E. Johnston on 04/26/1865. Paroled at Greensboro, North Carolina, on 05/01/1865. After the war, worked as a clerk in a dry goods store, a planter, and then a department store salesman in Jackson County, Georgia. Was married and the father of at least four children. Died after 1910.

535. Hartford, Frank: Enlisted as a private in Company K on 02/25/1863 at Camp Maynard, Georgia. Captured on 06/21/1863. Deserted to the enemy and took the Oath. Paroled at the Old Capitol Prison, Washington, D.C., on 06/25/1863. Sent to Philadelphia, Pennsylvania, on 07/16/1863.

536. Hartsfield, James M.: 18-year-old student from Cobb County, Georgia. Born on 01/10/1844 in Henry County, Georgia. Enlisted as a private in Company E on 04/09/1862 at Roswell, Georgia. Value of horse $165. Detailed as a scout in Prince William County, Virginia, in November/December 1863. On furlough beginning 02/19/1864. Was present on last record in September/October 1864. After the war, became a farmer in Cobb County, Georgia. Married (1) Martha Hadyn Jackson on 10/25/1866 in Henry County, Georgia, and they had at least seven children. Married (2) Inah Elizabeth Read on 07/21/1886 in Henry County, Georgia. Died on 10/12/1891.

537. Hatch, James A.: Resident of Georgia. Enlisted as a private in Company E on 03/25/1862 in Burke County, Georgia. Horse, owned by Needam Bullard, valued at $175. Transferred to Company F on 10/01/1862. Absent sick in March/April 1863. On furlough beginning 02/19/1864. Detailed as fisherman on 03/17/1864. Missing since 07/01/1864, changed to absent without leave. (Possibly the same person as James Hatcher, a carriage maker from Burke County, Georgia. Born in South Carolina. Listed in Company F in *Roster of the Confederate Soldiers of Burke County, Georgia: 1861–1865*.)

538. Hatfield, William H.: 26-year-old farmer resident from Richmond County, Georgia. Born on 03/09/1833 in Augusta, Georgia. Enlisted as a corporal in Company A on 08/17/1861 at Augusta, Georgia. Value of horse $200 and horse equipment $25. Last service record 12/1861. Hired a substitute and joined Capt. Allen's Co., State Troops, and served until the surrender. Married Elizabeth W. Chavous on 03/17/1858 and was the father of at least four children. Died on 11/27/1899 at Augusta, Georgia.

539. Hauser [Houser], William C.: From Jefferson County, Georgia. Born in Georgia ca. 1847. On a roster of Company F compiled by Glen Spurlock. No service records in Cobb's Legion. After the war, worked as an agent for the sale of patent medicine and then as a druggist in Jefferson County, Georgia. He and his wife, Laura, had seven children. Applied for a Confederate pension in Jefferson County, Georgia. Died in 1919. Buried in the Bethaney West Cemetery in Jefferson County, Georgia. His widow, L.C. Hauser, applied for a Confederate pension in Jefferson County, Georgia.

540. **Haynes, E.T. [G.]:** 27-year-old. Enlisted as a private in Company K on 02/07/1863 at Camp Maynard, Georgia. Returned to his regiment on 02/21/1863.

541. **Hays, A.D:** 25-year-old. Enlisted as a private in Company K on 02/08/1863 at Camp Maynard, Georgia. Returned to his regiment on 02/21/1863.

542. **Hays [Hayes], Dwight David:** Farm laborer from Dougherty County, Georgia. Born ca. 1842 in South Carolina or North Carolina. Enlisted as a private in Company D on 08/10/1861 at Albany, Georgia. Value of horse $200 and horse equipment $20. Captured near Malvern Hill, Virginia, and sent to Fort Monroe, Virginia, on 07/11/1862. Transferred to Fort Delaware 07/15/1862. Exchanged on steamer *Katskill* at Aiken's Landing, Virginia, on 08/05/1862. Described as having a fair complexion, dark hair, blue eyes, and being 5' 9" tall and 20 years of age. Detailed as a teamster beginning January/February 1863. Admitted to C.S.A. General Hospital in Danville, Virginia, with smallpox on 04/24/1863. Returned to duty on 05/08/1863. On furlough of indulgence beginning 02/20/1864. Sent to Georgia with Capt. Bostick to get a horse on 09/20/1864. Was surrendered by Gen. Joseph E. Johnston on 04/26/1865. Paroled at Greensboro, North Carolina, on 05/01/1865. After the war, worked as a farm laborer in Mitchell County, Georgia. He and his wife, Mary, had at least ten children. Died after 1910.

543. **Hays [Hayes], John B.:** Enlisted as a private in Company A on 08/17/1861 at Augusta, Georgia. Value of horse $160 and horse equipment $25. Lost horse on 01/01/1863. Captured at Westminster, Maryland, on 06/24/1863. Sent from Baltimore, Maryland, to Fort McHenry, Maryland, on 07/03/1863. Transferred to Fort Delaware on 07/08/1863. Paroled at Point Lookout, Maryland, and exchanged at Venus Point, Savannah River, on 11/15/1864. Last record was a receipt for clothing dated 11/18/1864.

544. **Head, George W.:** 22-year-old from Lumpkin County, Georgia. Born in 10/1839 in Georgia. Enlisted as a private in Company H on 03/03/1862 at Athens, Clarke County, Georgia. Without a horse from 11/1863 to 02/1864. Detailed as a teamster on 02/23/1864 due to not having a horse. Sent home to get a horse with Lt. Sinquefield under Special Order No. 27 from corps headquarters on 02/23/1864. Deserted to the enemy and dropped from muster roll in 04/1864. Took the Oath on 04/22/1864. Described as having a light complexion, brown hair, blue eyes, and being 5' 6" tall. After the war, became a farmer in Lumpkin County, Georgia. Married Lucie Ann Wehunt on 11/30/1868 in Lumpkin County, Georgia, and they had at least four children. Died in 1926.

545. **Head, James M.:** Farmer from Gwinnett County, Georgia. Born in Elbert County, Georgia, on 09/11/1825. Enlisted as a private in Company E on 04/09/1862 at Lawrenceville, Gwinnett County, Georgia. Value of horse $250 and horse bridle $7. Transferred to the 12th Georgia Artillery on 02/08/1863. Captured at Fisher's Hill, Virginia, on 09/22/1864. Imprisoned at Point Lookout, Maryland. Exchanged on 03/17/1865. Furloughed for 30 days on 03/21/1865. Discharged at Richmond in 03/1865 for being sick. After the war, became a farmer in Gwinnett County, Georgia. Married (1) Susan ca. 1854 and (2) Sarah Ann Moore on 04/07/1878 in Walton County, Georgia and (3) Louisa. Was the father of at least five children. Applied for a Confederate pension on 01/12/1888 in Gwinnett County due to deafness. Was a resident of Loganville at the time of application. Died on 05/09/1910 in Gwinnett County, Georgia. Buried in the Chestnut Grove Baptist Church Cemetery.

546. **Head, Joshua J.:** 21-year-old. Enlisted as a private in Company C on 08/15/1861 at Athens, Clarke County, Georgia. Discharged on 11/22/1861.

547. **Heffernan, William D.:** Student from Richmond County, Georgia. Born ca. 1845 in Ireland. Enlisted as a private in Company I on 03/25/1862 at Augusta, Georgia. Value of horse $200. Captured at Brandy Station, Virginia, on 08/01/1863. Sent to Old Capitol Prison in Washington, D.C., and then transferred to Point Lookout, Maryland, on 08/23/1863. Exchanged on 05/03/1864. Last record September/October 1864, sent to recruiting/infirmary camp at Stony Creek, Virginia, on 10/11/1864.

548. **Helton, William J.[T.]:** Farm laborer from Jackson County, Georgia. Born ca. 1840. Enlisted as a private in Company C on 08/01/1861 at Athens, Clarke County, Georgia. Died on 01/17/1862.

549. **Henderson, James:** Enlisted as a private in Company I on 01/16/1863 at Atlanta, Georgia. Appointed Captain and AQM of 1st SC Cavalry. Last

record in Cobb's Legion Cavalry dated March/April 1863. Married Harriett C. Smith in 1855. Died in 1895 in South Carolina, but was a resident of Georgia.

550. Henry [Hergrod], James E.[D.]: 20-year-old from Georgia. Enlisted as a private in Company B on 05/06/1862 at Atlanta, Georgia. Value of horse $175. Transferred to Company G in May/June 1862. Captured at Barbee's Cross Roads on 11/05/1862. Paroled on 11/09/1862 near Warrenton, Virginia. No horse beginning 02/21/1863. Sent to Georgia to get a horse on 02/21/1863. Was surrendered by Gen. Joseph E. Johnston on 04/26/1865. Paroled at Greensboro, North Carolina, on 05/01/1865.

551. Hewit [Hewitt, Huett], John J.: 27-year-old from Jackson County, Georgia. Born on 06/01/1834. Enlisted as a private in Company H on 04/24/1862 at Atlanta, Georgia. Listed as company blacksmith in January/March 1863. Sent home to get a horse with Lt. Sinquefield under Special Order No. 27 from corps headquarters on 02/23/1864. Last record September/October 1864, sent to Georgia to get a horse with Capt. Bostick on 09/20/1864. After the war, worked as a farm laborer in Jackson County, Georgia. Married (1) Drucilla Chandler on 12/22/1859 in Jackson County, Georgia and (2) Francis, and was the father of at least four children. Died on 06/24/1895. Buried in the Pentecost United Methodist Church Cemetery in Barrow County, Georgia.

552. Higdon [Higden], John T.[H.]: 28-year-old from Douillville, South Carolina. Enlisted on 02/01/1861 at Camp Pickens, South Carolina, in a South Carolina regiment. Transferred to Cobb's Legion Cavalry as a corporal in Company K on 02/15/1863 at Camp Maynard, Georgia. Reduced in rank to private on 02/28/1863. Admitted to C.S.A. General Hospital in Charlottesville, Virginia, on 06/10/1863 with a wound received at Brandy Station, Virginia. Returned to duty on 07/27/1863. Admitted to General Hospital No. 13 in Richmond, Virginia, on 11/02/1863 with lumbago. Admitted to Jackson Hospital in Richmond, Virginia, on 01/16/1864 with a wound in the right hip from a minié ball. Admitted to General Hospital No. 13 in Richmond, Virginia, on 01/24/1864 with inflammation of the nose and throat. Last hospital record states that he escaped on 01/04/1864.

553. Higgons [Higgins], Dan: 18-year-old from Savannah, Georgia. Enlisted as a private in Company K on 02/15/1863 at Camp Maynard, Georgia. Mortally wounded during battle at Brandy Station, Virginia, on 06/09/1863. Admitted to General Hospital No. 19 in Richmond, Virginia. Furloughed for 60 days on 06/14/1863. Died from the effects of the wound.

554. High, E.D.: Resident of Georgia. Enlisted as a private in Company D on 08/10/1861 at Albany, Georgia. Captured at Hanover Court House, Virginia, on 05/31/1864. Sent to White House, Virginia, on 06/11/1864. Transferred to Elmira Prison, New York, on 07/17/1864. Transferred to Point Lookout, Maryland, for exchange 10/11/1864. Last record, exchanged on 10/29/1864.

555. Hill, George B.[P.]: 20-year-old from Richmond County, Georgia. Born in Richmond County, Georgia, in 1842. Enlisted as a private in Company I on 03/25/1862 at Augusta, Georgia. Value of horse $225. Admitted to General Hospital No. 19 in Richmond, Virginia, on 12/02/1862. Given a 30 day furlough beginning 12/05/1862. Admitted to Jackson Hospital in Richmond, Virginia, with neuralgia on 10/17/1863. Furloughed for 30 days beginning 10/28/1863. Discharged and paid off on 12/22/1863.

556. Hill, James: 32-year-old from Georgia. Enlisted as a private in Company E on 03/22/1862 at Roswell, Georgia. Value of horse $185 and bridle $7. Admitted to Winder Hospital, Richmond, Virginia, on 09/25/1862. Returned to duty on 10/03/1862. Sent to Georgia to get a horse in March/April 1863. Sent home to get a horse with Lt. Sinquefield under Special Order No. 27 from corps headquarters on 02/23/1864. Last record September/October 1864, sent to Georgia to get a horse with Capt. Bostick on 09/20/1864.

557. Hill, James A.: Listed on a roster of Company D published in *The History of Dougherty County*, but not with the *Civil War Soldiers and Sailors System*. No service records in Cobb's Legion.

558. Hill, John P.[B.]: Farm laborer from Jackson County, Georgia. Born on 12/22/1834 in Jackson County, Georgia. Brother of Moses R. Hill. Enlisted as a private in Company C on 03/04/1862 at Athens, Clarke County, Georgia. Admitted to Howard's Grove Hospital in Richmond, Virginia, on 12/28/1862. Died on 01/06/1863 of smallpox.

559. Hill, Joseph N.[M.]: 17-year-old from Fulton County, Georgia. Enlisted as a private in Company B on 04/08/1862 at Atlanta, Georgia. Transferred to Company G in May/June 1862. Value of horse $180. Sent to recruiting/infirmary camp in January/February 1864. Captured at Stoney Creek, Virginia, on 12/01/1864 and sent to City Point, Virginia. Transferred to Point Lookout, Maryland. Released 06/27/1865. Described as having a light complexion, dark brown hair, grey eyes, and being 5'8" tall.

560. Hill, Moses R.: 35-year-old farmer from Jackson County, Georgia. Born on 10/08/1826 in Jackson County, Georgia. Brother of John P. Hill. Enlisted as a private in Company C on 03/04/1862 at Athens, Clarke County, Georgia. Died in hospital at Richmond, Virginia, on 12/22/1862 of diarrhea.

561. Hill, R.D.: 23-year-old. Enlisted as a private in Company K on 02/10/1863 at Camp Maynard, Georgia. Returned to his regiment on 02/21/1863.

562. Hill, Simeon William: Farm laborer from Jackson County, Georgia. Born ca. 06/02/1840 in Georgia. Enlisted as a private in Company C on 03/04/1862 at Athens, Clarke County, Georgia. Captured 06/26/1863 at Brookville, Maryland. Sent to Old Capitol Prison in Washington, D.C., on 06/29/1863. Transferred to Point Lookout, Maryland, on 08/08/1863. Exchanged in March 1864. Last record September/October 1864, absent without leave since 06/01/1864. After the war moved near Boaz, Alabama. Married Mary Jane Beddingfield and they had at least sixteen children. Died on 02/14/1898.

563. Hillens [Hillins, Hittins], Henry: Enlisted as a private in Company A on 08/17/1861 at Augusta, Georgia. Value of horse $125 and horse equipment $30. Detailed as a musician in January/February 1862. Killed on 06/28/1862 in a skirmish at Malvern Hill during the battle of Cold Harbor. His widow, Antoinette Hillens (the mother of his three children, the oldest of which was seven years old), received his back pay.

564. Hines, John R.: 23-year-old. Born in 10/1838 in Georgia. Enlisted as a private in Company F on 03/25/1862 at Atlanta, Georgia. Value of horse $200. Admitted to Winder Hospital in Richmond, Virginia, on 09/04/1862 with diarrhea. Returned to duty on 09/23/62. On sick furlough in January/February 1863. Admitted to a hospital in Lynchburg, Virginia, in March/April 1863. Discharged on 09/20/1863. After the war, became a farmer in Burke County, Georgia. He and his wife, Mary, had nine children. Died after 1900.

565. Hinton, John Jefferson [G.]: 22-year-old from Georgia. Born in Walton County, Georgia on 01/19/1840. Enlisted as a private in Company E on 04/09/1862 at Lawrenceville, Georgia. Value of horse $165 and horse equipment $8. Sent home to get a horse in March/April 1863. Sent home to get a horse with Lt. Sinquefield under Special Order No. 27 from corps headquarters on 02/23/1864. Was surrendered by Gen. Joseph E. Johnston on 04/26/1865. Paroled at Greensboro, North Carolina, on 05/01/1865. After the war, became a farmer in Gwinnett County, Georgia. Married Martha Long Farr ca. 1866 and they had twelve children. Applied for a Confederate pension in Gwinnett County, Georgia. Died in Gwinnett County, Georgia, on 04/04/1937.

566. Hitt, D.W.: Muster Roll Commission roster places him in Company A. No service records in Cobb's Legion.

567. Hodo, Joel: 25-year-old student from Warren County, Georgia. Born in 1839 in Warren County, Georgia. Enlisted as a private in Company L on 04/05/1864 at Decatur, Georgia. Assigned from Camp Randolph, Georgia. Absent without leave beginning 05/12/1864. Sent to Georgia with Capt. Bostick to get a horse on 09/20/1864.

568. Hogan, Dennis: 18-year-old gas fitter from Augusta, Georgia. Enlisted as a private in Company E on 03/28/1862 at Augusta, Georgia. Value of horse $175. Admitted to Winder Hospital, Richmond, Virginia, on 01/09/1863. Captured at Williamsport, Maryland, on 07/17/1863. Sent to Atheneum Prison in Wheeling, [West] Virginia. Transferred to Camp Chase, Ohio, on 07/30/1863, and then to Fort Delaware Prison on 03/04/1864. Paroled in 02/1865. Described as having a fresh complexion, blue eyes, light hair, and being 5'8" tall.

569. Hogrefe [Hogrife, Hogriefe, Hogrel], Fred: 23-year-old from Hanover, Germany. Resident of Georgia. Enlisted as a private in Company A on 11/07/1861 at Augusta, Georgia, as a substitute for William R. Murphy. Detailed as ambulance driver beginning 05/28/1862. On hospital muster roll on 02/28/1863 with a hernia. Note states he was not improving. Sent to infirmary/recruiting camp on 11/12/1863. Captured on 10/27/1864 at Hatcher's Run, Virginia, and sent to Point Lookout, Maryland. Exchanged at Aiken's Landing, Virginia, 03/28/1865. After the war, worked as a retail grocer in Augusta, Georgia. Was married and the father of at least one child.

570. Holcombe: Enlisted as a private in Company A on 12/02/1862 at Decatur, Georgia, as a substitute for W.H. Robertson. He deserted on the same day that he enlisted.

571. Holeman, W.B.: 48-year-old. Enlisted as a private in Company K on 02/07/1863 at Camp Maynard, Georgia. Absent sick beginning 04/22/1863. Died 05/12/1863.

572. Hood, Richard: Listed on a roster of Company C in *These Men She Gave*. No service records in Cobb's Legion.

573. **Hood, William C.:** Resident of Georgia. Enlisted as a private in Company H on 03/04/1862 at Athens, Clarke County, Georgia. Sent to infirmary/recruiting camp on 01/08/1864. Last record September/October 1864, sent to Georgia to get a horse with Capt. Bostick on 09/20/1864.

574. **Hope, Alexander:** Enlisted as a private in Company A on 01/02/1862 at Yorktown, Virginia. Died on 07/10/1862.

575. **Hopkins, Cary J.:** Enlisted as a private in Company D on 08/10/1861 at Albany, Georgia. Substitute for John C. Matthews. On furlough in January/February 1863. Deserted on 03/14/1863.

576. **Hopkins, John D.:** Resident of Georgia. Enlisted as a private in Company H on 03/14/1862 at Athens, Clarke County, Georgia. Sent to Georgia to get a horse on 11/11/1863. Absent without leave beginning 01/23/1864. Sent to Georgia with Capt. Bostick to get a horse on 09/20/1864. Was surrendered by Gen. Joseph E. Johnston on 04/26/1865. Paroled at Greensboro, North Carolina, on 05/01/1865.

577. **Hough, John:** 36-year-old native of Georgia. Enlisted as a private in Company F on 03/25/1862 at Burke County, Georgia. Value of horse $230. Sent to Georgia with Capt. Bostick to get a horse on 09/20/1864. Surrendered at Augusta, Georgia, on 05/30/1862.

578. **House, James S.[F.]:** Enlisted as a private in Company H on 03/05/1862 at Athens, Clarke County, Georgia. Appointed company farrier on 03/05/1862. Died on 07/21/1862 at Richmond, Virginia.

579. **Houser, William C.:** 17-year-old native of Georgia. Enlisted as a private in Company F on 03/25/1862 at Burke County, Georgia. Value of horse $140. Admitted to General Hospital No. 16 in Richmond, Virginia, on 03/04/1863. Admitted to Winder Hospital in Richmond, Virginia, on 11/03/1863 with typhoid fever. Returned to duty on 11/27/1863. Detailed as a courier for Gen. McLaws in January/February 1863. Detailed for provost duty at Hanover Junction beginning 02/23/1864. Was surrendered by Gen. Joseph E. Johnston on 04/26/1865. Paroled at Greensboro, North Carolina, on 05/01/1865.

580. **Houston, John Dougherty:** 19-year-old from Georgia. Born on 01/06/1842 in Dooly County, Georgia. Enlisted as a private in Company D on 08/10/1861 in Dougherty County, Georgia. Value of horse $150 and horse equipment $20. Sent to recruiting/infirmary camp on 10/20/1863. Listed as a corporal in November/December 1863. Promoted to sergeant. Sent to Georgia with Capt. Bostick to get a horse on 09/20/1864. Wounded in the right calf on 03/01/1865 near Chesterfield Court House, South Carolina. Admitted to General Hospital No. 3 in High Point, North Carolina in 04/1865. Was surrendered by Gen. Joseph E. Johnston on 04/26/1865. Paroled at Greensboro, North Carolina, on 05/01/1865. Was a patient in General Hospital No. 3 in High Point, North Carolina, at the time of the surrender. After the war, became a farmer in Worth County, Georgia. Married (1) Jane and (2) Martha and was the father of at least eight children. Applied for a Confederate pension in Worth County, Georgia. Died on 07/06/1926. Buried in the Smoak Bridge Cemetery in Crisp County, Georgia.

581. **Howard, Francis [Frank] Reeves:** 25-year-old from Georgia. Born on 04/28/1836 in Oglethorpe County, Georgia. Brother of George Henry, Joseph Robert, and Wiley Chandler Howard. Enlisted as a private in Company C on 03/03/1862 at Athens, Clarke County, Georgia. Detailed for commissary duty on 08/10/1862. Admitted to General Hospital No. 11 in Charlotte, North Carolina, on 02/03/1865 with a fracture of the femur. After the war, worked as a farm laborer in Oglethorpe County, Georgia. Married Ida Eugenia Herndon on 02/13/1888 and they had at least three children. Applied for a Confederate pension in Oglethorpe County, Georgia. Died on 01/02/1917 in Oglethorpe County, Georgia. Buried in the Howard Burial Ground in Oglethorpe County, Georgia.

582. **Howard, George Henry [W.]:** 17-year-old. Born on 01/18/1847 in Oglethorpe County, Georgia. Brother of Francis Reeves, Joseph Robert, and Wiley Chandler Howard. Enlisted as a private in Company C on 04/01/1864 at Chesterfield, Georgia. Admitted to a hospital on 08/14/1864. Sent to Georgia with Capt. Bostick to get a horse on 09/20/1864. Was surrendered by Gen. Joseph E. Johnston on 04/26/1865. Paroled at Greensboro, North Carolina, on 05/01/1865. After the war, became a farmer in Oglethorpe County, Georgia. Married Frances Susan Tiller on 12/21/1871 and they had seven children. Applied for a Confederate pension in Oglethorpe County, Georgia. Died on 08/13/1933 in Oglethorpe County, Georgia. Buried in the Howard Burial Ground in Oglethorpe County, Georgia.

583. **Howard, Joseph [Francis] Robert:** Brother of Francis Reeves, George Henry, and Wiley Chandler Howard. Enlisted as a private in Company C. Died on May 31, 1864, at Spotsylvania, Virginia.

584. **Howard, Wiley Chandler [E.]:** 22-year-old from Georgia. Born on 11/23/1838 in Oglethorpe

County, Georgia. Brother of George Henry, Francis Reeves, and Joseph Robert Howard. Attended the University of Georgia, and studied law. Enlisted as a private in Company C on 08/015/1861 at Athens, Clarke County, Georgia. Listed as a sergeant in November/December 1863. On furlough of indulgence beginning 01/26/1864. Sent home to get a horse with Lt. Sinquefield under Special Order No. 27 from corps headquarters on 02/23/1864. Wounded at Trevilian Station. Elected lieutenant on 08/01/1864. Was surrendered by Gen. Joseph E. Johnston on 04/26/1865. Paroled at Greensboro, North Carolina, on 05/01/1865. After the war, became a lawyer in Jefferson, Jackson County, and then Fulton County, Georgia. After that, worked as a bill collector in Fulton County, Georgia. Married Frances Elizabeth Randolph on 01/22/1867 in Fulton County, Georgia, and they had five children. Died on 04/29/1930. Buried in the Oconee Hill Cemetery in Clarke County, Georgia.

585. **Howell, E.W.:** Resident of Georgia. Enlisted as a private in Company D on 08/10/1861 at Albany, Georgia. Value of horse $225 and horse equipment $25, saddle furnished by the State of Georgia. Deserted on 03/27/1863. In Virginia penitentiary on 05/01/1863.

586. **Howell, H.L:** Resident of Camilla, Georgia. Enlisted as a private in Company D on 08/10/1861 at Albany, Georgia. Value of horse $225 and horse equipment $25, furnished by State of Georgia. Absent sick in January/February 1863. Absent with dismounted men in March/April 1863. Admitted to Henningson Hospital, Richmond, Virginia, on 08/19/1863. Furloughed for 30 days beginning 08/28/1863 due to tuberculosis. Admitted to hospital on 09/28/1863 with pulmonary disease. Admitted to Winder Hospital in Richmond, Virginia, on 10/22/1863. Sent to recruiting/infirmary camp on 01/15/1864. Admitted to Jackson Hospital in Richmond, Virginia, on 04/21/1864 with scurvy. Able to perform duty as nurse while convalescing beginning 05/07/1864. Returned to duty on 06/25/1864. Last record September/October 1864, sent to Georgia to get a horse with Capt. Bostick on 09/20/1864.

587. **Howell, J.D.:** Enlisted as a private in Company I. His only record states that he was transferred from Camp Chase, Ohio, to Fort Delaware Prison on 03/17/1864. There is no record of his taking the Oath or being paroled. He may have died at Fort Delaware.

588. **Howse [Howze], Elisha S.:** 16-year-old from Georgia. Enlisted as a private in Company C on 08/01/1861 at Athens, Clarke County, Georgia. Sent home to get a horse on 11/11/1862. Courier for telegraph office beginning 01/1862. Wounded on 05/23/1864 at Hanover Junction, Virginia. Died from gunshot wound in hospital in Richmond, Virginia, on 06/18/1864.

589. **Howse [Howze], Martin V.B.:** 19-year-old from Georgia. Enlisted as a private in Company C on 08/01/1861 at Athens, Clarke County, Georgia. Courier for Gen. Stuart beginning 12/10/1862. Courier for Gen. Stuart during May–August 1864. Was surrendered by Gen. Joseph E. Johnston on 04/26/1865. Paroled at Greensboro, North Carolina, on 05/01/1865.

590. **Howse [Howze], Thomas:** 32-year-old. Enlisted as a private in Company C on 08/01/1861 at Athens, Clarke County, Georgia. Elected lieutenant on 06/02/1862. Last record, pay voucher dated 05/01/1863.

591. **Hoy, John R.:** Enlisted as a private in Company D on 08/10/1861 at Albany, Georgia. Value of horse $125 and horse equipment $25, furnished by State of Georgia. Discharged by order of Gen. Magruder on 11/30/1861.

592. **Hubbard, J.C.:** Enlisted as a private in Company K on 05/02/1864 at Decatur, Georgia. Last record September/October 1864, sent to Georgia to get a horse with Capt. Bostick on 09/20/1864.

593. **Hudson, John H.:** 22-year-old planter from Burke County, Georgia. Born in Georgia. Enlisted as a private in Company F on 03/25/1862 at Burke County, Georgia. Value of horse $150. Died in November 1862.

594. **Hudson, Lewis B.:** 21-year-old native of Georgia. Enlisted as a private in Company B on 05/02/1862. Value of horse $175. Detailed to commissary department in March/April 1863. Detailed as a teamster beginning 01/28/1864. Lost horse on 07/12/1864. Was surrendered by Gen. Joseph E. Johnston on 04/26/1865. Paroled at Greensboro, North Carolina, on 05/01/1865.

595. **Huff, James C.:** 17-year-old. Born in 04/1845 in Georgia. Enlisted as a private in Company B on 03/05/1863 at Stone Mountain, Georgia. Sent to recruiting/infirmary camp on 08/20/1863. Sent home to get a horse with Lt. Sinquefield under Special Order No. 27 from corps headquarters on 02/23/1864. Horse valued at $1,100 killed in action at Spotsylvania Court House on 05/10/1864. Huff admitted to Jackson Hospital, Richmond, Virginia, on 05/28/1864 with acute diarrhea. Returned to duty on 06/12/1864. Sent to Georgia with Capt. Bostick to get a horse on 09/20/1864. Was

surrendered by Gen. Joseph E. Johnston on 04/26/1865. Paroled at Greensboro, North Carolina, on 05/01/1865. After the war became a grocer and then a harness maker in Fulton County, Georgia. He and his wife, Jennie, had at least three children. Died after 10/1919. His widow applied for a Confederate pension in Fulton County, Georgia.

596. **Huff, Jeremiah Clayton:** 31-year-old. Born on 03/04/1831 in Newton County, Georgia. Enlisted as a private in Company B on 04/22/1862 at Atlanta, Georgia. Value of horse $150. Sent to recruiting/infirmary camp on 12/10/1863. Sent home to get a horse with Lt. Sinquefield under Special Order No. 27 from corps headquarters on 03/13/1864. Furloughed to Georgia on 08/10/1864. Sent to Georgia with Capt. Bostick to get a horse on 09/20/1864. Was surrendered by Gen. Joseph E. Johnston on 04/26/1865. Paroled at Greensboro, North Carolina, on 05/01/1865. Married (1) Elizabeth M. I. America Norton (2) Matilda Conrad (3) Elizabeth Norten Wells. Was the father of at least three children. After the war, became a farmer in Caseys, Fulton County, Georgia. Died on 06/01/1907 at Atlanta, Georgia.

597. **Huff, John Floyd [N.]:** 43-year-old from Georgia. Born on 05/29/1820 in Warren County or Newton County, Georgia. Enlisted as a private in Company G on 09/22/1863 at Decatur, Georgia. Sent home to get a horse with Lt. Sinquefield under Special Order No. 27 from corps headquarters on 02/23/1864. Transferred to Company B on 07/25/1864. Last record September/October 1864, sent to Georgia to get a horse with Capt. Bostick on 09/20/1864. After the war, became a farmer in Fulton County, Georgia, and then a grocer at Atlanta, Fulton County, Georgia. Married Effie Pamela A. Cowsert ca. 1845 in Warren County, Georgia. Died on 12/28/1890.

598. **Huff, William T.:** Born ca. 1843 in Georgia. Enlisted as a private in Company B on 03/04/1862 at Atlanta, Georgia. Value of horse $175. Detailed to fish in the Rappahannock on 02/25/1864. Sent to Georgia with Capt. Bostick to get a horse on 09/20/1864. Was surrendered by Gen. Joseph E. Johnston on 04/26/1865. Paroled at Greensboro, North Carolina, on 05/01/1865. After the war, became a farmer and then a blacksmith in Fulton County, Georgia. His wife's name was Ellen.

599. **Hughes, George William:** Born on 07/26/1841 or 1843 in Burke County, Georgia. Enlisted as a private in Company F on 05/09/1862 at Burke County, Georgia. Horse, owned by Jesse P. Green, valued at $175. Admitted to C.S.A. General Hospital in Charlottesville, Virginia, on 12/01/1863 with scabies. Transferred to Lynchburg, Virginia, on 12/03/1863. Captured at Beverly's Ford, Virginia, on 06/09/1863 and sent to the Old Capitol Prison in Washington, D.C. Exchanged to the navy on 09/03/1863. Sent to Georgia with Capt. Bostick to get a horse on 09/20/1864. Was surrendered by Gen. Joseph E. Johnston on 04/26/1865. Paroled at Greensboro, North Carolina, on 05/01/1865. Married Martha Eugenia Clark on 02/26/1868 and they had at least two children. Died on 09/14/1872 in Richmond County, Georgia.

600. **Hughey, Joseph B.:** Resident of Georgia. Enlisted in the 26th Georgia Infantry Company I as a private on 05/10/1862 at Savannah, Georgia. Transferred to Cobb's Legion Cavalry, Company C, on 02/29/1864. Last record September/October 1864, sent to Georgia to get a horse with Capt. Bostick on 09/20/1864.

601. **Hunt, Isaac C.:** Resident of Georgia. Enlisted as a private in Company C on 01/18/1863 at Athens, Clarke County, Georgia. On detail to Port Royal, Virginia, as a fisherman beginning 03/01/1864. Was surrendered by Gen. Joseph E. Johnston on 04/26/1865. Paroled at Greensboro, North Carolina, on 05/01/1865.

602. **Hunter, John M.:** 31-year-old from Georgia. Enlisted as a private in Company E on 04/09/1862 at Lawrenceville, Georgia. Value of horse $150 and bridle $8. Lost his horse on 03/25/1863. Sent to infirmary/recruiting camp on 10/06/1863. Sent home to get a horse with Lt. Sinquefield under Special Order No. 27 from corps headquarters on 02/23/1864. Admitted to Jackson Hospital in Richmond, Virginia, on 06/18/1864. Transferred to Winder Hospital, Richmond, Virginia, on 06/28/1864. Last record September/October 1864, sent to Georgia to get a horse with Capt. Bostick on 09/20/1864.

603. **Hunton [Hunter], James M. [H.]:** 40-year-old dentist. Born in Clarke County, Georgia. Enlisted as a private in Company B on 08/14/1861 at Atlanta, Georgia. Value of horse $170 and horse equipment $3.75, saddle furnished by State of Georgia. Detailed as a musician in November/December 1861. Given a medical discharge and paid off on May 6, 1862. Described as having a florid complexion, dark hair, gray eyes, and being 6 feet tall.

604. **Huntsinger, Robert:** 21-year-old from Georgia. Born in North Carolina. Enlisted as a private in Company B on 05/01/1862 at Atlanta, Georgia. Value of horse $150. Admitted to C.S.A. General Hospital in Charlottesville, Virginia, with a gunshot wound on 08/02/1863. Furloughed for 30 days to North Carolina on 08/25/1863. Sent to recruiting/infirmary camp in November 1863. Ad-

mitted to Jackson Hospital, Richmond, Virginia, on 08/15/1864 with acute diarrhea. Returned to duty on 08/29/1864. Sent to Georgia with Capt. Bostick to get a horse on 09/20/1864. Was surrendered by Gen. Joseph E. Johnston on 04/26/1865. Paroled at Greensboro, North Carolina, on 05/01/1865. After the war, became a farmer in Lumpkin County, Georgia. Married Elizabeth England on 12/06/1868 in Lumpkin County, Georgia.

605. Huser, W.C.: Listed in Company F in *Roster of the Confederate Soldiers of Burke County, Georgia: 1861–1865*. No service records in Cobb's Legion.

606. Inman, Jeremiah Shadrach: 34-year-old planter from Burke County, Georgia. Born on 07/26/1828 in Burke County, Georgia. Enlisted as a private in Company F on 05/09/1862 at Burke County, Georgia. Value of horse $275. Provided Newton J. Moxley as a substitute. After the war, became a farmer in Burke County, Georgia. Married Morning W. Frances on 01/2/1851 in Jefferson County, Georgia, and they had at least four children. Died on 10/22/1889. Buried at Bark Camp Church, Burke County, Georgia.

607. Irby, Daniel J.: Carpenter from Fulton County, Georgia. Born ca. 1835 in Georgia. Enlisted as a private in Company B on 08/14/1861 at Atlanta, Georgia. Value of horse $200 and horse equipment $6.75. Lost horse and sent on to Georgia to get a horse with Lt. James H. Johnson on 04/14/1863. Detailed as courier to Gen. Young beginning 10/01/1863. Admitted to Jackson Hospital in Richmond, Virginia, on 01/21/1864 with pleurisy. Returned to duty on 01/25/1864. Sent to infirmary/recruiting camp on 03/09/1864. Lost horse on 06/11/1864. Sent to recruiting/infirmary camp in Lynchburg, Virginia, on 08/28/1864. Last record September/October 1864, sent to Georgia to get a horse with Capt. Bostick on 09/20/1864. After the war, worked as a carpenter in Atlanta, Fulton County, Georgia. He and his wife, J.E.V., had at least four children.

608. Irvine: Enlisted as a private in Company A as a substitute for Joseph Cutter on 08/20/1862 at Malvern Hill, near Richmond, Virginia. Left camp the same day without permission and was not seen again. Listed as a deserter.

609. Isdal, John F. [T.]: 22-year-old farm laborer from Columbia County, Georgia. Enlisted as a private in Company A on 08/17/1861 at Augusta, Georgia. Value of horse $165 and horse equipment $25. Courier for Col. Montague in 01/1862. No horse 01/01/1863. Died 03/16/1863 of cerebritis (inflammation of the brain) at General Receiving Hospital (also known as Charity Hospital), Gordonsville, Virginia. His sister, Martha, collected his back pay, as he was not survived by his father, a wife, or children.

610. Ivey [Ivy], Michael J.: Born ca. 1827 in South Carolina. Enlisted as a private Company B on 08/14/1861 at Atlanta, Georgia. Value of horse $250 and horse equipment $5.50, saddle furnished by State of Georgia. Detailed as a teamster in 01/1862. Furloughed to Georgia for 25 days beginning 02/07/1862. Captured at Georgetown, Virginia, and sent to Fort McHenry, Maryland, on 10/20/1862. Sent to Fort Monroe, Virginia, for exchange on 10/27/1862. Lost horse and sent to Georgia to get a horse with Lt. James H. Johnson on 04/14/1863. Lost horse and captured at Plain View, Gloucester County, Virginia, on 02/03/1864 and sent to Fort Norfolk, Virginia. Transferred to Point Lookout, Maryland. Last record, exchanged at Aiken's Landing, Virginia, on 02/24/1865. Married (1) Ida about 1850. Married (2) Sally J. Turner on 02/26/1861 in Fulton County, Georgia. Possibly married (3) Ida. After the war, became a lawyer in Fulton County, Georgia.

611. Ivey, Richard T.: Enlisted as a private in Company C on 04/01/1864 at Chesterfield, Virginia. Last record, September/October 1864, sent to Georgia to get a horse with Capt. Bostick on 09/20/1864.

612. Jack, Doctor F.: Born ca. 1842 in Augusta, Richmond County, Georgia. Brother of George Washington, James Russell, and William F. Jack. Enlisted as a private in Company B on 04/19/1862 at Atlanta, Georgia. Transferred to Company G in May/June 1862. Promoted to corporal on 11/01/1863. Detailed to commissary department beginning 04/1864. Was surrendered by Gen. Joseph E. Johnston on 04/26/1865. Paroled at Greensboro, North Carolina, on 05/01/1865.

613. Jack, George Washington: Machinist from Fulton County, Georgia. Born ca. 1840 in Georgia. Brother of Doctor F., James Russell, and William F. Jack. Enlisted as a private in Company B on 08/14/1861 at Atlanta, Georgia. Value of horse $300 and horse equipment $33.50. Last record, on furlough for 25 days beginning 01/20/1862. Furnished Wiley P. Mangum as a substitute. After the war, became a confection manufacturer in Fulton County, Georgia. Married Josephine A. Wall on 06/20/1858 in Fulton County, Georgia.

614. Jack, James Russell: Clerk from Fulton County, Georgia. Born ca. 1836 in Georgia. Brother of Doctor F. Jack, George Washington Jack, and William F. Jack. Enlisted as a private Company B on 08/14/1861 at Atlanta, Georgia. Value of horse $175 and horse equipment $11.25, saddle furnished by State of Georgia. Promoted to corporal in March/April 1862. Transferred to Company G on 05/30/1862. Sent to Georgia to get a horse with Lt. James H. Johnson on 04/14/1863. Sent home to get a horse on 11/10/1863. Sent home to get a horse with Lt. Sinquefield under Special Order No. 27 from corps headquarters on 02/23/1864. Last record September/October 1864, sent to Georgia to get a horse with Capt. Bostick on 09/20/1864. Killed at Monroe's Crossroads, North Carolina, on 03/09/1865. Howard said, "I remember Jim Jack, one of Atlanta's truest, best men, fell dead and many horses in the charge leaped over his dead body with upturned face."*

615. Jack, William F.: Machinist from Fulton County, Georgia. Born ca. 1838 in Georgia. Brother of Doctor F. Jack, George Washington Jack, and James Russell Jack. Enlisted as a private in Company B on 04/28/1862 at Atlanta, Georgia. Value of horse $140. Transferred to Company G in May/June 1862. Sent to Georgia to get a horse with Lt. James H. Johnson on 04/14/1863. Sent home to get a horse on 08/12/1863. On furlough of indulgence beginning 03/06/1864. Last record September/October 1864, sent to Georgia to get a horse with Capt. Bostick on 09/20/1864. Was married.

616. Jackson, Arthur M.: Resident of Georgia. Enlisted in 3rd Georgia Infantry, Company K, as a corporal on 08/26/1861 at Athens, Clarke County, Georgia. Transferred into Cobb's Legion Cavalry, Company H, as a private on 12/17/1862. Listed in April/September 1864 as corporal. Sent to hospital on 07/06/1864. Last record April/September 1864, in Georgia on sick furlough since 07/06/1864.

617. Jackson, Green B.: 17-year-old student from Clarke County, Georgia. Born on 10/29/1843 in Clarke County, Georgia. Brother of Henry E. Jackson. Enlisted as a private in Company C on 08/01/1861 at Athens, Clarke County, Georgia. Detailed as musician beginning 12/21/1861. Died on March 23, 1862 at Suffolk, Virginia.

618. Jackson, Henry E.: Student from Clarke County, Georgia. Brother of Green B. Jackson. Enlisted as a private in Company C 08/01/1861 at Athens, Clarke County, Georgia. Became a bugler in November/December 1863. On furlough of indulgence beginning 02/18/1864. Admitted to hospital in Raleigh, North Carolina, with a wound on 07/01/1864. Sent to Georgia with Capt. Bostick to get a horse on 09/20/1864. Was surrendered by Gen. Joseph E. Johnston on 04/26/1865. Paroled at Greensboro, North Carolina, on 05/01/1865. After the war, became a farmer in Oconee County, Georgia, and was married.

619. Jackson, John F.: Resident of Georgia. Enlisted as a private in Company A on 08/17/1861 at Augusta, Georgia. Value of horse $225 and horse equipment $30. Admitted to General Hospital No. 9 on 11/24/1862. Returned to duty on 11/26/1862. No horse in November/December 1863. Detailed in Quartermaster's Department in Augusta, Georgia, beginning December 1863. Last record September/October 1864.

620. Jackson, Sherrod [Sherwood] W.: Born in Georgia ca. 1845. Enlisted as a private in Company C on 01/27/1864 at Athens, Clarke County, Georgia. Sent to Georgia with Capt. Bostick to get a horse on 09/20/1864. Was surrendered by Gen. Joseph E. Johnston on 04/26/1865. Paroled at Greensboro, North Carolina, on 05/01/1865. After the war, became a farmer in District 255, Jackson County, and then in Clarke County, Georgia. He and his wife, Nancy, had nine children. Applied for a Confederate pension in Jackson County, Georgia. Died after 1900.

621. Jackson, Stephen Everett [D.]F.: 27-year-old physician from Clarke County, Georgia. Born in Georgia on 05/12/1834. Enlisted as a private in Company H on 03/06/1862 at Athens, Clarke County, Georgia. Sent home to get a horse with Lt. Sinquefield under Special Order No. 27 from corps headquarters on 02/23/1864. Sent to Georgia with Capt. Bostick to get a horse on 09/20/1864. Was surrendered by Gen. Joseph E. Johnston on 04/26/1865. Paroled at Greensboro, North Carolina, on 05/01/1865. After the war, became a doctor in Clarke County, Georgia. Married Christina Barnett Elder on 04/28/1859. Died on 09/19/1881. His widow applied for a Confederate pension in Fulton County, Georgia.

622. Jackson, Thomas E.: Resident of Georgia. Enlisted as a private in Company H on 03/06/1862 at Athens, Clarke County, Georgia. Appointed company bugler on 03/06/1862. Sent to Georgia with Capt. Bostick to get a horse on 09/20/1864. Was surrendered by Gen. Joseph E. Johnston on 04/26/1865. Paroled at Greensboro, North Carolina, on 05/01/1865. Applied for a Confederate pension in Oconee County, Georgia.

623. Jackson, William H.: Enlisted as a private in Company A on 08/17/1861 at Augusta,

---

*Howard, page 13.

Georgia. Value of horse $175 and horse equipment $25. Lost horse on 01/01/1863. Horse killed in action at Upperville, Virginia, on 06/21/1863. Jackson sent home to get a horse with Lt. Sinquefield under Special Order No. 27 from corps headquarters on 02/23/1864. Last record September/October 1864, sent to Georgia to get a horse with Capt. Bostick on 09/20/1864. Applied for a Confederate pension in Tennessee in 1914.

624. Jackson, William W.: Farm laborer from Jackson County, Georgia. Born ca. 1839 in Georgia. Enlisted as a private in Company C on 12/21/1863 at Athens, Clarke County, Georgia. Sent home to get a horse with Lt. Sinquefield under Special Order No. 27 from corps headquarters on 02/23/1864. Listed as a sergeant on last record in September/October 1864, when he was sent to Georgia to get a horse with Capt. Bostick on 09/20/1864. His wife's name was Eliza.

625. Jacobs, John J.: Baker from Richmond County, Georgia. Born in Bavaria ca. 1840. Enlisted in 1st Georgia Infantry, Company I, as a private on 03/18/1861. Mustered out at Augusta, Georgia, on 03/18/1862. Enlisted as a private in Cobb's Legion Cavalry, Company I, on 03/31/1862. Value of horse $240. Sent to recruiting/infirmary camp on 10/20/1863. Present on last record, September/October 1864. After the war, became the owner of a bakery in Richmond County, Georgia. Was married and the father of at least two children. Applied for a Confederate pension in Richmond County, Georgia. Died after 1910.

626. James, T.J.: 25-year-old from Alabama. Enlisted as a sergeant in Company K on 01/16/1863 at Camp Maynard, Georgia. Sent home to get a horse on 08/23/1863. Absent without leave beginning 10/22/1863 until last record, March/April 1864. Rank reduced to private.

627. Jaudon, J.T.: Enlisted as a private in Company D on 08/10/1861 at Albany, Georgia. Value of horse $225 and horse equipment $25, furnished by government. Detailed as an orderly to Col. Julakowski beginning November/December 1861. Last record, absent with dismounted men in March/April 1863.

628. Jay, William H.B.: Resident of Georgia. Enlisted as a private in Company H on 03/03/1862 at Athens, Clarke County, Georgia. Captured at Brookville, Maryland, on 06/28/1863 and sent to the Old Capitol Prison in Washington, D.C. Transferred to Point Lookout, Maryland, on 08/08/1863. Exchanged on 03/03/1864. Detailed in Quartermaster Department in September/October 1864. Was surrendered by Gen. Joseph E. Johnston on 04/26/1865. Paroled at Greensboro, North Carolina, on 05/01/1865.

629. Jefferson, Thomas James: Enlisted as a lieutenant in Company A on 08/17/1861 at Augusta, Georgia. It was not stated if he was present on his only record, dated 08/28/1861. (He may be the same person as J. Jefferson Thomas.)

630. Jenkins, John: Resident of Georgia. Enlisted as a private in Company A on 08/17/1861 at Augusta, Georgia. Value of horse $160 and horse equipment $20. Appointed corporal on 05/01/1862. No horse on 01/01/1863. Detailed on extra duty during March/April 1863. Listed as sergeant in March/April 1863. Horse killed in action at Martinsville, Virginia, on 07/23/1863. Jenkins sent to Georgia to get a horse in November/December 1863. On furlough beginning 04/01/1864. On scouting detail and listed as a private, 05/01/1864–09/01/1864. Was present on last record, September/October 1864.

631. Jenkins, Thomas S.: Resident of Virginia. Enlisted as a private in Company E on 03/15/1863 at Dogtown, Virginia. Lost horse and captured at Hunterstown, Pennsylvania, on 07/02/1863. Sent to Harrisburg, Pennsylvania, on 07/09/1863. Transferred to Fort Delaware Prison. Deserted and took the Oath on 08/30/1863. Joined the 3rd Maryland Cavalry.

632. Jenkins, William J.: 25-year-old native of Georgia. Enlisted as a private in Company B on 04/27/1862 at Atlanta, Georgia. Value of horse $140. Admitted to C.S.A. General Hospital in Danville, Virginia, on 05/16/1862 with measles. Returned to duty on 05/28/1862. Admitted to C.S.A. General Hospital in Charlottesville, Virginia, on 02/19/1863. Returned to duty on 03/09/1863. On sick furlough to Georgia beginning 03/17/1863. Detailed as a shoemaker beginning 11/26/1863. Was surrendered by Gen. Joseph E. Johnston on 04/26/1865. Paroled at Greensboro, North Carolina, on 05/01/1865.

633. Jennings, W.P.: Listed on a roster of Company D published in *The History of Dougherty County*, but not with the *Civil War Soldiers and Sailors System*. No service records in Cobb's Legion.

634. Jester, William: 18-year old from Georgia. Enlisted as a corporal in Company K on 01/16/1863 at Camp Maynard, Georgia. Sent home to get a horse on 08/23/1863. Absent without leave beginning 10/23/1863. Still absent without leave on last record, 04/01/1864.

635. Johnson, A.E.: Resident of Georgia. Enlisted as a private in Company E on 04/24/1862 at Decatur, Georgia. No horse in May/September

1864. Last record September/October 1864, sent to Georgia to get a horse with Capt. Bostick on 09/20/1864. After the war, lived in Cobb County, Georgia. Married Fannie S. Applied for a Confederate pension in Cobb County, Georgia. His widow applied for a Confederate pension in Georgia.

636. Johnson, Archibald C.: 25-year-old from Georgia. Born in 02/1837 in Georgia. Enlisted as a private in Company B on 03/04/1862 at Atlanta, Georgia. Value of horse $200 and horse equipment $7. Transferred to Company G in May/June 1862. Sent home to get a horse with Lt. James H. Johnson on 04/14/1863. Sent home to get a horse with Lt. Sinquefield under Special Order No. 27 from corps headquarters on 02/23/1864. Sent to Georgia with Capt. Bostick to get a horse on 09/20/1864. Was surrendered by Gen. Joseph E. Johnston on 04/26/1865. Paroled at Greensboro, North Carolina, on 05/01/1865. After the war, worked as a bookkeeper in Fulton County, Georgia. Married Nannie (or Nancy) Wilson on 02/22/1858 in Fulton County, Georgia. Applied for a Confederate pension in Fulton County, Georgia. Died ca. 1923.

637. Johnson, E.B.: Enlisted as a private in Company D on 08/10/1861 at Albany, Georgia. Value of horse $150 and horse equipment $15, bridle furnished by government. Was present on last record, November/December 1861.

638. Johnson, George G.: Enlisted in 3rd Georgia Infantry, Company C, as a private on 04/24/1861. Transferred to Cobb's Legion Cavalry, Company F, on 10/01/1862. Admitted to C.S.A. General Hospital in Charlottesville, Virginia, on 12/01/1863. Transferred to Lynchburg, Virginia, hospital on 12/03/1863. Appointed sergeant on 06/01/1864. Last record September/October 1864, sent to Georgia with Capt. Bostick to get a horse on 09/19/1864.

639. Johnson, I.J.: Enlisted as a private in Company D on 08/10/1861 at Albany, Georgia. Value of horse $175 and horse equipment $25. Lost horse on 04/14/1863. Sent home to get a horse in March/April 1863. Absent without leave beginning 06/13/1863. Last record 04/1864, still absent without leave.

640. Johnson, J.D.: Enlisted as a corporal in Company B. In a Williamsburg hospital on only record, dated 01/15/1862.

641. Johnson, James C.: Not listed in Cobb's Legion with the *Civil War Soldiers and Sailors System*. On a roster of Company D compiled by Glen Spurlock. No service records in Cobb's Legion. His widow, Sarah A. Johnson, applied for a pension in Carroll County, Georgia.

642. Johnson, James H.: Enlisted as a private in Company B on 04/28/1862 at Atlanta, Georgia. Value of horse $225. Transferred to Company G as a sergeant in May/June 1862. Promoted to lieutenant on 11/21/1862. Admitted to Chimborazo Hospital, Richmond, Virginia, on 10/24/1862 with debility. Returned to duty on same day. In command of horse detail to Georgia on 04/14/1863. Wounded on 05/23/1864 at Chancellorsville, Virginia. Admitted to General Hospital No. 4, Richmond, Virginia, on 05/24/1864. Died on 05/25/1864.

643. Johnson, James M.: 18-year-old native of Georgia. Enlisted as a private in Company F on 05/09/1862 at Greensboro, Burke County, Georgia. Value of horse $231. Furloughed for 30 days from Jackson Hospital, Richmond, Virginia. Sent home to get a horse with Lt. Sinquefield under Special Order No. 27 from corps headquarters on 02/23/1864. Was present on last record, September/October 1864. After the war, lived in Jefferson County, Georgia. Applied for a Confederate pension in Jefferson County, Georgia.

644. Johnson, Jesse: Enlisted as a private in Company A on 01/06/1864 at Decatur, Georgia. Admitted to hospital in Augusta, Georgia, on 05/01/1864. Returned to duty on 09/01/1864. Absent without leave on last record September/October 1864.

645. Johnson, John A.: 28-year-old from Georgia. Enlisted as a private in Company E on 03/15/1862 at Roswell, Georgia. Value of horse $185 and horse equipment $6. Sent home to get a horse on 11/12/1863. Sent to Georgia to get a horse with Lt. Sinquefield under Special Order No. 27 from corps headquarters on 02/23/1864. Captured at Spotsylvania Court House on 05/09/1864. Sent to Belle Plain, Virginia, on 05/17/1864. Transferred to Point Lookout, Maryland, and then to Elmira Prison, New York, on 08/08/1864. Sent to the James River in Virginia for exchange on 02/20/1865. Was surrendered by Gen. Joseph E. Johnston on 04/26/1865. Paroled at Greensboro, North Carolina, on 05/01/1865. After the war, lived in Cobb County, Georgia. His widow, Jennie, applied for a Confederate pension in Cobb County, Georgia.

646. Johnson, Leonard E.[J.]: Resident of Georgia. Enlisted as a private in Company D on 08/10/1861 at Albany, Georgia. Value of horse $225 and horse equipment $25. Detailed in commissary department in November/December 1861. Detailed to repair carbines and pistols and to make cartridges in Richmond, Virginia, on 02/11/1862. Detailed to be in charge of baggage and stores for Cobb's Legion on 03/05/1862. Furloughed to Georgia for 24 days from beginning 02/11/1864. Detailed to commissary department beginning 08/01/1864. Was surrendered by Gen. Joseph E. Johnston on 04/26/1865. Paroled at Greensboro, North Carolina, on 05/01/1865.

647. **Johnson, Leonidas D.:** 28-year-old native of Georgia. Enlisted as a private in Company F. Transferred to Company L on 03/25/1862 at Burke County, Georgia. Value of horse $200 and horse equipment $35. Detailed as an assistant from 04/01/1862 to 06/01/1862. Sent home to get a horse with Lt. Sinquefield under Special Order No. 27 from corps headquarters on 02/23/1864. Admitted to C.S.A. General Hospital in Danville, Virginia, with a wound on 05/12/1864. Transferred from hospital on 06/21/1864. On furlough for 30 days beginning 09/01/1864. Sent to Georgia with Capt. Bostick to get a horse on 09/20/1864. Elected lieutenant on 12/28/1864. Was surrendered by Gen. Joseph E. Johnston on 04/26/1865. Paroled at Greensboro, North Carolina, on 05/01/1865.

648. **Johnson, Lorenzo D:** 35-year-old. Enlisted as a lieutenant in Company E on 03/22/1862 at Roswell, Georgia. Value of horse $175. Last record dated 04/22/1862.

649. **Johnson, Samuel Jack:** 21-year-old from Georgia. Born on 01/07/1840 in Madison County, Georgia. Enlisted as a private in Company C on 08/01/1861 at Athens, Clarke County, Georgia. Sent to Georgia with Capt. Bostick to get a horse on 09/20/1864. Was surrendered by Gen. Joseph E. Johnston on 04/26/1865. Paroled at Greensboro, North Carolina, on 05/01/1865. Married to Elmyra Jane Faulkner on 10/13/1868 in Madison County, Georgia. Died on 08/17/1869. Buried at Johnson/Old Hull, Madison County, Georgia.

650. **Johnson, T.J.:** 45-year-old. Enlisted as a private in Company K on 01/20/1863 at Camp Maynard, Georgia. Deserted on 02/20/1863.

651. **Johnson, Thomas D.:** Enlisted as a private in Company B on 08/14/1861 at Atlanta, Georgia. Value of horse $160 and horse equipment $9.50, saddle furnished by State of Georgia. Admitted to a hospital in Williamsburg, Virginia, in November/December 1861. Courier for Gen. Raines in 12/1861. Transferred to the 7th Georgia Infantry on 01/15/1863 as a drillmaster.

652. **Johnson, Wesley:** Listed on a roster of Company C in *These Men She Gave*. No service records in Cobb's Legion.

653. **Johnson, William Baldwin:** 24-year-old. Born on 08/12/1837 in Georgia. Enlisted as a private in Company F on 05/09/1862 at Burke County, Georgia. Value of horse $175. Horse killed in action on 09/13/1863 at Culpeper County, Virginia. Baldwin sent to Georgia with Capt. Bostick to get a horse on 09/20/1864. Was surrendered by Gen. Joseph E. Johnston on 04/26/1865. Paroled at Greensboro, North Carolina, on 05/01/1865. After the war, became a farmer in Burke County, Georgia. He and his wife, Julia, had at least two children. Died on 01/08/1912. Buried in Burke County, Georgia.

654. **Johnson, William H.:** Native of Georgia. Enlisted as a private in Company F on 05/09/1862 at Burke County, Georgia. Transferred from 44th Georgia Infantry. Value of horse $275. Sent home to get a horse with Lt. Sinquefield under Special Order No. 27 from corps headquarters on 02/23/1864. Furloughed for 30 days beginning 09/01/1864. Sent to Georgia with Capt. Bostick to get a horse on 09/20/1864. Admitted to hospital in Salisbury, North Carolina, on 03/19/1865. Returned to duty on 03/22/1865. The hospital record says that he was a prisoner of war at that time. Was surrendered by Gen. Joseph E. Johnston on 04/26/1865. Paroled at Greensboro, North Carolina, on 05/01/1865.

655. **Johnston, M.:** Enlisted as a private in Company K on 02/23/1863 at Camp Maynard, Georgia. Returned to his regiment in March/April 1863.

656. **Joiner [Joyner], John E.:** Enlisted as a private in Company D on 08/10/1861 at Albany, Georgia. Value of horse $150 and horse equipment $25, furnished by State of Georgia. Detailed as an ambulance driver. Given a discharge for disability on 12/02/1861. Paroled at Albany, Georgia, on 05/17/1865.

657. **Jones, C.A.:** Enlisted as a private in Company B on 10/01/1861 at Yorktown, Virginia. His single service record shows he was surrendered by Gen. Joseph E. Johnston on 04/26/1865. Paroled at Greensboro, North Carolina, on 05/01/1865.

658. **Jones, H.:** Enlisted on 08/10/1861 at Albany, Georgia. Transferred as a private to Company D on 07/15/1862. Deserted in 09/1862.

659. **Jones, Henry Francis [W. Frank] [L.]:** Born ca. 1841. Enlisted as a private in Company C on 08/01/1861 at Athens, Clarke County, Georgia. Sent to Georgia to recruit for company on 02/19/1862. Appointed sergeant on 06/15/1862. Promoted to lieutenant and adjutant on 04/15/1864. Killed at Trevilian Station on 06/12/1864. Howard described him as being "among the purest, gentlest, knightliest gentlemen whose wealth and blood were spent and poured out, a willing libation on the altar

of Southern liberty."* Buried in the Jones Family Cemetery in Thomas County, Georgia.

660. Jones, James W.: Enlisted as a private in Company B on 10/01/1861 at Yorktown, Virginia. Promoted to lieutenant on 01/07/1863. On furlough to Georgia for 24 days beginning 01/14/1864. Sent to Lynchburg, Virginia, in charge of disabled horses on 08/21/1864. Was surrendered by Gen. Joseph E. Johnston on 04/26/1865. Paroled at Greensboro, North Carolina, on 05/01/1865.

661. Jones, Jeremiah [Jerry] Berry: 18-year-old farmer from Lowndes County, Georgia. Born on 08/23/1844. Enlisted as a private in Company L on 12/15/1862 at Burke County, Georgia. Horse valued at $450 captured in battle at Brandy Station, Virginia, on 06/09/1863. Jones admitted to C.S.A. General Hospital in Charlottesville, Virginia, with a wound on 06/10/1863. Furloughed beginning 07/10/1863. Admitted to Jackson Hospital in Richmond, Virginia, on 05/12/1864. Home on wounded furlough on last record, summer 1864. Married Susan Elizabeth Young on 03/04/1868 and they had at least four children. Died in 1919 or 02/28/1924. Buried at the Sunset Hill Cemetery in Lowndes County, Georgia. His widow, Susan Young Jones, applied for a Confederate pension in Richmond County, Georgia.

662. Jones, Jerry: Listed as a private in Company F in *Roster of the Confederate Soldiers of Burke County, Georgia: 1861–1865*. No service records in Cobb's Legion. May be the same person as Jeremiah (Jerry) Berry Jones.

663. Jones, John T.: 22-year-old from Georgia. Enlisted as a private in Company I on 03/24/1862 at Augusta, Georgia. Value of horse $140. Horse killed in action near Mechanicsville, Virginia, on the Chickahominy River on 06/20/1862. Jones sent home to get a horse with Lt. Sinquefield under Special Order No. 27 from corps headquarters on 02/23/1864. Sent to Georgia with Capt. Bostick to get a horse on 09/20/1864. Was surrendered by Gen. Joseph E. Johnston on 04/26/1865. Paroled at Greensboro, North Carolina, on 05/01/1865. Applied for a Confederate pension in Richmond County, Georgia.

664. Jones, Malcom Daniel: Born ca. 1828 in Georgia. Enlisted as a captain in Company F on 03/25/1862 at Burke County, Georgia. Value of horses $250 and $230 and horse equipment $70. Promoted to major on 10/09/1863. On detached service for division court-martial in April–October 1864. In Georgia with Gen. Young on 11/28/ 1864. Last record dated 01/19/1865. Died on 09/29/1869. Buried at Inman Cemetery, Burke County, Georgia.

665. Jones, Mitchell T.: Native of Georgia. Enlisted in 26th Georgia Infantry, Company H, on 05/01/1862 at Savannah, Georgia. Transferred as a private to Cobb's Legion Cavalry, Company F, on 10/12/1862. Sent to Georgia with Capt. Bostick to get a horse on 09/20/1864. Was surrendered by Gen. Joseph E. Johnston on 04/26/1865. Paroled at Greensboro, North Carolina, on 05/01/1865.

666. Jones, Nathan: Enlisted as a private in Company A on 07/07/1864 at Stony Creek, Virginia. Last record was a receipt for clothing, dated 12/01/1864.

667. Jones, Shepard A.: Born ca. 1841 in Georgia. Enlisted as a private in Company B on 10/01/1861 at Yorktown, Virginia. Sent to Georgia to get a horse with Lt. James H. Johnson on 04/14/1863. Last record September/October 1864, sent to Georgia to get a horse with Capt. Bostick on 09/20/1864. After the war, lived in DeKalb County, Georgia. His wife's name was Mary. His widow applied for a Confederate pension in DeKalb County, Georgia.

668. Jones, Thomas P.: Enlisted in 20th Georgia on 02/05/1864 at Laurens County, Georgia. Transferred as a private to Cobb's Legion Cavalry, Company F. Sent to Georgia with Capt. Bostick to get a horse on 09/20/1864. Was surrendered by Gen. Joseph E. Johnston on 04/26/1865. Paroled at Greensboro, North Carolina, on 05/01/1865.

669. Jones, Thomas R. Washington: 23-year-old farmer. Born in Fayette County, Georgia. Enlisted as a private in Company B on 08/14/1861 at Atlanta, Georgia. Value of horse $175 and horse equipment $13.75, saddle furnished by State of Georgia. Discharged on 09/07/1861 due to epileptic seizures. Described as having a dark complexion, dark blue eyes, black hair and being 5'11" tall. Enlisted as a private in 1st Georgia Infantry, Company G, on 09/01/1861. Mustered out at Augusta, Georgia, on 03/18/1862. Enlisted as a private in 20th Georgia Cavalry, Company A, on 05/16/1862. Transferred from the 20th Georgia Cavalry to Cobb's Legion Cavalry, Company F, on 08/05/1864. Sent to Georgia with Capt. Bostick to get a horse on 09/20/1864. Surrendered and was paroled at Thomasville, Georgia, on 05/21/1865.

670. Jones, William Beamon: 20-year-old from Columbia County, Georgia. Enlisted as a private in Company A on 08/17/1861 at Augusta,

---

Howard, page 17.

Georgia. Value of horse $175 and horse equipment $35. Detailed to Quartermaster Department in 01/1862. Transferred to Company F on 07/01/1862. Discharged in 11/1862. After the war, became a farmer in Columbia County, Georgia. Was married and the father of at least five children.

671. Jones, William H.: 22-year-old from Georgia. Enlisted as a sergeant in Company I on 02/14/1862 at Winchester, Virginia. Value of horse $250. Sent to Georgia to get a horse in November/December 1863. Admitted sick to Jackson Hospital in Richmond, Virginia, on 01/25/1864. Admitted to Chimborazo Hospital in Richmond, Virginia, on 04/10/1864. Last record, returned to duty on 10/08/1864.

672. Jones, William Hemphill: Enlisted in the 8th Georgia Infantry, Company D, as a private on 02/20/1862 at Rome, Georgia. Transferred to Cobb's Legion Cavalry Company B on 01/07/1863. Sent to Georgia to get a horse on 08/25/1863. Sent home to get a horse with Lt. Sinquefield under Special Order No. 27 from corps headquarters on 02/23/1864. Sent to Georgia with Capt. Bostick to get a horse on 09/20/1864. Was surrendered by Gen. Joseph E. Johnston on 04/26/1865. Paroled at Greensboro, North Carolina, on 05/01/1865.

673. Jowers, John: Laborer from Richmond County, Georgia. Born ca. 1840 in South Carolina. Enlisted as a private in Company K on 02/07/1863 at Camp Maynard, Georgia. Returned to his regiment on 02/23/1863.

674. Jowers, John L.: 20-year-old. Enlisted as a private in Company I on 03/24/1862 at Augusta, Georgia. Value of horse $200. Killed in action at Jack's Shop, Virginia, on 09/22/1863. His wife, Sarah E. Jowers, received his back pay. They had one child.

675. Juhan, Daniel Bordeaux: 18-year-old. Born on 03/09/1845 in Gwinnett County, Georgia. Twin of Richard Nathaniel Juhan. Enlisted as a private Company in B on 03/05/1863 at Stone Mountain, Georgia. Left at Staunton, Virginia, sick on 03/26/1863. Returned to duty on 04/21/1863. Furloughed to Georgia for 24 days beginning 02/19/1864. Detailed to tear up railroad above Hamilton Crossing, Virginia, on 03/29/1864. Was surrendered by Gen. Joseph E. Johnston on 04/26/1865. Paroled at Greensboro, North Carolina, on 05/01/1865. After the war, became a farmer in DeKalb County, Georgia. Married Ann Duncan on 04/10/1873 in Norcross, Georgia, and they had at least two children. Died on 02/28/1908 in DeKalb County, Georgia. Buried in the Zoar Methodist Church Cemetery, DeKalb County, Georgia. His widow applied for a Confederate pension in Gwinnett County, Georgia.

676. Juhan, Francis Ferdinand [Frank]: 29-year-old lawyer from Gwinnett County, Georgia. Born 10/04/1832 or 10/14/1832 in Gwinnett County, Georgia, or Barnwell, South Carolina. Brother of Lewis Alexander and Oliver Hazard Perry Juhan. Enlisted as a private in Company B on 04/29/1862 at Atlanta, Georgia. Value of horse $185. Promoted to sergeant on 11/10/1863. Was surrendered by Gen. Joseph E. Johnston on 04/26/1865. Paroled at Greensboro, North Carolina, on 05/01/1865. After the war, became an attorney-at-law in Gwinnett County, Georgia. Married Narcissa Elizabeth Ivie on 01/21/1866 in Gwinnett County, Georgia, or Seneca, Ohio. They possibly had nine children.

677. Juhan, J.A.: Resident of Georgia. Enlisted as a private in Company A on 02/01/1864 at Decatur, Georgia. Last record September/October 1864, sent to Georgia to get a horse with Capt. Bostick on 09/20/1864.

678. Juhan, Lewis Alexander: 25-year-old farmer. Born on 01/11/1836 in Jones County, Georgia. Brother of Francis Ferdinand and Oliver Hazard Perry Juhan. Enlisted as a private Company B on 08/14/1861 at Atlanta, Georgia. Value of horse $200 and horse equipment $3, saddle furnished by State of Georgia. Horse killed in action at Barbee's Cross Roads, Virginia, on 11/06/1862. Juhan admitted to General Hospital No. 7 in Richmond, Virginia, with wound in left foot on 11/09/1862. Furloughed for 30 days beginning 11/12/1862. Sent to recruiting/infirmary camp on 01/15/1864. Last record September/October 1864, sent to Georgia to get a horse with Capt. Bostick on 09/20/1864. After the war, became a farmer in Gwinnett County, Georgia. Married Emily C. Humphries in 1858 and they had at least seven children. Died on 10/21/1927 in DeKalb County, Georgia. Buried at the Rockbridge Baptist Church Cemetery in Gwinnett County, Georgia.

679. Juhan, Oliver Hazard Perry: 30-year-old. Born on 09/07/1830 in Barnwell, South Carolina. Brother of Lewis Alexander and Francis Ferdinand Juhan. Enlisted as a private in Company B on 08/14/1861 at Atlanta, Georgia. Value of horse $175 and horse equipment $4.50, saddle furnished by State of Georgia. Sent to recruiting/infirmary camp on 03/05/1862. Promoted to lieutenant on 06/04/1862. Promoted to captain on 01/07/1863. Horse valued at $800 killed in action at Brandy Station, Virginia, on 08/01/1863. Another horse valued at $800 killed in action near Culpeper Court House, Virginia, on 09/13/1863. Juhan furloughed to Georgia for 24 days beginning 01/22/1864. Killed in action at Spotsylvania Court House (White Hall Plantation) on 05/07/1864. Married Mandolene (Amanda) Hutchinson on 10/24/1850 in Gwinnett County, Georgia, and they possibly had at least five children.

680. **Juhan, Richard Nathaniel [S.]:** 18-year-old. Born 03/09/1845 in Gwinnett County, Georgia. Twin of Daniel Bordeaux Juhan. Enlisted as a private in Company B on 03/05/1863 at Stone Mountain, Georgia. Left at Staunton, Virginia, sick on 03/26/1863. Captured at Milford Station, Virginia, on 05/21/1864 and sent to Port Royal, Virginia. Transferred to Point Lookout, Maryland. Exchanged at Camp Lee near Richmond, Virginia, on 01/17/1865. Last record states he reported from hospital on 01/25/1865.

681. **Karr, J.J.:** Resident of Laurenceville, Alabama. Enlisted as a private in Company K on 09/02/1863 at Stevensburg, Virginia. Admitted to Winder Hospital in Richmond, Virginia, on 09/17/1863 with a flesh wound in his left side received on 09/13/1863. Given a medical furlough for 30 days to a hospital in Alabama beginning 09/23/1863. Admitted to Floyd House and Ocmulgee Hospital, Macon, Georgia, on 12/13/1863 with a wound in his back and side. Sent home to get a horse with Lt. Sinquefield under Special Order No. 27 from corps headquarters on 02/23/1864. Found to be a deserter from the 15th Alabama Infantry and turned over to them on 05/03/1864.

682. **Keaton, Benjamin O.:** Planter from Dougherty County, Georgia. Born ca. 1805 in Washington County, Georgia. Enlisted as a private in 15th Georgia Cavalry (State Guards). Listed on a roster of Company D published in *The History of Dougherty County*, but not with the *Civil War Soldiers and Sailors System*. No service records in Cobb's Legion. Was married and the father of at least one child.

683. **Keefe, John:** 32-year-old from Georgia. Enlisted as a veterinary surgeon in Company I on 02/28/1862 at Augusta, Georgia. Value of horse $200. Admitted sick to hospital in Lynchburg, Virginia, on 08/12/1864. Was surrendered by Gen. Joseph E. Johnston on 04/26/1865. Paroled at Greensboro, North Carolina, on 05/01/1865.

684. **Kelley, Edward:** 25-year-old from Augusta, Georgia. Enlisted as a private in Company K on 02/10/1863 at Camp Maynard, Georgia. Admitted to hospital on 07/09/1863 with a wound. Absent without leave on 11/30/1863. Deserted to the enemy while in Georgia wounded on or about 02/01/1864.

685. **Kelly, John:** Enlisted as a private in Company F on 10/01/1863 at Orange Court House, Virginia, as a substitute for John Thomas Kenedy. Received a gunshot wound to his left leg at Mine Run, Virginia, on 11/24/1863. Admitted to Hospital No. 1 in Richmond, Virginia, on 12/03/1863. Furloughed for 30 days beginning 12/22/1863. Never returned to regiment and listed as absent without leave.

686. **Kelly, William:** Listed in Company F on *Roster of the Confederate Soldiers of Burke County, Georgia: 1861–1865*. No service records in Cobb's Legion. Possibly the same person as John Kelly.

687. **Kendrick, W.W.:** Born ca. 1822. Enlisted as a private in 15th Georgia Cavalry (State Guards). Listed on a roster of Company D published in *The History of Dougherty County*, but not with the *Civil War Soldiers and Sailors System*. No service records in Cobb's Legion.

688. **Kenedy [Kenady], John Thomas:** 31-year-old farmer. Born in Jefferson County, Georgia. Enlisted as a private in Company F on 01/01/1863 at Stevensburg, Virginia. Admitted to Confederate States Hospital in Petersburg, Virginia, on 09/15/1863. Returned to duty on 09/19/1863. Furnished John Kelly as a substitute. Discharged on 10/01/1863.

689. **Kennedy, James J.:** Brother of John Milton Kennedy. Enlisted as a private in Company F on 03/25/1862 at Burke County, Georgia. Value of horse $160. Admitted to General Hospital No. 9 in Richmond, Virginia, with debility on 11/08/1862. Discharged in 11/14/1862. Died in 11/1862.

690. **Kennedy [Kenady], John Milton:** Born ca. 1842 in Carroll County, Georgia. Brother of James J. Kennedy. Enlisted as a private in Company F on 03/25/1862 at Burke County, Georgia. Value of horse $225. Sent to Georgia with Capt. Bostick to get a horse on 09/20/1864. Was surrendered by Gen. Joseph E. Johnston on 04/26/1865. Paroled at Greensboro, North Carolina, on 05/01/1865. After the war, became a farmer in Jefferson County, Georgia. He and his wife, Susan, had at least two children. Applied for a Confederate pension in Jefferson County, Georgia. Died ca. 1937. Buried in the Moxley Community Cemetery in Jefferson County, Georgia.

691. **Kennedy, Joseph J.:** 16-year-old. Enlisted as a private in Company I on 03/31/1862 at Augusta, Georgia. Value of horse $150. Died 07/01/1862.

692. **Kennedy, Thomas B.:** Listed as a private in Company F in *Roster of the Confederate Soldiers of Burke County, Georgia: 1861–1865*. No service records in Cobb's Legion.

693. Kennemur, James S.: 18-year-old. Enlisted as a private in Company K on 02/09/1863 at Camp Maynard, Georgia. Returned to his regiment on 02/21/1863.

694. Kenney, Joseph: Listed on a roster of Company C in *These Men She Gave*. No service records in Cobb's Legion.

695. Keogh [Keough], John H.: 17-year-old born in County Tyrone, Ireland. Immigrated to Georgia on 09/08/1860. Enlisted as a private in Company A on 08/17/1861 at Augusta, Georgia. Value of horse $200 and horse equipment $25. Horse killed in battle at Barbee Cross Roads on 11/08/1862. On furlough in November/December 1863. Detailed on scouting party with Lt. Shivers of the 2nd South Carolina Cavalry in Culpeper County, Virginia, 12/14–12/17/1863. Lost horse on 01/01/1863. Sent home to get a horse with Lt. Sinquefield under Special Orders No. 36 Corps Headquarters 01/01/1864. Last record September/October 1864, sent to Georgia to get a horse with Capt. Bostick on 09/20/1864. His Confederate pension application states he was captured 9 miles from Orangeburg, South Carolina, and sent to prison in Savannah, from which he escaped. Lived in Savannah, Chatham County, Georgia, after the war. Was married but had no children, and worked as a peddler of dry goods. Was granted a Confederate pension in 1900 when he was 56, due to blindness, cancer of the throat, and poverty. Died on 01/20/1901. Buried on 01/21/1901 at Laurel Grove Cemetery, Lot 1309, Savannah, Georgia. (His cemetery record says he was 55.)

696. Keyes, John C.: 34-year-old mechanic resident of Washington County, Georgia. Enlisted as a private in Company A on 08/17/1861 at Augusta, Georgia. Value of horse $160 and horse equipment $25. Detailed as musician in 01/1862. Sick at hospital in November/December 1863. Detailed as a carpenter at Lynchburg, Virginia, in 01/1864. In hospital in Lynchburg, Virginia, on 02/11/1864. Furloughed for 60 days in March/April 1864. Detailed in Quartermaster Department on 04/01/1864. No horse on 07/01/1864. Furloughed for 60 days beginning 05/01/1864. Sent to infirmary/recruiting camp to work with the horses on 10/08/1864. Was surrendered by Gen. Joseph E. Johnston on 04/26/1865. Paroled at Greensboro, North Carolina, on 05/01/1865. After the war, was married and worked as a carpenter in Sandersville, Washington County, Georgia.

697. King, Barrington Simeral: 28-year-old physician from Richland County, South Carolina. Born on 10/17/1833 in Liberty County, Georgia. Enlisted as a private in Company C on 08/01/1861 at Athens, Clarke County, Georgia. Value of two horses $275. Served as acting surgeon for company beginning 11/01/1861. On furlough for 25 days beginning 01/20/1862. Elected captain on 03/22/1862. Was promoted to lieutenant colonel on 10/09/1863. Admitted to General Hospital No. 4 with dysentery on 05/28/1864. Absent with leave on 12/24/1864. Killed in action on 03/10/1865 near Averasboro, North Carolina. Mentioned in Colonel Young's Report of the Battle of Brandy Station on 06/09/1863: "King also deserves praise for the manner in which he commanded his sharpshooters." Wiley Howard described his death as follows: "The Cobb Legion gallantly charged upon that splendidly equipped battle line of dismounted Westerners, steadily advancing while their artillery, which we ought to have looked after better at the start, was playing upon our support murderously. We got within fifteen to twenty paces from their front line, our men and horses falling fast. Col. King, by whose side I happened to be, my youngest brother being on the other side, was mortally wounded, the artery of his thigh being severed. Blood spouted onto my shoulder as I leaned over to grasp him, and we held him and wheeled about, managing to take him off under a most terrific fire. My brother and Bugler Jackson afterwards buried him, taking note of the place, etc., so that after the war I was enabled to direct his brother to the spot and his remains were removed and reinterred at Roswell, where he had lived."* Married Sarah Elizabeth Macleod in 1859. Buried at Presbyterian Cemetery, Roswell, Georgia. The Mercer University Press published his letters in 2003.

698. King, Mark W.: Enlisted as a private in Company K on 05/18/1864 at Decatur, Georgia. Last record September/October 1864, sent to Georgia to get a horse with Capt. Bostick on 09/20/1864.

699. King, William J.: Resident of Georgia. Enlisted in 11th Georgia Infantry, Company A, as a private on 07/03/1861. Transferred Cobb's Legion Cavalry, Company H, on 03/01/1862 at Athens, Clarke County, Georgia. Wounded at 2nd Manassas, Virginia, on 08/30/1862. Horse valued at $160 killed in action at Brandy Station, Virginia, on 08/01/1863. On provost duty on 01/04/1864. Detailed for extra duty by order of the brigade commander on 04/01/1864. Sent to Georgia with Capt.

---

*Howard, page 14.

Bostick to get a horse on 09/20/1864. Was surrendered by Gen. Joseph E. Johnston on 04/26/1865. Paroled at Greensboro, North Carolina, on 05/01/1865.

700. Kirkland, George W.: Born ca. 1846 in Georgia. Enlisted as a private in Company F on 03/25/1862 at Atlanta, Georgia. Value of horse $200. Horse killed in action on 07/19/1862 while on picket duty on the James River below Malvern Hill, Virginia. Kirkland admitted sick to U.S.A. General Military Hospital No. 4 in Wilmington, North Carolina, on 05/17/1862. Returned to duty on 05/25/1862. Sent to Georgia with Capt. Bostick to get a horse on 09/20/1864. Was surrendered by Gen. Joseph E. Johnston on 04/26/1865. Paroled at Greensboro, North Carolina, on 05/01/1865. After the war, became a physician in Burke County, Georgia, and then a farmer in Emanuel County, Georgia. He and his wife, Ella, had five children. Died after 1900. His widow, Ella G. Kirkland, applied for a Confederate pension in Emanuel County, Georgia.

701. Kitchens, J.J.: Resident of Georgia. Enlisted as a private in Company D on 08/10/1861 at Albany, Georgia. Value of horse $200 and horse equipment $25, furnished by State of Georgia. Promoted to corporal on 11/01/1862. No horse from November 1863 to February 1864. Last record 11/01/1864, detailed to brigade provost guard with the use of a public horse beginning 09/15/1864.

702. Knight, Frank: Resident of Georgia. Enlisted as a private in Company K on 08/25/1863 at Stevensburg, Virginia. Sent home to get a horse with Lt. Sinquefield under Special Order No. 27 from corps headquarters beginning 03/13/1864. Found to be a deserter from the 5th Alabama Infantry and turned over to them on 05/10/1864.

703. Knight, George L.: 16-year-old from Georgia. Born in Georgia in 11/1845. Enlisted as a private in Company E on 04/09/1862 at Lawrenceville, Georgia. Value of horse $125. Sent home to get a horse in March/April 1863. Admitted sick to Jackson Hospital in Richmond, Virginia, on 02/14/1864. Returned to duty on 02/25/1864. Last record September/October 1864, sent to Georgia to get a horse with Capt. Bostick on 09/20/1864. After the war, became a farmer in Gwinnett County, Georgia. He and his wife, Isabella, had thirteen children. Died in 1938.

704. Knight, John W.: 17-year-old. Enlisted as a private in Company E on 04/03/1862 at Atlanta, Georgia. Value of horse $150. Last record dated 04/22/1862 does not state if he were present or absent.

705. Laffew, T.R.: 23-year-old from Virginia. Enlisted as a private in Company K on 01/20/1863 at Camp Maynard, Georgia. Wounded on 06/09/1863. Last record September/October 1864, still absent wounded.

706. Lambert, George A.: 17-year-old farm hand from Burke County, Georgia. Born on 05/18/1845 in Georgia. Enlisted as a private in Company F on 03/25/1862 at Burke County, Georgia. Value of horse $175. On sick furlough for 15 days beginning 11/10/1862. Admitted to Winder Hospital, Richmond, Virginia, on 10/11/1863. Lost horse in 03/1864. Sent to Georgia with Capt. Bostick to get a horse on 09/20/1864. Was surrendered by Gen. Joseph E. Johnston on 04/26/1865. Paroled at Greensboro, North Carolina, on 05/01/1865. After the war, became a druggist in Burke County, Georgia. Married Mary E. Watkins on 12/20/1868 and they had three children. Died on 10/17/1908. Buried in Bark Camp Baptist Church Cemetery, Burke County, Georgia.

707. Lamkin [Lampkin], James T. [G.][P.]: 28-year-old carpenter from Gwinnett County, Georgia. Born in Gwinnett County, Georgia, in 04/1833. Enlisted as a private in Company B on 08/14/1861 at Atlanta, Georgia. Value of horse $150 and horse equipment $1.25, saddle furnished by State of Georgia. Promoted to corporal on 03/27/1863. Detailed as a guard at Port Royal, Virginia, in 01/1864. Wounded in both legs by gunshot at Burgess Mill, Virginia, and sent to General Hospital in Petersburg, Virginia, on 10/27/1864. The lower third of his right leg was amputated and his left leg was fractured. Transferred to Richmond on 03/30/1865. Captured at Jackson Hospital, Richmond, Virginia, on 04/03/1865. Sent to Point Lookout, Maryland, on 05/02/1865 on hospital transport Thomas Powell. Released at U.S.A. General Hospital, Point Lookout, Maryland, on 07/08/1865. Described as having a fair complexion, light hair, blue eyes, and being 5'6" tall. After the war, became a merchant in Gwinnett County, Georgia. Married (1) Lou, and they had at least three children. Married (2) Rebecca in 1899 or 1900. Applied for a Confederate pension in Turner County, Georgia.

708. Lampkin, Robert A.: Native of Georgia. Enlisted as a private Company B 08/27/1861 at Lawrenceville, Georgia. Horse valued at $275 killed in action at Upperville, Virginia, on 06/21/1863. Lampkin sent to recruiting/infirmary camp on 12/01/1863. Killed in action at Samaria Church on 06/24/1864.

709. Lampkin, William F.: 38-year-old. Enlisted as a private in Company B on 04/30/1862. Value of horse $170. Admitted to Institute Hospital in Richmond, Virginia, with a gunshot wound. Returned to duty 09/04/1862. Sent to recruiting/infirmary camp on 10/25/1863. Died on 05/05/1864.

710. Lander, Thomas: 22-year-old from Georgia. Born in Scotland in 06/1839. Immigrated in 1860. Enlisted as a private Company I on 02/27/1862 at Augusta, Georgia. Value of horse $200. Admitted to Winder Hospital, Richmond, Virginia, on 11/17/1862. Admitted to General Hospital, Staunton, Virginia, on 03/13/1863 with a hydrocele. Admitted to Jackson Hospital, Richmond, Virginia, on 03/04/1864. Was using a public horse on 04/01/1864. Note on 04/30/1864 said he had been operated on four times for hydrocele. Detailed as a nurse at Jackson Hospital, Richmond, Virginia, on 05/17/1864. Furloughed for 15 days beginning 08/06/1864. Detailed to Quartermaster Department in Augusta, Georgia, on 09/01/1864. Detailed as a nurse at Jackson Hospital in Richmond, Virginia, on 12/23/1864. Captured at Jackson Hospital in Richmond, Virginia, on 04/03/1865. Paroled at Richmond, Virginia, on 05/03/1865. After the war, worked as a compositor and printer in Richmond County, Georgia. He and his wife, Julia, had 19 children. Married (2) Hattie. Died after 1920.

711. Landrum, Benjamin: 38-year-old from Georgia. Born on 05/20/1824 in Georgia. Enlisted as a private in Company H on 03/01/1863 in Stevensburg, Virginia. Substitute for Michajah Monroe Landrum. Mentioned in Colonel Young's Report of the engagement at Brandy Station on 06/09/1863: "I desire also to mention the most distinguished gallantry of Privates McCroan and Landrum, who, on foot, refused to surrender when surrounded by the enemy, but cut their way through safely."* Sent to Georgia to get a horse on 11/11/1863. Absent without leave beginning 01/23/1864. Last record September/October 1864, sent to Georgia to get a horse with Capt. Bostick on 09/20/1864. After the war, became a farmer in Lumpkin County, Georgia. Married Jane Kilpatrick on 07/13/1844 in Lumpkin County, Georgia. Died on 06/12/1893 in Floyd County, Georgia.

712. Landrum, Michajah Monroe: Born ca. 1828 in Hall County, Georgia. Enlisted as a private in Company C on 05/12/1862 at Hall County, Georgia. Enlisted in Company H on 03/12/1862 at Athens, Clarke County, Georgia. The enlistment dates seem to be in disagreement but he served in Company H. Last record, January/February/1863. Furnished Benjamin Landrum as a substitute. After the war, became a farmer in Hall County, and then Floyd County, Georgia. Married Agnes E. Tate in Hall County Georgia, on 02/09/1846 and they had at least eight children. Died on 04/07/1897 in Floyd County, Georgia.

713. Landrum, Thomas Jefferson: 22-year-old. Born on 02/15/1839. Enlisted as a private in Company B on 08/14/1861 at Atlanta, Georgia. Value of horse $200 and horse equipment $6.75, saddle furnished by State of Georgia. Detailed in March/April 1863 to stay behind and capture deserters in Franklin County, Virginia. Sent home to get a horse with Lt. Sinquefield under Special Order No. 27 from corps headquarters on 02/23/1864. Detailed at brigade headquarters on 07/28/1864. Was admitted to C.S.A. General Hospital in Danville, Virginia, on 11/29/1864 with an earache. Returned to duty on 12/02/1864. There is a handwritten note in his records that states, "Deserted from hospital and is absent without leave." After the war, became a farmer in Fayette County, Georgia, and then a schoolteacher in Cullman County, Alabama. Married Josephine J. Davine or Davis on 09/20/1865 in Fayette County, Georgia, and they had at least seven children.

714. Langston, Jeptha N.: 25-year-old from Georgia. Enlisted in 1st Georgia Infantry, Company F, as a private on 03/18/1861. Mustered out on 03/18/1862 at Augusta, Georgia. Enlisted as a private in Company B, Cobb's Legion Cavalry, on 04/28/1862 at Atlanta, Georgia, at the age of 25. Value of horse $190. Transferred to Company G in May/June 1862. Sent home to get a horse with Lt. Sinquefield under Special Order No. 27 from corps headquarters on 02/23/1864. Horse valued at $1,300 killed in action at Trevilian Station on 06/11/1864. Langston was present on last record, September/October 1864. After the war, became a retail grocer and then a justice of the peace in Fulton County, Georgia. He and his wife, M.E., had at least six children. Died after 1910.

715. Lankford, James R.: 18-year-old farmer. Resident of Tennessee. Enlisted as a private in Company K on 01/18/1863 at Camp Maynard, Georgia. Promoted to corporal on 04/18/1863. Horse valued at $400 killed in action at Brandy Station, Virginia, on 06/06/1863. Lankford captured at Clear Spring, Maryland, on 07/09/1863 and sent to Atheneum Military Prison in Wheeling, [West] Virginia. Transferred to Camp Chase, Ohio,

---

*OR, *Series 1, Vol. 27, pt. 2, pages 732–733.*

on 07/22/1863. Transferred to Fort Delaware Prison on 02/29/1864. Described as having a florid complexion, black eyes, dark hair, and being 5'6" tall. There is no record of his taking the Oath or being released from Fort Delaware. Since he could not be identified on a later U.S. census, he may have died at Fort Delaware, but he is not listed in *They Died at Fort Delaware: 1861–1865*.

716. Lassiter, R.W.: Enlisted as a private Company I on 09/05/1862 at Augusta, Georgia. Substitute for McKinne Law. Transferred to the 48th Georgia Infantry on 01/01/1864.

717. Lataste, E.G.: Born ca. 1842 in Georgia. Enlisted as a private in Company A on 11/07/1861 at Augusta, Georgia. No horse on 01/01/1863. Another horse, appraised at $450, killed at Hunterstown, Pennsylvania, on 07/03/1863. Admitted to Jackson Hospital, Richmond, Virginia, on 09/23/1863. Returned to duty on 10/27/1863. Admitted to Chimborazo Hospital No. 3, Richmond, Virginia, with debility on 05/26/1864. Returned to duty on 06/11/1864. Admitted to Jackson Hospital, Richmond, Virginia, with ascites (liver disease) on 07/01/1864. Returned to duty on 07/06/1864. Sent home to get a horse with Capt. Bostick on 09/20/1864. Last record is a receipt for clothing at 3rd General Hospital, Augusta, Georgia, dated 11/14/1864. After the war, worked as a carpenter and then as a postmaster in St. Clair County, Alabama. Was married to Margaritte and was the father of at least one child. Died before 1910.

718. Law, McKinne: 25-year-old. Born in 11/1836 in Georgia. Enlisted as a private Company I on 04/21/1862 at Augusta, Georgia. Furnished R.W. Lassiter as a substitute on 09/05/1862. After the war, became a retail grocer in Richmond County, Georgia. He and his wife, Mary, had one child. Died after 1900.

719. Lawrence, William E.: Enlisted as a private in Company L on 10/16/1863 at Augusta, Georgia. Paroled on 05/19/1865 at Augusta, Georgia.

720. Lawson, John M.: 18-year-old. Enlisted as a private in Company F on 03/25/1862 at Burke County, Georgia. Value of horse $160. Admitted to Jackson Hospital, Richmond, Virginia, on 02/14/1864 with typhoid fever. Died on 02/22/1864 at Jackson Hospital, Richmond, Virginia. His father, Robert M. Lawson, received his back pay, as he was not survived by a wife or children.

721. Lawson, Roger McGill: 51-year-old. Born on 04/15/1810. Enlisted as a sergeant in Company F on 03/15/1862 at Burke County, Georgia. Value of horse $160. Admitted to Chimborazo Hospital No. 3, Richmond, Virginia, on 11/24/1862. Admitted to General Hospital No. 14, Richmond, Virginia, on 02/02/1862. In Jefferson County on sick furlough in January/February 1863. Admitted to Winder Hospital, Richmond, Virginia, on 04/04/1863 with debility. Returned to duty on 04/06/1863. Discharged on 08/01/1863. Served in Indian War in Florida. Was a member of the Associate Reformed Presbyterian Church. Married (1) Mary Alexander (2) Sarah Jane Marsh. Died on 03/11/1887. Buried in old part of the Bethany Cemetery near Wadley, Georgia.

722. Lawton, Alexander Cater: Born ca. 1841 in Georgia or South Carolina. Enlisted as a sergeant in Company D on 08/10/1861 at Albany, Georgia. Value of horse $200 and horse equipment $30. Reduced in rank to private on 12/28/1861. Last record, March/April 1863, on horse detail since January/February 1863. After the war, became a hotel keeper in Turner County, Georgia. Married Sarah A. Godfrey on 11/29/1866 and they had three children. Applied for a Confederate pension in Turner County, Georgia. Died on 07/26/1921 in Turner County, Georgia.

723. Lawton, B.H. [W.T.]: Enlisted as a private in Company D on 08/10/1861 at Albany, Georgia. Value of horse $175 and horse equipment $25, furnished by State of Georgia. Absent without leave beginning 04/01/1862. Still absent without leave on last record, March/April 1863.

724. Lawton, George M.: Planter from Dougherty County, Georgia. Born, ca. 1822 in South Carolina. Enlisted as a private in the 15th Georgia Cavalry (State Guards). Listed on a roster of Company D published in *The History of Dougherty County*, but not with the *Civil War Soldiers and Sailors System*. No service records in Cobb's Legion.

725. Lawton, Winburn J.: Planter from Dougherty County, Georgia. Born ca. 1812 in South Carolina. Enlisted as a private in the 2nd Georgia Cavalry. Enlisted as a captain in Cobb's Legion Cavalry, Company D, on 08/10/1861 at Albany, Georgia. Value of horses $300, $200, $250, and horse equipment $25, $25, $35. On furlough without limit beginning 01/18/1862 by order of Gen. Magruder. Last record, promoted to colonel on 05/02/1862. He and his wife, Sarah, had at least three children.

726. Lay, Elijah [Elisha] Columbus: Born ca. 1844. Brother of Marcus L. Lay. Enlisted as a private in Company H on 03/18/1862 at Athens, Clarke County, Georgia. Was listed in Company C on 04/25/1862, but in Company H on the rest of his records. Admitted to C.S.A. General Hospital, Danville, Virginia, on 07/23/1862 with a fever. Returned to duty on 07/30/1862. Was present on last record, September/October 1862.

727. **Lay, Marcus L. [C.]:** 23-year-old from Georgia. Born on 03/17/1838 in Jackson County, Georgia. Brother of Elijah Columbus Lay. Enlisted as a private in the 16th Georgia Infantry, Company G, in 07/19/1861 in Jefferson, Georgia. Transferred into Cobb's Legion Cavalry, Company H, on 08/18/1862 at Athens, Clarke County, Georgia. Sent home to get a horse with Lt. Sinquefield under Special Order No. 27 from corps headquarters on 02/23/1864. Shot with minié ball at Battle of Spotsylvania Court House on 05/08/1864. Admitted to Jackson Hospital, Richmond, Virginia, on 05/17/1864 with a minié ball wound in right arm. Furloughed for 60 days beginning 05/23/1864. Given a disability discharge on 02/17/1864. Described as 28 years of age, having a fair complexion, blue eyes, light hair, and being 5'8 1/2" tall. Was on muster roll of Retired Men at the Post of Athens, Georgia, on 10/31/1864. After the war, lived in Milam County, Texas. Married Elizabeth Pike on 01/26/1860 in Jackson County, Georgia. Died on 06/15/1912 in Columbia County, Georgia.

728. **Lazenby, Artemus M.:** 27-year-old schoolteacher from Columbia County, Georgia. Born 06/19/1832 in Columbia County, Georgia. Enlisted as a private in Company A on 09/21/1861 at Williamsburg, Virginia. Sent to infirmary/recruiting camp on 02/01/1864 and on 02/23/1864. Sent to hospital 09/01/1864. Last record September/October 1864, was still in hospital. On his Confederate pension application, he stated that he had been scouting with Gen. P.M.B. Young and was at Augusta, Georgia, when the company surrendered. After the war, became a farmer, then a merchant in Columbia County, Georgia. Married Mary (Mollie) Isabel J. Fuller on 04/16/1868 in Columbia County, Georgia, and was the father of at least eight children. Died on 06/15/1912 and buried in Harlem Memorial Cemetery in Columbia County, Georgia.

729. **Leach [Leech], James M.:** Laborer from Fulton County, Georgia. Born in Alabama. Enlisted in 21st Georgia Volunteer Infantry, Company C, as a private on 06/26/1861 at Atlanta, Georgia. Appointed corporal. Wounded at 2nd Manassas, Virginia, on 08/28/1862. Transferred to Company B, Cobb's Legion Cavalry, as a private on 11/08/1862. Detailed as a teamster on 03/16/1864. Admitted to Wilson Hospital (probably in North Carolina) on 08/06/1864. Last record 10/31/1864, was still at Wilson Hospital.

730. **Leach, John:** Resident of Fulton County, Georgia. Enlisted as a private Company B 07/20/1864. Was present on last record, September/October 1864 at Stony Creek, Virginia. After the war, became a merchant in Fulton County, Georgia, and was married.

731. **Leach, Thomas [Leech]:** Carpenter from Fulton County, Georgia. Born ca. 1826 in North Carolina. Enlisted as a private Company B on 08/14/1861 at Atlanta, Georgia. Value of horse $200. Horse equipment, owned by W.B. Cox, valued at $18. Lost horse on 02/10/1863. Sent to recruiting/infirmary camp on 12/01/1863. Sent home to get a horse with Lt. Sinquefield under Special Order No. 27 from corps headquarters on 02/23/1864. Sent to Georgia with Capt. Bostick to get a horse on 09/20/1864. Admitted to Pettigrew General Hospital, Raleigh, North Carolina, on 02/17/1865 with a flesh wound in his left arm. Last record, returned to duty on 03/01/1865. He and his wife, Elizabeth, had at least five children. Applied for a Confederate pension in Fulton County, Georgia.

732. **Leatherwood [Letherwood], Wiley M.:** 20-year-old from Georgia. Enlisted as a private in 1st Georgia Infantry, Company C, as a private on 06/01/1861. Mustered out on 03/18/1862 at Augusta, Georgia. Enlisted as a private in Company B, Cobb's Legion Cavalry, on 04/04/1862 at Atlanta, Georgia. Value of horse $175. Transferred to Company G in May/June 1862. Detailed as a courier to Gen. McLaws on 08/24/1862. Lost horse on 12/31/1862. Forfeited pay for 6 months by order of court-martial on 04/01/1863. Horse valued at $700 killed in action at Raccoon Ford on 09/14/1863. Leatherwood was present on last record, October 1864.

733. **Leckie, Alexander:** 28-year-old from Georgia. Born in 09/1833 in Scotland. Enlisted as a private in Company H on 03/07/1862 at Athens, Clarke County, Georgia. Sent home to get a horse with Lt. Sinquefield under Special Order No. 27 from corps headquarters on 02/23/1864. In Georgia on sick furlough beginning 05/01/1864. Last record September/October 1864, still on sick furlough in Georgia. After the war, became a farmer in Hall County, Georgia. He and his wife, Sarah, had at least one child. Died after 1910.

734. **Lee, A.B.:** Enlisted as a private in Company L on 04/25/1864 at Decatur, Georgia. Absent without leave on 05/12/1864. Still absent without leave on last record, September/October 1864.

735. **Lepole:** Listed in Company F in *Roster of the Confederate Soldiers of Burke County, Georgia: 1861–1865*. No service records in Cobb's Legion.

736. **Lewellyn, C.E.:** 18-year-old. Enlisted as a private in Company K on 01/18/1863 at Camp Maynard, Georgia. Last record 09/1863–01/1864, absent without leave since 07/14/1863.

737. **Lewis, Milton H.:** Wheelwright from Burke County, Georgia. Born ca. 1817 in Georgia. Enlisted as a sergeant in Company F on 03/25/1862 at Burke County, Georgia. Value of horse $125. Listed as a private in March/April 1864. Admitted to Jackson Hospital, Richmond, Virginia, on 05/27/1864 with chronic rheumatism. Returned to duty on 05/28/1864. Admitted to C.S.A. General Hospital, Farmville, Virginia, on 06/02/1864 with chronic rheumatism. Transferred to Jackson Hospital, Richmond, Virginia. Returned to duty on 07/21/1864. Sent to Georgia with Capt. Bostick to get a horse on 09/20/1864. Was surrendered by Gen. Joseph E. Johnston on 04/26/1865. Paroled at Greensboro, North Carolina, on 05/01/1865. After the war, became a farmer in Emanuel County, Georgia. Married Rosetta Nasworthy on 11/07/1844 in Laurens County, Georgia, and they had at least one child. Died after 1880.

738. **Lewis, W.C.:** 33-year-old. Enlisted as a private in Company K on 02/06/1863 at Camp Maynard, Georgia. Returned to his regiment on 02/21/1863.

739. **Light, Wiley R.:** Enlisted as a private in Company L on 04/19/1864 at Decatur, Georgia. Last record September/October 1864, sent to Georgia to get a horse with Capt. Bostick on 09/20/1864.

740. **Linsey [Lindsey], Elijah:** 21- or 22-year-old from Georgia. Enlisted as a private in Company E on 03/27/1862 at Roswell, Georgia. Value of horse $200. Admitted to C.S.A. General Hospital in Charlottesville, Virginia, on 05/31/1863 with chronic kidney disease. Returned to duty on 06/08/1863. Sent to recruiting/infirmary camp on 10/15/1863. Admitted to Jackson Hospital, Richmond, Virginia, on 08/20/1864. Returned to duty on 10/12/1864. Was present on last record, September/October 1864. After the war, worked as a farm laborer in Cherokee County and then Milton County, Georgia. He and his wife, Emaline, had at least four children. Died after 1880.

741. **Lippitt, W.H.:** Exchange-merchant in Dougherty County, Georgia. Born ca. 1838. Enlisted as a private in Company D on 08/10/1861 at Albany, Georgia. Value of horse $200 and horse equipment $25. On sick furlough in 12/1861. Absent with dismounted men in March/April 1863. Captured at Ream's Station, Virginia, on 08/25/1864. Sent to City Point, Virginia. Listed as a "Rebel deserter" by the Army of the Potomac on 09/06/1864. (Note: This is probably in error as there is no record of his taking the Oath, and he was exchanged and allowed to return to Georgia after being released from prison.) Transferred to Point Lookout, Maryland, on 09/23/1864. Exchanged on 11/01/1864. Paroled at Albany, Georgia, on 05/16/1865.

742. **Lively, Charles Pinkney:** 21-year-old. Born on 08/08/1840 in DeKalb County, Georgia. Enlisted as a private Company B on 08/14/1861 at Atlanta, Georgia. Value of horse $200 and horse equipment $4, saddle furnished by State of Georgia. Sent home to get a horse with Lt. Sinquefield under Special Order No. 27 from corps headquarters on 02/23/1864. Last record, September/October 1864, sent to Georgia to get a horse with Capt. Bostick on 09/20/1864. After the war, became a farmer and then a retail merchant in Gwinnett County, Georgia. Married Marcella E. Walker on 03/14/1872 and they had at least three children. Applied for a Confederate pension in Gwinnett County, Georgia. Died on 04/08/1926 in Gwinnett County, Georgia. Buried in Norcross Cemetery, Gwinnett County, Georgia.

743. **Liverman, William N.:** Resident of Richmond County, Georgia. Born in Georgia. Enlisted in the 1st Georgia Infantry, Company I, as a private on 03/18/1861. Mustered out at Augusta, Georgia, on 03/18/1862. Enlisted as a private in Cobb's Legion Cavalry, Company I, on 02/13/1862 at Winchester, Virginia. Value of horse $180. Admitted to Jackson Hospital, Richmond, Virginia, on 09/21/1863 with chronic diarrhea. Admitted to Pettigrew Hospital, Raleigh, North Carolina, with chronic diarrhea on 10/12/1864. On furlough beginning 10/15/1864. Admitted to Jackson Hospital, Richmond, Virginia, on 10/20/1864 with a fever. Returned to duty on 10/27/1864. Other records indicate he was killed while on scout duty in South Carolina on 04/09/1865.

744. **Lord, William R:** 26-year-old from Georgia. Enlisted as a private in Company C on 08/01/1861 at Athens, Clarke County, Georgia. Transferred to Company H in July/August 1862. On sick furlough beginning 08/14/1863. Sent to recruiting/infirmary camp on 02/23/1863. On sick furlough in 10/1864. Paroled at Athens, Clarke County, Georgia, on 05/08/1865. After the war, became a farmer in Troup County, Georgia. Was married to Buena V. Applied for a Confederate pension in Troup County, Georgia. His widow applied for a Confederate pension in Troup County, Georgia.

745. Lowe, John D.: 24-year-old from Georgia. Enlisted as a private in Company E on 04/09/1862 at Lawrenceville, Georgia. Value of horse $200. Admitted to C.S.A. General Hospital, Farmville, Virginia, on 05/07/1863 with acute rheumatism. Returned to duty on 05/18/1863. Captured at Battle of Spotsylvania Court House, Virginia, on 05/09/1864 and sent to Belle Plain, Virginia. Transferred to Point Lookout, Maryland, on 05/17/1864. Transferred to Elmira Prison, New York, on 08/08/1864. Died at Elmira Prison Camp, New York, on 05/3/1865 from chronic diarrhea. Buried in the Woodlawn Cemetery in Elmira, New York.

746. Lowery, Melvin K.: 16-year-old. Born in South Carolina. Enlisted as a private in Company A on 08/17/1861 at Augusta, Georgia. Value of horse $225 and horse equipment $25. Was present on last record, July/August 1862. After the war, became a farmer in Edgefield County, South Carolina. Was married and the father of at least three children.

747. Lowry, David P.: 38-year-old. Born on 09/03/1824. Enlisted as a private in Company L on 12/15/1862 at Burke County, Georgia. Sent to Georgia with Capt. Bostick to get a horse on 09/20/1864. Was surrendered by Gen. Joseph E. Johnston on 04/26/1865. Paroled at Greensboro, North Carolina, on 05/01/1865. Married (1) Selina Ruth Darley on 10/14/1854 in Jefferson County, Georgia, (2) Eleanor J.A.C. Netherland on 03/11/1858 in Jefferson County, Georgia. Died on 08/31/1868. Buried in the Lowry-Alexander Cemetery in Jefferson County, Georgia.

748. Loyd, John H.: Farmer. Born in Walker County, Georgia. Enlisted as a private in Company B on 08/14/1861 at Atlanta, Georgia. Value of horse $225 and horse equipment $9. Saddle furnished by State of Georgia. On sick furlough for 30 days beginning 12/04/1861. Admitted to General Hospital No. 17, Richmond, Virginia, in 10/1861. Was given a medical discharge on 10/22/1862. Described as being 21 years old and having a light complexion, gray eyes, sandy hair, and being 5'11" tall.

749. Lumpkin, Miller Grieve: Merchant from Clarke County, Georgia. Born ca. 1837 in Georgia. Brother of Robert C. Lumpkin. Enlisted as a private in the 3rd Georgia Infantry, Company K on 04/25/1861. Transferred to Cobb's Legion Cavalry, Company C, as a private on 08/01/1861 at Athens, Clarke County, Georgia. Appointed assistant commissary in 1861. Resigned on 02/23/1862. Promoted to A.C.S. on 05/15/1862. Last record, appointed major and commissary sergeant and ordered to report to General Young on 01/14/1865.

750. Lumpkin, Robert C.[S.]: Student from Clarke County, Georgia. Born ca. 1840 in Georgia. Brother of Miller Grieve Lumpkin. Enlisted as a private in Company C on 08/01/1861 at Athens, Clarke County, Georgia. Given a medical discharge on 09/10/1861.

751. Lutes, David F.: Farmer from Gordon County, Georgia. Born in North Carolina. Enlisted as a private in Company L on 04/22/1864 at Decatur, Georgia. Absent without leave beginning 05/12/1864. Still absent without leave on last record, September/October 1864. After the war, became a farmer in Gordon County, Georgia. Married Cynthia C. Hoyle ca. 1859 in Gordon County, Georgia, and they had at least five children.

752. Lyle, James Ray: Attorney from Clarke County, Georgia. Born ca. 1833. Enlisted as a lieutenant in Company C on 08/14/1861 at Athens, Clarke County, Georgia. Last record, a pay receipt dated 08/28/1861. After the war, became a lawyer in Clarke County, Georgia. He and his wife, Clara, had at least three children. Died in 1899. Buried in the Oconee Hill Cemetery in Clarke County, Georgia.

753. Lyle, Lee M.: Resident of Georgia. Enlisted as a private in the Troup Artillery on 04/24/1861 at Athens, Georgia. Was listed on a roll of prisoners of war on 09/30/1862. Transferred as a private in Cobb's Legion Cavalry, Company C, on 06/01/1863. No horse on 01/01/1864. On scouting detail on 02/18/1864 and 07/14/1864. Was present on his last record, September/October 1864. In recommending him as a cadet, Gen. Young called him a "good and faithful soldier" and Lt. C.W. Motes of the Troup Artillery said, "He served faithfully, always attending to his duty cheerfully."

754. Lyons, Thomas: 25-year-old from Richmond County, Georgia. Enlisted as a private in Company I on 03/26/1862 at Augusta, Georgia. Value of horse $200. Sent to Georgia to get a horse in November/December 1863. Sent to Georgia with Capt. Bostick to get a horse on 09/20/1864. Captured at Cheraw, South Carolina, on 03/04/1865 and sent to New Bern, North Carolina. Transferred to Point Lookout, Maryland, on 03/30/1865. Released on 06/30/1865. Described as having a fair complexion, auburn hair, blue eyes, and being 5' 8½" tall. Buried in the Memory Hill Cemetery in Baldwin County, Georgia.

755. Magby, D.: Listed on a roster of Company D published in *The History of Dougherty County*, but not with the *Civil War Soldiers and Sailors System*. No service records in Cobb's Legion.

756. Mahaffey, W.H.C.: Resident of Georgia.

Enlisted as a private in Company E on 09/21/1863 at Atlanta, Georgia. Sent to recruiting/infirmary camp on 10/27/1864. Last record September/October 1864, sent home to get a horse with Capt. Bostick on 09/20/1864. After the war, lived in Jackson County, Georgia. Applied for a Confederate pension in Jackson County, Georgia.

757. **Mahaffy, Emory V.W.:** Teacher, resident of Georgia. Born ca. 1839 in Georgia. Enlisted as a private in Company E on 04/09/1862 at Lawrenceville, Georgia. Value of horse $125 and horse equipment $30. Admitted to General Hospital No. 4, Richmond, Virginia, on 11/21/1862 with general debility. On furlough to Atlanta, Georgia, for 30 days beginning 11/25/1862. Absent sick in March/April 1863. Sent to recruiting/infirmary camp on 12/12/1863. Was present on last record, September/October 1864. After the war, became a farmer in Jackson County, Georgia, and then lived in Gwinnett County, Georgia. Was married. Applied for a Confederate pension in Gwinnett County, Georgia.

758. **Mahaffy, James A.B.:** 19-year-old. Born in 04/1843 in Georgia. Enlisted as a private in Company E on 04/09/1862 at Lawrenceville, Georgia. Value of horse $225 and horse equipment $30. Sent home to get a horse with Lt. Sinquefield under Special Order No. 27 from corps headquarters on 02/23/1864. Last record September/October 1864, sent to Georgia to get a horse with Capt. Bostick 09/20/1864. After the war, became a lawyer in Jefferson, Jackson County, Georgia. Married Evaline Callahan and they had seven children. Died after 1910. His widow applied for a Confederate pension in Jackson County, Georgia.

759. **Mahaffy [Mehaffey], John W.S.:** 27-year-old from Cobb County, Georgia. Enlisted as a private in Company E on 04/09/1862 at Lawrenceville, Georgia. Value of horse $200 and horse equipment $35. Sent home to get a horse in March/April 1863. Wounded on 05/08/1864. Deserted and took the Oath at Chattanooga, Tennessee, on 08/22/1864. Described as having a dark complexion, black hair, dark eyes, and being 5'10" tall.

760. **Mahany [Mahaney], Martin:** 29-year-old native of Georgia. Enlisted as a private in Company F on 03/25/1862 at Burke County, Georgia. Value of horse $140. Horse died on 06/01/1862. Mahany sent to Georgia with Capt. Bostick to get a horse on 09/20/1864. Was surrendered by Gen. Joseph E. Johnston on 04/26/1865. Paroled at Greensboro, North Carolina, on 05/01/1865.

761. **Mallory, Elisha S.:** 33-year-old farmer. Born in New Brunswick, British America. Enlisted as a corporal in Company F on 03/25/1862 at Waynesboro, Burke County, Georgia. Value of horse $275. Listed as a bugler in March/April 1862. Granted a discharge on 07/23/1862, due to a fracture. The discharge was not approved by Gen. Lee, so he was detailed as a nurse in the Division Field Hospital of Gen. McLaw's infantry command. Admitted to Moore Hospital (General Hospital No. 24), Richmond, Virginia, with chronic inflammation of the knee joint from the fracture on 09/15/1862. Given a medical discharge on 09/17/1862. Described as having a light complexion, blue eyes, light brown hair, and being 5'7 1/2" tall.

762. **Malone, Robert G.:** 48-year-old from Augusta, Georgia. Born in South Carolina and lived in Barnwell, South Carolina, before moving to Georgia. Enlisted as a blacksmith in Company A on 08/17/1861 at Augusta, Georgia. Value of horse $125 and horse equipment $25. Discharged due to a rupture on 02/15/1862. Surrendered at Augusta, Georgia, 05/27/1865 and paroled 06/02/1865. Was married and the father of at least eight children. Buried on 03/22/1883, age 72, at Magnolia Cemetery, Augusta, Georgia.

763. **Mangum, Wiley P.:** Native of Georgia. Enlisted as a private in Company B on 03/01/1862 at Camp Marion, Yorktown, Virginia, as a substitute for George W. Jack. Promoted to corporal on 06/01/1862. Without a horse in January/February 1863. Admitted to C.S.A. General Hospital, Charlottesville, Virginia, on 06/18/1863. Furloughed for 40 days beginning 06/30/1863. Lost horse on 09/01/1863. Admitted to a hospital in Lynchburg, Virginia, on 09/13/1863. Got another horse on 07/20/1864. Sent to recruiting/infirmary camp in Lynchburg, Virginia, on 08/18/1864. Sent to Georgia with Capt. Bostick to get a horse on 09/20/1864. Was surrendered by Gen. Joseph E. Johnston on 04/26/1865. Paroled at Greensboro, North Carolina, on 05/01/1865.

764. **Mann, J.M.:** 34-year-old from Georgia. Enlisted as a private in Company K on 02/10/1863 at Camp Maynard, Georgia. Absent without leave beginning 07/22/1863. Last record March/April 1864, still absent without leave.

765. **Manning, James [Jeremiah] H.:** 22-year-old. Born in Indiana. Enlisted as a private in Company I on 03/12/1862 at Augusta, Georgia. Value of horse $180. Detailed as a teamster in 12/1862. Captured near Gettysburg, Pennsylvania, on 07/03/1863. Sent to Fort Delaware Prison. Deserted and took the Oath. Applied to join Federal army on 08/30/1863.

766. **Marchman, Coleman W.:** Farmer from Fulton County, Georgia. Born ca. 1836 in Newton County, Georgia. Brother of John H. Marchman. Enlisted as a private in Company B on 04/30/1862 at Atlanta, Georgia. Value of horse $175. Died on 07/29/1862 at Camp Winder near Richmond, Virginia. Buried in Hollywood Cemetery, Richmond, Virginia. Described as having a sallow complexion, grey eyes, light hair and being 5'7" tall. His widow, Martha C. Durham Marchman, with whom he had at least one child, received his back pay.

767. **Marchman, John H.:** 19-year-old farmer from Fulton County, Georgia. Born on 02/02/1843 in DeKalb County, Georgia. Brother of Coleman Marchman. Enlisted as a private in Company B on 03/01/1662 at Camp Marion, Yorktown, Virginia. Lost horse on 03/14/1863. Sent to Georgia to get a horse in 04/1863. Sent to Georgia to get a horse on 11/13/1863. Detailed to pack forage for brigade in Essex County, Virginia, beginning 02/24/1864. Wounded on 03/01/1864 in Essex County, Virginia. Admitted to Jackson Hospital, Richmond, Virginia, on 03/13/1864 with a wound from a minié ball in right arm. Furloughed to Georgia for 60 days beginning 03/16/1864. Last record September/October 1864, listed as absent without leave since 10/14/1864. After the war, became a farmer in Carroll County, Georgia. Married Mary Elizabeth ca. 1869 in Carroll County, Georgia, and they had at least one child. On 1910 Census of Fulton County, Georgia, was resident of the Confederate Soldiers Home. Died on 07/10/1910. Was buried in the Westview Cemetery in Fulton County, Georgia. His widow applied for a Confederate pension in Carroll County, Georgia.

768. **Marshall, Henry:** 22-year-old native of England. Enlisted as a private in Company K on 02/25/1863 at Richmond, Virginia. Captured at Upperville, Virginia, on 06/21/1863 and sent to the Old Capitol Prison, Washington D.C. Deserted and took the Oath on 07/17/1863. A note said he had friends in the North.

769. **Marshall, James F.:** Enlisted as a sergeant in Company D on 08/10/1861 at Albany, Georgia. Value of horse $300 and horse equipment $60. Elected lieutenant on 12/31/1861. Killed in action near Middletown, Maryland (probably at Quebec Schoolhouse), on 09/13/1862.

770. **Marshall, William H.:** 22-year-old from Georgia. Enlisted as a private in Company B on 05/01/1862 at Atlanta, Georgia. Value of horse $135. Transferred to Company G in May/June 1862. Admitted to General Hospital No. 9, Richmond, Virginia, on 10/19/1863. Returned to duty on 10/20/1863. Sent to recruiting/infirmary camp in 12/1863. Last record, admitted to C.S.A. General Hospital No. 3, Greensboro, North Carolina, in 04/1865.

771. **Martin, John C.:** Resident of Georgia. Enlisted as a private in Company H on 09/03/1862 at Athens, Clarke County, Georgia. Absent without leave beginning 11/01/1863. Drew cash at hospital in November/December 1863 and January/February 1864. Last record September/October 1864, still absent without leave. His widow, Mrs. S.M. Martin, applied for a Confederate pension in White County, Georgia.

772. **Martin, Malachi Chappell:** 31-year-old. Born on 02/08/1831 in Jackson County, Georgia. Enlisted as a private in Company H on 03/12/1862 at Athens, Clarke County, Georgia. Sent to infirmary/recruiting camp on 11/12/1863. Was present on last muster roll, September/October 1864. Paroled at Athens, Clarke County, Georgia, on 05/08/1865.

773. **Mass [Maas], Richard L.:** 28-year-old. Enlisted as a private in Company I on 02/27/1862 at Augusta, Georgia. Value of horse $175. Captured in 11/1862 before 11/08/1862. Deserted and took the Oath on 11/08/1862.

774. **Mathews, C.W.:** Enlisted as a private in Company L on 05/10/1864 at Decatur, Georgia. Last record September/October 1864, sent to Georgia with Capt. Bostick to get a horse on 09/20/1864. There is a certificate of disability for discharge dated 09/12/1862 in his records, but it is so faded that the name could not be verified and the details could not be read.

775. **Mathews [Matthews], James H.:** 24-year-old. Enlisted as a private in Cobb's Legion Infantry, Company G, on 07/24/1861 at Madison, Morgan County, Georgia. Elected sergeant on 12/01/1861. Admitted to General Hospital No. 17, Richmond, Virginia. Returned to duty on 11/26/1862. Furnished Asbury A. Vaughn as a substitute on 12/20/1862. Enlisted in Cobb's Legion Cavalry, Company K, on 02/11/1864 at Decatur, Georgia. No horse in March/April 1864. Last record September/October 1864, sent to Georgia to get a horse with Capt. Bostick on 09/20/1864.

776. **Mattax [Mattox], John:** 17-year-old. Enlisted as a private in Company I on 03/01/1862 at Augusta, Georgia. Value of horse $175. Was listed as present in January/February 1863. On last record March/April 1863, it is not stated if he were present or absent.

777. **Matthews, John C.:** Enlisted as a corpo-

ral in Company D on 08/10/1861 at Albany, Georgia. Value of horse $225 and horse equipment $30. Listed as a private in November/December 1861. Furnished Cary J. Hopkins as a substitute on 12/06/1861.

778. Matthews, William J.A.: Resident of Georgia. Enlisted as a private in Company H on 03/27/1862 at Athens, Clarke County, Georgia. Value of horse equipment $50. Admitted to C.S.A. General Hospital, Danville, Virginia, on 08/06/1862 with debility. Returned to duty on 09/09/1862. Sent to infirmary/recruiting camp on 06/13/1864. Was surrendered by Gen. Joseph E. Johnston on 04/26/1865. Paroled at Greensboro, North Carolina, on 05/01/1865.

779. Mayo, Cranford M.: Planter from Dougherty County, Georgia. Born ca. 1825 in Pulaski County, Georgia. Enlisted as a private in the 15th Georgia Cavalry (State Guards). Listed on a roster of Company D published in *The History of Dougherty County*, but not with the *Civil War Soldiers and Sailors System*. No service record in Cobb's Legion. He and his wife, H.B., had at least one child. Buried in the Oakview Cemetery in Dougherty County, Georgia.

780. Mayo, J.J.: Listed on a roster of Company D published in *The History of Dougherty County*, but not with the *Civil War Soldiers and Sailors System*. Elected captain. No service records in Cobb's Legion.

781. Mayo, J.W.[G.]: Enlisted in Company D as a lieutenant on 08/10/1861 at Albany, Georgia. Value of horses $180 and $200 and horse equipment $30 and $25, one saddle furnished by State of Georgia. Resigned on 12/30/1861.

782. McAuliffe, John: 18-year-old from Georgia. Enlisted as a private in Company I on 03/24/1862 at Augusta, Georgia. Value of horse $150. Sent to recruiting/infirmary camp on 10/20/1863. Received a gunshot wound to his right arm on 10/27/1864. Admitted to General Hospital, Petersburg, Virginia, on 10/29/1864 where his arm was amputated at the elbow. Furloughed for 60 days on 11/18/1864. Last record, pay receipt received at Richmond, Virginia, dated 03/07/1865.

783. McBride, Robert Boyd: Farmer from Jefferson County, Georgia. Born ca. 1820 in Georgia. Enlisted as a lieutenant in Company F on 03/25/1862 at Burke County, Georgia. Value of horse $175. Transferred from Lynchburg to C.S.A. General Hospital, Danville, Virginia, on 08/22/1862 with debility. On sick furlough beginning 09/01/1862. Resigned in 01/1863. After the war, became a farmer in Jefferson County, Georgia. He and his wife, Delia, had at least six children. Died after 1880. Buried in the Boyd-McBride Cemetery in Burke County, Georgia.

784. McCale [McHale], John: 26-year-old from Georgia. Born on 06/10/1835 in Ireland. Enlisted as a private in Company I on 03/07/1862 at Augusta, Georgia. Value of horse $150. Captured on 06/24/1863 at Upperville, Virginia, and sent to Old Capitol Prison, Washington D.C. No date given for his release. Lost horse on 04/02/1864. Was surrendered by Gen. Joseph E. Johnston on 04/26/1865. Paroled at Greensboro, North Carolina, on 05/01/1865. After the war, lived in Wilkes County, Georgia. Applied for a Confederate pension in Wilkes County, Georgia. Died on 02/25/1913.

785. McCall [McColl], Henry Hugh: Resident of Georgia. Enlisted as a private in Company A on 08/17/1861 at Augusta, Georgia. Value of horse $150 and horse equipment $25. Sent to Georgia with Lt. James H. Johnson to purchase a horse on 04/18/1863. Detailed on scouting party with Lt. Shivers of the 2nd South Carolina Cavalry in Culpeper County, Virginia, on 12/14/1863. Captured at Plain View, Virginia, on 02/03/1864 and sent to Fort Norfolk. Transferred to Point Lookout, Maryland. Paroled 02/18/1865 and exchanged at Boulwares & Cox Wharf in the James River, Virginia, on 02/20–21/1865.

786. McCall, William H.: 21-year-old from Georgia. Enlisted as a private in Company E on 03/22/1862 at Roswell, Georgia. Value of horse $150. Appointed corporal on 04/22/1863. Absent sick behind enemy lines beginning 11/12/1863. Last record September/October 1864, still absent sick behind enemy lines. Applied for a Confederate pension in Douglas County, Georgia.

787. McCollum, Joseph P.C.: 20-year-old farm laborer from Dougherty County, Georgia. Born on 12/24/1840 in North Carolina. Brother of Josiah F. and Moses W. McCollum. Enlisted as a private in Company D on 08/10/1861 at Albany, Georgia. Value of horse $175 and horse equipment $15. Sent to Georgia with Capt. Bostick to get a horse on 09/20/1864. Was surrendered by Gen. Joseph E. Johnston on 04/26/1865. Paroled at Greensboro, North Carolina, on 05/01/1865. After the war became a farmer in Thomas County, Georgia. Married (1) Hannah (2) Lou. Was the father of at least two children. Applied for a Confederate pension in Thomas County, Georgia. Died after 1900.

788. McCollum [McCollom], Josiah F.: 22-year-old. Born on 09/08/1838 in Union County,

North Carolina. Brother of Joseph P.C. and Moses W. McCollum. Enlisted as a private in Company D on 08/10/1861 at Albany, Georgia. Detailed at fishery near Fredericksburg, Virginia, on 04/01/1864. Promoted to lieutenant on 01/01/1864. Was surrendered by Gen. Joseph E. Johnston on 04/26/1865. Paroled at Greensboro, North Carolina, on 05/01/1865.

789. **McCollum, Moses W.:** 20-year-old farm laborer from Dougherty County, Georgia. Born on 12/24/1840 in North Carolina. Brother of Josiah F. and Joseph P.C. McCollum. Enlisted as a private in Company D on 08/10/1861 at Albany, Georgia. Value of horse $200 and horse equipment $25, saddle furnished by State of Georgia. Given a medical discharge on 12/09/1861. Died in 12/1863.

790. **McCorkle, Mark:** Resident of Georgia. Enlisted as a private in Company D on 08/10/1861 at Albany, Georgia. Value of horse $250 and horse equipment $25, saddle furnished by State of Georgia. Admitted to Winder Hospital, Richmond, Virginia, on 09/25/1862. Furloughed for 25 days beginning 10/15/1862. Furloughed to Georgia for 24 days beginning 01/16/1864. Was surrendered by Gen. Joseph E. Johnston on 04/26/1865. Paroled at Greensboro, North Carolina, on 05/01/1865.

791. **McCoy, John:** Resident of Georgia. Enlisted as a private in Company G on 09/28/1863 at Atlanta, Georgia. Admitted to Jackson Hospital, Richmond, Virginia, on 04/30/1864 with erysipelas (an acute, infectious, streptococcus disease which causes inflammation of the skin). Returned to duty on 05/23/1864. Admitted to Jackson Hospital, Richmond, Virginia, on 08/17/1864 with chronic diarrhea. Returned to duty on 08/29/1864. Furloughed for 60 days beginning 09/04/1864. Was surrendered by Gen. Joseph E. Johnston on 04/26/1865. Paroled at Greensboro, North Carolina, on 05/01/1865.

792. **McCoy, John Milledge:** 37-year-old stock-minder in Burke County, Georgia. Born on 08/20/1824 in Burke County, Georgia. Enlisted as a private in Company F on 08/04/1862 at Burke County, Georgia, as a substitute for Jesse P. Green. On sick furlough in November/December 1862. Detailed as brigade butcher beginning 06/15/1863. Was surrendered by Gen. Joseph E. Johnston on 04/26/1865. Paroled at Greensboro, North Carolina, on 05/01/1865. Married Martha W. Perkins ca. 1852 and they had at least four children. Died on 04/09/1894. Buried in the Green Fork Baptist Church Cemetery in Jenkins County, Georgia.

793. **McCrary, Alex N.:** On a roster of Company C compiled by Glen Spurlock. No service records in Cobb's Legion.

794. **McCrary [McCreary], James M.:** Resident of Georgia. Enlisted as a private in Company C on 03/16/1862 at Athens, Georgia. Sent home to get a horse with Lt. Sinquefield under Special Order No. 27 from corps headquarters on 02/23/1864. Last record September/October 1864, sent to Georgia with Capt. Bostick to get a horse on 09/20/1864. After the war, lived in Fulton County, Georgia.

795. **McCroan [McCrone], Augustus Owen [C.]:** From Jefferson County, Georgia. Born ca. 1848 in Georgia. Enlisted as a private in Company F on 09/01/1862 at Burke County, Georgia, as a substitute for R.J. Peterson. Sent home to get a horse with Lt. Sinquefield under Special Order No. 27 from corps headquarters on 02/23/1864. Was surrendered by Gen. Joseph E. Johnston on 04/26/1865. Paroled at Greensboro, North Carolina, on 05/01/1865. After the war, became a farmer in Jefferson County, Georgia, and then in Eastland County, Texas. He and his wife had nine children. Died after 1910. His widow received a Confederate pension in Eastland County, Texas.

796. **McCroan [McCrone], Henry M.:** Student from Jefferson County, Georgia. Born ca. 1844 in Georgia. Enlisted as a private in Company F on 04/18/1862 at Burke County, Georgia. Horse, owned by Thomas A. Pierce, valued at $200. Detailed as a courier in October 1862. Wounded in the eye at Brandy Station, Virginia, on 06/09/1863. Admitted to C.S.A. General Hospital in Charlottesville, Virginia, on 06/10/1863. Furloughed for 40 days beginning 07/01/1863. Detailed in sub-enrolling office in Jefferson, Georgia, in November/December 1863. Sent to Georgia with Capt. Bostick to get a horse on 09/20/1864. Was surrendered by Gen. Joseph E. Johnston on 04/26/1865. Paroled at Greensboro, North Carolina, on 05/01/1865. Mentioned in Colonel Young's Report of the Battle of Brandy Station on 06/09/1863: "I desire also to mention the most distinguished gallantry of Privates McCroan and Landrum, who, on foot, refused to surrender when surrounded by the enemy, but cut their way through safely."* After the war, became a farmer in Jefferson County, Georgia. Married Fannie E. Lawrence on 06/20/1872 in Columbus, Muscogee County, Georgia. Died in 06/1885 in Columbus, Muscogee County, Georgia. His widow, Fannie E. McCroan, received a Confederate pension from Muscogee County, Georgia.

*OR, Series 1, Vol. 27, pt. 2, pages 732–733.

797. McCroan, John J.: Student from Jefferson County, Georgia. Born ca. 1841 in Georgia. On a roster of Company F in *Roster of the Confederate Soldiers of Burke County, Georgia: 1861–1865*. No service records in Cobb's Legion.

798. McCullough [McCollough], W.H. [W.J.] [B.H.]: Resident of Georgia. Enlisted as a private in Company A on 11/07/1861 at Augusta, Georgia. Admitted to C.S.A. General Hospital, Charlottesville, Virginia, on 12/02/1862. Returned to duty on 12/11/1862. Admitted to C.S.A. General Hospital, Charlottesville, Virginia, on 01/20/1863 with haemophisis (spitting blood). Returned to duty on 02/16/1863. Detailed on a scouting party with Lt. Shivers of the 2nd South Carolina Cavalry in Culpeper County, Virginia, 12/15/1863–12/17/1863. Admitted to Jackson Hospital, Richmond, Virginia, on 02/28/1864 with pneumonia. Admitted to Jackson Hospital, Richmond, Virginia, on 03/29/1864 with typhoid fever. Returned to duty on 04/12/1864. Admitted to Jackson Hospital, Richmond, Virginia, on 06/18/1864 with chronic diarrhea. Returned to duty on 06/21/1864. Sent to Georgia with Capt. Bostick to get a horse on 09/20/1864. Admitted to General Hospital No. 9, Richmond, Virginia, on 03/12/1865. Last record, furloughed for 30 days beginning 03/14/1865.

799. McCullough, W.V.: Enlisted as a lieutenant in Company E. Was a patient in Jackson Hospital, Richmond, Virginia, on 03/18/1864. Paroled at Augusta, Georgia, on 05/24/1865.

800. McCullum, James N.: Enlisted as a private in Company D on or before 09/01/1861. Value of horse $200 and horse equipment $25, furnished by State of Georgia. Died on 10/21/1861 at Yorktown, Virginia. His father, Daniel W. McCullum, of Baker County, Georgia, received his back pay, as he was not survived by a wife or children.

801. McCullum, John: Listed on a roster of Company D in *The History of Dougherty County*, but not with the *Civil War Soldiers and Sailors System*. No service records in Cobb's Legion.

802. McCune [McCun], John L.: Enlisted as a private in Company K on 05/02/1864 at Decatur, Georgia. Admitted to General Hospital No. 2, Wilson, North Carolina, on 09/03/1864 with malaria. Died on 09/19/1864. His father, John McCune, of Clarke County, Georgia, received his back pay.

803. McCurry, M. Rufus [Rufus R.] [K.R.]: Resident of Georgia. Enlisted as a private in Company C on 03/12/1862 at Athens, Clarke County, Georgia. Captured on 06/11/1864 at Trevilian Station. Sent to Fortress Monroe, Virginia, on 06/20/1864. Transferred to Elmira Prison, New York, on 07/25/1864. Died on 10/11/1864 of chronic diarrhea at Elmira Prison Camp, New York. Buried in Woodlawn Cemetery in Elmira, New York.

804. McCurry, S. Marcus: 18-year-old from Georgia. Born on 08/14/1843 in North Carolina. Enlisted as a private in Company C on 08/01/1861 at Athens, Clarke County, Georgia. Detailed as a forage master on 05/07/1863. Detailed as a scout on 08/25/1864. Was absent scouting on last record, September/October 1864. After the war, became a farmer in Lumpkin County, Georgia, and then moved to Jackson County, Georgia. Married Sarah E. on 12/24/1865 in Lumpkin County, Georgia, and they had at least four children. Applied for a Confederate pension in Jackson County, Georgia. Died on 03/25/1915. Buried at the Concord Baptist Creek Cemetery, Hall County, Georgia. His widow applied for a Confederate pension in Hall County, Georgia, from 1916 to 1929.

805. McCurry, Thomas J.: 20-year-old from Georgia. Enlisted as a private in Company C on 08/01/1861 at Athens, Clarke County, Georgia. Detailed as forage receiver in 01/1862. Listed as a sergeant in September/October 1862. Listed as a private in November/December 1863. Sent to recruiting/infirmary camp on 02/23/1864. Last record September/October 1864, sent to Georgia with Capt. Bostick to get a horse on 09/20/1864.

806. McDade, Robert F.: Stonecutter from Augusta, Georgia. Born ca. 1843 in Georgia. Enlisted as a private in Company A on 08/17/1861 at Augusta, Georgia. Value of horse $175 and horse equipment $30. Discharged on 10/12/1861 at Yorktown, Virginia. The Muster Roll Commission lists him as being permanently detailed with the Southern Express Company. After the war, worked as a fireman on the Georgia Railroad. Married LeAnna Evans and was the father of at least one child.

807. McDaniel, W.: Enlisted as a private in Company D on 03/04/1862 at Albany, Georgia. His only service record is dated 05/07/1862.

808. McDaniel [McDonald], William H.: 20-year-old from Atlanta, Georgia. Enlisted as a private in Company B on 05/06/1862 at Atlanta, Georgia. Value of horse $175 and horse equipment $5. Sent to Georgia to get a horse with Lt. James H. Johnson on 04/14/1863. Sent home to get a horse with Lt. Sinquefield under Special Order No. 27 from corps headquarters on 02/23/1864. Captured at King George County, Virginia, on 05/13/1864 and sent to Belle Plain, Virginia. Transferred to Elmira Prison, New York, on 07/03/1864. Released on 06/21/1865. Described as having a dark complexion, dark hair, blue eyes, and being 5'10" tall.

809. McDaniel, William J.: 28-year-old from Georgia. Enlisted as a private in Company G on 04/19/1862 (or 03/22/1862) at Atlanta, Georgia. Sent to Georgia to get a horse with Lt. James H. Johnson on 04/14/1863. Sent home to get a horse with Lt. Sinquefield under Special Order No. 27 from corps headquarters on 02/23/1864. Admitted to Jackson Hospital, Richmond, Virginia, on 06/13/1864 with dysentery and hemorrhoids. Returned to duty on 06/22/1864. Last record September/October 1864, sent to Georgia with Capt. Bostick to get a horse on 09/20/1864.

810. McDermont, Marcus [Marquis] L.: 20-year-old. Enlisted as a sergeant in Company E on 03/15/1862 at Roswell, Georgia. Value of horse $150. Given a medical furlough for 60 days beginning 11/13/1862. Last known rank was lieutenant. Died on 10/01/1863 from wounds received in battle. His widow, Rebecca McDermont, received his back pay.

811. McDonald, W.: Enlisted as a private in Company D on 03/02/1862 at Albany, Georgia. Died on 07/07/1862.

812. McElhanon [McElhannon, McAlhennon], George W.: Farmer from Jackson County, Georgia. Born ca. 1832. Enlisted as a private in Company H on 03/04/1862 at Athens, Clarke County, Georgia. Listed in May/June 1862 as a sergeant. Captured on 08/05/1862 at Malvern Hill, Virginia. Paroled at Fort Wool, Virginia, on 08/26/1862. On provost duty on 02/23/1864. Died on 08/11/1864 at a General Hospital No. 8, Raleigh, North Carolina, from chronic diarrhea. Buried at Oakwood Cemetery in Raleigh, North Carolina. Married Mary Trout on 02/01/1854 in Jackson County, Georgia, and they had at least two children.

813. McGinness, Edward: About 22 years old. Born in Alleghany County, Maryland. Enlisted as a private in Company K. Captured at Upperville, Virginia, on 06/21/1863 and sent to the Old Capitol Prison, Washington, D.C. Deserted and took the Oath.

814. McJunkin, James: 28-year-old. Enlisted as a private in Company K on 02/09/1863 at Camp Maynard, Georgia. Returned to his regiment on 02/21/1863.

815. McJunkin, Thomas: 26-year-old. Enlisted as a private in Company K on 02/09/1863 at Camp Maynard, Georgia. Returned to his regiment on 02/21/1863.

816. McKnight, E.: Enlisted as a private in Company I. Wounded, captured, and paroled at Crampton's Pass, Maryland, on 09/14/1862.

817. McLelland [McLellan], D.: Farmer from Worth County, Georgia. Enlisted as a private in Company D on 08/10/1861 at Albany, Georgia. Value of horse $150 and horse equipment $25. Last record, November/December 1861 states that he was confined sick with rheumatism.

818. McNair, James M.: Resident of Georgia. Enlisted as a private in Company G on 07/03/1861 at Atlanta, Georgia. Sent to Georgia to get a horse on 11/10/1863. Sent home to get a horse with Lt. Sinquefield under Special Order No. 27 from corps headquarters on 02/23/1864. Absent without leave beginning 05/01/1864. Deserted and took the Oath. Described as having a dark complexion, black hair, hazel eyes, and being 5' 6" tall.

819. McWhorter, David S. [D.F.]: Resident of Georgia. Enlisted as a private in Company H on 03/18/1862 at Athens, Clarke County, Georgia. On provost duty beginning 12/15/1863. Sent to Georgia with Capt. Bostick to get a horse on 09/20/1864. Was surrendered by Gen. Joseph E. Johnston on 04/26/1865. Paroled at Greensboro, North Carolina, on 05/01/1865.

820. Mead, Lemuel S.: Enlisted as a private in Company B on 08/14/1861 at Atlanta, Georgia. Value of horse $250 and horse equipment $25. Detailed as a courier for Col. Cobb in November/December 1861. Provided Henry North as a substitute and was discharged on 02/03/1862.

821. Meaders [Meders], Barney R.: Born ca. 1831 in Georgia. Enlisted as a private in Company H on 06/01/1864 in Dahlonega, Georgia. Last record September/October 1864, sent to Georgia with Capt. Bostick to get a horse on 09/20/1864. After the war, lived in Lumpkin County, Georgia. Applied for a Confederate pension in Lumpkin County, Georgia.

822. Means, Samuel D.: Resident of Mill Creek, Banks County, Georgia. Enlisted as a private in Company C on 03/14/1862 at Athens, Clarke County, Georgia. Transferred to Company H. Died at General Hospital No. 13 in Richmond, Virginia, on 09/07/1862 of typhoid fever complicated by inflammation of kidneys and pneumonia.

823. Meldon [Melden], J.J.: From Dougherty County, Georgia. Born ca. 1817 in Ireland. Enlisted as a private in Company D on 08/10/1861 at Albany, Georgia. Value of horse $200 and horse equipment $20. Detailed as a blacksmith in November/December 1861. Detailed as a veterinary surgeon for company in November/December 1862. Admitted to Winder Hospital, Richmond, Virginia, on 11/01/1863. Detailed in the Adjutant and Inspector General's Office in 01/1864. Admitted to Jackson Hospital, Richmond, Virginia, on 03/26/1864 with bronchitis. Last record dated 09/09/1864, still detailed at Richmond, Virginia.

824. Melton, J.H.: Resident of Georgia. Enlisted as a private in Company D on 08/10/1861 at Albany, Georgia. Value of horse $100 and horse equipment $15. Admitted to C.S.A. General Hospital, Charlottesville, Virginia, on 01/09/1863 with typhoid fever. Returned to duty on 02/05/1863. Was sent home to get a horse in March/April 1863. Detailed as an ambulance driver beginning 11/17/1863. Was surrendered by Gen. Joseph E. Johnston on 04/26/1865. Paroled at Greensboro, North Carolina, on 05/01/1865.

825. Merchant, Rufus B.: Possibly 23 years old, from Georgia. Enlisted as a private in Company A on 08/17/1861 at Augusta, Georgia. Value of horse $140 and horse equipment $25. Detailed as a scout 09/01/1863 by order of Gen. Wade Hampton. Surrendered at Augusta, Georgia, and paroled on 05/26/1865. Possibly Rufus Bainbridge Merchant, born in Prince William, Virginia, on 04/02/1838. After the war, became the editor of the *Fredericksburg Star* in Fredericksburg, Virginia. Married Henrietta Wina Mills on 04/03/1866 at Fredericksburg, Virginia, and was the father of nine children. Died on 10/06/1905 and is buried in the Fredericksburg City Cemetery, Fredericksburg, Virginia. His tombstone says, "A Brave Confederate Soldier."

826. Merriman [Merryman], Montague: From Georgia. Born ca. 1832. Enlisted as a private in Company D on 08/10/1861 at Albany, Georgia. Value of horse $200 and horse equipment $25. Bridle furnished by State of Georgia. Absent with horses and promoted to sergeant in March/April 1863. Detailed to company commissary beginning 08/13/1863. Sent to Georgia with Capt. Bostick to get a horse on 09/20/1864. Was surrendered by Gen. Joseph E. Johnston on 04/26/1865. Paroled at Greensboro, North Carolina, on 05/01/1865.

827. Mershew, W.W.: Enlisted as a private in Company D. Died of disease on 02/25/1862.

828. Milhollen, D.: Enlisted in Company L on 05/11/1864 at Decatur, Georgia. Absent without leave beginning 05/12/1864. Still absent without leave on last record, September/October 1864.

829. Miller, Edwin J.: Resident of Georgia. Enlisted as a private in Company D on 05/12/1862 at Albany, Jasper County, Georgia. Absent sick, never reported for duty, January/February 1864. Admitted to City Hall Hospital, Macon, Georgia, on 03/28/1864. Admitted to Jackson Hospital, Richmond, Virginia, on 08/21/1864. Last record 11/01/1864, absent sick, never reported for duty.

830. Miller, John J.: 17-year-old native of Georgia. Enlisted as a private in Company F on 03/25/1862 at Burke County, Georgia. Value of horse $225. Admitted to Winder Hospital, Richmond, Virginia, on 09/25/1863. Admitted to Jackson Hospital, Richmond, Virginia, on 01/26/1864 with scabies. Returned to duty on 02/02/1864. Sent home to get a horse with Lt. Sinquefield under Special Order No. 27 from corps headquarters on 02/23/1864. Admitted to Jackson Hospital on 08/17/1864 with chronic diarrhea. Returned to duty on 08/25/1864. Sent to Georgia with Capt. Bostick to get a horse on 09/20/1864. Was surrendered by Gen. Joseph E. Johnston on 04/26/1865. Paroled at Greensboro, North Carolina, on 05/01/1865.

831. Miller, Josiah: Born ca. 1843 in Burke County, Georgia. Enlisted in 1st Georgia Infantry, Company D, as a private on 03/18/1861. Mustered out at Augusta, Georgia, on 03/18/1862. Enlisted as a private in Cobb's Legion Cavalry, Company I, on 04/14/1862 at Augusta, Georgia. Detailed as a courier for Gen. Stuart beginning 09/14/1862. Horse valued at $200 killed in action on 09/22/1862 at Williamsport, Maryland. Captured at Beverly's Ford, Virginia, on 06/09/1863 and sent to the Old Capitol Prison, Washington, D.C. Paroled on 06/25/1863. Sent home to get a horse with Lt. Sinquefield under Special Order No. 27 from corps headquarters on 02/23/1864. Last record September/October 1864, sent to Georgia with Capt. Bostick to get a horse on 09/20/1864. After the war, became a grocer in Richmond County, Georgia. Married on 01/15/1868 to Richardine Hayes in Richmond County, Georgia. Applied for a Confederate pension in Richmond County, Georgia. Died on 01/20/1910 in Richmond County, Georgia. Buried in the Magnolia Cemetery in Richmond County, Georgia.

832. Miller, Thomas K.: 19-year-old. Enlisted as a private in Company I on 03/19/1862 at Augusta, Georgia. Value of horse $175. It is not stated if he was present on his last record, 05/01/1862.

833. Millican, Lewis A.: 22-year-old from Georgia. Enlisted as a private in Company E on 04/09/1862 at Lawrenceville, Georgia. Value of horse $185 and horse equipment $30. On furlough beginning 02/19/1864. Was surrendered by Gen. Joseph E. Johnston on 04/26/1865. Paroled at Greensboro, North Carolina, on 05/01/1865.

834. Milligan [Miligan, Millican], Joseph C.: Resident of Georgia. Enlisted as a private in Company H on 07/10/1863 in Stevensburg, Virginia. Sent to Georgia with Capt. Bostick to get a horse on 09/20/1864. Was surrendered by Gen. Joseph

E. Johnston on 04/26/1865. Paroled at Greensboro, North Carolina, on 05/01/1865. Applied for a Confederate pension in Crisp County, Georgia.

835. Mills, James W.: 28-year-old from Georgia. Enlisted as a private in Company E on 04/09/1862 at Lawrenceville, Georgia. Detailed as a hospital steward beginning 06/25/1862. Sent to Georgia with Capt. Bostick to get a horse on 09/20/1864. Was surrendered by Gen. Joseph E. Johnston on 04/26/1865. Paroled at Greensboro, North Carolina, on 05/01/1865. A letter in his records from a surgeon said that he was "possessed of steady habits and unimpeachable moral character." The letter also mentioned "his complimentary gallant conduct on the battlefield" and "his prompt and unwearying attentions to the wounded." After the war, lived in Fulton County, Georgia. Applied for a Confederate pension in Fulton County, Georgia.

836. Mills, William Hugh: Resident of Yellow River, Georgia. Born in Georgia. Enlisted in 7th Georgia Volunteer Infantry, Company E, as a private on 07/17/1861. Transferred to Cobb's Legion Cavalry, Company B, on 08/11/1861 at Decatur, Georgia. Received a gunshot wound in his right thigh at Culpeper, Virginia, on 09/13/1863. Furloughed for 40 days beginning 09/15/1863. Detailed in Medical Department on 03/05/1864. Was surrendered by Gen. Joseph E. Johnston on 04/26/1865. Paroled at Greensboro, North Carolina, on 05/01/1865.

837. Millsaps, W.W.: Enlisted as a private in Company L on 05/03/1864 at Decatur, Georgia. Last record September/October 1864, sent to Georgia with Capt. Bostick to get a horse on 09/20/1864.

838. Mince, Newton A.[M.]: Enlisted as a private in Company C on 05/11/1862 at Athens, Georgia. Sent home to get a horse with Lt. Sinquefield under Special Order No. 27 from corps headquarters on 02/23/1864. Admitted to a hospital on 07/15/1862. Last record, furloughed 30 days from General Hospital No. 14, Richmond, Virginia, beginning 10/25/1862.

839. Minchen [Minchew], W.: Enlisted as a private in Company D on 08/10/1861 at Albany, Georgia. Value of horse $175 and horse equipment $15, bridle furnished by State of Georgia. Absent sick on last record in November/December 1861.

840. Minchener [Minchiner], Joseph: 25-year-old native of Georgia. Enlisted as a private in Company F on 03/25/1862 at Burke County, Georgia. Value of horse $175 and horse equipment $35. Detailed to work in Jones Wodley & Co. Mill in Herndon, Georgia, without pay from government, beginning January/February 1863. Admitted to hospital at Hanover Junction, Virginia, on 01/05/1864. Admitted to Jackson Hospital, Richmond, Virginia, with pneumonia on 01/21/1864. Admitted to Jackson Hospital, Richmond, Virginia, with pneumonia on 03/20/1864. Returned to duty on 03/29/1864. Transferred to C.S.A. Navy on 04/25/1864.

841. Mitchell, Henry Alex: 22-year-old from Georgia. Born on 03/23/1841 in Georgia. Brother of William P. Mitchell. Enlisted 1st Georgia Infantry, Company F, as a private in 03/18/1861. Mustered out at Augusta, Georgia, on 03/18/1862. Enlisted as a private in Cobb's Legion Cavalry, Company G, on 04/05/1862 at Atlanta, Georgia. Value of horse $190. Detailed as a courier to Gen. Cobb in November/December 1862. Horse killed in action at the Battle of Fredericksburg on 12/13/1862. Sent to Georgia to get a horse on 11/10/1863. Sent home to get a horse with Lt. Sinquefield under Special Order No. 27 from corps headquarters on 02/23/1864. Was surrendered by Gen. Joseph E. Johnston on 04/26/1865. Paroled at Greensboro, North Carolina, on 05/01/1865. After the war, became a cotton merchant in Fulton County, Georgia. Died on 01/04/1901 or 1907. Buried in Oakland Cemetery in Fulton County, Georgia.

842. Mitchell, John E.: From Bells, Cherokee County, Georgia. Born ca. 1843 in Georgia. Enlisted as a private in Company E on 03/22/1862 at Roswell, Georgia. Value of horse $150. Killed in battle at Barbee's Cross Roads, Virginia, on 11/05/1862. His back pay was given to Martha Ann Mitchell.

843. Mitchell, Roland P.: Resident of Fulton County, Georgia. Enlisted as a private in Company E on 03/15/1862 at Roswell, Georgia. Value of horse $160. Detailed as a teamster beginning 12/01/1863. Admitted to Episcopal Church Hospital in Williamsburg, Virginia, on 07/13/1864 with lumbago. Admitted to Episcopal Church Hospital, Williamsburg, Virginia, on 08/14/1864 with chronic diarrhea. Returned to duty on 08/27/1864. Sent to Georgia with Capt. Bostick to get a horse on 09/20/1864. Was surrendered by Gen. Joseph E. Johnston on 04/26/1865. Paroled at Greensboro, North Carolina, on 05/01/1865.

844. Mitchell, Thomas J.: 39-year-old from Georgia. Enlisted as a private in Company E on 04/09/1862 at Lawrenceville, Georgia. Value of horse $140. Wounded at Jack's Shop on 09/22/1863. Admitted to Winder Hospital, Richmond, Virginia, on 09/25/1863. Lost horse on 10/01/1863. Last record September/October 1864, still absent wounded. After the war, lived in Gwinnett County, Georgia. Applied for a Confederate pension in Gwinnett County, Georgia.

845. Mitchell, W.S.: From Georgia. Born ca. 1838. Enlisted as a private in the infantry on 05/31/1861 at Atlanta, Georgia. Transferred to Cobb's Legion Cavalry Company E on 06/01/1864 in exchange for A.M. Quarles. Last record September/October 1864, sent to Georgia with Capt. Bostick to get a horse on 09/20/1864. After the war, lived in Polk County and then Bartow County, Georgia. Applied for a Confederate pension in Polk County, Georgia. Transferred it to Bartow County, Georgia. Received a Confederate pension in Bartow County from 1901 through 1907.

846. Mitchell, William P.: 17-year-old. Born on 10/18/1846 in Henry County, Georgia. Brother of Henry Alex Mitchell. Enlisted as a private in Company G on 05/22/1864 at Atlanta, Georgia. Sent to Georgia with Capt. Bostick to get a horse on 09/20/1864. Was surrendered by Gen. Joseph E. Johnston on 04/26/1865. Paroled at Greensboro, North Carolina, on 05/01/1865. After the war, worked in the cotton business in Fulton County, Georgia. Died on 08/24/1901. Buried in the Oakland Cemetery in Fulton County, Georgia.

847. Mock, George W.: From Georgia. Born ca. 1844. Enlisted as a private in Company D on 08/10/1861 at Albany, Georgia. Value of horse $150 and horse equipment $25, saddle furnished by State of Georgia. Wounded on 11/28/1863. Admitted to C.S.A. General Hospital, Charlottesville, Virginia, on 12/01/1863. Furloughed to Georgia for 60 days beginning 12/28/1863. Sent to Georgia with Capt. Bostick to get a horse on 09/20/1864. Was surrendered by Gen. Joseph E. Johnston on 04/26/1865. Paroled at Greensboro, North Carolina, on 05/01/1865. After the war, lived in Dougherty County, Georgia. Applied for a Confederate pension in Dougherty County, Georgia. Died after 1913.

848. Mollere [Mollier], J.F.: Enlisted as a private in Company L on 11/19/1863 at Orange Court House, Virginia. Captured on 11/25/1863. No further records.

849. Montgomery, George Cicero: 31-year-old. Born 08/13/1830. Enlisted as a private in Company B on 08/14/1861 at Atlanta, Georgia. Value of horse $250. Horse equipment furnished by company. Died on 11/01/1863.

850. Montgomery, Joseph: Enlisted in 1st Georgia Infantry, Company F, as a private on 08/01/1861. Mustered out at Augusta, Georgia, on 03/18/1862. On a roster of Company G compiled by Glen Spurlock. No service records in Cobb's Legion.

851. Moon, George M.D.: Student from Jackson County, Georgia. Born in Jackson County, Georgia, ca. 1843. Brother of Thomas J. Moon. Enlisted as a private in Company C on 04/01/1862 at Athens, Georgia. Sent to Stony Creek recruiting/infirmary camp beginning 10/12/1864. Captured at Stony Creek on 12/01/1864 and sent to City Point, Virginia. Transferred to Point Lookout, Maryland. Released on 06/29/1864. Described as having a light complexion, brown hair, hazel eyes, and being 5'10" tall. After the war, became a farmer in Jackson County, Georgia. Was married. Died after 1880.

852. Moon, Thomas J.: Student from Jackson County, Georgia. Born ca. 1841 in Georgia. Brother of George M.D. Moon. Enlisted as a private in Company C on 04/01/1862 at Athens, Georgia. Sent home to get a horse on 11/10/1863. Admitted to Jackson Hospital, Richmond, Virginia, on 06/02/1864 with rheumatism. Returned to duty on 06/17/1864. Last record, sent to Georgia with Capt. Bostick to get a horse on 09/20/1864. After the war, lived in Jackson County, Georgia. Married Ella Randolph and they had at least seven children. His widow received a Confederate pension in Jackson County, Georgia.

853. Moony [Mooney], James: Resident of Georgia. Enlisted as a private in Company K on 02/08/1863 at Camp Maynard, Georgia. Admitted to Winder Hospital, Richmond, Virginia, with a wound on 10/16/1863. Furloughed for 30 days beginning 12/04/1863. Sent to recruiting/infirmary camp beginning 02/23/1864. Deserted on 05/25/1864.

854. Moore, J.J.: Enlisted as a private in Company K on 05/10/1864 at Augusta, Georgia. Admitted to hospital on 08/18/1864. Last record, sent to Georgia with Capt. Bostick to get a horse on 09/20/1864.

855. Moore, John: Listed as a private in Company F in *Roster of the Confederate Soldiers of Burke County, Georgia: 1861–1865*. No service records in Cobb's Legion.

856. Moore, John: Enlisted as a private in Company L on 12/17/1863 at Fredericksburg, Virginia. Transferred to the Navy Department before 05/21/1864.

857. Moore, John A.: Resident of Georgia. Enlisted as a private in Company H on 04/03/1862 at Atlanta, Georgia. Admitted to C.S.A. General Hospital in Charlottesville, Virginia, on 06/14/1862 with typhoid fever. Returned to duty on 07/07/1862. Admitted to Chimborazo Hospital No. 2, Richmond, Virginia, on 01/09/1863 with pneumonia. Returned to duty on 01/11/1863. Sent to infirmary/recruiting camp beginning 01/08/1864. Admitted to Winder Hospital, Richmond, Virginia, on 01/14/1864 with chronic diarrhea. Returned to duty on 01/21/1864. Captured on 06/11/1864 at Louisa Court House (Trevilian Station) and sent to Fort Monroe, Virginia. Transferred to Point Lookout, Maryland, on 06/20/1864, and then to Elmira Prison, New York, on 07/25/1864. Died on 01/10/1865 of pneumonia. Buried in the Woodlawn Cemetery in Elmira, New York.

858. Moore, Joseph A.: Resident of Murry County, Georgia. Enlisted as a private in Company C on 03/04/1862 at Thomas County, Georgia. Deserted and took the Oath on 04/17/1865 at Chattanooga, Tennessee. Was paroled at Louisville, Kentucky, to remain north of the Ohio River during the war. Described as having a fair complexion, dark hair, brown eyes, and being 5'10" tall.

859. Moore, Joseph L.: 27-year-old from Georgia. Born on 01/26/1835. Enlisted as a private in Company G on 04/28/1862 at Atlanta, Georgia. Value of horse $225. Listed as a corporal in May/June 1862. Captured 10/20/1862 at Georgetown, Virginia. Paroled at Fort McHenry, Maryland, on 11/03/1862. Promoted to sergeant on 11/21/1862. In November/December was elected lieutenant in a Georgia company and reduced to private in Cobb's Legion until his discharge because of his absence. Married Sarah Louise Rogers on 04/14/1864 in Forsyth County, Georgia. Died on 12/26/1917. His widow, Sarah A. Moore, received a Confederate pension in Gwinnett County, Georgia.

860. Moore, Richard: Born ca. 1831. Enlisted as a private in Company C on 08/01/1861 at Athens, Clarke County, Georgia. On sick furlough to Georgia in 12/1861. Courier for the telegraph office beginning in 01/1862. Horse died on 08/15/1862. Moore transferred to Troup Artillery on 01/15/1863. Admitted to General Hospital, Howard's Grove, Richmond, Virginia, on 05/09/1863 with a wound in his right foot. Died on 07/03/1863 at General Hospital, Howard's Grove, Richmond, Virginia, of acute dysentery. Buried in the Oakwood Cemetery in Richmond, Virginia.

861. Moore, William C.: 19-year-old from Georgia. Enlisted as a private in Company G on 04/28/1862 at Atlanta, Georgia. Value of horse $180. Sent to Georgia to get a horse with Lt. James H. Johnson on 04/14/1863. Furloughed for 24 days in 03/1864. Was present on last record in September/October 1864.

862. Moran, John J.: About 17 years old. Enlisted as a private in Company L on 03/21/1864 at Waynesboro, Burke County, Georgia. Sent to Georgia with Capt. Bostick to get a horse on 09/20/1864. Deserted on 01/17/1865 at Hilton Head Island, South Carolina, and sent to New York City on the steamer *Fulton*. He may have been a prisoner of war at the time, as there was a notorious Federal prison-of-war camp on Hilton Head Island where prisoners were being deliberately starved in retaliation for the Andersonville Prison Camp. He gave his age as 19 and his residence as Virginia when he deserted and was described as having a light complexion, dark hair, dark eyes, and being 5'4½" tall.

863. Morgan, Daniel: Enlisted as a private in Company G on 04/18/1864 at Atlanta, Georgia. Sent to Georgia with Capt. Bostick to get a horse on 09/20/1864. Was surrendered by Gen. Joseph E. Johnston on 04/26/1865. Paroled at Greensboro, North Carolina, on 05/01/1865.

864. Morgan, Hampton W.: Enlisted as a private in Company B on 02/20/1862 at Atlanta, Georgia. Value of horse $175. Discharged and paid off on 07/19/1862 at Camp Meadow, Virginia.

865. Morris, Edwin Pierce [Pearce]: From Appling, Columbia County, Georgia. Born ca. 1846 in Georgia. Enlisted as a private in Company A on 02/01/1863 at Augusta, Georgia, as a substitute for James W. Boyd. Last record September/October 1864, sent to Georgia with Capt. Bostick to get a horse on 09/20/1864. On his Confederate Pension Application, he stated that he had been given a thirty-day furlough to go home and get a horse. Was on his way back to the army when he met members of his company, and he found they had surrendered before his thirty days were out. After the war he became a farmer. Was married and the father of at least three children. Died on 12/27/1922. His wife, Ida, died on 04/01/1954, the last Confederate pensioner for Columbia County.

866. Morris, Elisha F.: About 31 years old, a farmer. Born in Habersham County, Georgia. Enlisted as a private in Company H on 03/03/1862 at Athens, Clarke County, Georgia. Listed in May/June 1862 as a corporal. On furlough beginning 07/01/1862. Returned to duty on 11/01/1862. Admitted to Chimborazo Hospital No. 4, Richmond, Virginia, and given a medical furlough for 40 days beginning 11/02/1862. Discharged from service on 10/08/1863 in Madison County, Virginia, due to a gunshot wound which caused him to lose the use of his left arm. Described as having a fair complexion, blue eyes, dark hair, and being 5'11" tall.

867. Morris, O.: Captured near Madison Court House, Virginia (the Battle of Jack's Shop), on

09/23/1863. There is no record of his being released or taking the Oath. He may have died as a prisoner of war.

868. **Morris, Robert Stockton:** Born ca. 1838 in Georgia. Enlisted as a private in Company B on 08/14/1861 at Atlanta, Georgia. Value of horse $200 and horse equipment $11, saddle furnished by State of Georgia. Admitted to College Hospital in Williamsburg, Virginia, in November/December 1861. Lost horse on 03/15/1863. Sent to Georgia to get a horse on 04/01/1863. Lost horse on 09/22/1863. Captured at Jack's Shop, Virginia, on 09/22/1863 and sent to Washington, D.C. Transferred to Elmira Prison, New York, on 08/16/1864. Paroled 03/10/1865 and sent to the James River in Virginia to be exchanged. After the war, became a farmer in Columbia County, Georgia, and was married. Applied for a Confederate pension in Columbia County, Georgia.

869. **Moseley, Benjamin R.:** 19-year-old. Enlisted as a private in Company C on 08/01/1861 at Athens, Georgia. Transferred to Company F on 06/01/1862. Given furlough of indulgence for 30 days beginning 02/19/1864. Last record September/October 1864, under surgical treatment in Florida for dementia since 02/19/1864.

870. **Moseley, John D.:** Enlisted as a private in Company L on 12/15/1862 at Burke County. Sent to Georgia with Capt. Bostick to get a horse on 09/20/1864. Paroled at Augusta, Georgia, on 05/13/1865. After the war, lived in Bibb County, Georgia. Applied for a Confederate pension in Bibb County, Georgia.

871. **Moss, J. Winchester:** 24-year-old from Georgia. Enlisted as a private in Company E on 03/15/1862 at Roswell, Georgia. Value of horse $125. Horse valued at $400 killed in action at Culpeper Court House, Virginia, on 09/13/1863. Moss sent home to get a horse on 11/12/1863. Last record September/October 1864, sent to Georgia with Capt. Bostick to get a horse on 09/20/1864.

872. **Moxley, Green Young:** 17-year-old. Born in 03/1845 in Georgia. Enlisted as a private in Company F on 03/25/1862 at Burke County, Georgia. Value of horse $125. Last record September/October 1864, sent to Georgia with Capt. Bostick to get a horse on 09/20/1864. Married Margaret Jane Williams on 11/12/1884 in Travis County, Texas, and they had at least two children. Received a Confederate pension from Bexar County, Texas. Died on 11/08/1911 in Hamilton County, Texas.

873. **Moxley, Newton J.:** Resident of Jefferson County, Georgia. Enlisted as a private in Company F on 05/09/1862 at Burke County, Georgia. On sick furlough 09/1862–02/1863. Transferred to Company L on 03/01/1863. Admitted to Jackson Hospital, Richmond, Virginia, on 01/07/1864 with kidney disease. Furloughed for 30 days beginning 02/03/1864. Listed as a farrier beginning 03/01/1864. Last record September/October 1864, sent to Georgia with Capt. Bostick to get a horse on 09/20/1864.

874. **Murdock, Charles A.:** Born ca. 1843 in Georgia. Enlisted as a private in Company E on 04/14/1862 at Atlanta, Georgia. Last service record dated 04/27/1862. After the war, lived in Burke County, Georgia.

875. **Murdock, Thomas M.:** 19-year-old native of Georgia. Enlisted as a private in Company F on 03/25/1862 at Burke County, Georgia. Value of horse $150. Captured near Brandy Station, Virginia, on 10/12/1863 and sent to the Old Capitol Prison in Washington, D.C. Exchanged 03/03/1864. Sent to Georgia with Capt. Bostick to get a horse on 09/20/1864. Was surrendered by Gen. Joseph E. Johnston on 04/26/1865. Paroled at Greensboro, North Carolina, on 05/01/1865.

876. **Murphee [Murphree], Augustus Wright:** 30-year-old. Born on 05/28/1831 in Georgia. Enlisted in 3rd Georgia Infantry. Company A as a private on 04/26/1861. Transferred to Cobb's Legion Cavalry, Company F on 03/25/1862. Value of horse $225. On sick furlough in September/October 1862. Detailed as a nurse March–May 1863. Sent home to get a horse with Lt. Sinquefield under Special Order No. 27 from corps headquarters on 02/23/1864. Last record September/October 1864, sent to Georgia with Capt. Bostick to get a horse on 09/20/1864. Married Eliza T. Jordan on 06/11/1857 in Jefferson County, Georgia. Died on 12/29/1883. Buried in the Midville Cemetery in Burke County, Georgia.

877. **Murphey, Moses Collins [G.]:** 23-year-old native of Georgia. Enlisted as a private in Company F on 04/30/1862 at Burke County, Georgia. Value of horse $200. Detailed as a courier beginning 06/01/1864. Was surrendered by Gen. Joseph E. Johnston on 04/26/1865. Paroled at Greensboro, North Carolina, on 05/01/1865.

878. **Murphey, Nelson Wright:** From Jefferson County, Georgia. Born ca. 1830. Enlisted as a private in Company F on 04/30/1862 at Burke County, Georgia. Value of horse $225. On sick furlough in September/October 1862. Still on sick furlough on last record, November/December 1862. Furnished Cuthbert C. Torrance as a substitute on 01/01/1863. After the war, became a shoe dealer in Richmond County, Georgia, and was married.

879. **Murphey, Robert A.:** From Burke County, Georgia. Born ca. 1834. Enlisted as a private in Company F on 03/25/1864 at Burke County, Georgia. Value of horse $350. On sick furlough in September/October 1862. Provided Maurice Whalin as a substitute on 06/01/1863. After the war, became a farmer in Burke County, Georgia. He and his wife, Henry, had at least three children. Died after 1880. Buried in the Bark Camp Baptist Cemetery in Burke County, Georgia.

880. **Murphy, Bartholomew J.:** 22-year-old from Georgia. Enlisted as a private in Company I on 04/01/1862 at Augusta, Georgia. Value of horse $140. Captured in Maryland on 06/20/1863 and sent to Harrisburg, Pennsylvania. Transferred to Fort Delaware Prison on 07/04/1863. Paroled on 05/05/1865. Described as having a light complexion, light hair, and blue eyes. His parole gave his residence as New York, New York.

881. **Murphy [Murphey], Thomas J.:** 19-year-old from Georgia. Enlisted in 1st Georgia Infantry, Company I, as private on 03/18/1861. Transferred to Cobb's Legion Cavalry, Company I, as a sergeant on 02/13/1862 at Winchester, Virginia. Value of horse $190. Last record September/October 1864, sent to Georgia with Capt. Bostick to get a horse on 09/20/1864.

882. **Murphy [Murphey], William R.:** 23-year-old railroad foreman from Augusta, Georgia. Born in Ireland. Enlisted as a private in Company A on 08/17/1861 at Augusta, Georgia. Value of horse $235 and horse equipment $30. Detailed as Acting Quartermaster in 12/1861. Last service record dated 02/25/1862. Furnished Fred Hogrefe as a substitute.

883. **Muse, E. N.:** 18-year-old from Augusta, Georgia. Born in Virginia. Enlisted as a private in Ramsey's Georgia Infantry, Company A, on 11/07/1861. The Muster Roll Commission roster places him in Cobb's Legion Cavalry, Company A, but he has no service records in Cobb's Legion. He may have served in Cobb's Legion after November 1864.

884. **Nabers, William:** Enlisted as a private in Company H on 03/03/1862 at Athens, Clarke County, Georgia. Transferred to the 3rd Georgia Infantry, Company K, on 01/30/1863. Wounded at Weldon Railroad, Virginia, on 08/21/1864. Died on 09/08/1864 of wounds.

885. **Nash, Charles T.:** Medical student from Jackson County, Georgia. Born ca. 1838 in Georgia. Brother of John J. and Reuben Long Nash. Enlisted as a private in Company C on 08/01/1861 at Athens, Clarke County, Georgia. On furlough for 25 days beginning 01/20/1862. Sent home to get a horse with Lt. Sinquefield under Special Order No. 27 from corps headquarters on 02/23/1864. Sent to Georgia with Capt. Bostick to get a horse on 09/20/1864. Was surrendered by Gen. Joseph E. Johnston on 04/26/1865. Paroled at Greensboro, North Carolina, on 05/01/1865. After the war, became a farmer in Jackson County, Georgia. Married Georgia M. Borders on 08/25/1858 in Jackson County, Georgia, and they had at least five children. Applied for a Confederate pension in Jackson County, Georgia. His widow applied for a Confederate pension in Fulton County, Georgia.

886. **Nash, James Rutherford Polk:** 24-year-old farm laborer from Jackson County, Georgia. Born on 03/10/1837 in Georgia. Brother of Reuben T. Nash. Enlisted as a private in Company C on 08/01/1861 at Athens, Clarke County, Georgia. Detailed as a courier beginning 01/1862. Detailed as a teamster beginning 11/11/1863. Was surrendered by Gen. Joseph E. Johnston on 04/26/1865. Paroled at Greensboro, North Carolina, on 05/01/1865. After the war, became a farmer in Jackson County, Georgia. Married Louela Collins on 08/03/1865 in Jackson County, Georgia, and they had at least five children. Died on 06/06/1913. Buried in Jackson County, Georgia.

887. **Nash, John J.:** Farm laborer from Jackson County, Georgia. Born ca. 1839 in Georgia. Brother of Charles T. and Reuben Long Nash. Enlisted in 3rd Georgia Infantry, Company K, as a private on 05/25/1861. Transferred to Cobb's Legion Cavalry, Company C, as a private on 10/06/1862. Sent to Georgia with Capt. Bostick to get a horse on 09/20/1864. Captured at Anderson, South Carolina, in 1865. Paroled at Anderson, South Carolina.

888. **Nash, Reuben Long:** Farm laborer from Jackson County, Georgia. Born ca. 1842 in Georgia. Brother of Charles T. and John J. Nash. Enlisted as a private in Company C on 08/01/1861 at Athens, Clarke County, Georgia. Listed as a corporal in November/December 1861. Captured at Jack's Shop, Virginia, on 09/22/1863 and sent to the Old Capitol Prison, Washington D.C. Transferred to Point Lookout, Maryland, on 09/26/1863. Listed as a sergeant in November/December 1863. Exchanged in 11/1864. Was surrendered by Gen. Joseph E. Johnston on 04/26/1865. Paroled at Greensboro, North Carolina, on 05/01/1865. Married Nancy Catherine (Kate) Chandler ca. 1885. (Some records list this marriage for Reuben T. Nash.)

889. **Nash, Reuben T.:** Farm laborer from Jackson County, Georgia. Born ca. 1833 in Georgia.

Brother of James Rutherford Polk Nash. Enlisted as a private in Company C on 05/01/1863 at Athens, Georgia. Sent home to get a horse on 11/10/1863. Absent without leave beginning 02/01/1864. Admitted to Jackson Hospital, Richmond, Virginia, on 05/30/1864 with deafness. Returned to duty on 06/01/1864. Discharged on 07/20/1864. After the war, became a farmer in Jackson County, Georgia. Married Elizabeth A. Nunn on 10/09/1859 in Jackson County, Georgia, and they had at least two children. Died after 1880.

890. Nasworthy, Thomas J.: Born ca. 1843 in Georgia. Enlisted as a private in Company F on 03/25/1862 at Burke County, Georgia. Value of horse $200. Admitted to General Hospital, Petersburg, Virginia, on 10/29/1862. Admitted to Henningsen Hospital, Richmond, Virginia, on 10/31/1862. Returned to duty on 02/01/1863. Captured at Beverly's Ford, Virginia, on 06/09/1863 and sent to the Old Capitol Prison, Washington, D.C. Paroled on 06/25/1863. Admitted to Winder Hospital, Richmond, Virginia, on 10/10/1863. Sent home to get a horse with Lt. Sinquefield under Special Order No. 27 from corps headquarters on 02/23/1864. Admitted to Jackson Hospital, Richmond, Virginia, on 08/15/1864 with dysentery. Returned to duty on 08/29/1864. Last record September/October 1864, wounded on 10/27/1864 and admitted to a hospital in Petersburg, Virginia. After the war, became a farmer in Burke County, Georgia, and was married. Died after 1880.

891. Neal, Samuel C.: Enlisted as a private in Company A 05/01/1862 at Augusta, Georgia. No horse beginning 01/01/1863. Admitted to a hospital in Gordonsville, Virginia, on 02/17/1863 with smallpox. On sick furlough in March/April 1863. Last record March/April 1863.

892. Neese, William J.: 23-year-old from Georgia. Enlisted as a private in Company E on 03/22/1862 at Roswell, Georgia. Value of horse $200. Detailed as an ambulance driver beginning 02/20/1863. Detailed to Quartermaster Department at Orange Court House beginning 11/11/1863. Lost horse on 11/14/1863. Last record September/October 1864, detailed at Stony Creek, Virginia. After the war, lived in Cobb and Forsyth counties, Georgia. Was married to S.A. Applied for a Confederate pension in Cobb and Forsyth counties, Georgia. His widow applied for a Confederate pension in Cobb County, Georgia.

893. Nelson, Charles H.: Native of Georgia. Enlisted as a private in Company B on 07/10/1863 at Atlanta, Georgia. Without a horse beginning 07/1864. Captured at Gold Mine Ford on the Rapidan River on 02/06/1864 and sent to the Old Capitol Prison, Washington D.C. Admitted to Old Capitol Prison Hospital on 04/14/1864. Transferred to Fort Delaware Prison on 06/17/1864. Last record, paroled at Fort Delaware and sent to Washington on 02/11/1865. After the war, lived in Fulton County, Georgia, and was married to Mary. His widow received a Confederate pension in Fulton County, Georgia.

894. Nelson [Neilson], James Hamilton: Enlisted as a private in Company A on 08/17/1861 at Augusta, Georgia. Value of horse $200 and horse equipment $25. Detailed as an orderly to Gen. Magruder beginning 11/07/1861. Courier for Gen. Raines beginning 02/1862. Detailed in Quartermaster Department as a brigade clerk in March/April 1863. Extra duty as a forager beginning 05/07/1863. Sent home to get a horse on 04/01/1864 under Special Order No. 27 from corps headquarters. No horse in the summer of 1864. Was surrendered by Gen. Joseph E. Johnston on 04/206/1865. Paroled at Greensboro, North Carolina, on 05/01/1865.

895. Nesbitt, Robert Taylor: Enlisted as a private in Company B on 08/14/1861 at Atlanta, Georgia. Discharged with a surgeon's certificate of disability on 09/03/1861.

896. Netherland, James A.: 20-year-old from Georgia. Enlisted as a private in Company E on 03/24/1862 at Roswell, Georgia. Value of horse $185. Captured at Malvern Hill, Virginia, on 08/05/1862 and sent to Fort Monroe, Virginia. Paroled at Fort Wool, Virginia, on 08/26/1862. Captured at Beverly's Ford, Virginia, on 06/09/1863 and sent to the Old Capitol Prison, Washington, D.C. Paroled on 06/25/1863. Lost horse on 07/04/1863. Absent without leave beginning 09/15/1863. Still absent without leave on last record, September/October 1864. However, since he was eligible for a Confederate pension, he must have returned to his regiment. After the war, lived in Fulton County, Georgia, and was married. Received a Confederate pension from Fulton County, Georgia. His widow received a Confederate pension in DeKalb County, Georgia.

897. Netherland, William Patterson: 18-year-old. Born on 09/21/1843 in Georgia. Enlisted as a private in Company F on 05/09/1862. Value of horse $225. Detailed as a teamster beginning 10/25/1863. Admitted to Jackson Hospital, Richmond, Virginia, on 12/15/1863 with a wound in his right foot. Furloughed for 30 days beginning 12/30/1863. Listed as a corporal beginning March/April 1864. Was present on his last record, September/October 1864. After the war, became a farmer in Burke County, Georgia. Married Mary Jane Robinson on 10/18/1866 in Burke County, Georgia. Died on 06/29/1901. Buried in the Bark Camp Baptist Cemetery in Burke County, Georgia.

898. Newbolt, T.: Enlisted as a private in Company K on 02/17/1863 at Camp Maynard, Georgia. Deserted 03/24/1863.

899. Newton, B.F.: 26-year-old. Enlisted as a sergeant in Company K on 02/06/1863 at Camp Maynard, Georgia. Returned to his regiment on 02/23/1863.

900. Nichols, John W.: 23-year-old. Enlisted in the 1st Georgia Infantry, Company I, as a private on 03/18/1861. Mustered out at Augusta, Georgia on 03/18/1862. Enlisted as a corporal in Cobb's Legion Cavalry, Company I, on 03/26/1862 at Atlanta, Georgia. Value of horse $200. Discharged because of disability on 08/23/1862. Survived the war. Married Elsie E. She received a Confederate pension in Richmond County, Georgia.

901. Nicholson, J. Roger: 26-year-old from South Carolina. Enlisted as a private in Company I on 03/25/1862 at Augusta, Georgia. Sent home to get a horse with Lt. Sinquefield under Special Order No. 27 from corps headquarters on 02/23/1864. Last record, September/October 1864 states that he was detailed in the ambulance corps.

902. Nolan [Noland], J.T.: 18-year-old from Mississippi. Enlisted as a private in Company K on 02/04/1863 at Camp Maynard, Georgia. Last record March/April 1864, missing or absent without leave from 07/02/1863.

903. Noose, J.F.: Enlisted as a private in Company B. Captured at Georgetown, Virginia, on 10/20/62 and sent to Fort McHenry, Maryland. Exchanged at Fort Monroe, Virginia, on 10/27/1862.

904. Norman, Henry: Enlisted as a private in Company D on 08/10/1861 at Albany, Georgia. Value of horse $165, saddle furnished by State of Georgia. Detailed as a hospital cook beginning 11/15/1861. Detailed as a cook for Col. Wright beginning 02/01/1863. Sent to recruiting/infirmary camp in March/April 1863. Was surrendered by Gen. Joseph E. Johnston on 04/26/1865. Paroled at Greensboro, North Carolina, on 05/01/1865.

905. Norris, James T.: Enlisted as a private in Company D on 08/10/1861 at Albany, Georgia. Value of horse $200 and horse equipment $25. Detailed as a teamster on 11/24/1861. Promoted to sergeant on 11/01/1862. Appointed lieutenant and adjutant on 06/15/1864 to replace Henry Francis "Frank" Jones who was killed at Trevilian Station. Was wounded 3½ miles from Stony Creek, Virginia, on 11/30/1864. Was wounded near Hicks Ford on 12/31/1864. Was surrendered by Gen. Joseph E. Johnston on 04/26/1865. Paroled at Greensboro, North Carolina, on 05/01/1865.

906. Norris, Thomas O.: 21-year-old farmer. Born in Morgan County, Georgia. Enlisted as a private in Company E on 04/09/1862 at Lawrenceville, Georgia. Value of horse $150 and bridle $5. Discharged on 07/25/1862 due to rheumatism. Described as having a fair complexion, blue eyes, sandy hair, and being 5' 6" tall. After the war, lived in Gwinnett County, Georgia. Received a Confederate pension from Gwinnett County, Georgia.

907. North, Henry: Native of Georgia. Enlisted as a private in Company B on 02/03/1862 at Yorktown, Virginia. Lost his horse on 01/24/1864. Detailed as a teamster beginning 03/23/1864. Admitted to Jackson Hospital, Richmond, Virginia, on 08/17/1864 with a sprained ankle. Furloughed to Georgia for 30 days beginning 08/21/1864. Was surrendered by Gen. Joseph E. Johnston on 04/26/1865. Paroled at Greensboro, North Carolina, on 05/01/1865 and at Augusta, Georgia, on 05/18/1865. After the war lived in Fulton County, Georgia. Received a Confederate pension from Fulton County, Georgia.

908. Nunn, E.T. [E.K.]: Resident of Georgia. Enlisted as a private in Company D on 08/10/1861 at Albany, Georgia. Value of horse $200 and horse equipment $25. Sent to Georgia with Capt. Bostick to get a horse on 09/20/1864. Was surrendered by Gen. Joseph E. Johnston on 04/26/1865. Paroled at Greensboro, North Carolina, on 05/01/1865.

909. Oates [Oats], James L.: 18-year-old farm overseer. Born in 1845 in Georgia. Enlisted as a private in Company F on 03/25/1862 at Burke County, Georgia. Value of horse $140. Detailed as a teamster on 03/14/1864. Captured at Beverly's Ford, Virginia, on 06/09/1863. Paroled at the Old Capitol Prison, Washington, D.C., on 06/25/1863. Was surrendered by Gen. Joseph E. Johnston on 04/26/1865. Paroled at Greensboro, North Carolina, on 05/01/1865. After the war, lived in Emanuel County, Georgia. Married Emma Catherine Odom. Applied for a Confederate pension in Emanuel County, Georgia. His widow, Emma Catherine Odom, applied for a Confederate pension in Emanuel County, Georgia.

910. Oates, Joseph L.: Born ca. 1844 in Burke County, Georgia. Listed on a roster of Company F compiled by Glen Spurlock. No service records in Cobb's Legion. After the war, became a farmer in Jefferson County, Georgia. Died after 1880.

911. Oates [Oats], L.H: Resident of Georgia. Enlisted as a private in the 10th Georgia Infantry. Transferred to Cobb's Legion Cavalry, Company D, on 11/01/1862. Lost horse on 11/01/1861. Sent to Georgia with Capt. Bostick to get a horse on 09/20/1864. Was surrendered by Gen. Joseph E. Johnston on 04/26/1865. Paroled at Greensboro, North Carolina, on 05/01/1865.

912. Oats [Oates], Andrew B.: 32-year-old. Born on 09/21/1830 in Georgia. Enlisted as a private in Company F on 05/05/1862 at Burke County, Georgia. Value of horse $150. Captured with his horse at Beverly's Ford, Virginia, on 06/09/1863. Paroled at the Old Capitol Prison, Washington, D.C., on 06/25/1863. Admitted to Confederate States Hospital, Petersburg, Virginia, on 07/02/1863. Returned to duty on 07/15/1863. Detailed to tear up tracks on the R. F. & P. Railroad between Fredericksburg and Hamilton's Crossing, Virginia, on 04/01/1864. Admitted to Jackson Hospital, Richmond, Virginia, on 05/16/1864 with a fever. Admitted to Jackson Hospital, Richmond, Virginia, on 05/25/1864. Returned to duty on same day. Last record September/October 1864, sent to Georgia with Capt. Bostick to get a horse on 09/20/1864. After the war, became a farmer in Burke County, Georgia, and was married. Died on 11/14/1901. Buried in the Boyd McBride Cemetery in Burke County, Georgia.

913. O'Connor [O'Conner], Daniel: 27-year-old from Hall County, Georgia. Enlisted as a private in Company C on 08/01/1861 at Athens, Clarke County, Georgia. Wounded by minié ball shattering the bone of his left leg. Captured at Jack's Shop on 09/22/1863. Sent to the Old Capitol Prison, Washington, D.C. Lower third of his left leg was amputated. Leg was further amputated at Staunton Hospital, Washington D.C., on 04/10/1864 because the old flap did not cover the bone. Transferred to depot for wounded prisoners at Lincoln Hospital on 06/03/1864. Was still at hospital on 09/30/1864. Transferred to Elmira Prison, New York, on 10/27/1864. Paroled on 02/09/1865 and sent to the James River, Virginia, for exchange. Admitted to Jackson Hospital, Richmond, Virginia, on 02/22/1865. Transferred to Camp Lee on 03/03/1865. Returned to duty on 03/09/1865. Admitted to Jackson Hospital, Richmond, Virginia, on 03/08/1865. Last record, furloughed for 60 days beginning 03/17/1865. After the war, became a farmer in Montgomery County, Illinois. Was married. Died after 1880.

914. O'Connor [O'Conner], Owen [Eugene J.]: 18-year-old farmer and grocer from Augusta, Richmond County, Georgia. Born on 03/31/1845 in County Cork, Ireland. Enlisted as a private in Company I on 03/28/1862 at Augusta, Georgia. Value of horse $190. Family records indicate he received saber cut at Little Washington, Virginia, on 11/08/1862, and was wounded at Brandy Station, Virginia, on 06/09/1863. Wounded on 07/02/1863 at Hunterstown, Pennsylvania. Admitted to Chimborazo Hospital No. 2, Richmond, Virginia, on 07/14/1863. Furloughed to Augusta, Georgia, for 25 days. Detailed at works in Augusta, Georgia, on 02/05/1864. Was surrendered by Gen. Joseph E. Johnston on 04/26/1865. Paroled at Greensboro, North Carolina, on 05/01/1865. His parole papers described him as having a light complexion, dark hair, grey eyes, and being 5' 9" tall and 19 years old. After the war, worked as a bookkeeper, business manager, and the owner of a wholesale liquor store in Augusta, Georgia. Also served in the Spanish-American War and World War I. Was a member of the Catholic Layman's Association, the Knights of Columbus, Richmond County Board of Education, St. Vincent de Paul Society, charter member of Sacred Heart Church, and charter member of the United Confederate Veterans, Augusta Camp. Married Margaret M. Magarahan on 06/30/1868 in Augusta, Georgia, and they had four children. Applied for a Confederate pension in Richmond County, Georgia. Died on 12/07/1927 in Augusta, Richmond County, Georgia. Buried on 12/08/1927 in Augusta, Richmond County, Georgia. The *Augusta Chronicle* said he was "a valiant soldier, an upright man, a true Christian, and a devoted husband and father, a loyal friend and a patriotic citizen."

915. O'Donnell [O'Dunold], John B.: 25-year-old, born in Ireland. Enlisted as a private in Company A on 08/17/1861 at Augusta, Georgia. Value of horse $200 and horse equipment $25. Detailed permanently by Col. Cobb as a telegraph operator at Yorktown, Virginia, and sent to Greensboro, North Carolina, on 12/18/1861. Sent to Augusta, Georgia, on 04/24/1862. No horse from 01/01/1863. Sent to Waynesboro, Georgia, in 12/1864. Remained at Waynesboro until Gen. Sherman left Savannah. Went to Augusta, Georgia, and remained until the surrender. Paroled on 05/19/1865 at Augusta, Georgia. After the war, worked as a freight agent for the railroad in Savannah, Georgia. Married Catherine Larkin on 07/03/1862 at Augusta, Georgia, and they had at least one child. Died on 10/03/1878 at Little Rock, Arkansas.

916. O'Donohoe [O'Donoho], Martin: Resident of Richmond County, Georgia. Enlisted as a private in Company I on 04/07/1862 at Augusta, Georgia. Value of horse $146. Died on 03/07/1863 at General Hospital No. 2, Lynchburg, Virginia.

917. O'Hara [O'Harra], James: 28-year-old from Georgia. Enlisted as a private in Company I on 03/06/1862 at Augusta, Georgia. Value of horse $150. Listed as a corporal in September/October 1862. Sent to infirmary/recruiting camp on 01/15/1864. Was surrendered by Gen. Joseph E. Johnston on 04/26/1865. Paroled at Greensboro, North Carolina, on 05/01/1865.

918. O'Keefe, Owen: Enlisted in the 1st Georgia Infantry, Company I, as a private on 03/18/1861. Discharged and enlisted as a corporal in Cobb's Legion Cavalry, Company I, on 03/19/1862 at Augusta, Georgia. Value of horse $205. Horse killed in action at Sharpsburg, Maryland, on 09/17/1862. O'Keefe admitted to hospital in Lynchburg, Virginia, on 10/16/1863. Detailed as a scout on 03/23/1864. Captured at Falmouth, Stafford County, Virginia, on 03/31/1864 and sent to the Old Capitol Prison, Washington, D.C. Transferred to Fort Delaware Prison. Paroled at Fort Delaware, Delaware, in 02/1865. Sent to City Point, Virginia, on 03/07/1865. Exchanged at Boulware & Cox's Wharves, James River, Virginia, on 03/10–12/1865.

919. Oliver, James C.: Farmer from Jackson County, Georgia. (Prisoner of war record states he was from Athens, Georgia.) Born ca. 1828 in Georgia. Enlisted as a private in Company C on 04/22/1862 at Athens, Clarke County, Georgia. Detailed as a teamster in March/April 1863. Captured at Spotsylvania Court House, Virginia, on 02/29/1864. Sent to Yorktown, Virginia, for transfer to Point Lookout, Maryland. Transferred to Elmira Prison, New York, on 07/17/1864. Released on 06/16/1865. Was described as having a florid complexion, auburn hair, blue eyes and being 5'9" tall. After the war, became a farmer in Jackson County, Georgia. Married Susan Pinson on 01/08/1854 in Jackson County, Georgia, and they had at least four children. Died after 1880. His widow applied for a Confederate pension in Jackson County, Georgia.

920. Oliver, R.L.: Enlisted as a private in Company D on 04/22/1863 at Meadsville, Virginia. Admitted sick to Chimborazo Hospital, Richmond, Virginia, on 12/20/1863. No horse beginning 11/10/1863. Admitted to Chimborazo Hospital No. 3, Richmond, Virginia, on 01/06/1864. Transferred to Petersburg, Virginia, on 04/04/1864. Was present on last record, 11/01/1864.

921. O'Neal, Pat: Resident of Georgia. Enlisted as a private in Company K on 02/25/1862 at Camp Maynard, Georgia. Sent to infirmary/recruiting camp on 01/17/1864. Last record September/October 1864, admitted to hospital on 09/13/1864.

922. Orr, William C.: From Jackson County, Georgia. Born in Alabama ca. 1846. Enlisted as a private in Company C on 12/21/1863 at Jefferson, Georgia. Admitted to Jackson Hospital, Richmond, Virginia, on 08/17/1864 with a wound to his left eye from a minié ball. Furloughed for 30 days beginning 08/25/1864. Was surrendered by Gen. Joseph E. Johnston on 04/26/1865. Paroled at Greensboro, North Carolina, on 05/01/1865. After the war, became a cotton shipper in Clarke County, Georgia. He and his wife, Emma, had at least one child. Applied for a Confederate pension in Clarke County, Georgia. Died after 1880.

923. Orrison, C. W.: Enlisted as a private in Company K. His one record is a prisoner of war parole, but the writing is illegible.

924. O'Shields [O'Sheals], John B.: Born ca. 1837 in Georgia. Enlisted as a private in Company H on 03/04/1862 at Athens, Clarke County, Georgia. Other records indicate he was wounded on 06/09/1863 during the cavalry battle at Brandy Station, Virginia. Sent to infirmary/recruiting camp on 08/12/1863. Was surrendered by Gen. Joseph E. Johnston on 04/26/1865. Paroled at Greensboro, North Carolina, on 05/01/1865. After the war, became a farmer from Jackson County, Georgia, and was married.

925. Owens, Ira W.: From Georgia. Born ca. 1835 in Georgia. Enlisted as a private in Company E on 03/15/1862 at Roswell, Georgia. Value of horse $175. Sent home to get a horse on 11/13/1863. Absent without leave beginning 01/17/1864. Last record September/October 1864, still absent without leave. After the war, became a carpenter in Calhoun County, Alabama, and was married.

926. Owens, Jacob: Resident of Georgia. Enlisted as a private in Company E on 05/12/1862 at Atlanta, Georgia. Lost horse on 04/12/1863. Sent home to get a horse on 11/12/1863. Absent without leave beginning 01/17/1864. Last record September/October 1864, still absent without leave.

927. Owens, John A.: Transferred to Cobb's Legion Cavalry, Company D, as a private on 04/01/1863. Transferred to Company L on or after 09/01/1863. Deserted during action at Raccoon Ford, Virginia, on 09/14/1863. Sent to the Old Capitol Prison, Washington, D.C., on 09/19/1863. Transferred to Point Lookout, Maryland, on 10/27/1863 where he was listed as a Rebel deserter.

928. Owens, John W.: 23-year-old from Georgia. Enlisted as a private in Company E on 03/22/

1862 at Roswell, Georgia. Sent home to get a horse with Lt. Sinquefield under Special Order No. 27 from corps headquarters on 02/23/1864. Last record September/October 1864, still absent on horse detail. After the war, lived in Cobb County, Georgia. Applied for a Confederate pension in Cobb County, Georgia.

929. Ownby, Gaines [James] C.[B.]: Enlisted as a private in Company H on 03/15/1862 at Athens, Clarke County, Georgia. Admitted to C.S.A. General Hospital at Charlottesville, Virginia, on 07/03/1863 with an ulcer in the cornea. Admitted to C.S.A. General Hospital, Danville, Virginia, with diarrhea on 07/13/1862. Returned to duty on 07/30/1862. Discharged from service on 09/11/1863.

930. Ozburn [Osburn], George H.[D.H.]: About 17 years old. Enlisted as a private in Company I on 03/23/1864 at Guiney's (Guinea's) Station, Virginia. Sent to Georgia to get a horse with Capt. Bostick on 09/20/1864. Was surrendered by Gen. Joseph E. Johnston on 04/26/1865. Paroled at Greensboro, North Carolina, on 05/01/1865.

931. Ozburn [Osborne, Ozborne], James R.D.: Enlisted as a corporal in Company B on 08/14/1861 at Atlanta, Georgia. Value of horse $175, and horse equipment $30. Supplied James G. Ringgold as a substitute and was discharged on 11/20/1861. Was married to Eliza Mangum on 12/10/1854 in Fulton County, Georgia.

932. Ozburn [Osburne, Osburn, Osburne], James Robert: Resident of Conyers Station, Newton County, Georgia. Enlisted in the 18th Georgia Infantry, Company B, as a private on 04/30/1861. Transferred to Cobb's Legion Cavalry, Company I, on 06/26/1863 at Camp McDonald, Georgia. Sent to Georgia to get a horse with Lt. Sinquefield under Special Order No. 27 from corps headquarters on 02/23/1864. Admitted to hospital sick on 08/03/1864. Furloughed beginning 10/04/1864. Admitted to C.S.A. General Hospital, Charlotte, North Carolina, on 01/15/1865. Returned to duty on 01/24/1865. Admitted to Pettigrew General Hospital No. 13, Raleigh, North Carolina, on 02/18/1865. Returned to duty on 02/24/1865. Was surrendered by Gen. Joseph E. Johnston on 04/26/1865. Paroled at Greensboro, North Carolina, on 05/01/1865.

933. Ozburn [Ozborne], Thomas Ozias: Born ca. 1833 in Georgia. Enlisted as a private in Company B on 08/14/1861 at Atlanta, Georgia. Value of horse $150 and horse equipment $7. Furloughed for 20 days beginning 11/14/1861. Lost horse and was captured at Gold Mine Ford, Rapidan River, Virginia, on 02/06/1864. Sent to Old Capitol Prison, Washington, D.C., on 02/11/1864. Transferred to Fort Delaware Prison on 06/15/1864. Paroled at Fort Delaware Prison in 02/1865. After the war, lived in Fulton County and then Morgan County, Georgia. Married Olive Fielder on 02/03/1854 in Newton County, Georgia. Applied for a Confederate pension in Fulton County, Georgia. Transferred the pension to Morgan County, Georgia.

934. Packard, Cyrus: Resident of Georgia. Enlisted as a private in Company D on 03/04/1862 at Albany, Georgia. Value of horse $250 and horse equipment $40. Absent sick in March/April 1863. Lost horse in 11/1863. Discharged on 09/05/1864.

935. Paden, Samuel D.: From Georgia. Born ca. 1845 in Georgia. Enlisted as a private in Company E on 04/18/1862 at Roswell, Georgia. Lost horse on 09/01/1863. Admitted to Jackson Hospital, Richmond, Virginia, on 10/23/1863. Sent home to get a horse on 11/12/1863. Lost horse and captured at Milford Station, Virginia, on 05/18/1864. Sent to Point Lookout, Maryland. Exchanged on the James River, Virginia, on 10/11/1864. Admitted to Jackson Hospital, Richmond, Virginia, on 10/16/1864 with chronic diarrhea. Last record, furloughed for 20 days beginning 10/20/1864. After the war, became a farmer in Gwinnett County, Georgia, and then lived in Cobb County, Georgia. Was married to Joanna. Applied for a Confederate pension in Cobb County, Georgia.

936. Palmer, Benjamin Brown: 22-year-old farmer. Born on 11/20/1839 in Burke County, Georgia. Enlisted as a private in Company F on 05/09/1862 at Burke County, Georgia. Value of horse $225. Wounded by gunshot in right arm at Mine Run, Virginia, on 11/29/1863. Admitted to C.S.A. General Hospital, Charlottesville, Virginia, on 12/03/1863. Arm was amputated at the shoulder. Furloughed to Georgia on 01/18/1864. Was given a disability discharge on 03/18/1865. Described as having a light complexion, gray eyes, light hair, and being 6 feet tall. Died on 08/20/1870.

937. Palmer, William C: 25-year-old planter. Born in Burke County, Georgia. Enlisted as a private in Company F on 05/09/1862 at Burke County, Georgia. Value of horse $225. Wounded in the right arm, resulting in loss of use of the arm, at Barbee's Cross Roads, Virginia, on 11/05/1862. Furloughed for 40 days beginning 11/13/1862 1862. Discharged on 08/19/1863. Described as having a light complexion, dark gray eyes, dark hair, and being 6'1" tall.

938. Park [Parks], Byrd: Resident of Coweta

County, Georgia. Enlisted as a private in Company L on 05/06/1864 at Decatur, Georgia. Transferred to Phillips Legion on 08/02/1864 in exchange for B.H. Couch. Admitted to Pettigrew General Hospital No. 12, Raleigh, North Carolina, on 08/02/1864 with debility from pneumonia. Died of typhoid fever on 08/16/1864. Buried in the Oakwood Cemetery in Raleigh, Wake County, North Carolina.

939. **Park, Hiram P.:** Enlisted as a private in Company C on 02/28/1862 at Athens, Clarke County, Georgia. Was listed as present on last record, March/April 1863.

940. **Park, J.A.:** Born ca. 1828. Enlisted as a private in Company D on 08/10/1861 at Albany, Georgia. Value of horse $225 and horse equipment $25, furnished by State of Georgia. Detailed as a nurse for company sick in camps in November/December 1861. Furloughed for 30 days beginning 02/14/1862. Discharged in 04/1862.

941. **Parker, J.P.:** Enlisted as a private in Company D on 08/10/1861 at Albany, Georgia. Value of horse $112, and horse equipment $25, furnished by State of Georgia. Sick at Richmond in 12/1861. Last record, detailed as a nurse to the sick in 01/1862.

942. **Parker, James A.:** About 17 years old. Enlisted as a private in Company D on 05/01/1864 at Guiney's (Guinea's) Station, Virginia. Transferred to Company L. Wounded on 06/24/1864. Admitted to Jackson Hospital, Richmond, Virginia, on 06/26/1864. Both legs were amputated. Furloughed for 60 days on 08/09/1864. Died on 08/16/1864 at General Hospital No. 3, Columbia, South Carolina.

943. **Parker, N.C.:** Enlisted as a private in Company C. Captured at Stony Creek, Virginia, in 12/05/1864 and sent to Point Lookout, Maryland. Released on 06/16/1865.

944. **Parker, Robert [H.] J.:** Born in Georgia ca. 1845. Enlisted as a private in Company F on 04/15/1862 at Burke County, Georgia. Horse, owned by Lt. Thomas A. Pierce, valued at $250. Admitted to Winder Hospital, Richmond, Virginia, on 09/25/1863. Transferred to Company L in March/April 1864. On wounded furlough beginning 04/01/1864. Appointed sergeant on 06/01/1864. Last record September/October 1864, sent to Georgia to get a horse with Capt. Bostick on 09/20/1864. After the war, worked as an inspector in Screven County, Georgia, and then lived in Jefferson County, Georgia. Was married to Sarah Emmaline. Applied for a Confederate pension in Jefferson County, Georgia. Died after 1880. His widow, Sarah Emmaline Parker, applied for a Confederate pension in Jefferson County, Georgia.

945. **Parker, W.H.:** Enlisted as a lieutenant in Company L on 12/15/1862 at Jefferson County, Georgia. Admitted to General Hospital No. 4, Richmond, Virginia, on 02/16/1864 with typhoid fever. Returned to duty on 03/05/1864. Wounded on 10/27/1864. Admitted to General Hospital, Petersburg, Virginia, on 10/29/1864. Died on 12/01/1864.

946. **Parker, William M.[L]:** 23-year-old native of Georgia. Enlisted as a private in Company F on 03/25/1862 at Burke County, Georgia. Value of horse $200. Detailed to attend horses at the infirmary/recruiting camp on 01/20/1864. Sent to Georgia to get a horse with Capt. Bostick on 09/20/1864. Was surrendered by Gen. Joseph E. Johnston on 04/26/1865. Paroled at Greensboro, North Carolina, on 05/01/1865.

947. **Parker, William R.:** 17-year-old. Enlisted as a private in Company F on 04/18/1862 at Burke County, Georgia. Horse, owned by Lt. Thomas A. Pierce, valued at $200. Transferred to Company L in March/April 1863. Last record, transferred to 20th Georgia Infantry, Company C on 04/01/1864.

948. **Parks, David Rives:** 20-year-old from Georgia. Born on 11/09/1840 in Hall County, Georgia. Brother of Harvey Calhoun and Samuel S. Parks. Enlisted as a private in Company C on 08/01/1861 at Athens, Clarke County, Georgia. Detailed as a forage master in January/February 1863. Sent to infirmary/recruiting camp in January/February 1864. Last record September/October 1864, sent to Georgia to get a horse with Capt. Bostick on 09/20/1864. After the war, became a farmer in Banks County, Georgia. Died on 01/26/1918 in Banks County, Georgia. Buried in the Gillsville Cemetery in Hall County, Georgia. His widow received a Confederate pension in Banks County, Georgia, in 1918.

949. **Parks, Harvey Calhoun:** 18-year-old from Georgia. Born on 09/24/1844 in Lumpkin County, Georgia. Brother of David Rives and Samuel S. Parks. Enlisted as a private in Company C on 01/18/1863 at Athens, Clarke County, Georgia. Sent to infirmary/recruiting camp in November/December 1863. Sent to infirmary/recruiting camp in 10/1864. Captured on 12/01/1864 at Stony Creek, Virginia, and sent to Point Lookout, Maryland. Released on 06/15/1865. After the war, became a farmer in Lumpkin County, Georgia. Married Sarah Elizabeth Cain on 12/08/1867. Received a Confederate pension in Hall County, Georgia, from 1908 to 1914. Died on either 07 or 08/21/1914.

Buried in the Yellow Creek Cemetery in Hall County, Georgia. His widow received a Confederate pension in Hall County, Georgia, from 1915 to 1937.

950. Parks, Isaac Glenn: From Georgia. Born in DeKalb County, Georgia, on either 08/28/1840 or 1841. Enlisted as a private in Company H on 03/03/1862 at Athens, Clarke County, Georgia. Sent home to get a horse with Lt. Sinquefield under Special Order No. 27 from corps headquarters on 02/23/1864. Sent to infirmary/recruiting camp on 06/13/1864. Surrendered at Augusta, Georgia, and paroled there on 05/18/1865. After the war, became a Methodist minister in Meriwether County, Georgia. Married Jimmie Tarver on 10/09/1877 in Whitfield County, Georgia. Died on 06/18/1885 in DeKalb County, Georgia. Buried in the Ebenezer Methodist Church Cemetery.

951. Parks, Marion: Born ca. 1847 in Jackson County, Georgia. On a roster of Company C compiled by Glen Spurlock. No service records in Cobb's Legion. After the war, became a farmer in DeKalb County, Georgia, and was married. Died after 1880.

952. Parks, Samuel S.: 32-year-old from Georgia. Born on 05/27/1831 in Hall County, Georgia. Brother of David Rives and Harvey Calhoun Parks. Enlisted as a private in Company C on 09/06/1862 at Calhoun, Georgia. Transferred from the 24th Georgia Infantry on 10/28/1862. Admitted to Winder Hospital, Richmond, Virginia, sick on 01/04/1864. Returned to duty on 01/05/1864. Admitted to Jackson Hospital, Richmond, Virginia, on 01/21/1864 with pneumonia. Returned to duty on 03/11/1864. Captured at Trevilian Station, Virginia, on 06/11/1864 and sent to Point Lookout, Maryland, on 06/20/1864. Transferred to Elmira Prison, New York, on 07/25/1864. Died of pneumonia at Elmira Prison Camp, New York, on 01/04/1865. His effects consisted of $14.12 in U.S. currency. Buried in the Woodlawn Cemetery in Elmira, New York.

953. Parrish, Charles T.: Enlisted as a corporal in Company E on 08/24/1861 at Atlanta, Georgia. Sent home to get a horse in March/April 1863. Sent to Georgia to get a horse with Lt. Sinquefield under Special Order No. 27 from corps headquarters on 02/23/1864. Sent to infirmary/recruiting camp on 06/21/1864. Still at infirmary/recruiting camp on last record, September/October 1864.

954. Parrish, George W.: 19-year-old clerk from Chatham County, Georgia. Enlisted as a private in Company A on 08/17/1861 at Augusta, Georgia. Value of horse $180 and horse equipment $25. Lost horse and was captured on 07/17/1863 at Hedgesville, [West] Virginia, and held at Atheneum Prison, Wheeling, [West] Virginia. Sent to Camp Chase, Ohio, on 07/22/1863, and then to Fort Delaware Prison on 02/29/1864. Paroled at Fort Delaware in 02/1865. Exchanged at Boulware's & Cox's Wharf between 03/10/1865 and 03/12/1865. Described as being 5'10½" tall, with a light complexion, blue eyes, and light hair.

955. Paschal [Paschill], Thomas A. Holliday: 21-year-old from Columbia County, Georgia. Born on 08/31/1839 in Lincoln County, Georgia. Enlisted as a private in Company A on 08/17/1861 at Augusta, Georgia. Value of horse $225 and horse equipment $35. Detailed as a courier for Gen. Toombs before 09/1862. Gen. Toombs wrote in his report of the Battle of Sharpsburg that "The conduct of one of my couriers, Mr. Thomas Paschal, of Cobb's Legion, deserves special mention for courage and fidelity to duty under circumstances of peculiar difficulties and dangers." Requested permission on 05/04/1863 to raise a company of partisan cavalry rangers from Columbia and surrounding counties in Georgia, who were aged 16–18 years-of-age, and owned their own horses. Request was approved by Col. P.M.B. Young. Admitted to Jackson Hospital, Richmond, Virginia, on 08/02/1863 with organic stricture of urethra of 12 years' duration due to an injury as the result of a fall. Furloughed for 30 days from Jackson Hospital, Richmond, Virginia, beginning 08/15/1863. Admitted to Jackson Hospital, Richmond, Virginia, on 09/21/1863. Returned to duty on 01/11/1864. Sick at a hospital on 01/25/1864. Detailed permanently as a steward at Jackson Hospital in Richmond, Virginia, on 01/30/1864 by the secretary of war. Employed as a steward and a guard at Louisiana Hospital, Richmond, Virginia, beginning 02/02/1864. No horse in March/April 1864. Last record, name appears on a purchase order for groceries on 09/30/1864 at Louisiana Hospital, Richmond, Virginia. After the war, became a farmer and a doctor in Columbia County, Georgia. Married Lucy Smith on 12/04/1866 in Columbia County, Georgia, and was the father of at least six children. Died on 04/10/1904 at Harlem, Georgia, and was buried in Harlem Memorial Cemetery. His widow stated on her Confederate pension application that he was at a hospital in Richmond, Virginia, when the war ended, and that he had sustained a wound to the left side of his head.

956. Pass, William H.: Born ca. 1841 in Hall County, Georgia. Enlisted as a private in Company C on 09/28/1861 at Athens, Clarke County, Georgia. No horse in March/April 1863. Captured at Stevensburg, Culpeper County, Virginia, on 11/09/1863 and sent to the Old Capitol Prison, Washington, D.C. Transferred to Point Lookout, Maryland, on 02/03/1864. Exchanged on 09/18/1864. Arrived at Receiving and Wayside Hospital, Richmond, Virginia, on 09/23/1864 where he died on 09/24/1864 from acute dysentery.

957. **Pate, M.M.:** Enlisted in Nelson's Independent Company, Georgia Cavalry. Listed on a roster of Company D published in *The History of Dougherty County*, but not with the *Civil War Soldiers and Sailors System*. No service records in Cobb's Legion.

958. **Patterson, James [Joseph] S. [M.]:** 23-year-old. Born on 05/22/1839 in Spartanburg, South Carolina. Enlisted as a private in Company H on 03/03/1862 at Athens, Clarke County, Georgia. Captured at Crampton's Pass, Maryland, on 09/14/1862 and paroled on 09/26/1862. Discharged from service in 03/1863. After the war, became a farmer in Lumpkin County, Georgia. Received a Confederate pension from Hall County, Georgia, from 1908 to 1920. Died on 09/13/1920. Buried in the Airline Baptist Cemetery in Hall County, Georgia.

959. **Patterson [Paterson], William L.:** Enlisted as a private in Company L on 03/12/1864 at Louisville, Georgia. Sent to Georgia to get a horse with Capt. Bostick on 09/20/1864. Was surrendered by Gen. Joseph E. Johnston on 04/26/1865. Paroled at Greensboro, North Carolina, on 05/01/1865.

960. **Paul, Neal B.:** Enlisted as a private in Company L on 09/24/1863 at Sawdust, Georgia. Last record September/October 1864, sent to Georgia to get a horse with Capt. Bostick on 09/20/1864.

961. **Payne, Alfred F.:** From Georgia. Born in Georgia ca. 1836. Enlisted as a private in Company E on 04/09/1862 at Lawrenceville, Georgia. Value of horse $140. Sent to infirmary/recruiting camp on 02/04/1864. Was surrendered by Gen. Joseph E. Johnston on 04/26/1865. Paroled at Greensboro, North Carolina, on 05/01/1865.

962. **Payne, David H.:** 47-year-old. Enlisted as a private in Company E on 03/17/1862 at Roswell, Georgia. Value of horse $285 and horse equipment $20. Last record dated 04/22/1862.

963. **Payne, William H.:** 23-year-old. Enlisted as a private in Company B on 05/06/1862 at Atlanta, Georgia. Value of horse $275. Transferred to Company G and listed as a sergeant in May/June 1862. Promoted to lieutenant in 03/1863. Sent to Georgia in charge of 64 men from Cobb's Legion Cavalry to procure fresh horses by order of Gen. Stuart on 04/12/1864. At the end of 30 days, they were to march back to Virginia and rejoin their regiment. Was surrendered by Gen. Joseph E. Johnston on 04/26/1865. Paroled at Greensboro, North Carolina, on 05/01/1865.

964. **Peck, Leroy M.:** Born ca. 1835 in Georgia. Enlisted in the 1st Georgia Infantry, Company I, as private on 03/18/1861. Appointed corporal and later sergeant. Mustered out at Augusta, Georgia, on 03/18/1862. Enlisted as a private in Cobb's Legion Cavalry, Company I, on 03/27/1862. Value of horse $200. Detailed as a fisherman at Fredericksburg, Virginia, on 04/01/1864. Sent to Georgia to get a horse with Capt. Bostick on 09/20/1864. Was surrendered by Gen. Joseph E. Johnston on 04/26/1865. Paroled at Greensboro, North Carolina, on 05/01/1865. After the war, became a farmer in Aiken County, South Carolina, and was married. Died after 1880.

965. **Peek, R.C.:** 18-year-old. Enlisted as a private in Company K on 02/10/1863 at Camp Maynard, Georgia. Returned to his regiment on 03/23/1863.

966. **Peel, E.L.:** resident of Georgia. Enlisted as a private in Company D on 08/10/1861 at Albany, Georgia. Value of horse $160 and horse equipment $20. Admitted to Winder Hospital, Richmond, Virginia, on 09/26/1862. Sent home to get a horse in January/February 1863. Detailed as a teamster on 06/01/1863. Was surrendered by Gen. Joseph E. Johnston on 04/26/1865. Paroled at Greensboro, North Carolina, on 05/01/1865.

967. **Peel, John P.:** Native of Georgia. Born ca. 1840. Enlisted as a private in Company F on 03/25/1862 at Burke County, Georgia. Value of horse $175. Detailed to tear up railroad tracks between Hamilton's Crossing and Fredericksburg, Virginia, on 03/27/1864. Captured at Milford Station, Virginia, on 05/16/1864 and sent to Point Lookout, Maryland. Exchanged at Aiken's Landing, Virginia, on 03/14/1865. After the war, became a farmer in Burke County, Georgia. Married Lucy ca. 1870 in Burke County, Georgia. Died after 1880.

968. **Pendleton, B.A.:** Native of Georgia. Enlisted as a private in Company B on 05/08/1862 at Buckingham, Virginia. Sent to Georgia to get a horse on 11/13/1863. Last record September/October 1864, sent to Georgia to get a horse with Capt. Bostick on 09/20/1864.

969. **Penick [Pennick, Perrick], Lucas T.:** Resident of Georgia. Enlisted as a private in Cobb's

Legion Infantry, Company G, on 07/29/1861 at Madison, Morgan County, Georgia. Promoted to sergeant on 06/01/1862. Given a disability discharge on 07/23/1862 for debility, chronic diarrhea, and tuberculosis. Enlisted as a private in Cobb's Legion Cavalry, Company A, on 02/11/1864 at Decatur, Georgia. Admitted to a hospital, wounded, in March/April 1864. Admitted to Jackson Hospital, Richmond, Virginia, on 08/17/1864 with a wound in his right shoulder. Furloughed for 30 days on 08/25/1864. Was surrendered by Gen. Joseph E. Johnston on 04/26/1865. Paroled at Greensboro, North Carolina, on 05/01/1865.

970. **Penrow [Penroe], William E.[C.]:** Born ca. 1834 in Georgia. Enlisted as a private in Company F on 03/25/1862 at Burke County, Georgia. Value of horse $175. Captured at Beverly's Ford, Virginia, on 06/09/1863 and sent to the Old Capitol Prison, Washington, D.C. Paroled on 06/25/1863. Detailed as a fisherman on 03/01/1864. Was surrendered by Gen. Joseph E. Johnston on 04/26/1865. Paroled at Greensboro, North Carolina, on 05/01/1865. After the war, became a farmer in Jefferson County, Georgia, and was married. Died after 1880.

971. **Pentecost [Penticost], H.F.:** resident of Louisiana. Enlisted as a sergeant in Company K on 01/20/1863 at Camp Maynard, Georgia. Sent home to get a horse on 11/11/1863. Absent without leave beginning 01/23/1864. Still Absent without leave beginning on last record March/April 1864.

972. **Perkins, John A.:** Enlisted as a private in the 7th Georgia Infantry. Transferred to Cobb's Legion Cavalry, Company B, on 01/15/1863. Transferred to Phillip's Legion on 04/01/1863.

973. **Perryman, R.N.:** Enlisted as a private in Company A on 04/15/1864 at Macon, Georgia. Last record September/October 1864, sent to Georgia to get a horse with Capt. Bostick on 09/20/1864.

974. **Perryman, Thomas J.[J.T.]:** 26-year-old from Georgia. Enlisted as a private in Company E on 04/08/1862 at Atlanta, Georgia. Value of horse $140. Detailed as a teamster on 07/20/1862. Sent to infirmary/recruiting camp on 11/28/1863. Was surrendered by Gen. Joseph E. Johnston on 04/26/1865. Paroled at Greensboro, North Carolina, on 05/01/1865. After the war, lived in Cobb County, Georgia, and was married to Martha. His widow received a Confederate pension in Cobb County, Georgia.

975. **Peterson, Ransom J.:** Born ca. 1837 in Georgia. Enlisted as a private in Company F on 03/25/1862. Value of horse $175. Furnished Augustus Owen McCroan as a substitute and was discharged on 09/08/1862. After the war, became a farmer in Burke County, Georgia, and was married to Elmira. Died after 1880.

976. **Peterson, SeaBorn H.:** From Burke County, Georgia. Born ca. 1832 in Georgia. Enlisted as a corporal in Company F on 03/05/1862 at Burke County, Georgia. Value of horse $230. Detailed to attend horses at the infirmary/recruiting camp on 11/25/1863. Admitted to Way Hospital at Weldon, North Carolina, on 09/01/1864 and died there on 09/12/1864 of acute colitis. His widow, Francis Peterson, was given his back pay, his effects of $11.30, and his sundries. They had several children.

977. **Pettis, Harrison J.:** Native of Georgia. Enlisted as a veterinary surgeon in Company B on 08/14/1861 at Atlanta, Georgia. Horse, owned by O.H. Jones, valued at $300 and horse equipment $7, saddle furnished by the State of Georgia. Detailed as a teamster in 12/1861. Sent to Georgia to get a horse with Lt. James H. Johnson on 04/14/1863. Lost horse on 11/06/1863. Sent home to get a horse on 11/13/1863. No horse and detailed on light duty at Atlanta, Georgia, on 03/11/1864. Last record September/October 1864, still in Atlanta, Georgia, on light duty.

978. **Phelps, A.B. [A.D.]:** Enlisted as a private in Company L on 10/13/1864 at Dinwiddie Court House, Virginia. Admitted to C.S.A. General Hospital, Danville, Virginia, on 11/03/1864 with pleuritis. Returned to duty on 11/11/1864. Detailed as a courier. Was surrendered by Gen. Joseph E. Johnston on 04/26/1865. Paroled at Greensboro, North Carolina, on 05/01/1865.

979. **Phillips, James R.:** 16-year-old from Columbia County, Georgia. Enlisted as a private in Company A on 08/17/1861 at Augusta, Georgia. Value of horse $225 and horse equipment $40. Sent to infirmary/recruiting camp on 11/20/1863. On sick furlough for 60 days beginning 12/25/1861. Horse killed in action near Richmond, Virginia, on 07/28/1862. Sent home to get a horse with Capt. Bostick on 09/20/1864. Was surrendered by Gen. Joseph E. Johnston on 04/26/1865. Paroled at Greensboro, North Carolina, on 05/01/1865. Possibly the James Phillips who was a farm laborer from Richmond County in 1880. Was married and the father of at least three children.

980. **Pierce [Pearce], George W.:** Enlisted as a private in Company C on 02/25/1862 at Athens, Clarke County, Georgia. Died at Richmond, Virginia, on 12/20/1862.

981. **Pierce [Peirce], John A.:** 24-year-old na-

tive of Georgia. Enlisted as a private in Company F on 03/05/1862 at Burke County, Georgia. Value of horse $185. On sick furlough in Georgia but had not returned to regiment when the furlough expired on 09/07/1864. Still absent without leave on last record September/October 1864.

982. Pierce, Reuben J.: 20-year-old farmer. Born on 06/12/1840 in Hall County, Georgia. Enlisted as a private in Company C on 02/25/1862 at Athens, Clarke County, Georgia. Admitted to Institute Hospital, Richmond, Virginia, on 02/02/1862 with chronic diarrhea. Furnished a substitute and discharged on 09/03/1862. Described having a fair complexion, light hair, blue eyes, and being 5'6" tall. After the war, lived in Hall County, Georgia. Married (1) Sarah S. Eubanks on 05/14/1879 (2) Janie Lawson on 02/12/1905. Died on 07/25/1921. Buried at Mount Vernon Baptist Church Cemetery in Hall County, Georgia. His widow received a Confederate pension in Hall County, Georgia, from 1938 to 1941.

983. Pierce, Thomas A.: 32-year-old. Enlisted as a lieutenant in Company F on 03/25/1862 at Burke County, Georgia. Value of horses $300 and $175, and horse equipment $70. Resigned on 10/30/1862 due to an affliction of the kidneys which rendered him unfit for military service.

984. Pinson, Joseph Newton [A.]: Boot maker from Jackson County, Georgia. Born ca. 1833 in Georgia. Enlisted as a private in Company C on 04/25/1862 at Athens, Clarke County, Georgia. Sent home to get a horse in November/December 1863. Detailed as a shoemaker on 12/01/1862. Paroled at Athens, Georgia, on 05/05/1865. After the war, became a farmer in Jackson County, Georgia. He and his wife, Mary, had at least two children. Died after 1880. His widow received a Confederate pension from Jackson County, Georgia.

985. Pinson, William: On a roster of Company C compiled by Glen Spurlock. No service records in Cobb's Legion.

986. Pittard [Pittle], Isham Humphrey [J.]: 24-year-old from Clarke County, Georgia. Born on 05/21/1837 in Winterville, Clarke County, Georgia. Enlisted as a lieutenant in Company H on 03/03/1862 at Athens, Clarke County, Georgia. Served as the acting commanding officer of the company after the capture of Capt. Ritch on 06/09/1863. Captured on 02/21/1864 at Ely's Ford, Virginia, on the Rapidan River. Sent to the Old Capitol Prison in Washington, D.C. Transferred to Fort Delaware Prison on 06/17/1864. Released on 06/16/1865. Described as having a dark complexion, dark hair, blue eyes, and being 5'10" tall.

After the war, became a farmer in Oglethorpe County, Georgia. Married (1) Sarah Rebecca Pittard on 07/10/1877 (2) Maymie Mary C. Bishop. Died on 01/29/1914 at Athens, Clarke County, Georgia.

987. Pittard, R.T.: Born ca. 1845 in Georgia. On a roster of Company A compiled by Glen Spurlock. No service records in Cobb's Legion. After the war, became a farm worker in Clarke County, Georgia, and was married. Received a Confederate pension in Clarke County, Georgia. Although he had no service records, he had to prove he served in order to receive a pension.

988. Pittman [Pitman, Pittman], Marcus de Lafayette: 26-year-old farmer from Madison County, Georgia. Born on 09/25/1835 in Madison County, Georgia. Enlisted as a private in Company C on 08/01/1861 at Athens, Clarke County, Georgia. Received a gunshot wound through calf of right leg on 08/01/1863. Admitted to Robertson Hospital, Richmond, Virginia, on 09/20/1863 with gangrene. Furloughed for 60 days beginning 10/02/1863. Detailed in the Invalid Corps, Augusta, Georgia, on 04/01/1865. Described as having a dark complexion, dark eyes, dark hair, and being 6'3" tall. After the war, worked as a farm laborer and then a farmer in Clarke County, Georgia. Moved to Madison County, Georgia. Married Elizabeth Letitia Yerby on 12/18/1867 and they had at least one child. Died on 01/24/1916 in Morgan County, Georgia. Buried in the Pittman Family Cemetery in Madison County, Georgia. His widow received a Confederate pension from Madison County, Georgia.

989. Poland, Thomas N.: Born ca. 1836 in Georgia. Enlisted as a private in Company F on 03/25/1862 at Burke County, Georgia. Value of horse $200. Was surrendered by Gen. Joseph E. Johnston on 04/26/1865. Paroled at Greensboro, North Carolina, on 05/01/1865. Listed as a corporal at the time of the surrender. After the war, became a farmer in Burke County, Georgia. Married (1) Evaline V. Cason on 01/10/1861 in Jefferson County, Georgia (2) Caroline M. Whigham on 01/04/1866 in Jefferson County, Georgia. Died after 1880.

990. Pool [Poole], Benjamin J.B.: Resident of Fulton County, Georgia. Enlisted as a private on 04/22/1864 at Decatur, Georgia. Assigned to Company L from Camp Randolph, DeKalb County, Georgia, on 05/12/1864. Sent to Georgia to get a horse with Capt. Bostick on 09/20/1864. Deserted and took the Oath at Chattanooga, Tennessee, on 11/24/1864. Described as having a dark complexion, black hair, blue eyes, and being 5'10" tall.

991. Pope, Jesse: Enlisted as a private in Company G at Hanover, Virginia. First record, 05/01/1864–09/01/1864. Admitted to Jackson Hospital, Richmond, Virginia, on 06/10/1864 with measles. Returned to duty on 07/08/1864. Last record September/October 1864, sent to Georgia to get a horse with Capt. Bostick on 09/20/1864.

992. Poppin [Poppen], Richard S.: 26-year-old. Enlisted as a private in Company B. Value of horse $180. Transferred to Company G on 03/01/1862 at Atlanta, Georgia. Given a medical discharge on 08/22/1862.

993. Porter, Drury W.: Born ca. 1818. Enlisted in the 12th Regiment, Georgia Cavalry. Listed on a roster of Cobb's Legion Cavalry, Company D, published in *The History of Dougherty County*, but not with the *Civil War Soldiers and Sailors System*. No service records in Cobb's Legion.

994. Pounds [Ponnas], Sylvester: 19-year-old from Georgia. Born on 12/23/1848. Enlisted as a private in Company B on 03/22/1862 at Atlanta, Georgia. Value of horse $175. Transferred to Company G in May/June 1862. Sent to Georgia get a horse with Lt. James H. Johnson on 04/14/1863. Furloughed for 24 days beginning 02/20/1864. Was surrendered by Gen. Joseph E. Johnston on 04/26/1865. Paroled at Greensboro, North Carolina, on 05/01/1865. After the war, worked as a laborer in DeKalb County, Georgia. Married Mary Elizabeth Ragsdale on 06/08/1865 in DeKalb County, Georgia. Died on 09/20/1920. Buried in the Chamblee Cemetery in DeKalb County, Georgia. His widow received a Confederate pension from DeKalb County, Georgia.

995. Powell, Benjamin C.: 35-year-old. Enlisted as a private in Company I on 02/27/1862 at Augusta, Georgia. Value of horse $165. Admitted to C.S.A. General Hospital, Danville, Virginia, on 08/02/1862 with nephritis. Returned to duty on 09/01/1862. Discharged on 12/12/1862.

996. Powell, D.A.: Enlisted as a private in Company D on 08/10/1861 at Albany, Georgia. Value of horse $125 and horse equipment $15. Listed as a corporal in May/June 1862. Listed as a sergeant in November/December 1862. Admitted to Jackson Hospital, Richmond, Virginia, sick on 01/13/1864. Furloughed for 30 days beginning 02/03/1864. Admitted to Jackson Hospital, Richmond, Virginia, on 02/15/1864. Died of pneumonia on 03/02/1864 at Jackson Hospital, Richmond, Virginia.

997. Prater, W.T.: 21-year-old. Enlisted as a corporal in Company K on 01/16/1863 at Camp Maynard, Georgia. Deserted while on horse detail on 08/23/1863.

998. Price, James W.: 24-year-old. Enlisted as a private in Company K on 02/10/1863 at Camp Maynard, Georgia. Deserted on 04/23/1863.

999. Price, John L.: 19-year-old from Georgia. Enlisted as a private in Company B on 05/06/1862 at Atlanta, Georgia. Value of horse $225. Transferred to Company G in May/June 1862. Lost horse in 08/1862. Sent to Georgia to get a horse with Lt. James H. Johnson on 04/14/1863. Was present on last record, September/October 1864.

1000. Prince, J.W.: Enlisted as a private in Company L on 05/11/1864 at Decatur, Georgia. Assigned from Camp Randolph, DeKalb County, Georgia, on 05/12/1864. Sent to Georgia to get a horse with Capt. Bostick on 09/20/1864. Was surrendered by Gen. Joseph E. Johnston on 04/26/1865. Paroled at Greensboro, North Carolina, on 05/01/1865. After the war, lived in Richmond County, Georgia. Received a Confederate pension from Richmond County, Georgia.

1001. Prince, Oliver H.: On a roster of Company C compiled by Glen Spurlock. No service records in Cobb's Legion.

1002. Pritchard [Prichard], Matthew Clifford: 25-year-old. Born on 02/25/1837 in Jefferson County, Georgia. Enlisted as a private in Company F on 05/05/1862 at Burke County, Georgia. Value of horse $185. Detailed as a teamster beginning 03/23/1864. Admitted to Winder Hospital, Richmond, Virginia, on 07/14/1863. Admitted to Jackson Hospital, Richmond, Virginia. Returned to duty on 09/24/1863. Sent to Georgia to get a horse with Capt. Bostick on 09/20/1864. Was surrendered by Gen. Joseph E. Johnston on 04/26/1865. Paroled at Greensboro, North Carolina, on 05/01/1865. Married Sarah Jane Ingram on 02/18/1869 in Screven County, Georgia. Died on 04/30/1903 at the age of 66 in Chatham County, Georgia, and was buried on 05/01/1903 in Laurel Grove Cemetery, Lot 2560, Savannah, Georgia.

1003. Pritchard [Prichard], Thomas W.: 37-year-old. Enlisted as a private in Company F on 05/04/1862 at Burke County, Georgia, as a substitute for Samuel Jordan Smith. Sent to Georgia to get a horse with Lt. Sinquefield under Special Order No. 27 from corps headquarters on 02/23/1864. Sent to Georgia to get a horse with Capt. Bostick on 09/20/1864. Was surrendered by Gen. Joseph E. Johnston on 04/26/1865. Paroled at Greensboro, North Carolina, on 05/01/1865.

1004. Province [Provence, Prosince], Hiram: Native of Georgia. Enlisted as a private in Company B on 08/14/1861 at Atlanta, Georgia. Value of horse $200 and horse equipment $5.25. Sent home to get a horse with Lt. James H. Johnson on 04/14/1863. Lost horse on 08/13/1863. Sent home to get a horse on 08/25/1863. Absent without leave in November/December 1863. Sent to Georgia to get a horse with Lt. Sinquefield under Special Order No. 27 from corps headquarters on 02/23/1864. Last record September/October 1864, sent to Georgia to get a horse with Capt. Bostick on 09/20/1864.

1005. Pruett, Benjamin: 20-year-old. Enlisted as a private in Company K on 02/08/1863 at Camp Maynard, Georgia. Returned to his regiment on 03/23/1863.

1006. Pugh, Nathan S.: Enlisted in the 1st Georgia Infantry, Company I, as a corporal on 03/18/1861. Mustered out at Augusta, Georgia, on 03/18/1862. Enlisted as a private in Cobb's Legion Cavalry, Company I, on 04/10/1862 at Augusta, Georgia. Elected lieutenant on 09/10/1862. Horse valued at $600 killed in action at Rector's Cross Roads, Fauquier County, Virginia, on 06/21/1863. Last record was a claim for the horse dated 06/30/1863. Other records indicate that he was killed at Hunterstown, Pennsylvania, on 07/02/1863. Buried in the National Cemetery, Gettysburg, Pennsylvania, and reinterred on 08/21/1871 at Laurel Grove Cemetery, Gettysburg Section, Lot 853, Savannah, Georgia.

1007. Pugsley [Pugely], Sidney A.: Enlisted as a private in Company L on 12/15/1864 at Burke County, Georgia. Sent to infirmary/recruiting camp in 04/1864. Admitted to Jackson Hospital, Richmond, Virginia, on 06/20/1864 with chronic diarrhea. Returned to duty on 07/10/1864. Sent to Georgia to get a horse with Capt. Bostick on 09/20/1864. Was surrendered by Gen. Joseph E. Johnston on 04/26/1865. Paroled at Greensboro, North Carolina, on 05/01/1865.

1008. Pylant, Edwin: 28-year-old native of Georgia. Enlisted as a private in Company B on 04/19/1862 at Atlanta, Georgia. Value of horse $190. Sent to infirmary/recruiting camp on 03/09/1864. Sent to Georgia to get a horse with Capt. Bostick on 09/20/1864. Was paroled at Augusta, Georgia, on 05/19/1865.

1009. Quarles, A.M.: Resident of Georgia. Enlisted as a private in Company E on 07/09/1863 at Atlanta, Georgia. Sent to Georgia to get a horse with Lt. Sinquefield under Special Order No. 27 from corps headquarters on 02/23/1864. Transferred to the 4th Georgia Infantry on 06/01/1864 in exchange for W.S. Mitchell and was killed in action.

1010. Ramsey, S. Thomas: 24-year-old. Enlisted as a private in Company E on 03/15/1862 at Roswell, Georgia. Received in 12/1862 gunshot wound in left hand, causing permanent contracture of the tendons of the hand and rendering it useless. Furloughed for 40 days beginning 02/02/1863 from General Hospital, Liberty, Virginia. Found unfit for military service by medical board on 07/23/1863

1011. Rasbury, Mansel W.: Photographer from Fulton County, Georgia. Born ca. 1836 in Georgia. Enlisted as a private in Company A on 02/14/1864 at Atlanta, Georgia. Transferred to Company G on 02/26/1864. Last record September/October 1864, sent to Georgia to get a horse with Capt. Bostick on 09/20/1864. Married (1) Amanda W. Witcher on 08/23/1857 in Paulding County, Georgia. His widow, Mary B. Rasbury, received a Confederate pension from Fulton County, Georgia.

1012. Rasbury, Reuben L.: 21-year-old from Fulton County, Georgia. Born in 11/1842 in Paulding County, Georgia. Enlisted as a private in Company B on 04/08/1862 at Atlanta, Georgia. Value of horse $200. Transferred to Company G. Admitted to Winder Hospital, Richmond, Virginia, on 07/25/1863. Sent to Georgia to get a horse on 04/15/1863. Last record September/October 1864, sent to Georgia to get a horse with Capt. Bostick on 09/20/1864. After the war, became a photographer in Floyd County, Georgia, and then in Talladega County, Alabama. He and his wife, Nena or Nonie, had at least three children. Died after 1880.

1013. Ray, John R.: 32-year-old blacksmith from Jackson County, Georgia. Born on 01/06/1830 in Jackson County, Georgia. Enlisted as a private in Company H on 03/04/1862 at Athens, Clarke County, Georgia. Discharged from service and paid off on 07/17/1862. After the war, became a farmer and a blacksmith in Jackson County, Georgia. Married Martha Ann on 04/12/1852 in Jackson County, Georgia, and they had at least four children. Received a Confederate pension from Banks County, Georgia, from 1895 to 1904. Died on 01/01/1905 in Fulton County, Georgia. His widow, Martha Ann Ray, received a Confederate pension from Banks County, Georgia, from 1905 to 1907.

1014. Ray [Wray], William A.: Farm laborer from Jackson County, Georgia. Born ca. 1845. Enlisted as a private in Company C on 07/15/1863 at Strasburg, Virginia. Received clothing at General Hospital No. 3 Lynchburg, Virginia, on 11/18/1863. Detailed as a fisherman on 03/01/1864. Last record September/October 1864, sent to Georgia to get a horse with Capt. Bostick on 09/20/1864.

1015. Raynes [Rains], J.M.: Resident of Baldwin County, Georgia. Enlisted as a private in Company K on 02/19/1863 at Camp Maynard, Georgia. Detailed as a teamster in 02/1863. Sent home to get a horse on 08/23/1863. Absent without leave beginning 10/22/1863. Still absent without leave on last record, March/April 1864.

1016. Reader [Reeder], J.N.: Resident of Georgia. Enlisted as a private in Company A on 02/11/1864 at Decatur, Georgia. Sent to Georgia to get a horse with Capt. Bostick on 09/20/1864. Was surrendered by Gen. Joseph E. Johnston on 04/26/1865. Paroled at Greensboro, North Carolina, on 05/01/1865.

1017. Reese, Henry C.: 17-year-old from Thompson, Columbia County, Georgia. Enlisted as a private in Company A on 03/26/1862 at Augusta, Georgia. Value of horse $210. Transferred to Company B on 04/22/1862, and to Company I around 01/1863. Wounded on 08/25/1864. Admitted to Pettigrew General Hospital No. 13, Raleigh, North Carolina, on 08/28/1864 with a gunshot wound in the right shoulder. Was surrendered by Gen. Joseph E. Johnston on 04/26/1865. Paroled at Greensboro, North Carolina, on 05/01/1865.

1018. Reese, W.M.: About 17 years old. From Georgia. Enlisted as a private in Company I on 01/13/1864 at Augusta, Georgia. Sent to Georgia to get a horse with Capt. Bostick on 09/20/1864. Was surrendered by Gen. Joseph E. Johnston on 04/26/1865. Paroled at Greensboro, North Carolina, on 05/01/1865.

1019. Reeves, William: On a roster of Company C compiled by Glen Spurlock. No service records in Cobb's Legion.

1020. Reid, A.R.: Enlisted in Nelson's Independent Company, Georgia Cavalry. Listed on a roster of Company D published in *The History of Dougherty County*, but not with the *Civil War Soldiers and Sailors System*. No service records in Cobb's Legion.

1021. Reid [Read], J.L. [J.S., L.R.]: Resident of Georgia. Enlisted as a private in Company A on 10/08/1862 at Bunker Hill, [West] Virginia. Listed as absent on detail in March/April 1863. Sent to infirmary/recruiting camp on 12/22/1863. Was present on last record, September/October 1864.

1022. Reid [Reed], Jonas G.B.: Farmer from Emanuel County, Georgia. Born ca. 1828 in Georgia. Enlisted as a private in Company F on 05/05/1862 at Burke County, Georgia. Value of horse $125. Given furlough of indulgence for 24 days beginning 02/19/1864. Detailed to tear up railroad tracks between Hamilton's Crossing and Fredericksburg, Virginia, on 03/27/1864. Sent to Georgia to get a horse with Capt. Bostick on 09/20/1864. Was surrendered by Gen. Joseph E. Johnston on 04/26/1865. Paroled at Greensboro, North Carolina, on 05/01/1865. After the war, became a farmer in Emanuel County, Georgia. He and his wife, Martha, had at least one child. Died after 1880.

1023. Reid, William Halum: 24-year-old from Georgia. Born on 09/23/1838 in Hall County, Georgia. Enlisted as a private in Company C on 08/15/1861 at Athens, Clarke County, Georgia. Was surrendered by Gen. Joseph E. Johnston on 04/26/1865. Paroled at Greensboro, North Carolina, on 05/01/1865. After war, worked as a farm laborer and then a farmer in Lumpkin County, Georgia. Married (1) Nancy M. Anderson on 10/21/1869 in Lumpkin County, Georgia, and they had at least five children. Married (2) Jennie or Jane Thompson on 07/10/1890 in Lumpkin County, Georgia, and they had at least two children. Applied for a Confederate pension in Lumpkin County, Georgia. Died on 01/10/1911 in Lumpkin County, Georgia. Buried in Pecks Chapel Cemetery in Lumpkin County, Georgia. His widow applied for a Confederate pension in Lumpkin County, Georgia.

1024. Reidling, Joseph W.M.: Teacher from Jackson County, Georgia. Born ca. 1835 in Georgia. Enlisted as a private in Company H on 02/27/1862 at Athens, Clarke County, Georgia. Died in 09/1862. His back pay was given to his father as he had no wife or children.

1025. Reynolds, Joseph Jones: 24-year-old planter from Burke County, Georgia. Born on 01/25/1838. Enlisted as a private in Company F on 03/25/1862 at Burke County, Georgia. Value of horse $325. Admitted to Henningsen Hospital, Richmond, Virginia, on 11/03/1862. On sick furlough to Burke County, Georgia, in 11/1862. Returned to duty in 02/1863. Sent to Georgia to get a horse with Capt. Bostick on 09/20/1864. Was surrendered by Gen. Joseph E. Johnston on 04/26/1865. Paroled at Greensboro, North Carolina, on 05/01/1865. Married (1) Rosa V. Anderson ca. 1860 (2) Lizzie W. Anderson ca. 1870. Was the father of at least one child. Died on 03/16/1900. Buried in the Waynesboro Confederate Cemetery in Burke County, Georgia.

1026. Reynolds, Robert Augustus.: 16-year-old from Lincoln County, Georgia. Born in Lincoln County, Georgia, on 06/30/1836. Enlisted as a private in Company A on 08/17/1861 at Augusta, Georgia. Value of horse $200 and horse equipment $25. No horse and detailed as a teamster for Maj.

Goodwin on 01/01/1863. Given public horse in November/December 1863. Was present in September/October 1864. His last record is a receipt for clothing dated 12/01/1864. After the war, became a farmer in Lincoln County, Georgia. Married Elizabeth A. Tillery on 12/22/1870 in Lincoln County, Georgia, and was the father of eight children. On his Confederate pension application, he stated that he surrendered at Appomattox Court House. His physician stated that the tibia in his left leg had been fractured and he had suffered a gunshot wound of the right leg. In addition, his skull had been fractured by a saber. He was not able to stand the sun because the head wound caused violent attacks of neuralgia. Received a Confederate pension from Lincoln County, Georgia. Died after 1907.

1027. Reynolds, Robert Augustus [J.]: Born ca. 1836 in Burke County, Georgia. Enlisted as a private in Company F on 03/25/1862 at Burke County, Georgia. Value of horse $225. Wounded at Barbee's Cross Roads, Virginia, on 11/05/1862. Admitted to a hospital in Richmond, Virginia, on 11/11/1862. Furloughed to Georgia for 40 days beginning 11/14/1862. Detailed as brigade forage master on 03/30/1864. Last record September/October 1864, sent to Georgia to get a horse with Capt. Bostick on 09/20/1864. Married to Laura Morgan. Died in 1867.

1028. Reynolds, Thomas: 22-year-old from Richmond County, Georgia. Enlisted as a private in Company I on 03/05/1862 at Augusta, Georgia. Value of horse $185. Killed in action at Brandy Station, Culpeper County, Virginia, on 08/01/1863. His back pay was given to his mother, Bridgette Thomas, as he was not survived by his father, a wife, or children.

1029. Reynolds, Walter C.: Overseer from Dougherty County, Georgia. Born ca. 1844 in Georgia. Enlisted as a private in Company D on 08/10/1861 at Albany, Georgia. Value of horse $160, and horse equipment $20, furnished by State of Georgia. Furloughed beginning 09/13/1862. Admitted to C.S.A. General Hospital, Charlottesville, Virginia, on 09/28/1862 with a gunshot wound in the thigh. Furloughed beginning 10/07/1862. Promoted to corporal in November/December 1862. Listed as a sergeant in November/December 1863. Sent to infirmary/recruiting camp on 12/08/1863. Listed as a private in March/April 1864. Was surrendered by Gen. Joseph E. Johnston on 04/26/1865. Paroled at Greensboro, North Carolina, on 05/01/1865. After the war, became an overseer in Dougherty County, Georgia. Died after 1870.

1030. Rheney, Elisha Anderson: Farmer from Jefferson County, Georgia. Born in Richmond County, Georgia, ca. 1826. Enlisted as a private in Company L on 12/15/1862 at Burke County, Georgia. Sent to Georgia to get a horse with Lt. Sinquefield under Special Order No. 27 from corps headquarters on 02/23/1864. Admitted to Jackson Hospital, Richmond, Virginia, on 06/06/1864. Furloughed for sickness. Last record, admitted to C.S.A. General Hospital, Danville, Virginia, on 11/29/1864 with paralysis. After the war, became a planter in Richmond County, Georgia. Married Julia Agnes Rhodes on 03/31/1858 in Richmond County, Georgia, and they had at least five children. Received a Confederate pension from Richmond County, Georgia. Died after 1880.

1031. Rhodes, Henry N. [H.L.]: 18-year-old student from Augusta, Georgia. Born on 01/01/1843 in Richmond County, Georgia. Enlisted as a private in Company A on 08/17/1861 at Augusta, Georgia. Value of horse $200 and horse equipment $25. Detailed as a courier in 05/1862. Killed in action on 11/05/1862 at Barbee's Cross Roads. His father, Thomas R. Rhodes, received his back pay as he was not survived by a wife or children.

1032. Rhodes, Radford C.: 32-year-old farmer. Resident of Allens, Warren County, Georgia. Born on 05/20/1829. Enlisted as a private in Company A on 08/17/1861 at Augusta, Georgia. Wounded in the arm while on picket duty 08/01/1862. Appointed sub-enrolling (conscript) officer of Warren County, Georgia, on 01/15/1863. Last record, 06/09/1864. After the war, became a farmer in Hello or Red Lick, Warren County, Georgia. He married Mary J. Holden, and they had no children. Received a Confederate pension from Warren County, Georgia.

1033. Rice, Calvin C.: 36-year-old overseer from Burke County, Georgia. Born in South Carolina. Enlisted as a private in Company F on 03/25/1862 in Burke County, Georgia. Value of horse $175. Horse killed in action at Barbee's Cross Roads on 11/05/1862. Detailed as a teamster and sent home for a horse in January/February 1863. Detailed to attend horses at recruiting/infirmary camp on 02/22/1864. Was surrendered by Gen. Joseph E. Johnston on 04/26/1865. Paroled at Greensboro, North Carolina, on 05/01/1865. Married Susan C. Beasley on 01/09/1856 in Chatham County, Georgia. He and his wife, Susan, had at least two children.

1034. Rice, J.W.: About 17 years old. From Georgia. Enlisted as a private in Company E on 04/24/1864 at Chesterfield, Virginia. Sent to Georgia with Capt. Bostick to get a horse on 09/20/

1864. Was surrendered by Gen. Joseph E. Johnston on 04/26/1865. Paroled at Greensboro, North Carolina, on 05/01/1865.

1035. Rice, Zachariah A.: 38-year-old from Atlanta, Georgia. Retail merchandiser, part owner of the newspaper *Southern Miscellany* (which became the *Weekly Atlanta Intelligencer*) and a slave dealer. Born on 09/22/1822 in Spartanburg, South Carolina. Participated in the "Cherokee Removal" in North Georgia in 1837. Enlisted as a lieutenant in Company B on 08/14/1861. Value of horse $250 and horse equipment $30. Furloughed for 25 days beginning 11/27/1861. Elected captain on 12/17/1861. Promoted to major on 11/01/1862. Resigned on 06/10/1863 for family and business reasons. After the war, became a farmer in Campbell County, Georgia, and then a businessman, judge, and city councilman in Atlanta, Fulton County, Georgia. Married Louisa R. Green in Fulton, County, Georgia, on 05/15/1855 and they had at least five children. Died on 07/02/1890 at Atlanta, Georgia. Buried in Oakland Cemetery, Atlanta, Fulton County, Georgia. His papers are at the Atlanta Historical Society.

1036. Rich, James L.: 20-year-old from Webbville, Newton County, Georgia. Enlisted as a private in Company B on 04/10/1862 at Atlanta, Georgia. Value of horse $225 and horse equipment $25. Transferred to Company G in May/June 1862. Detailed as a teamster beginning 02/21/1863. Admitted to Pettigrew General Hospital No. 13, Raleigh, North Carolina, on 12/07/1864 with chronic rheumatism. Returned to duty on 12/31/1864. Was surrendered by Gen. Joseph E. Johnston on 04/26/1865. Paroled at Greensboro, North Carolina, on 05/01/1865.

1037. Riden [Readen, Rieden], Martin W.: 31-year-old from Georgia. Born on 09/30/1830. Enlisted as a private in Company C on 08/01/1864 at Athens, Clarke County, Georgia. Courier for Col McKenny, Col Zoulueski, and Col. Johnson beginning 12/1861. Detailed in Commissary Department beginning 12/01/1863. Clerk for brigade commissary beginning 07/07/1864. Was surrendered by Gen. Joseph E. Johnston on 04/26/1865. Paroled at Greensboro, North Carolina, on 05/01/1865. Died on 05/21/1882. Buried in the Alta Vista Cemetery in Hall County, Georgia.

1038. Ridgway, James N.: Farmer from Gwinnett County, Georgia. Enlisted as a private in Company C on 04/28/1862 at Athens, Georgia. Transferred to Company H in January/February 1863. Fined $12 by court-martial in January/February 1863. Sent home to get a horse on 11/11/1863. Absent without leave beginning 01/23/1864, but was present in March/April 1864. Sent to Georgia with Capt. Bostick to get a horse on 09/20/1864. Was surrendered by Gen. Joseph E. Johnston on 04/26/1865. Paroled at Greensboro, North Carolina, on 05/01/1865. He and his wife, Martha, had at least five children.

1039. Ridgway [Rigway], John N.: Farmer from Clarke County, Georgia. Enlisted as a private in Company C. Transferred to Company H. Sent to Georgia to get a horse on 11/11/1863. Absent without leave in 01/1864. Sent to Georgia with Capt. Bostick to get a horse on 09/20/1864. Was surrendered by Gen. Joseph E. Johnston on 04/26/1865. Paroled at Greensboro, North Carolina, on 05/01/1865. After the war, became a farmer in Clarke and Oconee Counties, Georgia. He and his wife, Sarah, had at least eight children. Died after 1880. His widow received a Confederate pension from Walton County, Georgia.

1040. Ridings, George: 18-year-old from Georgia. Born in North Carolina or in Cobb County, Georgia. Enlisted as a private in Company E on 03/22/1862 at Roswell, Georgia. Value of horse $125. Sent to recruiting/infirmary camp on 01/19/1864. Last record September/October 1864, sent to Georgia with Capt. Bostick to get a horse on 09/20/1864.

1041. Ridley, W.B.: Resident of Georgia. Enlisted as a private in Company D on 03/04/1862 at Albany, Georgia. Value of horse $250 and horse equipment $12. Last record September/October 1864, sent to Georgia with Capt. Bostick to get a horse on 09/20/1864.

1042. Ridlin, J.W.M.: On a roster of Company C compiled by Glen Spurlock. No service records in Cobb's Legion.

1043. Ridling, J.K.P.: Resident of Jackson County, Georgia. Native of Georgia. Enlisted as a private in Company B on 07/10/1863 at Atlanta, Georgia. Wounded at Spotsylvania Court House on 05/07/1864. Admitted to Jackson Hospital, Richmond, Virginia, on 05/12/1864 with a wound in his left shoulder from a carbine ball. Furloughed to Georgia for 60 days on 05/25/1864. Returned to duty on 08/08/1864. Was surrendered by Gen. Joseph E. Johnston on 04/26/1865. Paroled at Greensboro, North Carolina, on 05/01/1865.

1044. Rigand [Regan, Regand], L.[S.]: 25-year-old from Holly Springs, Mississippi. Enlisted as a private in Company K on 02/09/1863 at Camp Maynard, Georgia. Admitted to C.S.A. General Hospital, Charlottesville, Virginia, on 03/04/1863 with debility. Returned to duty on 03/05/1863 without a regular hospital discharge. Captured at Totopotomoy Creek, Virginia, on 06/04/1864 and sent to Elmira Prison, New York. Released on 07/03/1865. Described as having a fair complexion, dark hair, blue eyes, and being 5'8" tall.

1045. Ringgold [Ringold], James G. [A.G.]: Resident of Fulton County, Georgia. Native of Georgia. Enlisted as a private in Company B on 11/20/1861 at Yorktown, Virginia, as a substitute for James R.D. Ozborne. Admitted to Winder Hospital, Richmond, Virginia, on 07/22/1862 with dysentery. Returned to duty on 08/04/1862. Lost horse on 01/01/1863. Detailed on provost guard beginning 04/18/1864. Captured at Columbia, South Carolina, on 02/19/1865 and sent to New Bern, North Carolina. Transferred to Hart's Island, New York Harbor, on 04/10/1865. Released on 06/14/1865. Described as having a light complexion, dark hair, blue eyes and being 5'6½" tall. His name was on a list of invalids able to travel.

1046. Ritch [Rich], James L.[S.]: Enlisted as a private in Company B. Transferred to Company G. No service records in Cobb's Legion. After the war, lived in Fulton County, Georgia, with his wife, Sarah F. His widow received a Confederate pension in Fulton County, Georgia.

1047. Ritch [Rich], Jeremiah E.: Merchant from Clarke County, Georgia. Born ca. 1828 in Georgia. Brother-in-law of John James Alexander. Enlisted as a lieutenant in Company C on 08/01/1861 at Athens, Clarke County, Georgia. On furlough to Georgia for 30 days beginning 02/18/1862. Elected captain of Company H on 05/26/1862. Served as commanding officer, inspector, and mustering officer. Captured on 06/09/1863 at Beverly's Ford, Virginia, while leading the company as dismounted sharpshooters, and sent to the Old Capitol Prison, Washington D.C. Transferred to Johnson's Island Prison, Ohio, on 08/02/1863. Transferred to City Point, Virginia, for exchange on 02/24/1865. Colonel P.M.B. Young's report of the 06/09/1863 engagement at Brandy Station mentioned that "Among others whose distinguished conduct came under my personal observation, was ... Capt. J.E. Ritch commanding sharpshooters (who, I regret to say, while dismounted, was captured by a cavalry charge)...." After the war, became a dealer in ready-made clothing in Clarke County, Georgia. He and his wife, Jane, had at least five children. Applied for a Confederate pension in Clarke County, Georgia. Died after 1870. His widow received a Confederate pension in Clarke County, Georgia.

1048. Rives [Reaves], Burwell [Burrell] G.: Merchant from Hall County, Georgia. Born ca. 1839 in Georgia. Enlisted as a private in Company H on 03/01/1863 in Brownsburg, Virginia, as a substitute for Aaron H. Boggs. Sent to infirmary/recruiting camp on 11/01/1863. Last record September/October 1864, sent to Georgia with Capt. Bostick to get a horse on 09/20/1864. Was married to Elizabeth.

1049. Rives [Reaves], Reuben P.: 32-year-old farmer from Lumpkin County, Georgia. Born on 02/11/1830 in Hall County, Georgia. Enlisted as a private in Company H on 09/03/1862 at Athens, Clarke County, Georgia. Horse killed in battle at Raccoon Ford on 09/18/1863. Sent to Georgia to get a horse on 11/11/1863. Sent to infirmary/recruiting camp on 02/23/1864. Last record September/October 1864, sent to Georgia with Capt. Bostick to get a horse on 09/20/1864. After the war, became a farmer in Lumpkin County, Georgia. He and his wife, Nancy J., had at least four children. Died on 01/19/1908 in Hall County, Georgia. Buried in Yellow Creek Cemetery in Hall County, Georgia.

1050. Rives [Reaves], Thomas J.: 18-year-old farmer/student from Lumpkin County, Georgia. Born on 02/11/1843 in Hall County, Georgia. Enlisted as a private in Company C on 08/01/1861 at Athens, Clarke County, Georgia. Transferred into Company H on 01/01/1863. Admitted to Jackson Hospital, Richmond, Virginia, on 11/30/1863 with a minié ball wound to the mouth. Sent to Georgia on 60 days wounded furlough beginning 12/16/1863. Still in Georgia wounded on last record, September/October 1863. After the war, became a farmer in Hall County, Georgia. He and his wife, Malinda C., had at least seven children. Received a Confederate pension from Jackson County, Georgia. Died on 02/15/1896 in Jackson County, Georgia. Buried in Walnut Fork Cemetery in Jackson County, Georgia.

1051. Roach, William H.: Native of Georgia. Enlisted as a blacksmith in Company B on 08/14/1861 at Atlanta, Georgia. Furloughed for 25 days on 11/29/1861. Sent home to get a horse with Lt. Sinquefield under Special Order No. 27 from corps headquarters on 02/23/1864. Sent to Georgia with Capt. Bostick to get a horse on 09/20/1864. Paroled at Augusta, Georgia, on 05/20/1865. His rank was listed as a private on his parole.

1052. Roark, Page Jefferson: Student from Hall County, Georgia. Born ca. 1845 in Hall County, Georgia. Enlisted as a private in Company H on 03/01/1863 at Athens, Clarke County, Georgia. Admitted to C.S.A. General Hospital in Charlottesville, Virginia, on 05/04/1863 with intermittent fever (probably malaria). Returned to duty on 05/11/1863. Wounded in the left forearm in Maryland on 07/10/1863. The arm was "unjointed" at the wrist joint and about six inches of small bone in the forearm dissected. Sent to Georgia on furlough awaiting retirement. Retired on 08/19/1864. After the war, became a farmer in Hall County, Georgia. Married (1) Nancy A. Prather in 12/1863 in Hall County, Georgia, and they had at least five children. Married (2) Julia V. Smith on 12/12/1884 in Hall County, Georgia. Received a Confederate pension from Hall County, Georgia, in 1908. Died on 04/09/1910 in Hall County, Georgia. Buried in the Antioch Methodist Cemetery in Hall County, Georgia.

1053. Robbins, Francis (Frank): About 22 years old, farmer. Enlisted as a private in Company A 09/01/1862 at Richmond, Virginia. Value of horse $125 and horse equipment $20. Deserted in March/April 1863. Described by the Federal Provost Marshal's Office, 4th Dist., Richmond, Virginia, as age 23, 5 feet 4 1/2 inches tall, dark complexion, dark eyes, and dark hair, occupation farmer.

1054. Robert, Alexander J.: Planter from Dougherty County, Georgia. Born on 10/08/1828 in South Carolina. Enlisted in the 4th Regiment, Georgia Infantry. Listed on a roster of Company D published in *The History of Dougherty County*, but not with the *Civil War Soldiers and Sailors System*. No service records in Cobb's Legion. Married Virginia Simms on 10/18/1863.

1055. Robert, Benjamin F.: Resident of Dougherty County, Georgia. Born on 09/12/1835 in South Carolina. Listed on a roster of Company D published in *The History of Dougherty County*, but not with the *Civil War Soldiers and Sailors System*. No service records in Cobb's Legion. After the war, became a farmer in Dougherty County, Georgia. Married Mary Isabel Patot on 01/31/1866 in Dougherty County, Georgia, and they had at least two children. Died after 1870.

1056. Robert, Jehu Stoney: Physician from Dougherty County, Georgia. Born on 11/09/1833 in South Carolina. Listed on a roster of Company D published in *The History of Dougherty County*, but not with the *Civil War Soldiers and Sailors System*. No service records in Cobb's Legion. After the war, became a physician in Dougherty County, Georgia. Married Catherine J. Patot and they had at least nine children. Died after 1870.

1057. Robert, Ulysses M.: Born in South Carolina ca. 1820–1830. Enlisted in the 4th Regiment, Georgia Infantry. Listed on a roster of Company D published in *The History of Dougherty County*, but not with the *Civil War Soldiers and Sailors System*. No service records in Cobb's Legion.

1058. Roberts, George W.: Resident of Georgia. Enlisted as a private in Company A on 02/17/1862 at Yorktown, Virginia, as a substitute for William H. Robertson. Admitted to C.S.A. General Hospital, Danville, Virginia, on 06/04/1864 with a wound. Given a medical furlough on 06/09/1864. Last record September/October 1864, sent to Georgia with Capt. Bostick to get a horse on 09/20/1864.

1059. Roberts, Richard E.: 17-year-old from Lincoln County, Georgia. Born on 02/28/1846. Enlisted as a private in Company A on 02/26/1864 at Augusta, Georgia. Sent to Georgia with Capt. Bostick to get a horse on 09/20/1864. Was surrendered by Gen. Joseph E. Johnston on 04/26/1865. Paroled at Greensboro, North Carolina, on 05/01/1865. After the war, became a farmer in Lincoln County, Georgia. Was married and the father of at least one child. Died on 03/11/1936 in McDuffie County, Georgia. Buried in Salem Cemetery, Lincolnton, Georgia.

1060. Roberts, W.: Enlisted as a private in Company D on 04/14/1862 at Griffin, Georgia. Transferred to 2nd North Carolina Cavalry, Company K, on 08/01/1863.

1061. Roberts, William R. (Bill): Attorney-at-law in Burke County, Georgia. Born ca. 1839 in Georgia. Enlisted as a private in Company F on 03/25/1862 at Burke County, Georgia. Value of horse $225 and horse equipment $65. Horse valued at $800 killed in action at Jack's Shop on 09/22/1863. Roberts promoted to lieutenant on 11/04/1863. Given a 24-day furlough of indulgence beginning 02/11/1864. Was acting A.A. for Jeff Davis Legion in 1864. Was surrendered by Gen. Joseph E. Johnston on 04/26/1865. Paroled at Greensboro, North Carolina, on 05/01/1865. Rank listed as captain on his parole.

1062. Robertson, Isaac: 18-year-old. Enlisted as a private in Company K on 02/09/1863 at Camp Maynard, Georgia. Returned to his regiment on 02/21/1863.

1063. Robertson, William H.: Enlisted as a private in Company A on 8/17/1861 at Augusta, Georgia. Value of horse $240 and horse equipment $40. On sick furlough in 12/1861. Temporarily assigned as an assistant surgeon on 06/09/1862. Last record January/February 1863, lists rank as sergeant. Furnished Holcombe, who deserted, and then George W. Roberts as substitutes.

1064. Robertson, William S.: 32-year-old

from Georgia. Enlisted as a private in Company B on 04/28/1862. Value of horse $175. Transferred to Company G in May/June 1862. Wounded and horse valued at $375 killed in battle at Hunterstown, Pennsylvania, on 07/02/1863. Admitted to Chimborazo Hospital, Richmond, Virginia, on 07/21/1863. Furloughed for 40 days to Atlanta, Georgia, on 08/08/1863. Detailed at hospital in Atlanta, Georgia, beginning 04/01/1864 due to inability to perform field service. Last record 04/30/1864, detailed at hospital in Atlanta.

1065. **Roch, E.J.:** Enlisted as a private in Company B on or before 09/03/1861. Horse, owned by company, valued at $175. Only one service record in Cobb's Legion.

1066. **Rodgers [Rogers], Alpheus M.:** From Waynesboro, Burke County, Georgia. Born in South Carolina ca. 1833. Brother of Charles Edward Rodgers. Enlisted in 12th Georgia Infantry in 04/1862. Transferred to Cobb's Legion Cavalry, Company L, in 12/1862 at Augusta, Georgia. Elected captain on 01/10/1863. Admitted to Pettigrew General Hospital, Raleigh, North Carolina, on 08/29/1864 with debility (possibly wounded). Last record, at home on sick furlough beginning 10/05/1864.

1067. **Rodgers [Rogers], Charles Edward:** From Richmond County, Georgia. Born ca. 1842 in South Carolina. Brother of Alpheus M. Rodgers. Enlisted in 48th Georgia Infantry, Company C, as a private on 02/28/1862 at Augusta, Georgia. Transferred to Cobb's Legion Cavalry, Company L, as a private on 02/17/1864. Sent home to get a horse under Special Order No. 36 Corps Headquarters 04/01/1864. Was present on his last record, September/October 1864.

1068. **Roebuck, Henry A.:** 21-year-old lawyer from Elbert County, Georgia. Born on 01/01/1839 in Georgia. Enlisted as a private in Company C on 08/01/1861 at Athens, Clarke County, Georgia. Appointed postmaster for the legion on 11/01/1861 by Col. Cobb. On furlough of indulgence beginning 01/17/1864. Was surrendered by Gen. Joseph E. Johnston on 04/26/1865. Paroled at Greensboro, North Carolina, on 05/01/1865. After the war, became a lawyer in Elbert County, Georgia. Received a Confederate pension from Elbert County, Georgia. Died on 12/07/1914. Buried in the Elmhurst Cemetery in Elbert County, Georgia.

1069. **Roesel, G.E.:** Born ca. 1842 in Saxony. On a roster of Company C compiled by Glen Spurlock. No service records in Cobb's Legion. After the war, became a baker in Fulton County, Georgia. He and his wife, Lena, had at least three children. Received a Confederate pension in Cobb County, Georgia. Transferred to Fulton County, Georgia. Died after 1880.

1070. **Roesel [Roasel], Herman [Hermon]:** Resident of Georgia. Enlisted as a private in Company H on 03/25/1862 at Augusta, Georgia. Value of horse $150. Sent to Georgia to get a horse 01/15/1864. Last record September/October 1864, sent to Georgia with Capt. Bostick to get a horse on 09/20/1864.

1071. **Rogers, Charles H.:** 21-year-old from Augusta, Richmond County, Georgia. Enlisted as a corporal in Company I on 03/02/1862 at Augusta, Georgia. Value of horse $250. Received a bullet wound in the right knee at Mine Run, Virginia, on 11/27/1863. Admitted to C.S.A. General Hospital, Charlottesville, Virginia, for an amputation above the knee. Admitted to Jackson Hospital, Richmond, Virginia, on 01/30/1864. Furloughed for 60 days. Last record September/October 1864, still absent due to wound. After the war, lived in Richmond County, Georgia. Received a Confederate pension from Richmond County, Georgia.

1072. **Rogers, G. Washington:** Listed as a private in Company F in *Roster of the Confederate Soldiers of Burke County, Georgia: 1861–1865*. No service records in Cobb's Legion.

1073. **Rogers, Jethro W.:** 32-year-old native of Georgia. Enlisted as a private in Company F on 05/09/1862. Value of horse $175. Lost his horse and was sent to the recruiting/infirmary camp to tend to the horses in November/December 1863. Sent home to get a horse with Lt. Sinquefield under Special Order No. 27 from corps headquarters on 02/23/1864. Killed in action at Trevilian Station, Virginia, on 06/11/1864. Mrs. Mary T. Rogers was his legal representative.

1074. **Rogers, John Blake:** 15-year-old from Jackson County, Georgia. Born on 03/27/1847. Enlisted as a private in Company C 03/17/1863 at Athens, Clarke County, Georgia. Was surrendered by Gen. Joseph E. Johnston on 04/26/1865. Paroled at Greensboro, North Carolina, on 05/01/1865. After the war, became a farmer in Jackson County, Georgia, and was married to Lucy A. Received a Confederate pension from Jackson County, Georgia. Died on 06/17/1929. Buried in the Rogers Family Cemetery in Jackson County, Georgia.

1075. **Rogers, John J.:** Painter from Fulton County, Georgia. Born ca. 1842 in Georgia. Enlisted as a private in Company B on 04/20/1862 at Atlanta, Georgia. Transferred to Company G in May/June 1862. Sent to Georgia to get a horse in March/April 1863. Last record September/October 1864, sent to Georgia with Capt. Bostick to get a horse on 09/20/1864.

1076. Rogers, Thomas A.: Farm laborer from Jackson County, Georgia. Born ca. 1842 in Georgia. Enlisted as a private in Company C on 03/17/1862. Admitted to General Hospital No. 7 in Raleigh, North Carolina, on 06/15/1864. Admitted to Jackson Hospital, Richmond, Virginia, on 06/21/1864 with German measles. Returned to duty on 07/06/1864. Sent to Georgia with Capt. Bostick to get a horse on 09/20/1864. Was surrendered by Gen. Joseph E. Johnston on 04/26/1865. Paroled at Greensboro, North Carolina, on 05/01/1865. After the war worked as a farm laborer in Jackson County, Georgia. Died after 1870.

1077. Rollins, Thomas: Enlisted as a private in Company C. Captured at Amissville (Amosville [sic] or Arnorsville [sic]), Virginia, on 08/26/1863. Sent to the Old Capitol Prison, Washington, D.C., on 08/28/1863. Transferred to Point Lookout, Maryland, on 09/26/1863. Died at Point Lookout, Maryland, on 09/16/1864.

1078. Roper, James: 24-year-old. Enlisted as a private in Company K on 02/09/1863 at Camp Maynard, Georgia. Deserted on 02/17/1863.

1079. Ross, John: Resident of Georgia. Enlisted as a private in Company A on 01/17/1863 at Decatur, Georgia. Mortally wounded in the thigh and groin at Jack's Shop, Virginia, 09/22/1863. Admitted to Camp Winder Hospital, Richmond, Virginia, 09/25/1863. Listed with rank of corporal in November/December 1863. No horse in March/April 1864. Admitted to Jackson Hospital, Richmond, Virginia, on 03/06/1864 with a gunshot wound in the left thigh and groin. Released from hospital on 04/11/1864. Sent to Georgia with Capt. Bostick to get a horse on 09/20/1864. Surrendered and paroled at Augusta, Georgia, on 05/22/1865. After the war, his wound never healed. Was an invalid and walked on two crutches. Married in 1857. Died on 11/30/1867 in Augusta, Georgia, of gangrene from his wound. His widow, Annie Ross, received a pension in Chatham County, Georgia.

1080. Ross, Perryman: 22-year-old. Enlisted as a private in Company K on 02/10/1863 at Camp Maynard, Georgia. Returned to his regiment on 02/23/1863.

1081. Rountree [Roundtree], James A.: 28-year-old farmer from Emanuel County, Georgia. Born on 04/16/1834 in Emanuel County, Georgia. Enlisted as a private in Company F on 05/09/1862 at Burke County, Georgia. Value of horse $250. Sent home to get a horse with Lt. Sinquefield under Special Order No. 27 from corps headquarters on 02/23/1864. Sent to Georgia with Capt. Bostick to get a horse on 09/20/1864. Was surrendered by Gen. Joseph E. Johnston on 04/26/1865. Paroled at Greensboro, North Carolina, on 05/01/1865. Listed as a sergeant on his parole. After the war, became a farmer in Emanuel County, Georgia. Married Lavinia Lane on 10/10/1866 and they had at least four children. Died on 09/15/1914.

1082. Rountree, William R.: Clerk from Screven County, Georgia. Born ca. 1839. Enlisted as a private in Company F on 03/25/1862 at Burke County, Georgia. Value of horse $200 and horse equipment $35. Admitted to General Hospital No. 2, Lynchburg, Virginia, in 08/1863 with typhoid fever. Died in hospital on 08/27/1863. Buried in the Old City Cemetery, Lynchburg, Virginia.

1083. Rucker, Alexander Randolph: Born ca. 1831 in Ruckersville, Elbert County, Georgia. Attended Franklin College at Athens, Clarke County, Georgia, and the Dane Law School, Harvard University. Enlisted as a private in Company A on 08/17/1861 at Augusta, Georgia. Value of horse $200 and horse equipment $45. Promoted to lieutenant on 07/04/1863. Absent without leave beginning 09/13/1864. Furloughed by Gen. Lee 09/25/1864. Absent without leave in Georgia beginning 10/07/1864. Paroled at Charlotte, North Carolina, on 05/23/1865. After the war, worked as a farmer and a merchant. Married Aurelia Calhoun on 11/22/1859. Died on 08/16/1900 in Elberton, Georgia, and was buried in the city cemetery. His obituary in the *Elberton Star* said that his last request "was that he be shrouded in the flag of the Confederacy, which request was granted."

1084. Ruddell, John Henry: 21-year-old from Burke County, Georgia. Enlisted as a private in Company A in 11/1861 at Camp Marion, Yorktown, Virginia. Served with Company A for 10 days, and then was detailed as an assistant surgeon with the 24th Georgia Infantry. After the war, became a farmer in Beaufort County, South Carolina, and then Hampton County, South Carolina. Married (1) Hattie C. Turner in 1866 and was the father of at least three children. Married (2) Catherine T. Hallahan on 11/19/1878 at Augusta, Georgia. Died on 05/07/1908 at Augusta, Georgia.

1085. Rushin, John: Enlisted as a private in Company H on 04/03/1862 at Athens, Clarke County, Georgia. Discharged from service and paid off on 07/17/1862.

1086. Rushin, Joseph A.: Enlisted as a private in Company C on 05/04/1862 at Thomas County, Georgia. Had only one muster roll record.

1087. Rusk, David: Farmer from Cherokee

County, Georgia. Born ca. 1840 in Georgia. Enlisted as a private in Company E on 03/15/1862 at Roswell, Georgia. Value of horse $175. Listed with rank of Bugler in January/February 1863. Last record September/October 1864, sent to Georgia with Capt. Bostick to get a horse on 09/20/1864. After the war, worked as a farm laborer in Cherokee County, Georgia. Married Barltuna or Barthina ca. 1865 and they had at least seven children.

1088. Rusk, Dempsy P.: Farmer from Cherokee County, Georgia. Born ca. 1845 in Georgia. Enlisted as a private in Company E on 03/25/1863 at Roswell, Georgia. Last record September/October 1864, sent to Georgia with Capt. Bostick to get a horse on 09/20/1864. After the war, became a farmer in Forsyth County, Georgia, and later lived in Milton County, Georgia. He and his wife, Martha, had at least four children. Received a Confederate pension from Milton County, Georgia. Died after 1880.

1089. Rutherford, John Cobb: 19-year-old student at the University of Georgia. Resident of Clarke County, Georgia. Born on 04/13/1842 in Crawford County, Georgia. Enlisted as a sergeant in Company C on 08/01/1861 at Athens, Clarke County, Georgia. Appointed adjutant with rank of lieutenant on 11/16/1861. Served on Thomas R.R. Cobb's brigade staff as a volunteer aide-de-camp. Later, served on Howell Cobb's staff as an assistant adjutant and inspector general with the rank of captain. Also, served on the staffs of Finegan and Garner in the same position. Paroled on 05/18/1865 in Florida. After the war, became a lawyer in Decatur County and then Bibb County, Georgia. Married and was the father of at least three children. Died on 03/10/1891 in Florida. Buried in Oconee Hill Cemetery in Clarke County, Georgia.

1090. Rutherford, Robert R.: Enlisted as a private in Company L on 06/24/1864 at Macon, Georgia. Admitted to Jackson Hospital, Richmond, Virginia, on 07/06/1864 with sore feet. Returned to duty on 07/08/1864. Sent to Georgia with Capt. Bostick to get a horse on 09/20/1864. Admitted to Jackson Hospital, Richmond, Virginia, on 11/12/1864 with scabies. Returned to duty on 12/08/1864 and sent to Augusta, Georgia, to report to Gen. Young. Was surrendered by Gen. Joseph E. Johnston on 04/26/1865. Paroled at Greensboro, North Carolina, on 05/01/1865.

1091. Rutledge, M.B.: On a roster of Company I compiled by Glen Spurlock. No service records in Cobb's Legion.

1092. Rylee, Andrew Jackson: 28-year-old farmer from Banks County, Georgia. Born in Columbia County, Georgia, on 03/09/1833. Enlisted as a private in Company C on 08/15/1861 at Athens, Clarke County, Georgia. Detailed as a courier in 10/62. Listed as a corporal in November/December 1863. Sent home to get a horse with Lt. Sinquefield under Special Order No. 27 from corps headquarters on 02/23/1864. Was surrendered by Gen. Joseph E. Johnston on 04/26/1865. Paroled at Greensboro, North Carolina, on 05/01/1865. Married Sarah Amanda Fortenberry on 12/22/1856. Died on 03/28/1905.

1093. Rylee, James B.: 28-year-old farmer from Banks County, Georgia. Born on 01/18/1833 in Banks County, Georgia. Enlisted as a private in Company C on 08/01/1861 at Athens, Clarke County, Georgia. Sent home to get a horse under Special Order No. 36 Corps Headquarters on 04/01/1864. Last record September/October 1864, sent to Georgia with Capt. Bostick to get a horse on 09/20/1864. After the war, became a farmer in Banks County, Georgia. He and his wife, Nancy, had at least three children. Received a Confederate pension from Oconee County, Georgia. Transferred to Gwinnett and then Jackson County, Georgia. Died after 1880.

1094. Salter, Thomas W.: Tinner from Clarke County, Georgia. Born ca. 1828 in South Carolina. Enlisted as a private in Company H on 03/05/1862 at Athens, Clarke County, Georgia. Listed in May/June 1862 as a sergeant. Elected lieutenant on 03/25/1863. Was killed in a skirmish on 07/19/1863 near Martinsburg, [West] Virginia. Wiley stated, "We assisted in tearing up the Baltimore & Ohio Railroad beyond Martinsburg as far as a little place called Funktown, I think, where in a brisk and hot little fight Lieut. Salter, of Company H, was killed."* He and his wife, Nancy W., had at least five children.

1095. Sanford, Allen: Deserted at Clarksburg, [West] Virginia, on 10/12/1863. Sent north via Hancock, Maryland.

1096. Saunders, B.F.: Enlisted as a private in Company B on 04/29/1864 at Hamilton's Crossing, Virginia. Lost his horse and was captured on 05/12/1864 at King George County, Virginia. Sent to the Old Capitol Prison, Washington, D.C. Transferred to Fort Delaware Prison on 06/17/1864 and exchanged on 10/31/1864.

1097. Saunders [Sanders, Lander], William: Enlisted as a private in Company L on 09/24/1863

---

*Howard, page 4.

at Sawdust, Georgia. Admitted to Jackson Hospital, Richmond, Virginia, on 02/26/1864. Transferred to 2nd Georgia Infantry, Company D, on 03/02/1864. Returned to duty 04/18/1864.

1098. Scammell, E.W.: Enlisted as a private in Company D. Captured at Ashland, Virginia, on 03/14/1865. Sent to Fortress Monroe, Virginia, on 03/25/1865 and transferred to Point Lookout, Maryland.

1099. Schlesinger, Gustavus: Enlisted as a private in Company B on 08/14/1861 at Atlanta, Georgia. Value of horse $180 and horse equipment $12.75. Detailed as a courier to Col. Thomas R.R. Cobb beginning 02/03/1862. Mortally wounded in action at Fredericksburg, Virginia, on 12/13/1862.

1100. Sconyers, Andrew J.: Farmhand from Burke County, Georgia. Born ca. 1834 in Georgia. Enlisted as a private in Company F on 03/25/1862 at Burke County, Georgia. Value of horse $200. Transferred to Company L in March/April 1863. Sent to Georgia with Capt. Bostick to get a horse on 09/20/1864. Was surrendered by Gen. Joseph E. Johnston on 04/26/1865. Paroled at Greensboro, North Carolina, on 05/01/1865. After the war, became a farmer in Burke County, Georgia. Died after 1880.

1101. Sconyers, Richard: Farmhand from Burke County, Georgia. Enlisted as a private in Company L on 12/15/1862 at Burke County, Georgia. Killed in action at Brandy Station, Virginia, on 06/09/1863. His back pay was given to his father, Richard B. Sconyers, as he was not survived by a wife or children.

1102. Scott, A.F.: 25-year-old from Georgia. Born on 09/27/1835. Enlisted as a private in Company D on 08/10/1861 at Albany, Georgia. Value of horse $200 and horse equipment $25, saddle furnished by State of Georgia. Detailed as a teamster in September/October 1862. Detailed as a blacksmith beginning 08/13/1863. Admitted to Jackson Hospital, Richmond, Virginia, on 08/13/1864 with chronic diarrhea. Returned to duty on 08/18/1864. Sent to Georgia with Capt. Bostick to get a horse on 09/20/1864. Was surrendered by Gen. Joseph E. Johnston on 04/26/1865. Paroled at Greensboro, North Carolina, on 05/01/1865. After the war, lived in Dooly County, Georgia, and then Crisp County, Georgia. Received a Confederate pension from Dooly County, Georgia, and then Crisp County, Georgia. Died on 09/15/1903. Buried in the Zion Hope Cemetery in Crisp County, Georgia.

1103. Scott, Alfred D.: 19-year-old. Enlisted as a private in Company I on 03/19/1862 at Augusta, Georgia. It was not stated if he were present on his last record, 05/01/1862.

1104. Scott, James D.: From Bibb County, Georgia. Born ca. 1832 in Bibb County, Georgia. Enlisted as a private in Company D on 08/10/1861 at Albany, Dougherty County, Georgia. Value of horse $175 and horse equipment $25, saddle furnished by State of Georgia. Detailed packing forage in 12/1861. Promoted to sergeant on 11/01/1862. Wounded on 10/12/1863. Admitted to C.S.A. General Hospital, Charlottesville, Virginia, on 10/15/1864 with a fracture of the forearm. Furloughed for 60 days beginning 11/22/1863. Transferred to the Brigade Ambulance Train in March/April 1864. Assigned to the Provost Guard on 09/25/1864. Was surrendered by Gen. Joseph E. Johnston on 04/26/1865. Paroled at Greensboro, North Carolina, on 05/01/1865.

1105. Scruggs, Joseph L.: Student from Jefferson County, Georgia. Born ca. 1844 in Georgia. Enlisted as a private in Company L on 12/15/1862 at Burke County, Georgia. Sent home to get a horse under Special Order No. 36 Corps Headquarters on 04/01/1864. Sent to Georgia with Capt. Bostick to get a horse on 09/20/1864. Was surrendered by Gen. Joseph E. Johnston on 04/26/1865. Paroled at Greensboro, North Carolina, on 05/01/1865. After the war, worked as a farm laborer in Jefferson County, Georgia. Married (1) Emily F. Thompson on 12/09/1862 in Jefferson County, Georgia (2) Sarah J. and was the father of at least five children. Received a Confederate pension from Jefferson County, Georgia. Died after 1880. His widow, Mrs. M.L. Stevens, received a Confederate pension from Jefferson County, Georgia.

1106. Scudder, Jacob McCarty: 24-year-old. Born on 11/23/1836. Brother of Lewis Blackburn and William Henry Harrison Scudder. Enlisted as a private in Company B on 08/14/1861 at Atlanta, Georgia. Value of horse $150, saddle furnished by State of Georgia. Killed in action near Little Washington, Virginia, on 11/08/1862.

1107. Scudder, Lewis Blackburn: 21-year-old from Forsyth County, Georgia. Born in Georgia or South Carolina on 10/27/1839. Brother of Jacob McCarty and William Henry Harrison Scudder. Enlisted as a private in Company B on 08/14/1861 at Atlanta, Georgia. Value of horse $175 and horse equipment $5.50, saddle furnished by State of Georgia. Listed as a sergeant in March/April 1862, but declined serving and went back to ranks on 03/15/1862. Lost his horse on 03/13/1863. Sent to Georgia to get a horse with Lt. James H. Johnson on 04/14/1863. Detailed as a courier to Gen. Young on 10/30/1863. Was present on last record, September/October 1864. After the war, became a farmer in Forsyth County, Georgia. Married Malinda Elmira Kelly on 04/05/1870 in Forsyth County, Georgia. Died on 10/18/1902.

1108. Scudder, William Henry Harrison: 21-year-old. Born on 08/08/1840 in Georgia. Brother of Jacob McCarty and Lewis Blackburn Scudder. Enlisted as a private in Company B on 05/06/1862 at Atlanta, Georgia. Value of horse $200. Furloughed to Georgia for 24 days beginning 02/19/1864. Lost horse and sent to Georgia to get another horse on 04/21/1864. Sent to Georgia with Capt. Bostick to get a horse on 09/20/1864. Was surrendered by Gen. Joseph E. Johnston on 04/26/1865. Paroled at Greensboro, North Carolina, on 05/01/1865. After the war, became a farmer in Forsyth County, Georgia. Married Margaret (Maggie) Josephine Garmany on 02/161869 and they had at least six children. Died on 08/02/1911 in Rogers County, Oklahoma.

1109. Seagers [Segars], Francis Graves: 36-year-old farmer from Jackson County, Georgia. Born on 02/01/1825. Enlisted as a private in Company H on 04/22/1862 at Athens, Clarke County, Georgia. Sent to Georgia to get a horse on 11/11/1863. Detailed as a shoemaker on 02/06/1864. Sent to Georgia with Capt. Bostick to get a horse on 09/20/1864. Paroled at Augusta, Georgia, on 05/20/1865. After the war, became a farmer in Jackson County, Georgia. Married (1) Permelia or Amanda C. Shaw on 10/20/1842 in Jackson County, Georgia (2) Margarette. Was the father of at least five children. Died on 01/29/1879. Buried at the Segars Cemetery in Barrow County, Georgia.

1110. Seago, James Franklin: 19-year-old from Richmond County, Georgia. Born on 11/24/1842. Brother of Josiah Middleton Seago. Enlisted as a private in Company I on 03/04/1862 at Augusta, Georgia. Value of horse $210. Admitted sick to hospital in Lynchburg, Virginia, on 10/18/1863. Wounded on 06/01/1864. Admitted to Jackson Hospital, Richmond, Virginia, on 06/03/1864 with a gunshot wound in the right leg. Furloughed for 30 days beginning 06/09/1864. Sent to Georgia with Capt. Bostick to get a horse on 09/20/1864. Was surrendered by Gen. Joseph E. Johnston on 04/26/1865. Paroled at Greensboro, North Carolina, on 05/01/1865. After the war, became a farmer in Richmond County, Georgia. Married (1) Sarah Netherland on 12/24/1868 in Richmond County, Georgia (2) Anna Harley on 12/17/1874 and was the father of at least three children. Received a Confederate pension from Richmond County, Georgia. Died after 1880. His widow received a Confederate pension from Fulton County, Georgia.

1111. Seago, Josiah Middleton: 24-year-old farmer from Richmond County, Georgia. Born in Georgia on 04/16/1837. Brother of James Franklin Seago. Enlisted as a private in Company I on 03/04/1862 at Augusta, Georgia. Value of horse $225. Captured on 07/17/1863 at Martinsburg, [West] Virginia and sent to Military Prison, also known as Atheneum Prison, in Wheeling, [West] Virginia. Transferred to Camp Chase, Ohio, on 07/23/1863. Transferred to Fort Delaware Prison on 02/27/1864. Exchanged on 03/07/1865. Sent to a hospital at Fort Lee, Virginia, on 03/11/1865. Described as having a dark complexion, dark hair, dark eyes, being 24-years-old and 5' 4" tall. After the war, worked as a farm hand in Richmond County, Georgia. Married Florence K. Stiles on 12/24/1874 in Richmond County, Georgia, and they had at least three children. Received a Confederate pension from Richmond County, Georgia. Died after 1880. His widow received a Confederate pension from Richmond County, Georgia.

1112. Seay, Marshall N.: 23-year-old laborer from Fulton County, Georgia. Born on 06/09/1841. Enlisted as a private in Company K on 05/10/1864 at Atlanta, Fulton County, Georgia. Wounded on 08/16/1864. Admitted to Jackson Hospital, Richmond, Virginia, on 08/18/1864. Transferred to Company G after 10/1864. Was surrendered by Gen. Joseph E. Johnston on 04/26/1865. Paroled at Greensboro, North Carolina, on 05/01/1865. After the war, became a boot- and shoemaker in Hall County, Georgia. Married Margaret D. Chandler on 05/13/1877. Received a Confederate pension for infirmity and poverty in Hall County, Georgia. Died on 02/03/1911. Buried in the Alta Vista Cemetery in Hall County, Georgia.

1113. Seay, Osborne A.: Laborer from Fulton County, Georgia. Born ca. 1844 in Georgia. Enlisted as a private in Company B on 04/28/1862 at Atlanta, Georgia. Value of horse $175. Transferred to Company G in May/June 1862. Furloughed for 24 days beginning 02/23/1864. Absent without leave beginning 03/15/1864. Wounded near Spotsylvania Court House, Virginia, in 05/1864. Admitted to a hospital at Huguenot Springs, Virginia. Was surrendered by Gen. Joseph E. Johnston on 04/26/1865. Paroled at Greensboro, North Carolina, on 05/01/1865. After the war, lived in the Georgia Lunatic Asylum at Milledgeville, Baldwin County, Georgia. Died after 1870.

1114. Segars, Dub: On a roster of Company C compiled by Glen Spurlock. No service records in Cobb's Legion.

1115. Segars [Seagars], William Richey: 35-year-old farmer from Jackson County, Georgia. Born on 07/27/1827. Enlisted as a private in Company H on 03/27/1863 at Decatur, Georgia. Detailed as a shoemaker beginning 10/16/1863. Was surrendered by Gen. Joseph E. Johnston on 04/26/1865. Paroled at Greensboro, North Carolina, on 05/01/1865. After the war, became a farmer in Jackson County, Georgia. Married Susan Caroline Arnold on 10/14/1847 in Jackson County, Georgia, and they had at least six children. Died on 02/06/1904. Buried at the Segars Cemetery in Barrow County, Georgia.

1116. Sego [Seago], Calvin Cephus: 17-year-old student from Richmond County, Georgia. Born 10/22/1845 in Richmond County, Georgia. Enlisted as a private in Company A on 08/17/1861 at Augusta, Georgia. Value of horse $125 and horse equipment $25. On detail in March/April 1863. Ordered to Georgia to get a horse in November/December 1863. Detailed as a Provost Guard by order of Gen. Lee in March/April 1864. Admitted to Jackson Hospital, Richmond, Virginia, with scabies on 06/11/1864. Returned to duty on 06/24/1864. Last record, absent without leave beginning 10/10/1864 at the time of the Battle of Arthur's Swamp, Virginia. After the war, became a wheelwright in Emanuel County, Georgia, and then a farmer in Richmond County, Georgia. Married Margaret Frances Wiggins. Was the father of at least four children. Died on 01/16/1917.

1117. Sewel, Thomas A.: 27-year-old from Georgia. Enlisted as a private in Company E on 04/09/1862 at Lawrenceville, Georgia. Value of horse $175, saddle and muzzle furnished by State of Georgia. Listed as a farrier beginning January/February 1863. Sent to recruiting/infirmary camp on 09/20/1863. Sent home to get a horse with Lt. Sinquefield under Special Order No. 27 from corps headquarters on 02/23/1864. Sent to recruiting/infirmary camp on 07/05/1864. Paroled at Meridian, Mississippi, on 05/14/1865.

1118. Shackleford, Charles William: 37-year-old farmer from Jackson County, Georgia. Born on 03/15/1826 in Jackson County, Georgia. Brother of Thomas Jefferson Shackleford. Enlisted as a private in Company C on 02/14/1863 at Gainesville, Georgia. Sent to recruiting/infirmary camp in November/December 1863. Sent home to get a horse with Lt. Sinquefield under Special Order No. 27 from corps headquarters on 02/23/1864. Absent without leave beginning 05/01/1864. Still absent without leave on last record, September/October 1864. After the war, became a farmer in Jackson County, Georgia. Married Nancy Carolyn Chandler on 07/19/1860 and they had at least six children. Died on 03/06/1915.

1119. Shackleford, Thomas Jefferson: From Jackson County, Georgia. Born ca. 1838 in Jackson County, Georgia. Brother of Charles William Shackleford. Enlisted as a private in Company C on 04/22/1862 at Athens, Georgia. Sent home to get a horse with Lt. Sinquefield under Special Order No. 27 from corps headquarters on 02/23/1864. Detailed as a teamster beginning March/April 1863. Sent to Georgia with Capt. Bostick to get a horse on 09/20/1864. Was surrendered by Gen. Joseph E. Johnston on 04/26/1865. Paroled at Greensboro, North Carolina, on 05/01/1865. After the war, became a farmer in Jackson County, Georgia. Married Georgia A. Davenport on 12/26/1891 in Jackson County, Georgia. Received a Confederate pension in Hall County, Georgia, from 1916 to 1921. Died on 05/20/1921. His widow received his 1921 pension.

1120. Sharpe, Jarrell G.: 21-year-old from Georgia. Enlisted as a private in Company C on 08/01/1861 at Athens, Clarke County, Georgia. Detailed building officer's quarters from 11/1861 until 01/1862. Admitted to Jackson Hospital, Richmond, Virginia, on 08/18/1864 with debility. Furloughed to Athens, Georgia, for 30 days beginning 09/01/1864. On detail service with Capt. Lumpkin in September/October 1864. Was surrendered by Gen. Joseph E. Johnston on 04/26/1865. Paroled at Greensboro, North Carolina, on 05/01/1865.

1121. Sharpe [Sharp], John H. [Jack]: Student from Pennfield, Greene County, Georgia. Enlisted as a private in Company F on 04/18/1864 at Decatur, Georgia. Wounded in battle on 08/25/1864 at Reams Station, Virginia. Admitted to Pettigrew Hospital, Raleigh, North Carolina, on 08/28/1864 with right foot torn off above the ankle by a shell fragment, necessitating amputation at middle third of right leg. Furloughed for 60 days beginning 10/17/1864. Was surrendered by Gen. Joseph E. Johnston on 04/26/1865. Paroled at Greensboro, North Carolina, on 05/01/1865.

1122. Sharpe, Milton C.: Born ca. 1832 in Georgia. Enlisted as a private in Company C on 03/17/1863 at Decatur, Georgia. Sent to recruiting/infirmary camp on 12/15/1863. Last record September/October 1864, sent to Georgia with Capt. Bostick to get a horse on 09/20/1864.

1123. Shaw, J. Sidney: 28-year-old from

Georgia. Enlisted as a private in Company E on 04/03/1862 at Lawrenceville, Georgia. Sent to Georgia to get a horse in March/April 1863. Sent to recruiting/infirmary camp on 02/04/1864. Last record September/October 1864, sent to Georgia with Capt. Bostick to get a horse on 09/20/1864. His widow, Malissa Shaw, received a Confederate pension from Cobb County, Georgia.

1124. Shaw, William M.: Resident of Georgia. Enlisted as a private in Company E on 01/17/1864 at Roswell, Georgia. He had no horse until 05/14/1864. Was wounded on 06/20/1864. Admitted to Jackson Hospital, Richmond, Virginia, on 06/22/1864 with a gunshot wound in his left arm, necessitating a resection of 3½" of the lower humerus bone. Furloughed for 40 days beginning 07/31/1864. Was absent on furlough on last record, September/October 1864.

1125. Shead [Shed], Loring [Low] Wheeler: From Richmond County or Savannah, Georgia. Born ca. 1839 in Maine. Lived in Eastport, Maine, before migrating south. Enlisted in the 1st Georgia Infantry, Company D, as a private in 03/18/1861. Appointed corporal. Mustered out at Augusta, Georgia, on 03/18/1862. Served in the Augusta Fire Battalion. Enlisted as a private in Cobb's Legion Cavalry, Company I, on 02/14/1864. Deserted to the enemy while on picket duty on the Vaughn Road on 09/10/1864. Took the Oath in Washington, D.C., and was transferred to Eastport, Maine. Described as having a dark complexion, black hair, dark eyes, and being 5' 4½" tall. After the war, became an artist and photographer in Windham County, Connecticut, and then a farmer in northeast Connecticut. Claimed he either had to fight for the South or go to prison, so he joined; nevertheless, he wore his Confederate uniform in parades around Boston. Married Ellen Coman Aldrich, who was the widow of Captain Aldrich, captain of a colored unit from Connecticut, who died of consumption acquired while in Libby prison. Died suddenly in 1915 after caring for his uncle, who was sick, in Eastport, Maine.

1126. Shed, J.A.: Resident of Gwinnett County, Georgia. Enlisted as a private in Company E on 06/01/1864 at Hanover County, Virginia. Was present on his last record, September/October 1864. According to Wiley, he was mortally wounded in action at the Battle of Bentonville in 03/1865. Wiley mentions him in his sketch. He said, "Passing one of our men (at Monroe's Cross Roads) who was shot through the ear on his horse, the Yankee getting the advantage, I was enabled, by a right parry blow, striking the back of the head, to floor his antagonist, and relieve him. His name was Shed, from Gwinnett County. He afterwards thanked me for relieving him, and a little later I saw the poor fellow brought off the skirmish line at Bentonville mortally wounded."*

1127. Sheffield, James M.: Enlisted as a private in Company D on 08/10/1861 at Albany, Georgia. Value of horse $225 and horse equipment $25, furnished by State of Georgia. Was present on his last record, March/April 1863.

1128. Shelby, William Alexander: 27-year-old physician from Fulton County, Georgia. Born on 02/20/1835 in Georgia. Enlisted as a private in Company B on 04/28/1862 at Atlanta, Georgia. Value of horse $275. Transferred to Company G in May/June 1862. Discharged on 11/26/1862. Appointed assistant surgeon in C.S.A. Army in January/February 1863. After the war, became a physician in Calhoun County, Georgia, and then in Orange County, Florida. Married Mary Louisa Floyd on 01/20/1860 in Covington, Newton County, Georgia, and they had at least three children. Died on 02/24/1889 at Orlando, Orange County, Florida.

1129. Sherman, George W.: Farmer from DeKalb County, Georgia. Born in South Carolina. Enlisted as a private in Company B on 08/14/1861 at Atlanta, Georgia. Value of horse $125, saddle furnished by State of Georgia. On sick furlough beginning 10/07/1861. Discharged on 06/19/1862.

1130. Shinall, Benjamin F.: From Georgia. Born in 1836 in Edgefield County, South Carolina. Enlisted as a private in Company I on 03/31/1862 at Augusta, Georgia. Value of horse $150. Admitted to Chimborazo Hospital No. 2, Richmond, Virginia, on 01/10/1863 with rheumatism. Returned to duty on 02/02/1863. Admitted to Chimborazo Hospital No. 2, Richmond, Virginia, on 03/08/1863 with rheumatism. Transferred to a hospital in Augusta, Georgia, on 04/16/1863. Sent home to get a horse with Lt. Sinquefield under Special Order No. 27 from corps headquarters on 02/23/1864. Absent on sick furlough beginning 09/20/1864. Paroled at Augusta, Georgia, on 05/25/1865. After the war, lived in Burke County, Georgia. Received a Confederate pension in Burke County, Georgia.

1131. Shivers, J.W.: Enlisted in the 9th Virginia Infantry. Transferred as a private to Cobb's Legion Cavalry, Company K, on 01/06/1864 at Richmond, Virginia. Admitted to Chimborazo Hospital No. 1 on 04/20/1864 with a skin disease.

---

*Howard, page 14.

Returned to duty on 06/27/1864. Admitted to Howard's Grove Hospital, Richmond, Virginia, on 08/21/1864. Transferred on 09/07/1864 to Castle Thunder. Sent home to get a horse on 10/26/1864. Admitted to Jackson Hospital, Richmond, Virginia, on 11/08/1864. Deserted from Jackson Hospital on 11/16/1864.

1132. Shurdon [Sherdon], John W.: Enlisted as a private in Company I on 08/06/1862 at Augusta, Georgia. Deserted on 11/04/1862 near Martinsburg, [West] Virginia.

1133. Sibley, Benjamin F.: Farmer from Dougherty County, Georgia Born ca. 1834 in North Carolina. Enlisted as a sergeant in Company D on 08/10/1861 at Albany, Georgia. Value of horse $225, and horse equipment $25, saddle furnished by State of Georgia. Furloughed for 60 days beginning 11/27/1861. Listed as absent without leave with rank of private beginning 03/01/1862. Admitted to Confederate States Hospital, Petersburg, Virginia, on 09/15/1863. Returned to duty on 09/19/1863. Sent home to get a horse with Lt. Sinquefield under Special Order No. 27 from corps headquarters on 02/23/1864. He had been without a horse for 22 days. Absent without leave beginning 04/26/1864 until his last record, 11/01/1864. Paroled on 05/15/1865 at Albany, Georgia. After the war, became a farmer in Dougherty County, Georgia. He and his wife, E., had at least two children. Died after 1880.

1134. Sibley, C.L.: Farm laborer from Dougherty County, Georgia. Born ca. 1843 in Georgia. Enlisted as a private in Company D on 08/10/1861 at Albany, Georgia. Value of horse $225, and horse equipment $25, saddle furnished by State of Georgia. Detailed as an orderly to Col. McKinney in November/December 1861. Sent home to get a horse in March/April 1863. Detailed as a clerk for Capt. Eadlin beginning 01/14/1864. Last record 11/01/1864, sent to Georgia with Capt. Bostick to get a horse on 09/20/1864.

1135. Sibley, E.L. [E.S.]: Resident of Georgia. Enlisted as a private in Company D on 08/10/1861 at Albany, Georgia. Value of horse $175 and horse equipment $25. On furlough in January/February 1863. Detailed as an ambulance driver beginning 08/25/1863. No horse in January/February 1864. Paroled at Bainbridge, Georgia, on 05/20/1865. Described as having a dark complexion, dark eyes, black hair, and being 5'10" tall.

1136. Sibley, Samuel Hale: 25-year-old merchant from Augusta, Georgia. Born on 09/09/1835 in Augusta, Georgia. Enlisted as a private in Company A on 04/17/1864 at Decatur, Georgia. Last record September/October 1864, sent to Georgia with Capt. Bostick to get a horse on 09/20/1864. After the war, became a cotton merchant and then a saddle maker and harness maker. Married Sarah Virginia Hart 11/15/1865 at Augusta, Georgia, and was the father of six children. Died on 12/11/1883 at Atlanta, Georgia.

1137. Sibley, William H.: Overseer from Dougherty County, Georgia. Born ca. 1830 in North Carolina. Enlisted as a private in Company D on 08/10/1861 at Albany, Georgia. Died of sickness on 03/17/1862 at Smithfield, Virginia. He back pay was given to his widow, D.A. Sibley.

1138. Simmons, Henry J.: Farmer from Jackson County, Georgia. Born ca. 1836 in Georgia. Enlisted as a private in the 3rd Georgia Infantry, Company K, in 06/10/1861 at Athens, Clarke County, Georgia. Transferred to Cobb's Legion Cavalry, Company H, on 01/08/1863. Wounded on 08/01/1863. Admitted to General Hospital No. 1, Richmond, Virginia, and had arm amputated. Furloughed for 60 days beginning 09/15/1863. Retired on 09/08/1864. After the war, became a farmer in Jackson Parish, Louisiana. Married Harmoline Grambling on 05/21/1874 in Vienna, Lincoln Parish, Louisiana. Died at Atlanta, Winn Parish, Louisiana, after 1920. Buried at Atlanta, Winn Parish, Louisiana. Received a Confederate pension from Louisiana.

1139. Simmons, James Overton [A.]: 18-year-old student from Hall County, Georgia. Born on 09/03/1843 in Hall County, Georgia. Brother of Moses Taliaferro Simmons. Enlisted as a private in Company C on 06/10/1862 at Richmond, Virginia. Captured on 08/01/1863 at Brandy Station, Virginia, and sent to the Old Capitol Prison, Washington, D.C. Transferred to Point Lookout, Maryland, on 08/23/1863. Exchanged on 02/24/1865. Was surrendered by Gen. Joseph E. Johnston on 04/26/1865. Paroled at Greensboro, North Carolina, on 05/01/1865. After the war, lived in Clarke County, Georgia. Received a Confederate pension in Clarke County, Georgia. Died on 02/28/1921. Buried in the Simmons Family Cemetery in Hall County, Georgia.

1140. Simmons, Jesse A.: Student from Jackson County, Georgia. Born ca. 1839. Enlisted as a private in Company H on 03/01/1862 at Athens, Clarke County, Georgia. Sent home to get a horse with Lt. Sinquefield under Special Order No. 27 from corps headquarters on 02/23/1864. Sent to Georgia with Capt. Bostick to get a horse on 09/20/1864. Was surrendered by Gen. Joseph E. Johnston on 04/26/1865. Paroled at Greensboro, North Carolina, on 05/01/1865. Married (1) Nancy

G. Morris in Vienna, Lincoln Parish, Louisiana, on 03/18/1875. Married (2) Mrs. Eliza Greer on 07/09/1889 in Gregg County, Texas. Was the father of at least three children. Died on 03/26/1920 at Atlanta, Winn Parish, Louisiana, and is buried there. He and subsequently his widow received a Confederate pension from Louisiana.

1141. Simmons, Moses Sylvanus [N.S.]: 19-year-old student from Hall County, Georgia. Born on 04/18/1843 in Hall County, Georgia. Enlisted as a private in Company H on 03/19/1862 at Athens, Clarke County, Georgia. Horse valued at $175 killed in the action at Malvern Hill, Virginia, on 08/05/1862. Simmons captured on 06/09/1863 at Beverly's Ford, Virginia, during the cavalry battle at Brandy Station and sent to the Old Capitol Prison, Washington, D.C., on 06/25/1863. Exchanged on 06/30/1863 at City Point, Virginia. Sent to Georgia to get a horse on 11/11/1863. On provost duty in 02/1864. Was surrendered by Gen. Joseph E. Johnston on 04/26/1865. Paroled at Greensboro, North Carolina, on 05/01/1865.

1142. Simmons, Moses Taliaferro: From Georgia. Born ca. 1839. Brother of James Overton Simmons. Enlisted as a sergeant in Company C 08/14/1861 at Athens, Clarke County, Georgia. On sick furlough in 12/1861 and 01/1862. Admitted to C.S.A. General Hospital, Charlottesville, Virginia, on 07/02/1863. Transferred to Lynchburg, Virginia, on 09/21/1863. Detailed as sergeant of brigade provost guard in March/April 1864. Last record September/October 1864, sent to Georgia with Capt. Bostick to get a horse on 09/20/1864. Married Mary E.E. Morris ca. 1868. Died in 1883.

1143. Simmons, W.S. [W.A.]: Enlisted as a private in Company H on 03/03/1862 at Athens, Georgia. Discharged at Staunton, Virginia, on 09/20/1862. His widow, Sarah E. Simmons, received a Confederate pension from Fulton County, Georgia.

1144. Simmons, William D.: 23-year-old from Georgia. Enlisted as a corporal in Company C on 08/14/1864 at Athens, Clarke County, Georgia. Sent home to get a horse with Lt. Sinquefield under Special Order No. 27 from corps headquarters on 02/23/1864. Listed as a private beginning March/April 1864. Detailed as a scout beginning 05/01/1864. Last record September/October 1864, sent to Georgia with Capt. Bostick to get a horse on 09/20/1864.

1145. Simon [Simmons], Isaac: Merchant from Richmond County, Georgia. Born in Prussia ca. 1837. Enlisted as a private in Company I on 02/27/1862 at Augusta, Georgia. Detailed on scouting party with Lt. Shivers of the 2nd South Carolina Cavalry in Culpeper County, Virginia from 12/14 to 12/17, 1863. Absent without leave beginning 01/01/1864. Last record September/October 1864, on sick furlough beginning 09/14/1864. After the war, became a dry goods merchant in Richmond County, Georgia. Married Johanna Hertz on 05/30/1869 in Richmond County, Georgia, and they had one child. Died before 1880.

1146. Simon, Nathan: Merchant's clerk from Augusta, Georgia. Born in Prussia ca. 1832. Enlisted as a private in Company A on 08/17/1861 at Augusta, Georgia. Value of horse $200 and horse equipment $20. Discharged on 10/12/1861 at Yorktown, Virginia. After the war, worked as a retail clothing merchant in Mobile County, Alabama. Married Amalia on 10/03/1867 in Mobile County, Alabama, and was the father of at least two children.

1147. Simpkins, William H.: 19-year-old student from Jackson County, Georgia. Born on 04/24/1842 in Georgia. Enlisted as a private in Company H on 02/28/1862 at Athens, Clarke County, Georgia. Sent to Georgia to get a horse on 11/11/1863. Sent to infirmary/recruiting camp on 03/08/1864. Listed in May/September 1864 as a corporal. Sent to Georgia with Capt. Bostick to get a horse on 09/20/1864. Was surrendered by Gen. Joseph E. Johnston on 04/26/1865. Paroled at Greensboro, North Carolina, on 05/01/1865. After the war, became a lawyer in Jackson County, Georgia. Died on 04/23/1898. Buried in the Eastview Cemetery in Rockdale County, Georgia. His widow, Fannie B. Simpkins, received a Confederate pension from Rockdale County, Georgia.

1148. Sinquefield, Francis A.: Merchant clerk from Richmond County, Georgia. Born ca. 1836 in Georgia. Enlisted as a private in Company F on 03/25/1862 at Burke County, Georgia. Value of horse $200. Elected lieutenant on 02/01/1863. Wounded on 06/09/1863 at Brandy Station. Mentioned in Wade Hampton's report on 06/12/1863: "I have never seen any troops display greater coolness, bravery, and steadiness. In the list of wounded are ... Singuefield [sic], of the Cobb Legion."* Admitted to General Hospital No. 4, Richmond, Virginia, on 06/16/1863. Furloughed to Augusta, Georgia, on 06/19/1863. In command of a detail of 142 men sent home to get horses under Special Order No. 27 from corps headquarters on 02/23/1864. On detached service as adjutant on 10/01/

---

*OR, *Vol. 27, pt. 2, page 723.*

1864. Ordered to Georgia with Gen. Young on 11/23/1864. Was surrendered by Gen. Joseph E. Johnston on 04/26/1865. Paroled at Greensboro, North Carolina, on 05/01/1865. After the war, became a merchant in a country store in Jefferson County, Georgia. Married Mary Laura Brown on 03/08/1869 or 03/09/1869 in Jefferson County, Georgia, and they had at least four children. Died after 1880.

1149. Slatern [Slaton, Slayton], George W.: 20-year-old from Fayette County, Georgia. Born on 11/12/1840 in Fayette County, Georgia. Enlisted as a private in Company B on 08/14/1861 at Atlanta, Georgia. Value of horse $175 and horse equipment $2.75, saddle furnished by State of Georgia. Admitted to Chimborazo Hospital, Richmond, Virginia, on 12/18/1861. Returned to duty on 12/19/1861. Lost horse and was captured on 09/22/1863 at Jack's Shop, Virginia. Sent to Old Capitol Prison, Washington, D.C., and then transferred to Point Lookout, Maryland, on 09/26/1863. Transferred to Elmira Prison on 08/16/1864. Exchanged on 10/11/1864. Was surrendered by Gen. Joseph E. Johnston on 04/26/1865. Paroled at Greensboro, North Carolina, on 05/01/1865. After the war, became a farmer in Fayette County, Georgia. Married Ivy E. Chandler on 02/03/1871 in Fayette County, Georgia, and they had at least three children. Received a Confederate pension in Fayette County, Georgia. Died on 03/29/1910. His widow received a Confederate pension from Fayette County, Georgia.

1150. Smith, Alexander [Augustus] P.[R.]: 19-year-old from Columbia County, Georgia. Enlisted as a corporal in Company A on 08/17/1861 at Augusta, Georgia. Value of horse $175 and horse equipment $25. Rank reduced to private in May/June 1862. Detailed by Gen. D.H. Hill to accompany him as a courier to Mississippi in January/February 1863. On last record 07/10/1863, he still was detailed as a courier with Gen. Hill.

1151. Smith, Andrew J.: 18-year-old from Georgia. Enlisted as a private in Company I on 03/21/1862 at Augusta, Georgia. Value of horse $200. Transferred to Company G on 03/31/1863. Sent to Georgia to get a horse on 04/01/1863. Killed at Battle of Ream's Station on 08/25/1864.

1152. Smith, David [Davis] E.: Teacher from Hall County, Georgia. Born ca. 1833 in Georgia. Enlisted as a sergeant in Company C on 08/01/1861 at Athens, Clarke County, Georgia. On furlough in 02/1862. Listed as a private in November/December 1863. Sent home to get a horse with Lt. Sinquefield under Special Order No. 27 from corps headquarters on 02/23/1864. Detailed as a scout on 05/01/1864. Still detailed as a scout on last record, September/October 1864. After the war, became a teacher in Hall County, Georgia.

1153. Smith, Ebenezer B.: 26-year-old planter from Burke County, Georgia. Born in Georgia. Enlisted as a sergeant in Company F on 03/25/1862 at Burke County, Georgia. Admitted to C.S.A. General Hospital, Danville, Virginia, on 08/20/1862 with debility. Returned to duty on 08/22/1862. Admitted to Winder Hospital, Richmond, Virginia, on 10/18/1862. Returned to duty on 10/20/1862. Sent home to get a horse under Special Order No. 36 from corps headquarters on 03/13/1864. Sent to Georgia with Capt. Bostick to get a horse on 09/20/1864. Was surrendered by Gen. Joseph E. Johnston on 04/26/1865. Paroled at Greensboro, North Carolina, on 05/01/1865. He and his wife, Jane, had at least one child.

1154. Smith, Ebenezer F.(T.): 22-year-old. Enlisted as a corporal in Company E on 03/15/1862 at Roswell, Georgia. Value of horse $140. Listed as a private in January/February 1863. Died at Gettysburg, Pennsylvania. (Was probably either killed or mortally wounded on 07/02/1863.) Buried in the National Cemetery, Gettysburg, Pennsylvania, and reinterred on 08/21/1871 at Laurel Grove Cemetery, Gettysburg Section, Lot 854, Savannah, Georgia.

1155. Smith, Henry W.: 16-year-old from Georgia. Enlisted as a private in Company E on 04/05/1862 at Roswell, Georgia. Value of horse $150. Wounded at Upperville, Virginia, on 06/21/1863. Last record September/October 1864, sent to Georgia with Capt. Bostick to get a horse on 09/20/1864.

1156. Smith, Isaac T. [J.S.]: About 17 years old, from Virginia. Enlisted as a private in Company D on 02/01/1864 at Hamilton Crossing, Virginia. Captured in King George County, Virginia, on 05/14/1864 and sent to the Old Capitol Prison, Washington, D.C. Transferred to Fort Delaware Prison on 06/17/1864. Died on 02/13/1865 at Fort Delaware Prison of consumption (tuberculosis).

1157. Smith, J.D.: Listed on a roster of Company D published in *The History of Dougherty County*, but not with the *Civil War Soldiers and Sailors System*. No service records in Cobb's Legion. Possibly same person as Isaac T.[J.S.] Smith.

1158. Smith, James B.: Resident of Georgia. Enlisted as a private in Company C on 04/25/1862 at Athens, Clarke County, Georgia. Transferred to Company H in 03/1862. Admitted to Chimborazo Hospital, Richmond, Virginia, on 11/22/1862.

Transferred to General Hospital, Farmville, Virginia, on 12/16/1862 to convalesce. Returned to duty on 01/06/1863. Admitted to C.S.A. General Hospital, Charlottesville, Virginia, on 08/25/1863 with chronic rheumatism. Returned to duty on 09/07/1863. Admitted to Winder Hospital, Richmond, Virginia, on 09/17/1863. Returned to duty on 09/18/1863. Admitted to General Hospital No. 11, Richmond, Virginia. On furlough to Georgia beginning 02/19/1864. Sent to Georgia with Capt. Bostick to get a horse on 09/20/1864. Was surrendered by Gen. Joseph E. Johnston on 04/26/1865. Paroled at Greensboro, North Carolina, on 05/01/1865.

1159. Smith, Job: Farm laborer from Hall County, Georgia. Born in South Carolina. Enlisted as a private in Company C on 04/06/1863 at Athens, Clarke County, Georgia, as a substitute for Thomas C. Gower. Sent to a hospital on 07/16/1864. Sent home to get a horse with Lt. Sinquefield under Special Order No. 27 from corps headquarters on 02/23/1864. Admitted to C.S.A. General Hospital, Charlotte, North Carolina, on 01/01/1865. Returned to duty on 04/14/1865. After the war, worked as a farm laborer in Hall County, Georgia. Married to Malissa and they had at least nine children. Died after 1880.

1160. Smith, John: Possibly 22-year-old carpenter, resident of Richmond County, Georgia. Muster Roll Commission roster places him in Company A as a private. Killed at Ream's Station, Virginia, in 06/1864.

1161. Smith, Joseph: Resident of Georgia. Enlisted as a private in Company A on 08/17/1861 at Augusta, Georgia. Value of horse $175 and horse equipment $20. On detail in March/April 1863. Horse was killed and Smith was captured at Upperville, Virginia, on 06/21/1863. Paroled at Old Capitol Prison, Washington, D.C., on 06/25/1863. Was listed as present on last record, September/October 1864.

1162. Smith, Robert F.: 27-year-old from Georgia. Enlisted as a private in Company I on 04/25/1862 at Augusta, Georgia. Patient at General Hospital No. 14, Richmond, Virginia, in 1862. Detailed at Port Royal, Virginia, with Lt. T.J. Dunnahoo on 04/01/1864. Sent to Georgia with Capt. Bostick to get a horse on 09/20/1864. Paroled at Augusta, Georgia, on 05/29/1865.

1163. Smith, Russell: 22-year-old from Georgia. Born on 07/03/1839. Enlisted as a private in Company E on 04/09/1862 at Lawrenceville, Georgia. Value of horse $160 and saddle $20. Listed as a sergeant in January/February 1863. Wounded on 07/09/1863 at Boonsboro, Maryland, by a minié ball, which penetrated the right shoulder joint and severed it, breaking the bones of the right arm and necessitating a resection of four inches of the bone of the arm and rendering the arm useless. No horse on 09/20/1863. Still absent due to wound on last record, September/October 1864. After the war, lived in Hall County, Georgia. Received a disability pension because of the shoulder wound from Hall County, Georgia, from 1908 to 1920. Died on 09/20/1920. Buried in the Alta Vista Cemetery in Gainesville, Hall County, Georgia.

1164. Smith, Samuel Jordan: Farmer from Washington County, Georgia. Enlisted as a private in Company F on 05/09/1862 at Burke County, Georgia. Value of horse $318. Furnished Thomas W. Pritchard as a substitute in 05/1862. After the war, became a farmer in Washington County, Georgia. He and his wife, Susan A., had at least six children. Died after 1880.

1165. Smith, T.H.: Enlisted as a private in Company H on 02/25/1862 at Athens, Georgia. Admitted to Howard's Grove Hospital, Richmond, Virginia, on 03/31/1864. Was surrendered by Gen. Joseph E. Johnston on 04/26/1865. Paroled at Greensboro, North Carolina, on 05/01/1865.

1166. Smith, Thomas A.: Enlisted as a private in Company H on 04/02/1862 at Athens, Clarke County, Georgia. Elected lieutenant on 06/02/1862. Died on 03/15/1863.

1167. Smith, W.W.: Enlisted as a private in Company K on 02/24/1863 at Camp Maynard, Georgia. Deserted on 05/03/1863. Horse valued at $425 killed in action at Brandy Station, Virginia, on 06/09/1863. Was paid for loss of horse on 09/18/1863. The facts are problematic, as it does not make sense that his horse was killed in battle a month after his desertion, and he collected for the loss of the horse four months later.

1168. Smith, Wilber F.: 20-year-old. Born on 12/20/1839 in Anderson County, South Carolina. Enlisted as a private in Company B on 08/14/1861 at Atlanta, Georgia. Detailed as provost guard on 11/22/1863. Sent to recruiting/infirmary camp on 01/15/1863. Sent to Georgia with Capt. Bostick to get a horse on 09/20/1864. Was surrendered by Gen. Joseph E. Johnston on 04/26/1865. Paroled at Greensboro, North Carolina, on 05/01/1865. After the war, lived in South Carolina. Applied for a South Carolina Confederate pension on 09/26/1919. Died after 09/26/1919.

1169. Smith, William W.: Student from DeKalb County, Georgia. Born ca. 1845 in Georgia. Enlisted as a private in Company C on 03/08/

1862 at Athens County, Georgia. Died on 08/28/1862 at Hanover Court House, Virginia.

1170. Smith, Zachariah H.: From Georgia. Born ca. 1837 in North Carolina. Enlisted as a private in Company H on 02/25/1862 at Athens, Clarke County, Georgia. Admitted to Winder Hospital, Richmond, Virginia, on 09/21/1862. Furloughed for 30 days beginning 11/15/1862. Admitted to Howard's Grove Hospital on 02/16/1864 with small pox. Admitted to Jackson Hospital in Richmond, Virginia, on 08/23/1864 with dysentery. Returned to duty on 08/26/1864. Last record September/October 1864, sent to Georgia with Capt. Bostick to get a horse on 09/20/1864. Other sources indicate he was surrendered by Gen. Joseph E. Johnston on 04/26/1865 and paroled at Greensboro, North Carolina, on 05/01/1865. After the war, became a farmer in Jackson County, Georgia. He and his wife, Sarah, had at least four children. Received a Confederate pension in Jackson County, Georgia.

1171. Snelling, James M.: 27-year-old merchant from Atlanta, Georgia. Born in Barnwell, South Carolina. Enlisted as a private in Company A on 08/17/1864 at Augusta, Georgia. Value of horse $200 and horse equipment $30. Appointed corporal on 05/01/1862. On furlough for 25 days beginning 01/02/1862. Discharged at Richmond, Virginia, due to heart disease on 11/20/1862. Described as having a dark complexion, dark eyes, dark hair, and being 6'1" inch tall. After the war, worked as a painter. Married Sarah on 01/18/1860 in Richmond County, Georgia, and they had at least seven children. Died on 03/31/1910 at Atlanta, Georgia. His widow received a Confederate pension from Fulton County, Georgia.

1172. South, Amaziah: From Georgia. Born ca. 1827 in South Carolina. Enlisted as a private in Company E on 03/15/1862 at Roswell, Georgia. Listed as a corporal in January/February 1863. Promoted to sergeant on 11/01/1863. Sent home to get a horse on 11/12/1863. Absent sick beginning 01/17/1864. Last record September/October 1864, sent to Georgia to get a horse with Capt. Bostick on 09/20/1864. After the war, worked as a farm laborer in Cobb County, Georgia. He and his wife, Laura, had at least five children. Died after 1880. His widow received a Confederate pension from Fulton County, Georgia.

1173. Spain, Francis [Frank] J.: About 17 years old. Enlisted as a private in Company F on 06/24/1864 at Augusta, Georgia. Admitted to a hospital on 09/13/1864. Was surrendered by Gen. Joseph E. Johnston on 04/26/1865. Paroled at Greensboro, North Carolina, on 05/01/1865.

1174. Spain, William: Listed as a private in Company F in *Roster of the Confederate Soldiers of Burke County, Georgia: 1861–1865*. No service records in Cobb's Legion.

1175. Speer, Francis A.: Enlisted as a private in the 2nd Georgia Infantry. Transferred as a private to Cobb's Legion Cavalry, Company A, on 09/06/1862. No service records in Cobb's Legion.

1176. Spencer, John W.: 18-year-old from Lumpkin County, Georgia. Enlisted as a private in Company G on 05/01/1862 at Atlanta, Georgia. Value of horse $125. Horse killed in action at Gettysburg (Hunterstown), Pennsylvania, on 07/02/1863. Listed as a corporal in November/December 1863. Sent home to get a horse on 10/10/1863. Sent to the infirmary/recruiting camp on 02/23/1864. Admitted to Jackson Hospital, Richmond, Virginia, on 04/03/1864 with a fracture of his right thigh. Last record, furloughed for 30 days beginning 06/15/1864.

1177. Sponsler, Henry (Harry) L.[N.]: 43-year-old veterinarian from Augusta, Georgia. Born in Pennsylvania. Enlisted as a veterinary surgeon in Company A on 08/17/1861 at Augusta, Georgia, for the duration on the war. Value of horse $200 and horse equipment $25. Sent to infirmary/recruiting camp on 05/03/1863. Sent to pasture in charge of horses on 10/08/1864. Was surrendered by Gen. Joseph E. Johnston on 04/26/1865. Paroled at Greensboro, North Carolina, on 05/01/1865. After the war, became a veterinarian in Augusta, Georgia.

1178. Sprague, Chauncy A.: Enlisted as a private in Company B on 08/14/1861 at Atlanta, Georgia. Horse, owned by J.M Nealbrook, valued at $250 and horse equipment $8.50, saddle furnished by the State of Georgia. Transferred to the *Virginia* (the warship that became the *Merrimac*) on 03/28/1862. Had to pay the government $25 for the pistol he lost.

1179. Stanford, Allen R.: Farmer from Columbia County, Georgia. Born ca. 1838 in Taliaferro County, Georgia. Enlisted as a private in Company I on 04/21/1862 at Augusta, Georgia. Captured near Martinsburg, [West] Virginia, on 07/18/1863 and sent to Atheneum Military Prison, Wheeling, [West] Virginia. Deserted and took the Oath. Sent to Ohio on 07/30/1863. Described as having a dark complexion, blue eyes, dark hair, and being 5' 8½" tall. After the war, worked as a teamster in Columbia County, Georgia. Married Sarah C. Brown on 04/22/1858 in Columbia County, Georgia. Died after 1880.

1180. Stanley, John C.: 41-year-old from Georgia. Enlisted as a private in Company E on 04/09/1862 at Lawrenceville, Georgia. Value of horse $185. Absent without leave in March/April 1863. Sent home to get a horse on 11/12/1863. Sent to the infirmary/recruiting camp on 02/23/1864. Detailed to ambulance corps on 08/01/1864. Last record, September/October 1864, absent without leave beginning 10/04/1864.

1181. **Stanton, J.B.:** Enlisted as a private in Company K on 06/06/1864 at Macon, Georgia. Absent without leave beginning 06/16/1864. Still absent without leave on last record September/October 1864.

1182. **Staunton [Stanton], A.A.:** 19-year-old from Virginia. Enlisted as a private in Company K on 02/08/1863 at Camp Maynard, Georgia. Appointed corporal on 02/28/1863. Admitted to hospital on 07/08/1864. Last record September/October 1864, sent home to get a horse on 10/27/1864.

1183. **Steen [Stein], Henry:** From Georgia. Born in Georgia ca. 1835. Enlisted as a private in Company E on 03/22/1862 at Roswell, Georgia. Value of horse $250. Detailed as a teamster in 05/1863. Applied for a transfer to a command of disabled soldiers, fit for light duty but unfit for field duty on 07/28/1863 due to chronic bronchitis. Captured on 02/07/1864 at the Rapidan River and sent to the Old Capitol Prison, Washington, D.C., on 02/11/1864. Transferred to Fort Delaware Prison on 06/17/1864. Exchanged at Aiken's Landing, Virginia, on 09/30/1864. Admitted to Jackson Hospital, Richmond, Virginia, on 10/07/1864 with a pulmonary disease. Last record, furloughed for 30 days beginning 10/16/1864.

1184. **Stephens, Harvey:** Listed on a roster of Cobb's Legion Cavalry, Company C in *These Men She Gave*. No service records in Cobb's Legion.

1185. **Stephens [Stevens], W.J.H.:** Resident of Georgia. Enlisted as a private in Company H on 03/03/1862 at Athens, Clarke County, Georgia. Listed as corporal in May/June 1862. Listed as sergeant in April/September 1864. Sent home to get a horse with Lt. Sinquefield under Special Order No. 27 from corps headquarters on 02/23/1864. Last record September/October 1864, sent to Georgia with Capt. Bostick to get a horse on 09/20/1864.

1186. **Sterling [Starling], Isaac:** Farmer from Jackson County, Georgia. Enlisted as a private in Company H on 03/07/1862 at Athens, Clarke County, Georgia. Died on 10/17/1862 of chronic diarrhea at General Hospital No. 2, Lynchburg, Virginia. Buried in the Old City Cemetery, Lynchburg, Virginia. His back pay and effects were given to his wife, Sarah.

1187. **Stevens [Stephens], Edward N.:** Farmer from Jefferson County, Georgia. Born ca. 1828 in Georgia. Enlisted as a private in Company L on 12/15/1862 at Burke County, Georgia. Sent to Georgia to get a horse with Lt. Sinquefield under Special Order No. 27 from corps headquarters on 02/23/1864. Last record September/October 1864, sent to Georgia to get a horse with Capt. Bostick on 09/20/1864. He and his wife, Mary, had at least two children.

1188. **Stevens, W.C.:** Enlisted as a private in Company L on 04/20/1864 at Decatur, Georgia. Assigned from Camp Randolph, DeKalb County, Georgia, on 05/12/1864. Last record September/October 1864, sent to Georgia to get a horse with Capt. Bostick on 09/20/1864.

1189. **Stewarder, H.J.:** Enlisted as a private in Company I. Captured at the Battle of South Mountain, Maryland, on 09/14/1862 and sent to Fort Delaware Prison. Exchanged at Aiken's Landing, Virginia, on 10/02/1862. No further records.

1190. **Stewart, Hugh Henderson:** 24-year-old farm laborer from Butts County, Georgia. Born on 07/09/1837 in Georgia. Enlisted as a private in Company B 04/28/1862 at Atlanta, Georgia. Value of horse $150. Transferred to Company G in May/June 1862. Detailed as a teamster in July/August 1862. No horse on 08/15/1862. Furloughed for 30 days beginning 12/16/1863. Was surrendered by Gen. Joseph E. Johnston on 04/26/1865. Paroled at Greensboro, North Carolina, on 05/01/1865. After the war, became a farmer and then a blacksmith in Henry County, Georgia. He and his wife, Ann, had at least six children. Received a Confederate pension in Butts County, Georgia. Died after 1910. His widow received a Confederate pension in Butts County, Georgia.

1191. **Stewart, J. Lafayette:** 29-year-old from Georgia. Enlisted as a private in Company E on 03/22/1862 at Roswell, Georgia. Value of horse $185. Listed as a sergeant in January/February 1863. Lost horse on 09/20/1863. Sent to Georgia to get a horse with Lt. Sinquefield under Special Order No. 27 from corps headquarters on 02/23/1864. Last record September/October 1864, sent to Georgia to get a horse with Capt. Bostick on 09/20/1864.

1192. **Stewart [Stuart], William A.:** 41-year-old from McDonough, Georgia. Enlisted as a private in Company G on 03/31/1862 at Atlanta, Georgia. Value of horse $200 and horse equipment $30. Admitted to Winder Hospital, Richmond, Virginia, on 07/22/1862. Transferred to a hospital at Lynchburg, Virginia, on 07/24/1862. No horse on 08/01/1862. Detailed as a teamster for the Commissary Department in 04/1864. Last record September/October 1864, sent to Georgia to get a horse with Capt. Bostick on 09/20/1864.

1193. Stewart, William T.M.: 27-year-old. Born in Georgia on 03/22/1835. Enlisted as a private in Company E on 03/15/1862 at Roswell, Georgia. Value of horse $150. Only service record dated 04/03/1862. After the war, became a farmer in Carroll County, Arkansas. Married Maria Sophia Dalton ca. 1858. Died in Waco, Texas, on 06/18/1906.

1194. Stokes, James W.: 21-year-old from Georgia. Enlisted as a private in Company G on 03/29/1862 at Atlanta, Georgia. Value of horse $160. Sent to Georgia to get a horse in March/April 1863. Detailed as a scout in 01/1864. Captured at King George County, Virginia, on 05/18/1864 and sent to Belle Plain, Virginia. Transferred to Point Lookout, Maryland, and then to Elmira Prison, New York, on 07/06/1864. Exchanged on 10/29/1864. Was surrendered by Gen. Joseph E. Johnston on 04/26/1865. Paroled at Greensboro, North Carolina, on 05/01/1865.

1195. Stone, Edward Preston: 19-year-old farmer from Jefferson County, Georgia. Born on 11/25/1842 in Jefferson County, Georgia. Brother of William L. Stone. Enlisted as a private in Company F on 03/25/1862 at Burke County, Georgia. Value of horse $225. He and his horse were killed in action at Jack's Shop, Virginia, on 09/22/1863. Described as having a fair complexion, gray eyes, light hair, and being 5'10" tall. His mother, Martha L. Stone, was given his back pay, as he had no wife, children, or father surviving him.

1196. Stone, William L.: 18-year-old student from Jefferson County, Georgia. Born in 11/1844 in Jefferson County, Georgia. Brother of Edward Preston Stone. Enlisted as a private in Company F on 11/02/1862 at Jefferson County, Georgia. Died on 08/13/1864 at Stony Creek, Virginia. His mother, Martha L. Stone, was given his back pay, as he had no wife, children, or father surviving him.

1197. Stovall, Bolling Anthony: 33-year-old merchant clerk from Augusta, Georgia. Born 08/19/1827 in Sparta, Hancock County, Georgia. Brother of Thomas P. Stovall. Enlisted as a sergeant in Company A on 08/17/1861 at Augusta, Georgia. Value of horse $225 and horse equipment $40. Engineer for Gen. McLaws in 12/1861. Last record, discharged on 05/01/1862 to accept appointment in ordnance department in charge of Nitre Bureau in Richmond. Elected captain of engineer corps. After the war, was an "Agent Government Chs Work" at Athens, Clarke County, Georgia. Married Martha Smithey Wilson on 09/19/1856 in Washington, D.C., and was the father of at least six children. Died on 08/24/1887 at Athens, Clarke County, Georgia. Buried in the Oconee Hill Cemetery in Clarke County, Georgia.

1198. Stovall, Francis (Frank) Marion: 19-year-old student from Augusta, Georgia. Born in 11/1841 in Georgia. Enlisted as a private in 8th Georgia Infantry, Company A, on 05/18/1861. Transferred to Cobb's Legion Cavalry, Company C, on 08/15/1861 at Athens, Clarke County, Georgia. Captured at Malvern Hill, Virginia, on 08/05/1862 and sent to Fort Wool, Virginia. Exchanged at Fort Monroe, Virginia, on 08/26/1862. Record states that he lost his money and all of his belongings, dated 08/29/1862. Admitted to Hospital No. 16, Richmond, Virginia, on 10/28/1862. Returned to duty on 11/05/1862. Transferred to Troup Artillery on 11/13/1862. Wounded at Fredericksburg on 12/13/1862. Last record January/February 1864, on detail in Quartermaster Dept. at Augusta, Georgia. After the war, worked as a coal merchant, and then as a bookkeeper in Augusta, Georgia. Died on 12/17/1905. Buried in the Magnolia Cemetery in Richmond County, Georgia.

1199. Stovall, J.F.: Resident of Georgia. Enlisted as a private in Company A on 02/11/1864 at Decatur, Georgia. Sent to Georgia to get a horse with Capt. Bostick on 09/20/1864. Was surrendered by Gen. Joseph E. Johnston on 04/26/1865. Paroled at Greensboro, North Carolina, on 05/01/1865.

1200. Stovall, Thomas P.: Miller from Augusta, Georgia. Born ca. 1833 in Hancock County, Georgia. Brother of Bolling Anthony Stovall. Enlisted as a captain in Company A on 08/17/1861 at Augusta, Georgia. Value of horses, $325, $225, and $225. Value of horse equipment $40 and $12. Resigned on 05/30/1862. Married Valinnia A. Cooper on 01/14/1846 in Murray County, Georgia, and was the father of at least two children.

1201. Strickland, E.: Enlisted as a private in Company E on 10/02/1864 at Lawrenceville, Georgia. Was surrendered by Gen. Joseph E. Johnston on 04/26/1865. Paroled at Greensboro, North Carolina, on 05/01/1865.

1202. Strickland, Henry: Resident of Georgia. Enlisted as a private in Company D on 08/10/1861 at Albany, Georgia. Value of horse $200 and horse equipment $13. Bridle valued at $3 furnished by State of Georgia. On detached service in January/February 1863. Absent with the colonel's horses in March/April 1863. Detailed as a courier for Col. Wright beginning 11/22/1863. Given furlough of indulgence for 24 days beginning 09/20/1864. Last record September/October 1864, absent without leave beginning 10/14/1864.

1203. Strickland, J.F.: Resident of Barbour County, Alabama. Enlisted as a private in Company K. Received flesh wounds in both hips on 09/09/1863. Furloughed from General Hospital No. 19, Richmond, Virginia, for 40 days beginning 06/14/1864. No other records.

1204. Strickland, Noah C.: Farm laborer from Jackson County, Georgia. Born ca. 1837 in Georgia. Enlisted in 3rd Georgia Infantry, Company K, as a private on 06/10/1861. Wounded at Malvern Hill, Virginia, on 07/01/1862. Transferred to Cobb's Legion Cavalry, Company C, on 10/06/1862. Last record, March/April 1863. Other records indicate that he was killed at Gettysburg, Pennsylvania, on 07/03/1863. (His tombstone says 07/01/1863.) Buried in the National Cemetery, Gettysburg, Pennsylvania, and reinterred on 08/21/1871 at Laurel Grove Cemetery, Gettysburg Section, Lot 853, Savannah, Georgia.

1205. Strickland, T.J.: 18-year-old from Alabama. Enlisted as a private in Company K on 01/17/1862 at Camp Maynard, Georgia. Detailed as a teamster on 02/25/1864. Was present on last record, September/October 1864.

1206. Strickland, William M.: Resident of Georgia. Enlisted as a private in Company E on 03/23/1864 at Augusta, Georgia. Sent to Georgia to get a horse with Capt. Bostick on 09/20/1864. Was surrendered by Gen. Joseph E. Johnston on 04/26/1865. Paroled at Greensboro, North Carolina, on 05/01/1865. Received a Confederate pension in Chattooga County, Georgia.

1207. Suddeth [Sudduth], George A.: From Georgia. Born ca. 1845. Enlisted as a private in Company G on 05/02/1862 at Atlanta, Georgia. Value of horse $200. Listed as a corporal in May/June 1862. Listed as a sergeant in November/December 1862. Detailed in the Quartermaster Department in 02/21/1863. In charge of horses for Gen. Young beginning November/December 1863 at Albemarle County, Virginia. Furloughed for 30 days beginning 04/01/1864. Sent to Georgia to get a horse with Capt. Bostick on 09/20/1864. Was surrendered by Gen. Joseph E. Johnston on 04/26/1865. Paroled at Greensboro, North Carolina, on 05/01/1865. Married Ellen in 1888. Died in 1907. His widow applied for a South Carolina widow's pension on 12/08/1919.

1208. Sutton, Leander: Born in Georgia ca. 1843. Enlisted as a private in the 5th Georgia State Troops, Company E, on 10/12/1861. Sick at home on 04/09/1862. Mustered out in 05/1862. Enlisted as a private in 32nd Georgia Infantry, Company G, on 05/07/1862. Transferred to Cobb's Legion Cavalry, Company L, on 12/15/1862. Last record September/October 1864, sent to Georgia to get a horse with Capt. Bostick on 09/20/1864. After the war, became a farmer in Emanuel County, Georgia. Married Sarah Rountree on 01/23/1862 in Emanuel County, Georgia, and they had at least seven children. Received a Confederate pension in Emanuel County, Georgia. Died on 09/30/1915 in Emanuel County, Georgia.

1209. Sutton, William E: Resident of Georgia. Enlisted as a private in Company B on 08/10/1861 at Albany, Georgia. Value of horse $200 and horse equipment $25, saddle valued at $20 furnished by State of Georgia. Captured at Middletown, Maryland, on 09/13/1862 and sent to Fort Delaware Prison. Exchanged at Aiken's Landing, Virginia, on 11/10/1862. Sent home to get a horse in March/April 1863. Promoted to sergeant on 01/01/1864. Sent to Georgia to get a horse with Capt. Bostick on 09/20/1864. Was surrendered by Gen. Joseph E. Johnston on 04/26/1865. Paroled at Greensboro, North Carolina, on 05/01/1865.

1210. Swan, Henry J.: Enlisted as a private in Company L on 12/15/1862 at Burke County, Georgia. Appointed corporal on 06/01/1864. Last record September/October 1864, sent to Georgia to get a horse with Capt. Bostick on 09/20/1864. Married to Jane E. Died before 1880. His widow received a Confederate pension from Jefferson County, Georgia.

1211. Swan, John C: Mechanic from Jefferson County, Georgia. Born ca. 1830 in Georgia. Enlisted as a private in Company F on 03/25/1862 at Burke County, Georgia. Value of horse $225. Sent to the infirmary/recruiting camp on 09/15/1863. Captured and paroled, but not exchanged, at Cheraw, South Carolina, on 03/05/1865. After the war, became a farmer in Jefferson County, Georgia. Died after 1880. Buried at the Ways Baptist Church Cemetery in Jefferson County, Georgia.

1212. Syler [Siler, Silver], Joseph: Resident of New Orleans, Louisiana. Enlisted as a private in Company I on 06/18/1862 at Richmond County, Georgia, as a substitute for Davis Thomas. Captured at Cheraw, South Carolina, on 03/04/1865 and sent to New Bern, North Carolina. Transferred to Point Lookout, Maryland, on 03/30/1865. Released on 06/19/1865. Described as having a dark complexion, brown hair, light hazel eyes, and being 5'6½" tall.

1213. Tabb, Thomas J.: Farmer from Richmond County, Georgia. Born ca. 1834 in Georgia. Enlisted as a private in Company I on 03/05/1862 at Augusta, Georgia. Value of horse $140. Forfeited one month's pay by order of court-martial in March/April 1863. Detailed as a teamster on 11/08/1863. Sent to Georgia to get a horse with Capt. Bostick on 09/20/1864. Was surrendered by Gen. Joseph E. Johnston on 04/26/1865. Paroled at Greensboro, North Carolina, on 05/01/1865. After the war, became a farmer in Richmond County, Georgia. He and his wife, Elizabeth (Betsy), had at least one child. Received a Confederate pension in Richmond County, Georgia. Died after 1880. His widow received a Confederate pension from Richmond County, Georgia.

1214. Tank, Charles N.: Native of Georgia. Enlisted as a private in Company B on 03/01/1862 at Camp Marion, Yorktown, Virginia. Admitted to a hospital in Richmond, Virginia, on 07/15/1862. Admitted to Winder Hospital, Richmond, Virginia, on 07/22/1862 with an injury to the thigh. Returned to duty on 09/30/1862. Admitted to a hospital in Charlottesville, Virginia, on 02/15/1863. Admitted to a hospital in Gordonsville, Virginia, on 02/21/1863. Admitted to Buchanan Hospital on 04/08/1863. Lost horse on 06/08/1863. Sent to Georgia to get a horse on 06/08/1863. Absent without leave beginning 07/08/1863. Detailed to Nitre & Mining Bureau, Rome, Georgia, for 60 days beginning 02/09/1864, and to draw no pay during detail. Last record September/October 1864, still detailed at Nitre Bureau.

1215. Tanner, Daniel F.: 28-year-old from Georgia. Enlisted as a private in Company I on 03/04/1862 at Augusta, Georgia. Value of horse $255. Last record September/October 1864, was detailed as a scout on 08/25/1864.

1216. Tanner, Francis D.: 26-year-old from Georgia. Enlisted as a private in Company I on 03/04/1862 at Augusta, Georgia. Value of horse $140. Detailed as a courier for Gen. Semmes on 06/08/1862. Admitted to C.S.A. General Hospital, Charlottesville, Virginia, on 08/25/1863 with orchitis. Transferred to Winder Hospital, Richmond, Virginia, on 09/14/1863. Returned to duty on 10/16/1863. Sent to Georgia to get a horse with Capt. Bostick on 09/20/1864. Was surrendered by Gen. Joseph E. Johnston on 04/26/1865. Paroled at Greensboro, North Carolina, on 05/01/1865.

1217. Tanner [Turner], George C.: 17-year-old from Georgia. Enlisted as a bugler in Company I on 04/01/1862 at Augusta, Georgia. Listed as a private in 05/1862. Captured at Gettysburg, Pennsylvania, on 07/05/1863 and sent to Fort McHenry, Maryland. Paroled and transferred to Fort Delaware Prison on 07/10/1863. Last record September/October 1864, sent to Georgia to get a horse with Capt. Bostick on 09/20/1864.

1218. Tanner, William Avery [H.]: Gas fitter from Augusta, Georgia. Born ca. 1842 in North Carolina. Enlisted as a bugler in Company on A on 08/17/1861 at Augusta, Georgia. Value of horse $180 and horse equipment $25. Detailed as bugler for Col. Cobb in 01/1862. Detailed as chief bugler for staff in January/February 1863. Sent to infirmary/recruiting camp 02/01/1864. Admitted to General Hospital No. 3, Goldsboro, North Carolina, on 09/01/1864. Returned to duty on 09/12/1864. Was surrendered by Gen. Joseph E. Johnston on 04/26/1865. Paroled at Greensboro, North Carolina, on 05/01/1865. After the war, worked as a tinner in Augusta, Georgia. Married Isabella and was the father of at least three children.

1219. Tatum, J.D.: 18-year-old. Enlisted as a private in Company K on 01/25/1863 at Camp Maynard, Georgia. Returned to his regiment on 02/18/1863.

1220. Taylor, B.F.: Enlisted as a private in Company A on 09/25/1863 at Decatur, Georgia. Admitted to Jackson Hospital, Richmond, Virginia, on 08/21/1864 with a fever and diarrhea. Returned to duty on 08/29/1864. Last record September/October 1864, admitted to hospital on 09/12/1864.

1221. Taylor, Calvin C.: Farmer from Lumpkin County, Georgia. Born in North Carolina. Enlisted as a private in Company H on 03/03/1862 at Athens, Clarke County, Georgia. Detailed as a teamster in 06/1863. Lost horse in November/December 1863. Furloughed to Georgia on 02/19/1864. Last record September/October 1864, sent to Georgia with Capt. Bostick to get a horse on 09/20/1864. After the war, became a farmer in Hall County, Georgia. Married Harriett Turner on 09/08/1870 in White County, Georgia. His widow received a Confederate pension from White County, Georgia.

1222. Taylor, Lemuel: Enlisted as a private in Company D on 03/04/1862 at Albany, Georgia. Value of horse $200 and horse equipment $5. Absent without leave beginning 03/01/1863. Last record, January/February 1864, states that he had transferred to Company D on 03/04/1/863 but had never been present.

1223. Thayer, Curtis J.: From Atlanta, Georgia. Born in New York ca. 1833. Enlisted as a private in Company B on 08/14/1861 at Atlanta, Georgia. Value of horse $175 and horse equipment $7, saddle furnished by the State of Georgia. Listed as a musician in November/December 1861. Admitted to C.S.A. General Hospital, Charlottesville, Virginia, on 08/03/1863 with confusion. Transferred to General Hospital, Lynchburg, Virginia, on 09/21/1863. Furloughed to Georgia for 24 days beginning 02/19/1864. Sent to infirmary/recruiting camp on 05/26/1864. Deserted and took the Oath on 03/28/1865 at Louisville, Kentucky, and sent north of the Ohio River. Described as having a fair complexion, light hair, blue eyes and being 5' 8 1/2" tall. After the war, became a silversmith and a jeweler in Gordon County, Georgia. He and his wife, Mary, had at least one child. Died after 1880.

1224. Thomas, Andrew Jackson: Student from Newton County, Georgia. Born ca. 1845 in Georgia. Enlisted as a private in Company A on 08/17/1861 at Augusta, Georgia. Value of horse $250 and horse equipment $35. Wounded in the head on 11/08/1862 at Little Washington, Virginia. Admitted to Richmond Hospital No. 11 on 11/12/1862. Transferred to Exchange Hotel on 11/15/1862. Furloughed for 30 days beginning 11/16/1862. Admitted to hospital in Augusta, Georgia, in 01/1863. Released from hospital in 08/1864. Discharged 08/17/1864. After the war, became a farm worker.

1225. Thomas, Davis: Farmer from Richmond County, Georgia. Born ca. 1829 in Georgia. Enlisted as a private in Company I on 03/15/1862 at Augusta, Georgia. Value of horse $167. Provided Joseph Syler as a substitute on 06/18/1862. After the war, became a farmer and then a grocer in Richmond County, Georgia. He and his wife, Sarah Eliza, had at least three children. Died after 1880. His widow received a Confederate pension from Richmond County, Georgia.

1226. Thomas, Isma W.: 30-year-old from Georgia. Born on 01/01/1832 in Clarke County, Georgia. Enlisted as a sergeant in Company E on 04/09/1862 at Atlanta, Georgia. Value of horse $200 and horse equipment $30. Captured near Warrenton, Virginia, on 11/12/1862. Paroled on 11/14/1862. Other records indicate he received a fractured skull from a saber cut in an engagement in 12/1862. Last record September/October 1864, sent to Georgia to get a horse with Capt. Bostick on 09/20/1864. Other records indicate that he also was sent home to get a horse in 02/1865. After the war, lived in Hall County, Georgia. Married F. Marion Horton on 10/21/1852. Received a Confederate pension in Hall County, Georgia, in 1901. Died on 06/05/1908 in Hall County, Georgia. Buried in the Oakwood Cemetery.

1227. Thomas, J.F.: Resident of Georgia. Enlisted as a private in Company E on 07/09/1863 at Roswell, Georgia. Sent to Georgia to get a horse with Lt. Sinquefield under Special Order No. 27 from corps headquarters on 02/23/1864. Detailed as an ambulance driver on 04/02/1864. No horse on 09/01/1864. Was surrendered by Gen. Joseph E. Johnston on 04/26/1865. Paroled at Greensboro, North Carolina, on 05/01/1865.

1228. Thomas, J. Jefferson: 29-year-old. Born in 1831. Enlisted as a lieutenant in Company on A on 08/17/1861 at Augusta, Georgia. Value of horses $350 and $225, and horse equipment $65 and $16. Furloughed for 25 days beginning 02/22/1862. Elected captain in Company I in 1862. Resigned on 07/23/1862 due to physical and mental debility. Given a medical discharge due to chronic gastritis. After the war, lived in Fulton County, Georgia. Received a Confederate pension in Fulton County, Georgia. Died in 1919.

1229. Thomas, J.N. [J.M.]: 38-year-old farmer. Enlisted as a private in Company L on 12/15/1862 at Burke County, Georgia. Lost horse on 09/15/1863. Wounded on 07/12/1863. Admitted to Winder Hospital, Richmond, Virginia, on 08/01/1863. Last record September/October 1864, home on wounded furlough since 10/1863. Was paroled at Augusta, Georgia, on 05/18/1865.

1230. Thomas, J.R. [J.T.]: Enlisted as a private in Company D on 08/10/1861 at Albany, Georgia. Value of horse $200 and horse equipment $25, furnished by State of Georgia. Detailed as an orderly of Col T.R.R. Cobb in November/December 1861. Detailed as a courier for telegraph office in 01/1862. Transferred to artillery on 07/15/1862.

1231. Thomas, James: Resident of Louisiana. Enlisted as a private in Company K on 02/25/1863 at Camp Maynard, Georgia. Was present on last record, September/October 1864.

1232. Thomas, James M.: Enlisted as a private in Company L on 12/15/1862 at Burke County, Georgia. Wounded at Brandy Station, Virginia, on 06/09/1863. Admitted to Winder Hospital, Richmond, Virginia, on or before 06/30/1863. Still on wounded furlough on last record in 05/1864.

1233. Thomas, John W.: About 17 years old. Enlisted as a private in Company L on 09/24/1863 at Sawdust, Georgia. Was surrendered by Gen. Joseph E. Johnston on 04/26/1865. Paroled at Greensboro, North Carolina, on 05/01/1865.

1234. Thomas, Johnathan Pinckney: Planter from Augusta, Georgia. Born ca. 1840 in Georgia. Enlisted as a private in Company A on 05/01/1862 at Augusta, Georgia. Wounded in the arm and left chest in 11/1862 near Hamlet, Little Washington, Virginia. Gen. Wright said that he had been "gallantly fighting at the head of his company." Ball was never removed from his chest. Admitted to Hospital No. 11, Richmond, Virginia, on 11/15/1862. Furloughed for 30 days beginning 11/16/1862. Reentered service after about a year although was found unfit for service in the field. Detailed as a clerk for Gen. Young in 11/1863. Gen Young said he was "a most excellent man." Sent to Georgia to get a horse with Lt. Sinquefield under Special Order No. 27 from corps headquarters on 02/23/1864. Was present on last record, September/October 1864. After the war, became a farmer in Waynesboro, Burke County, Georgia. Married to Mary on 02/23/1860 and was the father of at least six children. Died on 06/11/1888 from effects of his wound, when the ball suddenly fell into his abdomen. His widow received a Confederate pension from Fulton County, Georgia.

1235. Thomas, Lovick P.: 50-year-old. Enlisted as a private in Company C on 08/01/1861 at Athens, Clarke County, Georgia. It was not stated if he were present on his only record dated 08/15/1861.

1236. Thomas, Robert F.: 24-year-old farmer from Richmond County, Georgia. Enlisted as a private in Company I on 05/04/1862 at Augusta, Georgia. Value of horse $300 and horse equipment $10. Sent to Georgia to get a horse with Lt. Sinquefield under Special Order No. 27 from corps headquarters on 02/23/1864. Last record September/October 1864, sent to Georgia to get a horse with Capt. Bostick on 09/20/1864. After the war, lived in Columbia County, Georgia, and then became a farmer in Augusta, Georgia. Was married and the father of at least three children.

1237. Thompson, Alfred R.: Student from Hall County, Georgia. Born ca. 1843 in Georgia. Enlisted as a private in Company C on 08/01/1861 at Athens, Clarke County, Georgia. Sent to Georgia to get a horse with Lt. Sinquefield under Special Order No. 27 from corps headquarters on 02/23/1864. Admitted to C.S.A. General Hospital, Danville, Virginia, on 06/15/1864 with a wound in his arm. Returned to duty on 06/20/1864. Last record September/October 1864, sent to Georgia to get a horse with Capt. Bostick on 09/20/1864. After the war, became a farmer in Johnson County, Texas. He and his wife, Betty, had at least six children.

1238. Thompson, George W.: Farm laborer from Dougherty County, Georgia. Born ca. 1845 in Alabama. Enlisted as a private in Company D on 08/10/1861 at Albany, Georgia. Value of horse $150 and horse equipment $25. No horse on 11/01/1863. Last record dated 11/01/1864, detailed as a brigade provost guard on 09/01/1864. After the war, became an overseer in Dougherty County, Georgia, and was married to Martha. Died before 1880. His widow received a Confederate pension from Mitchell County, Georgia.

1239. Thompson, Jackson S.: Enlisted as a private in Company A on 09/01/1861 at Richmond, Virginia. Became sick at Williamsburg, Virginia. Admitted to Chimborazo Hospital, Richmond, Virginia, on 12/18/1861. Last record, returned to duty 01/11/1862.

1240. Thompson, James F.: Printer from Augusta, Georgia. Born ca. 1838 in Georgia. Enlisted as a private in Company I on 02/27/1862 at Augusta, Georgia. Value of horse $200. Sent to Georgia to get a horse with Lt. Sinquefield under Special Order No. 27 from corps headquarters on 02/23/1864. Last record September/October 1864, sent to Georgia to get a horse with Capt. Bostick on 09/20/1864. After the war, worked as a journeyman printer in Augusta, Georgia. Was married to Laura H. and they had at least eight children. Buried in Magnolia Cemetery, Augusta, Georgia, on 08/15/1882. His widow received a Confederate pension from Richmond County, Georgia.

1241. Thompson, Lewis B.: 32-year-old. Enlisted as a private in Company I on 03/31/1862 at Augusta, Georgia. Discharged on 07/31/1862.

1242. Thornton, James Madison: Native of Georgia. Enlisted as a private in Company B on 08/14/1861 at Atlanta, Georgia. Value of horse $160 and horse equipment $5.50, saddle furnished by the State of Georgia. Furloughed for 30 days beginning 02/15/1863. No horse on 04/01/1863. Sent home to get a horse with Lt. James H. Johnson on 04/14/1863. No horse, sent to infirmary/recruiting camp on 10/13/1863. Sent to Georgia to get a horse under Special Order No. 36 on 03/13/1864. Last record September/October 1864, sent to Georgia to get a horse with Capt. Bostick on 09/20/1864.

1243. Thornton, Simeon Willis: Bailiff from Fulton County, Georgia. Born ca. 1828 in Georgia. Enlisted as a private in Company B on 08/14/1861 at Atlanta, Georgia. Value of horse $175 and horse equipment $18.50, equipment in name of company. Discharged and paid off on 12/01/1861 at Yorktown, Virginia. He and his wife, Mary R., had at least eight children. Died ca. 1869.

1244. Thrash, John S.: Laborer from Mitchell County, Georgia. Born ca. 1842 in Alabama. Enlisted as a private in Company D on 08/10/1861 at

Albany, Georgia. Value of horse $150 and horse equipment $20. Confined, sick in November/December 1861. Sent home to get a horse in March/April 1863. No horse in November/December 1863. Admitted to a hospital in Raleigh, North Carolina, on 01/22/1864. Admitted to Jackson Hospital, Richmond, Virginia, on 06/07/1864 with a wound in his right hand. Returned to duty on 07/06/1864. Last record 11/01/1864 sent to Georgia to get a horse with Capt. Bostick on 09/20/1864. After the war, became a farm laborer in Mitchell County, Georgia, and then in Decatur County, Georgia. Received a Confederate pension in Decatur County, Georgia. Died after 1880.

1245. Thurman [Thurmond], Joseph W. [W.L.]: 22-year-old from South Carolina. Enlisted as a private in Company A on 09/01/1861 at Richmond, Virginia. Value of horse $125 and horse equipment $20. Admitted to C.S.A. General Hospital, Charlottesville, Virginia, with a fractured arm on 12/02/1862. Furloughed on 12/11/1862. No horse beginning 01/01/1863. Detailed in Quartermaster Department on 12/15/1863. Sent to infirmary/recruiting camp in March/April 1864. Paroled at Augusta, Georgia, on 05/23/1865.

1246. Tinsley, Thomas Haywood: Silversmith from Newton County, Georgia. Born ca. 1834 in Georgia. Enlisted as a private in Company B on 08/14/1861 at Atlanta, Georgia. Value of horse $180 and horse equipment $7, saddle furnished by the State of Georgia. Listed as a musician in November/December 1861. Furloughed for 30 days beginning 02/15/1863. Sent to the infirmary/recruiting camp on 10/13/1863. Sent to Georgia to get a horse with Capt. Bostick on 09/20/1864. Was surrendered by Gen. Joseph E. Johnston on 04/26/1865. Paroled at Greensboro, North Carolina, on 05/01/1865.

1247. Todd, James H.: Resident of Fulton County, Georgia. Enlisted as a private in Company B on 08/14/1861 at Atlanta, Georgia. Value of horse $150 and horse equipment $5, saddle furnished by the State of Georgia. Detailed as a teamster in November/December 1861. Died on 04/25/1862 at Goldsboro, North Carolina. His back pay was given to his mother, Martha Todd, as he was not survived by his father, a wife, or children.

1248. Todd [Tood], Thomas B.F.: Born ca. 1845 in South Carolina. Enlisted as a private in Company H on 04/28/1862 at Atlanta, Georgia. Admitted to C.S.A. General Hospital, Charlottesville, Virginia, on 08/31/1863 with a wound. Transferred to General Hospital No. 9, Richmond, Virginia, on 12/07/1863. Furloughed for 60 days beginning 12/07/1863. Captured at Totopotomoy Creek near Hanover Court House, Virginia, on 06/04/1864 and sent to White House, Virginia. Transferred to Point Lookout, Maryland. Exchanged on 10/30/1864. Other records indicate he was wounded eight times during the war. After the war, became a schoolteacher in Cherokee County, Georgia. He and his wife, Maggie L., had at least four children. Received a Confederate pension in Gwinnett, Oconee, Jackson, and Clarke counties, Georgia. Died after 1910. His widow, Martha L. Todd, received a Confederate pension from Clarke County, Georgia.

1249. Tollison [Tallison], Healey [Halley] A.: Well-digger from Fulton County, Georgia. Enlisted as a private in Company K. Captured near Flat Rock, Georgia, on 07/26/1864 and sent to Nashville, Tennessee. Transferred to Louisville, Kentucky, on 08/11/1864. Transferred to Camp Chase, Ohio, on 08/13/1864. Deserted and took the Oath, and was released on 11/02/1864 with orders to remain north of the Ohio River. Married to E.R.

1250. Tompkins, Eubanks B.: Resident of Georgia. Enlisted as a private in Company D on 03/04/1862 at Albany, Georgia. Value of horse $300 and horse equipment $8. Admitted sick to City Hall Hospital, Macon, Georgia, on 06/20/1864. On detail duty under Special Order 185/30 on 08/06/1864. Was paroled at Albany, Georgia, on 05/29/1865.

1251. Tompson, Charles: Enlisted as a private in Company D on 03/04/1862 at Albany, Georgia. Single record dated 05/07/1862 at Camp Stephens, Georgia, does not state if he was present.

1252. Toole, James M.: Resident of Georgia. Enlisted in the 48th Georgia Infantry on 03/04/1862 at Appling, Georgia. Transferred as a private in Cobb's Legion Cavalry, Company I, on 01/11/1864. Sent to Georgia to get a horse with Lt. Sinquefield under Special Order No. 27 from corps headquarters on 02/23/1864. Sent to Georgia to get a horse with Capt. Bostick on 09/20/1864. Was surrendered by Gen. Joseph E. Johnston on 04/26/1865. Paroled at Greensboro, North Carolina, on 05/01/1865.

1253. Torrance [Torrence], Cuthbert C.: Native of Georgia. Enlisted as a private in Company F on 01/01/1863 at Stevensburg, Virginia, as a substitute for Nelson Wright Murphey. Admitted to Winder Hospital, Richmond, Virginia, on 12/23/1863 with a wound. Transferred to Jackson Hospital, Richmond, Virginia, on 01/21/1864 with neuralgia. Returned to duty on 04/19/1864. Detailed as an ambulance driver on 04/18/1864. Admitted to

Jackson Hospital, Richmond, Virginia, with neuralgia on 04/20/1864. Declared permanently disabled on 03/30/1864 at Jackson Hospital, Richmond, Virginia. Sent to Georgia to get a horse with Capt. Bostick on 09/20/1864. Was surrendered by Gen. Joseph E. Johnston on 04/26/1865. Paroled at Greensboro, North Carolina, on 05/01/1865.

1254. Truitt, James C.: Resident of Georgia. Enlisted as a private in Company A on 09/01/1861 at Richmond, Virginia. Mustered on 09/14/1861. Value of horse $225 and horse equipment $20. Appointed sergeant on 05/01/1862. Sent to Georgia to get a horse with Lt. Sinquefield under Special Order No. 27 from corps headquarters on 02/23/1864. Admitted to Jackson Hospital, Richmond, Virginia, on 05/13/1864 with pneumonia. Returned to duty on 05/21/1864. Last record September/October 1864, absent, sent to hospital on 09/01/1864. (Note: His records and those of James Riley Truitt were mixed together, but they could be sorted because the men held different ranks.)

1255. Truitt, James Riley: 38-year-old farmer from Wilkes County, Georgia. Born on 12/22/1822 in Wilkes, Georgia. Enlisted in 11th Georgia Infantry, Company C, on 10/01/1861. Transferred to Cobb's Legion, Company A, as a private on 05/01/1862 at Richmond, Virginia. Admitted to Chimborazo Hospital No. 3, Richmond, Virginia, on 11/24/1862 with rheumatism. Admitted to Hospital No. 17, Richmond, Virginia, on 12/02/1862. Transferred to 4th Georgia Hospital on 12/03/1862. Admitted to Winder Hospital in Richmond, Virginia, on 02/13/1863. Sent to Georgia to get a horse in November/December 1863. Sent to the infirmary/recruiting camp on 03/14/1864. Was surrendered by Gen. Joseph E. Johnston on 04/26/1865. Paroled at Greensboro, North Carolina, on 05/01/1865. Was listed as a blacksmith at the time of the surrender. Married Sarah (Sallie) A. Smith on 02/01/1870 in Wilkes County, Georgia, and they had at least three children. Died on 03/12/1896 in Wilkes County, Georgia. His widow received a Confederate pension from Wilkes County, Georgia. (Note: His records and those of James C. Truitt were mixed together, but they could be sorted because the men held different ranks.)

1256. Tuck, James J.[I.]: 17-year-old student from Clarke County, Georgia. Born on 01/09/1845 in Oglethorpe County, Georgia. Son of Robert Tuck. Enlisted as a private in Company C on 05/03/1862 at Athens, Clarke County, Georgia. Detailed as a teamster in 08/1862. Died on 02/16/1863 at Stevensburg, Virginia. His back pay was given to his father.

1257. Tuck, Robert: Farmer from Clarke County, Georgia. Born ca. 1815 in Halifax, Virginia. Father of James J. Tuck. On a roster of Company C in *These Men She Gave*. No service records in Cobb's Legion. After the war, became a farmer in Clarke County, Georgia. Married Dicey Louisa O'Kelly on 01/21/1844 in Oglethorpe County, Georgia, and they had at least ten children.

1258. Tuck, Thomas Ransom: 22-year-old farmer from Clarke County, Georgia. Born on 11/23/1838 in Halifax, Virginia. Enlisted as a private in Company C on 08/01/1861 at Athens, Clarke County, Georgia. Wounded on 11/29/1863. Admitted to C.S.A. General Hospital, Charlottesville, Virginia, on 12/01/1863 with a wound. Furloughed on 01/14/1864. Detailed in the Quartermaster Department in March/April 1864. Was surrendered by Gen. Joseph E. Johnston on 04/26/1865. Paroled at Greensboro, North Carolina, on 05/01/1865. After the war, became a farmer in Clarke County and then Oglethorpe County, Georgia. He returned to Clarke County, Georgia, later in life. Married Sarah E.S. Mathews on 09/26/1867 in Clarke County, Georgia, and they had at least four children. Received a Confederate pension in Clarke County, Georgia. Died on 02/15/1914 in Clarke County, Georgia. Buried in the Oconee Hill Cemetery in Clarke County, Georgia.

1259. Tuck, William Boyd: 23-year-old from Jackson County, Georgia. Born on 01/01/1839 in Georgia. Enlisted as a private in Company H on 03/03/1862 at Athens, Clarke County, Georgia. Died before the end of 03/1862. His back pay and bounty were given to his father, E.B. Tuck.

1260. Tucker, William J.: Merchant from Emanuel County, Georgia. Born ca. 1837 in Richmond County, Georgia. Enlisted as a private in Company A on 08/17/1861 at Augusta, Georgia. Value of horse $200 and horse equipment $20. Furloughed for 25 days beginning 02/22/1862 due to sickness. Captured at Martinsburg, [West] Virginia, on 07/15/1863 and hospitalized in Martinsburg, [West] Virginia. Sent to U.S. General Hospital, Baltimore, Maryland, on 09/21/1863. Paroled at City Point, Virginia, 09/25/1863. Admitted to Jackson Hospital, Richmond, Virginia, 09/29/1863 with typhoid fever. Transferred to Camp Lee, Virginia, on 10/06/1863. Absent, a paroled prisoner sick in Georgia, in January/February 1864. Admitted to Jackson Hospital, Richmond, Virginia, with chronic diarrhea on 08/23/1864. Returned to duty on 09/20/1864. Was surrendered by Gen. Joseph E. Johnston on 04/26/1865. Paroled at Greensboro,

North Carolina, on 05/01/1865. After the war, became a school teacher in Emanuel County, Georgia. Married Gincy A. Rountree on 12/05/1868 in Emanuel County, Georgia.

1261. Tullis, James M.: Enlisted as a private in the 46th Georgia Infantry, Company F, on 03/04/1862. Transferred to Cobb's Legion Cavalry, Company D, on 05/07/1862. Discharged on 05/13/1862. No service records in Cobb's Legion.

1262. Turner, Absalom B.: 20-year-old farmer from Emanuel County, Georgia. Born in Emanuel County, Georgia, on 01/25/1842. Enlisted as a private in Company L on 12/15/1862 at Burke County, Georgia. Absent without leave beginning 02/01/1863. Still absent without leave on last record, 09/01/1864. After the war, became a farmer in Emanuel County, Georgia. Married Sarah Jane Coleman on 06/27/1861 and they had at least nine children. Died on 10/25/1926.

1263. Turner, Calhoun H.: Student from Cobb County, Georgia. Born ca. 1846 in Georgia. Enlisted as a private in Company B on 08/14/1861 at Atlanta, Georgia. Value of horse $180 and horse equipment $4.25, saddle furnished by the State of Georgia. Detailed as a courier for Col. Johnston in November/December 1861. Transferred to Company G on 05/30/1862. Detailed as a courier for Gen. McLaws in 07/1862. Lost horse on 01/08/1863. Sent to Georgia in 01/1863 because of an application by his father for his discharge (probably because he was underage). However, he returned to his unit. Sent home to get a horse on 11/10/1863. Last record September/October 1864, sent to Georgia to get a horse with Capt. Bostick on 09/20/1864. After the war, lived in Cobb County, Georgia, and was married to F.E. Died after 1910. His widow received a Confederate pension from Fulton County, Georgia.

1264. Turner, Cornelius [Christopher] C.: Resident of Georgia. Enlisted as a private in Company H on 09/03/1862 at Athens, Clarke County, Georgia. Admitted Winder Hospital, Richmond, Virginia, in 08/1863. Admitted to C.S.A. General Hospital, Charlottesville, Virginia, on 08/25/1863 with a wound. Transferred to Winder Hospital, Richmond, Virginia, on 09/14/1863. Returned to duty on 10/16/1863. Furloughed to Georgia beginning 02/19/1864. Absent without leave beginning 08/01/1864. Captured in Hall County, Georgia. Deserted and took the Oath on 08/29/1864 at Chattanooga, Tennessee. Transferred to military prison in Louisville, Kentucky, in 09/1864. Released north of the Ohio River. Described as having a light complexion, light hair, dark eyes, and being 6 feet tall.

1265. Turner, James: Enlisted as a private in Company L on 12/20/1862 at Burke County, Georgia. Value of horse $250. Mortally wounded and horse lost in action at Brandy Station, Virginia, on 06/09/1863. Died at Henningsen Hospital, Richmond, Virginia, on 06/24/1863. His father, John L. Turner, was reimbursed for the horse and given his back pay, as he was not survived by a wife or children.

1266. Turner, James J.: 26-year-old from Georgia. Enlisted in 1st Georgia Infantry, Company F, as a private on 03/18/1861. Mustered out at Augusta, Georgia, on 03/18/1862. Enlisted as a private in Cobb's Legion Cavalry, Company B, on 04/08/1862. Value of horse $160. Transferred to Company G in May/June 1862. Sent to infirmary/recruiting camp on 11/01/1863. Absent sick beginning 10/10/1864. Captured at Sussex Court House, Virginia, on 12/12/1864 and sent to City Point, Virginia. Transferred to Point Lookout, Maryland, on 12/13/1864. Died in the hospital of disease at Point Lookout, Maryland, on 01/20/1865. Buried in grave number 834. (Note: His death certificate is misfiled with the records of Jefferson J. Turner.)

1267. Turner, Jefferson J.: From Georgia. Born ca. 1840 in White County, Georgia. Enlisted as a private in Company C on 08/01/1861 at Athens, Clarke County, Georgia. Sent home to get a horse on 11/10/1863. Absent without leave beginning 02/01/1864. Listed as an artificer at the surrender. Was surrendered by Gen. Joseph E. Johnston on 04/26/1865. Paroled at Greensboro, North Carolina, on 05/01/1865. After the war, became a farmer in Hall County, Georgia. Married Rosella Dyar on 10/09/1864 in White County, Georgia, and they had at least six children. Received a Confederate pension from Hall County, Georgia, from 1908 to 1920. Died on 10/15/1920.

1268. Turner, Stephen: 18-year-old from Georgia. Enlisted in 1st Georgia Infantry, Company F, as a private on 03/18/1861. Mustered out at Augusta, Georgia, on 03/18/1862. Enlisted as a private in Cobb's Legion Cavalry, Company B, on 04/19/1862 at Atlanta, Georgia. Transferred to Company G in May/June 1862. Detailed as a courier for Gen. Semmes in 06/1862. Lost horse on 01/09/1863. Wounded at Funkstown, Maryland, on 07/10/1863. Admitted to hospital and furloughed to Georgia. Lost horse on 08/02/1863. Admitted to Winder Hospital, Richmond, Virginia, on 08/04/1863 with malaria. Furloughed for 30 days beginning 08/13/1863. Sent to Georgia to get a horse with Lt. Sinquefield under Special Order No. 27 from corps headquarters on 02/23/1864. Last record September/October 1864, sent to Georgia to get a horse with Capt. Bostick on 09/20/1864.

1269. Tweedy, Ephraim, Jr.: 30-year-old retail merchant from Augusta, Georgia. Born in Ireland. Enlisted as a lieutenant in Company A on 08/17/1861. Value of horses $200 and $225, and horse equipment $40 and $15. Horse killed in battle on 10/13/1861. Tweedy resigned on 10/22/1862. Furnished John Christman as a substitute. After the war, worked as a jeweler in Augusta, Georgia. Married Jesse and was the father of at least two children.

1270. Twitty, W.W.: Listed in a roster of Company D published in *The History of Dougherty County*, but not with the *Civil War Soldiers and Sailors System*. No service records in Cobb's Legion.

1271. Tyus, C.: Enlisted as a private in Company D on 08/10/1861 at Albany, Georgia. Was surrendered by Gen. Joseph E. Johnston on 04/26/1865. Paroled at Greensboro, North Carolina, on 05/01/1865.

1272. Usry, Joshua F.[Y.]: 27-year-old physician from Warren County, Georgia. Born in Warren County, Georgia. Enlisted as a private in Company A on 8/17/1861 at Augusta, Georgia. Value of horse $225, and horse equipment $35. Horse killed in action on the Peninsula in 02/1862 (or 12/11/1861). Usry on sick furlough for 60 days beginning 12/25/1861. Furlough was extended. Discharged on 06/20/1862 due to chronic hepatitis. Described as being 5'11" tall, with a light complexion, blue eyes, and light hair. After the war, became a farmer, physician, and miller in Glascock County, Georgia.

1273. Vasser, Richard A.: Farmer from Elbert County, Georgia. Born ca. 1842 in Georgia. Enlisted as a private in Company C on 08/01/1861 at Athens, Clarke County, Georgia. On furlough of indulgence beginning 02/18/1864. Admitted to Jackson Hospital, Richmond, Virginia, on 08/21/1864 with acute diarrhea. Returned to duty on 08/29/1864. Last record September/October 1864, sent to Georgia to get a horse with Capt. Bostick on 09/20/1864. After the war, worked as a farm laborer in Wilkes County and then Lincoln County, Georgia. He and his wife, Mary, had at least five children. Received a Confederate pension in Lincoln County, Georgia. Died after 1930.

1274. Vaughan, George W.: 30-year-old from Carrollton, Georgia. Enlisted as a private in Company E on 03/15/1862 at Roswell, Georgia. Value of horse $125. Transferred to Company F in July/August 1862. Wounded on 09/14/1862. Admitted to Winder Hospital, Richmond, Virginia, on 09/30/1862. Furloughed for 20 days beginning 10/11/1862. Captured at Cold Harbor, Virginia, on 06/01/1864 and sent to Point Lookout, Maryland. Deserted and took the Oath on 06/27/1864.

1275. Vaughn, Claborn: Hireling from Lumpkin County, Georgia. Born ca. 1832 in Georgia. Brother of Thomas R. Vaughn. Enlisted as a corporal in Company E on 03/15/1862 at Roswell, Georgia. Value of horse $160. Admitted to Winder Hospital, Richmond, Virginia, on 09/10/1862 with rheumatism. Furloughed for 25 days beginning 10/20/1862. Absent sick in March/April 1863. Admitted to Winder Hospital, Richmond, Virginia, on 07/29/1863. Detailed at the Medical Department on 10/14/1863. Sent to Georgia to get a horse under Special Order No. 36 from corps headquarters on 03/13/1864. Sent to the infirmary/recruiting camp on 06/03/1864. Still at the infirmary/recruiting camp on last record, September/October 1864. Married Frances Avaline (or Evaline or Elender) Bowman on 09/28/1848 in Forsythe County, Georgia.

1276. Vaughn, Thomas R.: Born in Forsyth County, Georgia, in 1838 or 1839. Brother of Claborn Vaughn. Enlisted as a private in Company E on 04/03/1862 at Roswell, Georgia. Last record dated 04/22/1862.

1277. Vigis [Visis], Thomas: Native of Georgia. Enlisted as a private in Company B on 08/14/1861 at Atlanta, Georgia. Horse, owned by Thomas H. Williams, valued at $180 and horse equipment $6.50, saddle furnished by the State of Georgia. On detached service in November/December 1861. Last record September/October 1864, sent to Georgia to get a horse with Capt. Bostick on 09/20/1864.

1278. Voss, James A.: 36-year-old farmer from Fannin County, Georgia. Born in Cobb County, Georgia, on 11/22/1825. Enlisted as a private in Company E 03/15/1862 at Roswell, Georgia. Value of horse $175. Sent home to get a horse in March/April 1863. Horse killed in action at Upperville, Virginia, on 06/21/1863. Voss detailed as a blacksmith beginning 06/26/1863. Lost horse on 10/29/1863. Sent home to get a horse with Lt. Sinquefield under Special Order No. 27 from corps headquarters on 02/23/1864. Last record September/October 1864, sent to Georgia to get a horse with Capt. Bostick on 09/20/1864. After the war, became a blacksmith and then a farmer from Milton County, Georgia. Later, lived in Fulton County, Georgia. Married Rebecca Naylor on 03/04/1847 in Cobb County, Georgia, and they had at least two children. Received a Confederate pension in Fulton County, Georgia. Died after 1880. His widow received a Confederate pension from DeKalb County, Georgia, and Milton County, Georgia.

1279. Voss, John A.: Carpenter from Cobb County, Georgia. Born ca. 1828 in Georgia. Enlisted as a private in Company E on 03/15/1862 at Roswell, Georgia. Value of horse $200. Detailed as an ordnance wagon driver on 04/08/1863. Lost horse on 04/25/1863. On furlough sometime after 05/01/1864. Captured in Cobb County, Georgia, on 09/01/1864 and sent to Military Prison, Louisville, Kentucky. Deserted and took the Oath on 09/16/1864 and was sent north of the Ohio River. Described as having a fair complexion, brown hair, blue eyes, and being 5'11" tall. He and his wife, Susan, had at least five children. Died before 1880.

1280. Voss, William A.: Brick mason from Pickens County, Georgia. Born ca. 1833 in Georgia. Enlisted as a private in Company E on 03/15/1862 at Roswell, Georgia. Value of horse $250. Detailed as a teamster on 08/17/1862. No horse in January/February 1864. Last record September/October 1864, sent to Georgia to get a horse with Capt. Bostick on 09/20/1864. After the war, became a brick mason in Fulton County, Georgia. Later, lived in Cobb and DeKalb counties, Georgia. Married Lucy Paul on 10/06/1856 in Pickens County, Georgia, and they had at least two children. Received a Confederate pension in Cobb County, Georgia. His widow received a Confederate pension from Fulton County, Georgia.

1281. Wadlee, H.S.: Enlisted as a private in Company C. Only record, furloughed for 25 days in 01/1862.

1282. Waggins, L.D.: Listed on a roster of Company D published in *The History of Dougherty County*, but not with the *Civil War Soldiers and Sailors System*. No service records in Cobb's Legion.

1283. Wait, Nickolas C.: Enlisted as a private in Company C on 03/01/1862 at Clark County, Georgia. Only record dated 04/25/1862.

1284. Waldrup, J.J.: 18-year-old. Enlisted as a private in Company K on 02/08/1863 at Camp Maynard, Georgia. Returned to his regiment on 03/23/1863.

1285. Walker, James F.[Y.]: Native of Georgia. Enlisted as a private in Company B on 08/14/1861 at Atlanta, Georgia. Value of horse $200 and horse equipment $5.25, saddle furnished by the State of Georgia. Detailed as a wagon master beginning 10/01/1861. Sent to Georgia to get a horse on 11/13/1863. Sent to Georgia to get a horse under Special Order No. 36 from corps headquarters on 03/13/1864. Sent to Georgia to get a horse with Capt. Bostick on 09/20/1864. Was surrendered by Gen. Joseph E. Johnston on 04/26/1865. Paroled at Greensboro, North Carolina, on 05/01/1865.

1286. Walker, Persons (Pat): Farmer from Warren County, Georgia. Born ca. 1830 in Georgia. Enlisted as a private in Company A on 2/10/1862 at Augusta, Georgia. Lost horse on 01/01/1863. Admitted to hospital in 04/1863. Returned to duty in 06/1863. Detailed on Orange and Alexandria Railroad beginning 07/01/1863. On detached service beginning 09/10/1863. Admitted to Jackson Hospital, Richmond, Virginia, with pneumonia on 01/20/1864. Returned to duty on 01/25/1864. No horse, detailed to Quartermaster Department, Car Corps, in March/April 1864. Last record, sent to Georgia to get a horse with Capt. Bostick on 09/20/1864. Married Elizabeth (or Julia) Darden in 01/1845 in Warren County, Georgia, and they had at least seven children. Died after 1880.

1287. Walkin, H.H.: Enlisted as a private in Company A. Captured at Stony Creek, Virginia, on 12/01/1864 and sent to City Point, Virginia. Transferred to Point Lookout, Maryland. Released on 06/22/1865.

1288. Wall, William Carter: Teacher from Burke County, Georgia. Born ca. 1839 in Georgia. Enlisted as a private in Company F on 05/09/1862 at Burke County, Georgia. Value of horse $150. Detailed as a teamster in January/February 1863. Admitted to a hospital in January/February 1863. Detailed as a teamster in the Commissary Department on 08/02/1863. Was surrendered by Gen. Joseph E. Johnston on 04/26/1865. Paroled at Greensboro, North Carolina, on 05/01/1865. After the war, became a farmer in Burke County, Georgia. He and his wife, Frances, had at least six children. Died after 1880.

1289. Wallace, Charles: 18-year-old. Enlisted as a private in Company B on 04/19/1862 at Atlanta, Georgia. Value of horse $235. Last record November/December 1862, wounded and sent to Richmond, Virginia, on 09/15/1862. Furloughed to Atlanta, Georgia, for 60 days.

1290. Wallace, Patrick: 23-year-old baker from Augusta, Georgia. Born in Ireland. Enlisted as a private in Company A on 08/17/1861 at Augusta, Georgia. Value of horse $150 and horse equipment $25. Detailed as an ambulance driver beginning 05/01/1862. Listed as a corporal in January/February 1863. Listed as a sergeant in March/April 1863. No horse, on furlough, wounded in November/December 1863. Detailed at government bakery in Augusta, Georgia, in 01/1864. Last record September/October 1864, still detailed as baker in Augusta, Georgia. After the war, was a baker in

Richmond County, Georgia, and was married to Maggie.

1291. Walsh, Michael: On a roster of Company I compiled by Glen Spurlock. No service records in Cobb's Legion.

1292. Walter [Walters], Fred W.: Resident of Georgia. Enlisted as a bugler in Company C on 08/01/1861 at Athens, Clarke County, Georgia. Appointed chief bugler on 12/01/1862. Was wounded in the scalp by a saber at Dispatch Station, Virginia, on 06/28/1862.* Sent home to get a horse with Lt. Sinquefield under Special Order No. 27 from corps headquarters on 02/23/1864. Last record September/October 1864, sent to Georgia to get a horse with Capt. Bostick on 09/20/1864.

1293. Walter, Jerry: Listed on a roster of Company D published in *The History of Dougherty County*, but not with the *Civil War Soldiers and Sailors System*. No service records in Cobb's Legion.

1294. Ward, Calvin D.: 28-year-old planter from Burke County, Georgia. Born on 12/16/1833 in Pickens County, South Carolina. Enlisted as a private in Company F on 05/09/1862 at Augusta, Georgia. Value of horse $150. Sent home to get a horse with Lt. Sinquefield under Special Order No. 27 from corps headquarters on 02/23/1864. Sent to Georgia to get a horse with Capt. Bostick on 09/20/1864. Paroled at Augusta, Georgia, on 05/18/1865. After the war, became a farmer in Burke County, Georgia. Married Aljarona on 12/28/1851 and they had at least eight children. Died on 03/11/1892. Buried at old McBean Church Cemetery, Burke County, Georgia. His widow received a Confederate pension from Burke County, Georgia.

1295. Ward, James M.: Resident of Georgia. Enlisted as a private in Company D on 03/04/1862 at Albany, Georgia. Value of horse $200 and horse equipment $8. Admitted to C.S.A. General Hospital, Charlottesville, Virginia, sick on 12/09/1863. Sent to Georgia to get a horse with Capt. Bostick on 09/20/1864. Was surrendered by Gen. Joseph E. Johnston on 04/26/1865. Paroled at Greensboro, North Carolina, on 05/01/1865.

1296. Ware, Nicholas C.: Farmer from Madison County, Georgia. Born in Georgia or Alabama ca. 1832. Enlisted as a private in Company H on 03/01/1862 at Athens, Clarke County, Georgia. Killed on 06/09/1863 during the cavalry battle at Brandy Station, Virginia. Married Frances Antoinette Yerby ca. 1862 in Georgia.

1297. Warwick, Edwin [Edward] A.: From Fulton County, Georgia. Born ca. 1846 in Georgia. Enlisted as a private in Company G on 04/19/1862 at Atlanta, Georgia. Value of horse $200. Admitted to hospital in Richmond, Virginia, in 08/1862. Returned to duty in 12/1862. Sent home to get a horse with Lt. Sinquefield under Special Order No. 27 from corps headquarters on 02/23/1864. Sent to Georgia to get a horse with Capt. Bostick on 09/20/1864. Paroled at Charlotte, North Carolina, on 05/23/1865. After the war, became a Railroad Conductor in Fulton County, Georgia. Married (1) Mary L. (2) Gertrude, and was the father of at least two children. Received a Confederate pension in DeKalb County, Georgia. Died after 1920.

1298. Warwick, John N.: From Georgia. Born ca. 1846 in Georgia. Enlisted as a private in Company B on 04/29/1862 at Atlanta, Georgia. Value of horse $185. On extra duty beginning 03/01/1863. Captured at King George County, Virginia, on 05/21/1864 and sent to Belle Plain, Virginia. Transferred to Point Lookout, Maryland. Exchanged on 11/01/1864 and sent to Camp Lee, Virginia. Was given a 30 days' furlough beginning 12/06/1864 to go home and get a horse, blanket, and adequate winter clothing, and then to join his command in Georgia. Was surrendered by Gen. Joseph E. Johnston on 04/26/1865. Paroled at Greensboro, North Carolina, on 05/01/1865. After the war, worked as a railroad conductor in DeKalb County, Georgia, and was married.

1299. Waters, Charles L.: Student from Baker County, Georgia. Enlisted as a private in Company D on 03/02/1863 at Albany, Georgia. Admitted to Jackson Hospital, Richmond, Virginia, on 06/22/1864. Paroled at Albany, Georgia, on 05/19/1865.

1300. Waters, James B.: 21-year-old farmer from Lumpkin County, Georgia. Born on 09/30/1840. Enlisted as a private in Company C on 03/08/1862 at Lumpkin County, Georgia. Courier for Gen. Stuart beginning 08/01/1863. Deserted and took the Oath on 02/01/1864. After the war, worked as a farm laborer in Murray County and then Lumpkin County, Georgia. His wife's name was Emeline and they had eight children. Died on 10/26/1918.

1301. Watkins [Wadkins], Benjamin H.: From Georgia. Born ca. 1840 in Georgia. Brother of Charles D. Watkins. Enlisted in the 1st Georgia Infantry, Company D, as a private in 03/18/1861. Transferred to Cobb's Legion Cavalry, Company I, as a sergeant on 02/14/1862. Value of horse $230. Pay stopped for one month by court-martial in Jan-

*Howard, page 2.

uary/February 1863. Sent to infirmary/recruiting camp in November/December 1863. Horse valued at $1,500 killed in action at Trevilian Station, Virginia, on 06/11/1864. Watkins sent to Georgia to get a horse with Capt. Bostick on 09/20/1864. Was surrendered by Gen. Joseph E. Johnston on 04/26/1865. Paroled at Greensboro, North Carolina, on 05/01/1865.

1302. Watkins, Charles D: 19-year-old from Georgia. Brother of Benjamin H. Watkins. Enlisted in the 1st Georgia Infantry, Company D, as a private in 03/18/1861. Appointed corporal on 02/01/1862. Mustered out at Augusta, Georgia, on 03/18/1862. Enlisted as a private in Cobb's Legion Cavalry, Company I, on 03/25/1862. Detailed in Quartermaster Department beginning 01/01/1863. Was present on last record, September/October 1864. After the war, became a farmer in Abbeville County, South Carolina. Married Fannie Hodges on 03/29/1866 in Abbeville, South Carolina, and they had at least six children. Died after 1880.

1303. Watkins Henry A.[H.]: Merchant's clerk from Augusta, Georgia. Born ca. 1844. Enlisted as a private in Company A on 09/17/1861 at Augusta, Georgia. Lost horse on 01/01/1863. Admitted to C.S.A. General Hospital, Charlottesville, Virginia, with debility on 02/07/1863. Returned to duty on 04/03/1863. Admitted to C.S.A. General Hospital in Charlottesville, Virginia, on 04/09/1863. Returned to duty on 04/30/1863. Admitted to C.S.A. General Hospital, Charlottesville, Virginia, with stricture of the urethra on 05/08/1863. Returned to duty on 06/17/1863. Admitted to Jackson Hospital, Richmond, Virginia, with stricture of the urethra on 03/20/1864. Returned to duty on 04/12/1864. Sent to infirmary/recruiting camp at Stony Creek, Virginia, on 10/12/1864. Captured sometime after 10/12/1864 and sent to Point Lookout, Maryland. Released on 06/22/1865. Described as being 5'10" tall, with a dark complexion, black hair, and dark eyes.

1304. Watson, James B.: 22-year-old from Georgia. Enlisted as a corporal in Company E on 03/15/1862 at Roswell, Georgia. Value of horse $250. Admitted to Winder Hospital, Richmond, Virginia, on 09/10/1862 with lumbago. Returned to duty on 11/10/1862. Sent home to get a horse in March/April 1863. Wounded by a gunshot in the left thigh at Gettysburg, Pennsylvania, on 07/04/1863. Captured on 07/05/1863 at Gettysburg, Pennsylvania. Admitted to Letterman General Hospital, Gettysburg, Pennsylvania, where his left leg was amputated. Transferred to U.S.A. General Hospital, West's Buildings, Baltimore, Maryland, on 10/06/1863. Sent to City Point, Virginia, on 11/12/1863 for exchange. Admitted to Winder Hospital, Richmond, Virginia, on 11/18/1863. Furloughed for 60 days beginning 11/28/1863. Still absent wounded on last record, September/October 1864.

1305. Weaver, H.F.[T.]: 25-year-old. Enlisted as a private in Company K on 01/27/1863 at Camp Maynard, Georgia. Deserted on 03/11/1863.

1306. Weaver, W. T.: Enlisted as a private in Company D on 03/03/1864 at Atlanta, Georgia. Last record September/October 1864, sent to Georgia to get a horse with Capt. Bostick on 09/20/1864.

1307. Webb, Joseph M.: Student from Emanuel County, Georgia. Born ca. 1845 in Georgia. Enlisted as a private in Company L on 05/06/1864 at Decatur, Georgia. Absent without leave beginning 05/12/1864. Deserted and took the Oath on 07/27/1864 at Chattanooga, Tennessee. Ordered to stay north of the Ohio River during the remainder of the war. Described as having a light complexion, light hair, blue or gray eyes, and being 5'10" tall. After the war, became a farmer in Emanuel County, Georgia. He and his wife, Margaret, had at least one child. Died after 1880.

1308. Weir [Wier], Nathan Hoyt: Farmer from Clarke County, Georgia. Born ca. 1832 in Georgia. Enlisted as a private in Company H on 04/29/1862 at Atlanta, Georgia. Sent home to get a horse under Special Order No. 36 on 04/01/1864. In Georgia on sick furlough beginning 05/01/1864. Paroled at Athens, Clarke County, Georgia, on 05/08/1865. Died after 1870.

1309. Weir [Wier], Samuel B.: Farmer from Jackson County, Georgia. Born ca. 1823 in Georgia. Enlisted as a private in Company C on 03/01/1862 at Jackson County, Georgia. Discharged on 07/16/1862 at Richmond, Virginia. Was present beginning January/February 1864. Sent home to get a horse under Special Order No. 36 on 03/13/1864. Admitted to a hospital on 08/24/1864. Returned to duty on 08/29/1864. Sent to Georgia to get a horse with Capt. Bostick on 09/20/1864. Paroled at Athens, Georgia, on 05/08/1865. After the war, became a farmer in Jackson County, Georgia. Later lived in Clarke County, Georgia. His wife's name was Cinthia (or Cynthia) and they had at least six children. Received a Confederate pension in Jackson County, Georgia. Transferred to Clarke County, Georgia. Died after 1870.

1310. Welch, Michael: 23-year-old from Augusta, Georgia. Enlisted as a private in Company I on 04/14/1862 at Augusta, Georgia. He was issued clothing at General Hospital No. 3, Lynchburg, Virginia, on 10/12/1863. Sent to the infirmary/recruiting camp in November/December 1863. He was issued clothing at General Hospital No. 3, Lynchburg, Virginia, on 02/01/1864. Sent to Georgia to get a horse on 04/20/1864. Admitted to a hospital in North Carolina on 07/20/1864. Admitted to C.S.A. General Hospital No. 11, Charlottesville, Virginia, on 02/14/1865. Transferred to Pettigrew General Hospital No. 13, Raleigh, North Carolina, on 02/16/1865. Paroled at Raleigh, North Carolina, on 06/11/1865. On his parole, he gave his home address as Boston.

1311. Wellborn, Olive: Enlisted as a private in Company B on 08/14/1861 at Atlanta, Georgia. Value of horse $225 and horse equipment $7.50, saddle furnished by the State of Georgia. Promoted to lieutenant in Col. Hunt's Cavalry on 05/23/1862. Discharged from Cobb's Legion Cavalry on 05/14/1862.

1312. Wells, Thomas B.: Coach driver from Jefferson County, Georgia. Born ca. 1843 in Jefferson County, Georgia. Enlisted as a private in Company F on 03/25/1862 at Burke County, Georgia. Value of horse $160. Admitted to Henningsen Hospital, Richmond, Virginia, sick on 10/28/1862. Sent home to get a horse with Lt. Sinquefield under Special Order No. 27 from corps headquarters on 02/23/1864. Admitted to Winder Hospital, Richmond, Virginia, with a wound on 08/17/1863. Returned to duty on 08/22/1863. Last record September/October 1864, sent to Georgia to get a horse with Capt. Bostick on 09/20/1864. After the war, worked as a clerk in Burke County, Georgia. He and his wife, Adelia, had at least two children. Died after 1880.

1313. Weston, Edward H.: Merchant's clerk from Augusta, Georgia. Born in Maine. Enlisted as a private in Company I on 02/14/1864 at Augusta, Georgia. Deserted to the enemy while on picket duty on the Vaughan Road in Virginia, and was sent to City Point, Virginia, on 09/05/1864. Took the Oath on 10/09/1864, and was sent to Eastport, Maine. Described as having a fair complexion, black hair, black eyes, and being 5'10" tall.

1314. Weston, J.H.: Listed on a roster of Company D published in *The History of Dougherty County*, but not with the *Civil War Soldiers and Sailors System*. No service records in Cobb's Legion.

1315. Whaley, Caleb A.: Enlisted as a sergeant in Company B on 08/14/1861 at Atlanta, Georgia. Value of horse $25 and horse equipment $25. Furloughed for 25 days beginning 11/29/1861. Promoted to captain in Col. Lawton's Cavalry on last record, March/April 1862. His widow, Mary P. Whaley, received a Confederate pension from Jones County, Georgia.

1316. Whalin [Whalen, Whelen], Maurice: Native of Georgia. Enlisted as a private in Company F on 06/01/1863 at Culpeper County, Virginia, as a substitute for Robert A. Murphey. Received a gunshot wound at Mine Run, Virginia, on 11/27/1863 and was sent to a hospital in Gordonsville, Virginia. Furloughed for 40 days beginning 01/17/1864. Detailed to attend horses at the infirmary/recruiting camp on 03/10/1864. Was surrendered by Gen. Joseph E. Johnston on 04/26/1865. Paroled at Greensboro, North Carolina, on 05/01/1865.

1317. Wharton, J.T.M.: Enlisted as a private in Company G on 05/20/1864 at Atlanta, Georgia. Admitted to Jackson Hospital, Richmond, Virginia, on 12/11/1864 with a wound from a minié ball in the left arm. Returned to duty on 01/30/1865. Was surrendered by Gen. Joseph E. Johnston on 04/26/1865. Paroled at Greensboro, North Carolina, on 05/01/1865.

1318. Whelchel, Alexander S.: From Hall County, Georgia. Born ca. 1844 in Georgia. Enlisted as a private in Company C on 08/01/1861 at Athens, Clarke County, Georgia. Detailed as an assistant forage master in March/April 1863. Had a receipt for clothing at Winder Hospital, Richmond, Virginia, in 09/1863. Sent home wounded on 09/22/1863. Returned to duty on 02/10/1864. Sent to infirmary/recruiting camp on 02/23/1864. Last record September/October 1864, sent to Georgia to get a horse with Capt. Bostick on 09/20/1864. After the war, became a county merchant and then a farmer in Hall County, Georgia. Married Margaret M. Garner in Hall County, Georgia, on 12/17/1868 and they had at least five children. Died after 1880.

1319. Whelchel [Welchel], Francis Marion: Student from Hall County, Georgia. Born ca. 1842 in Georgia. Enlisted as a private in Company C on 08/01/1861 at Athens, Clarke County, Georgia. Detailed as a forage master in March/April 1863. Sent home to get a horse with Lt. Sinquefield under Special Order No. 27 from corps headquarters on 02/23/1864. Listed as a corporal in September/October 1864. On sick furlough on last record, September/October 1864. Other records indicate that he injured his back and kidneys while on horse detail on 02/23/1864. After the war, became a farm laborer in Hall County, Georgia. Married Mary F. Patterson on 02/08/1866 and they had at least five children. Received a Confederate pension in Hall County, Georgia, in 1901. Died on 01/09/1907 in Hall County, Georgia.

1320. Whelchel, Stephen T.: Student from Hall County, Georgia. Born ca. 1840 in Georgia. Enlisted as a corporal in Company C on 08/01/1861 at Athens, Clarke County, Georgia. Listed as a sergeant in November/December 1861. Detailed as an assistant forage master in January/February 1863. Listed as a private in November/December 1863. Sent to Georgia to get a horse with Lt. Sinquefield under Special Order No. 27 from corps headquarters on 02/23/1864. Was surrendered by Gen. Joseph E. Johnston on 04/26/1865. Paroled at Greensboro, North Carolina, on 05/01/1865. After the war, became a farmer in Hall County, Georgia. He and his wife, Mary E., had at least two children.

1321. Whisenant [Whistenance], Henry: From Hall County, Georgia. Born ca. 1841 in Georgia. Enlisted as a private in Company H on 03/03/1862 at Athens, Clarke County, Georgia. Died on 02/26/1863 at Mt. Hope, Virginia. His back pay was given to his father, Joseph Whisenant, of Hall County, Georgia.

1322. White, Alexander R.: Enlisted as a corporal in Company B on 08/10/1861 at Atlanta, Georgia. Discharged on 04/22/1862.

1323. White, C.C.: Enlisted as a private in Company B on 05/06/1864 at Guiney's (Guinea's) Station, Virginia. Was present on last record, September/October 1864.

1324. White, George B.: Butcher from Augusta, Georgia. Born in Georgia ca. 1841. Enlisted as a private in Company A on 08/17/1861 at Augusta, Georgia. Value of horse $175 and horse equipment $20. On furlough for 25 days beginning 01/22/1862. Appointed bugler on 05/01/1862. Transferred to Company G. Sent to Georgia to get a horse in November/December 1863. Killed in action at Ream's Station, Virginia, on 08/25/1864.

1325. White, Henry: Enlisted as a sergeant in Company L on 12/15/1862 at Burke County, Georgia. Admitted to Winder Hospital, Richmond, Virginia, on 07/21/1863. Sent to Georgia to get a horse with Capt. Bostick on 09/20/1864. Was paroled at Augusta, Georgia, on 05/18/1865.

1326. White, Henry Clay: 13-year-old from Georgia. Born 12/30/1848. Enlisted as a private in Company H on 03/04/1862 at Athens, Clarke County, Georgia. Listed in May/June 1862 as a sergeant. Horse, valued at $500, killed in action at Jack's Shop, Virginia, on 09/22/1863. White sent home to get a horse with Lt. Sinquefield under Special Order No. 27 from corps headquarters on 02/23/1864. Last record September/October 1864, sent to Georgia with Capt. Bostick to get a horse on 09/20/1864. Received a Confederate pension in Newton County, Georgia. Died on 11/13/1895. Buried in Hill Cemetery, Oconee, Clarke County, Georgia.

1327. White, James K. Polk: Enlisted as a private in Company B on 08/14/1861 at Atlanta, Georgia. Horse, owned by Thomas H. Williams, valued at $225, and equipment $6.50, saddle furnished by the State of Georgia. Discharged due to disability on 02/06/1862.

1328. White [Whyte], Joseph: Resident of Georgia. Enlisted as a private in Company I on 07/03/1863 at Augusta, Georgia. Had use of a public horse. Admitted to Robinson Hospital on 10/07/1863. Detailed as a clerk at brigade headquarters on 01/12/1864. Still on detail at brigade headquarters on last record September/October 1864.

1329. White, Lawson V.: Resident of Fulton County, Georgia. Enlisted as a private in Company B on 01/07/1862 at Camp Marion, Virginia, as a substitute for James R. Glenn. Detailed to work in a rolling mill in Atlanta, Georgia, for 60 days beginning 08/02/1862. Lost horse on 05/01/1863. Deserted and took the Oath on 03/05/1864 at Chattanooga, Tennessee. Was described as having a fair complexion, dark hair, blue eyes, and being 6' 2" tall. After the war, became a heater in a rolling mill in Mercer County, New Jersey, and then Hamilton County, Tennessee. Married (1) Hetty (2) Junie, and was the father of one child.

1330. White, Robert: Farm laborer from Jackson County, Georgia. Born in Georgia ca. 1840. Enlisted as a private in Company C on 04/02/1862 at Jackson County, Georgia. Transferred to Company H in 04/1862 at Athens, Clarke County, Georgia. Discharged from service on 07/17/1862. After the war, became a farmer in Jackson County, Georgia. Married Nancy Helen Smith ca. 1865 in Jackson County, Georgia, and they had at least seven children. Died on 11/17/1903. Buried in the White Family Cemetery in Jackson County, Georgia.

1331. White, W.J.: 32-year-old. Enlisted as a private in Company K on 02/09/1863 at Camp Maynard, Georgia. Returned to his regiment on 02/21/1863.

1332. White, William Augustus (Gus): Elected a lieutenant in Company K. Was under arrest for desertion from the 10th Georgia Infantry and imprisoned on 02/15/1863, but no charges were brought against him. Listed as absent without leave beginning 05/12/1863, but he has a signed pay voucher dated 07/07/1863. Resigned on 07/15/1863.

1333. White, William H.: Enlisted as a private in Company B on 03/31/1864 at Calhoun, Georgia. No horse until 07/15/1864. Was present on last record, September/October 1864. After the war, lived in Fulton County, Georgia. He and his wife, Joyce G., had at least one child. Received a Confederate pension in Fulton County, Georgia. His widow received a Confederate pension from Fulton County, Georgia.

1334. White, William R.: Resident of Georgia. Enlisted as a private in Company A on 08/17/1861 at Augusta, Georgia. Value of horse $175 and horse equipment $27.50. Detailed as a musician in 01/1862. Listed as a corporal in March/April 1863. Horse killed at Hunterstown, Pennsylvania, on 07/02/1863. Sent to infirmary/recruiting camp on 10/20/1863. Listed as a sergeant in November/December 1863. Last record September/October 1864, at infirmary/recruiting camp.

1335. Whitehead, David A.: Farmer from Polk County, Georgia. Born ca. 1837 in Virginia. Enlisted as a private in Company B on 05/05/1862 at Atlanta, Georgia. Value of horse $275. Transferred to Company G in May/June 1862. Lost horse on 02/21/1863. Sent to Georgia to get a horse with Lt. James H. Johnson on 04/14/1863. Sent home to get a horse on 11/10/1863. Sent home to get a horse with Lt. Sinquefield under Special Order No. 27 from corps headquarters on 02/23/1864. Last record September/October 1864, sent to Georgia to get a horse with Capt. Bostick on 09/20/1864. After the war, became a farmer in Polk County, Georgia. Married Martha C. Whatley on 02/25/1862 in Polk County, Georgia, and they had at least eight children. Died on 09/16/1923. Buried in Polk County, Georgia.

1336. Whitehead, F.[H.] Jasper: Student from Jackson County, Georgia. Born ca. 1841 in Georgia. Enlisted as a private in Company C on 08/01/1861 at Athens, Clarke County, Georgia. Last record, was furloughed to Georgia beginning 02/18/1862. After the war, became a farmer in Walton County, Georgia. Married N.E. and they had at least one child. Applied for a Confederate pension in Georgia ca. 10/03/1929.

1337. Whitt, A.R.: Enlisted as a corporal in Company B before 09/03/1861. Value of horse $160 and horse equipment $3, saddle furnished by the State of Georgia.

1338. Wicket, J.S.: Enlisted in the 18th Georgia Infantry. Listed on a roster of Company D published in *The History of Dougherty County*, but not with the *Civil War Soldiers and Sailors System*. No service records in Cobb's Legion.

1339. Wier, Nicholas C.: On a roster of Company C in *These Men She Gave*. No service records in Cobb's Legion.

1340. Wier, Robert W.: Enlisted as a private in Company H on 07/29/1863 at Athens, Clarke County, Georgia. Died from disease on 01/10/1864. Was forty-five years old. Married Sarah J. Kirkpatrick on 07/14/1849 in Clarke County, Georgia. His widow received a Confederate pension from Clarke County, Georgia. Later she transferred the pension to Jackson County, Georgia.

1341. Wiggins, William David: 18-year-old farm hand from Richmond County, Georgia. Born at Augusta, Georgia, on 10/12/1842. Enlisted as a private in Company A on 08/17/1861 at Augusta, Georgia. Value of horse $170, and horse equipment $20. Promoted to corporal in November/December 1863. Absent on horse detail under Special Order No. 36 on 04/01/1864. Listed as a sergeant at the surrender. Was surrendered by Gen. Joseph E. Johnston on 04/26/1865. Paroled at Greensboro, North Carolina, on 05/01/1865. After the war, became the manager of rice mills in Savannah, Georgia; Charleston, South Carolina; Wilmington, North Carolina; Washington, North Carolina; and Goldsboro, North Carolina. Was a member of the McLaws Camp of Confederate Veterans in Savannah, Georgia. Married Frances Adelle Dodge in St. James Methodist Church in Augusta, Georgia, on 12/31/1874 and they had eight children. Died at Savannah, Georgia, on 10/20/1905. Buried in Laurel Grove Cemetery, Lot 2096, Savannah, Georgia. His obituary said that he had been wounded several times during the war. His widow received a Confederate pension in Jacksonville, Florida. She lived to be over one hundred years in age and died in 1948. She was one of last surviving widows of Cobb's Legion Cavalry. A note from John W. Clark in her pension application said, "We all recall Wiggins with pleasure — as a good soldier and citizen."

1342. Wilborn [Wilburn], James C.: 35-year-old farm laborer from Jackson County, Georgia. Born on 09/13/1836. Enlisted as a private in Company H on 04/03/1862 at Athens, Clarke County, Georgia. Captured on 06/11/1864 at Trevilian Station, Virginia. Sent to Point Lookout, Maryland. Transferred to Elmira Prison, New York, on 07/25/1864. Released on 06/21/1865. He gave his place of residence as Marietta, Georgia. Described as having a fair complexion, dark hair, blue eyes, and being 6'1½" tall. After the war, became a farmer in Forsyth County, Georgia. Married Mary Jane Shadburn on 07/06/1866 in Forsyth County, Georgia, and they had at least six children. Died on 08/12/1889.

1343. Wild, George: 26-year-old from Maryland. Enlisted as a private in Company K on 01/24/1863 at Camp Maynard, Georgia. Absent sick beginning 04/22/1863. Horse, valued at $325, killed in action at Brandy Station, Virginia, on 06/09/1863. Wild transferred to Maryland line on 04/18/1864.

1344. Wilder, C.W.: Enlisted as a private in Company D on 08/10/1861 at Albany, Georgia. Value of horse $175 and horse equipment $25, saddle furnished by the State of Georgia. Died of disease at Camp Marion, Virginia, on 02/05/1862.

1345. Wilkinson [Wilkenson, Wilkerson], Thomas J.: Born ca. 1830 in Georgia. Enlisted as a private in Company I on 03/04/1862 at Augusta, Richmond County, Georgia. Value of horse $150. Listed as absent without leave beginning 08/01/1862 and as a deserter beginning 10/09/1863, but the dates overlap his hospitalizations. Admitted to Robinson Hospital (Winder Hospital, Richmond, Virginia) on 10/07/1863. Admitted to Episcopal Church Hospital, Williamsburg, Virginia, on 02/22/1864 with nephritis. Transferred to General Hospital, Petersburg, Virginia, on 05/07/1864 with cystitis. Transferred to P.L. Hospital on 05/21/1864. Paroled at Augusta, Georgia, on 05/23/1865. After the war, became a carpenter in Richmond County, Georgia. He and his wife, Louisa J., had at least four children. Died after 1880. His widow, Louisa J. Wilkinson, received a Confederate pension from Richmond County, Georgia, which proves that he was not a deserter.

1346. Willard, John Larkin: 20-year-old farm laborer from Butts County, Georgia. Born 04/15/1841 in Butts County, Georgia. Enlisted in the 27th Georgia Infantry, Company H, as a private in 09/1861. Enlisted as a private in Cobb's Legion Cavalry, Company B, on 02/01/1862 at Camp Marion, Yorktown, Virginia. Admitted to C.S.A. General Hospital, Danville, Virginia, with chronic diarrhea on 07/30/1862. Returned to duty on 10/10/1862. Admitted to General Hospital No. 16, Richmond, Virginia, on 10/12/1862. Transferred to Winder Hospital, Richmond, Virginia, on 10/22/1862. Returned to duty on 11/13/1862. Lost horse on 04/01/1863. Lost horse on 12/01/1863. Returned to camp on 12/24/1863. Sent to Georgia to get a horse with Lt. Sinquefield under Special Order No. 27 from corps headquarters on 02/23/1864. Was surrendered by Gen. Joseph E. Johnston on 04/26/1865. Paroled at Greensboro, North Carolina, on 05/01/1865. Married Therca (or Teresa) Frances Lummus in 1865 in Butts County, Georgia, and they had at least eight children. Died on 04/04/1914 in Butts County, Georgia.

1347. Willbanks, Richard H.: Laborer from Cherokee County, Georgia. Born in South Carolina ca. 1833. Enlisted as a private in Company E on 03/12/1862 at Roswell, Georgia. Value of horse $150. Detailed as a teamster beginning 12/22/1862. No horse in March/April 1863. Sent to the infirmary/recruiting camp on 11/15/1863. Was present on last record, September/October 1864. After the war became a farmer in Cobb County and then Cherokee County, Georgia. He and his wife, Margaret, had at least four children. Received a Confederate pension in Cherokee County, Georgia. Died after 1880.

1348. Williams, A.J.: Enlisted as a private in Company G sometime between 05/01/1861 and 09/01/1861 at Dinwiddie County, Virginia. Last record September/October 1864, sent home to get a horse with Capt. Bostick on 09/20/1864.

1349. Williams, Andrew [Anderson] B.: 23-year-old clerk from Augusta, Georgia. Enlisted as a private in Company A on 08/17/1861 at Augusta, Georgia. Discharged because of disability on 10/19/1861. Described as having a light complexion, dark hair, blue eyes, and being 5'7½" tall.

1350. Williams, Dilmus P.: Fisherman from Jackson County, Georgia. Born ca. 1826. Enlisted in the 3rd Georgia Infantry, Company K as a private on 04/25/1861. Transferred to Cobb's Legion Cavalry, Company C on 10/06/1862. Transferred from Winder Hospital, Richmond, Virginia, to Petersburg, Virginia, on 10/09/1862. Was present on last record, January/February 1863.

1351. Williams, George A.: 24-year-old from Georgia. Enlisted in the 1st Georgia Infantry, Company I as a corporal on 03/18/1861. Mustered out at Augusta, Georgia, on 03/18/1862. Enlisted as a private in Cobb's Legion Cavalry, Company I, on 03/15/1862 at Augusta, Georgia. Value of horse $210. Horse killed in action at Upperville, Virginia, on 06/21/1863. Listed as a scout on 04/01/1864. Wounded on 06/11/1864. Elected lieutenant on 08/11/1864. Absent sick at Caroline County, Virginia, on 10/12/1864. Other records indicate he was wounded at Columbia, South Carolina, on 04/09/1865. Was surrendered by Gen. Joseph E. Johnston on 04/26/1865. Paroled at Greensboro, North Carolina, on 05/01/1865.

1352. Williams, Henry F.: Native of Georgia. Enlisted as a private in Company B on 08/14/1861 at Atlanta, Georgia. Value of horse $200 and horse equipment $4.50, saddle furnished by the State of Georgia. (Admitted to C.S.A. General Hospital, Charlottesville, Virginia, on 02/12/1863 with tuberculosis. Returned to duty on 06/15/1863. This may be hospital records of Henry M. Williams below.) Wounded at Upperville, Virginia, on 06/21/1863. Furloughed to Georgia beginning on 09/10/1863. Absent without leave beginning 04/01/1864. Still absent without leave on last record, September/October 1864.

1353. Williams, Henry M.: 27-year-old from North Carolina. Enlisted in the 1st Georgia Infantry, Company I as a private in 03/18/1861. Mustered out at Augusta, Georgia, on 03/18/1862. Enlisted as a private in Cobb's Legion Cavalry, Company I, on 04/14/1862 at Augusta, Georgia. (Admitted to C.S.A. General Hospital, Charlottesville, Virginia, on 02/12/1863 with tuberculosis. Furloughed beginning 06/15/1863. This may be hospital records of Henry F. Williams above.) Last record, detailed at headquarters in September/October 1864. Other records indicate that he was wounded in 1863 and wounded at Columbia, South Carolina, on 04/09/1865.

1354. Williams, J.B.: Resident of Georgia. Enlisted as a private in Company D on 08/10/1861 at Albany, Georgia. Value of horse $175 and horse equipment $20, saddle furnished by the State of Georgia. Detailed as a butcher in January/February 1863. Detailed in charge of horses at infirmary/recruiting camp beginning 11/20/1863. No horse and detailed as a teamster for brigade commissary department beginning 04/30/1864. Was surrendered by Gen. Joseph E. Johnston on 04/26/1865. Paroled at Greensboro, North Carolina, on 05/01/1865.

1355. Williams, Thomas C.: Farmer from Jackson County, Georgia. Born ca. 1831 in Georgia. Enlisted as a lieutenant in Company C on 08/01/1861 at Athens, Clarke County, Georgia. Promoted to captain on 04/25/1862. Horse valued at $400 lost on retreat from Martinsburg, [West] Virginia, in 10/1862. It was left at Bunker Hill, [West] Virginia, by order of Lt. Early. Furloughed for 30 days from Hospital No. 16, Richmond, Virginia, beginning 10/15/1862. Horse valued at $400 was lost on 07/10/1864 during retreat from Gettysburg, Pennsylvania. Admitted to General Hospital No. 4, Richmond, Virginia, on 12/22/1863 with neuralgia and rheumatism. On sick furlough beginning 12/27/1863. Admitted to Episcopal Church Hospital, Williamsburg, Virginia, on 05/06/1864 with rheumatism and inflammation of bladder (another record says diarrhea). Transferred to General Hospital, Petersburg, Virginia, on 05/08/1864. Transferred to hospital at Warm Springs on 05/27/1864. Wounded (another record says rheumatism) and admitted to Jackson Hospital, Richmond, Virginia, on 08/27/1864. Returned to duty on 09/07/1864. On sick furlough beginning 10/21/1864. On wounded furlough beginning 11/30/1864. Retired to Invalid Corps at Macon, Georgia, on 11/15/1864 and was assigned to Gen. Howell Cobb. After the war became a farmer in Jackson County, Georgia. He and his wife, Sarah, had at least three children. Received a Confederate pension in Jackson County, Georgia. Died after 1880.

1356. Williams, Thomas H.: Enlisted in the 38th Georgia Infantry, Company M, as a private. Enlisted as a private in Cobb's Legion Cavalry, Company B, on 03/04/1862 at Atlanta, Georgia. Value of horse $275 and horse equipment $45. Detailed in Quartermaster Department beginning 03/1862. Last record was a receipt dated 05/07/1863.

1357. Williams, William M.: 38-year-old born on 01/28/1823. Enlisted as a lieutenant in Company G on 08/14/1861 at Atlanta, Georgia. Value of horses $250 and $275, and horse equipment $30 and $20. Admitted to Episcopal Church Hospital, Williamsburg, Virginia, on 10/28/1861 with malaria. Transferred to another hospital on 11/19/1861. Furloughed to Georgia for 20 days, extended, beginning 02/04/1862. Elected captain on 05/26/1862. Detailed as acting brigade commissary beginning 04/01/1864. Admitted to General Hospital No. 4, Richmond, Virginia, on 08/25/1864 with dysentery and hemorrhages. Furloughed on 08/30/1864. Wounded and furloughed on 11/30/1864. Last record is a typed note that states a letter from May Hospital, Madison, Georgia, dated 04/10/1865 says that he was released from the hospital on that day and furloughed for 60 days. Died on 03/06/1896. Buried in Oconee Hill Cemetery in Clarke County, Georgia.

1358. Williams, William S.: Enlisted as a private in Company L on 10/16/1863 at Augusta, Georgia. Sent to Georgia to get a horse under Special Order No. 36 on 04/01/1864. Discharged because of disability on 09/07/1864.

1359. Williams, Willis B. [A.]: From Georgia. Born ca. 1847 in Georgia. Enlisted as a private in Company E on 03/23/1864 at Augusta, Georgia. Last record September/October 1864, sent to Georgia to get a horse with Capt. Bostick on 09/20/1864. After the war, became a farmer in Hall County, Georgia, and then a house carpenter in Gwinnett County, Georgia. Later, he lived in Fulton County, Georgia. He and his wife, Emily A., had at least four children. Applied for a Confederate pension in Gwinnett County, Georgia. Died after 1920. His widow received a Confederate pension from Fulton County, Georgia.

1360. **Williamson, James R.:** 24-year-old merchant from Emanuel County, Georgia. Enlisted as a private in Company F on 05/09/1862 at Burke County, Georgia. Value of horse $225. Admitted to Henningsen Hospital, Richmond, Virginia. On sick furlough in September/October 1862. Discharged on 10/31/1862 because of rheumatism and nephritis. Described as having a fair complexion, blue eyes, brown hair, and being 5'10" tall.

1361. **Williard [Willard], George W.:** 34-year-old farmer from Gwinnett County, Georgia. Born in South Carolina. Enlisted as a private in Company E on 04/04/1862 at Lawrenceville, Georgia. Value of horse $160 and horse equipment $22. Absent without leave in 04/1862. Admitted to Winder Hospital, Richmond, Virginia, on 08/27/1862 with debility. Transferred to General Hospital No. 21, Richmond, Virginia, on 09/06/1862. Sent to infirmary/recruiting camp on 09/25/1863. Last record September/October 1864, sent to Georgia to get a horse with Capt. Bostick on 09/20/1864. After the war, became a farmer in Gwinnett County and then Forsyth County, Georgia. He and his wife, Nica (or Nicey), had at least four children. Died after 1880.

1362. **Willis, Alonzo D.:** 32-year-old overseer from Columbia County, Georgia. Born in Oglethorpe County, Georgia, in 1829. Enlisted as a private in Company A on 08/17/1861 at Augusta, Georgia. Value of horse $200 and horse equipment $20. Admitted to Hospital No. 12 in Richmond, Virginia, on 11/15/1862. Furloughed to Georgia for 30 days beginning 11/22/1862. Sent to infirmary/recruiting camp on 02/01/1864. Last record September/October 1864, sent to Georgia to get a horse with Capt. Bostick on 09/20/1864. On his Confederate pension application, he swore that he was at the surrender in Greensboro, North Carolina. After the war, became a farmer in Madison, Warren, and Oglethorpe counties, Georgia. Married Palatiah Ryan in Columbia County on 08/25/1853 and was the father of at least three children. Received a Confederate pension in Oglethorpe County, Georgia.

1363. **Willis, Josiah N.[M.]:** Resident of Georgia. Enlisted as a private in Company H on 03/08/1862 at Athens, Clarke County, Georgia. Admitted to General Hospital, Farmville, Virginia, with diarrhea on 07/06/1862. Returned to duty on 07/28/1862. Horse, valued at $200, killed in action at Urbana, Maryland, on 09/11/1862. Willis sent to infirmary/recruiting camp on 11/13/1863. Was surrendered by Gen. Joseph E. Johnston on 04/26/1865. Paroled at Greensboro, North Carolina, on 05/01/1865. A second parole was dated 05/23/1865 at Augusta, Georgia. After the war, became a farmer in Tarrant County, Texas. His wife's name was Mary.

1364. **Willis, T.J.:** Resident of Virginia. Enlisted as a private in Company K on 02/10/1863 at Camp Maynard, Georgia. Was present on last record, September/October 1864.

1365. **Wilson, E.J.:** Resident of Georgia. Enlisted as a private in Company H on 03/03/1862 at Athens, Clarke County, Georgia. Sent home to get a horse with Lt. Sinquefield under Special Order No. 27 from corps headquarters on 02/23/1864. Was present on last record, September/October 1864. Other records indicate he died on 01/25/1865 after being wounded and having one of his legs amputated at the thigh. Buried at Magnolia Cemetery in Charleston, South Carolina.

1366. **Wilson, E.N.:** Enlisted as a private in Company D on 08/10/1861 at Albany, Georgia. Value of horse $175 and horse equipment $20, furnished by State of Georgia. Wounded on 09/13/1863. Admitted to Winder Hospital, Richmond, Virginia, on 09/19/1863. Died on 10/09/1863 from blood poisoning from gunshot wound. His back pay and effects were given to Francis Wilson.

1367. **Wilson, Frank R.:** Enlisted as a private in Company A 08/17/1861 at Augusta, Georgia. Value of horse $200 and horse equipment $20. Detailed in Quartermaster Department beginning 07/1863. Detailed as a courier beginning 01/01/1864. Last record, a receipt for clothing dated 11/26/1864. After the war, became a farmer in Burke County, Georgia. His wife's name was Laura.

1368. **Wilson, J.A.:** 25-year-old. Enlisted as a private in Company K on 02/09/1863 at Camp Maynard, Georgia. Returned to his regiment on 02/21/1863.

1369. **Wilson, James L.:** Resident of Georgia. Enlisted as a private in Company G on 10/28/1862 at Camp Randolph, DeKalb County, Georgia. Sent to Georgia to get a horse with Lt. Sinquefield under Special Order No. 27 from corps headquarters on 02/23/1864. Was surrendered by Gen. Joseph E. Johnston on 04/26/1865. Paroled at Greensboro, North Carolina, on 05/01/1865.

1370. **Wilson, Joseph R.[P.]:** Resident of Georgia. Enlisted as a private in Company A on 08/14/1861 at Augusta, Georgia. Captured at Danville, Kentucky, on 01/02/1863 and sent to Lexington, Kentucky. Transferred to Campbell County, Tennessee, and then to Vicksburg, Mississippi, for exchange on 01/14/1863. Last record 04/01/1864 states he was detailed as a clerk at Division Headquarters in 1863.

1371. Wimberly, E.: Enlisted as a lieutenant in Company D on 08/10/1861 at Albany, Georgia. Value of horses $350 and $150, and horse equipment $30 and $25, one saddle furnished by the State of Georgia. Resigned on 12/30/1861.

1372. Wimberly, E.M.: Enlisted as a private in Cobb's Legion Infantry, Company E, on 08/08/1861 at Waynesboro, Georgia. Admitted to Winder Hospital, Richmond, Virginia, in 05/1863. Found unfit for field service. Transferred to Cobb's Legion Cavalry, Company L, on 04/27/1864. Admitted to General Hospital, Kittrell Springs, North Carolina, in 08/1864. Sent to Georgia to get a horse with Capt. Bostick on 09/20/1864. Was surrendered by Gen. Joseph E. Johnston on 04/26/1865. Paroled at Greensboro, North Carolina, on 05/01/1865.

1373. Wimpy, John A.: 24-year-old. Enlisted as a sergeant in Company C on 08/14/1861 at Athens, Clarke County, Georgia. Furloughed to Georgia for 25 days in 12/1861. Elected lieutenant on 12/28/1862 to replace Elijah D. Cowen, deceased. Resigned on 10/07/1863 due to disability. A laceration on his left elbow caused loss of power and shrinking of the muscles of his left arm. His widow, Emily J. Wimpy, received a Confederate pension from Fulton County, Georgia.

1374. Winchester, J.: Listed on a roster of Company D in *The History of Dougherty County*, but not with the *Civil War Soldiers and Sailors System*. No service records in Cobb's Legion.

1375. Winder, Charles C.: Resident of Georgia. Enlisted as a private in Company A on 08/17/1861 at Augusta, Georgia. Value of horse $150 and horse equipment $20. Courier for Maj. Yancey beginning 02/1862. Detailed on a scouting party with Lt. Shivers of the 2nd South Carolina Cavalry in Culpeper County, Virginia, on 12/14–12/17 1863. Listed as a corporal in March/April 1863. Listed as a sergeant on 09/01/1864. Used a public horse beginning 10/01/1864. Was surrendered by Gen. Joseph E. Johnston on 04/26/1865. Paroled at Greensboro, North Carolina, on 05/01/1865.

1376. Winder, J.P.S.: 27-year-old merchant resident of Eatonton, Putnam County, Georgia. Born in New York. Enlisted as a sergeant in Company A on 08/17/1861 at Augusta, Georgia. Value of horse $175 and horse equipment $25. On furlough for 25 days beginning 01/02/1862. Elected lieutenant on 06/12/1862. Last record, returned to duty from Hospital No. 18 in Richmond, Virginia, on 11/15/1862. Elected major of an Alabama Regiment.

1377. Winfrey [Wemphrey, Wormfry], George W.[J.W.]: 26-year-old farmer from Madison County, Georgia. Born on 04/06/1835 in Oglethorpe County, Georgia. Enlisted as a private in Company H on 03/03/1862 at Athens, Clarke County, Georgia. Detailed as a driver for Gen. J.E.B. Stuart in 08/1863. Sent to Georgia to get a horse with Capt. Bostick on 09/20/1864. Paroled at Athens, Clarke County, Georgia, on 05/08/1865. After the war, became a farmer in Madison County, Georgia. Married Missouri Adaline Johnson on 08/01/1852 in Madison County, Georgia, and they had at least five children.

1378. Winfrey, John A.: Farmer from Madison County, Georgia. Born ca. 1832 in Georgia. On a roster of Company C in *These Men She Gave*. No service records in Cobb's Legion. After the war, became a farmer in Madison County, Georgia. He and his wife, Eliza A., had at least eight children. Died after 1880.

1379. Winship [Windship], George: 26-year-old foundry worker from Fulton County, Georgia. Born on 12/20/1835 in Massachusetts. Enlisted as a private in Company G on 03/03/1862 at Atlanta, Georgia. Value of horse $285 and horse equipment $45. Listed as a sergeant in May/June 1862. Received a gunshot wound to the hip near Burkettsville, Maryland, on 09/10/1862. Admitted to C.S.A. General Hospital Charlottesville, Virginia, on 09/23/1862. Furloughed on 10/09/1862. Returned to duty on 11/21/1862. Lost horse in 01/1863. Wounded on 08/01/1863 at Brandy Station, Virginia. Admitted to hospital, C.S.A. General Hospital, Charlottesville, Virginia, on 08/04/1863. Furloughed to Atlanta, Georgia, on 08/21/1863. Admitted to Ocmulgee Hospital, Macon, Georgia, on 10/20/1864 with a gunshot flesh wound in the left thigh. Transferred to Fort Valley, Houston County, Georgia, on 10/24/1864. Given a disability discharge from the service on 01/31/1865. Described as having a fair complexion, gray eyes, dark hair, and being 5'10" tall. After the war, worked as an iron founder in Fulton County, Georgia. Elected as a trustee of Emory College in 1899. Married (1) Mary Eugenia Speer on 11/14/1860 in Fulton County, Georgia (2) Lula (or Helen T.) Lane in Bibb County, Georgia (3) Elizabeth Thiot in 1896. Was the father of at least two children. Died after 1899.

1380. Winters, Merriman: Farmer from Richmond County, Georgia. Enlisted as a private in Company I. Captured at Burkettsville, Maryland, on 11/01/1862. Paroled at Fort McHenry, Maryland, on 11/06/1862. No further records. Married Martha Ann Collins in Hall County, Georgia, on 12/02/1860.

1381. Witcher, Charles N.[W.]: Resident of Georgia. Enlisted as a private in Company G on 02/20/1864 at Atlanta, Georgia. Last record September/October 1864, sent to Georgia to get a horse with Capt. Bostick on 09/20/1864.

1382. Wivins, W.R.: 30-year-old. Enlisted as a private in Company K on 02/11/1863 at Camp Maynard, Georgia. Returned to his regiment on 02/21/1863.

1383. Wolfe, Herman: Resident of Georgia. Enlisted as a private in Company I on 02/27/1862 at Augusta, Georgia. Value of horse $175. Was surrendered by Gen. Joseph E. Johnston on 04/26/1865. Paroled at Greensboro, North Carolina, on 05/01/1865.

1384. Wood, Green C.[J.C.]: 17-year-old from Georgia. Enlisted as a private in Company A on 08/17/1861 at Augusta. Value of horse $75 and horse equipment $25. Sent to Georgia to get a horse with Lt. Sinquefield under Special Order No. 27 from corps headquarters on 02/23/1864. Was surrendered by Gen. Joseph E. Johnston on 04/26/1865. Paroled at Greensboro, North Carolina, on 05/01/1865. The Muster Roll Commission roster says he was wounded during the war. After the war, worked as a farm laborer in Davids, Banks County, Georgia, and then as a farmer at Athens, Clarke County, Georgia. Was married and the father of at least seven children.

1385. Wood, J.F.: Enlisted as a private in Company A on 02/01/1864 at Decatur, Georgia. Last record September/October 1864, sent to Georgia to get a horse with Capt. Bostick on 09/20/1864. May be the same person as J.W. Wood, below.

1386. Wood, J.G.: Enlisted as a private in Company K on 02/04/1863 at Camp Maynard, Georgia. Returned to his regiment on 03/23/1863.

1387. Wood, J.W.: Enlisted as a private in Company A on 02/01/1864 at Decatur, Georgia. Last record September/October 1864, at a hospital in Augusta, Georgia. May be the same person as J.F. Wood, above.

1388. Wood, James R.: Enlisted as a private in Company B on 08/14/1861 at Atlanta, Georgia. Value of horse $175 and horse equipment $7.50, saddle furnished by the State of Georgia. Detailed as a blacksmith in 10/1862 and as a teamster in 01/1863. Last record, a receipt dated 05/07/1863.

1389. Wood, John N.[H.]: Born ca. 1833 in Georgia. Enlisted as a private in Company B on 08/14/1861 at Atlanta, Georgia. Value of horse $200 and horse equipment $20, equipment owned by the company. Wounded and captured at South Mountain, Maryland, on 09/14/1862 and sent to Fort McHenry, Maryland. Paroled at Fortress Monroe, Virginia, on 12/08/1862. Admitted to General Hospital, Petersburg, Virginia, on 12/10/1862 with a wound in his leg. Furloughed for 90 days beginning 12/19/1862. Detailed as an ambulance driver in March/April 1863. Sent to infirmary/recruiting camp on 10/22/1863. Sent to the infirmary/recruiting camp in Lynchburg, Virginia, on 08/28/1864. Was surrendered by Gen. Joseph E. Johnston on 04/26/1865. Paroled at Greensboro, North Carolina, on 05/01/1865. After the war, became a farmer in Fulton County, Georgia. He and his wife, Mary F., had at least four children. Died after 1880. His widow received a Confederate pension from Fulton County, Georgia.

1390. Wood, John R.: Enlisted as a private in the 16th Georgia Infantry, Company G, on 07/20/1861 at Jefferson, Georgia. Transferred into Cobb's Legion Cavalry, Company C, in March/April 1862. Lost horse on 01/01/1864. Sent home to get a horse with Lt. Sinquefield under Special Order No. 27 from corps headquarters on 02/23/1864. Transferred to Company H on 08/01/1864. Last record September/October 1864, sent to Georgia to get a horse with Capt. Bostick on 09/20/1864.

1391. Wood, John T.: 23-year-old from Georgia. Born in 1841 in Georgia. Enlisted in 10/1861 in the Georgia State Troops, Company E, at Greensboro, Georgia. Appointed sergeant. Mustered out at Savannah, Georgia, on 5/20/1862. Enlisted as a private in Cobb's Legion Cavalry, Company A, on 02/11/1864 at Decatur, Georgia. Was surrendered by Gen. Joseph E. Johnston on 04/26/1865. Paroled at Greensboro, North Carolina, on 05/01/1865. After the war, became a farmer in Kingston (Buckhead), Morgan County, Georgia. Married Rebecca Louise Harris on 10/28/1868 and was the father of at least seven children. Died on 01/26/1916 at Buckhead, Morgan County, Georgia. An interesting letter to his father describing his experiences in Cobb's Legion Cavalry is included in his service records.

1392. Wood, Moses: 27-year-old farm tenant from Fulton County, Georgia. Born in 1834 in Georgia. Enlisted as a private in Company B on 08/14/1861 at Atlanta, Georgia. Value of horse $150 and horse equipment $7, saddle furnished by the State of Georgia. Admitted to Winder Hospital, Richmond, Virginia, on 07/22/1862 with dysentery. Returned to duty on 08/01/1862. Sent to Georgia to get a horse with Lt. Sinquefield under Special Order No. 27 from corps headquarters on 02/23/1864. On sick furlough to Georgia beginning 10/03/1864. Was surrendered by Gen. Joseph E. Johnston on 04/26/1865. Paroled at Greensboro,

North Carolina, on 05/01/1865. After the war, became a farmer in Fulton County, Georgia. Married Julia Walker on 11/10/1857 in Carroll County, Georgia, and they had at least six children. Died after 1880.

1393. Wood, R.W.: Enlisted as a private in Company K on 02/08/1863 at Camp Maynard, Georgia. Returned to his regiment on 03/23/1863.

1394. Woodruff, Berrimon: 29-year-old resident to Cherokee County, Georgia. Enlisted as a private in Company E on 03/22/1862 at Roswell, Georgia. Value of horse $150. Died at C.S.A. General Hospital, Danville, Virginia, on 07/14/1862 of typhoid fever. Was married to Narcepa Woodruff.

1395. Woods [Wood], Marcus V. [B.]: 21-year-old grocer from Atlanta, Georgia. Enlisted as a private in Company G on 04/08/1862 at Atlanta, Georgia. Value of horse $185. Appointed corporal on 10/01/1862. Captured at Barbee's Cross Roads, Virginia, on 11/05/1862. Paroled at City Point, Virginia, on 11/18/1862. Captured at Hedgesville, [West] Virginia, on 07/17/1863 and sent to Military Prison, also known as Atheneum Prison, Wheeling, [West] Virginia. Transferred to Camp Chase, Ohio, on 07/23/1863. Deserted and took the Oath on 07/25/1863. Described as having a florid complexion, blue eyes, light hair, and being 5'7½" tall.

1396. Woody, Alex: 35-year-old. Enlisted as a private in Company K on 01/29/1863 at Camp Maynard, Georgia. Deserted on 03/14/1863.

1397. Woolley, George: Native of Virginia. Enlisted as a private in Company F on 01/01/1863 at Stevensburg, Virginia. Captured at Kelly's Ford, Virginia, on 08/15/1863 and sent to the Old Capitol Prison, Washington, D.C. Listed as a deserter by the provost marshall general of the Union army.

1398. Wooten [Wootten], Powhattan Bolling: Day laborer from Catoosa County, Georgia. Born on 06/06/1844 in Catoosa County, Georgia. Enlisted as a private in Company B on 08/14/1861 at Atlanta, Georgia. Transferred to Company G on 05/30/1862. Detailed as a teamster beginning 02/1863. Sent to Georgia to get a horse with Lt. James H. Johnson on 04/14/1863. Detailed in Quartermaster Department as a forager beginning 10/1863. Sent to Georgia to get a horse with Lt. Sinquefield under Special Order No. 27 from corps headquarters on 02/23/1864. Sent to infirmary/recruiting camp during the summer of 1864. Last record September/October 1864, detailed in the ambulance corps. After the war, married Katherine Lynch, on 10/05/1873 in Fulton County, Georgia. Died on 03/31/1880. May be the same person as S.B. Wooten below.

1399. Wooten, S.B.: Enlisted as a private in Company B on or before 09/03/1861. Value of horse $250 and horse equipment $35. No other records. May be the same person as Powhatton Bolling Wooten above.

1400. Wooten [Wootten], William J.: From Georgia. Born ca. 1831 in Georgia. Enlisted as a private in Company G on 05/06/1862 at Atlanta, Georgia. Value of horse $300. Detailed as a veterinary surgeon for company in May/June 1862. Listed as a corporal in January/February 1863. Sent to Georgia to get a horse in March/April 1863. Sent to Georgia to get a horse with Lt. Sinquefield under Special Order No. 27 from corps headquarters on 02/23/1864. It was not stated if he were present on his last record, September/October 1864.

1401. Worrison, W.C.: 24-year-old from Virginia. Enlisted as a private in Company K on 02/09/1863 at Camp Maynard, Georgia. Appointed sergeant on 02/23/1863. Furloughed for 15 days beginning 02/20/1864. Last record September/October 1864, sent to Georgia to get a horse with Capt. Bostick on 09/20/1864.

1402. Worsham, E.J.: Resident of Georgia. Enlisted as a private in Company E on 07/23/1863 at Cherokee County, Georgia. Sent to the infirmary/recruiting camp on 02/23/1864. Paroled at Tate House Hospital, North Carolina, on 05/01/1865.

1403. Wray, John R.: On a roster of Company C in *These Men She Gave*. No service records in Cobb's Legion.

1404. Wray, Philip: 23-year-old student from Clarke County, Georgia. Born on 06/01/1838 in Georgia. Enlisted as a private in Company C on 08/01/1861 at Athens, Clarke County, Georgia. Appointed musician on 12/21/1861. Lost horse on 07/01/1862. Discharged on 12/05/1862. After the war, became a farmer in Greene County, Georgia. He and his wife, Jesse, had at least one child. Died after 08/02/1914. Buried in Hill Cemetery, Oconee, Clarke County, Georgia.

1405. Wray, Walter A.: 16-year-old. Born on 06/09/1844. Enlisted as a private in Company C on 08/01/1861 at Athens, Clarke County, Georgia. Discharged because of disability in 02/1862. Rejoined Company C on 07/15/1863 at Stevensburg, Virginia. Was surrendered by Gen. Joseph E. Johnston on 04/26/1865. Paroled at Greensboro, North Carolina, on 05/01/1865. Died on 10/22/1909. Buried in Hill Cemetery, Oconee, Clarke County, Georgia.

1406. Wright, B.E.: Enlisted as a private in Company L on 03/18/1864 at Waynesboro, Georgia. Sent to Georgia to get a horse with Capt. Bostick on 09/20/1864. Was surrendered by Gen. Joseph E. Johnston on 04/26/1865. Paroled at Greensboro, North Carolina, on 05/01/1865.

1407. Wright, William D.: 37-year-old farmer. Born in South Carolina. Enlisted as a private in Company B on 08/14/1861 at Atlanta, Georgia. Value of horse $150 and horse equipment $10, saddle furnished by the State of Georgia. Given a medical discharge for rheumatism on 09/01/1861. Described as having a fair complexion, brown hair, blue eyes and being 5' 9½" tall.

1408. Wynne [Winn, Wynn], William Joseph [I.]: 16-year-old from Georgia. Enlisted as a private in Company A on 08/17/1861 at Augusta, Georgia. Value of horse $175 and horse equipment $25. Horse killed in battle at Cold Harbor, Virginia, on 06/27/1862. Wynne received a wound in his left shoulder at Brandy Station, Virginia, on 06/10/1863. Admitted to Chimborazo Hospital, Richmond, Virginia, with a gunshot wound to the left shoulder 06/12/1863. Transferred to Augusta Hospital on 06/23/1863. Sent to Georgia to get a horse in November/December 1863. Last record September/October 1864, sent to Georgia to get a horse with Capt. Bostick on 09/20/1864. After the war, became a carpenter in Richmond County, Georgia, and was married.

1409. Yancey, Benjamin Cudworth: Planter from Fulton County, Georgia. Born in Charleston, South Carolina, on 03/27/1817. Graduated from the University of Georgia and Harvard. Enlisted as a captain in Company B on 08/14/1861 at Atlanta, Georgia. Value of horses $275, $300, and $400, and horse equipment $20, $20, and $50. Appointed major on 11/15/1861. Resigned on 05/23/1862. After the war, became a lawyer and then a farmer in Clarke and Floyd counties, Georgia. Was a trustee of the University of Georgia 1860–1886; president of the Georgia State Agricultural Society 1867–1871, and legislator for Clarke County, Georgia, for one term. Married (1) Laura Hines in Floyd County, Georgia, on 07/20/1841. Married (2) Sarah Paris Hamilton on 11/04/1846 and they had at least three children. Died on 10/25/1891 in Floyd County, Georgia.

1410. Yerby [Yearby], Burrell Henry: Farmer from Clarke County, Georgia. Born in Coweta or Madison County, Georgia, on 04/01/1836. Enlisted as a private in Company H on 03/01/1862 at Athens, Clarke County, Georgia. Detailed as a driver for Gen. J.E.B. Stuart in 10/1863. Without a horse in 12/1863. Sent home to get a horse under Special Order No. 36 Corps Headquarters on 03/13/1864. Sent to Georgia to get a horse with Capt. Bostick on 09/20/1864. Was surrendered by Gen. Joseph E. Johnston on 04/26/1865. Paroled at Greensboro, North Carolina, on 05/01/1865. After the war, became a farmer in Clarke County, Georgia. Married Mary Frances Pittard in Clarke County, Georgia, on 01/12/1854 and they had at least nine children. Died on 08/03/1890 in Clarke County, Georgia. Buried in the Yerby Family Cemetery in Clarke County, Georgia.

1411. Young, Milton B.: Pattern maker from Augusta, Georgia. Born ca. 1839 in Georgia. Enlisted as a private in Company A on 08/17/1861 at Augusta, Georgia. Value of horse $175 and horse equipment $20. Elected lieutenant on 07/28/1862. Transferred to Shanks' Virginia Horse Artillery on 01/12/1863. Returned to Cobb's Legion Cavalry and served through the war. Admitted to Jackson Hospital, Richmond, Virginia, on 05/27/1864 with dysentery. Admitted to Jackson Hospital, Richmond, Virginia, 08/20/1864 with a gunshot wound in the right foot. Returned to duty 09/13/1864. Detailed as a "maker" in September/October 1864. Surrendered on 05/04/1865 at Citronelle, Alabama, and paroled on 05/21/1865 at Mobile, Alabama. After the war, became a machinist and moulder in Savannah, Georgia, and was married to Jennie.

1412. Young, Stanley: Teacher from Burke County, Georgia. Born in Kentucky. Enlisted as a private in Company L on 12/15/1864 at Burke County, Georgia. Sent to infirmary/recruiting camp on 04/01/1864. Admitted to C.S.A. General Hospital, Danville, Virginia, on 11/16/1864 with acute dysentery. Returned to duty on 11/25/1864. Was surrendered by Gen. Joseph E. Johnston on 04/26/1865. Paroled at Greensboro, North Carolina, on 05/01/1865.

1413. Young, William [Hughes, Frank]: 24-year-old. Born in Ireland. Enlisted as a private in Company K on 02/25/1863 at Camp Maynard, Georgia. Captured at Upperville, Virginia, on 06/21/1863 and sent to the Old Capitol Prison, Washington, D.C. Deserted and took the Oath on 07/11/1863 and was sent to Philadelphia, Pennsylvania.

1414. Young, William Benjamin: 24-year-old from Richmond, County, Georgia. Enlisted as a corporal in Company A on 08/17/1861 at Augusta, Georgia. Value of horse $250 and horse equipment $25. Listed as a lieutenant in May/June 1862. Furloughed for 25 days beginning 02/22/1862. Promoted to captain on 08/08/1862. Listed in Company I in January/February 1863. Captured at Ely's Ford on the Rapidan River on 02/29/1864. Sent to Washington, D.C., on 03/01/1864. Transferred to

Fort Delaware Prison on 06/15/1864. Released on 06/10/1865. Described as having a dark complexion, dark hair, gray eyes, and being 5'8" tall. Married Mary E. Ivey on 01/30/1868. Died on 07/04/1898 in Columbia County, Georgia.

It could not be determined if the following men were in Cobb's Legion Cavalry, or Cobb's Legion Infantry:

1415. Ashmand, H.B.: Enlisted as a private in Company B. Captured at Frederick, Maryland, and imprisoned at Fort Delaware on 09/14/1862. Exchanged on 11/10/1862 at Aiken's Landing, Virginia. His single service record does not indicate if he served with the cavalry or the infantry, but both were in the area of Frederick, Maryland, at the time of his capture.

1416. Donnan, M.T.: Enlisted as a private in Company G. Admitted to General Hospital No. 21, Richmond, Virginia, on 11/26/1862. Died 11/30/1862 of smallpox. No pay vouchers or records other than the hospital records.

1417. Doubleday, G.: Enlisted as a private, company unknown. Wounded at Crampton's Gap, Maryland, on 09/14/1862, captured, and paroled. His single record does not indicate if he was in the cavalry or the infantry.

1418. Harris, William: Enlisted as a private in Company B. Died in Confederate States Hospital, Petersburg, Virginia, on 06/02/1862 of pneumonia. His record does not indicate if he was in the cavalry or the infantry.

1419. Huckabee, J.D: Enlisted as a private in Company F. Received a gunshot wound of left forearm, which necessitated amputation. Discharged on 05/29/1862. His records do not give any additional information.

1420. Joie, William R.: Enlisted as a private, company unknown. Wounded at Crampton's Gap, Maryland, on 09/14/1862, captured, and paroled. His single record does not indicate if he was in the cavalry or the infantry.

1421. Kennedy, J.F: Born in Clarke County, Georgia. Enlisted as a private in Company D. Killed in battle on 09/14/1862, probably at the Battle of South Mountain. His record does not indicate if he was in the cavalry or the infantry.

1422. Mowan, J.E.: Enlisted as a private in Company A. Deserted at Martinsburg, [West] Virginia, on 07/23/1863 and took the Oath at Fort Mifflin, Pennsylvania. His record does not indicate if he was in the cavalry or the infantry.

1423. Newton, B.: Enlisted as a private in Company E. Captured at Gettysburg, Pennsylvania, on 07/03/1863 and sent to Fort Delaware Prison. Transferred to Point Lookout, Maryland, 10/18/1863. There is no record of his taking the Oath or being paroled. He may have died in prison. Both the infantry and the cavalry were at Gettysburg, Pennsylvania.

1424. Parish, J.S.: Enlisted as a private, company unknown. Paroled at Athens, Clarke County, Georgia, on 05/18/1865.

1425. Pemberton, J.C.: Rank and company unknown. Wounded, captured and paroled at Crampton's Pass, Maryland, on 09/14/1862. His single record does not indicate if he was in the cavalry or the infantry.

1426. Poss, William H.: Listed On a roster of Company C compiled by Glen Spurlock. No service records in Cobb's Legion.

1427. Powell, Ambrose: On a roster of Company B compiled by Glen Spurlock. No service records in Cobb's Legion.

1428. Powell, G.M.: On a roster of Company A compiled by Glen Spurlock. No service records in Cobb's Legion.

1429. Price, George F.: Enlisted as a lieutenant in Company G. No service records in Cobb's Legion.

1430. Reeves, James: Resident of Richmond County, Georgia. Deserted and took the Oath on 09/09/1864 at City Point, Virginia, and sent to Washington, D.C. Described as having a black complexion, black hair, black eyes, and being 5'5" tall. Probably in the cavalry, as the cavalry was near City Point, Virginia, but the infantry was in the Shenandoah Valley, Virginia, at the time of his desertion.

1431. Rockman [Rockmon], J.H.: Enlisted as a private in Company A. Admitted to U.S.A. Field Hospital in Burkettsville, Maryland, in 1862 with severe wounds in both arms. Probably captured at South Mountain. May have died in captivity as there is no record of his release. Both the infantry and the cavalry were in the area of Burkettsville, Maryland, at that time.

1432. Smith, C.H.: Enlisted as a private in Company B. Admitted to Winder Hospital, Richmond, Virginia, on 09/25/1862. No other records.

1433. Smith, C.N.: Enlisted as a private in Company C. Has a pay receipt for 05/01/1862–09/01/1862 at Richmond, Virginia. He may have been in the infantry, as there is a clothing allowance included but no pay for the use of a horse. Both the cavalry and the infantry were near Richmond, Virginia, at the time.

1434. Smitzer, Edward G.: On a roster of Company A compiled by Glen Spurlock. No service records in Cobb's Legion.

1435. Statham, W.R.: Enlisted as a private in Company B. Discharged from the service at Winder Hospital, Richmond, Virginia, on 01/09/1863 for total deafness.

1436. Suggs, R.E.: Paroled on 05/22/1865 at Albany, Georgia.

1437. Thompson, Charles: On a roster of Company D compiled by Glen Spurlock. No service records in Cobb's Legion.

1438. Thompson, E.: On a roster of Company D compiled by Glen Spurlock. No service records in Cobb's Legion.

1439. Thornton, J.T: Enlisted as a private in Company D. Admitted to Jackson Hospital, Richmond, Virginia, on 12/14/1864. No further records.

1440. Tredell, J.: Enlisted as a private, company unknown. Wounded, captured, and paroled at Crampton's Pass, Maryland, on 09/14/1862. His single record does not indicate if he was in the cavalry or the infantry.

1441. Turner, S. Otis: Wounded at the battle of Crampton's Pass, Maryland, captured and paroled on 09/14/1862. His single record does not indicate if he was in the cavalry or the infantry.

1442. Wabrey, P.: His single record is his parole at Athens, Georgia, on 05/05/1865.

1443. Wade, H.: Enlisted as a private in Company C in 10/1862 at Decatur, Georgia. Admitted to General Hospital No. 23, Richmond, Virginia, on 05/09/1863 with a wound. His right leg was amputated at the thigh. Died on 06/25/1863 at the hospital in Richmond, Virginia. His record does not indicate if he was in the cavalry or the infantry.

1444. Waiott, J.J.: Paroled at Athens, Georgia, on 05/08/1865.

1445. Wells, Jasper: Enlisted as a private. Died at General Hospital No. 16, Richmond, Virginia, of typhoid fever on 09/09/1862. His single does not indicate if he were in the cavalry or the infantry.

1446. White, H.D: On a roster of Company D compiled by Glen Spurlock. No service records in Cobb's Legion.

1447. White, H.H. [M.M.]: Paroled at Albany, Georgia, on 05/18/1865.

1448. White, H.J.: Enlisted as a private in Company B. Furloughed for 60 days beginning 09/29/1862 from General Hospital No. 9, Richmond, Virginia. His record does not indicate if he was in the cavalry or the infantry.

1449. White, James M.: Enlisted as a quartermaster sergeant. Captured near Petersburg, Virginia, on 10/27/1864 and sent to City Point, Virginia. Transferred to Point Lookout, Maryland. Released on 05/13/1865 and transferred to Martinsburg, [West] Virginia. Was probably in the cavalry, because of where he was captured. The infantry was in the Shenandoah Valley, Virginia, and the cavalry was near Petersburg, Virginia, at the time of his capture.

1450. Whitney, W.M.: Enlisted as a private. Paroled at Athens, Georgia, on 05/08/1865.

1451. Williams, Carlos: Resident of Clark County, Georgia. Enlisted as a private in Company D. Died on 07/19/1862. His record does not indicate if he was in the cavalry or the infantry.

1452. Williams, W.H.: On a roster of Company D compiled by Glen Spurlock. No service records in Cobb's Legion.

1453. Wimperly, G.: Captured at Crampton's Pass, Maryland, on 09/14/1862. On list of unwounded prisoners who were paroled 09/26/1862. His single record does not indicate if he was in the cavalry or the infantry.

1454. Wise, J.J.: Born in Clark County, Georgia. Enlisted as a private in Company D. Died 07/11/1862. His record does not indicate if he was in the cavalry or the infantry.

1455. Wittson, R.S.: Enlisted as a private. Paroled at Athens, Clarke County, Georgia, on 05/08/1865.

1456. Wynn, K.A.: On a roster of Company D compiled by Glen Spurlock. No service records in Cobb's Legion.

1457. Young, T.B.: Enlisted as a private in Company C. On enrolling duty in Georgia for 11 days during 02/1864. No other records.

Appendix C

Original Members of Cobb's Legion Cavalry

Enlisted on or Before September 1, 1861

†Killed in action, mortally wounded in action, or died of disease
†Discharged as a result of severe wounds
•Prisoner of war
*Deserted or absent without leave on last record

J.T. Adams
S.D. Adams
†Thomas Adams
W.H. Adams
Francis M.C. Aiken
†Augustus Alford
Ira Allen
†Edward A. Anderson
•†John M. Anderson
†Miles A. Anderson
Nicholas M. Anderson
William E. Anderson
Young J. Anderson
Walter H. Anthony
†Edward J. Appling
Thomas B. Archer
David A. Armistead
Charles M. Arnold
Jesse Asbury
J.M. Ashfield
†James H. Bailey
Oscar W. Bailey
Samuel W. Bailey
James A. Bale
†Green B. Barksdale
Thomas E. Barnwell
James Riley Barrett
†Thomas R. Barrett
†Walton T. Barrett
Jefferson Bassett
Charles E. Bassford
•†Daniel C. Baxter

Ethelbert Penn Bedell
Madison M. Bell
Marlin M. Bell
James A. Bennett
John W. Bennett
John J. Bishop
Josiah E. Blackburn
Josiah S. Blackwell
†Uriah Blanchard
†Bennett Boler
Willis C. Bone
Samuel D. Bostick
James R. Bowen
Charles L. Bowie
John W. Bowie
George G. Bowman
•Henry S. Bradley
•†James H. Brent
•†James T. Broadway
William A. Broadway
†R.J. Brown
†Aquilla Bruce
Matthew L. Bryan
George B. Bryce
Hill Bunch
Drewry Burford
D.C.N. Burkhalter
•†John Howard Burr
J.J. Butler
Caleb H. Camfield
J.P. Carpenter
Robert C. Carroll

†Albert W.J. Carter
Noah B. Cash
William F. Cavanaugh
Frank Chandler
†James F. Chavous
†John W. Cheesboro
†John P. Cherry
John Christman
William Lee Church
James Luke Clanton
John William Clark
J.T. Cochran
†William B. Cochran
William T. Cone
Wm. Curran Connelly
George W.D. Cook
Joshua C. Cook
John M. Cooper
R.E. Cooper
Charles H. Costello
John Coston
†Elijah D. Cowen
†John H. Cowen
James A. Cox
*Joseph S. Cutter
•Theodore F. Daniel
•†John W. David
Cyrus C. Davis
L. B. Davis
•†William G. Delony
†Abel B. C. Densmore
J.D. Deriso

•B.L. Dickens
Walter M. Dickinson
J.S. Dosier
G.C. Douglas
John W. Drinkwater
Alfred W. Early
William H. Early
†Williamson F. Early
Edward H. Edwards
J.B. Everett
Marcus C. Few
•Julius J. Fields
Levi C. Fields
Richard J. Fields
†William Finch
Andrew J. Fish
†J.D. Ford
Lewis R. Ford
•†H.M. Fowler
†Julius Michael Frix
William Gabbett
†Patrick Gallaher
W.L. Gallaway
Nathaniel E. Gardner
†James H. Garner
John S. Garron
•Jesse C. Gibson
James R. Glenn
Joseph T. Glenn
•†David P. Godfrey
Robert W. Gondelock
Nathan Goodman

- •Thomas C. Gower
- Eli Griffin
- †Berry T. Grindle
- Daniel Grindle
- Alexander C. Guedron
- John C. Guedron
- William T. Gunby
- •Samuel B. Haesler
- John Schley Haines
- Jacob W. Hamilton
- Robert J. Hancock
- William D. Hancock
- James W. Hanlon
- George W. Hardwick
- Anselin L. Harper
- •Charles R. A. Harris
- Henry S. Harris
- William H. Hatfield
- •Dwight David Hays
- •John B. Hays
- Joshua J. Head
- †William J. Helton
- •E.D. High
- †Henry Hillens
- *Cary J. Hopkins
- John D. Houston
- Wiley C. Howard
- *E.W. Howell
- H.L. Howell
- †Elisha S. Howse
- Martin V. B. Howse
- Thomas Howse
- John R. Hoy
- James M. Hunton
- Daniel J. Irby
- †John F. Isdal
- •Michael J. Ivey
- George W. Jack
- †James Russell Jack
- Green B. Jackson
- Henry E. Jackson
- John F. Jackson
- William H. Jackson
- J.T. Jaudon
- Thomas J. Jefferson
- John Jenkins
- E.B. Johnson
- *I.J. Johnson
- Leonard E. Johnson
- Samuel Jack Johnson
- Thomas D. Johnson
- John E. Joiner
- †Henry Francis Jones
- Thomas R. W. Jones
- William B. Jones
- Lewis A. Juhan
- †Oliver H. P. Juhan
- •John H. Keogh
- John C. Keyes
- †Barrington S. King
- J.J. Kitchens
- •James T. Lamkin
- †Robert A. Lampkin
- *Thomas J. Landrum
- Alexander C. Lawton
- *B.H. Lawton
- Winburn J. Lawton
- Thomas Leach
- •W.H. Lippitt
- Charles P. Lively
- William R. Lord
- Melvin K. Lowery
- John H. Loyd
- Miller G. Lumpkin
- Robert C. Lumpkin
- James Ray Lyle
- Robert G. Malone
- †James F. Marshall
- John C. Matthews
- J.W. Mayo
- •Henry Hugh McCall
- Jos. P.C. McCollum
- Josiah F. McCollum
- Moses W. McCollum
- Mark McCorkle
- †James N. McCullum
- S. Marcus McCurry
- Thomas J. McCurry
- Robert F. McDade
- D. McLelland
- *James M. McNair
- Lemuel S. Mead
- J.J. Meldon
- J.H. Melton
- Rufus B. Merchant
- Montague Merriman
- William Hugh Mills
- W. Minchen
- George W. Mock
- †Geo. C. Montgomery
- †Richard Moore
- •Robert S. Morris
- Benjamin R. Moseley
- William R. Murphy
- Charles T. Nash
- James R. Polk Nash
- •Reuben Long Nash
- James H. Nelson
- Robert Taylor Nesbitt
- Henry Norman
- James T. Norris
- E.T. Nunn
- •Daniel O'Connor
- John B. O'Donnell
- James R. D. Ozburn
- •Thomas O. Ozburn
- J.A. Park
- J.P. Parker
- David Rives Parks
- Charles T. Parrish
- •George W. Parrish
- Thomas A.H. Paschal
- E.L. Peel
- Harrison J. Pettis
- James R. Phillips
- Marcus De L. Pittman
- †D.A. Powell
- Hiram Province
- William Halum Reid
- R.A. Reynolds (Co. A)
- Walter C. Reynolds
- †Henry N. Rhodes
- Radford C. Rhodes
- Zachariah A. Rice
- Martin W. Riden
- •Jeremiah E. Ritch
- Thomas J. Rives
- William H. Roach
- William H. Robertson
- Henry A. Roebuck
- Alexander R. Rucker
- John Cobb Rutherford
- Andrew Jackson Rylee
- James B. Rylee
- †Gustavus Schlesinger
- A.F. Scott
- James D. Scott
- †Jacob McC. Scudder
- Lewis B. Scudder
- *Calvin C. Sego
- Jarrell G. Sharpe
- James M. Sheffield
- George W. Sherman
- *Benjamin F. Sibley
- C.L. Sibley
- E.L. Sibley
- †William H. Sibley
- Moses T. Simmons
- William D. Simmons
- Nathan Simon
- •George W. Slatern
- Alexander P. Smith
- David E. Smith
- •Joseph Smith
- Wilber F. Smith
- James M. Snelling
- Henry L. Sponsler
- Chauncy A. Sprague
- Bolling A. Stovall
- Francis M. Stovall
- Thomas P. Stovall
- *Henry Strickland
- •William E. Sutton
- William Avery Tanner
- *Curtis J. Thayer
- †Andrew J. Thomas
- J. Jefferson Thomas
- J.R. Thomas
- Lovick P. Thomas
- Alfred R. Thompson
- George W. Thompson
- James M. Thornton
- Simeon W. Thornton
- John S. Thrash
- Thomas H. Tinsley
- †James H. Todd
- Thomas Ransom Tuck
- •William J. Tucker
- Calhoun H. Turner
- Jefferson J. Turner
- Ephraim Tweedy
- C. Tyus
- Joshua F. Usry
- Richard A. Vasser
- Thomas Vigis
- James F. Walker
- Patrick Wallace
- Fred W. Walter
- Olive Wellborn
- Caleb A. Whaley
- Alexander S. Whelchel
- Francis M. Whelchel
- Stephen T. Whelchel
- Alexander R. White
- †George B. White
- James K. Polk White
- William R. White
- F. Jasper Whitehead
- William D. Wiggins
- †C.W. Wilder
- Andrew B. Williams
- *Henry F. Williams
- J.B. Williams
- Thomas C. Williams
- William M. Williams
- Alonzo D. Willis

†E.N. Wilson
Frank R. Wilson
•Joseph R. Wilson
E. Wimberly
†John A. Wimpy

Charles C. Winder
J.P.S. Winder
Green C. Wood
James R. Wood
•John N. Wood

Moses Wood
Powhatton B. Wooten
Phillip Wray
Walter A. Wray
William D. Wright

Wm. Joseph Wynne
Benjamin C. Yancey
Milton B. Young
William Benj. Young

Appendix D

Greensboro Roster

Those Who Were Surrendered with Cobb's Legion Cavalry on April 26, 1865, at Greensboro, North Carolina

The men who fought in Cobb's Legion Cavalry were in every major action in the East and skirmished with the enemy almost daily between those major actions. We will never know the extent of their heroism and sacrifices, especially during the last year of the war when their records were burned. The following men should be remembered and honored for fighting for the independence and freedom of the Southern States against tremendous odds until the end of the hostilities.

*Original member of Cobb's Legion Cavalry

A.J. Abercrombie
James Adams
*S.D. Adams
*W.H. Adams
Thomas J. Agerton
Frank J. Ahern
*Francis M.C. Aiken
Emanuel Aiman
Charles H. Allen
*Ira Allen
John C. Allen
*Nic. M. Anderson
*David A. Armistead
Owen H. Arrington
*Jesse Asbury
Archer Avery
*Samuel W. Bailey
*James Riley Barrett
George J. Barwick
*Jefferson Bassett
*Charles E. Bassford
Solomon L. Bassford
*James A. Bennett
William A. Blount
Milton Alonza Boggs
*Willis C. Bone
Daniel M. Born
*Samuel D. Bostick
*Charles L. Bowie
William H. H. Bowie
*George G. Bowman

George W. Brady
*William A. Broadway
Thomas D. Brooks
Joseph Broome
Matthew L. Brown
George W. Brumley
John H. Bulloch
Causby D. Burnett
Robert H. Burton
John R. Byne
Jesse Calaway
Joseph W. B. Calaway
Alfred Webb Cantrell
Silas Jennings Carey
Oscar L. Carter
John J. Cates
Thomas Cates
Wm. F. Cavanaugh
Walter H. Chavous
James E. Christian
James Thomas Clark
Thomas S. Clark
George Clitt
J.S. Cochran
James A. Coleman
Pleasant Coleman
William Coleman
William J. Collins
*John M. Cooper
Wiley R. Copeland
Thomas J. Cosnahan

*John Coston
Samuel L. Cowart
Stephen D. Cowen
Joshua Crawley
Rufus Cross
Elisha J. Dagnell
Charles F.S. Dalvigny
Julius Foster Daniel
Joseph T. Davenport
William L. Davis
William S. Davis
William W. Davis
Alexander F. Dent
*J.D. Deriso
James A. Dixon
James Anison Dodgen
John W. Dodgen
Martin Donohue
*J.S. Dosier
Henry R. Dougherty
Augustus Dover
Elias C. Downs
*John W. Drinkwater
Berry T. Duckett
James H. Duke
Berrien W. Durden
*Alfred W. Early
Joseph G. Early
*William H. Early
Samuel Edward
William Edward

Columbus Emanuel
Joseph A. Epps
Justinian Evans
Richard Jones Evans
J.B. Everett
John Hayes Farr
Daniel Fesler
Jacob Fesler
John Fesler
*Marcus C. Few
*Levi C. Fields
*Richard J. Fields
Robert A. Fife
*Andrew J. Fish
John A.W. Fleming
Samuel P. Fleming
William W. Fleming
*Lewis R. Ford
Felix Walker Foster
Morris Friedenthal
William Fulcher
*W.L. Gallaway
John L. Gamblin
James E. Gibson
Jasper Norman Gilbert
George W. Givens
Dudley C. Gleaton
William E. Goodwin
James Gordon
James A. Gordon
Samuel J.L. Gordon

Joseph Simeon Gough
John R. Gramling
William M. D. Gray
Allen T. Grimes
James Grubbs, Jr.
*Alex. C. Guedron
*William T. Gunby
*Samuel B. Haesler
John Dalton Ham
*James W. Hanlon
*Anselin L. Harper
Tira L. Harris
William O. Harrison
William H. Hatfield
*Dwight David Hays
James E. Henry
John Jefferson Hinton
John D. Hopkins
William C. Houser
*John D. Houston
George H. Howard
*Wiley C. Howard
*Martin V. B. Howse
Lewis B. Hudson
James C. Huff
Jeremiah Clayton Huff
William T. Huff
George W. Hughes
Isaac C. Hunt
Robert Huntsinger
Doctor F. Jack
*Henry E. Jackson
Sherrod W. Jackson
Stephen E. Jackson
Thomas E. Jackson
William H.B. Jay
William J. Jenkins
Archibald C. Johnson
John A. Johnson
*Leonard E. Johnson
Leonidas D. Johnson
*Samuel Jack Johnson
Wm. Baldwin Johnson
William H. Johnson
C.A. Jones
James W. Jones
John T. Jones
Mitchell T. Jones
Thomas P. Jones
Wm. Hemphill Jones
Daniel B. Juhan
Francis F. Juhan
John Keefe

John Milton Kennedy
*John C. Keyes
William J. King
George W. Kirkland
George A. Lambert
Milton H. Lewis
David P. Lowry
Martin Mahany
Wiley P. Mangum
Wm. J.A. Matthews
John McCale
*Jos. P.C. McCollum
*Josiah F. McCollum
*Mark McCorkle
John McCoy
John Milledge McCoy
Augustus O. McCroan
Henry M. McCroan
David S. McWhorter
*J.H. Melton
*Montague Merriman
John J. Miller
Lewis A. Millican
Joseph C. Milligan
James W. Mills
*William Hugh Mills
Henry Alex Mitchell
Roland P. Mitchell
William P. Mitchell
*George W. Mock
Daniel Morgan
Thomas M. Murdock
Moses C. Murphey
*Charles T. Nash
*James R. Polk Nash
*Reuben Long Nash
*James H. Nelson
*Henry Norman
*James T. Norris
Henry North
*E.T. Nunn
James L. Oates
L.H. Oates
Owen O'Connor
James O'Hara
William C. Orr
John B. O'Shields
George H. Ozburn
James Robert Ozburn
William M. Parker
William L. Patterson
Alfred F. Payne
William H. Payne

Leroy M. Peck
*E.L. Peel
Lucas T. Penick
William E. Penrow
Thomas J. Perryman
A.B. Phelps
*James R. Phillips
Thomas N. Poland
Sylvester Pounds
J.W. Prince
Matthew C. Pritchard
Thomas W. Pritchard
Sidney A. Pugsley
J.N. Reader
Henry C. Reese
W.M Reese
Jonas G.B. Reid
*William Halum Reid
Jos. Jones Reynolds
*Walter C. Reynolds
Calvin C. Rice
J.W. Rice
James L. Rich
*Martin W. Riden
James N. Ridgway
John N. Ridgway
J.K.P. Ridling
Richard E. Roberts
William R. Roberts
*Henry A. Roebuck
John Blake Rogers
Thomas A. Rogers
James A. Rountree
Robert R. Rutherford
*Andrew J. Rylee
Andrew J. Sconyers
*A. F. Scott
*James D. Scott
Joseph L. Scruggs
William H.H. Scudder
James Franklin Seago
Marshall N. Seay
Osborne A. Seay
William Richey Segars
Thomas J. Shackleford
*Jarrell G. Sharpe
John H. Sharpe
James O. Simmons
Jesse A. Simmons
Moses S. Simmons
William H. Simpkins
Francis A. Sinquefield
*George W. Slatern

Ebenezer B. Smith
James B. Smith
T.H. Smith
*Wilber F. Smith
Zachariah H. Smith
Francis J. Spain
*Henry L. Sponsler
Hugh H. Stewart
James W. Stokes
J.F. Stovall
E. Strickland
William M. Strickland
George A. Suddeth
*William E. Sutton
Thomas J. Tabb
Francis D. Tanner
*William Avery Tanner
J.F. Thomas
John W. Thomas
*Thomas H. Tinsley
James M. Toole
Cuthbert C. Torrance
James Riley Truitt
*Thomas R. Tuck
*William J. Tucker
*Jefferson J. Turner
*C. Tyus
*James F. Walker
William Carter Wall
James M. Ward
John N. Warwick
Benjamin H. Watkins
Maurice Whalin
J.T.M. Wharton
*Stephen T. Whelchel
*William D. Wiggins
John Larkin Willard
George A. Williams
*J.B. Williams
*Alonzo D. Willis
Josiah N. Willis
James L. Wilson
E.M. Wimberly
*Charles C. Winder
Herman Wolfe
*Green C. Wood
*John N. Wood
John T. Wood
*Moses Wood
*Walter A. Wray
B.E. Wright
*Burrell Henry Yerby
Stanley Young

APPENDIX E

Killed in Action, Mortally Wounded in Action, or Death Attributed to Disease

*Original member of Cobb's Legion Cavalry
†Died as a prisoner of war
•May have been in the infantry

1. *1861, September 16, Miles A. Anderson, died at Yorktown, Virginia.
2. *1861, October 21, James N. McCullum, died at Yorktown, Virginia.
3. *1861, December 08, Uriah Blanchard, died at Williamsburg, Virginia.
4. *1862, January 17, William J. Helton, died.
5. *1862, February 1, Julius Michael Frix, died of disease at Richmond, Virginia.
6. *1862, February 2, William B. Cochran, died of disease.
7. *1862, February 5, C.W. Wilder, died of disease.
8. *1862, February 17, Edward A. Anderson died of disease at Camp Marion, Yorktown, Virginia.
9. 1862, February 25, W.W. Mershew, died of disease.
10. *1862, March 15, James H. Garner, died at Camp Marion, Yorktown, Virginia.
11. *1862, March 17, William H. Sibley, died of disease at Smithfield, Virginia.
12. *1862, March 23, Green B. Jackson, died at Suffolk, Virginia.
13. *1862, March 28, Bennett Boler, died at Suffolk, Virginia.
14. *1862, March, James F. Chavous, died near Goldsboro, North Carolina.
15. 1862, March, William Boyd Tuck, died.
16. *1862, April 17, Abel B.C. Densmore, died at Garysburg, North Carolina.
17. *1862, April 22, Walton T. Barrett, died at Suffolk, Virginia.
18. *1862, April 25, James H. Todd, died at Goldsboro, North Carolina.
19. •1862, June 2, William Harris, died at Petersburg, Virginia, of pneumonia.
20. 1862, June 26, Stephen Franklin Burnley, died.
21. 1862, June 28, Henry N. Ash died at Camp Meadow near Richmond, Virginia, of typhoid fever.
22. *1862, June 28, Henry Hillens, killed in action at Malvern Hill, Virginia.
23. 1862, July 1, Joseph J. Kennedy, died.
24. 1862, July 7, W. McDonald, died.
25. 1862, July 8, James Brian, died at Camp Meadow, Virginia.
26. 1862, July 10, Alexander Hope, died.
27. •1862, July 11, J.J. Wise, died.
28. 1862, July 12, Aaron Brian, died at Camp Meadow, Virginia.
29. 1862, July 14, Berrimon Woodruff, died at Danville, Virginia, of typhoid fever.
30. 1862, July 18, O.M. Buffington, died at Richmond, Virginia.
31. •1862, July 19, Carlos Williams, died.
32. 1862, July 21, James S. House, died at Richmond, Virginia.
33. 1862, July 25, Ezekiel Francis Gilmer, died at Richmond, Virginia.
34. 1862, July 25, James A. Harris, died of disease at Richmond, Virginia.
35. 1862, July 29, Coleman W. Marchman, died at Camp Winder near Richmond, Virginia.

36. 1862, August 9, Pickens Noble Calhoun, died of typhoid fever near Richmond, Virginia.

37. *1862, August 22, John H. Cowen, died at Richmond, Virginia.

38. *1862, August 24, Aquilla Bruce, died at Hanover Court House, Virginia.

39. 1862, August 28, William W. Smith, died at Hanover Court House, Virginia.

40. *1862, September 7, Berry T. Grindle, died at Richmond, Virginia, from severe burns.

41. 1862, September 7, Samuel D. Means, died at Richmond, Virginia, of typhoid fever.

42. •1862, September 9, Jasper Wells, died at Richmond, Virginia, of typhoid fever.

43. 1862, September 13, Barksdale, killed in action at Middletown, Maryland.

44. *1862, September 13, Green B. Barksdale, killed in action at Middletown, Maryland.

45. *1862, September 13, James F. Marshall, killed in action near Middletown, Maryland.

46. *†1862, September 14, Seaborn W. Chisolm, mortally wounded at Crampton's Pass, Maryland.

47. •1862, September 14, J.F. Kennedy, killed in action.

48. 1862, Before September 20, Robert T. Clingan, killed in action during the Maryland campaign.

49. *1862, September, James T. Broadway, mortally wounded at Crampton's Pass, Maryland.

50. 1862, September, Joseph W.M. Reidling, died.

51. •†1862, September, J.H. Rockman, may have died at Burkettsville, Maryland.

52. 1862, October 7, James H. Foster, died of chronic diarrhea at Staunton, Virginia.

53. 1862, October 17, Isaac Sterling, died of chronic diarrhea at Lynchburg, Virginia.

54. 1862, November 5, John E. Mitchell, killed in action at Barbee's Cross Roads, Virginia.

55. *1862, November 5, Henry N. Rhodes, killed in action at Barbee's Cross Roads, Virginia.

56. *1862, November 8, Jacob McCarty Scudder, killed in action near Little Washington, Virginia.

57. •1862, November 30, M.T. Donnan, died of smallpox at Richmond, Virginia.

58. 1862, November, John H. Hudson, died.

59. 1862, November, James J. Kennedy, died.

60. *1862, December 13, Gustavus Schlesinger, mortally wounded in action at Fredericksburg, Virginia.

61. *1862, December 17, Augustus Alford, died in Hancock County, Georgia.

62. 1862, December 20, George W. Pierce, died at Richmond, Virginia.

63. 1862, December 22, Moses R. Hill, died of diarrhea at Richmond, Virginia.

64. *1862, before December 28, Elijah D. Cowen, died.

65. 1863, January 6, John P. Hill, died of smallpox at Richmond, Virginia.

66. *1863, January 21, Thomas Adams, died.

67. 1863, January 31, David Glenn Blackwell died of chronic diarrhea at Liberty, Virginia.

68. 1863, February 16, James J. Tuck, died at Stevensburg, Virginia.

69. 1863, February 26, Henry Whisenant, died at Mt. Hope, Virginia.

70. 1863, March 7, Martin O'Donohoe, died at Lynchburg, Virginia.

71. 1863, March 10, William L. Galaway, died at Richmond, Virginia, of smallpox.

72. 1863, March 14, J. Henry Donor, died at Gordonsville, Virginia, of typhoid fever.

73. 1863, March 15, Thomas A. Smith, died.

74. *1863, March 16, John F. Isdal, died at Gordonsville, Virginia, of cerebritis.

75. 1863, before March 30, A. John Freeman, died.

76. *1863, April 12, R.J. Brown, died at Buchanan, Virginia.

77. 1863, May 12, W.B. Holeman, died.

78. *1863, May 28, Albert W.J. Carter died at Gordonsville, Virginia.

79. 1863, June 9, Bennett H. Carter, killed in action at Brandy Station, Virginia.

80. 1863, June 9, T.W. Cates, killed in action at Brandy Station, Virginia.

81. 1863, June 09, James Dunahoo, killed in action at Brandy Station, Virginia.

82. 1863, June 9, William Hardwick, killed in action at Brandy Station, Virginia.

83. 1863, June 9, Augustus F. Hardy, killed in action at Brandy Station, Virginia.

84. 1863, June 9, Richard Sconyers, killed in action at Brandy Station, Virginia.

85. 1863, June 9, Nicholas C. Ware, killed in action at Brandy Station, Virginia.

86. 1863, died after June 14, Dan Higgons, mortally wounded at Brandy Station, Virginia.

87. 1863, June 24, James Turner, mortally wounded in action at Brandy Station, Virginia. Died at Richmond, Virginia.

88. •1863, June 25, H. Wade, mortally wounded in action. Died at Richmond, Virginia.

89. *1863, July 1, John Weaver Cheesboro, mortally wounded at Hunterstown, Pennsylvania.

90. *1863, July 2, Thomas C. Barrett, killed in action at Hunterstown, Pennsylvania.

91. 1863, July 2, Cicero C. Brooks, killed in action at Hunterstown, Pennsylvania.
92. 1863, July 2, Charles Harrington, killed in action, probably at Hunterstown, Pennsylvania.
93. *1863, July 2, Nathan S. Pugh, killed in action at Hunterstown, Pennsylvania.
94. 1863, July 2, Ebenezer F. Smith, killed in action at Gettysburg, Pennsylvania.
95. 1863, July 3, James M. Evans, listed as missing. May have been killed in action.
96. *1863, July 3, Richard Moore, died in Richmond, Virginia, of acute dysentery.
97. 1863, July 3 or 1 Noah C. Strickland, killed at Gettysburg, Pennsylvania.
98. 1863, about July 10, James M. Glaze, killed in action in Maryland.
99. 1863, July 12, Richard P. Burtz, mortally wounded at Funkstown, Maryland, and died at Williamsport, Maryland.
100. 1863, July 19, Thomas W. Salter, killed in action near Martinsburg, West Virginia.
101. 1863, August 1, Thomas Reynolds, killed in action at Brandy Station, Virginia.
102. 1863, August 27, William R. Rountree, died of typhoid fever in Lynchburg, Virginia.
103. 1863, September 22, John L. Jowers, killed in action at Jack's Shop, Virginia.
104. 1863, September 22, Edward Preston Stone, killed in action at Jack's Shop, Virginia.
105. †1863, after September 23, O. Morris, may have died as a prisoner of war.
106. 1863, October 1, John James Alexander, died of blood poisoning at hospital in Gordonsville, Virginia.
107. 1863, October 1, Marcus L. McDermont, mortally wounded in action.
108. *†1863, October 2, William Gaston Delony, mortally wounded in action at Jack's Shop, Virginia. Died in Washington, D.C. as a prisoner-of-war.
109. *1863, October 8, J.D. Ford, mortally wounded in action. Died in Richmond, Virginia.
110. *1863, October 9, E.N. Wilson, mortally wounded in action and died at Richmond, Virginia.
111. 1863, October 13, James Curran, stabbed to death in Georgia.
112. •†1863, after October 18, B. Newton, may have died as a prisoner of war at Point Lookout, Maryland.
113. *1863, November 1, George Cicero Montgomery, died.
114. 1863, November 4, William Boyd died near Stevensburg, Virginia.
115. 1863, November 9, Tilman H. Brown, killed in action near Stevensburg, Virginia.
116. †1863, November 17, William N. Bryant, died of smallpox at Point Lookout, Maryland.
117. †1863, December 2, Thomas J. Chatham, died of smallpox at Point Lookout, Maryland.
118. *1863, December, Moses W. McCollum, died after being given a medical discharge.
119. 1864, January 10, Robert W. Wier, died of disease.
120. *1864, February 17, James Holcomb Bailey, died of typhoid fever at Richmond, Virginia.
121. 1864, February 22, John M. Lawson, died of typhoid fever at Richmond, Virginia.
122. †1864, after February 29, James R. Lankford, presumably died as prisoner of war.
123. *1864, March 2, D.A. Powell, died at Richmond, Virginia, of pneumonia.
124. 1864, March 9, C. H. Barden died at the infirmary camp.
125. †1864, after March 17, J.D. Howell, may have died at Fort Delaware Prison.
126. 1864, May 5, William F. Lampkin, died.
127. *1864, May 7, Oliver Hazard Perry Juhan, killed in action at Spotsylvania Court House, Virginia.
128. 1864, May 25, James H. Johnson, mortally wounded at Chancellorsville, Virginia.
129. *1864, May 29, Williamson F. Early, killed in action at Hanover Court House, Virginia.
130. 1864, May 31, Joseph Robert Howard, died at Spotsylvania, Virginia.
131. After 06/01/1864, A.M. Quarles, transferred to the infantry and was killed in action.
132. 1864, June 11, Thomas Jefferson Colvin, killed in action at Trevilian Station, Virginia.
133. 1864, June 11, Jethro W. Rogers, killed in action at Trevilian Station, Virginia.
134. *1864, June 12, H.M. Fowler, killed in action at Trevilian Station, Virginia.
135. *1864, June 12, Henry Francis Jones, killed in action at Trevilian Station, Virginia.
136. †After June 12, Daniel C. Baxter, mortally wounded at Trevilian Station, Virginia.
137. *†1864, after June 17, James H. Brent, may have died at Fort Delaware Prison.
138. *1864, June 18, Elisha S. Howse, mortally wounded in action at Hanover Junction, Virginia, and died at Richmond, Virginia.
139. *1864, June 24, Robert A. Lampkin, killed in action at Samaria Church, Virginia.
140. 1864, June 25, C.J. Blundell, mortally wounded in action at Trevilian Station, Virginia, and died at Charlottesville, Virginia.

141. 1864, June [29], John Smith, killed in action at Ream's Station, Virginia.

142. 1864, August 11, George W. McElhanon, died at Raleigh, North Carolina, of chronic diarrhea.

143. 1864, August 13, William L. Stone, killed in action at Stony Creek, Virginia.

144. 1864, August 16, James A. Parker, mortally wounded in action and died at Columbia, South Carolina.

145. 1864, August 16, Byrd Park, died of typhoid fever at Raleigh, North Carolina, after transferring to the Phillips Legion.

146. 1864, August 18, Josiah N. Clayton, died at Wilson, North Carolina.

147. 1864, August 25, Andrew J. Smith, killed in action at Ream's Station, Virginia.

148. *1864, August 25, George B. White, killed in action at Ream's Station, Virginia.

149. 1864, August 26, Napoleon B. Algers, died of intermittent fever at Richmond, Virginia.

150. 1864, September 7, William H. Byrd, mortally wounded in action near Charles City, Virginia, and died in Georgia.

151. 1864, September 8, William Nabers, mortally wounded in action on August 21, 1864, at Weldon Railroad after transferring to the 3rd Georgia Infantry, Company K.

152. 1864, September 12, SeaBorn H. Peterson, died at Weldon, North Carolina, from acute colitis.

153. †1864, September 16, Thomas Rollins, died at Point Lookout, Maryland.

154. 1864, September 19, John L. McCune, died of malaria at Wilson, North Carolina.

155. 1864, September 24, William H. Pass, died at Richmond, Virginia, of acute dysentery.

156. 1864, September 30, John H. Abercrombie, died in Richmond, Virginia.

157. †1864, October 11, M. Rufus McCurry, died of chronic diarrhea at Elmira Prison, New York.

158. *†1864, October 17, John M. Anderson, died of remittent fever at Elmira Prison, New York.

159. 1864, October 19, Edward W. Cowen, died at Weldon, North Carolina, from enteritis.

160. 1864, December 1, W.H. Parker, mortally wounded in action and died at Petersburg, Virginia.

161. 1864, December 29, J. Harvey Fraser, died in Bedford County, Virginia.

162. 1864, William H. Bird, died.

163. *1865, January 1, John Howard Burr, mortally wounded in action and died of blood poisoning at Petersburg, Virginia.

164. †1865, January 4, Samuel S. Parks, died of pneumonia at Elmira Prison, New York.

165. †1865, January 10, John A. Moore, died of pneumonia at Elmira Prison Camp, New York.

166. †1865, January 20, James J. Turner, died at Point Lookout, Maryland.

167. 1865, January 25, E.J. Wilson, mortally wounded in action

168. 1865, ca. February 11, John W. Hammond, killed in action at Orangeburg, South Carolina.

169. †1865, February 13, Isaac T. Smith, died of consumption at Fort Delaware Prison, Delaware.

170. *†1865, February 16, John W. David, died of typhoid fever at Elmira Prison Camp, New York.

171. *1865, March 9, James Russell Jack, killed in action at Monroe's Crossroads, North Carolina.

172. *1865, March 10, Barrington Simeral King, killed in action near Averasboro, North Carolina.

173. 1865, March, J.A. Shed, mortally wounded in action at Bentonville, North Carolina.

174. 1865, April 9, William N. Liverman, killed in action in South Carolina.

175. 1865, April 12, Thomas Jordan Dunnahoo, killed during the action at Swift Creek near Raleigh, North Carolina.

176. †1865, May 5, John D. Lowe, died at Elmira Prison, New York, of chronic diarrhea.

177. 1867, November 30, John Ross, mortally wounded at Jack's Shop, Virginia. Died in Augusta, Georgia.

178. 1888, June 11, Johnathan Pinckney Thomas, mortally wounded near Hamlet, Little Washington, Virginia.

Appendix F

Prisoners of War

*Original member of Cobb's Legion Cavalry
†Died as a prisoner of war
◆Deserted as a prisoner of war
•May have been in the infantry

1. *1862, July 7, John Howard Burr, captured near Harrison's Landing (Carter's Farm), Virginia.
2. 1862, July 10, Michael Hanlon, captured at Harrison's Landing, Virginia.
3. 1862, July 11, James Buregard Chambers, captured near Malvern Hill, Virginia.
4. *1862, July 11, Dwight David Hays, captured near Malvern Hill, Virginia
5. 1862, August 5, William P. Dearing, captured at Malvern Hill, Virginia.
6. 1862, August 5, George W. McElhanon, captured at Malvern Hill, Virginia.
7. 1862, August 5, James A. Netherland, captured at Malvern Hill, Virginia.
8. *1862, August 5, Francis Marion Stovall, captured at Malvern Hill, Virginia.
9. *1862, September 13, James T. Broadway, captured at Crampton's Pass, Maryland.
10. *1862, September 13, H.M. Fowler, captured at Crampton's Gap, Maryland.
11. *1862, September 13, David P. Godfrey, captured at Crampton's Gap, Maryland.
12. *1862, September 13, William E. Sutton, captured at Middletown, Maryland.
13. •1862, September 14, H.B. Ashmand, captured at Frederick, Maryland.
14. †1862, September 14, Seaborn W. Chisolm, captured at Crampton's Pass, Maryland.
15. *1862, September 14, Theodore Floyd Daniel, captured at South Mountain.
16. •1862, September 14, G. Doubleday, captured at Crampton's Gap, Maryland.
17. •1862, September 14, William R. Joie, captured at Crampton's Gap, Maryland.
18. 1862, September 14, E. McKnight, captured at Crampton's Gap, Maryland.
19. 1862, September 14, James S. Patterson, captured at Crampton's Pass, Maryland.
20. •1862, September 14, J.C. Pemberton, captured at Crampton's Pass, Maryland.
21. 1862, September 14, H.J. Stewarder, captured at South Mountain, Maryland.
22. •1862, September 14, J. Tredell, captured at Crampton's Pass, Maryland.
23. • 1862, September 14, S. Otis Turner, captured at Crampton's Pass, Maryland.
24. •1862, September 14, G. Wimperly, captured at Crampton's Pass, Maryland.
25. *1862, September 14, John N. Wood, captured at South Mountain, Maryland.
26. 1862, September 15, James M. Evans, captured at South Mountain, Maryland.
27. 1862, September 29, Thomas C. Gower, captured at Warrenton, Virginia.
28. •†1862, September, J.H. Rockman, probably captured at South Mountain or Quebec Schoolhouse.
29. *1862, October 20, Michael J. Ivey, captured at Georgetown, Virginia.
30. 1862, October 20, Joseph L. Moore, captured at Georgetown, Virginia.
31. 1862, October 20, J. F. Noose, captured at Georgetown, Virginia.
32. 1862, November 1, Merriman Winters, captured at Burkettsville, Maryland.
33. 1862, November 5, James E. Henry, captured at Barbee's Cross Roads, Virginia.
34. 1862, November 5, Marcus V. Woods, captured at Barbee's Cross Roads, Virginia.
35. ◆1862, before November 8, Richard L. Mass, captured.
36. 1862, November 12, Isma W. Thomas, captured near Warrenton, Virginia.

37. *1862, November 13, David P. Godfrey, captured at Burkittsville, Maryland.
38. 1862, November 16, Andrew T. Baugh.
39. *1863, January 2, Joseph R. Wilson, captured at Danville, Kentucky.
40. *1863, April 18, Samuel Burchardt Haesler, captured at Waterloo, Virginia.
41. 1863, June 7, John W. Hammond, captured at Brandy Station, Virginia.
42. ◆1863, June 9, Lewis W. Barrett, captured at Beverly's Ford, Virginia.
43. 1863, June 9, John N. Brooks, captured at Beverly's Ford, Virginia.
44. 1863, June 9, Thomas D. Brooks, captured at Beverly's Ford, Virginia.
45. 1863, June 9, John H. Bulloch, captured at Beverly's Ford, Virginia.
46. 1863, June 9, Oscar L. Carter, captured at Beverly's Ford, Virginia.
47. 1863, June 9, Samuel L. Cowart, captured at Beverly's Ford, Virginia.
48. *1863, June 9, Julius J. Fields, captured at Beverly's Ford, Virginia.
49. 1863, June 9, Samuel J.L. Gordon, captured at Beverly's Ford, Virginia.
50. 1863, June 9, George William Hughes, captured at Beverly's Ford, Virginia.
51. 1863, June 9, Josiah Miller, captured at Beverly's Ford, Virginia.
52. 1863, June 9, Thomas J. Nasworthy, captured at Beverly's Ford, Virginia.
53. 1863, June 9, James A. Netherland, captured at Beverly's Ford, Virginia.
54. 1863, June 9, James L. Oates, captured at Beverly's Ford, Virginia.
55. 1863, June 9, Andrew B. Oats, captured at Beverly's Ford, Virginia.
56. 1863, June 9, William E. Penrow, captured at Beverly's Ford, Virginia.
57. 1863, June 9, Jeremiah E. Ritch, captured at Beverly's Ford, Virginia.
58. 1863, June 9, Moses Sylvanus Simmons, captured at Beverly's Ford, Virginia.
59. 1863, June 20, Bartholomew J. Murphy, captured in Maryland.
60. ◆1863, June 21, B.A. Ball, captured at Upperville, Virginia.
61. 1863, June 21, Solomon L. Bassford, captured at Upperville, Virginia.
62. 1863, June 21, D.R. Davis, captured at Upperville, Virginia.
63. 1863, June 21, James Walter Day, captured at Upperville, Virginia.

64. ◆1863, June 21, Frank Hartford, captured probably at Upperville, Virginia.
65. ◆1863, June 21, Henry Marshall, captured at Upperville, Virginia.
66. ◆1863, June 21, Edward McGinness, captured at Upperville, Virginia.
67. *1863, June 21, Joseph Smith, captured at Upperville, Virginia.
68. ◆1863, June 21, William Young, captured at Upperville, Virginia.
69. *1863, June 24, John B. Hays, captured at Westminster, Maryland.
70. 1863, June 24, John McCale, captured at Upperville, Virginia.
71. 1863, June 26, Simeon William Hill, captured at Brookville, Maryland.
72. 1863, June 28, William H.B. Jay, captured at Brookville, Maryland.
73. ◆1863, June 30, Othniel E. Cory, captured at Brookville, Maryland.
74. ◆1863, July 2, John T. Adams, captured at Gettysburg, Pennsylvania.
75. ◆1863, July 2, Francis M. Goss, captured at Gettysburg, Pennsylvania.
76. ◆1863, July 2, Thomas S. Jenkins, captured at Hunterstown, Pennsylvania.
77. †1863, July 3, Thomas J. Chatham, captured at Hunterstown, Pennsylvania.
78. ◆1863, July 3, James H. Manning, captured near Gettysburg, Pennsylvania.
79. •†1863, July 3, B. Newton, captured at Gettysburg, Pennsylvania.
80. 1863, between July 4 and 10, James M. Harris, captured at Williamsport, Maryland.
81. 1863, July 5, George C. Tanner, captured at Gettysburg, Pennsylvania.
82. 1863, July 5, James B. Watson, captured at Gettysburg, Pennsylvania.
83. †1863, July 9, James R. Lankford, captured at Clear Spring, Maryland.
84. 1863, July 10, Morris Harris, captured near Williamsport, Maryland.
85. *1863, July 15, William J. Tucker, captured at Martinsburg, [West] Virginia.
86. 1863, July 17, John D.D. Harben, captured near Martinsburg, [West] Virginia.
87. 1863, July 17, Dennis Hogan, captured at Williamsport, Maryland.
88. *1863, July 17, George W. Parrish, captured at Hedgesville, [West] Virginia.
89. 1863, July 17, Josiah Middleton Seago, captured at Martinsburg, [West] Virginia.
90. ◆1863, July 17, Marcus V. Woods, captured at Hedgesville, [West] Virginia.

91. 1863, July 18, Allen Chavous, captured near Martinsburg, [West] Virginia.
92. 1863, July 18, James M. Cobb, captured near Martinsburg, [West] Virginia on 07/18/1863.
93. ♦1863, July 18, Allen R. Stanford, captured at Martinsburg, [West] Virginia.
94. ♦1863, July 25, Andrew J. Graffan, captured and sent to Fort Mifflin, Pennsylvania, on 07/27/1863.
95. 1863, August 1, William D. Heffernan, captured at Brandy Station, Virginia.
96. 1863, August 1, James Overton Simmons, captured at Brandy Station, Virginia.
97. ♦1863, August 15, George Woolley, captured at Kelly's Ford, Virginia.
98. ♦1863, August 25, Martin J. Frie, captured at Culpeper, Virginia.
99. †1863, August 26, Thomas Rollins, captured at Amissville, Virginia.
100. *1863, September 22, Henry Stiles Bradley, captured at Jack's Shop, Madison County, Virginia.
101. †1863, September 22, William N. Bryant, captured at Jack's Shop, Madison County, Virginia.
102. *†1863, September 22, William Gaston Delony, captured at Jack's Shop, Virginia.
103. *1863, September 22, Robert Stockton Morris, captured at Jack's Shop, Virginia.
104. *1863, September 22, Reuben Long Nash, captured at Jack's Shop, Madison County, Virginia.
105. *1863, September 22, Daniel O'Connor, captured at Jack's Shop, Madison County, Virginia.
106. *1863, September 22, George W. Slatern, captured at Jack's Shop, Madison County, Virginia.
107. †1863, September 23, O. Morris, captured near Madison Court House, Virginia.
108. 1863, October 12, Thomas M. Murdock, captured near Brandy Station, Virginia.
109. 1863, November 9, William H. Pass, captured at Stevensburg, Culpeper County, Virginia.
110. 1863, November 25, J.F. Mollere, captured.
111. 1863, November 26, Noah Allison, captured at Mine Run, Virginia.
112. *1864, February 3, Michael J. Ivey, captured at Plain View, Gloucester County, Virginia.
113. *1864, February 3, Henry Hugh McCall, captured at Plain View, Virginia.

114. 1864, February 6, Charles H. Nelson, captured at Gold Mine Ford, Virginia.
115. 1864, February 6, Thomas Ozias Ozburn, captured at Gold Mine Ford, Virginia.
116. 1864, February 7, Henry Steen, captured at the Rapidan River.
117. 1864, February 21, Isham Humphrey Pittard, captured at Ely's Ford, Virginia.
118. *†1864, February 27, James H. Brent, captured at Stafford, Virginia.
119. 1864, February 29, James C. Oliver, captured at Spotsylvania Court House, Virginia.
120. *1864, February 29, William Benjamin Young, captured at Ely's Ford, Virginia.
121. 1864, March 01, Charles L. Camback, captured at Fauquier County, Virginia.
122. *1864, March 15, Charles R. A. Harris, captured at Fauquier County, Virginia.
123. †1864, March 17, J.D. Howell.
124. 1864, March 31, Owen O'Keefe, captured at Falmouth, Stafford County, Virginia.
125. 1864, May 9, John A. Johnson, captured at Spotsylvania Court House.
126. †1864, May 9, John D. Lowe, captured at Spotsylvania Court House.
127. 1864, May 12, B.F. Saunders, captured at King George County, Virginia.
128. 1864, May 13, William H. McDaniel, captured at King George County, Virginia.
129. *1864, May 14, Jesse C. Gibson, captured at King George County, Virginia.
130. †1864, May 14, Isaac T. Smith, captured at King George County, Virginia.
131. 1864, May 15, Edward Wyatt Collier, captured at Stafford, Virginia.
132. 1864, May 15, William Capers Dickson, captured at Stafford County, Virginia.
133. 1864, May 16, James A. Bryan, captured at Bowling Green, Stafford County, Virginia.
134. 1864, May 16, John P. Peel, captured at Milford Station, Virginia.
135. 1864, May 18, Samuel D. Paden, captured at Milford Station, Virginia.
136. 1864, May 18, James W. Stokes, captured at King George County, Virginia.
137. 1864, May 21, Richard Nathaniel Juhan, captured at Milford Station, Virginia.
138. 1864, May 21, John N. Warwick, captured at King George County, Virginia.
139. *†1864, May 29, John M. Anderson, captured at Hanover Court House, Virginia.
140. *†1864, May 29, John White David, captured at Hanover Court House, Virginia.

141. *1864, May 31, B.L. Dickens, captured at Hanover Court House, Virginia.

142. *1864, May 31, E.D. High, captured at Hanover Court House, Virginia.

143. ◆1864, June 1, George W. Vaughan, captured at Cold Harbor, Virginia.

144. 1864, June 4, L. Rigand, captured at Totopotomoy Creek, Virginia.

145. 1864, June 4, Thomas B.F. Todd, captured at Totopotomoy Creek, Virginia.

146. *†1864, June 11, Daniel C. Baxter, captured at Trevilian Station, Virginia.

147. †1864, June 11, M. Rufus McCurry, captured at Trevilian Station, Virginia.

148. †1864, June 11, M. John A. Moore, captured at Trevilian Station, Virginia.

149. †1864, June 11, Samuel S. Parks, captured at Trevilian Station, Virginia.

150. 1864, June 11, James C. Wilborn, captured at Trevilian Station, Virginia.

151. 1864, June 24, John McCale, captured at Upperville, Virginia.

152. *1864, August 25, W.H. Lippitt, captured at Ream's Station, Virginia.

153. 1864, before August 29, Cornelius C. Turner, captured at Hall County, Georgia.

154. ◆1864, September 1, John A. Voss, captured at Cobb County, Georgia.

155. 1864, September 22, James M. Head, captured at Fisher's Hill, Virginia.

156. 1864, September, Isaac G. Allbritten, captured.

157. 1864, after October 12, Henry A. Watkins, captured.

158. 1864, October 27, Fred Hogrefe, captured at Hatcher's Run, Virginia.

159. •1864, October 27, James M. White, captured near Petersburg, Virginia.

160. 1864, December 1, Joseph N. Hill, captured at Stoney Creek, Virginia.

161. 1864, December 1, George M.D. Moon, captured at Stoney Creek, Virginia.

162. 1864, December 1, Harvey Calhoun Parks, captured at Stoney Creek, Virginia.

163. 1864, December 1, H.H. Walkin, captured at Stoney Creek, Virginia.

164. 1864, December 5, N.C. Parker, captured at Stoney Creek, Virginia.

165. †1864, December 12, James J. Turner, captured at Sussex Court House, Virginia.

166. ◆1865, before January 17, John J. Moran.

167. *1865, ca. February 11–14, John H. Keogh, captured 9 miles from Orangeburg, South Carolina.

168. 1865, February 17, John Dorris, captured at Columbia, South Carolina.

169. 1865, February 19, James G. Ringgold, captured at Columbia, South Carolina.

170. 1865, February 22, William Givens, captured at Waynesboro, North Carolina.

171. *1865, February 25, Julius J. Fields, captured at Lynches Creek, South Carolina.

172. 1865, ca. March 1, Augustus C. Baker, captured near Cheraw, South Carolina.

173. 1865, March 4, Thomas Lyons, captured at Cheraw, South Carolina.

174. 1865, March 4, Joseph Syler, captured at Cheraw, South Carolina.

175. 1865, March 5, John C. Swan, captured at Cheraw, South Carolina.

176. 1865, March 14, E.W. Scammell, captured at Ashland, Virginia.

177. 1865, March 19, William H. Johnson, captured at Salisbury, North Carolina.

178. *1865, April 3, James T. Lamkin, captured at Richmond, Virginia.

179. 1865, April 3, Thomas Lander, captured at Richmond, Virginia.

180. *1865, April 6, Theodore Floyd Daniel, captured at Sailor's Creek, Virginia.

181. 1865, April 10, James A. Allbritten, captured near Raleigh, North Carolina.

182. 1865, April 12, William W. Dunn, captured at Salisbury, North Carolina.

183. 1865, April 13, William F.K. Garvin, captured at Raleigh, North Carolina.

184. 1865, John J. Nash, captured at Anderson, South Carolina.

185. Date unknown, C.W. Orrison.

Appendix G

Those Who Went on Horse Detail to Georgia with Capt. Bostick on September 20, 1864

*Original member of Cobb's Legion Cavalry
†Was present at the surrender and on the Greensboro Roster
•Deserted

†A.J. Abercrombie
Clement Abercombie
John H. Abercrombie
Wm. W. Abercrombie
*†S.D. Adams
*†W.H. Adams
†Thomas J. Agerton
James A. Allbritten
Pleasant G. Allbritten
William A. Allbritten
Jo. N. Allexander
*†Nic. M. Anderson
Robert B. Anderson
*Walter H. Anthony
*Edward J. Appling
John H. Archer
*David A. Armistead
Owen H. Arrington
*Jesse Asbury
Darling C. Atterberry
Augustus C. Baker
*†James Riley Barrett
*†Charles E. Bassford
A.J. Bates
William N. Bates
Andrew T. Baugh
*Marlin M. Bell
Daniel Bennett
*Josiah S. Blackwell
A.H. Blount
†Milton A. Boggs
*Samuel D. Bostick
Isaac Bowen
†William H.H. Bowie

*†George G. Bowman
William Burr Brian
Alonzo A. Brooks
John N. Brooks
Green W. Brookshear
Jesse T. Brown
† Matthew L. Brown
Wellington L. Bryant
*D.C.N. Burkhalter
† Causby D. Burnett
†John Randolph Byne
† J.W.B. Calaway
Edward L. Calhoun
Dilmus McP. Camp
†Alfred Webb Cantrell
John H. Cantrell
†Silas Jennings Carey
†Oscar L. Carter
Michael G. Casey
*Noah B. Cash
E.T. Cassell
†John J. Cates
†Thomas Cates
James B. Chambers
Robert Chandler
J.W. Chatham
John L. Chavous
†Walter H. Chavous
†James E. Christian
*John Christman
†James Thomas Clark
†William Coleman
†William J. Collins
†Wiley R. Copeland

†Thomas J. Cosnahan
*†John Coston
Edward W. Cowen
†Stephen D. Cowen
†Rufus Cross
†Elisha J. Dagnell
Daniel Davis
†William L. Davis
†William S. Davis
†William W. Davis
*†J.D. Deriso
James M. Deriso
A.C. Dickerson
James S. Dill
†James A. Dixon
†John W. Dodgen
Bernard Doris
†Elias C. Downs
James Madison Drake
*†John W. Drinkwater
†Berry T. Duckett
†Berrien W. Durden
*†William H. Early
J.F. Edwards
†Richard Jones Evans
*†J.B. Everett
William P. Fanning
Lorenzo D. Ferguson
†Daniel Fesler
*Julius J. Fields
*†Levi C. Fields
*Andrew J. Fish
†John A.W. Fleming
†Samuel P. Fleming

†William W. Fleming
Richard E. Fortson
†Felix Walker Foster
†William Fulcher
*†W.L. Gallaway
William F.K. Garvin
†Jasper N. Gilbert
William P. Gillespie
William Givens
Jacob Harris Glaze
†Dudley C. Gleaton
William T. Godbee
James H. Goff
William Henry Goff
†William E. Goodwin
†James Gordon
†Samuel J.L. Gordon
†Jos. Simeon Gough
†William M.D. Gray
Henry N. Greer
Robert Simeon Greer
William A. Greer
John J. Gregory
Jasper B. Groves
†James Grubbs, Jr.
*†Alex. C. Guedron
*†Samuel B. Haesler
†John Dalton Ham
Archi. N. Hamilton
*Robert J. Hancock
*†James W. Hanlon
*†Anselin L. Harper
George W. Harris
*Henry S. Harris

James M. Harris
Richard D. Harris
*†Dwight David Hays
John J. Hewit
James Hill
Joel Hodo
William C. Hood
†John D. Hopkins
John Hough
*†John D. Houston
†George H. Howard
*H.L. Howell
J.C. Hubbard
†James C. Huff
†Jeremiah C. Huff
John Floyd Huff
†William T. Huff
†George Wm. Hughes
Joseph B. Hughey
John M. Hunter
†Robert Huntsinger
*Daniel J. Irby
Richard T. Ivey
*James Russell Jack
William F. Jack
*†Henry E. Jackson
†Sherrod W. Jackson
†Stephen E. Jackson
†Thomas E. Jackson
*William H. Jackson
William W. Jackson
A.E. Johnson
†Archibald C. Johnson
George G. Johnson
†Leonidas D. Johnson
*†Samuel Jack Johnson
†William B. Johnson
†William H. Johnson
†John T. Jones
†Mitchell T. Jones
Shepard A. Jones
†Thomas P. Jones
*Thomas R.W. Jones
†Wm. Hemphill Jones
J.A. Juhan
*Lewis A. Juhan
†John M. Kennedy
*John H. Keogh
Mark W. King
†William J. King
†George W. Kirkland
George L. Knight
†George A. Lambert
Benjamin Landrum

E.G. Lataste
*Thomas Leach
†Milton H. Lewis
Wiley R. Light
*Charles P. Lively
†David P. Lowry
Thomas Lyons
W.H.C. Mahaffey
James A.B. Mahaffy
†Martin Mahany
†Wiley P. Mangum
C.W. Mathews
James H. Mathews
*†Jos. P.C. McCollum
James M. McCrary
†Henry M. McCroan
W.H. McCullough
*Thomas J. McCurry
William J. McDaniel
†David S. McWhorter
Barney R. Meaders
*†Montague Merriman
†John J. Miller
Josiah Miller
†Joseph C. Milligan
†James W. Mills
W.W. Millsaps
†Roland P. Mitchell
W.S. Mitchell
†William P. Mitchell
*†George W. Mock
Thomas J. Moon
J.J. Moore
•John J. Moran
†Daniel Morgan
Edwin Pierce Morris
John D. Moseley
J. Winchester Moss
Green Young Moxley
Newton J. Moxley
†Thomas M. Murdock
Augustus W. Murphee
Thomas J. Murphy
*†Charles T. Nash
John J. Nash
*†E.T. Nunn
†L.H. Oates
Andrew B. Oats
†George H. Ozburn
Robert J. Parker
†William M. Parker
*David Rives Parks
†William L. Patterson
Neal B. Paul

†Leroy M. Peck
*†E.L. Peel
B.A. Pendleton
R.N. Perryman
*†James R. Phillips
•Benjamin J. B. Pool
Jesse Pope
†J.W. Prince
†Matthew C. Pritchard
†Thomas W. Pritchard
*Hiram Province
†Sidney A. Pugsley
Edwin Pylant
Mansel W. Rasbury
Reuben L. Rasbury
William A. Ray
†J.N. Reader
†W.M. Reese
†Jonas G. B. Reid
†Jos. Jones Reynolds
R.A. Reynolds (Co. F)
†J.W. Rice
†James N. Ridgway
†John N. Ridgway
George Ridings
W.B. Ridley
Burwell G. Rives
Reuben P. Rives
*William H. Roach
George W. Roberts
†Richard E. Roberts
Herman Roesel
John J. Rogers
†Thomas A. Rogers
John Ross
†James A. Rountree
David Rusk
Dempsy P. Rusk
†Robert R. Rutherford
*James B. Rylee
†Andrew J. Sconyers
*†A.F. Scott
†Joseph L. Scruggs
†Wm. H.H. Scudder
Francis G. Seagers
†James Franklin Seago
†Thom. J. Shackleford
Milton C. Sharpe
J. Sidney Shaw
*C.L. Sibley
Samuel Hale Sibley
†Jesse A. Simmons
*Moses T. Simmons
*William D. Simmons

†William H. Simpkins
†Ebenezer B. Smith
Henry W. Smith
†James B. Smith
Robert F. Smith
*†Wilber F. Smith
†Zachariah H. Smith
Amaziah South
W.J.H. Stephens
Edward N. Stevens
W.C. Stevens
J. Lafayette Stewart
William A. Stewart
†J.F. Stovall
†Wm. M. Strickland
†George A. Suddeth
Leander Sutton
*†William E. Sutton
Henry J. Swan
†Thomas J. Tabb
†Francis D. Tanner
George C. Tanner
Calvin C. Taylor
Isma W. Thomas
Robert F. Thomas
*Alfred R. Thompson
James F. Thompson
*James M. Thornton
*John S. Thrash
*†Thomas H. Tinsley
†James M. Toole
†C. C. Torrance
*Calhoun H. Turner
Stephen Turner
*Richard A. Vasser
*Thomas Vigis
James A. Voss
William A. Voss
*†James F. Walker
Persons Walker
*Fred W. Walter
Calvin D. Ward
†James M. Ward
Edwin A. Warwick
†Benjamin H. Watkins
W.T. Weaver
Samuel B. Weir
Thomas B. Wells
*Alex. S. Whelchel
Henry White
Henry Clay White
David A. Whitehead
A.J. Williams
Willis B. Williams

George W. Williard	George W. Winfrey	John R. Wood	*Wm. Joseph Wynne
*Alonza D. Willis	Charles N. Witcher	W.C. Worrison	†Burrell Henry Yerby
†E.M. Wimberly	J.F. Wood	†B.E. Wright	

APPENDIX H

Last Record: Deserted or Absent Without Leave

Men from Cobb's Legion Cavalry who took the Oath of Allegiance to the United States were listed as deserters. Those who simply left their company — perhaps to go home — without taking the Oath were listed as Absent Without Leave. In other Confederate regiments they would have been listed as deserters. The cavalry was more lax about punishing those who were sent home to get horses and they were listed as Absent Without Leave. A man could not always go home, procure a horse, and return to his regiment in the allotted time given to him. Among those listed as Absent Without Leave, there may be some who had legitimate reasons for being absent or who rejoined their companies during the last six months when the records were burned. Those who did not have legitimate reasons for being absent from their companies at the surrender were not eligible for Confederate pensions.

*Original Member of Cobb's Legion Cavalry
•May have been in the infantry

Deserted

John T. Adams
Valentine Angle
Thomas J. Ash
N.D. Ashe
H.S. Autry
B.A. Ball
Lewis W. Barrett
James Bates
F. Booker
Othniel E. Cory
*Joseph S. Cutter
John Dougherty
William W. Downs
Martin J. Frie
Francis M. Goss
Andrew J. Graffan
Joseph Gray
Joseph H. Gulick
Frank Hartford
George W. Head
Unknown Holcombe
Cary J. Hopkins
*E.W. Howell
Unknown Irvine
Thomas S. Jenkins
T.J. Johnson
H. Jones
Edward Kelley
John W.S. Mahaffy
James H. Manning
Henry Marshall
Richard L. Mass
Edward McGinness
*James M. McNair
James Moony
Joseph A. Moore
John J. Moran
•J.E. Mowan
T. Newbolt
John A. Owens
Benj. J.B. Pool
W.T. Prater
James W. Price
•James Reeves
Francis Robbins
James Roper
Allen Sanford
Loring Wheeler Shead
J.W. Shivers
John W. Shurdon
Allen R. Stanford
*Curtis J. Thayer
Healey A. Tollison
Cornelius C. Turner
Edward H. Weston
George W. Vaughan
John A. Voss
James B. Waters
H.F. Weaver
Joseph M. Webb
Edward H. Weston
Lawson V. White
Marcus V. Woods
Alex Woody
George Woolley
William Young

Absent Without Leave

William Adams
N.D. Ashe
S.W. Bothwell
Charles E. Bowers
Allen Brown
James F. Brown
J.M. Calloway
Thomas M. Childers
D.R. Davis
R.G. Davis
H.E. Dempsey
Thomas Gay
Benjamin D. Gilstrap
James S. Graham
T. Moore Harman
James A. Hatch
Simeon William Hill
T.J. James
William Jester
*I.J. Johnson
Jesse Johnson
John Kelly
*Thomas J. Landrum
*B.H. Lawton
A.B. Lee
C.E. Lewellyn
David F. Lutes
J. M. Mann
John H. Marchman
D. Milhollen
J.T. Nolan
Ira W. Owens
Jacob Owens
H.F. Pentecost
John A. Pierce
J.M. Raynes
*Calvin Cephus Sego
Chas. W. Shackleford
*Benjamin F. Sibley
John C. Stanley
J.B. Stanton
*Henry Strickland
Lemuel Taylor
Absalom B. Turner
*Henry F. Williams

Chapter Notes

Preface
1. Edward L. Wells, *Hampton & His Cavalry in '64* (Richmond, VA: B. F. Johnson Publishing Co.,1899), 82.

Chapter 1
1. Capt. Francis Edgeworth Eve, address on Confederate Memorial Day, April 26, 1893, to the Ladies of the Memorial Association, Athens, Georgia. Published in *The (Athens) Weekly Banner,* May 2, 1893, and *The Athens Banner*, April 30, 1893.
2. Wells, 82–97, 131.

Chapter 2
1. *Compiled Service Records of Confederate Soldiers Who Served in Organizations from the State of Georgia* (National Archives Microfilm Publications, Young A. Anderson records, requisition dated April 22, 1862).

Chapter 3
1. W.W. Blackford, *War Years with Jeb Stuart* (New York: Charles Scribner's Sons, 1945), 71.
2. Wiley C. Howard, *Sketch of Cobb Legion Cavalry and Some Incidents and Scenes Remembered* (Prepared and read under appointment of Atlanta Camp 159, U.C.V., August 19, 1901), 2.
3. Blackford, 76.
4. Eve.
5. Ibid.
6. *War of the Rebellion: A Compilation of the Official Records of the Union and Confederate Armies,* vol. 11 (pt. 3) of 128 vols. (Washington, D.C.: Government Printing Office, 1880–1901), 660. (Hereafter referred to as OR.)

Chapter 4
1. Eve.
2. Burke Davis, *Jeb Stuart: The Last Cavalier* (New York: Wings Books, 1957), 183.
3. Eve.

Chapter 5
1. OR, vol. 19, pt. 1, p. 815.
2. Howard, 3.
3. *The (Middletown, Maryland) Valley Register,* April 8, 1898, cited in Timothy J. Reese, "The Cavalry Clash at Quebec Schoolhouse: Cobb's Legion, CSA, and Medill's Union Horsemen Fight in the Shadow of South Mountain, Maryland, September 13, 1862," *Blue & Gray,* February 1993, 24–29.
4. Howard, 3.
5. OR, vol. 19, pt. 1, p. 818.
6. Reese, 28.
7. Howard, 3.
8. Davis, 207–208.
9. Howard, 4.
10. Davis, 209.
11. OR, vol. 19, pt. 1, p. 821.

Chapter 6
1. Howard, 3.
2. John F. Stegeman, *These Men She Gave: The Civil War Diary of Athens, Georgia* (Athens, GA: Iberian Publishing, 2000), 65–66.
3. Blackford, 162–163.
4. Song sung by Southerners after the raid.
5. OR, vol. 19, pt. 2, p. 55.
6. U.R. Brooks, ed., *Butler and His Cavalry in the War of Secession, 1861–1865* (Columbia, SC: State Co., 1909), 173. (Hereafter referred to as Brooks, *Butler.*)
7. Davis, 218.
8. U.R. Brooks, *Stories of the Confederacy* (Columbia, SC: State Co., 1912), 100–101. (Hereafter referred to as Brooks, *Stories of the Confederacy.*) Walter Brian Cisco, *Wade Hampton: Confederate Warrior, Conservative Statesman* (Washington, D.C.: Brassey's Inc., 2004), 101. (Hereafter referred to as Cisco.)
9. J. Melchior Sheads, "Border Raids into Pennsylvania During the Civil War" (Thesis, Gettysburg College, 1933). Sheads cites the *Gettysburg Compiler.*
10. OR, vol. 19, pt. 2, p. 59.
11. Blackford, 173.
12. Ibid., 176–177.
13. Wells, 68.
14. Major Henry B. McClellan, *I Rode With Jeb Stuart: The Life and Campaigns of Major General J.E.B. Stuart* (New York: Da Capo Press, 1958), 161.

Chapter 7

1. Eve.
2. Howard, 10.
3. Ibid.
4. Ibid.
5. Ibid.

Chapter 8

1. OR, vol. 19, pt. 2, p. 145.
2. Ibid., vol. 21, pt. 1, p. 16.
3. Ibid., 15.
4. Ibid., 15–16.
5. Howard, 4.
6. Ibid.
7. Ibid., 5.
8. OR, vol. 21, pp. 689–691.
9. Howard, 5–6.
10. Brooks, *Stories of the Confederacy,* 120–121.
11. OR, vol. 21, pt. 1, p. 695.
12. Ibid.
13. Ibid., 735.
14. Wade Hampton to Mary Fisher Hampton, January 2, 1863, Hampton Family Papers, University of South Carolina. (Hereafter referred to as WH to MFH.)
15. Ibid., November 22, 1862.
16. Ibid., December 25, 1862.
17. Ibid., January 12, 1863.
18. McClellan, 258–259.
19. Ibid., 261.
20. Charles E. Cauthen, ed., *Family Letters of the Three Wade Hamptons, 1782–1901* (Columbia, SC: University of South Carolina Press, 1953), 91.
21. Edward G. Longacre, *Gentleman and Soldier: The Extraordinary Life of General Wade Hampton* (Nashville: Rutledge Hill Press, 2003), 127.
22. Hampton to Senator Lewis Wigfall of Texas, February 16, 1863, Hampton Family Papers, South Carolinian Library, University of South Carolina, Columbia, South Carolina.
23. Howard, 8.

Chapter 9

1. Howard, 6.
2. Col. Wilbur S. Nye, "The Affair at Hunterstown," *Civil War Times,* February 1971, 23.
3. Nye, 28.
4. Joseph Frederick Waring, diary entry for April 12, 1864.
5. Ted Alexander, "Gettysburg Cavalry Operations," *Blue & Gray* 6, no. 1, p. 10.
6. Nye, 23.
7. Wells, page 72
8. Ibid.
9. Howard, 6.
10. William Gaston Delony, letter dated June 10, 1863, William Gaston Delony Papers, Hargrett Library, University of Georgia.
11. Frances H. Kennedy, *The Civil War Battlefield Guide* (New York, Boston: The Conservation Fund, Houghton Mifflin Co., 1998), 204.
12. Blackford, 215–216.
13. Howard, 7.
14. Delony, June 10, 1863.
15. OR, vol. 27, pt. 2, p. 723.
16. Howard, 7–8.
17. OR, vol. 27, pt. 2, pp. 732–733.
18. Ibid., 723.
19. Delony, letter dated June 12, 1863, Hargrett Library, University of Georgia.
20. Howard, 2.
21. OR, vol. 27, pt. 2, 687.
22. Eve.
23. McClellan, 313.
24. OR, vol. 27, pt. 2, pp. 690–691.
25. McClellan, 316.
26. S.A.J. Creekmore Diary, Mississippi Department of Archives and History, Jackson, Mississippi.
27. Blackford, 225.
28. OR, vol. 27, pt. 2, p. 696.
29. *Confederate Veteran,* September 1899, 415. (Hereafter referred to as *CV.*)
30. Ibid.
31. Delony, letter dated July 4, 1863.
32. OR, vol. 27, pt. 2, p. 697.
33. Ibid., 725.
34. Ibid., 724.
35. H.E. Jackson, untitled letter, *CV* 7 (September 1899): 415.
36. Howard, 9.
37. Manly Wade Wellman, *Giant in Gray: A Biography of Wade Hampton of South Carolina* (New York: Charles Scribner's Sons, 1949), 121.
38. Blackford, 234–235.
39. Eve.

Chapter 10

1. Eve.
2. Ibid.
3. Howard, 11.

Chapter 11

1. Blackford, 241.
2. OR, Vol. 28, pt. 1, p. 452.
3. Ibid.

Chapter 12

1. Wellman, 130.
2. WH to MFH, November 20, 1863.
3. Ibid., November 29, 1863.

Chapter 13

1. Eleanor D. McSwain, ed., *Crumbling Defenses, or Memoirs and Reminiscences of John Logan Black, Colonel, C.S.A.* (Macon, GA: J.W. Burke Co., 1960), 70.
2. Wells, 99.
3. The original letter is in the possession of Mr. George F. Scheer of Chapel Hill, North Carolina, and was cited in Wellman, 136–137.
4. Waring, entry for April 7, 1864.

Chapter 14

1. Wells, 126–127.
2. Longacre, 182.
3. Waring, entry for May 11, 1864.
4. Wells, 138–139.
5. Howard, 8.
6. Waring, entry for May 15, 1864.
7. Howard, 8.
8. Waring, entry for May 13, 1864.
9. Waring, entry for May 15, 1864.
10. Wells, 155.
11. Howard, 6.
12. F.M. Myers, *The Comanches: A History of White's Battalion, Virginia Cavalry, Laurel Brigade, Hampton Division, A.N.V., C.S.A.* (Baltimore: Kelly, Piet & Co, 1891), 292.
13. Wells, 172.
14. Blackford, 258.

Chapter 15

1. Wells, 194.
2. Brooks, *Butler*, 239.
3. Howard, 16.
4. Brooks, *Butler*, 245.
5. Howard, 17.
6. Robert U. Johnson and Clarence C. Buel, eds., *Battles and Leaders of the Civil War*, 4 vols. (New York: Century, Co., 1884–88) 239.
7. Brooks, *Butler*, 205.
8. WH to MFH, June 14, 1864.
9. Wells, 213.
10. Walter Brian Cisco, *Wade Hampton: Confederate Warrior, Conservative Statesman* (Washington D.C.: Brassey's, 2004), 139.
11. Brooks, *Stories of the Confederacy*, 392.
12. Brooks, *Butler*, 212.
13. Howard, 17.
14. Ibid.
15. Ibid., 17
16. Waring, entry for June 14, 1864.
17. Ibid., entry for June 15, 1864.
18. Ibid., entry for June 19, 1864.
19. Ibid., entry for June 26, 1864.
20. OR, Vol. 36, pt. 1, p. 1096.
21. William M. Davis, "St. Mary's Church, Va.: A Rattling Fight by One of Gregg's Cavalry Brigades," Washington, D.C.: *The National Tribune*, June 12, 1890.
22. Wells, 219.
23. Stanton P. Allen, *Down in Dixie: Life in a Cavalry Regiment in the War Days* (Boston: D. Lothrop Co., 1892, 390–391.
24. Howard, 6.
25. OR, vol. 36, pt. 1, p. 1097.

Chapter 16

1. Howard, 6.
2. Wade Hampton to Edward L. Wells, February 22, 1900, Wells Manuscript papers, Charleston Library Society.
3. Wells, 242.
4. Ibid., 247.
5. Ibid., 250–251.
6. Douglas Southall Freeman, *Lee's Dispatches* (New York: Putnam, 1919), 268.
7. WH to MFH, Oct. 5, 1864..
8. Wells, 274.
9. WH to MFH, August 20, 1864.
10. Wells, 279.
11. Howard, 12.
12. Ibid.
13. OR, vol. 42, pt. 2, pp. 1204–1205.
14. Wells, 285–286.
15. OR, vol. 42, pt. 1, pp. 943–44.
16. Wells, 283.
17. Howard, 12.
18. OR, vol. 42, pt. 2, pp. 1204–1205.
19. Myers, 330.
20. Olin Fulmer Hutchinson, Jr., ed., "*My Dear Mother & Sisters*": *Civil War Letters of Capt. A.B. Mulligan, Co. B, 5th South Carolina Cavalry–Butler's Division–Hampton's Corps* (Spartanburg, SC: Reprint Co., 1992), 151.
21. Wells, 302.
22. Wellman, 159.
23. Brooks, 437.
24. Waring, entry for October 1, 1864.
25. Ibid., entry for October 16, 1864.
26. Wells, 329.
27. Brooks, *Stories of the Confederacy*, 270–271.
28. Brooks, *Butler*, 358.
29. Wellman, 160.
30. Longacre, 219.
31. Brooks, *Butler*, 386.
32. Waring, entry for December 18, 1864.

Chapter 17

1. *Freeman*, 317.
2. John T. Wood, letter to his father dated March 29, 1865, Confederate Pension Application, John T. Wood. (Hereafter referred to as Wood to father.)
3. Ibid.
4. Mary Boykin Chesnut, *A Diary from Dixie*, ed. Ben Ames Williams (Boston: Houghton, Mifflin, 1949), 512.
5. Wood to father.
6. Matthew Calbraith Butler, address given to the Reunion of the Division U.C.V. on July 26, 1899, in *CV*, January 1900, 30–33.
7. Wood to father.
8. William Tecumseh Sherman, *Memoirs of General W.T. Sherman*, vol. 2 of 2 vols. (New York: Appleton, 1875), 287.
9. Sherman, 288.
10. Johnson & Buel, 686.
11. Butler, 31.
12. OR, vol. 47, pt. 2, p. 546.
13. Ibid., 597.
14. Chesnut, 496.
15. Butler, 32.
16. Brooks, *Butler*, 425.
17. Wells, 404.
18. Brooks, *Butler*, 446–447.
19. Wood to father, March 29, 1865.

20. Wells, 412–413.
21. Ibid., 414.
22. Wood to father March 29, 1865.
23. Wellman, 178.
24. Ibid.
25. Butler, 33.
26. Wood to father, March 29, 1865.
27. Howard, 18.
28. Ibid.
29. Ibid.
30. Committee appointed by the Reunion Committee of the 92nd Illinois Infantry Regiment. *Ninety-Second Illinois Volunteers* (Freeport, IL: Journal Steam Publishing House and Bookbindery, 1875), 235–236.
31. Howard, 19.
32. Ibid.
33. Wells, 423.
34. Waring, entry for April 14, 1865.
35. Ibid., entry for April 15, 1865.
36. Ibid., entry for April 19, 1865.
37. Charles P. Hansell, "Surrender of Cobb's Legion," *Confederate Veteran* 25, no. 10, October 1917, 463. (Hereafter referred to as Hansell in *CV.*)
38. Wells, 182.
39. Dunbar Rowland, *Jefferson Davis, Constitutionalist: His Letters, Papers and Speeches,* 10 vols. (Jackson, MS: Printed for the Mississippi Dept. of Archives and History, 1923), 552–553.
40. Hansell in *CV,* 463.
41. Butler, 33.

Afterword

1. Eve.
2. Ibid.

Bibliography

Manuscripts and Letters

Brooks, Noble. Diary. University of North Carolina, Southern Historical Collection, Chapel Hill, North Carolina.

Cobb, T.R.R. Letters to his wife dated September 24, 1861, and November 5, 1861. Privately owned Cobb Letters, cited in "Howell Cobb's Confederate Career" by Horace Montgomery, Confederate Publishing. Tuscaloosa, Alabama, 1959.

Creekmore, S.A.J. Diary. Mississippi Department of Archives and History, Jackson, Mississippi.

Delony, Lt. Col. William. Letters to his wife. Hargrett Library, University of Georgia.

Eve, Francis Edgeworth. Address to the Ladies of the Memorial Association, Athens, Georgia, on April 26, 1893. Hargrett Library, University of Georgia.

Hampton, Wade. Correspondence and Memoirs. Hampton Family Papers, University of South Carolina.

Howard, Wiley C. "Sketch of Cobb Legion Cavalry and Some Incidents and Scenes Remembered." Prepared and read under appointment of Atlanta Camp 159, U.C.V., August 19, 1901.

Sheads, J. Melchior. "Border Raids into Pennsylvania During the Civil War." Thesis, Gettysburg College, 1933.

Walter, John F. "Cobb's Georgia Legion — Cavalry." July 1981, Rev. March 1996.

_____. "Cobb's Georgia Legion — Official History." Compiled October 1999.

Waring, Joseph Frederick. Diaries, 1864–1865. Wilson Library, University of North Carolina.

Wells, Edward L. *Hampton & His Cavalry in '64.* Richmond, VA: B.F. Johnson, 1899.

_____. Papers. Charleston Library Society.

Wood, John T. Letter to his father dated March 29, 1865. Included in John T. Wood's Confederate Pension Application.

Published Works

Allen, Stanton P. *Down in Dixie: Life in a Cavalry Regiment in the War Days.* Boston: D. Lothrop, 1892.

Alexander, Ted. "Gettysburg Cavalry Operations," *Blue & Gray* 6, no. 1.

Blackford, W.W. *War Years with Jeb Stuart.* New York: Scribner's, 1945.

Brooks, U.R., ed. *Butler and His Cavalry in the War of Secession, 1861–1865.* Columbia, SC: State, 1909.

_____. *Stories of the Confederacy.* Columbia, SC: State, 1912.

Cauthen, Charles E., ed. *Family Letters of the Three Wade Hamptons, 1782–1901.* Columbia, SC: University of South Carolina Press, 1953.

Chesnut, Mary Boykin. *A Diary from Dixie.* Edited by Ben Ames Williams. Boston: Houghton Mifflin, 1949.

Cisco, Walter Brian. *Wade Hampton: Confederate Warrior, Conservative Statesman.* Washington, D.C.: Brassey's, 2004.

Civil War Soldiers and Sailors System. http://www.itd.nps.gov/cwss/soldiers.cfm

Daughters of the American Revolution, Thronateeska Chapter (Albany, Georgia). *History of Dougherty County, Georgia.* Albany, GA: Herald Publishing, 1924.

Davis, Burke. *Jeb Stuart: The Last Cavalier.* New York: Wings Books, 1957.

Davis, William C., and Julie Hoffman. *The Confederate General.* Harrisburg, PA: National Historical Society, 1991.

Emerson, W. Eric. *Sons of Privilege: The Charleston Light Dragoons in the Civil War.* Columbia: University of South Carolina Press, 2005.

Foote, Shelby. *The Civil War, a Narrative: Fredericksburg to Meridian.* New York: Random House, 1963.

_____. *The Civil War, a Narrative: Fort Sumter to Perryville.* New York: Random House, 1963.

Freeman, Douglas Southall, ed. *Lee's Dispatches.* New York: Putnam's, 1919.

Freeman, Douglas Southall. Abridgment by Stephen W. Sears. *Lee's Lieutenants IV.* New York: Scribner's, 1998.

_____. *R.E. Lee.* 4 vols. New York: Scribner's, 1934.

Grimsley, David A. *Actions in Culpeper County, Virginia, 1861–1865.* Culpepper, VA: Raleigh-Travers-Green, 1900.

Henderson, Lillian. (Director, Confederate Pension and Record Department, Georgia.) *Roster of the Confederate Soldiers of Georgia, 1861–1865.* 5 vols. Hapville, GA: Longina & Porter, 1960.

Henry, Robert Selph. *The Story of the Confederacy*. Indianapolis: Bobbs-Merrill, 1931.
Hutchinson, Olin Fulmer Jr., ed. *"My Dear Mother & Sisters,": Civil War Letters of Capt. A.B. Mulligan, Co. B, 5th South Carolina Cavalry–Butler's Division–Hampton's Corps*. Spartanburg, SC: Reprint, 1992.
Jamison, Jocelyn P. *They Died at Fort Delaware: 1861–1865, Confederate, Union and Civilian*. Fort Delaware Society, June 1997.
Johnson, Robert U., and Clarence C. Buel, eds. *Battles and Leaders of the Civil War*. 4 vols. New York: Century, 1884–88.
Johnston, Joseph E. *Narrative of Military Operations During the War Between the States*. New York: D. Appleton, 1872.
Kennedy, Frances H. *The Civil War Action Field Guide*. 2nd ed. New York and Boston: Conservation Fund, Houghton Mifflin, 1998.
Longacre, Edward G. *Gentleman and Soldier: The Extraordinary Life of General Wade Hampton*. Nashville: Rutledge Hill Press, 2003.
_____. *Custer and His Wolverines: The Michigan Cavalry Brigade, 1861–1865*. Conshohocken, PA: Combined Pub, 1997.
Lucas, Marion Brunson. *Sherman and the Burning of Columbia*. College Station: Texas A&M University Press, 1976.
McClellan, H.B. *The Life, Character and Campaigns of Major-Gen. J.E.B. Stuart*. Richmond: J.W. Randolph and English, 1880.
McClellan, Major Henry B. *I Rode with Jeb Stuart: The Life and Campaigns of Major General J.E.B. Stuart*. New York: Da Capo Press, 1958.
McSwain, Eleanor D., ed. *Crumbling Defenses, or Memoirs and Reminiscences of John Logan Black, Colonel, C.S.A*. Macon, GA: J.W. Burke, 1960.
Myers, F.M. *The Comanches: A History of White's Battalion, Virginia Cavalry, Laurel Brigade, Hampton Division, A.N.V., C.S.A*. Baltimore: Kelly, Piet, 1891.
Myers, Robert Manson, ed. *The Children of Pride: A True Story of Georgia and the Civil War*. New Haven and London: Yale University Press, 1972.
Ninety-Second Illinois Volunteers. Written by a committee appointed by the Reunion Committee of the 92nd Illinois Infantry Regiment. Freeport, IL: Journal Steam Publishing House and Bookbindery, 1875.
Pollard, E.A. *The Early Life, Campaigns and Public Services of Robert E. Lee, with a Record of the Campaigns and Heroic Deeds of His Companions in Arms*. Baton Rouge: LSU Press, 1870.
Priest, John Michael. *Antietam: The Soldier's Action*. New York: Oxford University Press, 1988.
Schenck, Martin. *Up Came Hill: The Story of the Light Division and Its Leaders*. Harrisburg, PA: Stackpole, 1958.
Sherman, William Tecumseh. *Memoirs of General W.T. Sherman*. Vol. 2 of 2 vols. New York: Appleton, 1875.
Stegeman, John F. *These Men She Gave: The Civil War Diary of Athens, Georgia*. Athens, GA: Iberian Publishing, 2000.
Swank, Walbrook D. (Col. USAF Ret.) *Eyewitness to War/1861–1865: Memoirs of Men Who Fought in the Action of Trevilian Station*. Charlottesville, VA: Papercraft Printing and Design, 1990.
Thomas, Emory M. *Bold Dragoon: The Life of J.E.B. Stuart*. Norman: University of Oklahoma Press, 1999.
Von Borcke, Heros. *Memoirs of the Confederate War for Independence*. Vol. 1. New York: Peter Smith, 1938.
War of the Rebellion: A Compilation of the Official Records of the Union and Confederate Armies. 128 vols. Washington, D.C.: United States Government Printing Office, 1880–1901.
Wellman, Manly Wade. *Giant in Gray: A Biography of Wade Hampton of South Carolina*. New York: Scribner's, 1949.
Wells, Edward L. *Hampton and His Cavalry in '64*. Richmond, VA: B.F. Johnson Publishing, 1899.
_____. *Hampton and Reconstruction*. Columbia, SC: State, 1907.
_____. *A Sketch of the Charleston Light Dragoons from the Earliest Formation of the Corps*. Charleston, SC: Lucas, Richardson, 1885.
Wheeler, Richard. *Voices of the Civil War: Antietam*. New York: NAL Dutton, 1990.
Wise, John S. *The End of an Era*. New York: Houghton Mifflin, 1899.
Wittenberg, Eric J. *Glory Enough for All: Sheridan's Second Raid and the Action of Trevilian Station*. Washington, D.C.: Brassey's, 2001.

Periodicals

The Athens (Georgia) Banner. Address given by Capt. Francis Edgeworth Eve on Confederate Memorial Day, April 26, 1893, to the citizens of Athens, Georgia (April 30, 1893)
Augusta (Georgia) Chronicle.
Blue & Gray 6, no. 1. "The Cavalry Clash at Quebec Schoolhouse: Cobb's Legion, CSA, and Medill's Union Horsemen Fight in the Shadow of South Mountain, Maryland, September 13, 1862" by Timothy J. Reese (February 1993) and "Gettysburg Cavalry Operations" by Ted Alexander
Civil War Times Illustrated. "The Real J.E.B. Stuart" by Emory M. Thomas (December 1989) and "The Affair at Hunterstown" by Col. Wilbur S. Nye (February 1971)
Confederate Veteran. Address given by Matthew Calbraith Butler to the Reunion of the Division U.C.V. on July 26, 1899 (January 1900), "Kilpatrick's Escape" by H.H. Scott, Scout for Hampton (Dec. 1904), and "Surrender of Cobb's Legion Cavalry" by Charles P. Hansell (October 1917)
Gettysburg: Historical Articles of Lasting Interest. "The Jeff Davis Legion at Gettysburg" (January 1995)

The National Tribune. "St. Mary's Church, Va.: A Rattling Fight by One of Gregg's Cavalry Brigades" by William M. Davis (June 12, 1890)

North & South. "The Cavalry Fight at Samaria Church: June 24, 1864" by Eric J. Wittenburg (February 2002)

Savannah Republican.

(Athens, Georgia) Southern Banner.

Southern Christian Advocate 1867–1878. Holcomb, Brent H., Columbia, SC (March, 1993)

Southern Historical Society Papers 8. "Address on the Life, Campaigns and Character of Gen'l J. E. B. Stuart" by H. B. McClellan (1880)

Other Sources

1850 United States Federal Census.
1860 United States Federal Census.
1870 United States Federal Census.
1880 United States Federal Census.
1900 United States Federal Census.
1910 United States Federal Census.
"8th GA Co A Rome Light Guards Roster." *www.home.earthlink.net/-larsrbl/CoA8thGARoster.htm.*
Administration of Estates and Wills Records, Georgia State Archives, Atlanta, Georgia.
Ancestry.com.
Compiled Service Records of Confederate Soldiers Who Served in Organizations from the State of Georgia, National Archives Microfilm Publications.
Florida Confederate Pension Records, www.floridamemory.com/collections/pensionfiles
"General Pierce Manning Butler Young, CSA." *History Central.* www.multied.com/Bio/CWcGENS/CSAYoung.html.
Georgia Confederate Pension Records, Georgia State Archives, Atlanta, Georgia.
Indexes of Vital Records for Georgia: Deaths, 1919–98. Georgia Health Department, Office of Vital Records, 1998.
Marcellus A. Stovall Collection, Reese Library, Augusta State University.
Memory Hill Cemetery Records, Baldwin County, Georgia.
Muster Roll Commission's Roster, Georgia State Archives, Atlanta, Georgia.
"Nelson's Sharps Carbine," www.talkingrelics.com/about2.html.
United Daughters of the Confederacy Cemetery Records, Helen Walpole Brewer Library, UDC Memorial Building, 328 North Boulevard, Richmond, Virginia 23220-4057.

Index

Abercrombie, Andrew Jackson 182, 329, 339
Abercrombie, Clement 182, 339
Abercrombie, John H. 144, 182–183, 334, 339
Abercrombie, William H. 183
Abercrombie, William Wiley 183, 339
Adams, C.H. 183
Adams, J.T. 14, 183, 326
Adams, James 183, 329
Adams, John T. 81, 183, 336, 342
Adams, S.D. 14, 183, 326, 329, 339
Adams, Thomas 57, 183, 326, 332
Adams, W.H. 183, 326, 329, 339
Adams, William 183, 342
Adcock, J.D. 183
Agerton, Thomas Jefferson 183–184, 329, 339
Ahern, Frank J. 184, 329
Aiken, Francis M.C. 184, 326, 329
Aiken, Hugh H. 144, 151, 159
Aiman, Emanuel 139, 184, 329
Albany, Georgia 6
Aldrich, Robert 123
Alexander, D.L. 184
Alexander, David J. 184
Alexander, John James 94, 184, 333
Alexander H. Stephens Museum 86
Alford, Augustus 53, 184, 326, 332
Algers, Napoleon B. 139, 184, 334
Allbritten, Isaac G. 144, 184–185, 338
Allbritten, James A. 10, 169, 185, 338, 339
Allbritten, Pleasant Griffin 185, 339
Allbritten, William A. 185, 339
Allen, Charles H. 185, 329
Allen, Ira 185, 326, 329
Allen, John C. 137, 185–186, 329
Allexander, Jo. Newton 186, 339
Allison, Noah 100, 186, 337
Americus, Georgia 92
Amissville, Virginia 44
Anderson, Edward A. 8, , 186, 326, 331
Anderson, John M. 113, 147, 186, 326, 334, 337
Anderson, Miles A. 7, 186, 326, 331
Anderson, Nicholas M. 186, 326, 329, 339
Anderson, Robert Branch 186, 339
Anderson, William E. 128, 135, 186–187, 326
Anderson, Young J. 187, 326

Anderson's Mill, South Carolina 156
Andrews, Thomas 187
Angle, Valentine 187, 342
Angley's Post Office, South Carolina 152–153
Anthony, Walter H. 187, 326, 339
Antietam Creek 25, 27–30
Appling, Edward Jones 164, 187, 326, 339
Appomattox (Court House), Virginia 169
Aquia Landing, Virginia 50, 53
Archer, John H. 187, 339
Archer, Thomas B. 6, 131, 187, 326
Armaments 5, 116
Armistead, David A. 187–188, 326, 329, 339
Armstrong's Mill 136, 145
Arnold, Charles M. 188, 326
Arnold, Givens W. 188
Arnold, Stephen T.B. 188
Armaments 5, 6, 105
Arrington, Owen H. 188, 339
Arthur's Swamp 144
Asbury, Jesse 188, 326, 329, 339
Ash, Henry N. 12, 331
Ash, John N. 131, 188
Ash, Thomas J. 188, 342
Ashby Gap 70
Ashe, N.D. 188, 342
Ashfield, J.M. 188, 326
Ashland, Virginia 11, 112
Ashmand, H.B. 27, 324, 335
Athens, Georgia 6
Atlanta, Georgia 6, 92, 151
Arlee's Station, Virginia 14, 111, 113, 116
Atterberry, Darling C. 188–189, 339
Atterberry, James D. 189
Auburn, Virginia 18, 96–97
Augusta Georgia 6, 148, 151, 174; Cavalry Survivors Association of Augusta 173; Museum of History 172–173; Powder Works 5
Autry, H.S. 189, 342
Avera, Thomas 189
Averell, Alfred M. 189
Avery, Archer 189, 329
Avery, John 189
Avery, Thomas 189
Aylett's (Station), Virginia 126

Bacon Race Church 53
Badger, Ralph Bostwick 189

Bailey, James H. 189
Bailey, James Holcomb 104, 189, 326, 333
Bailey, Oscar W. 189–190, 326
Bailey, Samuel W. 190, 326, 329
Bailey, William H. 190
Baker, Augustus C. 159, 190, 338, 339
Baker, Laurence Simmons 16, 69, 84, 88–89
Bale, James A. 190, 326
Ball, B.A. 61, 71, 190, 336, 342
Ball, J.C. 190
Ball, William B. 90
Baltimore & Ohio Railroad 21, 32, 34, 38, 75
Barbee's Cross Roads, Virginia 1, 41–42
Barber, Matthew S. 190
Barden, C.H. 105, 181, 190, 333
Barker, Elijah Henry Washington 190
Barker, Theodore G. 83
Barksdale 26, 190, 332
Barksdale, Green B. 26, 190–191, 326, 332
Barksdale, Samuel B. 191
Barnesville, Maryland 38, 191
Barnett's Ford, Virginia 102, 191
Barnwell, Thomas E. 191, 326
Barrett, James Riley 86, 191, 326, 329, 339
Barrett, Lewis Walton 14, 67, 191, 336, 342
Barrett, Thomas 81, 191, 326, 332
Barrett, Walton T. 10, 191, 326, 331
Barringer, Rufus 137
Barwick, George Ira 67, 191, 329
Bassett, Jefferson 172, 191, 326, 329
Bassford, Charles E. 45, 191–192, 326, 329, 339
Bassford, Solomon L. 71, 192, 329, 336
Bates, A.J. 192, 339
Bates, James 192, 342
Bates, William N. 192, 339
Battle's Bridge 169, 192
Baugh, Andrew T. 49, 160, 192, 336, 339
Baugh, Reuben P. 192
Baugh, Scott L. 192
Baxter, Daniel C. 120, 192, 326, 333, 338
Beale, R.L.T. 90

Beauregard, Pierre Gustave Toutant 151, 153–154
Beaverdam Station, Virginia 135
Beckham, Robert F. 61
Beckhamville, South Carolina 156
Bedell, Ethelbert Penn 14, 192, 326
Belches Mill 142
Belfield, Virginia 150
Bell, M.C. 192–193
Bell, Madison M. 193
Bell, Marlin M. 193, 326, 339
Bennett, Daniel 193, 339
Bennett, George W. 91, 193
Bennett, James A. 193, 326, 329
Bennett, John W. 193, 326
Bennett House 171, 193
Benton's Cross Roads, North Carolina 164–165
Bentonville, North Carolina 165–167
Bethel Church 94
Beverly, Joseph J. 193
Beverly's Ford, Virginia 60, 62–63, 66
Beverly's Ford Road 60, 63, 69
Big Black Creek 159
Big Lynch's Creek (Lynch's River) 159
Biles, Edwin R. 38
Bird, John P.M. 13, 193
Bird, William H. 150, 193, 334
Bishop, John J. 193, 326
Black, John Logan 64, 88, 90, 102
Black River 164
Black Soldiers 167
Blackburn, Josiah 193, 326
Blackford, William W. 27–28, 30, 36, 39, 75
Blackwater River 140–142
Blackwell, David Glenn 57, 194, 332
Blackwell, James M. 194
Blackwell, Josiah Sanford 194, 326, 339
Blakeny, South Carolina 159
Blanchard, Uriah 8, 194, 326, 331
Blount, A.H. 194, 339
Blount, William Augustus 194, 329
Blue Ridge Mountains 37, 41, 60, 69, 71
Blundell, C.J. 124, 194, 333
Blythewood, South Carolina 156
Boatright, Reuben 194
Boggs, Aaron H. 194
Boggs, Milton Alonza 194–195, 329, 339
Boler, Bennett 8, 195, 326, 331
Bolling, James 111, 195
Bonds, Flavius A. 195
Bone, Joseph H. 195
Bone, Willis C. 195, 326, 329
Booker, F. 195, 342
Boot Swamp 124
Born, Daniel M. 195, 329
Bostick, Samuel D. 6, 26, 31, 143, 163, 195, 326, 329, 339
Boston, Jerome M. 195
Bothwell, S.W. 195–196, 342
Bottom's Bridge 13, 102–103, 126
Bowen, Isaac 196 339

Bowen, James R. 196, 326
Bowers, Charles E. 196, 342
Bowie, Charles Lee 196, 326, 329
Bowie, John W. 196, 326
Bowie, William H.H. 196, 329, 339
Bowling Green, Virginia 102, 115
Bowman, George Grover 196, 326, 329, 339
Boyd, James William Walter 196–197
Boyd, Robert J. 197
Boyd, William 98, 197, 333
Boydton Plank Road 140, 145–147
Braddock's Gap 23
Bradford, J.A. 197
Bradley, Henry Stiles 92–93, 197, 326, 337
Brady, George W. 197, 329
Bragg, Braxton 104, 153, 165–166
Brandy Station, Virginia 1, 60–61, 63–64, 69, 71, 73, 88–89, 95, 175
Brent, James H. 46, 104, 197, 326, 333, 337
Brentsville, Virginia 73
Brian, Aaron 197, 331
Brian, Ezekiel 197
Brian, James 13, 197, 331
Brian, William Burr 197–198, 339
Brien, L. Tiernan 16
Brinson, N.M. 198
Bristoe Station, Virginia 73, 94, 97
Broad River 154
Broad Run 96
Broadway, James T. 27, 198, 326, 332, 335
Broadway, William A. 198, 326, 329
Bromley, George W. 198
Brook Turnpike 11
Brooks, Alonzo A. 102, 198, 339
Brooks, Cicero C. 81, 198, 333
Brooks, John N. 67, 198, 336, 339
Brooks, Thomas D. 67, 198–199, 329, 336
Brooks, U.R. 84, 123
Brookshear, Green W. 199, 339
Broom, James 199, 329
Broome, Joseph 199
Brown, Allen 199, 342
Brown, Henry 199
Brown, James F. 199, 342
Brown, Jesse T. 199, 339
Brown, Matthew L. 199, 329, 339
Brown, Milton A. 159
Brown, R.J. 58, 199, 326, 332
Brown, Ridgeley 90
Brown, Tilman H. 67, 99, 199, 333
Bruce, Aquilla 18, 199, 326, 332
Brumley, George W. 199, 329
Bryan, G.W. 199
Bryan, James A 112, 199–200, 337
Bryan, Matthew 200, 326
Bryant, Burrell 200
Bryant, Wellington L. 67, 200, 339
Bryant, William N. 93, 99, 200, 333, 337
Bryce, George B. 200, 326
Bryson, William 10, 200

Buckingame, L. 200
Buckland, Virginia 97
Buckland Ford 96
Buckland Mills, Virginia 73
Buckland Races 96–97
Buffington, O.M. 16, 200, 331
Buford, John 61, 63, 66, 69
Bull Run Creek 96–97
Bull Run Mountains 69, 71–72
Bull Run, Second Battle of 18
Bulloch, John Hawkins 67, 200, 329, 336
Bunch, S.J. 150, 200–201
Bunch Hill 200, 326
Bunker Hill, West Virginia 30, 41
Burford, Drewry 201, 326
Burgess, R.U. 201
Burgess Mill, Virginia 145–147
Burke County Georgia 6
Burke's Station, Virginia 54
Burkeville, Virginia 129
Burkhalter, David C.N. 201, 326, 339
Burkittsville, Maryland 1, 23–26
Burnett, Causby D. 201, 329, 339
Burnett, Daniel L. 68, 201
Burnley, Stephen Franklin 12, 201, 331
Burnside, Ambrose E. 44, 50, 52, 56–58
Burr, John Howard 6, 13, 147, 150, 201, 326, 334, 335
Burton, Robert H. 201–202, 329
Burtz, Richard P. 86, 87, 202, 333
Butler, Benjamin F. 133, 143, 145, 147, 149
Butler, Col. 63
Butler, J.J. 202, 326
Butler, Matthew Calbraith 16, 35–38, 50, 67, 89, 95, 105, 109–110, 113, 117–119, 120, 122–123, 126–128, 131, 134, 137, 140, 142–146, 148–149, 154–159, 161–162, 164, 167, 173, 177–178
Butler, Nat 146
Butler, Robert 202
Byne, John Randolph 43, 202, 329, 339
Byrd, John P.M. 202
Byrd, William H. 136, 202, 334

Cabell County, West Virginia 83
Calaway, Jesse 202, 329
Calaway, Joseph Woodson Brown 202, 329, 339
Calhoun, Edward Livingston 202–203, 339
Calhoun, Pickens Noble 16, 203, 332
Calloway, J.M. 203, 342
Camback, Charles L. 46, 105, 203, 337
Camden Road 154, 159
Camden, South Carolina 157
Camfield, Caleb Halstead 6, 203, 326
Camp, Dilmus McPherson 203, 339
Camp Marion, Virginia 7
Camp Maynard, Georgia 6

Camp Meadow, Virginia 8, 9, 10
Camp No Camp, Virginia 46
Camp Randolph, North Carolina 8
Camp Washington, Virginia 6
Campbell, John L. 203
Cane's Farm 124
Cannon, John 203
Cantey's Plantation 157–158
Cantrell, Alfred Webb 203, 329, 339
Cantrell, John H. 203, 339
Cantrell, Starlin Blackwell 203–204
Cape Fear River 161, 164
Capitol Dome 75
Carey, Silas Jennings 204, 329, 339
Carley, W.W. 204
Carlisle, Pennsylvania 77–78
Carpenter, J.P. 204, 326
Carpenter's Ford, Virginia 117, 120, 126
Carroll, J. 204
Carroll, Robert C. 204, 326
Carter, Albert W.J. 14, 59, 204, 326, 332
Carter, Bennett H. 67, 204, 332
Carter, Oscar L. 68, 136, 204, 329, 336, 339
Carter, R.W. 90
Carter's Wharf 9
Casey, Michael G. 204, 339
Cash, Noah B. 204, 326, 339
Cashtown, Pennsylvania 37
Cashtown Pass 78
Cassell, E.T. 204–205, 339
Catawba River 157
Cates, John (Co. F) 205
Cates, John (Co. L) 205
Cates, John J. 205, 329, 339
Cates, T.W. 68, 205, 332
Cates, Thomas 205, 329, 339
Catharpin Road 100, 109
Catoctin Creek Bridge 23
Catoctin Mountain 23, 37
Cattle Raid 140–143
Cattlet's Station, Virginia 18
Cavanaugh, William F. 205, 326, 329
Cedar Run 52
Cemetery Hill 84
Centreville, Virginia 71, 124
Chaffin's Bluff, Virginia 130, 135
Chambers, James Buregard 14, 205, 335, 339
Chambersburg, Pennsylvania 34, 36–38, 40, 41, 142
Chambliss, John Randolph 69, 71, 75–76, 83, 90, 127, 135
Chancellorsville, Virginia 55, 58
Chandler, Frank 205, 326
Chandler, Green W.W. 205
Chandler, Robert 205, 339
Chantilly Plantation, Virginia 19–20
Charles City (Court House), Virginia 14, 18, 127, 128, 135
Charles City Road 135
Charleston, South Carolina 151, 153–154, 159
Charlestown, West Virginia 41

Charlotte, North Carolina 156–157, 163, 170, 172
Charlotte & Columbia Railroad 156
Charlottesville, Virginia 87, 115
Charlottesville Road 120
Chastain, Anderson 205
Chatham, J.W. 205, 339
Chatham, Thomas J. 85, 101, 205, 333, 336
Chatham, William C. 206
Chavous, Allen 87, 206, 337
Chavous, James F. 8, 206, 326, 331
Chavous, John L. 206, 339
Chavous, Walter H. 148, 150, 206, 329, 339
Cheesboro, John Weaver 61, 206, 326, 332
Cheraw, South Carolina 156, 158–159
Cherry, John P. 206, 326
Chesapeake & Ohio Canal 74, 75
Chesapeake & Ohio Railroad 115
Chesnut, James B. 104–105, 154
Chesnut, Mary Boykin 154, 158
Chesterfield (Court House), South Carolina 159–160
Chesterfield Road 159
Chesterfield (Station), Virginia 111, 115, 124
Chestnut Hill 96
Chickahominy River 9, 11, 13, 102, 113, 126–127
Childers, Thomas M. 206, 342
Chilesburg, Virginia 124, 126
Chisolm, Seaborn W. 27, 206, 332, 335
Christian, James E. 206, 329, 339
Christman, John 207, 326, 339
Church, William Lee 66, 70, 172–173, 207, 326
The Citadel 119
City Point, Virginia 114, 140
Clanton, James Luke 44, 66, 68, 81, 87, 207, 326
Clark, James I. 207
Clark, James Thomas 207, 329, 339
Clark, John William 14, 207–208, 326
Clark, L. 208
Clark, T. 208
Clark, T.H. 52
Clark, Thomas Simmons 208, 329
Clark, W.H. 208
Clarke County, Georgia 6
Clarkson, William O. 208
Clayton, John M. 72, 208
Clayton, Josiah N. 137, 208, 334
Clayton's Store, Virginia 117
Clingan, Robert T. 14, 31, 208, 332
Clitt, George 208, 329
Cloud, Dr. 156
Cobb, Howell 8
Cobb, James M. 68, 87, 208–209, 337
Cobb, Thomas Reade Rootes 3, 7–8, 9, 11, 13, 32, 51, 180
Cobb County, Georgia 6
Cochran, J.S. 209, 329

Cochran, J.T. 209, 326
Cochran, John N. 209
Cochran, William B. 8, 209, 326, 331
Cockletown, Virginia 7
Coggin's Point, Virginia 140–142
Cold Harbor, Virginia 11–12, 110, 113, 114, 124, 170
Cole, J.P. 209
Coleman, Hosey W. 209
Coleman, James Augustus 209, 329
Coleman, Phil Newton 209
Coleman, Pleasant 209, 329
Coleman, Welcome Lafayette 209
Coleman, William 209, 329, 339
Cole's Store 52–53
Collier, Edward Wyatt 112, 210, 337
Collins, William J. 210, 329, 339
Columbia, South Carolina 151, 153–156
Columbia County, Georgia 6, 210
Colvin, Thomas Jefferson 210, 333
Comary, Col. 164
Company Shops, North Carolina 172
Cone, William T. 57, 210, 326
Confederate Artillery 63, 111, 114, 116, 120, 138, 159, 166; 1st Battery, MD Cavalry 90; 35th Battery, VA Cavalry 90; Beckham's Horse Artillery 60, 63; Cobb's Legion Troupe Artillery 7, 84; Fitz Lee's 96–97, 118; Hampton's Horse Artillery 126, 165, 166; Hardee's (Artillery and Engineers) 160; Hart's 66, 120, 122, 145–147, 149; Hill's 138; Jackson's 31, 58; Maryland 49; McGregor's 150; Stuart's Horse Artillery 35, 41, 74, 91, 95; Thompson's 120, 122
Confederate Cavalry: (Army of Northern Virginia) 69, 87–88, 108–111, 134, 138, 146–147, 160–161, 165; Barringer's 137; Butler's 39, 89, 97, 105, 112, 113–114, 116–120, 131, 133, 135–138, 140–141, 143–144, 146–151, 154–155, 156, 158–159, 162–164; Chambliss' 74, 81–83, 105, 127–128, 131, 137; Davis' 137–138; Dearing's 136, 140–143, 146, 149–150; Dulany's 128; Dunovant's 137; Ferguson's 82–83; Fitzhugh "Fitz" Lee's 41, 53, 55–56, 60, 63, 66, 71, 74, 77, 82, 84, 96–97, 102, 105, 108, 117–118, 120, 122–123, 126, 131, 133–134, 151; Gary's 128, 135; Georgia 79, 113, 156, (7th) 117, 119–120, (10th) 170–171, (20th) 120, (Cobb's [Cobb] Legion Cavalry) 3, 6, 65, 134, 160, 162, (Phillip's Legion) 3, 46, 53, 79, 83, 88, 89, 117, 119–120, 128, 134, 169–170; Gordon's 94–95, 97, 98, 100, 102, 104–105, 108, 115; Griffin's 143–144; Grumble Jones' 61, 63, 64, 69, 71, 115; Hampton's 5, 10, 14, 18, 21–23, 25–27, 32, 35–37, 41, 44, 46, 48, 54, 56–58,

61–64, 67, 69–71, 73, 75–83, 88, 91, 93–94, 96–97, 99–100, 102, 104–106, 108–109, 111–112, 115, 117, 122–123, 126–129, 131–134, 136–138, 140, 142–144, 146, 149–151, 154, 156, 158, 160–169, 172; Hardee's Corps 151, 153, 157, 165, 167; Jenkins' 82–83; Lomax's Brigade 127; Mississippi (Jeff Davis Legion) 1, 11, 16, 23, 50, 53–54, 62, 69–70, 89, 108, 110, 117, 119–120, 126, 128, 145, 158, 168–170; Munford's 23, 60; North Carolina 114, 138, 150, 156, (1st) 16, 46, 50, 53, 63, 67, 69–70, 83–84, 88–90, 109, (2nd) 76, 90, (4th) 90, (5th) 90; Robertson's 60, 62–63, 69–71; Rooney Lee's 32, 38, 41, 53, 56, 58, 60, 63, 71, 74, 76, 108, 112, 116, 127, 129–130, 135–137, 140, 143–144, 146–147, 150–151; Rosser's 95, 97, 100, 104–105, 108, 111–113, 116–117, 119–122, 131, 137, 140–142, 145; Shenandoah Valley Cavalry 35; South Carolina 69, 79, 112–113, 156, (1st) 46, 50, 53, 62, 64, 69, 88, 90, (2nd) 22, 46, 50, 52–53, 63, 67, 79, 88–89, (4th) 119–120, 158, (5th) 119–120, 146, (6th) 119–120, 123, (Charleston Light Dragoons) 110, 168, (Hampton Legion) 16; Stuart's Cavalry 14, 17, 20, 21–23, 28, 32, 37–39, 54, 60, 69–71, 73, 75–78, 108–109; Tennessee (4th) 166; Texas (8th) 166–167; Virginia 46, 49, 55–57, 79, 91, (1st) 11, 16, 90, 120, (2nd) 21, 26, 90, 120, (3rd) 16, 90, 120, (4th) 11, 16, 63, 90, 120, (5th) 16, 90, 95, 120, (6th) 64, 90, 120, (7th) 90, 120, (9th) 11 , 16, 90, (10th) 16, 90, (11th) 90, 120, (12th) 64, 90, 120, (13th) 90, (14th) 90, (15th) 90, 120, (35th) 64, 120; [West] Virginia (Laurel Brigade) 35, 119, 128, 137, 143; Wheeler's 151, 154, 156, 158, 163; Wickham's 63, 67, 112, 128; Wright's 116–117, 119, 120–122, 126; Young's 6, 85, 98, 100, 102, 104, 105–106, 108, 113, 115, 134, 137, 140–141, 146, 151, 154, 170

Confederate Forces 14, 18, 31, 76, 84, 129, 161, 166; Army of Northern Virginia 9, 19, 87, 94, 108, 134, 168, 175; Army of Tennessee 146, 151, 156; Army of the Peninsula 7, 9; Beauregard's Army 154, 157; Dubose's 3; Hood's Army 153, 156; Johnston's Army 9, 146, 157, 164–166, 169; Lee's Army 19, 21–22, 26, 28, 58, 69, 71, 74, 77, 85, 95, 108, 113, 114, 139, 140, 143, 145, 149, 171; Magruder's 9

Confederate Infantry 87, 88, 94, 97, 110–112, 114, 130–131, 138, 159, 165–166; Bragg's Corps 90, 153, 156; Cobb's Legion Infantry 7, 51, 58; Early's 108; Ewell's 60, 85, 87; Field's 136; Georgia 159, 166; Heth's 137, 144, 146; Hill's (A.P.) 60, 85, 88, 95, 136–137, 146, 149; Hill's (D.H.) 23; Hoke's 153, 156, 165, 166; Jackson's 11, 17, 20, 31, 41, 49, 109; Kershaw's 3; Lee's 142; Longstreet's 3, 17, 41, 44, 46, 49, 60, 85, 90; Mahone's 131; Pickett's 84; Stevenson's 153; Stonewall Brigade 113

Confederate Pensions 174, 181
Congaree River 151, 154
Connelly, William Curran 210, 326
Conococheague Creek 34, 36
Conrad's Ferry, Maryland 38
Cook, George W.D. 210, 326
Cook, Joshua C. 210, 326
Cook's Bridge 140
Cook's Mill 141
Cooley, John 210
Cooper, Fred L. 210–211
Cooper, John M. 211, 326, 329
Cooper, R.E. 211, 326
Copeland, Wiley R. 211, 329, 339
Corlew, Thomas 211
Corley, M. 211
Cory, Othniel E. 81, 211, 336, 342
Cosnahan, Thomas J. 211, 329, 339
Costello, Charles H. 211, 326
Coston, John 14, 211, 326, 329, 339
Cotter, Isaac 211
Couch, B.H. 212
Couparle, Leroy Isadore 58, 212
Cowart, Samuel L. 68, 212, 329, 336
Cowen, Edward W. 147, 212, 334, 339
Cowen, Elijah D. 53, 212, 326, 332
Cowen, John H. 18, 212, 326, 332
Cowen, Stephen D. 212, 329, 339
Cox, James A 133, 212, 326
Craby, Pat 212
Crampton's Gap, Maryland 26–27
Crawford, Capt. 76, 78–79
Crawfordville, Georgia 86
Crawley, Joshua 212, 329
Cress's Ridge 82–83
Crew's Bridge 167
Criglersville, Virginia 94
Cross, Rufus. 212–213, 329, 339
Crumley, William Macon 14, 213
Culpeper County, Virginia 50, 73, 91
Culpeper (Court House), Virginia 44, 46, 49, 54, 58, 60, 63, 91, 93–95, 97, 135
Cumberland Valley Railroad Bridge 34
Cunningham Farm 63
Curran, James 96, 213, 333
Custer, George Armstrong 62, 79, 83, 96–97, 112, 115, 118–120
Cutter, Joseph S. 213, 326, 342

Dagnell, Elisha J. 213, 329, 339
Dahlgren, Ulric 213
Dalvigny, Charles F.S. 213, 329
Dan River 171
Daniel, Julius Foster 213, 329
Daniel, Theodore Floyd 27, 169, 213–214, 326, 335, 338
Daniel, W.C. 214
Danville Railroad 129, 138
Darbytown Road 145
Darkesville, West Virginia 35
Darnestown, Maryland 75
Davenport, Joseph T. 214, 329
David, John White 113, 214, 326, 334, 337
Davies, Henry E. 142
Davis, Benjamin 139, 214
Davis, Benjamin F. "Grimes" 62–63
Davis, Benjamin J. 214
Davis, Cyrus C. 214, 326
Davis, D.R. 71, 214, 336, 342
Davis, Daniel 214–215, 339
Davis, J. Lucius 90, 137
Davis, Jefferson 56, 134, 151, 170–172
Davis, L.B. 215, 326
Davis, R.G. 215, 342
Davis, William L. 215, 329, 339
Davis, William S. 215, 329, 339
Davis, William W. 215, 329, 339
Davis, Zimmerman 146–147
Dawson, James B. 100, 215
Day, James Walter 71, 215, 336
Dead-line Camp 55, 69, 123, 133, 148
Dearing, James 136, 141
Dearing, William P. 18, 215, 335
Deep Bottom, Virginia 135
DeJarnette's Ford, Virginia 124
DeKalb County, Georgia 6
Delony, William Gaston 6, 12, 17, 32, 41, 43–44, 51, 65–67, 73, 79–81, 85, 89, 91–94, 215–216, 326, 333, 337
Dempsey, Harrington E. 216, 342
Densmore, Abel B.C. 10, 216, 326, 331
Dent, Albert F. 216
Dent, Alexander F. 216, 329
Dent, Stephen P. 216
Deriso, J.D. 216, 326, 339
Deriso, James M. 216, 329, 339
Dial, Tully John 216
Dial, William Choice 6, 45, 216–217
Dickens, B.L. 46, 114, 216–217, 326, 338
Dickerson, Augustus C. 217, 339
Dickinson, Walter M. 217, 326
Dickson, William Capers 112, 217, 337
Dill, James S. 217, 339
Dillsburg, Pennsylvania 78
Dinwiddie (Court House), Virginia 137
Dispatch Station Virginia 1, 12
Dixon, James A. 217, 329, 339
Dodgen, James Anison 217, 329
Dodgen, John W. 217, 329, 339
Doko, South Carolina 156
Donnan, M.T. 49, 324, 332
Donohue, Martin 217, 329
Donor, J. Henry 58, 217–218, 332

Doris, Bernard 218, 339
Dorkins Branch 18
Dorris, John 155, 218, 338
Dosier, J.S. 218, 326, 329
Double Bridge 149
Doubleday, G. 27, 324, 335
Dougherty, David H. 92–93, 218
Dougherty, Henry R. 218, 329
Dougherty, John 218, 342
Dougherty County, Georgia 6
Douglas, G.C. 218, 326
Dover, Augustus 218, 329
Dover, Pennsylvania 77
Downs, Elias Crockett 14, 218, 329, 339
Downs, Lindsey Warren 218–219
Downs, William W. 219, 342
Dozier, John Stapler 46, 93, 175, 219
Dozier, William L. 219
Drake, Augustus 150, 165, 219
Drake, James Madison 219, 339
Dranesville, Virginia 20, 73
Drinkwater, John W. 219, 326, 329, 339
Duckett, Berry T. 219, 329, 339
Duke, James H. 219–220, 329
Dulany, Richard H. 90, 128
Dumfries, Virginia 1, 50–51, 53, 55
Dunker Church 29
Dunn, William W. 170, 220, 338
Dunahoo, James 67, 220, 332
Dunnahoo, Thomas Jordan v, vii, 138, 161, 169–170, 220, 334
Dunovant, John 137, 141, 144
Durden, Berrien Walter 220, 329, 339
Durham Station, North Carolina 171
Dyes, John 220

Early, Alfred W. 220, 326, 329
Early, Joseph G. 220, 329
Early, Jubal Anderson 77, 108, 135
Early, Lemuel 220
Early, William H. 12, 220–221, 326, 329, 339
Early, Williamson F. 113, 221, 326, 333
Eason, Augustus 221
East Berlin, Pennsylvania 77
Eaton, Robert H. 221
Ebenezer Church 142
Eckles, Joel D. 221
Edward, Samuel 221, 329
Edward, William 221, 329
Edwards, Edward H. 221, 326
Edwards, J.F. 221, 339
Elk Ridge 26
Elmira Prison 120
Ely's Ford, Virginia 99, 106
Emanuel, Columbus 221, 329
Emmittsburg, Maryland 37–38
Epps, Joseph A. 221, 329
Essex County, Virginia 56
Evans, James M. 27, 85, 221, 333, 335
Evans, Jasper 147, 221
Evans, Justinian 221–222, 329
Evans, Richard Jones 222, 329, 339

Evans, Stephen B. 90
Eve, Francis Edgeworth 6, 14, 17, 18, 46, 65, 91–93, 112, 174, 179, 222
Everett, J.B. 222, 326, 329, 339
Everett, John G. 222
Ewell, Richard Stoddert 12, 60, 71, 77–78, 80, 111
Ezzard, John F. 221

Fairfax, Virginia 20, 54, 73
Fairfield, Pennsylvania 85
Falling Waters, West Virginia 28, 85
Falls Church, Virginia 54
Falmouth, Virginia 56
Fanning, William P. 222, 339
Farnsworth, John 23, 62, 76
Farr, John Hayes 222–223, 329
Farrow, Alfred A. 223
Fayetteville, North Carolina 1, 161, 163–164, 171
Fayetteville (Plank) Road 161
Felty's Barn 79–80
Fenn, E. 223
Ferebee, Dennis D. 90
Ferguson, Lorenzo D. 223, 339
Ferguson, Milton J. 82
Fesler, Daniel 223, 329, 339
Fesler, Jacob 223, 329
Fesler, John 223, 329
Few, Marcus C. 223, 326, 329
Field, Charles William 136
Fields, Julius J. 67, 158, 223, 326, 336, 338, 339
Fields, Levi C. 223–224, 326, 329, 339
Fields, Richard J. 224, 326, 329
Fife, Robert A. 224, 329
Finch, William 45, 224, 326
Fish, Andrew J. 54, 224, 326, 329, 339
Fishing Creek 156–157
Fitzjerrald, James 224
Fleetwood Hill 60, 63–66, 95
Fleming, James A. 224
Fleming, John A.W. 124, 224–225, 329, 339
Fleming, Samuel P. 93, 225, 329, 339
Fleming, William W. 225, 329, 339
Flint Hill Road 43
Force, Manning F. 152
Ford, J.D. 91, 94, 225, 326, 333
Ford, Lewis R. 14, 225, 326, 329
Ford, Thomas 225
Forge Bridge, Virginia 13
Forrest, Nathan Bedford 154
Fort Delaware Prison 34
Fort Monroe, Virginia 8, 10
Fort Powhatan, Virginia 141
Fortson, Richard Eaton 225–226, 339
Foster, Felix Walker 226, 329, 339
Foster, James H. 40, 226, 332
Foster, Robert Thomas 226
Foust, William 226
Fowler, H.M. 27, 124, 226, 326, 333, 335

Fox's Gap, Maryland 26
Francisco, John 226
Fraser, J. Harvey 150, 226, 334
Frederick City, Marylnd 1, 21–23, 26, 38
Fredericksburg, Virginia 17, 18, 44, 46, 49–51, 56–58, 60, 111
Fredericksburg Road 108
Freeman, A. John 58, 226, 332
Freeman's Ford, Virginia 142
Frie, Martin J. 88, 226, 337, 342
Friedenthal, Morris 226–227, 329
Frix, Julius Michael 8, 227, 326, 331
Frying Pan, Virginia 54
Frying Pan Church 1, 96
Fulcher, William 227, 329, 339
Fulton County, Georgia 6
Funkstown, Maryland 32
Funsten, O.R. 90
Fussell's Mill, Virginia 136

Gabbett, William 227, 326
Gaine's Cross-Roads, Virginia 44
Gaines Mill, Virginia 11
Gainesville, Virginia 73, 96–97
Galaway, William L. 58, 227, 332, 339
Gallaher, Patrick 45, 227, 326
Gallaway, George T. 71, 227
Gallaway, W.L. 227, 326, 329
Gamblin, John L. 227, 329
Gantt, Adolphus S. 14, 227
Gardner, Nathaniel Edward 227, 326
Garner, James H. 8, 228, 326, 331
Garron, John S. 228, 326
Garvin, William F.K. 167, 173, 228, 338, 339
Gary, Martin W. 127
Gay, Thomas 106, 228, 342
Gee House 63
General Store (Hunterstown) 81
Georgia Archives 175
Germanna Ford, Virginia 99, 111
Gettysburg, Pennsylvania 37, 58, 60, 75–81, 84–85, 87, 94
Gettysburg & Hanover Railroad 81
Gibson, C. 228
Gibson, James E. 228, 329
Gibson, Jesse C. 112, 228, 326, 337
Gilbert, Jasper Norman 228, 329, 339
Gilbert Home 81
Gillespie, Milton William 228
Gillespie, William P. 228, 339
Gilmer, Albert C. 229
Gilmer, Ezekiel Francis 16, 229, 331
Gilstrap, Benjamin D. 229, 342
Givens, George W. 229, 329
Givens, William 157, 229, 338, 339
Gladden's Grove, South Carolina 156
Glasscock's Gap 72
Glaze, Jacob Harris 229, 339
Glaze, James M. 86, 229
Glaze, John H. 229
Gleaton, Dudley C. 229–230, 329, 339

Glenn, James R. 230, 326
Glenn, Joseph T. 230, 326
Globe Tavern 136
Godbee, William T. 230, 339
Godfrey, David P. 27, 49, 230, 326, 336
Goff, James H. 124, 230, 339
Goff, William Henry 230, 339
Goldsboro, North Carolina 8, 155, 157, 165, 167, 168
Goldsboro Road 164
Gondelock, Robert W. 14, 230, 326
Goode, Thomas F. 16
Goodman, Nathan 14, 230, 326
Goodwin, Jacob 230
Goodwin, William E. 68, 230–231, 329, 339
Goose Creek 69
Goose Creek Bridge 69–70
Gordon, Elijah A. 231
Gordon, James 231, 329, 339
Gordon, James A. 231, 329
Gordon, James Byron 50, 66, 90, 109
Gordon, Samuel J.L. 67, 231, 329, 336, 339
Gordonsville, Virginia 17, 115, 123, 150
Gordonsville Road 116–117, 119, 120–122
Goss, Francis M. 81, 231, 336, 342
Goswick, W.H. 231
Gouche's Ferry, South Carolina 157
Gough, Joseph Simeon 231, 330, 339
Gower, Thomas C. 33, 231, 327, 335
Graffan, Andrew J. 88, 231, 337, 342
Graham, James S. 231–232, 342
Graham, J.W. 232
Gramling, John R. 232, 330
Grand Reviews 60, 89
Grant, Ulysses S. 4, 100, 104, 106, 108, 111, 113–115, 123–124, 129, 134–135, 140, 143, 145, 148, 151, 167–168
Grapevine Bridge 13
Grass Hotel 81
Gravelly Run 145–146, 148
Gray, Bessie Lee Humhreys vii
Gray, Joseph 232, 342
Gray, William M.D. 232, 330, 339
Green, Clement C. 31, 232
Green, G.C. 232
Green, G.M. 232
Green, John Shac 90
Green, James 232
Green, Jesse P. 232
Green, Lucius R. 232
Green, Sanders 232
Green, T.G. 232
Green County, Virginia 124
Green Spring, Virginia 123
Green Spring Valley 116
Green's House 63
Greensboro, North Carolina 143, 172–174
Greensboro Road 172
Greenwood Church 53

Greer, Henry N. 232–233, 339
Greer, Robert Simeon 233, 339
Greer, William A. 233, 339
Gregg, David McMurtrie 61, 63–64, 69–70, 112, 128–129, 142, 145, 148
Gregory, John Jefferson 233, 339
Griffeth, David Alexander 233
Griffin, Eli 233, 327
Griffin, Joel R. 143
Grimes, Allen T. 233, 330
Grimes, Newton J. 233–234
Grindle, Berry T. 21, 234, 327, 332
Grindle, Daniel 234, 327
Griswoldville, Georgia 5
Grove Church 57
Groves, Jasper B. 14, 234, 339
Groveton, Virginia 96
Groveton Heights, Virginia 18
Grubbs, James, Jr. 234, 330, 339
Guard, David S. 234
Guedron, Alexander C. 46, 234, 327, 330, 339
Guedron, John C. 234, 327
Guiney's [Guinea's] Station, Virginia 10, 102
Gulick, Joseph H. 234, 342
Gulley's, North Carolina 168
Gum Springs, Virginia 73, 96
Gunby, William T. 234, 327, 330
Guthrie, William M.R. 234–235
Gwinnett County, Georgia 6

Haesler, Samuel Burchardt 58, 235, 327, 330, 336, 339
Hagerstown, Maryland 37, 85
Haines, John Schley 46, 235, 327
Halifax Road 137
Ham, John Dalton 235, 330, 339
Hamby, John 235
Hamilton, Archibald N. 235, 339
Hamilton, George W. 235
Hamilton, Jacob W. 235, 327
Hammond, John W. 61, 153, 235, 334, 336
Hampton, D.B. 235
Hampton, Frank 67
Hampton, J.R. 235
Hampton, Mary Fisher 54, 56, 136
Hampton, Preston 64, 146–147
Hampton, Gen. Wade viii, 3, 16, 22–26, 32, 35–36, 46–48, 50–54, 56–57, 60, 64, 66–67, 69–70, 78–81, 83–85, 89–90, 94, 98–100, 103–105, 108–110, 111–113, 116–120, 122–124, 126–136, 138–147, 149–151, 153–159, 161–165, 167–172, 174–175, 177–179
Hampton, Wade, IV 146–147
Hancock, Robert Jackson 235–236, 327, 339
Hancock, William Dawson 236, 327
Hancock, Winfield Scott 137–139, 145–146
Hanging Rock, South Carolina 156–157
Hanlon, James W. 124, 236, 327, 330, 339
Hanlon, Michael 13, 150, 236, 335

Hannah's Creek 167
Hanover (Court House), Virginia 14, 114
Hanover Junction, Virginia 111
Hanover, Pennsylvania 76–77
Hanovertown Ferry 112
Hansell, Charles 171
Harben, John D.D. 87, 236, 336
Hardee, William Joseph 151, 159, 161, 165–167
Hardford, F. 236
Hardwick, George Washington 236, 327
Hardwick, William 67, 236, 332
Hardy, Augustus F. 67, 236, 332
Hardyman, B.L. 236
Harman, A.W. 90
Harman, T. Moore 237, 342
Harper, Anselin 237, 327, 330, 339
Harper, George 237
Harper, William 237
Harpers Ferry, West Virginia 26–27, 32, 41
Harrington, Charles 81, 237, 333
Harris, Charles R.A. 14, 46, 105, 237, 327, 337
Harris, George W. 237, 339
Harris, Henry S. 237, 327, 339
Harris, James A. 16, 237, 331
Harris, James M. 86, 237, 336, 340
Harris, Morris 86, 237–238, 336
Harris, P.S. 238
Harris, Richard D. 108, 238, 340
Harris, Tira 238, 330
Harris, William 10, 324, 331
Harrison, William O. 14, 238, 3330
Harrison's Landing 14, 18
Hart, James F. 116, 145–147
Hartford, Frank 71, 238, 336, 342
Hartsfield, James M. 46, 238
Hartwood Church 46
Hatch, James A. 81, 238, 342
Hatcher's Run 1, 143, 145–147, 149
Hatfield, William H. 238, 327, 330
Hauser, William C. 238–239
Haw's Shop 112–113
Haxall's Creek 13–14
Haymarket, Virginia 1, 72–73, 96–97
Haynes, E.T. 239
Hays, A.D. 239
Hays, Dwight David 14, 239, 327, 330, 335, 340
Hays, John B. 73, 239, 327, 336
Hazel River 60, 95
Hazel Run 49–50
Head, George W. 239, 342
Head, James M. 143, 239, 338
Head, Joshua J. 239, 327
Hedgesville, West Virginia 35
Heffernan, William D. 88, 239, 337
Heidlersburg, Pennsylvania 78
Helton, William J. 8, 239, 327, 331
Henderson, James 239–240
Henderson, R.J. 166
Henry, James E. 43, 240, 330, 335
Henry of Navarre 92
Herring Creek 13–14

Heth, Henry 137, 146
Hewit, John J. 240, 340
Hicksford, Virginia 148–150
Hicksford Road 133
Higdon, John T. 69, 102, 240
Higgons, Dan 69, 240, 332
High, E.D. 114, 240, 327, 338
High Point, North Carolina 172
Hill, Ambrose Powell 136–139, 146, 149–150
Hill, Daniel Harvey 87
Hill, George B. 240
Hill, James 240, 340
Hill, James A. 240
Hill, John P. 57, 240, 332
Hill, Joseph N. 148, 240–241, 338
Hill, Moses R. 53, 241, 332
Hill, R.D. 241
Hill, Simeon William 76, 241, 336, 342
Hillens, Henry 12, 241, 327, 331
Hillsboro, North Carolina 170–172
Hillsboro Road 165
Himsborough, South Carolina 159
Hines, John R. 241
Hine's Road 141
Hinton, John Jefferson 241, 330
Hitt, D.W. 241
Hodo, Joel 241, 340
Hogan, Dennis 87, 241, 336
Hogrefe, Fred 147, 241, 338
Hoke, Robert Frederick 153, 166
Holcombe 241, 342
Holeman, W.B. 59, 241, 332
Hood, John Bell 153
Hood, Richard 241
Hood, William C. 242, 340
Hooker, Joseph 58, 61, 109
Hope, Alexander 14, 242, 331
Hopewell Gap 71
Hopkins, Cary J. 242, 327, 342
Hopkins, John D. 242, 330, 340
Hopkins, William W. 119
Horses (condition of) 4, 41, 55–57, 91, 102, 104–105, 133, 150, 161, 172, 181
Hough, John 242, 340
House, James S. 16, 242, 331
House, Tom 22
Houser, William C. 14, 242, 330
Houston, John Dougherty 161, 242, 327, 330, 340
Howard, Francis Reeves 153, 242
Howard, George Henry 242, 330, 340
Howard, Joseph Robert 114, 242, 333
Howard, Oliver O. 166
Howard, Wiley Chandler 1, 22, 58, 65, 92, 109–110, 119, 123–124, 128, 131, 138–139, 163, 169–170, 179–181, 242–243, 327, 330
Howard's Grove Hospital 182
Howell, E.W. 243, 327, 342
Howell, H.L. 243, 327, 340
Howell, J.D. 105, 243, 333, 337
Howse, Elisha S. 14, 112, 127, 243, 327, 333
Howse, Martin V.B. 14, 243, 327, 330

Howse, Thomas 243, 327
Hoy, John R. 243, 327
Hubbard, J.C. 243, 340
Huckabee, J.D. 10, 324
Hudson, John H. 50, 243, 332
Hudson, Lewis B. 243, 330
Huff, James C. 243–244, 330, 340
Huff, Jeremiah Clayton 244, 330, 340
Huff, John A. 113
Huff, John Floyd 244, 340
Huff, William T. 244, 330, 340
Hughes, George William 67, 244, 330, 336, 340
Hughey, Joseph B. 244, 340
Hume, Virginia 41
Humphries 169
Hunt, Isaac C. 244, 330
Hunter, David 115, 123
Hunter, John M. 244, 340
Hunterstown, Pennsylvania 1, 77–81
Hunton, James M. 244, 327
Huntsinger, Robert 88, 244–245, 330, 340
Huser, W.C. 245
Hyattstown, Maryland 21, 38

Infirmary Camp 181
Inman, Jeremiah Shadrach 245
Irby, Daniel J. 14, 245, 327, 340
Iron Scouts 46, 50, 73, 104, 115, 116–117, 130–131, 140–141, 146, 149, 161–162
Irvine 245, 342
Isdal, John F. 14, 57, 245, 327, 332
Ivey, Michael J. 43, 102, 245, 327, 335, 337
Ivey, Richard T. 245, 340

Jack, Doctor F. 245, 330
Jack, George Washington 245, 327
Jack, James Russell 164, 181, 245–246, 327, 334, 340
Jack, William F. 246, 340
Jack's Shop 91
Jackson, Arthur M. 246
Jackson, Green B. 10, 246, 327, 331
Jackson, Henry E. 79–81, 133, 246, 327, 330, 340
Jackson, John F. 246, 327
Jackson, Sherrod W. 246, 330, 340
Jackson, Stephen Everett 246, 330, 340
Jackson, Thomas E. 246, 330, 340
Jackson, Thomas J. "Stonewall" 11, 13, 17, 18, 26–27, 34, 58, 109
Jackson, William H. 246–247, 327, 340
Jackson, William W. 247, 340
Jacobs, John J. 247
Jaconetta, Sandra Bey 174
James, T.J. 247, 342
James City, Virginia 94–95
James River 8, 9, 10, 13, 57–58, 104, 114–115, 124, 127, 129–131, 135–136, 140–141, 143, 145, 147, 149
James River Canal 115
Jamestown Island 9

Jamestown, Virginia 8
Jarratt Station (Depot), Virginia 132, 133
Jaudon, J.T. 247, 327
Jay, William H.B. 247, 330, 336
Jefferson, Thomas James 247, 327
Jefferson, Pennsylvania 77
Jeffries, Lt. 169–170
Jenkins, Albert Gallatin 83, 90
Jenkins, John 46, 247, 327
Jenkins, Thomas S. 81, 247, 336, 342
Jenkins, William J. 247, 330
Jennings, W.P. 247
Jerusalem Plank Road 142
Jesperson, Hal 81
Jester, William 247, 342
Johnson, A. F. 247–248, 340
Johnson, Archibald C. 248, 330, 340
Johnson, E.B. 248, 327
Johnson, George G. 248, 340
Johnson, I.J. 248, 327, 342
Johnson, J.D. 248
Johnson, James C. 248
Johnson, James H. 112, 248, 333
Johnson, James M. 248
Johnson, Jesse 248, 342
Johnson, John A. 110, 248, 330, 337
Johnson, Leonard E. 248–249, 327, 330
Johnson, Leonidas D. 112, 249, 330, 340
Johnson, Lorenzo D. 249
Johnson, Samuel Jack 249, 327, 330, 340
Johnson, T.J. 249, 342
Johnson, Thomas D. 16, 249, 327
Johnson, Wesley 249
Johnson, William Baldwin 249, 330, 340
Johnson, William H. 249, 330, 338, 340
Johnston, Joseph E. 9, 10, 156–157, 165–168, 170–173
Johnston, M. 249
Joie, William R. 27, 324, 335
Joiner, John E. 249, 327
Jones, C.A. 249, 330
Jones, Capt. 144
Jones, Frank 123
Jones, H. 249, 342
Jones, Henry Francis 124, 249–250, 327, 333
Jones, James W. 250, 330
Jones, Jeremiah Berry 68, 110, 250
Jones, Jerry 250
Jones, John T. 250, 330, 340
Jones, Malcolm Daniel 6, 250
Jones, Mitchell T. 250, 330, 340
Jones, Nathan 250
Jones, Shepard A. 250, 340
Jones, Thomas P. 250, 330, 340
Jones, Thomas R. Washington 250, 327, 340
Jones, William Beamon 250–251, 327
Jones, William Edmondson "Grumble" 35, 36, 60, 63, 66, 90, 115

Jones, William H. 251
Jones, William Hemphill 251, 330, 340
Jowers, John 93, 251
Jowers, John L. 251, 333
Juhan, Daniel Bordeaux 251, 330
Juhan, Francis Ferdinand 251, 330
Juhan, J.A. 251, 340
Juhan, Lewis Alexander 45, 251, 327, 340
Juhan, Oliver Hazard Perry 6, 108, 251–252, 327, 333
Juhan, Richard Nathaniel 112, 252, 337

Karr, J.J. 91, 102, 252
Kautz, August V. 129, 131, 133, 142
Keaton, Benjamin O. 252
Keefe, John 252, 330
Kelley, Edward 86, 252, 342
Kelly, John 100, 252, 342
Kelly, William 252
Kelly's Ford, Virginia 46–47, 49, 52–53, 55, 60, 62–64, 88, 98
Kelly's Ford Road 62–63
Kellytown, South Carolina 159
Kendrick, W.W. 252
Kenedy, John Thomas 252
Kennedy, J.F. 27, 324, 332
Kennedy, James J. 50, 252, 332
Kennedy, John Milton 252, 330, 340
Kennedy, Joseph J. 13, 252, 331
Kennedy, Thomas B. 252
Kennemur, James S. 253
Kenny, Joseph 253
Kentucky 8
Keogh, John H. 46, 153, 181, 253, 327, 338, 340
Kershaw, South Carolina 159
Keyes, John C. 253, 327, 330
Killian's Mill, South Carolina 155–156
Kilpatrick, H. Judson 62–65, 69, 77, 81, 91–92, 97, 161–164, 169–172
Kilpatrick's Shirttail Skedaddle 163
King, Barrington Simeral 6, 66, 162–164, 253, 327, 334
King, Mark W. 253, 340
King, William J. 19, 253–254, 330, 340
King House 81
King William County, Virginia 56, 126
King's Mill 8
Kirkland, George W. 254, 330, 340
Kitchens, J.J. 254, 327
Knight, Frank 254
Knight, George L. 254, 340
Knight, John W. 254

Ladd's Store 129
Laffew, T.R. 68, 254
Lambert, George A. 254, 330, 340
Lamkin, James T. 147, 169, 254, 327, 338
Lampkin, Robert A. 128, 254, 327, 333

Lampkin, William F. 20, 106, 254–255, 333
Lancaster (Court House), South Carolina 157
Lander, Thomas 169, 255, 338
Landrum, Benjamin 66, 255, 340
Landrum, Michajah Monroe 255
Landrum, Thomas Jefferson 255, 327, 342
Langston, Jeptha N. 255
Lankford, James R. 86, 104, 255–256, 333, 336
Lassiter, R.W. 256
Lataste, E.G. 256, 340
Laurel Hill, Virginia 108
Law, McKinne 256
Lawrence, William E. 256
Lawrenceville, Georgia. 6
Lawson, John M. 104, 256, 333
Lawson, Roger McGill 256
Lawton, Alexander Cater 256, 327
Lawton, B.H. 256, 327, 342
Lawton, George M. 256
Lawton, Winburn J. 6, 256, 327
Lawyer Road 141
Lay, Elijah Columbus 256–257
Lay, Marcus L. 110, 257
Lazenby, Artemus M. 46, 257
Leach, James M. 257
Leach, John 257
Leach, Thomas 155, 257, 327, 340
Leatherwood, Wiley M. 16, 257
Leckie, Alexander 257
Lee, A.B. 257, 342
Lee, Fitzhugh "Fitz" 32, 35, 53, 60, 66, 75, 89, 97, 98, 103–104, 108–111, 116, 119–120, 122, 126, 128, 130–135
Lee, Robert Edward 12, 16, 17, 23, 26–27, 31, 34–35, 41, 46, 48–52, 56, 58, 60, 71, 74, 77–78, 81, 83, 106, 108–109, 111–112, 114–115, 122–123, 128–130, 134–137, 139–140, 142, 145, 151, 169, 171, 175
Lee, William Henry Fitzhugh "Rooney" 12, 16, 32, 35, 53, 60, 66, 71, 83, 89–90, 105, 109, 131, 135, 141, 144, 146–147
Leesburg, Virginia 21, 39
Lepole 257
Lewellyn, C.E. 258, 342
Lewis, Milton H. 258, 330, 340
Lewis, W.C. 258
Liberty, Maryland 38
Liberty Mills, Virginia 91–92
Light, Wiley R. 258, 340
Lincoln, Abraham 44, 171
Linden, Virginia 41
Linsey, Elijah 258
Lippitt, W.H. 139, 258, 327, 338
Lipscomb, T.J. 88
Little Cohary River 165
Little Lynch's Creek 158
Little River 111
Little River Turnpike 20, 96
Little Washington, Virginia 1, 44
Lively, Charles Pinkney 258, 327, 340
Liverman, William N. 46, 169, 258, 334

Lomax, Lunsford Lindsay 89, 110
Long Bridge 127
Longstreet, James 18, 71
Lord, William R. 258, 327
Loudoun Valley, Virginia 41, 69
Louisa (Court House), Virginia 116–119
Love's Bridge 161
Lowe, John D. 110, 173, 259, 334, 337
Lowery, Melvin K. 259, 327
Lowndes, Rawlins 170–171
Lowry, David P. 259, 330, 340
Loyd, John H. 259, 327
Lumpkin, Miller Grieve 259, 327
Lumpkin, Robert C. 259, 327
Lunenburg County, Virginia 132
Lutes, David F. 259, 342
Lyle, James Ray 259, 327
Lyle, Lee M. 46, 259
Lynchburg, Virginia 6, 115, 124
Lynch's Creek 157
Lyons, Thomas 161, 259, 338, 340

Macon, Georgia 5
Madison (Court House), Virginia 91, 93–94
Madison, Georgia 6
Magby, D. 259
Magruder, John Bankhead 7, 8, 10
Magruder, Z.S. 16
Mahaffey, W.H.C. 259–260, 340
Mahaffy, Emory V.W. 260
Mahaffy, James A.B. 260, 340
Mahaffy, John W.S. 110, 260, 342
Mahany, Martin 260, 330, 340
Mahone, William 146
Mallory, Elisha S. 16, 260
Mallory's Ford, Virginia 120
Malone, Robert G. 260, 327
Malone's Bridge 137
Malone's Crossing, Virginia 137
Malone's Road 137
Malvern Hill, Virginia 13, 14–16, 129
Manassas, Virginia 9, 18–19
Manassas Gap 87
Manassas Station, Virginia 96
Mangum, Wiley P. 260, 330, 340
Mann, J.M. 260, 342
Manning, James H. 85, 260, 336, 342
March to the Sea 151
Marchman, Coleman W. 16, 261, 331
Marchman, John H. 105, 261, 342
Marker Road 24–25
Markham, Virginia 41
Marsh Road 47, 57
Marshall, Henry 71, 261, 336, 342
Marshall, James F. 261, 327, 332
Marshall, William H. 261
Martin, John C. 261
Martin, Malachi Chappell 261
Martin, William Thompson 16, 50, 53
Martinsburg, West Virginia 32, 41, 87
Mass, Richard L. 43, 261, 335, 342
Massaponnax Church, Virginia 17

Matadequin Creek 113
Mathew, James H. 261, 340
Mathews, C.W. 261, 340
Mathias Point, Virginia 124
Mattapony River 103, 124, 126
Mattax, John 261
Matthews, John C. 261–262, 327
Matthews, William J.A. 262, 330
Mayo, Cranford M. 262
Mayo, J.J. 262
Mayo, J.W. 262, 327
McAuliffe, John 147, 262
McBride, Robert Boyd 262
McCale, John 73, 128, 262, 330, 336, 338
McCall, Henry Hugh 46, 102, 262, 327, 337
McCall, William H. 262
McClellan, George B. 9, 11, 12, 26–27, 31, 37, 39, 44, 46
McClellan, Henry B. 25, 55, 70
McCollum, Joseph P.C. 262, 327, 330, 340
McCollum, Josiah F. 262–263, 327, 330
McCollum, Moses W. 102, 263, 327, 333
McCorkle, Mark 263, 327, 330
McCoy, John 263, 330
McCoy, John Milledge 263, 330
McCoy's Ford, West Virginia 35–36
McCrary, Alex N. 263
McCrary, James M. 263, 340
McCroan, Augustus Owen 263, 330
McCroan, Henry M. 16, 66–67, 263, 330, 340
McCroan, John J. 264
McCullough, W.H. 46, 264, 340
McCullough, W.V. 264
McCullum, James N. 8, 264, 327, 331
McCune, John L. 143, 264, 334
McCurry, M. Rufus 120, 144, 264, 334, 338
McCurry, S. Marcus 46, 264, 327
McCurry, Thomas J. 264, 327, 340
McDade, Robert F. 264, 327
McDaniel, W. 264
McDaniel, William H. 112, 264, 337
McDaniel, William J. 265, 340
McDermont, Marcus L. 93, 265, 333
McDonald, W. 14, 265, 331
McDowell's Farm 144
McElhanon, George W. 136, 265, 334, 335
McGinness, Edward 71, 265, 336, 342
McGrath, Andrew C. 151
McGregor, William 150
McJunkin, James 265
McJunkin, Thomas 265
McKnight, E. 26, 265, 335
McLaws, Lafayette 8
McLelland, D. 265, 327
McNair, James M. 265, 327, 342
McWhorter, David S. 265, 330, 340

Mead, Lemuel S. 16, 265, 327
Meade, George C. 71, 90, 97, 98, 100, 106, 108, 114, 127, 129
Meaders, Barney R. 265, 340
Means, Samuel D. 21, 265, 332
Mechanicstown, Maryland 38
Mechanicsville, Virginia 11
Medill, William H. 23–24
Meherrin River 148–149
Meigs, Montgomery 54
Meldon, J.J. 265, 327
Melton, J.H. 266, 327, 330
Mercersburg, Pennsylvania 36
Merchant, Rufus B. 46, 266, 327
Merriman, Montague 266, 327, 330, 340
Merritt, Wesley 62
Mershew, W.W. 8, 266, 331
Mesic, Harriet Bey 35
Mesic, Harry Randolph vii, 28–30, 41, 49, 51, 61
Middleburg, Virginia 54, 69
Middletown, Maryland 22–24
Middletown Valley, Maryland 23–24
Miles, Nelson A. 149
Milford, Virginia 103, 106, 108, 111
Milhollen, D. 266, 342
Military Road 146
Mill Creek 166–167
Millen, Col. 113
Miller, Edwin J. 266
Miller, John J. 266, 330, 340
Miller, Josiah 16, 68, 266, 336, 340
Miller, Thomas K. 266
Millican, Lewis A. 266, 330
Milligan, Joseph C. 266–267, 330, 340
Mills, James W. 267, 330, 340
Mills, William Hugh 91, 267, 327, 330
Millsaps, W.W. 267, 340
Millwood, Virginia 41
Mince, Newton A. 267
Minchen, W. 267, 327
Minchener, Joseph 267
Mine Road 109
Mine Run 98, 100, 106
Mitchell, Henry Alex 16, 267, 330
Mitchell, John E. 43, 267, 332
Mitchell, Roland P. 267, 330, 340
Mitchell, Thomas J. 93, 267–268
Mitchell, W.S. 268, 340
Mitchell, William P. 268, 330, 340
Moccasin Creek 167
Mock, George W. 101, 268, 327, 330, 340
Mollere, J.F. 99, 268, 337
Monck's Neck Bridge 136, 145
Money (value of) 104
Monocacy River 22, 38
Monroe's Cross Roads [Monroe's Crossing], North Carolina 161–164
Monrovia, Maryland 38
Montgomery, George Cicero 97, 268, 327, 333
Montgomery, Joseph 268
Moon, George M.D. 148, 268, 338
Moon, Thomas J. 268, 340

Moony, James 96, 268, 342
Moor, August 23
Moore, J.J. 268, 340
Moore, John (Co. F) 268
Moore, John (Co. L) 268
Moore, John A. 120, 150, 268–269, 334, 338
Moore, Joseph A. 269, 342
Moore, Joseph L. 43, 269, 335
Moore, Richard 16, 84, 269, 327, 333
Moore, William C. 269
Moran, John J. 150, 269, 338, 340, 342
Morgan, Daniel 269, 330, 340
Morgan, Hampton W. 269
Morris, Edwin Pierce 269, 340
Morris, Elisha F. 93, 269
Morris, O. 93, 269–270, 333, 337
Morris, Robert Stockton 93, 270, 327, 337
Morrisville, Virginia 47, 51, 53
Morton's Ford, Virginia 102
Moseley, Benjamin R. 270, 327
Moseley, John D. 270, 340
Moss, J. Winchester 270, 340
Mt. Eron Church 159
Mt. Olive, North Carolina 169
Mountain Church Road 23–25
Mowan, J.E. 424, 342
Mower, Joseph A. 166
Moxley, Green Young 266, 340
Moxley, Newton J. 266, 340
Mud March 57
Munford, Thomas T. 21, 26, 60, 63, 90, 110
Murdock, Charles A. 270
Murdock, Thomas M. 96, 270, 330, 337, 340
Murphee, Augustus Wright 270, 340
Murphey, Moses Collins 16, 270, 330
Murphey, Nelson Wright 270
Murphey, Robert A. 271
Murphy, Bartholomew J. 71, 271, 336
Murphy, Thomas J. 271, 340
Murphy, William R. 271, 327
Muse, E.N. 271
Myers, Frank M. 113

Nabers, William 143, 271, 334
Nance's Shop, Virginia 13, 113, 127–128
Nash, Charles T. 271, 327, 330, 340
Nash, James Rutherford Polk 16, 271, 327, 330
Nash, John J. 173, 271, 338, 340
Nash, Reuben Long 92–93, 271, 327, 330, 337
Nash, Reuben T. 271–272
Nasworthy, Thomas J. 67, 144, 272, 336
National Road 22
Neabsco Creek 52
Neal, Samuel C. 272
Neese, William J. 272
Negros 135

Nelson, Charles H. 102, 272, 337
Nelson, James Hamilton 16, 272, 327, 330
Nesbitt, Robert Taylor 272, 327
Netherland, James A. 67, 272, 335, 336
Netherland, William Patterson 102, 272–273
Neuse River 168
New Castle, Virginia 115
New Hope Church 99–100
New London, Maryland 38
New Market, Maryland 38
New Market, Virginia 126, 129
Newbolt, T. 273, 342
Newton, B. 85, 97, 324, 333, 336
Newton, B.F. 273
Nichols, John W. 273
Nicholson, J. Roger 273
Nolan, J.T. 273, 342
Noose, J.F. 43, 273, 335
Norfolk, Virginia 8
Norman, Henry 273, 327, 330
Norris, James T. 148, 150, 169, 273, 327, 330
Norris, Thomas O. 273
North, Henry 135, 273, 330
North Anna River 98, 110, 111, 115, 117, 124
North Carolina Railroad 169
North Edisto River 153
Nottoway River 133, 134–135, 142, 149–150
Nunn, E.T. 273, 327, 330, 340
Ny River 108

Oates, James L. 67, 273, 330, 336
Oates, Joseph L. 273
Oates, L.H. 274, 330, 340
Oats, Andrew B. 67, 274, 336, 340
Occoquan, Virginia 50, 52–53, 55
Occoquan River 53, 73
O'Connor, Daniel 22, 93, 274, 327, 337
O'Connor, Owen 1, 45, 68, 81, 274, 330
O'Donnell, John B. 274, 327
O'Donohoe, Martin 58, 274–275, 332
Ogg House 122
O'Hara, James 275, 330
O'Keefe, Owen 46, 105, 275, 337
Old Capitol Prison 34
Old Hillsboro, North Carolina 170
Old Stage Road 159
Oliver, James C. 104, 275, 337
Oliver, R.L. 275
O'Neal, Pat 275
Orange (Court House), Virginia 93, 98–100
Orange & Alexander Railroad 54, 57, 60
Orange Plank Road 100
Orange Springs, Virginia 98
Orangeburg, South Carolina 153
Orr, William C. 136, 170, 275, 330
Orrison, C.W. 173, 275, 338
O'Shields, John B. 67, 275, 330
Owen, Thomas H. 90
Owens, Ira 275, 342

Owens, Jacob 275, 342
Owens, John A. 275, 342
Owens, John W. 275–276
Ownby, Gaines C. 276
Ox Hill 19–20
Ozburn, George H. 276, 330, 340
Ozburn, James R.D. 276, 327
Ozburn, James Robert 276, 330
Ozburn, Thomas Ozias 102, 276, 327, 337

Packard, Cyrus 276
Paden, Samuel D. 112, 276, 337
Palmer, Benjamin Brown 101, 276
Palmer, William C. 43, 276
Pamunkey River 12, 111–113, 115, 126
Park, Byrd 136, 276–277, 334
Park, Hiram P. 277
Park, J.A. 277, 327
Parker, J.P. 277, 327
Parker, James A. 128, 277, 334
Parker, N.C. 148, 277, 338
Parker, Robert J. 105, 277, 340
Parker, W.H. 277, 334
Parker, William M. 277, 330, 340
Parker, William R. 277
Parker's Store, Virginia 1, 100
Parks, David Rives 277, 327, 340
Parks, Harvey Calhoun 148, 277–278, 338
Parks, Isaac Glenn 278
Parks, Marion 278
Parks, Samuel S. 120, 150, 278, 334, 338
Parrish, Charles T. 278, 327
Parrish, George W. 87, 278, 327, 336
Parrish, J.S. 324
Paschal, Thomas A. Holliday 14, 46, 278, 327
Pass, William H. 99, 143, 278–279, 334
Pate, M.M. 279
Patterson, James S. 27, 279, 335
Patterson, William L. 279, 330, 340
Paul, Neal B. 279, 340
Pay, for Cavalrymen 5
Payne, Alfred F. 279, 330
Payne, David H. 279
Payne, William H. 90, 105, 279, 330
Peach Orchard 64
Pearson, Frank 78
Peck, Leroy M. 279, 330, 340
Pee Dee River 159, 161
Peek, R.C. 279
Peel, E.L. 112, 279, 327, 330, 340
Peel, John P. 279, 337
Pelham, John 35, 39
Pemberton, J.C. 27, 324, 335
Pendleton, B.A. 279, 340
Penick, Lucas T. 105, 136, 279–280, 330
The Peninsula 7–10
Pennsville, Pennsylvania 76
Penrow, William E. 67, 280, 330, 336
Pentecost, H.F. 280, 342
Perkins, John A. 280

Perryman, R.N. 280, 340
Perryman, Thomas J. 280, 330
Petersburg, Pennsylvania 78
Petersburg, Virginia 4, 115, 124, 128, 130–131, 134–136, 140, 142, 144–145, 147–149, 168
Petersburg & Weldon Railroad 130
Peterson, Ransom J. 280
Peterson, SeaBorn H. 143, 280, 334
Pettis, Harrison J. 280, 327
Phelps, A.B. 16, 280, 330
Phillips, James R. 280, 327, 330, 340
Pickerill, William N. 24–26
Piedmont Virginia 115
Pierce, George W. 53, 280 332
Pierce, John A. 280–281, 342
Pierce, Reuben J. 281
Pierce, Thomas A. 281
Pierce's Bridge 159
Pinson, Joseph Newton 281
Pinson, William 281
Pittard, Isham Humphrey 104, 281, 337
Pittard, R.T. 281
Pittman, Marcus De Lafayette 88, 281
Pleasant Valley 26
Pleasonton, Alfred 23, 32, 38, 63, 69
Po River 108–110
Point of Rocks, Maryland 26
Poland, Thomas N. 281, 330
Pole Cat Creek 111, 115, 124
Pool, Benjamin J.B. 281, 340, 342
Poolesville, Maryland 21, 36, 38
Pope, Jesse 282, 340
Pope, John 17, 18
Poppin, Richard S. 282
Porter, Drury W. 282
Poss, William H. 324
Potomac River 21, 26–28, 31–32, 35–38, 41, 50, 71, 73–74, 78, 85, 124
Pounds, Sylvester 282, 330
Powell, Ambrose 324
Powell, Benjamin C. 282
Powell, D.A. 105, 282, 327, 333
Powell, G.M. 324
Prater, W.T. 282, 342
Presbyterian Church (Hunterstown) 81
Price, George F. 324
Price, James W. 282, 342
Price, John L. 282
Price, Nat 84
Prince, J.W. 282, 330, 340
Prince, Oliver H. 282
Pritchard, Matthew Clifford 282, 330, 340
Pritchard, Thomas W. 282, 330, 340
Province, Hiram 282–283, 327, 340
Pruett, Benjamin 283
Pugh, Nathan S. 81, 283, 333
Pugsley, Sidney A. 283, 330, 340
Pylant, Edwin 283, 340

Quaker Meeting House 146
Quaker Road 146
Quarles, A.M. 114, 283, 333
Quebec Schoolhouse 23–26

Raccoon Ford, Virginia 48, 91, 93, 98, 102
Railroads 8
Raines, George 5
Raleigh, North Carolina 169–170
Raleigh Railroad 168
Ramsey, S. Thomas 54, 283
Rape 158
Rapidan River 17, 56, 88, 91, 94, 97–99, 102–103, 106
Rapidan Station, Virginia 91
Rappahannock Bridge 57
Rappahannock River 17, 18, 41, 44, 46–47, 49–53, 56–58, 60–62, 67, 69, 88, 91, 95, 97–98, 111
Rappahannock Station, Virginia 57, 98
Rasbury, Mansel W. 283, 340
Rasbury, Reuben L. 283, 340
Rations 4, 13, 55, 109, 111, 115, 142, 149
Ray, John R. 283
Ray, William A. 283, 340
Raynes, J.M. 284, 342
Reader, J.N. 284, 330, 340
Ream's Station, Virginia 129, 130–134, 136–138, 148
Receiving and Wayside Hospital 182
Recruiting Camp 181
Rector's Cross Roads, Virginia 69, 71
Reese, Henry C. 139, 284, 330
Reese, W.M. 284, 330, 340
Reeves, James 324, 342
Reeves, William 284
Refugees 155
Reid, A.R. 284
Reid, J.L. 284
Reid, Jonas, G.B. 284, 330, 340
Reid, William Halum 284, 327, 330
Reidling, Joseph W.M. 33, 284, 332
Remington, Maj. 73
Reynolds, Joseph Jones 284, 330, 340
Reynolds, Robert Augustus (Co. A) 173, 284–285, 327
Reynolds, Robert Augustus (Co. F) 43, 285, 340
Reynolds, Thomas 88, 285, 333
Reynolds, Walter C. 31, 285, 327, 330
Rheney, Elisha Anderson 285
Rhodes, Henry N. 16, 43, 285, 327, 332
Rhodes, Radford C. 16, 285, 327
Rice, Calvin C. 285, 330
Rice, J.W. 285–286, 330, 340
Rice, John Andrew 179
Rice, Zachariah A. 6, 44, 286, 327
Rich, James L. 286, 330
Rich, William W. 88–89, 126
Richard's Ferry, Virginia 47–48

Richmond, Virginia 7, 9, 10, 13, 14, 17, 44, 60, 97, 102–105, 108–110, 113–114, 116, 129–130, 134–136, 143, 145, 147, 168, 170
Richmond County, Georgia 6
Richmond, Fredericksburg & Potomac Railroad 102
Riden, Martin W. 16, 286, 327, 330
Ridgeway, South Carolina 156
Ridgway, James N. 286, 330, 340
Ridgway, John N. 286, 330, 340
Ridings, George 286, 340
Ridley, W.B. 286, 340
Ridlin, J.W.M. 286
Ridling, J.K.P. 108, 286, 330
Rigand, L. 114, 286–287, 338
Ringgold, James G. 156, 287, 338
Ritch, James L. 287
Ritch, Jeremiah E. 6, 50, 66–67, 287, 327, 336
River Road 53
Rives, Burwell G. 287, 340
Rives, Reuben P. 287, 340
Rives, Thomas J. 101, 287, 327
Roach, William H. 287, 327, 340
Roark, Page Jefferson 86, 287–288
Robbins, Francis 288, 342
Robert, Alexander J. 288
Robert, Benjamin F. 288
Robert, Jehu Stoney 288
Robert, Ulysses M. 288
Roberts, George W. 114, 288, 340
Roberts, Richard E. 143, 288, 330, 340
Roberts, W. 288
Roberts, William R. 6, 288, 330
Robertson, Beverly 60, 69, 70, 90
Robertson, Isaac 288
Robertson, William H. 288, 327
Robertson, William S. 81, 288–289
Robertson's Ford, Virginia 91, 93
Robertson's River 94–95
Robinson, W.G. 90
Roch, E.J. 289
Rockingham, South Carolina 161
Rockman, J.H. 27, 324, 332, 335
Rockville, Maryland 73, 75–76
Rocky Ridge, Maryland 38
Rodgers, Alpheus M. 6, 167, 289
Rodgers, Charles Edward 289
Roebuck, Henry A. 289, 327, 330
Roesel, G.E. 289
Roesel, Herman 289, 340
Rogers, Charles H. 100, 289
Rogers, G. Washington 289
Rogers, Jethro W. 120, 289, 333
Rogers, John Blake 289, 330
Rogers, John J. 289–290, 340
Rogers, Thomas A. 290, 330, 340
Rollins, Thomas 88, 143, 290, 334, 337
Roper, James 290, 342
Ross, John 93, 173, 290, 334, 340
Ross, Perryman 290
Rosser, Thomas L. 16, 89, 90, 104, 109–110, 117, 119, 122–123, 133–134, 137–138, 141–142–143
Roswell, Georgia 6
Rountree, James A. 290, 330, 340

Rountree, William R. 88, 290, 333
Rowanty Creek 131, 136, 140
Rowanty Creek Bridge 132
Rowe, James Edward vii, 74, 75, 80, 86, 181
Rowser's Ford 73–74
Rucker, Alexander Randolph 290, 327
Ruddell, John Henry 290
Ruffin's Farm 126
Rummel's Farm 83
Rushin, John 290
Rushin, Joseph A. 290
Rushville, Virginia 73
Rusk, David 290–291, 340
Rusk, Dempsy P. 291, 340
Russell's Ford, Virginia 94
Rutherford, John Cobb 291, 327
Rutherford, Robert R. 291, 330, 340
Rutledge, B.H. 154
Rutledge, M.B. 291
Rylee, Andrew Jackson 16, 291, 327, 330
Rylee, James B. 291, 327, 340

St. James Church 60, 63–64
St. John's Church 132
St. Mary's Church 127
Salem Church 127
Salem Depot, Virginia 72
Salter, Thomas W. 87, 291, 333
Saluda River 154
Samaria Church 127–128
Sanford, Allen 291, 342
Sappony Church 129–131
Sappony Creek 130
Saunders, B.F. 112, 291, 337
Saunders, William 291–292
Savannah, Georgia 151
Scammell, E.W. 164, 292, 338
Schlesinger, Gustavus 16, 51, 292, 327, 332
Schweers, Owen 1
Schofield, John M. 157, 167
Sconyers, Andrew J. 292, 330, 340
Sconyers, Richard 68, 292, 332
Scott, A.F. 292, 327, 330, 340
Scott, Alfred D. 292
Scott, James D. 96, 292, 327, 330
Scruggs, Joseph L. 292, 330, 340
Scudder, Jacob McCarty 45, 292, 327, 332
Scudder, Lewis Blackburn 16, 292–293, 327
Scudder, William Henry Harrison 293, 330, 340
Seagers, Francis Graves 293, 340
Seago, James Franklin 114, 293, 330, 340
Seago, Josiah Middleton 87, 293, 336
Seay, Marshall N. 136, 293, 330
Seay, Osborne A. 112, 293, 330
Segars, Dub 294
Segars, William Richey 294, 330
Sego, Calvin Cephus 294, 327, 342
Selectman's Ford, Virginia 52–53
Service Records 181
Seven Pines, Virginia 126

Sewel, Thomas A. 294
Shackleford, Charles William 294, 342
Shackleford, Thomas Jefferson 294, 330, 340
Shadburne, George B. 140, 149
Shady Grove, Virginia 108
Sharpe, Jarrell G. 294, 327, 330
Sharpe, John H. 139, 294, 330
Sharpe, Milton C. 294, 340
Sharpsburg, Maryland 26–31
Shaw, J. Sidney 294–295, 340
Shaw, William M. 127, 295
Shead, Loring Wheeler 295, 342
Shed, J.A. 163–164, 167, 295, 334
Sheffield, James M. 295, 327
Shelby, William Alexander 295
Shenandoah Valley 11, 41, 46, 60, 104, 115, 123, 134–135, 140, 143
Shepherdstown, West Virginia 27–28, 32, 41
Sheridan, Philip H. 104, 108–113, 115–117, 120–123, 126–129, 132, 134, 140
Sherman, George W. 295, 327
Sherman, William Tecumseh 1, 62, 110, 151, 154–159, 161, 165–171
Shinall, Benjamin F. 295
Shirley Plantation 13
Shivers, J.W. 295–296, 342
Shriver Farm 76
Shurdon, John W. 296, 342
Sibley, Benjamin F. 296, 327, 342
Sibley, C.L. 296, 327, 340
Sibley, E.L. 296, 327
Sibley, Samuel Hale 296, 340
Sibley, William H. 8, 296, 327, 331
Simmons, Henry J. 88, 296
Simmons, James Overton 88, 296, 330, 337
Simmons, Jesse A. 296–297, 330, 340
Simmons, Mike 119
Simmons, Moses Sylvanus 67, 297, 330, 336
Simmons, Moses Taliaferro 297, 327, 340
Simmons, W.S. 297
Simmons, William D. 297, 327, 340
Simon, Isaac 46, 297
Simon, Nathan 297, 327
Simpkins, William H. 297, 330, 340
Sinquefield, Francis A. 67, 297–298, 330
Slatern, George W. 93, 298, 327, 330, 337
Slaughter's Hill 95
Slaves 132
Slocum, Henry W. 155, 165–166
Smith, Alexander P. 16, 298, 327
Smith, Andrew J. 139, 298, 334
Smith, C.H. 324
Smith, C.N. 324
Smith, David E. 46, 298, 327
Smith, Ebenezer B. 298, 330, 340
Smith, Ebenezer F. 85, 298, 333
Smith, Henry W. 71, 298, 340

Smith, Isaac T. 112, 153, 298, 334, 337
Smith, J.D. 298
Smith, James B. 298–299, 330, 340
Smith, Job 299
Smith, John 133, 299, 334
Smith, Joseph 71, 299, 327, 336
Smith, Robert F. 299, 340
Smith, Russell 86, 299
Smith, Samuel Jordan 299
Smith, T.H. 299, 330
Smith, Thomas A. 58, 299, 332
Smith, W.W. 299
Smith, Wilbur F. 299, 327, 330, 340
Smith, William W. 18, 299–300, 332
Smith, Zachariah H. 300, 330, 340
Smithfield, North Carolina 168
Smithfield, West Virginia 41
Smithfield Road 168
Smitzer, Edward G. 325
Snelling, James M. 300, 327
Soap, Making 140
South, Amaziah 300, 340
South Anna River 111–112, 135
South Carolina Military Academy 119
South Mountain 23, 25–27
Southside Railroad 129, 143–145
Spain, Francis J. 300, 330
Spain, William 300
Speer, Francis A. 300
Spencer, John W. 105, 300
Sperryville, Virginia 44
Sponsler, Henry L. 300, 327, 330
Spotsylvania (Court House), Virginia 58, 108, 110, 111–112
Sprague, Chauncy A. 300, 327
Spurlock, Glen vii, 181
Squirrel Level Road 143
Stanford, Allen R. 87, 300, 337, 342
Stanley, John C. 300–301, 342
Stanton, Edward McMasters 145
Stanton, J.B. 301, 342
Stark's Ford, Virginia 60, 63
Statham, W.R. 325
Staunton, A.A. 301
Staunton River 129
Staunton River Bridge 129
Steen, Henry 102, 301, 337
Stephens, Harvey 301
Stephens, W.J.H. 301, 340
Sterling, Isaac 43, 301, 332
Stevens, Edward N. 301, 340
Stevens, W.C. 301, 340
Stevensburg, Virginia 51, 61, 63, 90
Stevenson, Carter L. 153
Stewarder, H.J. 27, 301, 335
Stewart, Alexander P. 165–166
Stewart, Hugh Henderson 301, 330
Stewart, J. Lafayette 301, 340
Stewart, William A. 301–302, 340
Stewart, William T.M. 302
Stokes, James W. 46, 112, 302, 330, 337
Stone, Edward Preston 93, 302, 333

Stone, William L. 135, 302, 334
Stone Bridge 135
Stone Castle, Virginia 96
Stoneman, George 38, 58
Stony Creek 147–149
Stony Creek Station, Virginia 130–132, 139, 148
Stovall, Bolling Anthony 302, 327
Stovall, Francis Marion 18, 302, 327, 335
Stovall, J.F. 302, 330, 340
Stovall, Thomas P. 6, 302, 327
Strickland, E. 302, 330
Strickland, Henry 16, 302–303, 327, 342
Strickland, J.F. 68, 303
Strickland, Noah C. 84, 303, 333
Strickland, T.J. 303
Strickland, William M. 303, 330, 340
Stroud's Mills, South Carolina 158
Stuart, James Brown 1, 10, 11, 16, 18, 21–23, 25–31, 34–36, 38–41, 43–44, 46, 48, 51–54, 56–58, 60, 63–64, 66–67, 69–71, 73–74, 76–84, 89–91, 94–97, 100, 102, 104–106, 108–110, 113, 134, 142, 178
Stud Horse Battalion 123
Suddeth, George A. 303, 330, 340
Suffolk, Virginia 8
Sugar Loaf Mountain, Maryland 21
Suggs, R.E. 325
Susquehanna River 71, 77
Sussex (Court House) Road 149
Sutton, Leander 303, 340
Sutton, William E. 26, 303, 327, 330, 335, 340
Swan, Henry J. 303, 340
Swan, John C. 161, 303, 338
Swift Creek 169–170
Swift Run Gap, Virginia 124
Sycamore Church 140–142
Syler, Joseph 161, 303, 338

Tabb, Thomas J. 304, 330, 340
Tackett's Ford, Virginia 52
Tank, Charles N. 16, 304
Tanner, Daniel F. 46, 304
Tanner, Francis D. 16, 304, 330, 340
Tanner, George C. 86, 304, 336, 340
Tanner, William Avery 304, 327, 330
Tatum, J.D. 304
Taylor, B.F. 304
Taylor, Calvin C. 304, 340
Taylor, Giles 128
Taylor, Lemuel 304, 342
Telegraph Road 17, 46, 50, 52–53
Tennessee 8
Terry, Alfred H. 157, 167
Thayer, Curtis J. 304–305, 327, 342
Thomas, Andrew Jackson 45, 305, 327
Thomas, Davis 305
Thomas, Isma W. 49, 54, 305, 335, 340

Thomas, J.F. 305, 330
Thomas, J. Jefferson 6, 305, 327
Thomas, J.N. 87, 305
Thomas, J.R. 16, 305, 327
Thomas, James 305
Thomas, James M. 68, 305
Thomas, John W. 305, 330
Thomas, Jonathan Pinckney 45, 173, 305–306, 334
Thomas, Lovick P. 306, 327
Thomas, Robert F. 306, 340
Thompson, Alfred R. 127, 306, 327, 340
Thompson, Charles 325
Thompson, E. 325
Thompson, George W. 306, 327
Thompson, Jackson S. 306
Thompson, James F. 306, 340
Thompson, James W. 116
Thompson, Lewis B. 306
Thompson's Creek 159
Thornburg, Virginia 17
Thornton, J.T. 325
Thornton, James Madison 306, 327, 340
Thornton, Simeon Willis 306, 327
Thoroughfare Gap 17, 69, 72
Thrash, John S. 114, 306–307, 327, 340
Thurman, Joseph W. 44, 307
Tiller's Ferry, South Carolina 159
Tinsley, Thomas Haywood 307, 327, 330, 340
Todd, James H. 307, 327, 331
Todd, Thomas B.F. 88, 114, 307, 338
Todd's Tavern, Virginia 108
Tollison, Healey 307, 342
Tompkins, Eubanks B. 307
Tompson, Charles 307
Toole, James M. 307, 330, 340
Torbert, Alfred T.A. 117, 129, 134
Torrance, Cuthbert C. 102, 307–308, 330, 340
Totomoi Creek 113
Totopotomoy Creek 112
Trans-Mississippi 168, 172
Tredell, J. 27, 325, 335
Trevilian Station, Virginia 1, 115–124, 127–128, 134, 137, 140
Truitt, James C. 308
Truitt, James Riley 308, 330
Tuck, James J. 58, 308, 332
Tuck, Robert 308
Tuck, Thomas Ransom 101, 308, 327, 330
Tuck, William Boyd 10, 308, 331
Tucker, William J. 87, 309–309, 327, 330, 336
Tullis, James M. 309
Turner, Absalom B. 309, 342
Turner, Ashby 35
Turner, Calhoun H. 16, 309, 327, 340
Turner, Cornelius C. 88, 139, 309, 338, 342
Turner, James 68, 309, 332
Turner, James J. 150, 152, 309, 334, 338
Turner, Jefferson J. 309, 327, 330

Turner, S. Otis 27, 325, 335
Turner, Stephen 16, 86, 309–310, 340
Turner's Gap 23, 26
Tweedy, Ephraim, Jr. 310, 327
Twiggs, J.D. 50
Twitty, W.W. 310
Tyus, C. 310, 327, 330

Uniforms 5
U.S. Artillery 13, 17, 58, 73, 79, 85, 91, 94, 106, 113, 120, 128, 132, 149, 161, 163–164, 170; 10th Light Artillery 153; Gregg's 83; Horse Artillery 69, 108, 112, 115
U.S. Cavalry 12, 17, 18, 19, 52–53, 55, 57, 61, 65–67, 69, 71, 79–81, 85, 91, 94–96, 105–106, 108–109, 113, 115, 134, 137, 149; 1st U.S. Regulars 115; 5th OH 153, 162; 5th U.S. Regulars 44, 104, 115; 5th WI 153; Buford's 85, 91; Custer's Brigade 79, 81, 83, 120; Farnsworth's Brigade 76; Gregg's Cavalry 64, 112, 115, 127–128, 135, 137, 142, 145, 147; Illinois (8th) 23, (12th) 36; Indiana (3rd) 23–24; Kautz's Cavalry 131, 133, 137, 142; Kilpatrick's Cavalry 70, 76, 79, 91, 94, 96, 104, 158, 161, 163–164, 169; Massachusetts (1st) 128; Michigan (5th) 76, 113, (6th) 76–79, (Gray's) 77; New York 62, (2nd) 65, (5th) 76, (10th) 65; Pennsylvania 38, (18th) 76; Pleasonton's 32; Scott's Nine Hundred 73; Sheridan's Cavalry 108, 112, 116, 117, 122–123, 127–128, 131; Stoneman's Cavalry 58; Torbert's Division 115, 117, 127; Washington, D.C. Cavalry 65, 69, 75, 92, 126, 140, (1st) 141; Wilson's Cavalry 130, 131–133
U.S. Forces 10, 12, 13, 17, 18, 21, 26, 49, 58, 61, 74, 76, 83, 94, 100, 102, 104, 106, 110, 112–113, 113–114, 129, 132–133, 135, 139, 142, 144, 161, 164, 166; 1st Army Corps 97; 2nd Corps 136, 145; 5th Corps 98, 136, 143, 145, 149; 6th Corps 96; 9th Corps 145; 14th Corps 156–157, 165; 15th Corps 156–157; 17th Corps 156–157, 159, 165; 20th Corps 157, 165; 29th Corps 156; Army of the Potomac 100, 134, 140; Blair's Corps 156, 159; Burnside's 57; Force's Division 152–153; Grant's Army 111, 114–115, 126; Grimes Davis' 63; Hooker's Army 75; McClellan's Army 22, 35, 37; Meade's Army 71, 84, 95, 100; Pope's Army 19–20; Schofield's Corps 157; Sherman's Army 151, 154–159, 166–167, 170; Slocum's Division 165–166; Terry's Corps 157; Warren's Corps 136, 149–150
United States Ford, Virginia 57
U.S. Infantry 13, 31, 57, 71, 91, 95, 104, 106, 108, 111–113, 115, 127, 131, 134, 135–138, 149, 158, 163–164; French's Division 94; Hancock's 72–73, 137–138, 145–147; Illinois (92) 170; Mower's Division 166–167; New York 137; Ohio (28th) 23, (30th) 23; Pennsylvania (99th) 38; Vincent's Brigade 69
U.S. Mine Ford 57
Upperville, Virginia 41, 69, 71
Upperville Turnpike 69
Urbana, Maryland 21–22
Usry, Joshua F. 310, 327

Vance, Zebulon B. 139
Vasser, Richard A. 310, 327, 340
Vaughan, George W. 27, 114, 310, 338, 342
Vaughn, Claborn 310
Vaughn, Thomas R. 310
Vaughn Road 137, 143–146
Venable, A. Reid 146
Vienna, Virginia 54
Vigis, Thomas 310, 327, 340
Virginia Central Railroad 17, 111, 113, 115, 120, 124
Von Borcke, Maj. Heros 28, 30–31
Voss, James A. 310–311, 340
Voss, John A. 140, 311, 338, 342
Voss, William A. 311

Wabrey, P. 325
Wade, H. 59, 76, 325, 332
Wades, South Carolina 157
Waggins, L.D. 311
Waiott, J.J. 325
Wait, Nickolas C. 311
Waldrup, J.J. 311
Walker, James F. 311, 327, 330, 340
Walker, Persons 311, 340
Walkin, H.H. 148, 311, 338
Wall, William Carter 311, 330
Wallace, Charles 27, 311
Wallace, Patrick 97, 311–312, 327
Walsh, Michael 312
Walter, Fred W. 12, 312, 327, 340
Walter, Jerry 312
Wapping Heights 87
Ward, Calvin D. 312, 340
Ward, James M. 312, 330, 340
Ware, Nicholas C. 67, 312, 332
Waring, Joseph Frederick 1, 62, 89, 105, 109, 111, 124, 126, 135, 144–145, 150, 158, 171
Warren, Gouverneur K. 136, 148–150
Warrenton, Virginia 18, 41, 54, 69, 96–97
Warrenton Springs, Virginia 18
Warwick, Edwin A. 312, 340
Warwick, John N. 112, 312, 330, 337
Washington, D.C. 8, 19, 20, 34, 36, 50, 54, 71, 74
Wateree River 156
Waterloo Bridge 18
Waters, Charles L. 312
Waters, James B. 16, 312, 342

Watkins, Benjamin H. 312–313, 330, 340
Watkins, Charles D. 313
Watkins, Henry A. 147, 313, 338
Watson, James B. 86, 313, 336
Weaver, H.F. 313, 342
Weaver, W.T. 313, 340
Webb, Joseph M. 313, 342
Weir, Nathan Hoyt 313
Weir, Samuel B. 313, 340
Welch, Michael 313–314
Weldon Railroad 129, 131, 136, 139, 142–143, 148–150
Wellborn, Olive 314, 327
Wellford's Ford, Virginia 60
Wellman, Manly Wade 122
Wells, Edward L. 109–110, 112, 114, 117, 120, 122, 127, 134, 163, 171
Wells, Jasper 21, 325, 332
Wells, Thomas B. 88, 314, 340
Wesley, John William v, vii
West Point, Virginia 12
West Woods 29
Westminster, Maryland 76
Weston, Edward H. 314, 342
Weston, J.H. 314
West's Cross Roads, South Carolina 157
Whaley, Caleb A. 314, 327
Whalin, Maurice 100, 314, 330
Wharton, J.T.M. 150, 314, 330
Wheeler, Joseph 151, 162–163, 169
Whelchel, Alex. S. 91, 314, 327, 340
Whelchel, Francis Marion 104, 314, 327
Whelchel, Stephen T. 315, 327, 330
Whippy Swamp 152
Whisenant, Henry 58, 315, 332
White, Alexander R. 315, 327
White, B.S. 36–38
White, C.C. 315
White, E.V. 90
White, George B. 139, 315, 327, 334
White, H.D. 325
White, H.H. 325
White, H.J. 325
White, Henry 315, 340
White, Henry Clay 315, 340
White, James K. Polk 315, 327
White, James M. 147, 315, 338
White, Joseph 315
White, Lawson V. 315, 342
White, Robert 315
White, W.J. 315
White, William Augustus 315
White, William H. 315–316
White, William R. 316, 327
White Chimneys, Virginia 124
White House, Virginia 12, 13, 124, 126–127
White Oak Bridge 135
White Oak Road 145–147
White Post, South Carolina 153
White Ridge Road 1, 47
Whitehead, David A. 316, 340
Whitehead, F. Jasper 316, 327
White's Ford, Virginia 21, 38, 91
White's Tavern 135–136

Whitney, W.M. 325
Whitt, A.R. 316
Wicket, J.S. 316
Wickham, Williams C. 16, 110, 128
Wickham's Farm 126
Wier, Nicholas C. 316
Wier, Robert W. 102, 316, 333
Wiggins, William David v, vii, 174, 316, 327, 330
Wilborn, James C. 120, 316, 338
Wild, George 317
Wilder, C.W. 8, 317, 327, 331
The Wilderness 58, 106, 108–109, 112–113, 128
Wilkinson, Thomas J. 317
Wilkinson's Bridge 140
Willard, John Larkin 317, 330
Willbanks, Richard H. 317
Williams, A.J. 317, 340
Williams, Andrew B. 317, 327
Williams, Carlos 16, 325, 331
Williams, Dilmus P. 317
Williams, George A. 46, 120, 169, 173, 317, 330
Williams, Henry F. 71, 317–318, 327, 342
Williams, Henry M. 169, 318
Williams, J.B. 318, 327, 330
Williams, Thomas C. 6, 139, 148, 318, 327
Williams, Thomas H. 318
Williams, W.H. 325
Williams, William M. 6, 148, 318, 327
Williams, William S. 318
Williams, Willis B. 318, 340
Williamsburg Road 126, 135
Williamson, James R. 319
Williamsport, Maryland 28–32, 85, 87
Williard, George W. 319, 341
Willis, Alonzo D. 319, 327, 330, 341
Willis, Josiah N. 319, 330
Willis, T.J. 319
Williston, South Carolina 153
Wilmington, North Carolina 149
Wilmington & Weldon Railroad 8
Wilson, E.J. 152, 319, 334
Wilson, E.N. 91, 94, 319, 328, 333
Wilson, Frank R. 16, 319, 328
Wilson, J.A. 319
Wilson, James H. 129, 131–134
Wilson, James L. 319, 330
Wilson, Joseph R. 57, 319, 328, 336
Wimberly, E. 320, 328, 330
Wimberly, E.M. 320, 341
Wimperly, G. 27, 325, 335
Wimpy, John A. 94, 320, 328
Winchester, J. 320
Winchester, Virginia 32, 35, 41, 87
Winder, Charles C. 16, 46, 320, 328, 330
Winder, J.P.S. 320, 328
Winfrey, George W. 320, 341
Winfrey, John A. 320
Winnsboro, South Carolina 156
Winnsboro Road 154, 159
Winship, George 21, 88, 147, 320

Winters, Merriman 43, 320, 335
Wise, J.J. 14, 325, 331
Wise, John J. 179
Witcher, Charles N. 321, 341
Wittson, R.S. 325
Wivins, W.R. 321
W.J. McElroy Company. 5
Wolf Run Shoals 73
Wolfe, Herman 321, 330
Wood, Green C. 321, 328, 330
Wood, J.F. 321, 341
Wood, J.G. 321
Wood, J.W. 321
Wood, James R. 321, 328, 341
Wood, John N. 27, 328, 330, 335
Wood, John R. 321
Wood, John T. 153, 155, 164, 167, 179, 321, 330
Wood, Moses 321–322, 328, 330
Wood, R.W. 322
Woodruff, Berrimon 16, 322, 331
Woods, Marcus V. 43, 87, 322, 335, 336, 342
Woodsboro, Maryland 38
Woody, Alex 322, 342
Woolley, George 88, 322, 337, 342
Wooten, Powhattan Bolling 322, 328
Wooten, S.B. 322
Wooten, William J. 322
Worrison, W.C. 322, 341
Worsham, E.J. 322
Wray, John R. 322
Wray, Philip 322, 328
Wray, Walter A. 322, 328, 330
Wrenn, Lewis 35
Wright, B.E. 322–323, 330, 341
Wright, Gilbert "Gib" J. 6, 25–26, 110, 115, 118, 128, 138, 154, 162, 168, 170–172, 177–178
Wright, William D. 323, 328
Wyatt's Farm 144
Wyndham, Percy 62, 64
Wynn, K.A. 325
Wynne, William Joseph 67, 323, 328, 341

Yancey, Benjamin Cudworth 6, 323, 328
Yellow Chapel, Virginia 46–47
Yellow Tavern, Virginia 108–109, 140
Yerby, Burrell Henry 323, 330, 341
Yew Hills 63, 66
York, Pennsylvania 77, 81
York River 9, 126
York Road 84
York Springs, Pennsylvania 78
Yorktown, Virginia 7, 9, 10
Young, Milton B. 137, 323, 328
Young, Pierce Manning Butler "PMB" 6, 7, 14, 16, 24–26, 49–50, 63–66, 69, 79, 86, 88–89, 91–92, 95–97, 109–110, 114–115, 133, 137, 143–144, 148, 151, 178
Young, Stanley 323, 330
Young, T.B. 325
Young, William 71, 323, 336, 342
Young, William Benjamin 6, 104, 323–324, 328, 337

www.ingramcontent.com/pod-product-compliance
Lightning Source LLC
Chambersburg PA
CBHW081535300426
44116CB00015B/2637